D0500908

SASKATCHEWAN

A NEW
HISTORY

THE PROVINCE OF SASKATCHEWAN

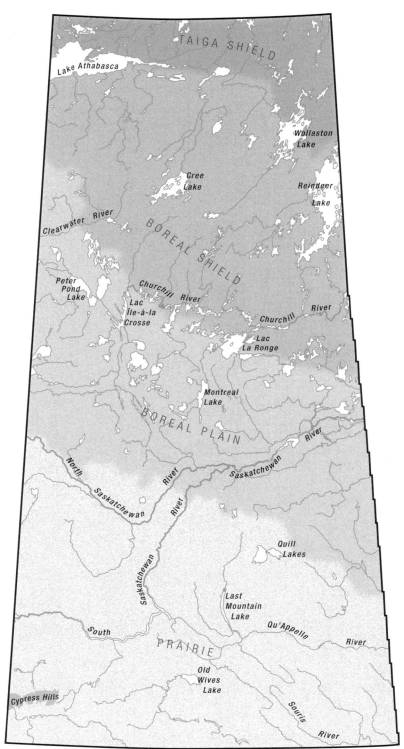

TAIGA SHIELD

Lake Athabasca

Wollaston Lake

Cree Lake

Reindeer Lake

Clearwater River

BOREAL SHIELD

Peter Pond Lake

Churchill River

Lac Île-à-la Crosse

Churchill River

Lac La Ronge

Montreal Lake

BOREAL PLAIN

River

North Saskatchewan River

Saskatchewan River

Saskatchewan River

Quill Lakes

Last Mountain Lake

Qu'Appelle River

South

PRAIRIE

Old Wives Lake

Cypress Hills

Souris River

SASKATCHEWAN

A NEW
HISTORY

BILL WAISER

COLOUR PHOTOGRAPHY
BY JOHN PERRET

FIFTH
HOUSE

Copyright © 2005 Bill Waiser

All rights reserved. No part of this publication may be reproduced, stored in a retrieval system, or transmitted, in any form or by any means, electronic, mechanical, recording, or otherwise, without the prior written permission of the publisher, except in the case of a reviewer, who may quote brief passages in a review to print in a magazine or newspaper, or broadcast on radio or television. In the case of photocopying or other reprographic copying, users must obtain a license from Access Copyright.

Cover and interior design by Articulate Eye
Cover photograph and interior colour photographs by John Perret
Edited by Lesley Reynolds
Proofread by Geri Rowlatt
Scans by St. Solo Computer Graphics

The publisher gratefully acknowledges the support of The Canada Council for the Arts and the Department of Canadian Heritage.

THE CANADA COUNCIL | LE CONSEIL DES ARTS
FOR THE ARTS | DU CANADA
SINCE 1957 | DEPUIS 1957

We acknowledge the financial support of the Government of Canada through the Book Publishing Industry Development Program (BPIDP) for our publishing activities.

Printed in Canada by Friesens

05 06 07 08 09 / 5 4 3 2 1

First published in the United States in 2006 by
Fitzhenry & Whiteside
121 Harvard Avenue, Suite 2
Allston, MA 02134

National Library of Canada Cataloguing in Publication Data

Waiser, W. A.

   Saskatchewan ; a new history / Bill Waiser

   Includes bibliographical references and index.

   ISBN 1-894856-43-0

   1. Saskachewan—History—1905–   I. Title.

FC3511.W325 2005   971.24   C2005-901913-1

Fifth House Ltd.
A Fitzhenry & Whiteside Company
1511, 1800-4 St. SW
Calgary, Alberta T2S 2S5

1-800-387-9776

www.fitzhenry.ca

FOR MARY MILLER,
A DEAR FRIEND WHO EMBRACED SASKATCHEWAN AS HER HOME
AND MADE IT A BETTER PLACE

A MESSAGE FROM THE PRESIDENT
OF THE UNIVERSITY OF SASKATCHEWAN

From the moment Saskatchewan's first government decided that a growing province with a promising future needed a first class university, the University of Saskatchewan has been involved in the life and aspirations of Saskatchewan people. We are proud to have been a sponsor of this book, which captures the spirit, drive, and vision of the people who built our province.

As I read through Professor Waiser's narrative, I was struck anew by three particular themes that seemed to recur throughout our history and, I think, epitomize the Saskatchewan experience.

First, the extraordinary vision and determination of our founders. They believed the future of this vast province was a great one, and they committed themselves to making that vision a reality, despite considerable challenges. As Professor Waiser observes, "If Saskatchewan had any advantage in 1905, it was confidence." I believe that confidence was well-founded then and even more appropriate as we look out on our second century.

Second, the truly diverse population that built Saskatchewan. As a destination for immigrants from a wide array of European and Asian nations, Saskatchewan represented a new life for thousands of people. If they were to succeed, they had to overcome language, cultural, religious, and economic differences. This was clearly not done without struggle, but with continuous progress toward a common goal. Our society today is richer for their efforts.

Finally, I was reminded of the tremendous role Aboriginal people—both First Nations and Métis—played in Saskatchewan's development. Though frequently misunderstood and mistreated, they were determined to find peaceful means of co-existence with those settling around them, including offering assistance to those who knew little about surviving on the harsh prairies. Their efforts were frequently overlooked, in spite of the impact they had on building a province.

With the benefit of 100 years to reflect upon, we can see Saskatchewan has a history of dreaming big, making diversity an advantage, and working together to achieve common goals. This look back is an opportunity to appreciate all we've achieved in our first century, but also a timely reminder of what we can accomplish in the future when we fully embrace the "Saskatchewan spirit."

Peter MacKinnon
President, University of Saskatchewan

A MESSAGE FROM
THE PREMIER OF SASKATCHEWAN

The Government of Saskatchewan is proud to be a sponsor of *Saskatchewan: A New History*. I extend sincere thanks and congratulations to Dr. Bill Waiser and his research team for this significant endeavour.

Saskatchewan's founders had a vision of a land full of opportunity. Through hard work, resourcefulness, and the strength of our people and communities, we have begun to realize this dream. We have beauty overhead and around us, and rich resources under our feet. We have fertile farmlands, bountiful forests, advanced technology, a growing manufacturing sector, and an ever-increasing number of value-added enterprises. We are especially proud of our publicly funded health care system, our education system, and our internationally recognized social programs.

Saskatchewan's motto is "From Many Peoples Strength" and there is no doubt that our people are, indeed, our greatest asset. Our 100th birthday offers a unique opportunity for us to look back with pride on our past accomplishments and to look forward with optimism and confidence in our province's future—a future built upon the solid foundation laid by our Aboriginal peoples and our pioneers, and revitalized by today's youth. As we look toward the future, it is important to remember our rich history. We have weathered some troubled times, but we have built on a legacy of growth, optimism, and achievement by Saskatchewan and her people.

I again congratulate Dr. Waiser for his efforts to document that rich history and place it within the context of the provincial events and issues of the day. It is through projects such as *Saskatchewan: A New History* that we make known our pride of place and tell the world that everyone needs a little more Saskatchewan.

Lorne Calvert
Premier

MESSAGE FROM THE PRESIDENT OF THE CELEBRATE CANADA! COMMITTEE FOR SASKATCHEWAN

The Celebrate Canada! Committee for Saskatchewan is excited to participate in the production of *Saskatchewan: A New History*.

The history contained within this volume is more than simply an interesting collection of facts but rather speaks to the experience of what it means to be from Saskatchewan. The stories and events it relates explain the development of our values, such as respect for diversity, community spirit, volunteerism, and tenaciousness in the face of adversity. As Tommy Douglas once suggested, it is through understanding our successes and our mistakes that we develop the confidence to face the challenges of the times in which we live.

Following the Saskatchewan tradition, this book is a popular history in the best sense of the word. Dr. Bill Waiser provides excellent scholarship written in accessible prose. It will provide a rich legacy, the influence of which will be felt for many years.

Connie McIntyre

Connie McIntyre
President
The Celebrate Canada! Committee for Saskatchewan

ÉBAUCHE – MESSAGE DU COMITÉ DES CÉLÉBRATIONS DU CANADA EN SASKATCHEWAN

Le Comité des célébrations du Canada en Saskatchewan est fier d'appuyer la publication d'un livre intitulé *Saskatchewan: A New History*, qui présente une version révisée de l'histoire de la province.

Bien plus qu'une simple accumulation de faits historiques intéressants, cet ouvrage décrit plutôt l'expérience de vivre en Saskatchewan. Les histoires et les événements qui y sont relatés expliquent l'évolution des valeurs des résidents de la province, telles que le respect de la diversité, la solidarité locale, le bénévolat, et la ténacité dans l'adversité. Conformément à ce que Tommy Douglas a déjà fait observer, c'est le fait de comprendre les succès et les erreurs du passé qui nous donne la confiance de relever les défis du présent.

Dans le respect de la tradition saskatchewanaise, ce livre relate la petite histoire de la province dans le meilleur sens du terme. Ainsi, M. Bill Waiser y présente les résultats d'excellents travaux de recherche dans une prose tout à fait accessible, dont l'héritage aura à son tour marqué l'histoire.

Connie McIntyre

Connie McIntryre,
Présidente
Comité des célébrations du Canada en Saskatchewan

Contents

CHAPTER ONE

THE BANNER PROVINCE

S IR WILFRID WAS LATE. Although Saskatchewan had officially entered Confederation on 1 September 1905, Prime Minister Laurier had chosen to be in Edmonton that day for Alberta's provincial inauguration. The Saskatchewan celebrations would have to wait. It was not the first time that controversy had overshadowed the creation of the province, especially over Ottawa's heavy hand in the process. The road to provincehood had been strewn with delay, acrimony, intrigue, confusion—even betrayal. These irritants, at another time or under different circumstances, might have provoked a new round of western alienation, but any frustration or disappointment in 1905 was effectively checked by the wheat province's ambitious enthusiasm for the future. These were heady days for the upstart Saskatchewan, and nothing—least of all delaying the formal ceremonies for three days—was going to stand in the way of the new province assuming its rightful place in Canada. Its destiny seemed to be limited only by the imagination, and if the mood at the 4 September inauguration party was any indication, anything was possible.

The Regina inauguration committee spent eight thousand dollars getting the "Queen City" ready for the big day. Four grand triumphal arches, adorned with sheaves of wheat and oats and evergreen boughs, were erected along the parade route on South Railway Street. Each was inscribed, in huge block letters, with a simple message: "World's Granary," "North West Forever," "Saskatchewan," and "God Save the King." Flags and bunting graced all public buildings and schools; many had colourful streamers or banners with the words "Prosperity and Progress" or "Peace." The committee also played upon the competitive spirit of Regina citizens by offering prizes for the best decorated residence and private business. Not to be outdone, city council provided free lamps, wire, and electricity to anyone who wanted to illuminate their home or building for the festivities. One of the more popular displays was the window of the Regina Trading Company, which featured an infant Saskatchewan in a baby carriage with the instructions "Watch the Baby Grow."[1]

Visitors began arriving in the city on Sunday, 3 September, many of them on special excursion trains offering discount fares for the event. Those unable to find accommodation were directed by the information bureau to bunkhouses that had been temporarily installed on Market Square. That afternoon in Victoria Park—what future premier Jimmy Gardiner described as "a block

Four grand triumphal arches, adorned with sheaves of wheat and oats and evergreen boughs, were erected along the Regina parade route. SASKATCHEWAN ARCHIVES BOARD R-A4110-2

of raw prairie"[2]—an estimated three thousand people, equivalent to half the population of Regina, attended an open-air church service. Many stayed on into the evening, picnicking to the sound of sacred music from the bandstand. Others joined the thousands of sightseers strolling the decorated city streets, enjoying the fine late summer weather. Above the din could be heard the cry of newsboys hawking a special inauguration edition of the *Regina Leader*. One seller alone sold 450 copies that weekend. An unexpected bonus would be two Monday performances by the Great Floto Shows; billed as the "Circus Beautiful and Mammoth Menagerie," the six-hundred-member carnival added to the party atmosphere.[3]

The Queen's representative, along with several current and former federal and territorial politicians and officials, travelled from Edmonton to Regina by train that same day. Governor General Earl Grey, an avid imperialist now best remembered for donating the trophy for Canadian football supremacy, was visiting western Canada for the first time. Sir Wilfrid, on the other hand, enjoyed a special attachment to the region. Elected to the House of Commons in 1874 and named leader of the opposition in 1887, Laurier had embarked on a campaign-style western tour in 1894 in order to raise his national profile. Two years later in the election that made him Canada's first French Catholic prime minister, he won in Quebec East and Saskatchewan (Prince Albert) at a time when it was possible to run in more than one riding at the same time. Although Laurier decided to represent the Quebec seat, his determination to settle the prairies and thereby complete one of the last great tasks of Confederation had made him one of the west's favourite sons. Not even the controversy over provincehood dulled his star.[4]

Securing provincial status for Saskatchewan had not been easy. When Canada acquired the western interior of British North America in 1870, the federal government intended to administer its vast new empire as little better than a colony. The Red River Resistance, however, forced these plans to be amended. Manitoba entered Confederation in May 1870, mockingly dubbed the "postage-stamp" province because of its size, while the remainder of the region was designated the North-West Territories.[5] It was a phenomenal parcel of land—seven times the original Canada of 1867—stretching from the forty-ninth parallel to the arctic coastline and from present-day northern Ontario and Quebec to the Alaska-Yukon boundary. No other country in the western hemisphere was larger, and only Russia controlled more arctic land.

Canada expected the rich agricultural soil of the prairie parkland to be easily converted into farms for the millions of immigrants expected to pour into the region; indeed, expanding westward promised greatness for the young dominion, whereas failure to do so meant stagnation, if not absorption by the aggressive United States. The federal government consequently wanted to manage and direct the region's settlement and development to ensure that it became an integral part of the emerging transcontinental economy. To prevent any interference with federal plans, Ottawa kept control of all public lands and resources—even in the new province of Manitoba. The 1875 North-West Territories Act also provided for a resident lieutenant-governor at the head of a small, appointed legislative council. The territorial government, based initially at Livingstone, then Battleford, and finally Regina, administered local affairs, but the real power rested with Ottawa and the federal Department of the Interior, which soon acquired a reputation, because of its apparent insensitivity to western concerns, as the department of indifference.

Ottawa's iron grip on the territories slowly began to lessen in the closing decades of the nineteenth century. In 1886, in an effort to quell the widespread discontent underlying the North-West Rebellion, the federal government finally awarded the territories parliamentary representation—a princely four seats in the 215-seat House of Commons. Two years later, the region was given two seats in the Senate, while the legislative council was converted into a legislative assembly of twenty-five elected members. But the real turning point came in October 1897, when Ottawa conferred responsible government on the territories. A territorial premier would now run the affairs of the region on the advice of an executive council or cabinet selected from the ranks of the territorial assembly. Any feeling of independence, though, was tempered by the fact Ottawa continued to hold the purse strings and grudgingly dispensed money to the territories in the form of annual grants.

The first and only territorial leader was the handsome, gentlemanly, forty-year-old Frederick Haultain. English-born but raised in southern Ontario, Haultain had come west to practise law at Fort Macleod in 1884. First elected to the territorial assembly three years later, he quickly emerged as a dominant player, a political gladiator renowned for his debating skills and stubborn sense of purpose. One contemporary likened him to a statesman, not a politician.[6] Haultain would need these qualities in wresting greater control over western affairs from Ottawa, especially better financial arrangements. Faced with thousands of immigrants pouring into the southern prairies in the late 1890s, the territorial government simply did not have enough money to meet the steadily growing service and infrastructure demands. "We are confronted with impossible conditions," Haultain pleaded with Clifford Sifton, the federal minister of the interior.[7] In fact, the funding shortfall was so desperate that a senior Regina official was sent to the Yukon during the Klondike gold rush to try to collect windfall liquor taxes in Dawson City.

Premier Haultain's strategy for securing concessions from the federal government was to adopt a non-partisan approach. Although a Conservative in

Frederick Haultain, the North-West Territories' first and only premier, wanted one large western province. UNIVERSITY OF SASKATCHEWAN ARCHIVES B-360

spirit, he believed that the region could deal most effectively with Ottawa, and avoid alienating whichever federal party was in power, if it spoke with a single, territorial voice. Getting the seemingly distant federal government to listen, however, was difficult at the best of times, and territorial politicians soon concluded that the only way to solve their financial woes was to secure provincial status for the region. Money, not political maturity, spurred the drive for autonomy. In 1900, at the urging of Premier Haultain, the territorial assembly unanimously approved a resolution calling on the new Liberal government to consider terms for provincehood. The following year in Ottawa, Haultain met with his federal counterpart, Liberal leader Sir Wilfrid Laurier, to pursue the matter. In the end, the Laurier government turned down the request as premature. It wanted more statistical information about the recent growth in the region. There was also no consensus in the territories over the number of provinces to be created.[8]

Haultain equated size with influence and steadfastly promoted the idea of one large western province from the international boundary to the fifty-seventh parallel, to be called Buffalo. "One big Province," he argued, "would

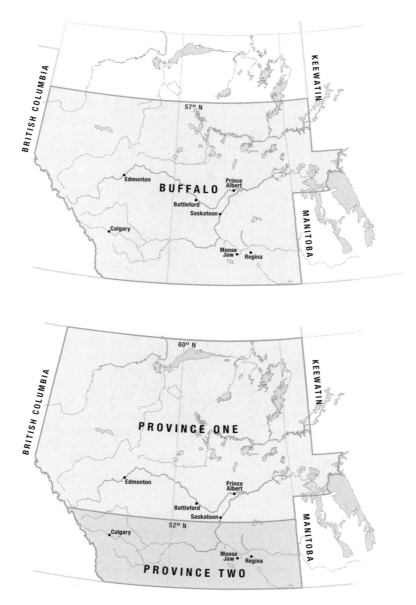

Territorial premier Frederick Haultain wanted one large western province, while Calgary had ambitions to be capital of a southern east-west "cattle" province.

be able to do things no other Province could."⁹ Several other possibilities were put forward. Manitoba premier Rodmond Roblin suggested that his province's western boundary be extended to create two roughly equal provinces between Ontario and British Columbia. Roblin and Haultain publicly debated this idea at Indian Head in December 1901. Saskatchewan senator

T. O. Davis proposed that northern and southern provinces running east-west be established, with capitals in Battleford and Regina respectively. Other variations reflected local identities. In 1882, the federal government had carved four provisional districts—Assiniboia, Saskatchewan, Athabasca, and Alberta—from the southern territories for administrative purposes. Each of these districts now considered itself provincial material. Calgary, in particular, had been calling for provincial status for Alberta as early as 1891.[10]

The Laurier government's procrastination in granting autonomy angered Haultain. He called a territorial election on the issue in 1902 and handily won. He also secured the public support of federal Conservative opposition leader Robert Borden, who called for provincehood during a western speaking tour that same year. Two years later, Haultain returned the favour and actively campaigned for the Conservatives during the 1904 general election. These actions only stiffened the resolve of Prime Minister Laurier. They also turned the autonomy question into a party issue—ironically, something that went against Haultain's philosophy of putting territorial interests before party considerations. But the territorial premier was so focused on achieving provincehood that he could not see the political repercussions of his actions. Western Liberals continued to work with Haultain in the territorial legislature, as if non-partisanship still mattered, but they were now leery of his motives and no longer trusted him.[11]

What eventually ended the standoff over provincehood was the unparalleled success of the federal immigration policy. So many prospective settlers were heading west that the Laurier government could no longer, in good conscience, hold off autonomy for the region. In January 1905, the prime minister invited Haultain to Ottawa, where the territorial leader outlined his vision of one province with full constitutional powers. But when the legislation was introduced by Laurier in the House of Commons on 21 February, Haultain's worst fears were realized. There was not one autonomy bill, but two, creating two north-south provinces, Saskatchewan and Alberta, named from two of the provisional districts. Saskatchewan—an anglicized version of a Cree word for swiftly moving water—was preferred to Assiniboia. Regina and Edmonton were named as temporary capitals, the final decision resting with the new provincial governments. The legislation also gave the federal government continued control over western lands and resources. Even more controversial, though, were the education clauses, which seemed to call for the restoration of separate school privileges dating back to 1875.[12] Publicly, the Laurier government insisted that one large western province would upset the balance of Confederation and that two provinces would satisfy regional aspirations. The greater fear, though, was that one province would give Haultain a tremendous power base, especially given the current rate of western immigration. Somehow his influence had to be minimized. What better way than to cut his fiefdom in half? Two new provinces, not one, guaranteed that Ottawa would not have a serious rival in western Canada.[13]

Instead of recognizing regional peculiarities, the borders of the new provinces were totally arbitrary and reflected little understanding of the geography of the western interior. In fact, Saskatchewan became the only Canadian province with completely artificial boundaries—an upright rectangle with two sides that narrowed from south to north. The sixtieth parallel was chosen as the northern boundary because it was understood to be the northern limit of agriculture. Although it exceeded territorial expectations—Haultain's one-province concept extended only to 57 degrees north—the Laurier government had initially toyed with the idea of setting the boundary at the shores of the Arctic Ocean. The fourth meridian (110 degrees west longitude), the north-south dividing line, was selected to create two provinces of roughly equal size. This interprovincial boundary upset western ranchers because it divided the southern range country. Lloydminster was worse off; straddling the border, the new community was split in two.[14]

At 251,700 square miles (651,903 square kilometres), Saskatchewan was less than half the area of Haultain's one big province and represented only 6.5 per cent of Canada's total area. But it was still huge by most standards. The proposed province was five times larger than the three Canadian maritime provinces and two-and-a-half times the United Kingdom. Even American western states did not measure up. Saskatchewan was three times larger than Minnesota, Nebraska, Oklahoma, or Kansas and only slightly smaller than Texas. These statistics, however, did little to dampen the province's desire for more territory. In 1906, landlocked Saskatchewan wanted its northeastern boundary extended along the Nelson River corridor to provide a port on Hudson Bay. Instead, the federal government moved the northern boundaries of Manitoba, Ontario, and Quebec to Hudson Bay in 1912. Curiously, the enlarged Quebec was bigger than Haultain's one large western province, even bigger than Saskatchewan and Alberta combined, while Ontario was one and two-thirds the size of either one of the new western provinces.[15]

The Laurier government was also proposing provincial status *with a difference*. Under the terms of the 1867 British North America Act, provinces exercised control over the public lands and resources within their boundaries. But this right was denied Manitoba in 1870, and denied Saskatchewan and Alberta in the autonomy bills. Ottawa justified the confiscation—some might argue theft—of this important source of provincial revenue on the grounds that the land was needed to promote immigration and settlement and that provincial control might jeopardize this national endeavour. Besides, as interior minister Clifford Sifton brusquely noted, "The Dominion owns

Twins. *Montreal Daily Star*, 23 February 1905

these lands."[16] One wonders whether Saskatchewan would have discontinued the federal policy of cheap homestead land; provincial control might have resulted in better land management through better understanding of local peculiarities. The federal government attempted to make up for the loss of revenue from lands and resources by awarding the new provinces generous subsidies based on population. Haultain, however, wanted no part of the compensation package and demanded the same rights as other Canadian provinces. He would be gamely supported by opposition leader Robert Borden, who tried to embarrass the Liberals by reminding them of their strong provincial rights stand in the past.[17]

The other contentious feature of the autonomy bills was the education clauses. The 1875 North-West Territories Act allowed the religious minority in any district to establish a separate school and support it through self-assessment. This system was formalized in 1884 with the establishment of a territorial Board of Education with distinct Roman Catholic and Protestant sections responsible for the supervision of their own schools. Then, in 1892, religious control of schools was discontinued in favour of a single, government-run Council of Public Instruction (replaced by a Department of Education in 1901). These modifications reflected a popular movement in the west toward secular education spearheaded by the largely Protestant population. But in the draft bills, the ambiguous phrase "existing system" suggested that Laurier wanted to restore the old territorial dual school system. Whether the prime minister realized what he was doing is debatable, but it is known that he was under incredible pressure from the Catholic hierarchy to avoid a repetition of the 1890 Manitoba schools legislation which had abolished state-supported denominational schools. The creation of Saskatchewan and Alberta gave him an unprecedented opportunity to secure legislative protection for Catholic minority rights, and the temptation seems to have been too great.[18]

The autonomy bills called for the entry of Saskatchewan and Alberta into Confederation on 1 July 1905, appropriately Canada's birthday, but the education provisions provoked a furor both within the government and on the opposition benches. Clifford Sifton, the pugnacious minister of the interior and ardent exponent of public schools, resigned without hesitation. Other cabinet ministers threatened to follow. Smelling blood, the Conservative opposition portrayed the legislation as a blatant invasion of provincial jurisdiction. Some even hinted at a papist conspiracy. Faced with a spiralling crisis that threatened to tear apart the administration and arouse latent Ontario-Quebec animosities, Prime Minister Laurier unceremoniously backed down and allowed a redrafting of the offending clauses to bring them in line with current practice in the territories. The damage, though, had been done. When Quebec nationalists, for example, learned of the prime minister's reversal, they countered by trying to have French recognized as an official language in the new provinces.[19]

The acrimony over the wording of the education clauses precipitated the longest debate in Canadian parliamentary history. Instead of a sense of accomplishment and spirit of celebration, the date of entry for the new provinces had to be postponed to 1 September because the bills did not receive royal assent until 20 July, a full five months after they had been tabled. The controversy also deflected attention away from the fact that Saskatchewan and Alberta were not to become full partners in Confederation. They, along with neighbouring Manitoba, were treated differently—unequally. What also got lost during the bitter debate was that the schools question was largely a non-issue in Saskatchewan. It was regarded as a problem of an older Canada, not the new west. Farmers, according to one commentator, were more interested in what they were going to seed that spring.[20] Sadly, the autonomy bill fiasco had unleashed the twin demons of religion and language, and future Saskatchewan governments would not escape them.[21]

Once the autonomy bills became law, the Liberal party turned its attention to securing power in Saskatchewan and displacing Haultain. This behind-the-scenes intrigue should have been risky, if not traitorous, given the territorial premier's defining role in the struggle for autonomy; however, Haultain's apparent assumption that the premiership of the province was his for the taking was naive at best. His spirited opposition to the legislation—even though he was defending the interests of western Canada—had made him the enemy of the Liberal party. Prime Minister Laurier, keenly aware of his adversary's stature, bypassed Haultain as premier or lieutenant-governor when he threatened to challenge the constitutionality of the autonomy terms in the courts.[22] As one western historian remarked, "The territorial premier was almost as much of an embarrassment to Laurier and his cabinet as the Métis leader [Louis Riel] to [Prime Minister J. A.] Macdonald and the Conservatives."[23]

While Haultain continued to fume about the provincial arrangements, Saskatchewan Liberals abandoned any pretense of non-partisanship and selected a leader at a convention in Regina in mid-August 1905. There was only one candidate: thirty-seven-year-old Walter Scott. Rakish in appearance and sporting a moustache characteristic of his generation, the Ontario-born Scott had arrived in Regina in 1886 to pursue a career in journalism and soon owned several Liberal newspapers. His business acumen was matched by a surprising victory at the polls in the federal constituency of Assiniboia West in 1900. Scott was initially an ally of Haultain and his one-province concept, but came to embrace the Liberal government's plans for the new provinces. When it came time to find a provincial leader and possible future premier for Saskatchewan, he was plucked from the House of Commons' backbenches. Scott was a logical choice for the job. Not only politically astute, thanks to his apprenticeship in Ottawa, he was a natural leader who had an uncanny ability to read the mood of the province in its early years. At the convention, the affable Scott predicted that Saskatchewan would be the "banner province of Canada."[24]

Regina's inauguration committee, headed by Mayor H. W. Laird, shared this outlook and had been meeting twice a week since May to prepare for Saskatchewan's formal entry into Confederation. It promised "as much to please the eye and the ear as well as to arouse the sentiment ... as can ... be crammed into one day."[25] Even though the province technically came into existence on Friday, 1 September 1905, the celebration would not be held until the following Monday to enable the governor general and the prime minister to come from the ceremonies in neighbouring Alberta. It was never officially explained why they chose Edmonton over Regina. Perhaps Laurier was troubled by the grumbling over the selection of Edmonton as the temporary

The day's program began with hundreds of schoolchildren marching through downtown Regina to Victoria Park. ONTARIO ARCHIVES 6184 S8906

capital of Alberta, especially among Calgary Conservatives such as future prime minister R. B. Bennett, and sought to bolster Liberal fortunes by going to Alberta first. He could also have been doing a political favour for his new minister of the interior and the MP for Edmonton, the feisty Frank Oliver. Then again, the prime minister might have assumed that slighting Regina would be less damaging because of Liberal strength in the new province. Whatever the reason, it was a fortuitous delay. Monday, 4 September was the Labour Day holiday, and more people were probably able to attend the ceremonies.

A brilliant, cloudless Monday morning, with only a light breeze, promised a perfect day for the festivities. It would be needed. The program, in the words of one commentator, "demanded true pioneer stamina."[26] At precisely 9 A.M., hundreds of schoolchildren, marching four abreast, circled downtown Regina in a long procession before sweeping into Victoria Park. Once they had formed up in neat rows before the bandstand, the governor general and prime minister arrived in separate carriages escorted by the Royal Northwest Mounted Police (RNWMP). The girls, wearing white, and the boys, sporting blue caps and sashes, then sang several patriotic songs while waving small Union Jack flags. Lady Evelyn Grey was so overwhelmed by the performance that "The Maple Leaf Forever" was sung again so she could take a photograph with her own camera. Her father, the governor general, delivered a solemn, at times wooden, address, reminding the children that they had to live up to Regina's namesake, the recently deceased Queen Victoria. Sir Wilfrid, who seemed to know just the right thing to say on such occasions, told the children he wished he could change places with them.[27]

The official party was then whisked away to watch the general parade from a special viewing stand erected on South Railway Street. The procession, interspersed with local bands, had been arranged to demonstrate "the evolution of Regina from darkness to light." A group of mounted Indians from nearby reserves, including eighty-nine-year-old Chief Piapot, leader of the southern Cree bands, led the way. The paint and feathers of their traditional outfits created quite a stir. They were trailed by members of Regina's Old Timers' Association, on horseback and in wagons, waving to the estimated ten thousand spectators. Next came "Our Fair Dominion," a boat-shaped float bearing Miss Canada and the nine provinces, all represented by local girls and women. Saskatchewan was portrayed by eight-year-old Dorothy Scott, coincidentally the adopted daughter of the new provincial Liberal leader. A long row of carriages followed, conveying former members of the territorial assembly and the House of Commons, as well as the mayor,

Governor General Earl Grey delivered a solemn address about Canadian citizenship to the hundreds of children gathered in Victoria Park. SASKATCHEWAN ARCHIVES BOARD R-B1030

A group of mounted Indians, headed by Chief Piapot, led the inauguration parade.
SASKATCHEWAN ARCHIVES BOARD R-A4131

aldermen, and other Regina civic officials. Among them was the elderly
David Laird, the first resident lieutenant-governor of the North-West
Territories in the late 1870s, and Sir George French, the first commissioner of
the North-West Mounted Police (NWMP). The end of the parade featured
Labour Day floats, a procession of recent immigrants representing different
nationalities, and, perhaps fittingly, an assortment of animals and performers from the touring Floto circus. Some were scandalized by this late
addition to the program, claiming it lowered the dignity of the occasion, but
the large crowd roared its approval as a string of elephants strode down
South Railway.[28]

No sooner had the last note been played by the Wolseley Silver Band
than the dignitaries were on the move again, this time to the exhibition
grounds for the swearing-in of Saskatchewan's first lieutenant-governor,
Amédée-Emmanuel Forget. Hundreds of spectators followed on foot or in
wagons or carriages, while thousands more took advantage of the fifteen-
minute train service provided by the Canadian Pacific Railway (CPR). Not
even a controversial fifty-cent admission fee discouraged attendance. The
crowd quickly filled the enlarged grandstand and spilled out around the
arena, where the viceregal party was treated to a special march-past by 200
mounted policemen and the 328 members of the 90th Regiment of Winnipeg,
more popularly known as the "Little Black Devils," who had fought in the
North-West Rebellion. Lord Grey's group, along with a number of special
guests, then made their way to a newly constructed pavilion for the formal

inauguration ceremony. In the distance, as far as the horizon, were fields of ripening grain.

The proceedings opened with an official welcome from the city. The governor general responded that Saskatchewan seemed "destined to become the happy and prosperous home of millions of Britons," all the more so since it was located in the "centre of a vast wheat belt." These sentiments were echoed in the congratulatory telegrams he read from the King and the British government. Forget was then called forward to be presented with his commission and administered his oath of office. It took only minutes to realize what the former territorial government had been actively seeking for the past five years. But there was little time for reflection, thanks to the booming of the 90th's guns and the shouting of three thunderous cheers through the immense crowd. The Quebec-born Forget seemed flattered by the honour and, after acknowledging the support of his wife, Henriette, spoke fondly of his first days in the North-West, almost three decades earlier. He was certainly well qualified for the position, having served as lieutenant-governor for the territories since 1898, but his most important attribute was that he was a Liberal. One of his first official duties would be to appoint someone as premier until an election could be called.[29]

Somewhat surprisingly, neither Haultain nor Laurier, the two men who had sparred over the creation of Saskatchewan, spoke at the outdoor ceremony. Haultain was never asked; nor did anyone publicly recognize his

Indians from nearby reserves joined hundreds of other visitors, many brought by special train, for the day's festivities. SASKATCHEWAN ARCHIVES BOARD R-A2746

A. E. Forget (centre, facing right) was sworn in as Saskatchewan's first lieutenant-governor at a special ceremony at Regina's exhibition grounds. SASKATCHEWAN ARCHIVES BOARD R-B1096

distinguished territorial career, even though his role in securing province-hood for Saskatchewan and Alberta effectively made him a father of Confederation. His shabby treatment that morning has been called "the big-gest political snub" in Canadian history.[30] It certainly signalled how the west's first and only territorial premier would be treated in the days ahead. Sir Wilfrid had originally been scheduled to speak at Forget's installation, but returned from Edmonton nursing a hoarse voice. At his request, he was moved to the luncheon program, where he would not have to shout to be heard. But the huge audience wanted to hear the noted orator and started to shout "Laurier, Laurier" at the end of Forget's remarks. The prime minister ignored the calls for as long as he could, but eventually stepped forward to the delight of the crowd. "Fellow citizens, citizens of the province of Saskatchewan," he announced jokingly, "if we pride ourselves upon anything we citizens of a British country, it is respect for the law and the law is that I am not to speak at this time." A ripple of laughter went through the spectators and then they began to disperse.[31]

It was well past noon when the formal inauguration ceremony ended, but the day's program offered much more. The women in the official party left for Government House, the residence of the lieutenant-governor, while the men headed to a civic luncheon at Regina's city hall. After the meal, Lord

Grey, in an expansive mood possibly because of the wine, speculated whether "at this very moment His Majesty is examining with pride and admiration the new leaves added to his maple crown." An equally effusive Laurier felt "a sense of pride thrilling through [my] whole body." The creation of the new provinces, the prime minister insisted, marked the coming of age of the dominion. Even former lieutenant-governor David Laird got caught up in the moment and boldly predicted there would soon be twenty-five to thirty million people in the great west. One can only wonder, though, what Haultain thought, for once again he was not called upon, but listened and applauded from his seat. Mayor Laird would later claim he turned down the invitation to make a toast and had no one to blame for being ignored but himself. Haultain, for his part, never spoke publicly about the inauguration.[32]

The afternoon sports program offered a choice between an equestrian exhibition or a lacrosse game between Regina and Brandon. Both events attracted large holiday crowds, despite competition from the visiting circus. At the exhibition grounds, sixteen mounties performed the famed musical ride to the repeated applause of the appreciative spectators, none more vocal than the governor general. The riders then doffed their tunics and played an amusing game of push soccer until one of the horses put its hoof through the

The official party spent the afternoon watching a sports program at the Regina exhibition grounds: from left to right, Wilfrid Laurier (1), Lady Grey (3), Earl Grey (4), Lady Laurier (5), and A. E. Forget (6). SASKATCHEWAN ARCHIVES BOARD R-B1095

ball. After the supper break, people gathered again at Victoria Park for a spectacular fireworks display that lit the night sky over Regina; estimates of the crowd ranged from five to ten thousand. Many then made their way along downtown city streets, marvelling at the illuminated homes and businesses and trees and ornamental gardens festooned with electric lights. Lord and Lady Grey, meanwhile, served as hosts for the inaugural ball at the new Auditorium Rink, which had been transformed into a grand salon. Bunting and flags, interspersed with sheaves of wheat and evergreen boughs, hid the rafters, while hundreds of lights brightened even the darkest corner of the cavernous structure. In keeping with the spirit of the day, admission was open to the public at a prohibitive five dollars per couple, but only invited guests were formally received, among them Miss Jessie Perry, the daughter of the RNWMP commissioner, who was making her debut. The dance was opened by the viceregal party and, except for a break for midnight lunch, continued until well past two when the last of the weary revellers said their goodbyes.[33]

As the official site for the provincial inauguration, Regina garnered most of the attention. But Moose Jaw, a CPR divisional point a mere forty miles to the west, also sponsored a children's parade followed by a rousing civic ceremony that morning. It was readily apparent from the Moose Jaw speeches, however, that the celebration had more to do with staking the city's claim to be the provincial capital—something that still had to be decided. Saskatoon, Regina's upstart rival to the north, also coveted the prize. The local paper, the *Phoenix*, made only passing mention of the Regina program—except to criticize it—preferring instead to trumpet Saskatoon's bright future as the province's capital. Press coverage in other parts of the country was mixed at best. The *Winnipeg Tribune* reproduced a *Brantford Expositor* article that mistakenly called Saskatchewan "Assiniboia," while the *Edmonton Evening Journal* story, perhaps foreshadowing the rivalry between the new provinces, carried a glaring typographical error—"Faskatchewan"—in the opening sentence. Further afield, the *Toronto Globe* warmly welcomed Saskatchewan to the Confederation family. The *Montreal Gazette* claimed the ceremonies "marked an epoch in the annals of the West," but then went on to charge that the muzzling of Haultain had marred an otherwise magnificent event.[34]

These comments, however intended, really made little difference to the new province's future in 1905. It was up to Saskatchewan—and Saskatchewan alone—to find its way. It had to unite the dispersed settlements, different peoples, and diverse regions into a single political entity. It had to generate and promote a provincial consciousness. And it had to find its own distinctive voice. These challenges would not be easy. The new province was essentially an artificial creation; its boundaries had nothing to do with the west's geography, let alone its history. But if Saskatchewan had any advantage in 1905, it was confidence. The new province not only believed it had a great future, but more importantly it could decide its own future.[35] Prime Minister Laurier learned this first-hand on the train ride to Regina for the ceremonies. During an informal conversation with some of the passengers about the new century, one man maintained that Saskatchewan would lead the way. "I stand for Saskatchewan," he repeatedly declared. When Sir Wilfrid reminded him that Ontario and Quebec were powerful provinces, the man insisted that Saskatchewan was destined to be the first province in Confederation. "After that," Sir Wilfrid explained to the inauguration luncheon, "there was nothing for me to do but to take a back seat."[36]

Regina spent eight thousand dollars on the provincial inauguration, including the production of a souvenir program. UNIVERSITY OF SASKATCHEWAN SPECIAL COLLECTIONS

CHAPTER TWO

ANOTHER COUNTRY ALTOGETHER

ONE OF THE HIGHLIGHTS of the Regina inauguration ceremonies was the mounted Indians, proudly decorated in traditional dress, riding at the head of the parade. Their placement that morning, however, had nothing to do with honour or status. Instead, they symbolized a dark, pre-modern past that the new province of Saskatchewan wanted to put behind it. "There they were," lampooned the *Moose Jaw Times*, "the remnants of a departing race ... peoples of an inferior civilization ... a motley crowd ... the true type of ... Indian as he is found today."[1] This conviction that First Nations had no place in the province's future was nowhere more evident than in the circumstances behind the signing of Treaty 10 in northern Saskatchewan. For more than two decades, the Indians of the region had actively sought a treaty with the Crown, but it was only after the creation of the province that the Canadian government hurriedly moved to extinguish Aboriginal title in areas not covered by earlier treaties. In reaching this agreement, federal representatives promised to protect the livelihood of the Indians and provide help in times of need. These obligations, though, were secondary to securing unrestricted access to the land and its resources in order to facilitate future development. If Saskatchewan was to fulfill its great destiny, Indians, like those in the inauguration parade, were expected to ride off into oblivion and never be heard from again.

When territorial premier Frederick Haultain began pushing for autonomy, he argued that one large province, brimming with resources, would best guarantee the west's future prosperity. "We do not want a province made up of one big wheat field, or one big cattle ranch and coal mine," he insisted. "We want wheat fields, cattle ranches, and coal mines, and every other thing that goes to make up a big, rich country."[2] Although Haultain's dream was not realized in 1905, the new province was certainly endowed with a diverse land base—ranging from open subarctic woodland and boreal forest in the north to aspen parkland and mixed-grass prairie in the south. In fact, by setting the northern boundary at the sixtieth parallel—well beyond that advocated by Haultain—the geographical centre of Saskatchewan was about one hundred miles north of Prince Albert, well into the boreal forest. It was seven hundred miles from Regina to the top of the province, double the distance from Regina to Winnipeg.

The northern half of the new province—generally considered the region north of an east-west line from Cumberland House to Meadow Lake—owed its creation to the same ice sheets that had deposited glacial till, sometimes in a thick mantle, on the southern plains ten to twelve thousand years ago. But in the north, the glaciers scoured the underlying bedrock, gouging out basins to produce a topography more in keeping with the area north of Lake Superior. Saskatchewan's shield country is a subdued landscape, characterized by a low, rolling relief, a heavy mixed-wood forest cover, and thousands of water bodies. There are fifteen lakes larger than 150 square miles in the region, including Reindeer (2,500 square miles) and Athasbasca (3,000 square miles), on the east and west side, respectively. Alberta has only three lakes of comparable size.

A provincial cabinet minister once called northern Saskatchewan "another country altogether."[3] But for the Woodland Cree and the Chipewyan, also known as the Dene, who had lived in the region for millennia, it was home. These hunter-gatherer societies enjoyed a diverse subsistence, moving from place to place depending on the season and the availability of resources. They were not aimless wanderers, but knew the land and its ecology intimately and followed a deliberate annual migration pattern. In the late spring, they gathered at favourite camping spots along lakes or rivers, where they fished, hunted large game animals, and harvested berries and roots throughout the

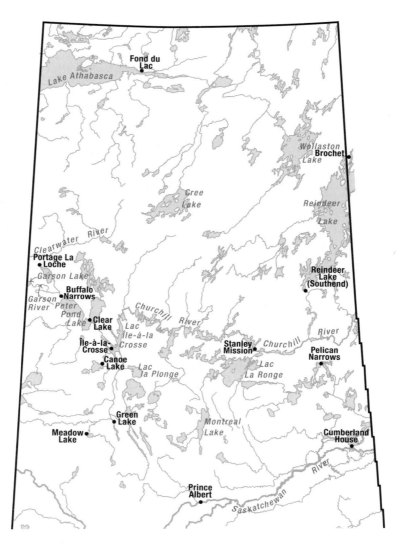

Many of Saskatchewan's earliest northern communities had fur trade beginnings.

summer. After the fall migration of waterfowl, they broke into smaller groups and departed for their winter territories. At first, they would hunt, trap, and put up provisions, but with the onset of cold weather, activity became severely restricted until the early spring when hunting and trapping would resume. Following breakup, they would rendezvous once again on the lakes and rivers.

This flexibility enabled the Cree and Dene to take advantage of the coming of the European fur trade. In the late seventeenth and early eighteenth centuries, the English-controlled Hudson's Bay Company (HBC) established posts

Women drying fish, a staple of the Aboriginal diet in northern Saskatchewan. SASKATCHEWAN ARCHIVES BOARD S-B9036

along the shores of Hudson and James bays and encouraged the interior Indians to come and trade with them. The French countered by pushing the St. Lawrence fur trade northwest beyond the Great Lakes, across present-day Manitoba to the North Saskatchewan River by the 1750s. The Cree and Dene, who generally lived south and north of the Churchill River, respectively, used their location to assume the lucrative middleman's role and expand their trapping and trading territories. But this dominant role came to an end in the late eighteenth century when the new Montreal-based Northwest Company decided to take the fur trade directly to the trapping Indians and extend its operations across the continent to the Pacific coast. To meet this challenge, the HBC, which had operated from bayside posts for over a century, had little alternative but to move inland as well.

This bitter struggle for commercial supremacy was played out along the province's two great rivers, the Churchill (or English) and the Saskatchewan. The HBC's first inland post (and Saskatchewan's oldest, continuously occupied settlement) was Cumberland House, located just inside the province's eastern boundary. Established by Samuel Hearne in 1774, the post heralded the beginning of a concerted effort by the HBC to secure direct access to interior Indians and their trapping areas. The Northwest Company, meanwhile, used Portage La Loche or Methye Portage, along the province's western boundary, to break out into the fur-rich Athabasca country in the late 1770s. Over the next few decades, a series of competing posts, often within view of one another, was established along the Saskatchewan and Churchill river corridors.

At first, rival traders fought ruthlessly to acquire the furs of local Indians. But as the trade advanced further inland and supply lines were stretched to their limit, the feeding of the posts and the annual fur brigades going in and out of the region assumed greater importance. The Saskatchewan posts consequently acted as a kind of pantry for the fur trade as local Indians were encouraged to bring in country provisions in exchange for trade items. Most of this food was secured in traditional hunting areas, including the millions of sloughs or "prairie potholes" in the parkland. Then, as now, these highly productive wetlands supported 50 to 80 per cent of the North American waterfowl population in any given year.

In 1821, the intense, at times violent, fur-trade rivalry came to an end with the amalgamation of the Hudson's Bay and Northwest companies. Thrift replaced the chaotic practices of the previous half century, and the number of posts was dramatically reduced to a few strategically located centres. All of the major settlements of northern Saskatchewan at this time—Cumberland House, Reindeer Lake (Southend), Lac La Ronge, Pelican Narrows, Green Lake, Île-à-la-Crosse, Buffalo Narrows, La Loche, Fond du Lac—began as fur-trade communities. Local Indian bands regularly visited these posts to obtain trade goods that had now become necessities, such as guns and ammunition, and food items to supplement their diet. Some, known as the

Loading York boats at the Hudson's Bay Company's Cumberland House in 1899. LIBRARY AND ARCHIVES CANADA PA053608

homeguard, even chose to stay in the vicinity year-round, providing furs and provisions in exchange for ongoing support. Many of the people who lived and worked at these communities were mixed-blood in origin, the result of decades of Indian-trader relationships. Collectively called Métis (from the French *métissage*) or half-breed, they were an invaluable source of labour—what one HBC official described as "very useful hands." They prepared the furs for shipment, manned the York boats and canoes, netted fish and hunted small game, tended the gardens, collected firewood, and performed other jobs around the post. Without them, the fur-trade system would not have worked so efficiently.[4]

Missionaries followed in the wake of the traders. Indeed, the mid-nineteenth-century rivalry between the Anglican and Roman Catholic churches was reminiscent of the old fur-trade wars. Believing they would have a better chance of converting Indian and Métis peoples to their faith by arriving first on the scene, the Anglicans sent Henry Budd, the first Native minister in western Canada, to establish a mission at Cumberland House in 1840. Five years later, James Settee, another ordained Native, founded a Church of England mission at the west end of Lac La Ronge; it was later relocated to Stanley Mission on the Churchill River, a region better suited for agriculture. The building of Holy Trinity Church at Stanley between 1854 and 1860—the oldest still-extant structure in Saskatchewan—led to the Anglican domination of the northeastern side of the province. Although the Gothic Revival church stands alone today on the north bank of the Churchill River, it was once the focal point of a large missionary complex, including a school, parsonage, barn, storeroom, warehouse, and gristmill.

The northwestern side of the province, on the other hand, was essentially a Roman Catholic stronghold. Oblates Louis Laflèche and Alexandre Taché established the St. Jean Baptiste mission at Île-à-la-Crosse in 1846, and within two decades mass was being celebrated throughout the area from Portage La Loche to Fond du Lac. Over the next half century, the Île-à-la-Crosse mission became known as the "Bethlehem of the North," especially with the arrival of the Grey Nuns of Montreal in 1860 and the building of a convent, orphanage, and school. It was also called the "nursery of bishops" because four future bishops (Laflèche, Taché, Grandin, and Faraud) did missionary work there.[5]

By the 1870s, a distinct society based on hunting and trapping and centred in water-based communities with a post and mission, had taken shape in northern Saskatchewan. It was largely Aboriginal in makeup and had its own unique rhythm of life. It was also separated from the prairie south. The major trade route ran east-west from Cumberland House up along the Churchill River through Île-à-la-Crosse and Portage La Loche to Fort

Aboriginal women with children gathered before Holy Trinity Church at Stanley Mission.
SASKATCHEWAN ARCHIVES BOARD S-B590

Chipewyan and the Mackenzie River. In fact, the region's isolation would become more pronounced in the early 1880s, when the new Canadian Pacific Railway, which was supposed to follow a northwesterly route through the parkland to the Pacific, was built directly west from Winnipeg through Regina and Calgary. This decision, one of the most controversial in western Canadian history, completely changed the axis of development in the region by focusing attention on the southern prairies—the North-West effectively became the west.[6] In the process, the future province of Saskatchewan became associated in Canadian minds with the flat, treeless prairie.

The rerouting of the transcontinental railway also coincided with a fundamental change in the old northern transportation system. In the mid-1880s, the HBC abandoned the century-old Portage La Loche route to the Mackenzie Basin in favour of accessing the region from Edmonton. It also cut a new overland supply route north from Prince Albert to Montreal Lake—thereby bypassing Cumberland House—in anticipation of the arrival of the Qu'Appelle, Long Lake, and Saskatchewan Railway in Prince Albert in 1890.[7] The railway and freight trail allowed local entrepreneurs to exploit the resources of the nearby boreal forest more intensively. By 1900, several hundred thousand pounds of fish were taken annually from northern lakes and exported to American markets. Lumbering experienced phenomenal growth as well. Prince Albert's sawmills supplied an increasing share of the western Canadian lumber market—16 per cent in 1904—as their winter cutting operations steadily pushed the timber frontier northward through the virgin white spruce stands. Scores of independent traders, in response to rising fur prices, also invaded the region. The greatest challenge to the HBC came from the Paris-based Revillon Frères, which opened a district post in Prince Albert in 1901 and established a number of competing posts throughout the north over the next three years.[7]

These outside forces posed a direct threat to the Aboriginal peoples of the region and their traditional lifestyle. Securing formal protection from the Canadian government, though, proved elusive. As early as February 1879, faced with depleted fur and game resources, the Indians of Stanley Mission, Lac La Ronge, and Pelican Narrows had asked the lieutenant-governor of the North-West Territories for a treaty. If the "Government [were to] witness the sights I have witnessed," implored the priest at Stanley Mission, "you would at once respond to their feeble petition."[8] Ottawa ignored the plea, beyond providing some ammunition and twine. The matter resurfaced four years later when the Île-à-la-Crosse Indians complained about surveyors investigating a possible route for a Hudson Bay railway through the region. This time, federal officials actually calculated what it would cost to conclude a northern treaty in order to avoid any interference with the project. But when the railway scheme collapsed in the late 1880s the treaty request was shelved with it—even though local missionaries reported the condition of people in several areas to be "wretched."[9]

Federal reluctance to offer a new northern treaty largely came down to dollars and cents. Between 1871 and 1877, the Canadian government, acting on behalf of the Crown, had negotiated seven numbered treaties with the First Nations of western Canada to prepare the way for commercial agriculture. Treaties 2 (1871), 4 (1874), 5 (1875), and 6 (1876) included territory in the future province of Saskatchewan. But by the mid-1880s the expected rush of settlers to the prairies had not materialized and Ottawa saw no need to extend the treaty process to northern Indians, especially when they occupied land of limited agricultural value. The federal government had also come to resent its existing treaty obligations, in particular the cost of feeding starving Indians following the destruction of the buffalo in the late 1870s, and balked at assuming additional duties. Many even questioned why money should be spent to keep a dying race alive. Canadian Indian policy consequently entered a new phase—what has been termed "best left as Indians"—whereby non-treaty Indians were encouraged to pursue their traditional lifestyle, without government assistance, for as long as possible. The alternative, Ottawa

Prince Albert's mills fed the growing western demand for lumber in the early twentieth century.
SASKATCHEWAN ARCHIVES BOARD S-B11880

believed, was to create a growing class of pampered idlers, a drain on the Canadian economy.[10]

The Indians did not relent in their quest for a northern treaty. As their condition steadily worsened through the 1890s, because of growing competition for the region's resources, northern First Nations called for the same kind of economic assistance that fell to treaty bands. Local missionaries supported these demands, as did the HBC, which had traditionally provided relief in time of need but was now anxious to divest itself of this growing responsibility. Ottawa, however, was reluctant to assume this role and acted only when it was in the government's interest to do so.

Such was the case in February 1889 when federal negotiators were dispatched to deal with the Montreal and Lac La Ronge Indians whose forested land was coveted by the voracious lumber industry. Even then, the Woodland Cree were not offered a separate agreement in keeping with their particular situation, but hurriedly encouraged to sign an adhesion to Treaty 6 (1876)—an agreement worked out at another time under different circumstances. Nor did the adhesion territory include other northern bands in need of help, but was deliberately confined to the area immediately north of Prince Albert. Ten years later, during the Klondike Gold Rush, the Canadian government negotiated

Treaty 8 (1899) after Indians blockaded the so-called "back door" route to the goldfields through their traditional lands in northern Alberta and British Columbia. Part of the treaty territory included Lake Athabasca in present-day northwestern Saskatchewan. A request from the Île-à-la-Crosse Indians to be included in the treaty deliberations was turned down.[11]

Treaty 8 placed the Indians of northern Saskatchewan in the anomalous position of being outside treaty—and they did not like it. Bishop Émile Pascal of Île-à-la-Crosse told a government official that it "makes them feel that they are being treated differently."[12] The logical solution would have been to continue the treaty process and work out an agreement with those bands living in the Hudson Bay drainage basin between treaties 5, 6, and 8. Besides, there was now an additional reason to act. In 1902, the Métis of Île-à-la-Crosse and Portage La Loche, destitute from several poor harvests and the loss of the main HBC trade route, petitioned the government for assistance. They qualified for what was known as scrip. First conceived by the Canadian government in 1879, scrip was a form of land grant, much like a promissory note, designed to extinguish any special land rights the Métis may have enjoyed because of their Aboriginal heritage. Claims were initially quite restricted, but by the beginning of the twentieth century people of mixed ancestry born in the territories between 1870 and 1885 were eligible. They had the option of taking scrip in one of two forms: a $240 certificate that could be redeemed for land or a certificate for 240 acres of dominion land in areas still open to homesteading. Those who chose land scrip over money scrip would have to leave the region to take up their homestead land; they were required to report in person to a Dominion Lands office to have their scrip coupon converted into land. The matter was further complicated by the fact that the government allowed people of mixed ancestry to elect whether they would take scrip or enter treaty as Indians. In other words, they had to choose an ethnicity—not an easy decision in a region where there was significant intermingling between the Indian and mixed-blood populations. Any decision was considered final.[13]

The government once again estimated what it would cost to sponsor a treaty and scrip commission, including the annuity payments, based on the 1901 census for the region. But like a decade earlier, it never took the next step. "The Indians and Halfbreeds," explained Indian Commissioner David Laird in 1904, "are better left to their hunting and fishing as a means of making a livelihood ... the matter [of a treaty] ... may very well stand over for the present." Only the resolution of the autonomy question in the territories or "an inrush of whites," reasoned Laird, would necessitate a treaty "without delay."[14] That time finally arrived in September 1905 with the creation of Saskatchewan and Alberta and the setting of their northern boundaries at the sixtieth parallel. There was now a need, if not an urgency, to extinguish all Aboriginal title in the new provinces in order to remove any obstacles to future development; indeed, the Laurier government deemed a treaty agreement to be in the "public interest." The question that dogged the federal Department of Indian Affairs, though, was how to proceed. One possibility was simply to extend Treaty 8 into Saskatchewan; after all, the northwestern corner of the province was already part of the treaty territory and Indians in the Île-à-la-Crosse area were familiar with its terms. Another proposal called for a new northern treaty that would include not only northern Saskatchewan, but eventually extend eastward into present-day northern Manitoba and northwestern Ontario. It was also suggested that the terms of any new treaty should deliberately exclude any form of agricultural assistance, since it was assumed that the Indians in the unceded territory lived largely by hunting and fishing; in this way, the financial obligations of the federal government would be reduced. Not surprisingly, the interests, let alone the wishes, of the affected Indians were never considered.[15]

It was not until 20 July 1906—more than a quarter century after the first Indian petition—that the Canadian government formally approved the terms for Treaty 10. A separate agreement would cover roughly eighty-six thousand square miles of shield country in northern Saskatchewan and a triangular wedge of adjoining land in east-central Alberta. The treaty included the standard gifts and annuities, as well as the option of living on reserve (based on the formula of one square mile for each family of five) or taking individual parcels of 160 acres (known as severalty). Schooling and agricultural assistance were to be provided only to the extent the government deemed "necessary" or "advisable," but were never precisely defined. Despite such vagueness, the treaty was not as tightfisted as originally contemplated and probably reflected the belief that the terms had to closely parallel those of Treaty 8 or it would have been rejected.[16]

The task of heading the treaty party fell to forty-four-year-old James McKenna, who had joined Indian Affairs in 1887 as private secretary to former Conservative prime minister John A. Macdonald. McKenna had been one of the Treaty 8 commissioners in 1899 and served on scrip commissions in 1900–02; consequently, he was no stranger to northern travel or working with Aboriginal peoples. Because of the lateness of his appointment, he had little time to organize the expedition and left for Saskatchewan almost immediately—without a formal treaty document! Working from an amended copy of Treaty 8, McKenna personally wrote out the text of the new treaty on fourteen pages of legal-size paper. The treaty medals and flags did not reach him until he was about to leave Winnipeg for Prince Albert. McKenna was to be assisted in the field by Superintendent J. V. Begin of the RNWMP and

Two young Indian men in the Waterhen Lake area, 1909. SASKATCHEWAN ARCHIVES BOARD S-B9035

Bishop Pascal, a revered Catholic leader. The mountie's presence was largely symbolic, but Pascal and other missionaries stationed in the region were expected to use their considerable influence to convince the Indians to take treaty. McKenna also depended heavily on the experience of the HBC, which had been contracted to transport the treaty party. Even then, the trip was "rather a difficult one" because of low water levels and stormy weather. Huge waves swamped the party's boats during the crossing of Buffalo Lake, resulting in the loss of supplies and baggage, including a good deal of money carried by the more than two dozen scrip buyers accompanying McKenna.[17]

The treaty commission intended to hold its first meeting at Portage La Loche on 3 September 1906—almost a year to the day after Saskatchewan's inauguration ceremonies—and then work its way back eastward. But by the time McKenna reached Île-à-la-Crosse, a predominantly Métis community of 357 people, all of the English River Dene and about ten Dene families from Clear Lake were anxiously waiting for him, even though their scheduled meeting was over two weeks away. Since the Indians were running out of supplies and still had to move to their winter hunting grounds, McKenna readily agreed to deal with them on 28 August. He quickly learned, though, that the deliberations would be anything but easy. "It appeared ... there would be some considerable difficulty," he confessed in his official report, "in effecting a settlement on the lines of the treaty."[18] It was quite an admission, especially when he could count on the authority of the local missionary, Father Rapet, a long-time resident of the region, who strenuously encouraged the Indians to accept the terms being offered.

The Dene had a clear sense of what had been offered in southern treaties, what they expected from this treaty—and equally important, what they feared about the treaty. "There was a marked absence of the old Indian style of oratory," McKenna observed, "the Indians confining themselves to asking questions and making brief arguments." Chief William Apisis, the middle-aged leader of the English River band, deftly began his remarks by suggesting that the Dene were owed arrears from the time of the signing of the first western treaty. He then asked for assistance in times of distress, care for the elderly and indigent, and improved education for children. Forty-year-old John Iron, chief of the Canoe Lake band, echoed the need for adequate schooling and requested a day school for the children from his area. He also called for agricultural support, prompting some of his people to put forward personal appeals for cattle and farming implements. But what concerned the Dene more than anything else during their meeting with McKenna was that the treaty appeared to be "a means of enslaving them." This anxiety was not idle speculation, the stuff of theatrics for the commissioner. They had already seen first-hand how the big commercial companies were draining the local lakes of fish and were worried that the treaty would end their traditional lifestyle. What they were seeking from the Crown's representative was the same kind of goodwill and assistance that the HBC had earlier provided.[19]

McKenna responded by staunchly defending the treaty and its purpose. He told the Dene that the government "expected" them to pursue their subsistence activities, that there would be "no interference" with their lifestyle. "I pointed out to them," he later reported, "that the same means of earning a livelihood would continue after the treaty ... as existed before ... I guaranteed [it]." McKenna also indicated that education and relief would be provided by the government—there was no need to amend the wording of the treaty—and promised to raise the matter of special help for the old and infirm. He was equally reassuring about the government's commitment to health care, but suggested that medicine placed at selected posts would make more sense than a resident doctor, given the dispersed nature of the Indian population. He was more resistant, however, to the idea of farming assistance, insisting

Children outside the Hudson's Bay Company post at Île-à-la-Crosse, 1908. SASKATCHEWAN ARCHIVES BOARD S-B8959

there would be no meaningful aid until the Dene were ready to take up agriculture seriously.[20]

McKenna's remarks were undoubtedly designed to secure swift approval of the treaty. He had a tight timetable and a considerable amount of territory to cover. But his verbal assurances were flatly contradicted by the actual wording of Treaty 10, which stipulated that "the [Indian] right to pursue their usual vocations ... throughout the territory" would be "subject to ... regulations" and excluded from "such tracts ... as may be taken up from time to time for settlement, mining, lumbering, trading or other purposes." This discrepancy between the official treaty terms and McKenna's promises raises serious questions about the integrity of the process. It would appear that McKenna placed acceptance of the treaty above anything else, including the truth. By telling the Dene that their subsistence activities would not be interfered with, McKenna failed to address the growing competition between Indians and outsiders for access to the region's resources. At the same time, his verbal assurances won over the Dene leaders; by the end of the day on 28 August, 199 Indians officially entered Treaty 10.[21]

McKenna's party headed next for Portage La Loche, arriving on 5 September, two days behind schedule. Once the HBC trans-shipment centre to the

Mackenzie Basin, the mostly mixed-blood community, numbering over two hundred people, had fallen on hard times in the twenty years the route had been abandoned. McKenna spent a week in the La Loche area, holding hearings in his other official capacity as scrip commissioner. It was his job to accept applications and issue scrip coupons to individual Métis, pending an interview and public declaration about their mixed-blood heritage. There was no shortage of applicants. Work was now difficult to find in the area, and many of the Métis gladly took what the government was offering. In fact, McKenna probably spent as much time dealing with scrip in 1906—investigating a total of 541 claims—as he did securing signatures to Treaty 10.[22] Unfortunately, most of the 498 awards he made were scooped up by speculators, acting on behalf of lawyers, bankers, businessmen, and other professionals, who travelled with the commission and secured scrip certificates for a fraction of what they were potentially worth. One such buyer was W. P. Fillmore, a Winnipeg law student, who had been "given $5,000 ... which I carried in my hip pocket." Fillmore reported that his fellow speculators sought to avoid competition by agreeing beforehand to offer only a dollar an acre for land scrip. He also later learned that scrip speculators hired people to impersonate the individuals named on the certificates and that these imposters would appear at a Dominion Lands office to apply for "their" land.[23]

From La Loche, the treaty commission headed back to Île-à-la-Crosse, stopping at Buffalo Narrows, between Buffalo and Clear lakes, to meet with the Clear Lake Dene. Since the chief had already agreed to the terms of the treaty three weeks earlier at Île-à-la-Crosse, McKenna's duties were a mere formality. One hundred and ten band members entered treaty on 17 September. McKenna's next stop was at Canoe Lake, southwest of Île-à-la-Crosse, two days later. Here, he secured the agreement of Chief John Iron and eighty-one members of his band, but only after he had given the Cree the same assurances about the treaty as he had given the Dene. At this point, the treaty party was supposed to move to the northeast, starting at Stanley Mission on 8 October. But both the HBC and Revillon Frères warned McKenna that low water levels would make it impossible to keep his scheduled meetings and that the Indians could not be expected to wait around during the fall hunting season. With freeze-up only weeks away, McKenna decided to cancel the second half of this treaty trip and head home, but not before notifying the bands he missed that they would be visited in the future. He had been in the region for less than a month.[24]

The job of completing Treaty 10 was handed to Thomas Borthwick, the Indian agent at Mistawasis, in the early spring of 1907. Borthwick not only had more time to make proper arrangements for the trip, including sending

Portage La Loche once served as a major fur-trade trans-shipment centre. LIBRARY AND ARCHIVES
CANADA PA44550

out notices about his commission, but arrived in the region in mid-June, a full two months earlier than the 1906 commission and a more convenient time for the Indians. Like McKenna, though, he had little leeway in dealing with the Cree and Dene. According to his instructions, there could be no revisions to the treaty document or any verbal or "outside" promises that departed from the terms of the treaty. Nor did the Laurier government want him chasing after Indians who had not entered treaty in 1906. The chiefs and headmen were to meet at specified posts at a prearranged date and, it was hoped, affix their marks in exchange for gifts and medals.[25]

Borthwick travelled first to Île-à-la-Crosse on 22 June in order to pay annuities and try to convince the nearby Lac La Plonge Indians—a band that McKenna missed the previous year—to come to the community to enter the treaty. That part of the trip was expected to take little more than two weeks. A number of Métis, however, still wanted to apply for scrip, and Borthwick was forced to hold lengthy sittings over several days; he even had to make a special trip to Portage La Loche. He would eventually consider a total of 202 claims and approve 178 awards. One of the applicants on 11 July 1907 was Lucia Janvier, a twenty-five-year-old mother with a two-year-old son, Pierre. She signed her X to receive 240 acres of land. More than two years later, on 18 January 1910, someone claiming to be Janvier redeemed her scrip at the Dominion Lands office in Moose Jaw; a cross served as her signature. The next day, ownership of the land passed to Frank Mason, a Lethbridge real estate agent who reportedly held almost twenty thousand acres in northern Métis scrip. This time, though, "Janvier" was able to write her name in full on the transfer document.[26]

Borthwick also found that the three bands that had entered treaty the previous year were still uneasy about what it meant for their future. At a meeting on 24 June, Chief Iron of the Canoe Lake Cree complained that McKenna had been in too much of a hurry to listen to their concerns about hunting and fishing. He also wondered why his people were receiving fewer supplies than the year before and called on Borthwick to host a feast or regale, much like the HBC had done in the past.[27] Several days later, during the meeting with the Clear Lake and English River Dene, similar concerns were voiced. The Clear Lake chief once again raised the question of help for the destitute—something that McKenna was supposed to secure on their behalf. Chief Apisis of the English River band stressed the need for a resident doctor to attend the sick and elderly. He also revealed that his people were "afraid" they would not be able to pursue their subsistence activities. "They would starve," Apisis bluntly declared, "if such should be the case." Like McKenna before him, Borthwick made every effort to ease these fears by presenting the treaty as a friendship agreement instead of a land transfer document. He told Apisis that "they would not at any time be prevented from hunting and fishing for their own use as heretofore." He also spoke of the government's "consideration for their circumstances" and how it would

Many Métis living in northern Saskatchewan applied for scrip during the visit of the treaty commissioners in 1906–07. SASKATCHEWAN ARCHIVES BOARD R-B2090-2

"treat them kindly." These statements suggested that Ottawa was interested in Indian well-being, and that the treaty symbolized a new partnership. That certainly seemed to be the message when they set aside their meetings and jointly celebrated the Dominion Day holiday.[28]

Borthwick's next meeting on 17 August was with the Barren Land and Lac La Hache bands at Brochet at the north end of Reindeer Lake in the northeast part of the province, just inside the Saskatchewan boundary. Resident Oblate priest Father Turquetil, who had an imperfect command of Dene, served as interpreter. Borthwick had clearly been influenced by his recent experience at Île-à-la-Crosse, for he indicated in his opening remarks that "the King was willing to ... help themselves and their children in the future," especially "their old and indigent people." Petit Casimir, speaking on behalf of the Barren Land band, wanted to know if the treaty would impinge on their hunting and fishing activities and whether it could be changed at some future date. Borthwick countered that the terms were fixed, but assured Casimir that there would be no interference with their lifestyle.[29]

The Dene asked for some time to discuss the treaty among themselves. When they returned to the parlay tent in the early afternoon, Casimir questioned whether the treaty money was meant to support them. Borthwick replied that the payments and gifts were intended to make their lives better; they were still expected to continue to live by hunting and fishing. With this assurance that they were not to be deprived of their traditional livelihood, the Barren Land Dene joined Treaty 10. Chief Benaouni of the Lac La Hache band deferred any decision until all of his followers were present. Three days later, after Borthwick explained the terms a second time through the interpreter, Benaouni placed his X on the treaty on behalf of this band.[30]

Borthwick spent two days in the area taking applications for Métis scrip before making his way back to Stanley, where he handled a few more scrip claims as his last official duty. By the time he returned to Mistawasis, he had spent more than three months in the north and travelled over two thousand miles by water to complete Treaty 10. But had he? At Brochet, Borthwick entered 329 Dene on the treaty roll. When this figure is added to the 394 Cree and Dene recorded by McKenna, a total of 723 Indians had taken treaty. But in 1905, Bishop Pascal had advised the federal government that there were approximately 1,800 Indians living in northern Saskatchewan. The total scrip applications (743) for 1906–07 also suggest that many Métis were excluded— as Borthwick himself discovered during his work in the Île-à-la-Crosse area in June 1907. According to the 1906 special western census, conducted the same year that McKenna was in the region, 2,988 people were counted in census district 17, an area slightly larger than that covered by Treaty 10.[31] Exactly how many were away in the bush and did not see the treaty/scrip

The front and back of the bronze Treaty 10 medal. LIBRARY AND ARCHIVES CANADA PA117761

commissioners is not easy to determine, but descendants of the Indians and Métis claim that "McKenna and Borthwick missed at least half the eligible residents of northern Saskatchewan."[32] This assertion may be exaggerated, but it certainly lends credence to the observation that "the whole affair was incredibly rushed."[33]

Even more important than the numbers involved were the timing and intent of Treaty 10. The Dene and Cree agreed to enter treaty in 1906–07 on the understanding that their subsistence activities would be secure from interference. They were deeply troubled about the future, about the threats to their traditional lifestyle, and looked to the Crown to provide protection and support. But if the Canadian government was genuinely concerned with preserving Indian hunting, fishing, and gathering practices in northern Saskatchewan, it could have acted much sooner, instead of waiting for the creation of the new province. It could also have offered more liberal terms— even allowed actual negotiations. Ottawa, however, had another motive. It wanted to extinguish Aboriginal title in the region in order to clear the way for future development and used the treaty to realize this goal. It amounted to "a gentleman's way to take without grabbing."[34] Ironically, the Dene and Cree—and not the two treaty commissioners—had the better understanding of the changes they would face in the coming years, but they could do little more than express their concerns before signing the treaty. The creation of Saskatchewan and Alberta had broken the old fur-trade north "into a number of powerless pieces ... [creating] northern colonies."[35] And the Indian and Métis people, as vestiges of that old North-West, were expected to have no part in the region's future. As Frank Oliver, the federal minister of the interior, bluntly told the House of Commons a year before Treaty 10 was introduced, "If it becomes a question between the Indians and the whites, the interests of the whites will have to be provided for."[36]

CHAPTER THREE

DEAD COWS HANGING

WHILE THE CREE AND DENE of northern Saskatchewan were grappling with the implications of Treaty 10, another major event was reshaping the face of the southwestern part of the province. In the early twentieth century, tens of thousands of head of cattle were feeding in the dry mixed-prairie district south of Swift Current from the Big Muddy Valley to the Cypress Hills. This open range country with its rich native grasses, sheltered creek bottoms, and relative isolation had everything a rancher needed. In fact, the manager of the T Bar Down outfit claimed the region "looked like the promised land."[1] That certainly appeared to be its destiny. By the time Saskatchewan entered Confederation, stock growers had millions of acres of federal land under lease, while cattle exports reached record levels. Then nature intervened. A fierce, three-day blizzard in mid-November 1906 signalled the beginning of a killing winter that held the region in its icy grip until late the following spring. When the snow finally melted, the sickening toll was everywhere to be seen—and smelled. Outfits lost on average half their stock, forcing many cattle producers to retreat from the area or adjust their ranching practices. The days of the open Saskatchewan range appeared to be over.

One of the groups most disappointed by the creation of two north-south provinces in 1905 was ranchers. Worried about becoming a powerless minority in any new political unit dominated by farmers, they had initially supported the idea of a horizontal province, with Calgary as the capital, made up of all the grazing land in the southern half of the provisional district of Alberta and the western half of Assiniboia. Once the federal government's autonomy plans became known, though, ranchers tried to get the proposed Alberta-Saskatchewan boundary adjusted to preserve the geographic integrity of the open range country. At the annual meeting of the Western Stock Growers' Association in Medicine Hat in May 1905, they formally recommended that Alberta's eastern boundary be moved three degrees eastward to the 107th meridian (roughly to the elbow of the South Saskatchewan River) so that a large block of ranching land in southwestern Saskatchewan would become part of Alberta instead. But like northern Aboriginal peoples, ranchers were a small group in a relatively isolated part of the North-West and their wishes for a separate stock-growing province were easily ignored.[2]

The question of what to do with the southern ranching country had been complicated by two conflicting views of the region—views that reflected little appreciation of the ecology of the dry mixed-prairie district. In the late 1850s, while the future of the North-West was being debated, the British and Canadian governments dispatched scientific exploring parties to the western interior to gather information about the potential for commercial agriculture. The Palliser (1857–60) and Hind (1857–58) expeditions, as they were called, readily appreciated the well-watered and wooded prairie parkland and believed it compared favourably with traditional farming land in Great Britain and Ontario. In their reports, they consequently extolled the merits of the "fertile belt," a broad band of land along the Assiniboine and North Saskatchewan rivers from present-day Winnipeg to Edmonton. Neither party, on the other hand, was impressed with the open prairies and declared that the area south of present-day Saskatoon to the international border formed a triangle of infertile lands—hence the name Palliser's Triangle.

This negative assessment was certainly understandable, since the expeditions had been asked to identify those areas best suited for agriculture; they did not even bother to examine the broken badlands region in the southwest part of the future province. Both Palliser and Hind were also outsiders, unfamiliar with the peculiar plains environment, who assumed that the treelessness of the South Saskatchewan country was a sure sign of aridity, if not barrenness. Fur traders, based in the northern boreal forest, had reached the same conclusion when they first ventured out onto the short-grass prairies in the

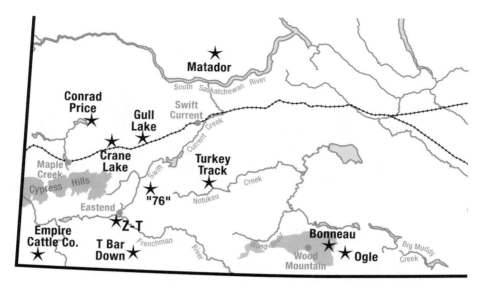

Much of the southwestern Saskatchewan range country was occupied by large American ranches before the killing winter of 1906–07.

eighteenth century. But the expeditions' sweeping resource generalizations unfairly condemned the entire southern district when the agricultural capabilities of the area actually varied from place to place and from year to year.[3]

Once Canada acquired the North-West in 1870, the southern grasslands were reassessed—but under completely different circumstances. Ottawa expected most, if not all, of its new western empire to be fertile and was anxious for government explorers to confirm this great vision. How else would it entice hundreds of thousands, possibly millions, of prospective farmers to the region? The potential of the dry mixed-prairie district therefore had to be reconsidered—the very idea of good and bad land was no longer acceptable. George Dawson, a geologist with the 1873–74 North American Boundary Commission survey, reported that the country along the forty-ninth parallel, except for a limited area, was not typical desert at all and was perfectly suited for stock raising. Plant geographer John Macoun, whose enthusiasm for the North-West and its future knew no bounds, took this reappraisal one step further when he explored the South Saskatchewan country during the 1879 and 1880 field seasons. Travelling during exceptionally wet summers, he found growing conditions ideal for the kind of large-scale agricultural colonization envisaged by Ottawa. He even challenged the common assumption that settlement should be initially confined to the parkland and instead promoted the virtues of homesteading the open prairie. Where Palliser and Hind had once found an irreclaimable desert, Macoun discovered a garden of unlimited potential.[4]

Building a boundary mound in 1873 to mark the international border between Canada and the United States. LIBRARY AND ARCHIVES CANADA C73304

This portrayal of the grasslands as a kind of agricultural Eden was reckless and potentially harmful. The failure to recognize the treeless prairie as a distinctive North American ecosystem had partly accounted for Palliser's and Hind's pessimistic findings. And although Macoun had reached completely opposite conclusions about the potential of the grasslands, he was equally guilty of misreading the landscape. Instead of recognizing the peculiar features of the region—light soils, scanty precipitation, and short growing season—Macoun saw what he wanted to see.

This dramatic re-evaluation of the dry mixed-prairie district is often cited as one of the key reasons why the new CPR syndicate abandoned the proposed Yellowhead route along the North Saskatchewan in 1881 in favour of sending the main line directly west from Winnipeg across the open grasslands and through a more southerly mountain pass. The location of the railway, however, had more to do with strategic business considerations than the quality of the land. The CPR syndicate was determined to build the main line as close to the international border as possible, even if the land was generally poor, in order to capture all of the traffic of the North-West and keep out American competitors. That's why the syndicate insisted that its twenty-five-million-acre land grant not be restricted to South Saskatchewan country. The contract specifically stipulated that the railway land had to be "fairly fit for settlement" and that it could fulfill its grant in other parts of the territories.[5] It also explains why the CPR evidently scheduled its passenger train service between Regina and Calgary at night in order to play down the marginal land along the route.[6]

The people who best understood the ecology of the dry mixed-prairie district were the Assiniboine, Gros Ventre, Cree, Saulteaux, and Blackfoot. In summer, they methodically stalked the great buffalo herds foraging on the nutrient-rich grasses of the region, sometimes using fire to influence their movements. Come winter, they would seek refuge in the Wood (sometimes Woody) Mountains, southwest of Moose Jaw, and the Cypress Hills, straddling the Saskatchewan-Alberta border.[7] These uplands of the third prairie steppe, stretching for more than one hundred miles from east to west and featuring the highest elevations in the province (over 3,900 feet/1,200 metres), feed streams that eventually flow south into the Missouri River system. They also provide some of the few sources of wood in the area, especially Cypress Hills, the only place in Saskatchewan where lodgepole pine is to be found. For the Indians, the uplands had always offered sanctuary from the harsh winters of the open plains, but once the number of buffalo began to decline precipitously because of overhunting in the mid-nineteenth century, they became one of the few areas where the animals could be found with any regularity.

It was the buffalo that also drew the Red River Métis to the Wood Mountain/Cypress Hills region. At first, the annual hunting brigades spent only the summer on the open plains before retreating to the Red River

A Métis camp in the early 1870s. LIBRARY AND ARCHIVES CANADA C4164

Settlement in the fall with their carts heavily laden with meat, tongues, and hides. But as the distance to the herds grew and trade increasingly shifted to buffalo robes, more and more Métis families began to winter inland in the 1850s and 1860s. These "hivernant" communities, often tucked in a coulee for shelter and water, were little more than temporary hunting camps, constantly on the move with the buffalo and oblivious to the international border. Some of the more permanent sites were located in southwestern Saskatchewan, especially along the eastern side of the Wood Mountain uplands. The boundary commission's Wood Mountain depot was a popular Métis wintering site, as was La Vieille near present-day Gravelbourg. By the 1870s, there were as many as five hundred families scattered throughout the region and a network of trails, many leading south to American posts. Some men turned to freighting and trading, but the hunt—and the freedom associated with it—still dominated their lives. The Métis also left their imprint on the land by giving many features French names, such as La Montagne de Bois (Wood Mountain) and La Rivière Blanche (Whitemud), later known as the Frenchman River.[8]

Although the Indians and Métis competed for the same resources, relations between the two groups were generally peaceful. Any incidents usually involved confrontations with American authorities, in most cases over hunting or horse stealing on the other side of the border. Not even the presence of American whisky traders, who peddled their vile concoctions from crude makeshift posts in the district, led to much violence. But in May 1873, a gang of drunken American wolf hunters, spoiling for a fight over a stolen horse, attacked a sleeping Assiniboine camp and ruthlessly murdered about twenty Indians. The Cypress Hills Massacre was a rare act of barbarity in a lawless land, but it forced the Canadian government to implement its plan to establish a special paramilitary force, the North-West Mounted Police, for the region. The following summer, about three hundred mounties marched west along the international border from southern Manitoba to the heart of the whisky trade country in southwestern Alberta. The 1874 March West, as it was dubbed, had more to do with sovereignty than survival—Ottawa could not have selected a more difficult route—and the mounted police reached their destination in no shape to deal with any resistance. But the whisky traders chose flight over confrontation, and within a year of their arrival in the west, the police had established Fort Walsh, a post along the southern flank of the Cypress Hills. Fort Walsh, the government's main supply depot in southwestern Saskatchewan, quickly emerged as a kind of crossroads. Because of the disappearance of buffalo from traditional hunting areas along the North Saskatchewan, Cree chiefs, such as Poundmaker and Big Bear, led their people south to the Cypress Hills where large game could still be secured. Here, they joined other equally desperate groups, such as the Assiniboine and Blackfoot, who had also turned to the region as a haven of last resort. By the end of the decade, up to three thousand starving Indians had gathered in the vicinity of Fort Walsh. Many followed the buffalo herds south to Montana's Milk River country, but were chased back across the line, like pilfering vagrants, by the United States Army. At Fort Walsh, meanwhile, Indian Affairs officials used the widespread hunger to gain the upper hand over the First Nations. They callously refused to feed any Indians who had not taken treaty or had left their reserves.[9]

Into this tense situation rode the renowned Lakota Sioux chief Sitting Bull with about one thousand followers. Fresh from their annihilation of the American 7th Cavalry at the Battle of the Little Big Horn in June 1876, the Sioux feared retribution at the hands of a vengeful American government and fled across the border, or medicine line as it was called, to Wood Mountain and the safety of Canada. Nearly five thousand would eventually

Lakota Sioux chief Sitting Bull sought refuge in Canada following the defeat of the American 7th Cavalry at the Little Big Horn. SASKATCHEWAN ARCHIVES BOARD R-A8660

seek sanctuary here. Alarmed by the arrival of the refugees and fearing trouble, Ottawa called on Major James Walsh of the NWMP to watch over the unwanted visitors. But instead of shooing the Sioux back to the United States, Walsh formed a close friendship with Sitting Bull and tried to help his people in whatever way he could; he even relocated his headquarters from Fort Walsh to Wood Mountain to be closer to the chief. The mountie could do little, however, to combat the Sioux's new enemy—hunger. With game resources exhausted and reduced to eating their horses, hundreds of Sioux began slipping back to Montana. In May 1880, Sitting Bull appealed to Walsh to help secure a permanent home in Canada for his starving people, but Walsh's request for a reserve only angered Ottawa authorities who wanted the Sioux to return home. The Canadian government soon decided that the mountie was the problem and transferred him to Fort Qu'Appelle that summer. Sitting Bull remained in Canada for another year, but starvation finally forced him to surrender to American authorities in July 1881. Walsh was powerless to help. Upset and disillusioned over how the great chief had been treated, he resigned from the NWMP in 1883.[10]

The situation for the Indians at nearby Fort Walsh was little better. In 1879, Cree chiefs Little Pine and Piapot and several Assiniboine leaders requested contiguous reserves in a sixteen-hundred-square-mile area stretching from present-day Medicine Hat to the Cypress Hills. This Indian territory would have allowed the bands to continue to hunt the area's remaining buffalo, as well as make a start at agriculture. Federal Indian commissioner Edgar Dewdney, who initially agreed to the idea, soon realized, however, that a concentration of Plains Cree in the Cypress Hills region would not be as easy to control as bands on isolated reserves. In addition, if Canadian Indians continued to pursue remnants of the great buffalo herds south of the border, it could lead to an ugly international incident. The rerouting of the CPR main line across the southern prairies further complicated matters; the vital transportation link, Canada's so-called national dream, would have skirted the proposed Indian territory. The Indian commissioner consequently decided not to honour the Indian requests—even though it was a breach of their treaty rights—and told the Cree that reserves had to be selected elsewhere. To back up his policy of submission, what he called "sheer compulsion," Dewdney refused to dispense rations unless the Indians agreed to leave. He then closed Fort Walsh in 1883, thereby eliminating the only source of provisions and one of the last inducements for remaining in the Cypress Hills. The Cree and Assiniboine had no choice but to accept the government offer—sweetened by the lure of rations—and left for their new homes to the east and north under police escort.[11]

The eviction of the Indians from their last refuge on the Canadian prairies

Major James Walsh of the North-West Mounted Police was sent to Wood Mountain to watch over Sitting Bull. SASKATCHEWAN ARCHIVES BOARD R-B626

did not mean that the Métis now had the uplands to themselves. In 1880, a fierce prairie fire consumed most of the timber and grass on Wood Mountain. This calamity was followed by an even bigger one the following summer, when the buffalo, for the first time in living memory, failed to appear north of the border. The hivernant camps were doomed. Many families, facing a future of destitution, went south in search of the herds to the Milk River, never to return, or migrated north to the parkland to join existing Métis communities. A few turned to ranching, while several others settled northeast of Wood Mountain and tried farming or worked as labourers, hauling freight, clearing brush, picking stones, and collecting buffalo bones. They generally remained an impoverished group on the margins of society, one whose presence steadily diminished as French-Canadian immigrants settled in the St. Victor/Willow Bunch area in the 1880s and 1890s.[12]

One prominent member of the emerging francophone community was Quebec-born Jean-Louis Légaré, a Wood Mountain trader since 1871. Légaré had supported Sitting Bull's Sioux during their days in Canada, expending thousands of dollars in food and supplies, but was never fully compensated by the Canadian and American governments, despite repeated appeals by his descendants to this day.[13] In 1880, he moved to Willow Bunch, where he erected the first store the following year, and started raising cattle and horses.

Métis cowboys in the Maple Creek area. GLENBOW ARCHIVES NA-1368-6

Soon a handful of ranches, some of them operated by Métis, sprang up along the Willow Bunch and Big Muddy valleys. Pascal Bonneau and his three sons, recent immigrants from Quebec, had one of the largest operations. Former mounties, such as Edward "Buffalo" Allen and Fred Brown, also tried ranching in the area. But the local market was extremely limited. There were no reserves in the area and police strength was being concentrated in the North Saskatchewan country in response to possible Indian unrest there.[14]

Ranching might have remained small-scale for some time if not for the active encouragement of the Canadian government. In 1879, in order to limit the spread of disease, Great Britain banned the import of live cattle from the United States. Anxious to cash in on its new preferred status in the British beef market and take advantage of the rerouting of the CPR across the prairies, Ottawa introduced a new grazing policy for western Canada in December 1881. For the ridiculously low sum of one cent per acre per year, prospective ranchers could lease up to one hundred thousand acres for a twenty-one-year period, provided they had one head of cattle on every ten acres within three years. These closed leases (homesteading was not permitted on the land) encouraged the flow of British and eastern Canadian capital to the Alberta range country south of Calgary, and in only a few short years, ten large companies controlled two-thirds of all stocked land. They were no ordinary cattlemen. A powerful, privileged elite, who had more in common with Montreal and London than Winnipeg, they played polo and tennis, hired Chinese cooks and English governesses, and wintered in Victoria or Great Britain.[15]

The ranching scene in southwestern Saskatchewan was quite different. In 1882, the CPR established Swift Current, on a creek bearing the same name, as its divisional point in the region; it was equidistant from other divisional centres at Moose Jaw and Medicine Hat and the closest shipping point from the railhead to Battleford, the former territorial capital. But despite the main line and endless miles of pasture in every direction, the 76 Ranch was the only major British-controlled operation in the area by 1888. It held three ten-thousand-acre leases: one immediately south of town, another at Rush Lake, and a third at Gull Lake.[16] American ranchers, on the other hand, jumped at the new lease arrangements. By the early 1880s, because of the great profits to be made supplying beef to industrial America, much of Montana's range country was overstocked and overgrazed. It was only natural for American producers to trail their cattle north across the border, up the wide river valleys, to feed on the same thick grasses that the buffalo once did. By 1886, Americans controlled three large leases near the Cypress Hills and shipped their stock to Chicago from the railhead at nearby Maple Creek. Further east that same year, the Home Land and Cattle Company of St. Louis drove 6,000 cattle and 250 horses into Wood Mountain. More would probably have followed, but the devastating winter of 1886–87 wiped out herds on both sides of the border.[17]

The "big die-up," as it was called locally, eased the pressure on the Montana range and the need to expand into Canada. Indeed, by 1891 south-western Saskatchewan had effectively become "an empty land." Census

Cattle round-up at the 76 Ranch near Gull Lake. GLENBOW ARCHIVES NA-3811-78

enumerators counted only 320 people in the sixteen-thousand-square-mile Swift Current subdistrict, only one person for every fifty square miles. Most were ranchers and their families, raising cattle and horses—or in a few cases, sheep. Even prospective farmers avoided the region, prompting the federal government to close temporarily the Dominion Lands office at Swift Current.[18] It was these very conditions—a vast, unsettled land with no fences and free grass—that brought American ranchers back as soon as they had rebuilt their stock in the early 1890s. This time, though, they did not bother with federal leases. Their herds were simply allowed to graze at will, back and forth across the border as if it never existed. Some reportedly ranged as far north as Old Wives Lake. Mounted police patrols regularly complained about the presence of cattle with American brands, but could do little about it except to suggest, in frustration, that the boundary be fenced. That certainly seemed tempting in 1897 when the mounties drove four thousand cattle back into the United States, only to have most of them return. Two years later, American cowboys rounded up twelve thousand cattle feeding along the south side of the Cypress Hills. They left behind any inferior animals, to the chagrin of local Canadian ranchers who worried about damage to their own stock.[19]

By the early 1900s, the invasion of the southwestern range had become an occupation. No less than twenty-five American ranches were established in the first five years of the new century. Several large firms, including many that had originated in Texas, drove tens of thousands of cattle and hundreds of horses across the line into areas that had never been stocked before. The Matador Land and Cattle Company, for example, started a Canadian division on a 150,000-acre lease north of Saskatchewan Landing on the South Saskatchewan River. Further west, the Conrad Price Cattle Company grazed cattle north of the CPR main line at Maple Creek into the Great Sand Hills. Other companies, which had been illegally grazing thousands of cattle in the district for years, formalized their activities by finally applying for federal leases. In 1902, the Cresswell Cattle Company (the Turkey Track ranch) secured control over a vast stretch of land between Swift Current and Seventy Mile Crossing (Val Marie), while the Bloom Cattle Company (the T Bar Down) operated a huge ranch from the Whitemud River west to Eastend. There were other, smaller Montana outfits as well, all anxious to cash in on the great beef bonanza. And bonanza it was. In 1903 alone, border inspectors reported the entry of 63,000 head. By 1906, there were 360,000 beef cattle in Saskatchewan, a whopping 70 per cent increase from 1901. More cattle, meanwhile, were being shipped from Swift Current than anywhere else in the new province.[20]

The ranchers who brought their cattle north in the early twentieth century were after the same kind of refuge the Indians had sought only a generation earlier. Alarmed by the growing tide of farmers—derisively called "nesters"—invading the American West, they looked to the less crowded Saskatchewan range as one of the few remaining places where they could simply turn their cattle loose to fend for themselves. There would be no fences, no haying, and, most importantly, no squabbles with settlers. Former Montana rancher T. B. Long fondly recalled riding through the Cypress Hills for the first time in 1904. "It is just impossible to describe the amount of grass we saw," he reminisced, "and there was free range everywhere."[21]

Ranching left little imprint on the land. Because most of their money was literally on the hoof, owners invested in local improvements only grudgingly. Ranch headquarters were invariably modest log structures, located along rivers and creeks, separated by vast stretches of grazing country, known as benches. Trails followed the natural contours of the land instead of being laid out in the grid system used in farming districts. And instead of putting up fences, larger outfits relied on topographical boundaries, be it a creek or ridge, to mark their range lines.[22]

It was also an isolated existence—something that ranchers, unlike farmers, deliberately sought. In mid-November 1906, Harry Otterson, manager of the T Bar Down, and his wife travelled 125 miles by buckboard from Malta, Montana, to ranch headquarters on the Whitemud River, just south of the

The Z-X outfit at Eastend was one of several American ranches in southwestern Saskatchewan.
SASKATCHEWAN ARCHIVES BOARD R-A6811

RNWMP post at Eastend. "My wife and I discussed many things," he recalled, as they crossed the border near the present-day town of Frontier, "and gazing at the great open country we wondered when it would ever be settled by families, and if it would be possible to live out on those bleak plains in winter time ...To the east, there was not a house until one reached Wood Mountain ... And to the west ... only a few isolated ranches ... So there was ample room to get lost, freeze, starve ... I was inclined to doubt the country would be settled or railroads built during our time."[23]

This isolation was compounded by the fact that the outfits were essentially self-contained units and could go for months without contacting the outside world. To break the monotony, ranching families would make social calls on one another, lasting from three days to a week. One of the more popular social centres was the Cutting ranch on the north fork of Swift Current Creek, where "cowboys for miles around" were always welcome. Another favourite home was that of Ben Rose, the postmaster for Eastend, where ranchers would gather for the weekly mail night. Sometimes Rose would host a dance "and the six or eight ladies, mostly all married, received plenty of attention and did not sit out any dances, for there would possibly be forty men present."[24] Robert and Winnie Hancock, who did a lot of reading and playing cards on their small ranch on Piapot Creek, never missed a dance in nearby Maple Creek, often staying up most of the night.[25]

It was the American cowboy who probably made the greatest impression on the region and its image. The way he performed his day-to-day chores, drawing on years of practical experience in the saddle south of the border, was widely admired and became the accepted manner of doing things in this male-dominated world. The imitation extended to how he dressed, handled his horse, and even the way he talked or rolled a cigarette. He was a cultural icon for the wide open range country with its short-grass prairie, steep coulees, and scruffy badlands, and often romanticized as a solitary figure whose best friend was his horse.[26]

This influence extended to the local Métis and French-Canadian cowboys. One young man, however, had difficulty fitting in. Edouard Beaupré, born in Willow Bunch in 1881, just wanted to be a cowhand, but his feet dragged on the ground when he rode his horse—and for good reason. He stood eight feet, three inches tall. At seventeen, Beaupré joined the circus and toured North America as the Willow Bunch Giant until his death at the 1904 St. Louis World's Fair. His preserved remains, placed on display in Montreal for several decades, returned home only in 1990.[27] Another French Canadian came to the region to find a new identity. Fifteen-year-old Ernest Dufault headed for southwestern Saskatchewan in 1907 in search of the mythical west that he had read about in dime novels during his childhood in St. Nazaire,

Quebec. Over the next four years he learned about horses, steers, and the range, and was transformed from a greenhorn Quebec teenager into a rugged cowboy and horse breaker. Dufault's obsession with becoming a cowboy spurred him to bury one past and adopt another. He assumed a new persona—Will James—and learned to speak English with a western accent to hide his francophone past. With this new identity, James rode into the United States in 1911 and eventually found considerable fortune as an artist/writer.[28]

Despite the pervasive American influence, the violence that once characterized the American western frontier in the immediate post–Civil War period did not follow the cattlemen north. One ranch hand suggested that "the alkali water they drinked [*sic*] up here took it out of them, and the winters froze out what was left."[29] But there were outlaws operating in the area. One of the most notorious was Joseph Erving Kelley, more popularly known as Sam Kelly or Charles "Red" Nelson. Born in Nova Scotia in 1859, the lanky Kelley, remembered today for his deadly aim as much as for his bright red beard, came to prominence in the Saskatchewan-Montana border country in the 1890s when he fell in with American Frank Jones and his criminal friends. Over the next few years, the Nelson-Jones gang, sometimes working with the rough-and-tumble Dutch Henry, terrorized local ranchers and settlers, stealing horses and rustling cattle when not robbing trains and businesses. The mounted police responded by setting up a detachment in the Big Muddy Valley, but the gang eluded capture by hiding in caves near Peake's Butte in the badlands or just slipping across the line. Sometime after 1902, perhaps tired of running, Kelley abandoned his life of crime and tried his hand at ranching before leaving the area in 1913 and taking up a homestead near Debden, several hundred miles to the north. He could not leave behind the memory of his unsavoury past, however, and died a broken man in the Battleford asylum in 1937.[30]

While Kelley and his ilk proved an irritant to ranchers, the more vexing problem was the weather. One author has called it the "one constant" of the frontier, if only because its unpredictable nature made life more difficult.[31] It also led to tragedy. In April 1906, Nellie and Ruth Hoffman, aged eleven and nine and the youngest of five sisters, disappeared during a freak sleet storm southeast of Wood Mountain while leading some horses home. Although the animals were found the next day, an exhaustive search of the nearby coulees and benches failed to locate the missing girls. Their remains would not be discovered for another nine years, near what is today known as Lost Child Creek.[32]

Ranchers constantly struggled against the weather, often adjusting their practices to fit local conditions. No one could have anticipated, however,

Quebec-born writer-illustrator Will James learned the cowboy trade on the Saskatchewan open range. GLENBOW ARCHIVES NA-862-1

what would befall the Saskatchewan range country in 1906. It had been a wetter than usual summer and the grass was stocked to capacity. "Altogether we were healthy, safe and prosperous," remarked Harry Otterson. "Little did we realize we were heading into the worst winter in the history of the range cattle business."[33]

The winter began with the first snowfall on 5 November 1906. Then, a little more than a week later, a brutal three-day blizzard raged across the west, dumping several feet of snow. Pioneers called it "the earliest, most violent, and longest storm in living memory."[34] December hinted at a return to normal weather, but a series of heavy snowfalls, accompanied by record low temperatures, pounded the region through most of January and February. Spring brought little relief. Storms continued to hit, while temperatures remained well below normal. It was as if winter would never let go.

After the first heavy snowfall, ranch hands spent all their days on horseback, trying to rescue stranded cattle, especially the calves. But as the bad weather continued and the snow blanketed the range in deep drifts, the men could do little more than hope that a warming chinook would expose the grass in time to keep the losses to a minimum. Many a hardened cowboy was shaken by the bellowing of the cold and hungry cattle searching in vain for food and shelter. At the end of March 1907, Otterson left the safety of his ranch headquarters to visit the Whitemud range. "It surely was a gruesome ride," he vividly recounted. "The cattle were in all stages of dying ... The live ones, at night, would lie down on the dead and many would not be able to get up again; consequently they were literally piled up, dead and dying together." The news was equally bad at other ranches. The men at the Turkey Track "reported cattle dying by the thousands as far as they could ride from their camp."[35]

Because of the late spring, the round-up did not start until almost June. Even then, searching for animals that had survived the winter was difficult because "the country was a mass of lakes."[36] The dead were everywhere, bloated and rotting in small groups where they had perished. It was particularly gruesome in the coulees, where "dead cows hanging in the tops of trees gave a clue to the depth of the snow."[37] Wallace Stegner, in his classic *Wolf Willow*, called it "carrion spring."[38] Rancher R. D. Symons was blunter—he spoke of "the Big Smell."[39] Whatever the term, the toll was truly appalling. The T Bar Down men rendezvoused with the Turkey Track outfit on the Whitemud in June 1907 in order to separate their cattle and take them to their respective summer ranges, but the herds were a mere shell of their former numbers. An initial estimate suggested that the two ranches had lost 60 to 65 per cent of their cattle. Other large ranches that depended on the open range, such as the Matador and 76, were hit just as hard. Only smaller outfits, which did some haying, were able to keep their casualties to about one-third. In the final tally, the average loss for ranches was pegged at around 50 per cent.[40]

The death of so many cattle in one winter was a heavy blow, especially since the large American operations had only recently stocked their land and had yet to recover their expenses. Several companies consequently sent their remaining cattle to market and gave up their leases. By 1910, the T Bar Down, Turkey Track, and 76 ranches had all been sold to the Winnipeg-based meat-packing company Gordon, Ironside, and Fares, which reduced and consolidated the former outfits' holdings.[41] Otterson of the T Bar Down had wanted to stay on, convinced that the company could make up its losses in a few years by making better winter preparations, but his counterpart at the Turkey Track, Tony Day, who had worked from Texas to Montana, had had enough. "I am through with range business," he told Otterson while surveying the carnage. "I believe I have enough left out of this wreck to keep myself and family. I have spent my entire life on the range and have been set back several times by hard winters ... I am ready to cash in and take my loss."[42]

The liquidation of the large outfits, together with the retirement or departure of seasoned cattlemen, signalled the end of the open range era. Thereafter, more leases were fenced and holdings were smaller. These changes, however, could not guarantee the continued vitality of the ranching industry in southwestern Saskatchewan. By a fluke of nature, the brutal winter of 1906–07 coincided with the "voracious appetite" for farmland in the new province, and as the ranchers withdrew, freeing up vast stretches of leased land, settlers poured into the semi-arid region in search of homestead land.[43] It was a doubly ironic turn of events. American stock producers had pushed their herds across the border to get away from the plough and barbed-wire fences. They yearned for open range and recognized—as did smaller Canadian ranching outfits—that the dry mixed-grass district of Palliser's Triangle was ideal grazing country. But in the end, there would be no escape from the homesteader. No sooner had ranchers been staggered by the ruinous winter than a new blizzard appeared on the horizon—this time a human one determined to break the virgin prairie sod and cultivate wheat.[44]

A horse ranch in the Cypress Hills in 1905. LIBRARY AND ARCHIVES CANADA PA11480

CHAPTER FOUR

THE GRAND ROUND-UP

SASKATCHEWAN was going to be big. That was the sentiment at the September 1905 inauguration ceremonies in Regina as speaker after speaker saw greatness on the horizon for the new province. Naturally, few would have predicted otherwise, given the spirit and enthusiasm of the occasion. But even Prime Minister Wilfrid Laurier, who once declared the twentieth century would be Canada's century, was probably surprised by the findings of the 1911 census. A mere six years after entering Confederation, the province's population had almost doubled to 492,432. It was larger than neighbouring Alberta (374,663), even larger than Manitoba (455,614), which had a thirty-five-year advantage over the upstart Saskatchewan. And the population was expected to climb by leaps and bounds. More settlers applied for homesteads in western Canada in the first decade of the twentieth century than during the entire previous century. In fact, for the years 1906 to 1911, three out of every five homestead entries in the three prairie provinces were in Saskatchewan.[1] But the news was not all good. At the inauguration party, the talk was of a British province, peopled by British immigrants. During the 1911 census, though, one-third of the Saskatchewan respondents indicated that they had been born in neither Canada nor Great Britain. This immigrant population—foreigners, as they were called at the best of times—would challenge the Anglo-Canadian identity of the new province and make cultural diversity one of the defining characteristics of Saskatchewan society.

If Canadian expansionists were to be believed in the 1860s, the North-West Territories were to be the future home of countless millions of Anglo-Canadian farmers, a land where the best features of British civilization would take root and flourish. By the 1890s, however, the reality was disappointing. Despite glowing reports about the unparalleled fertility of the soil and the ready availability of homestead land, the forecast flood of people never materialized. In 1881, four years before the CPR was finally completed, the entire territorial population was just over twenty-five thousand. Ten years later it had reached nearly sixty-seven thousand, but that was well below expectations. Only about 30 per cent of the immigrants who came to Canada in the closing decades of the nineteenth century headed west, and of these, most went to Manitoba, if they remained in the country at all.[2] The majority of Saskatchewan's first settlers were of British background and predominantly from English-speaking, Protestant Ontario. They had come to the future province in anticipation of the railroad, or during the boom precipitated by the building of the main line across the district of Assiniboia; others were simply part of the spillover from western Manitoba. The settlement pattern largely reflected these realities. By 1891, the non-Aboriginal population was largely confined to the CPR main line across the southern prairies, the Assiniboine and Qu'Appelle valleys in the southeast, and the North Saskatchewan River, especially in the Prince Albert and Battleford districts, where the railway was originally intended to run.

Despite the territories' failure to grow as expected, there had been no shortage of schemes to put people on the land. Beginning in 1881, Ottawa sold selected western tracts, generally north of the CPR main line, to colonization companies at a flat rate of two dollars per acre, with the promise of a $160 rebate (or a dollar per acre) for every bona fide settler placed on a homestead. Even with this incentive, the companies had trouble finding recruits. Only seven placed more than fifty settlers each in eastern Saskatchewan in the 1880s; many placed none. Two that did succeed were the York Farmers' Colonization Company and the Temperance Colonization Company, the forerunners of Yorkton and Saskatoon, respectively.[3] Another corporate experiment was the Qu'Appelle Valley Farming Company, popularly known as the Bell Farm. In May 1882, Major William Bell of Ontario purchased a

Tens of thousands of immigrants headed to Saskatchewan during Prime Minister
Wilfrid Laurier's tenure in office. *La Presse*, 8 July 1910

whopping fifty-three thousand acres—the equivalent of eighty square miles—
from the Canadian government and CPR along the proposed rail line at
Indian Head. By the end of the following summer, his "bonanza" farming
operation employed more than two hundred people and had broken seven
thousand acres. It reportedly took an entire morning to cut a single furrow
in one direction and all afternoon for the plough to return to its starting
point. But the 1885 North-West Rebellion, together with several poor harvests, undermined the operation's fragile financial stability, and the super-
farm was liquidated by the end of the decade. Today, a round fieldstone barn
with a central wooden silo is one of the few reminders of Bell's ambitious
undertaking.[4]

Other groups looked to Saskatchewan to provide a new start or preserve
old ways. Benevolent societies and individuals sponsored special colonies for
Scottish crofters, London artisans, and Russian Jews in the Moosomin area
in the early 1880s. Although these first Jewish refugees failed miserably and
abandoned the "New Jerusalem" settlement within a few years, subsequent
attempts at homesteading at Wapella (1886–88) and Hirsch (1892) were successful, especially in comparison to the experience of other groups. The first

batch of Hungarians, for example, who were moved from the United States to the area north of Whitewood in 1886 under a special arrangement between the Canadian government and Count Paul d'Esterhazy, drifted away and had to be replaced by immigrants directly from Hungary. The Jews, however, could not shake off the popular assumption that they were not suited to be farmers—something that the Moosomin colony only seemed to confirm.[5]

Two of the more curious Saskatchewan settlement experiments were Cannington Manor and La Rolanderie. In 1882, a group of British investors headed by Captain William Pearce bought over two thousand acres southeast of Moose Mountain to build a colony to train Britain's well-to-do in the rudiments of agriculture. Farming at Cannington Manor seemed secondary, though, to the cultural and sporting activities of the young Englishmen— they played at everything from London theatre to polo, cricket, and the hunt. The charade lasted until the early 1890s when the costs of running the resortlike colony became prohibitive, especially when it had been bypassed by the railway, and the "settlers" moved on to new pursuits.

The other remarkable venture was La Rolanderie, a haven for French aristocracy on Pipestone Creek just south of Whitewood. In 1885, feeling threatened by the changes sweeping republican France, at least thirteen counts headed to the wilds of southeastern Saskatchewan to recreate their sophisticated

Immigrants bound for Canada in 1903. WESTERN DEVELOPMENT MUSEUM 5-A(A)-2

lifestyle, complete with servants, impressive homes, and extravagant parties. Suddenly the area could boast more nobility than any other place in North America. But the counts' local business activities, which included a cheese factory and sugar beet plantation, failed because of arrogance and overconfidence. By 1900, most had returned to France, leaving behind their hired help who had decided to stay after their employers had given up.[6]

These various settlement initiatives, even if they survived and prospered, never resulted in the kind of immigrant numbers anticipated by the Canadian government. Part of the failure to attract settlers was the sluggish growth that kept the country in the doldrums for the better part of the 1880s and early 1890s. There was also a period of adjustment, as farmers learned how to contend with the different growing conditions in the region. But an even bigger factor was competition from the United States. As long as land could be secured there, the American frontier captured the lion's share of immigrants who came to North America. This pull even extended to Canada. During the last four decades of the nineteenth century, the country lost an estimated two-thirds of a million people. It was not until 1901 that more people came to Canada than left.[7]

What turned this bleak situation around was the return of prosperity, sparked by an unprecedented world demand for Canadian commodities, lower shipping costs, and the discovery of gold in the Klondike and South Africa. The United States had also exhausted its homestead land, prompting historian Frederick Jackson Turner to declare the end of an era in American history. Almost overnight, the Canadian prairies were transformed into "the last, best West." An advertiser could not have asked for a more enticing image.

It took one other crucial ingredient—the appointment of Clifford Sifton as the new Liberal minister of the interior in 1896—to make western Canada one of the most desired destinations for immigrants in search of land. Sifton, a no-nonsense lawyer-turned-politician with considerable private business interests, looked upon settlement of western Canada as the last great national task facing the young dominion; the region would be the engine driving Canada's growth and future well-being. Under his firm stewardship—he was nicknamed the young Napoleon—a streamlined Department of the Interior invested a substantial amount of time, energy, *and* money into the recruitment of experienced farmers. It circulated millions of promotional brochures, sponsored displays at exhibitions, financed western tours for journalists, and even struck secret deals with steamship agents to direct prospective immigrants to Canada. The demanding Sifton expected results, not excuses, and results would be measured in the number of settlers.[8]

These herculean efforts paid handsome dividends. So many immigrants began pouring into the region that Prime Minister Laurier ordered a special census of the three prairie provinces in 1906 to serve as a kind of statistical snapshot of the phenomenal growth. Even the normally reserved Sifton confidently bragged about "what is going on in the West where we have turned dismal failure into a magnificent success."[9] The statistics backed up his words. In Saskatchewan alone, the 1891 population (41,522) grew 127 per cent by 1901 (91,279) and then another 182 per cent just five years later (257,763). The immigrants effectively swamped the First Nations population. The 6,358 Indians counted in 1906 represented less than 3 per cent of Saskatchewan's population, down from just over 8 per cent at the start of the century. The chief census officer predicted that Canada would never be bedevilled by "the native problems that affect South Africa and other countries in the British Empire."[10] The provincial north also slipped into irrelevance, as less than 1 per cent of the population lived in the region. The other noteworthy data from the 1906 census were the sex and age breakdown. Men not only dominated Saskatchewan society—there were roughly three men to every two women (1.46 to 1)—but two of every three men were single. It was also a young population. Two-thirds were under forty-five, including a large number of people in their prime working years. This preponderance of single young men would characterize the Saskatchewan workforce into the 1930s.[11]

One statistic from the 1906 census would have particularly pleased Sifton: that over 80 per cent of Saskatchewan's population was rural. The minister of the interior believed, as did many of his contemporaries, that agriculture was the backbone of all great societies. He had consequently sought out immigrants who had a history of working the soil, settlers who possessed the determination to survive on their own and bring the prairies under cultivation, and whose children and grandchildren could be expected to take over the homestead.[12]

What this policy meant, however, is that certain groups were unwanted. Sifton had no use for English urban immigrants, Blacks, Asians, Jews, and southern Europeans, especially Italians. He simply assumed that they would never stay on the land, but migrate to cities and towns where they would take away jobs from Canadian workers. "They are hopelessly incapable," he once complained about British labourers, "of going on farms and succeeding."[13] He voiced similar reservations about Jews. In a 1901 memorandum prepared for the prime minister about a plan to establish a new Jewish settlement in the Lipton-Cupar area in the Qu'Appelle Valley, he argued, "Experience shows that the Jewish people do not become agriculturalists."[14] Nothing was therefore done by Sifton's department to encourage or facilitate the immigration of these peoples to Canada. If anything, roadblocks were placed in their way, especially the Chinese. No sooner had the CPR been completed in 1885 than the federal government imposed a "head" tax of fifty dollars on Chinese

The Canadian emigration offices in London advertised free western homesteads. LIBRARY AND ARCHIVES CANADA C063257

entering the country; this fee was later raised to one hundred dollars in 1900 and then five hundred dollars three years later.

Sifton's search for settlers with practical farming experience included people of peasant stock from central Europe, from what had traditionally been regarded as "non-preferred countries." These groups, from Doukhobors to Russian Germans to Ukrainians, were exactly the kind of immigrants Sifton believed were best suited to the challenging task of turning the prairie wilderness into productive farms. For Sifton the entrepreneur, they were one of the most important investments Canada could make in its future. Not everyone, however, shared Sifton's appreciation of these non-Anglo-Saxon settlers. They may have made good farmers, but would they make good citizens with their unpronounceable last names, pauperlike appearance, strange customs, and different religious beliefs? Indeed, central Europeans at the time were popularly associated with poverty, crime, ignorance, and immorality. One newspaper likened their immigration to a "grand 'round-up' of European freaks and hoboes."[15] Critics of Sifton's policies were genuinely worried that these foreign groups threatened to weaken, perhaps even ruin, the Anglo-Canadian fabric of the country. They also questioned why the backward dregs of European society were more welcome than English workers. Was not western Canada supposed to be home for the sons of Britain? Race, not agricultural experience, should have governed entry into Canada.

Sifton shrugged off this opposition and continued to champion the virtues of the "stalwart peasant in a sheepskin coat ... with a stout wife and a half-dozen children."[16] He had a job to do—in his mind, a region to build—and any public doubts about the wisdom of his strategy were not going to divert him from settling the Canadian prairies. It would be a mistake, however, to portray Sifton as an advocate of a multicultural west. Although he aggressively pursued what might generously be described as an "open door" immigration policy, he fully expected immigrants to accept and embrace the ways and traditions of their new country, to be "Canadianized" according to the popular terminology at the time. And the only way to bring about this transformation was to get them established on the land and interacting with British institutions. Settlement and assimilation, in Sifton's thinking, went hand in hand. Immigrant farmers, whatever their background, would eventually become valuable Canadian citizens.[17]

Because of the notoriety generated by the Doukhobors and to a lesser extent by the Ukrainians, it is often assumed that most settlers who came to Saskatchewan during Sifton's tenure as interior minister were from continental Europe. But according to the 1906 census returns, slightly more than half (128,879) of the new province's population was born in Canada, over 40 per cent in Ontario. The British (35,518), meanwhile, topped all other

The Schwartz family near Lipton around 1903. SASKATCHEWAN ARCHIVES BOARD R-B1781

immigrant groups during this period simply because the Department of the Interior spent more money promoting western Canada in Great Britain than anywhere else. In 1902–03, for example, over two hundred thousand dollars went to promotional literature in Britain, more than three times the amount for the rest of Europe. Among the foreign-born population (excluding Great Britain), those from the United States were clearly the majority at 35,464; they made up almost 40 per cent of the population born outside Canada and Great Britain. The next two largest "foreign" groups were Austro-Hungarians (21,188) and Russians (16,551). Together, they represented only 15 per cent of the total provincial population. Scandinavians (6,297) and Germans (5,827), considered "preferred" immigrants, were the fourth and fifth largest groups according to place of birth. Undoubtedly, some of the Canadian-born were children of immigrant parents; the same could be said for many of the American-born. But clearly, the central European numbers were significantly smaller than the totals for Great Britain and the United States.[18]

Most of the immigrants from English Canada or the British Isles settled throughout Saskatchewan in small groups or as individuals. Given their numerical dominance, there was little need to congregate. Still, a sense of continuity between their old world and their new homes was evident in the names of villages, rural municipalities, school districts, and local churches: Balliol, Birsay, Colonsay, Glaslyn, Limerick, Runnymede, Saltcoats, and Shamrock. For the Irish, this identity extended to the ultra-Protestant Orange Order and the English-speaking Roman Catholic Church. Those from Quebec, on the other hand, migrated to French-speaking communities in the southeastern (Forget, Oxbow, and Pipestone Valley) and southwestern (Lisieux, Coderre, and Ferland) corners of the province and in a central band from Hudson Bay and Saint-Brieux on the east through the Prince Albert district to the Battlefords and Paradise Hill on the west. These parishes, centred on the Catholic church, offered a kind of collective security for the minority francophone population. French-speaking newcomers, including those from the United States, Belgium, and France, represented only about 5 per cent of the provincial population in 1906.[19]

Some of the British settlers traded one exotic part of the world for another. In 1902, for example, about two hundred Welsh immigrants, who had initially tried farming in Argentina over three decades earlier, moved to Bangor in eastern Saskatchewan.[20] Hundreds of others were refugees from the streets and slums of British cities, orphans and abandoned children who were placed with Saskatchewan host families. Known as home children, many of these "little immigrants" were warmly accepted and built new lives for themselves. Others were harshly mistreated and worked like slaves. One, John Morrison, coldly murdered five members of the McArthur family with an axe at

Welwyn in June 1900 when the father forbade the hired hand from seeing his eldest daughter.[21]

Perhaps the most infamous group of British settlers to head for Saskatchewan in the early twentieth century was the Barr Colonists. Adopting the slogan, "Canada for the British," Anglican clergyman Isaac Barr had convinced—some might say hoodwinked—two thousand English recruits to join him in creating the Britannia Colony in the west-central part of the province near the future Saskatchewan-Alberta border. But the expedition soon began to flounder because of repeated foul-ups and scandals—Barr was a dreamer, not an organizer—and the thoroughly disillusioned settlers were ready to revolt by the time they reached Saskatoon in the spring of 1903. Only the intervention of the chaplain, George Exton Lloyd, saved "Barr's lambs," and they thankfully named their new community Lloydminster in his honour. Tough times were still ahead, though, since few of the settlers had any farm experience. During the trip from Saskatoon to the colony site, one man refused to unharness his horses for days, while another tied strings to the legs of his chickens to keep them from wandering off. Bob Holtby sheepishly admitted, "We could have done a lot better the first summer if we had not been so green."[22]

The largest "foreign" group to make Saskatchewan their new home came from the United States. What had started out as a trickle in the mid-1890s

The Barr Colonists purchased equipment and supplies in Saskatoon before the trek west to the Lloydminster area. SASKATCHEWAN ARCHIVES BOARD R-A2310

turned into a flood of biblical proportions by the end of the 1910s—what one historian has called "one of the greatest land rushes in the North American experience."[23] It is estimated that nearly six hundred thousand Americans crossed the border into Saskatchewan and Alberta between 1896 and 1914. What attracted them to Saskatchewan was the promise of cheap land, and they headed north with considerable equipment, money, and experience, especially in comparison to immigrants who came directly from Europe. Their movement into the region was greatly facilitated by the so-called Soo Line, a CPR branch line that ran northwestward from St. Paul, Minnesota, across the border at Portal through Estevan and Weyburn and on to Moose Jaw. It effectively served as a conduit, drawing prospective homesteaders from the Dakotas and Minnesota, and to a lesser extent, other midwest states. As early as 1898 Sifton was proudly claiming, "The exodus of Canadians to the United States has been stopped."[24]

About a third of the American immigrants were Yankee in origin. Another third were expatriate Canadians returning after an absence of a few years, or even one or two generations. The last third were originally from northern Europe, in particular Germany, Sweden, and Norway, and had immigrated to the northern central states after the American Civil War. Many American settlers came north on their own, disembarking throughout southern Saskatchewan along the Soo or CPR main line with one or two carloads of possessions. Others tended to follow and join people of the same ethnic heritage—what is known as chain migration. Germans, for example, concentrated in the Grenfell, Melville, Lanigan, and St. Walburg districts, while Scandinavians moved en masse into east-central Saskatchewan, especially from Naicam east through Buchanan to the Manitoba border. In a few cases, there was a desire to create distinct enclaves. The St. Peter's and St. Joseph's colonies were German-American Roman Catholic settlements in the Humboldt and Tramping Lake areas, respectively. By far the greatest success story was that of the Saskatchewan Valley Land Company. Buying over one million acres between Regina and Saskatoon in 1902, the Canadian-American syndicate sponsored a special promotional train from Chicago to Prince Albert for American journalists and other interested parties. Within a year, the towns of Craik, Davidson, and Hanley had not only been established, but hundreds of American farmers had purchased land in what had largely been regarded as a poor agricultural region. The Canadian government even maintained two immigration halls in the area to support settlers until they were on their land.[25]

Given their affinity with Anglo-Canadian traditions and institutions, and their experience farming the open plains, Americans generally had little difficulty blending into Saskatchewan society. But the Ukrainians, known at the time as Ruthenians, stood out as one of the most distinctive peoples of the settlement boom. The Department of the Interior actively began recruiting Ukrainians in the mid-1890s because of their reputation as a hard-working agricultural people inured to hardship and privation. And they responded in the thousands from the Hapsburg provinces of Galicia and Bukovyna in the Austro-Hungarian Empire—hence their contemporary names, Galicians and Bukovynians. To this day, turn-of-the-century Ukrainians have been tradition-ally portrayed as simple, ignorant peasants, more superstitious than religious, the poorest of the poor with one foot firmly rooted in the Middle Ages. Many of the immigrants, though, were more literate, more progressive, and more versatile than the popular stereotype. Like other groups, Ukrainians were seeking new economic opportunities and a better future for their children, and looked to western Canada as the land of opportunity.[26]

No exclusive areas for Ukrainians were set aside in Saskatchewan. Nor did they receive any special concessions. But in selecting a place to start their new lives, the first Ukrainians deliberately avoided the open prairies in favour of farms along the northern edge of the parkland through central Saskatchewan (Rosthern, Vonda, Yorkton). This bush country, although poorly suited for commercial grain production at first, offered a diverse subsistence base for the newcomers, especially when they arrived with few personal resources to fall back on. Those Ukrainians who followed naturally gravitated to the same areas. The Department of the Interior did little to discourage these block settlements, since they enabled recent immigrants to survive the difficult transition years with minimal assistance. It was also quite apparent that they wanted to live together. When a government colonization agent attempted to divert about fifty Ukrainian families, originally bound for Dauphin and Edmonton, to the Fish Creek district in the spring of 1898 in order to start a new settlement, the immigrants either stubbornly refused to leave their railway cars in Saskatoon or started to walk back to Regina. "They are wicked," the hapless agent plaintively declared.[27] Sifton's critics decried the block communities as an impediment to assimilation, yet at the same time, in a contradictory vein, they feared contamination of western society by these "disgusting creatures."[28] The Ukrainians certainly were different from the Anglo-Saxon ideal, which aroused much concern about their suitability as future citizens. But they had come to stay and did not see why their new attachment to Canada should come at the price of their language and cul-ture, especially when it meant the difference between survival and failure.

Another distinct group determined to live separately were the Mennonites, an Anabaptist Protestant group of Dutch-German origin. In 1874, some seven thousand Mennonites had fled Russia, largely because of persecution for their pacifist beliefs, and secured two large reserves of land in southern

Some questioned whether continental European immigrants should be
encouraged to settle in western Canada. *Montreal Daily Star*, 17 May 1905

Manitoba. Here, they reproduced their traditional farm villages thanks to the
addition of a special "hamlet clause" to the Dominion Lands Act. Although
individual Mennonites were required to hold title or patent to a particular
homestead, the fields were worked collectively in long strips (*kagel*), not quarter
sections, while animals grazed in common pastures. These German-speaking
villages, which doubled as religious or worship centres with their own
internal system of government and schools, flourished in the open prairies.
But the Mennonite desire to remain apart began to erode when individuals
decided to live outside the village system and farm their own land. Others
realized that future prosperity depended on integration into the commercial
grain industry.[29]

Mennonites first took up land around Rosthern in the Saskatchewan
Valley north of Saskatoon in the early 1890s. By the end of the decade, hundreds of immigrants from Manitoba, Russia, Prussia, and the United States,

representing more than half a dozen different Mennonite denominations, had settled in the region, creating a series of small village communities in such places as Dalmeny, Hepburn, Laird, and Waldheim. The federal government also agreed to establish Old Colony reserves in the province for those Mennonites most determined to resist acculturation. A block of land was set aside in the Hague-Osler area in 1895; a second reserve was created south of Swift Current in 1904 and a third near Carrot River two years later. Individual Mennonite homesteaders also took up land at Aberdeen, north of Rosthern, and in the Herbert area outside Swift Current. Sifton had no qualms about the farm villages, because they served to attract experienced agriculturalists who otherwise might not have come to western Canada. But like the Ukrainians, the Mennonites introduced a distinctive peasant culture to the wider prairie community.[30]

The most controversial group to be offered a new home in western Canada during this period was the Doukhobors, or "spirit wrestlers." A Protestant sect from Russia, organized along communist principles and practising an internalized religion (God resides in everyone), they first came to the attention of the Canadian government when word of their persecution by Czarist authorities became headline news in the late 1890s. Sifton agreed to provide religious sanctuary for the Doukhobors, a popular decision at the time, on the understanding that they were accomplished farmers. They were granted the same privileges as the Mennonites and awarded three-quarter million acres of land in three Saskatchewan blocks for their exclusive use: the South Colony (including the Good Spirit Lake annex) and North Colony, both north of Yorkton, and the Saskatchewan or Prince Albert Colony, northwest of Saskatoon near Blaine Lake. Between January and September 1899, some seventy-four hundred Doukhobors came to Canada under the special deal and quickly established nearly sixty Old World villages or communes, where they collectively worked the land and held all buildings and equipment in common. Their adjustment to their new surroundings, despite their initial poverty, was nothing short of astounding.[31]

Any goodwill initially enjoyed by the Doukhobors, however, was quickly dissipated. Not having enough farm animals during their first spring, and with the men away at Yorkton securing supplies, the women of the South Colony hitched themselves to a plough to get the ground ready for planting. A photograph of the women in harness caused a national outcry. Then, in the summer of 1902, some members of the South Colony began to believe that it was a sin to exploit animals in any manner and burned their leather shoes and released their cows and horses. Later that October two thousand converts began to march southeastward across the prairie to the supposed promised land. The NWMP were able to detain the women and children in Yorkton, but the barefooted men were not rounded up until they had reached Minnedosa, Manitoba, several weeks later, exhausted, hungry, and seemingly delirious. If that was not enough, a splinter group known as Freedomites insisted on demonstrating their opposition to material goods by destroying their belongings and holding nude demonstrations. These scandalous antics—and that's how they were regarded—earned the Doukhobors a reputation as a bizarre, if not fanatical, people, and turned the Canadian public against them. It could not have come at a worse time, since there were already rumblings that the Doukhobors were cultivating only the land immediately around their villages and not working their individual homesteads.

The person who decided what should be done about the Doukhobors was the new minister of the interior, the fiery, outspoken Frank Oliver. When Sifton resigned from the Laurier cabinet in February 1905 over the educational clauses in the autonomy bills, he was replaced by his rival, the Liberal MP for Edmonton and publisher of the *Bulletin*, Alberta's first newspaper. Oliver had been nothing less than a thorn in Sifton's side, constantly carping about his open door immigration policy and how it was populating the west with "scum." He once declared that a Ukrainian was "only a generation removed from a debased and brutalized serf" and deeply resented "this millstone of an alien Slav population hung about their necks."[32] The answer, according to Oliver, was to adopt a more selective, more restrictive policy that placed greater emphasis on racial origin. In other words, there would now be a clear pecking order: British immigrants would be given preference over all

The Doukhobors preferred to live in villages and farm their land communally. SASKATCHEWAN ARCHIVES BOARD R-B2113

other groups, followed by northern Europeans and Americans. Everyone else was unacceptable.

One of Oliver's first acts was to give the Doukhobors an ultimatum: they either had to fulfil their homestead obligations, including swearing allegiance to the Crown, or lose their land. It is not clear whether Oliver was trying to stamp out Doukhobor communism, clearly at odds with the ideal of an individualistic west, or simply responding to the intense public demand for homestead land. Whatever the case, he was not prepared to compromise. Nor were the Doukhobors. Their spiritual leader, Peter Veregin, interpreted Oliver's ruling as a betrayal of Sifton's agreement and refused to abide by government regulations that went against their most basic beliefs.[33] The Department of the Interior consequently went ahead with Oliver's threat and cancelled nearly fourteen hundred Doukhobor homestead entries on 1 May 1907; the only concessions were to allow each village to retain all land within a three-mile radius and to grant fifteen acres to those families who lost their homesteads.

The government's cancellation decision provoked a crisis in Doukhobor ranks. The Independents, a minority numbering about one thousand, decided to take up land as individual homesteaders. The majority, however, was not willing to forsake the dream of communal life—on its own terms—and about five thousand followed Veregin to British Columbia to begin anew on purchased land. It took more than a year to bring calm to the situation. The mounted police were kept busy evicting Community members from lands that had been withdrawn, when not dealing with nude demonstrations in protest of the government's action. They also had their hands full dealing with the mini land rush precipitated by the sudden availability of several thousand Doukhobor homesteads. One mountie confessed that he "never experienced a meaner job" than trying to keep order at the Yorkton land office.[34] But the real tragedy was the unhappy exodus of the Community Doukhobors and the gradual decay and disappearance of their thriving villages that had once graced the Saskatchewan landscape.

Oliver also tangled with another group—Blacks from Oklahoma. Starting around 1905, a handful of Black families, attracted by the Canadian advertising campaign in American midwest newspapers, entered the province and settled in the Maidstone and Rosetown districts in west-central Saskatchewan. Westerners initially took little notice of the new immigrants because there were so few of them, but once Black farmers began to move north in greater numbers to escape segregationist policies in the new state of Oklahoma, Anglo-Canadians grew alarmed. They were already uneasy about the influx of continental European immigrants and were not about to share the region with visible minorities. After all, it was supposed to be "white man's country." The western press spearheaded the campaign against Black immigration.

The *Saskatoon Daily Phoenix* carried a series of articles arguing that the Canadian prairies were no place for Blacks and insisting that the "Negro problem" was America's problem. Other newspapers revived Black stereotypes, suggesting that it was impossible for them to be assimilated into the Canadian way of life.[35]

The Department of the Interior was not immune to the racism behind this protest and initiated a number of measures to stem the flow of Blacks into western Canada, even though they never numbered more than a thousand. It pulled all advertising from newspapers in Black communities in the United States. It also subjected Blacks to more rigorous medical exams at the border, sometimes bribing doctors to turn them away. It even sent two agents—one a Black—to Oklahoma to talk about the hostile reception that Blacks could expect if they immigrated to Canada.[36] But the most far-reaching measure, undertaken at Oliver's urging, was a government order on 12 August 1911 banning Black immigration for a period of one year. The order-in-council, approved by Prime Minister Laurier and signed into law by the governor general, stated that the "Negro race ... is deemed unsuitable to the climate and requirements of Canada."[37] The order was never used and was repealed two months later because Blacks stopped coming to western Canada, yet it underscored the lengths to which the federal government was willing to go to slam the door on Black immigration.

Those Blacks who tried to make Saskatchewan their new home faced a difficult period of adjustment and acceptance. One of the problems they encountered was common to all settlers in the west-central part of the province at that time: railroad construction severely lagged behind the movement of people. Up until the early twentieth century, most settlers never strayed too far from the railway and were generally able to find land along or relatively near the various lines. But after 1905, as the number of immigrants skyrocketed, settlement swept across central Saskatchewan to the northwest in advance of the railway. The occupation of this region, beyond the so-called railway zone, was a sure sign of the seemingly insatiable demand for land.[38] So too was Oliver's decision in 1908 to amend the Dominion Lands Act to allow for the settlement of the range country in the southwest part of the province. Convinced that there were few areas in the west totally unsuited for agriculture, Oliver opened federal grazing leases to homesteading, even though much of the land held by ranchers had yet to be surveyed into sections. It did not matter. Thousands of people, mostly from the United States, poured in. The postmaster in the Pinto Creek area, along the north side of Wood Mountain, reported that every homestead was snapped up in less than six months, making it impossible for Norwegian Americans to try to settle together as they had done elsewhere. The story was the same further west at

Maple Creek, where the land office agent was so overworked that he quit until he got a pay raise. The census data for the district explains his frustration, for between 1906 and 1911 the local population jumped from twenty-eight hundred to just over eighteen thousand.[39]

Even with homesteading in the dry mixed-prairie district, the Department of the Interior was worried that the rate of immigration to Canada—over 260,000 people in 1907–08 alone—would soon exhaust the available supply of homestead land and that prospective settlers might go elsewhere. A special branch of the department consequently began to investigate the idea of starting a second settlement frontier north of the North Saskatchewan River. In the late summer of 1908, Frank Crean, a civil engineer by training and clerk with the department, examined a huge sweep of forested land south of the Churchill River between Stanley Mission on the east and Île-à-la-Crosse on the west, including present-day Prince Albert National Park. Although Treaty 10 Indians depended on this territory for their subsistence activities, Crean believed that the local Aboriginal population was squandering the land's great potential and suggested that the climate was ideal for raising any kind of cereal crop. To this end, he reported that almost one-quarter of the survey region of five million acres was ready for cultivation. He reached an even more favourable conclusion the following summer when he

Newspaper writers on tour in the Battleford area in 1908. LIBRARY AND ARCHIVES CANADA PA21123

continued his investigation westward from Portage la Loche into northeastern Alberta. Once again he found small garden plots and promising patches of wheat and oats, a fact confirmed by the splendid photographs he took at northern settlements, including one picture where the crop reached his shoulders. But even though Crean's findings nicely dovetailed with the needs of the moment, the Department of the Interior realized that settlement of the "New Northwest" would have to wait until the problem of accessibility had been resolved.[40]

Oliver, himself a great supporter of the northland's potential, had another solution to the pending shortage of homestead land: reduce, if not eliminate entirely, Indian reserves. This idea did not originate with the new minister of the interior, who also doubled as the superintendent general of Indian Affairs. The first surrender of reserve land in Saskatchewan was in 1901 when Clifford Sifton stripped the Pheasant's Rump and Ocean Man bands of their entire land base (46,720 acres) and moved them to the White Bear reserve in southeastern Saskatchewan. But it was during Oliver's tenure that the push for surrenders accelerated and gained momentum. Oliver, who was supposed to represent First Nations interests, had long doubted that Indians would ever become successful farmers or put their reserves to good use. Now, as Canada's most senior Indian official, he questioned why bands should continue to hold land in prime agricultural areas when that same land could be used to satisfy some of the demand for homesteads; at the very least, the amount of "idle" or "unused" land occupied by Indians should be reduced by persuading band members to surrender portions of their reserves.[41] To facilitate this process, Oliver proposed several amendments to the federal Indian Act. In 1906, the maximum amount that band members could expect to receive from the sale of any reserve land was raised from 10 to 50 per cent of the eventual proceeds. When this inducement proved ineffective, the Laurier government gave itself the power in 1911, in direct contravention of the Indian Act, to take reserve land without band consent if it was near a town or "needed for public purposes."[42]

Land surrenders in Saskatchewan during this period were justified on the grounds that some reserves were overly large and actually exceeded treaty provisions. It was also claimed that the steady decline in Indian numbers, because of chronic health problems and disease,[43] meant that most reserves had more land than they needed. In other words, there was "surplus" land for the taking. Oliver insisted that the government had a moral duty to correct "the disparity between the people and the land." In resolving this apparent inequity, however, his officials not only initiated the surrender process, including preparation of the formal "band" proposal, but used a mixture of intimidation and bribery to secure Indian approval.[44] Many of the surrenders involved the reduction of reserves in areas heavily settled by non-Indians or along existing or proposed railway lines. Cowessess, part of the Crooked Lakes agency just north of Indian Head, was reduced by 40 per cent in 1907, while at Muscowpetung, northwest of Regina in the Qu'Appelle Valley, almost half the reserve was withdrawn in 1909. A few Saskatchewan reserves lost slightly more, others much less, but at least ten reserves had their boundaries reduced during Oliver's tenure. Sometimes bands were able to resist government pressure, such as when Moscowequan in the Touchwood Hills foiled an attempt in 1908 to dissolve the reserve in favour of amalgamation with Poor Man. But Little Bone, which was once located south of Yorkton, will never be found on a provincial map. The seven-thousand-acre reserve was completely surrendered in 1907. Moosomin and Thunderchild in the Battlefords area were relocated in 1909 in order to make prized farming land available to settlers. Government officials maintained that the two reserves were the wrong size—one too small, the other too big—and that the bands should simply acquire new reserves in a different area. But it took visits from Oliver and Indian Commissioner David Laird, a stack of cash on the table at the surrender meeting, and three votes over a three-day period before Thunderchild approved the surrender by a narrow, one-vote margin.[45] In the end, the relocations represented a giant step backward. According to a senior Indian Affairs official, the new Moosomin reserve near Jackfish Lake was "practically useless as a farming proposition."[46]

Oliver's efforts—or excesses—certainly put people on the land in Saskatchewan. For the three-year period from 1909 to 1911 the number of homestead entries in the province averaged between twenty and twenty-five thousand, more than Manitoba and Alberta combined. The number of immigrants who came to Saskatchewan, meanwhile, jumped to 40,763 in 1910–11, an increase of ten thousand from the previous year; the figure would climb another five thousand for the next two years.[47] This rapid settlement of the prairies created a seemingly insatiable regional appetite for new railways and branch lines and demanded a steady supply of unskilled labourers to build the transportation network. And since Asians were no longer acceptable for this kind of work, while those of British background were generally not willing to do it, the Laurier government began to admit large numbers of central and southern Europeans, particularly Italians, to serve as railway navvies. Not even Oliver's vociferous objections could override the demands of the Canadian business community and its need for an industrial proletariat. This lifting of the restrictions on "alien" labour is readily discernible in immigration statistics for the period. Between 1907 and the start of the Great War in 1914, the percentage of unskilled workers entering Canada dramatically increased, as did the percentage of immigrants from central and southern Europe.[48]

A young married couple who pinned their hopes for a better future on western Canada. WESTERN DEVELOPMENT MUSEUM 5-C-20

The recruitment of these foreign navvies accentuated the already pronounced cultural diversity of Saskatchewan society. By the start of the war, almost half the provincial population had been born in another country. One observer in 1910 suggested that "the West is nothing less than a 'new nation'."[49] An American historian said much the same thing when he claimed that the northern plains were "the heir of many cultures, the copy of none."[50] Others have employed different images to depict Saskatchewan's cultural makeup in the early twentieth century, from a kaleidoscope to a giant checkerboard to the shuffling of two decks of playing cards.[51] This ethnically diverse society, however, was totally at odds with the Anglo-Canadian ideal for the province. Saskatchewan was supposed to be a bastion of British values, traditions, and institutions, not some multicultural amalgam. Assimilation consequently replaced immigration as western Canada's new necessity. As Methodist minister J. S. Woodsworth argued in *Strangers within Our Gates*, "Language, nationality, race, temperament, training are all dividing walls that must be broken down."[52] Many confidently assumed that the breaking down of these walls was not only desirable but possible, and that the newcomers would readily integrate over time. Little did they realize that Saskatchewan's spectacular settlement story jeopardized its Britishness.[53]

CHAPTER FIVE

SASKATCHEWAN FOREVER

A LITTLE MORE THAN FOUR YEARS after the Saskatchewan inauguration, Governor General Earl Grey was back in Regina, silver trowel in hand, laying the cornerstone for the new Legislative Building. The ceremony was no ordinary public event; nor was it any ordinary public building. More than anything else, the elegant, domed structure, rising from the treeless prairie south of Wascana Creek, expressed Saskatchewan's resolve to become Canada's most powerful and populous province. The political leaders of the day believed that the future belonged to the province, and more importantly, that the province could decide and shape that future. The Saskatchewan government consequently embarked on an ambitious province-building program, determined to leave behind the old territorial days and any lingering sense of colonialism, while cultivating a new and separate identity in keeping with the province's central place in Confederation.[1] Even the governor general, who had a special affinity with the province, was struck by this sense of destiny at the cornerstone ceremony. "I do not think I have ever been so greatly surprised," he confessed during a candid moment later that day. "I realized for the first time how extremely dignified your new parliamentary and executive buildings will be ... and the big ideas which they have ... given expression to."[2] It fell to Saskatchewan's first government to make this "big idea" come true.

Saskatchewan and controversy went hand-in-hand for the Wilfrid Laurier government. No sooner had the new province come into existence on 1 September 1905, after a long and bitter struggle over the terms of entry, than a new controversy erupted over the selection of Saskatchewan's first premier. Lieutenant-Governor A. E. Forget's first official duty was to call on someone to form a provincial government. He immediately chose Walter Scott, the new leader of the provincial Liberal party. The decision sparked howls of protest, even charges of federal interference, since the popular choice was Frederick Haultain, the first and only territorial premier and one of the region's dominant political figures. It appeared that Forget, in selecting Scott, was acting more like a federal civil servant than an impartial representative of the Crown. And he was. Laurier was still in Regina, actually staying at Government House, when the lieutenant-governor summoned Scott and asked him to form the first government.[3]

Haultain was no longer welcome. He had become a bloody nuisance to the federal government by 1905, if not earlier, because of his vehement opposition to the terms by which Saskatchewan entered Confederation. Indeed, Laurier, who at one time had considered offering Haultain the Alberta premiership, was deeply troubled by the westerner's repeated threat to challenge the legislation in the courts. Haultain's behaviour provided the federal government with the justification to do what it really wanted to do: appoint a "friendly" administration in Saskatchewan. What Forget's decision meant, though, was that the heavy hand of Ottawa continued to be exerted. Some even suggested that Scott's appointment was nothing less than an attempt by the federal government to keep Saskatchewan under its thumb.[4]

On 12 September 1905 Walter Scott, along with three other Liberal colleagues, was sworn into office: Scott as premier and minister of public works; James Calder as provincial treasurer and minister of education; W. R. Motherwell as provincial secretary and minister of agriculture; and J. H. Lamont as attorney general. Only Scott and Lamont had any political experience, but all had their own particular strengths and abilities, whether as spokesperson for government policy or party organizer. Their selection also followed the traditional parliamentary practice of trying to ensure that all regions were included in the cabinet. Lamont, an accomplished Prince Albert lawyer who had just been elected to the House of Commons a year earlier,

Frederick Haultain, leader of the new Provincial Rights party, threatened to challenge the constitutionality of the Saskatchewan Act. SASKATCHEWAN ARCHIVES BOARD R-B12887-2

was chosen in part because of the need to have a representative from outside the southern part of the province; he would eventually serve on the Supreme Court of Canada. The most noteworthy feature of this first Saskatchewan cabinet, however, was the appointment of Motherwell, a successful farmer from the Abernethy district and founding member of the Territorial Grain Growers' Association. He was the first in a succession of farm leaders to be brought into government, signalling the fundamental importance of agriculture to the new provincial administration.[5]

The first test of the fledgling Liberal government was Saskatchewan's first provincial election, called for 13 December 1905, the anniversary of Scott's arrival in Regina nineteen years earlier. Here, finally, was the chance for the electorate to voice its opinion on the passing over of Haultain as premier. The shrewd Scott concentrated on the practical issues facing the new province; his sense of optimism was nicely captured in the campaign slogan "Peace, Progress, and Prosperity."[6] Haultain, on the other hand, although nominally a Conservative, objected to the introduction of party politics and formed a new Provincial Rights party dedicated to securing full provincial rights for Saskatchewan. He promised, if he formed the government, to challenge the constitutionality of the Saskatchewan Act, especially federal control of the province's public lands and natural resources. The Provincial Rights party took dead aim at the Liberals and their seemingly servile relationship with Ottawa by playing up the province's shabby treatment at the hands of the Laurier government. But Scott's unbridled enthusiasm for Saskatchewan's future proved more attractive than Haultain's cry about violated rights, and the Liberals won sixteen of twenty-five seats in the legislature. It was the beginning of a Liberal reign that lasted a quarter century.[7]

The first legislative session was convened at the end of March 1906. The ethnicity of those charged with guiding Saskatchewan in the critical first few years contrasted sharply with the larger society taking shape at that time. Only one member—Gerhard Ens, a Mennonite from Rosthern—was of non-British, non-Canadian background. In fact, only two were *not* Anglican, Methodist, or Presbyterian. They were also all men; women would not secure the right to vote in Saskatchewan elections, let alone sit in the legislature, for another ten years.[8] The members quickly got down to work, passing sixty-six bills in less than two months. The heavy legislative agenda reflected the fact

A polling station near Fort Qu'Appelle during the 1904 federal election. SASKATCHEWAN ARCHIVES BOARD R-B1176

that the Scott government had to create the machinery to administer the rapidly growing province.[9] Ironically, the demands on this and subsequent governments could have been much heavier if Ottawa had not retained jurisdiction over Saskatchewan lands and resources, especially during the settlement boom. Nor did the provincial government have to attend to the needs of the First Nations, since they remained a federal responsibility under the 1867 British North America Act. The government's gaze also rarely extended to the northern half of the province, where it gladly abdicated any meaningful presence in favour of the Anglican and Roman Catholic churches, the RNWMP and the Hudson's Bay and Revillon Frères fur-trade companies.

The major issue of the first session was the selection of the permanent Saskatchewan capital. Regina had been named temporary capital in the Saskatchewan Act on the understanding that it would be confirmed by the legislature. Since Regina, or the Queen City as it was dubbed, had served as territorial capital since 1883, it was assumed that the question would be quickly resolved. Any controversy was expected in neighbouring Alberta, where Edmonton and Calgary were both spoiling for the prize. But if the Scott government looked upon the decision as a mere formality, other Saskatchewan cities did not. Part of the problem was Walter Scott's own doing. During the election campaign, he had vowed that major institutions would be distributed throughout the province, not housed in a single centre. Several cities took him at his word. The other difficulty was that Liberal strength was concentrated in the central part of the province, north of the CPR main line. The Scott government had to be careful not to alienate this support.[10]

The battle to secure the capital actually started in the early spring of 1905 while the Alberta and Saskatchewan autonomy bills were still being debated in the House of Commons. When it was learned that Regina had been named only the temporary capital, Moose Jaw, Prince Albert, and Saskatoon decided to try to capture the provincial crown. Moose Jaw and Regina, separated only an hour by train, had always been friendly adversaries, while Prince Albert was still smarting from the rerouting of the CPR main line across the southern prairies. The real skirmish, though, was between Regina and its rival Saskatoon, half the size but big on ambition. In a 30 June 1905 editorial, the *Saskatoon Phoenix* wondered what Regina had to offer: "It is the coldest point known in Western Canada, lying in an unhealthy depression whose mud is proverbial." The *Leader* gamely responded, "Yes, there is mud at Regina ... and it is that same mud at Regina which yields such abundant crops of wheat."[11]

Over the next few months Saskatoon, led by Mayor James Clinkskill, campaigned tirelessly, even bringing members of the legislature north by special train on 5 May 1906 to tour the city and "capital hill" in Nutana. The intense lobbying snared several government members. The night before the matter was to be decided in the legislature, Premier Scott informally canvassed his caucus at a secret meeting and was stunned to discover that two-thirds, including cabinet minister William Motherwell, favoured Saskatoon. The premier, who had confidently assumed that Regina would get the nod, made it known that he was not prepared to see the capital relocated. His caucus closed ranks. When W. C. Sutherland, the Liberal representative for Saskatoon, introduced a resolution on 23 May calling for the awarding of the seat of government to Saskatoon, claiming the city was destined to be "a second Ottawa," the motion was soundly defeated twenty-one to two. During the debate a somewhat contrite Scott tried to make his support of Regina a little more palatable to the losing cities by suggesting that the decision had not been an easy one for him. Haultain brushed his remarks aside, maintaining that the government's failure to make its position known months earlier had been the real problem.[12]

One of the main reasons Premier Scott was so anxious to see the capital remain in Regina was that he was already planning to build a new legislative building in the city. The first Saskatchewan government was housed in two buildings on Dewdney Avenue, holdovers from territorial days. These facilities were completely inadequate for the administrative and legislative needs of the province, especially at the rate at which it was growing. The premier also wanted a building that reflected the great expectations for Saskatchewan, a building that would meet the needs of the not-too-distant future when the provincial population was expected to top several million.[13] Wearing his other hat as minister of public works, Scott called on his trusted cabinet colleague Jim Calder to prepare a list of possible sites for the new building. Calder's investigation by horse and wagon produced seven options, including Victoria Park in downtown Regina and a property near Government House, the lieutenant-governor's official residence. His preference, and the site that best met the premier's insistence for a spacious setting, was a 168-acre parcel of land known as the Old Sinton property, south of the Wascana Creek reservoir. The cabinet accepted the recommendation in late June 1906, but not without protest from Regina's civic leaders, who complained that the proposed location was outside city limits and pitched Wascana Park as an alternative site. Scott politely turned down the offer, but agreed to develop the entire area into a public park to complement the Legislative Building.[14]

Once the site had been purchased at a cost close to one hundred thousand dollars, the Department of Public Works hired Frederick Todd, a noted Montreal landscape architect, to design the grounds and determine the site for the building. It was his recommendation that the structure face north.

Walter Scott served eleven years as Saskatchewan's first premier.
SASKATCHEWAN ARCHIVES BOARD
R-A245

Selecting an architect was more difficult, especially since any appointment had to avoid the appearance of patronage. Premier Scott simply wanted to hire an accomplished architect, even approaching F. M. Rattenbury, the designer of British Columbia's handsome legislative building, but the cabinet convinced him that there had to be a competition handled by an independent committee of recognized architectural experts. The proposed structure, however, still reflected Scott's vision and influence. The specifications called for a 125-seat legislative chamber—at a time when there were only twenty-five members—and provision for enlargement by the adding of two wings if necessary in the future. There was also to be a central dome, so that the building would serve as a central landmark, visible for miles in any direction. The assessment committee invited seven architectural firms, including one from New York and another from London, to submit plans; all were numbered to conceal their source. The winning design, by Edward and W. S. Maxwell of Montreal, was communicated to the government on 20 December 1907. It was an early Christmas present for the province, but it came at a cost. The projected price tag was now $1.75 million, twice the original estimate.[15]

While construction of the new Legislative Building was underway, the

Scott government tried to bring order and structure to Saskatchewan's disparate settlements in the southern half of the province. It also had to provide services to a largely rural community, scattered over thousands of square miles. The province's first royal commission, the Municipal Commission, was established in 1907 to examine the best way of delivering a system of local self-government that was both economical and comprehensive. The commission recommended that the existing local improvement districts be dissolved in favour of larger, nine-township rural municipalities (RMs) with broad local powers including fire protection and road maintenance, a uniform rate of land taxation, and the collection of local school taxes. This system was incorporated into the 1908–09 Rural Municipality Act, which also called for a Department of Municipal Affairs, the first in Canada. By 1912, nearly three hundred RMs (each 324 square miles in area) were organized in the province, a form of rural local government that exists to this day. But because the system was intended to be uniform, no allowance was made for varying population density or physical features such as small lakes or forested land. It was assumed that all districts would continue to grow, but even then some areas were less populated than others, a situation that would become more pronounced in the following decades.[16]

Another key infrastructure initiative during these formative years was telephone legislation. At first, the Scott government showed little interest in the existing telephone facilities, but when the public began to demand better, more efficient service, it hired Francis Dagger, a telephone expert, in 1907 to investigate the feasibility of introducing a government-owned system. Dagger found that only 22 of 121 urban centres had telephone service, that only 3,250 homes (310 rural) had telephones, and that there was no long-distance service effectively north of Regina. But instead of creating a wholly publicly owned telephone network in 1908, the government introduced a system, in the words of the first telephone minister, Jim Calder, "that would efficiently provide service for all sections of the province."[17] It purchased all long-distance or trunk-line facilities of private companies, while giving both urban centres and rural municipalities the authority to build their own systems subject to government standards and regulation. What made the Saskatchewan solution unique, though, was the rural telephone system whereby residents could form mutual or co-operative companies to provide service to subscribers. People living in the country would not have to wait for telephone service to reach them, but could proceed on their own, with assistance from the province in the form of free telephone poles and technical advice.[18]

The Scott government also took steps to improve transportation. In the late nineteenth century, except for the CPR main line, travel was by trail or steamboat on the Saskatchewan River system and Long Lake; in fact, by the

The S.S. *City of Medicine Hat* crashed into Saskatoon's new traffic bridge during high water in June 1908. LIBRARY AND ARCHIVES CANADA PA038502

1880s sternwheelers had replaced cart trains for the summer shipment of freight across the northern prairies. But the heyday of the river steamers, numbering around a dozen at one time, did not last more than a few decades because of the coming of the railway. It has been suggested that the era of the prairie steamer symbolically came to an end on 7 June 1908, when the 250-passenger *City of Medicine Hat*, hurtling down the swollen South Saskatchewan, crashed into Saskatoon's Victoria Bridge and capsized.[19] Most settlers used existing prairie trails or cut new ones, but as the land was occupied they increasingly used road allowances to get around. In 1906, the Scott government spent close to one hundred thousand dollars on road and highway construction; by the following year, this expenditure had increased four times and would soon exceed more than a million dollars annually.[20] The real need, though, was for more rail lines, especially for the burgeoning farming community which had to ship its grain to market. Some relief was forthcoming in the early twentieth century when two new transcontinental railways, the Canadian Northern and the Grand Trunk Pacific, were pushed across the northern prairies with the support of the Laurier government. Securing branch or feeder lines, on the other hand, became the responsibility of the province after 1905. To facilitate this work, the Scott government passed railway legislation in 1909 that promised provincial backing of the principal and interest of railway construction bonds. This guarantee, up to a limit of thirteen thousand dollars per mile, encouraged the Canadian Northern and Grand Trunk Pacific to build fourteen branch lines, or more than one thousand miles of track, by the start of the Great War.[21]

A road gang at work near Tisdale in 1908. SASKATCHEWAN ARCHIVES BOARD R-B215(12)

Another major task for the Scott government was meeting the province's educational needs. School districts, each covering from six to thirty square miles, had to be organized at a rate that kept pace with the steadily growing population of rural children, while teachers had to be found to staff the small, generally isolated, one-room schools. It was an extraordinary challenge. During the eight-year period from 1905 to 1913 the number of elementary schools in the province jumped from 405 to 2,747, an astounding 678 per cent. Nor did the demand lessen for several years. For the 1916–17 school year, one-half of all registered children in Saskatchewan were in grade one. The government opened normal schools in Regina and Saskatoon to train teachers, and established a system of high schools. This preparation and training may have helped teachers better deal with the difficulty of handling eight grades in one classroom, but they still had to contend with poor pay, inadequate facilities, and uneven attendance. Cold weather and the cost of keeping buildings heated often kept schools closed from Christmas until late February. Children also stayed home in the early fall to help with harvest. Students of all ages were consequently concentrated in the primary grades, while many quit before completing grade eight. The real sticking point, though, was finding teachers who were willing to work for any length of time in "foreign" districts.[22]

During the December 1905 election, Premier Scott also announced his intention to establish a provincial university and agricultural college, a decision that one political scientist has called "an act of supreme confidence in the future of the province."[23] Once again Saskatoon was an early entrant in the race. In early January 1906, even before the capital question had been resolved, the *Phoenix* suggested that the university would be admirably located on Caswell Hill, just across the river from the site for the capital buildings. When the *Moose Jaw Signal* responded, "You take one and we'll take the other," the Saskatoon newspaper shot back that the capital and university could not be separated. Moose Jaw citizens had their own scheme and tried unsuccessfully to secure a provincial charter for a "Saskatchewan College," believing that it would give the city an edge in the contest for the university. Indian Head, meanwhile, claimed that the agricultural school would be a natural fit with the town's federal experimental farm.[24] Then there was Prince Albert. In 1883, the Reverend Dr. John McLean, the first Anglican bishop of Saskatchewan and founder of Prince Albert's Emmanuel College, a training school for Native missionaries and catechists, had secured a federal charter for the "University of Saskatchewan." These degree-granting powers fell into disuse in 1887 when Emmanuel became an Indian boarding school. But in October 1906, when the diocese decided to open a theological college,

One of the many rural, one-room schools that dotted the prairies. SASKATCHEWAN ARCHIVES BOARD R-B803

the Prince Albert city council and board of trade called on Premier Scott to recognize the city's rightful claim to the provincial university.[25]

Prince Albert got its answer in the spring of 1907 when the Saskatchewan legislature refused to recognize the earlier dominion charter and unanimously approved the University Act. The legislation provided for a single, government-supported institution with exclusive degree-granting powers, except in theology; it was to be free from political interference, open to both men and women, and required no religious test for admission. The proposed university's defining feature, however, was that it was intended to serve the wider provincial community. This role was openly embraced by the university's first president, the affable Walter Murray, a philosophy professor from the Maritimes, who was appointed in August 1908.[26] "What is the sphere of the university?" he asked in his first annual report. "Its watchword is service— service of the state ... No form of that service is too mean or too exalted for the university."[27] Murray's infectious outlook for the university matched that of Scott for the province.

As in the case of the capital, the location of the university proved to be a contentious issue. The University Act was silent about the site question. And the Scott government, while not refuting its official policy of decentralization, publicly maintained that the decision would not be a political one, but would rest with the university's nine-member board of governors. Behind the scenes, though, it was a different story. When both Moose Jaw and Prince Albert returned Provincial Rights candidates in the August 1908 provincial election, the premier privately told a Liberal colleague that the two cities had eliminated themselves from the competition.[28] President Murray, also a member of the board of governors, wanted the university to be located in Regina, close to the seat of government, but had to wait patiently while the board visited several possible sites, now including Battleford, and received delegations from the competing cities. Regina, for example, offered one thousand acres of free land. The main contender, though, was Saskatoon, which had redoubled its efforts to win the university after losing the capital; the city could also count on the influence of Scott.[29] On the evening of 7 April 1909, the board met in Regina's new city hall and first agreed that the College of Agriculture should be part of the new university. It then turned to the question of the site and by secret ballot awarded the university to Saskatoon.[30] A. P. McNab, the new minister of public works and Saskatoon MLA, sent word of the victory to the city in what must rank as one of the most understated telegrams in Saskatchewan history: "Everything Ok. got university will be home tomorrow."[31]

President Murray was distressed with the decision—he bluntly told his wife, "The interests of the University were simply ignored"[32]—and contemplated

The telegram announcing that Saskatoon had won the competition for the provincial university.
UNIVERSITY OF SASKATCHEWAN ARCHIVES A2377

resigning. He was also worried that a rival institution would take root in Regina some day. But in mid-April he put these concerns behind him and headed north to Saskatoon with William Rutherford, the new dean of agriculture, to select the site for the university. There were two favoured locations: Caswell Hill (near present-day St. Paul's Hospital), and the east side of the South Saskatchewan River north of Nutana. The latter was chosen because it was the better farmland; in other words, agriculture—what Murray called "the sheet anchor of the university"[33]—determined the site. While negotiations for the land were underway, the president was busy hiring faculty and finding a temporary campus for the first students. Classes officially began on 29 September 1909 on the fourth floor of the Drinkle Building in downtown Saskatoon. It was probably just a coincidence that the first lecture was in history.[34]

Although Regina was miffed about the awarding of the university to Saskatoon, the Scott government refused to reconsider its decentralization policy and continued to distribute major institutions throughout the southern half of the province. One was an asylum to house the mentally ill. In 1907, Dr. David Low, the provincial health officer, toured the major mental health hospitals in eastern Canada and the United States to collect information about the most advanced forms of treatment and facility design. Several towns and cities, in the meantime, lined up to be home to the new Saskatchewan Hospital. It was eventually built in North Battleford in 1913.[35] Another coveted institution was the Saskatchewan penitentiary, which opened in Prince Albert in 1911. Although the new jail was a federal facility, it was undoubtedly given to Saskatchewan's most northerly city on the advice of the Scott government and prominent local Liberals, including Senator T. O. Davis and Judge J. H. Lamont.[36] There is no evidence, however, to support the popular myth that Prince Albert actually preferred the jail over the university. What also tends to be overlooked is that Moose Jaw was the perennial loser,[37] even though it was the largest urban centre in Saskatchewan at the time of the 1906 special western census. Despite its failed attempts to secure the capital and then the university, the city was never offered a consolation prize. In 1908, for example, the Scott government chose Moosomin, near the Saskatchewan-Manitoba border, for the site of a new provincial jail. It seemed as if Regina would brook no southern rival, especially one that was less than fifty miles away.

One sure sign of Regina's rise to prominence was the stately Legislative Building taking shape near Wascana Lake. In July 1908, P. Lyall and Sons of Montreal, one of Canada's foremost construction companies, began driving the first of over three thousand piles for the massive edifice; almost eighteen hundred would be needed to support the central dome. By the following spring, crews had completed the skeletal framework and were ready to start on the red brick exterior. But at Premier Scott's insistence, it was decided at the last moment to switch to Tyndall stone—a design change that resulted in additional cost and delay, but ultimately enhanced the graceful appearance of the structure.[38] A further slowdown was experienced in the late summer of 1909 when the local men working on the project left for harvest. Construction had reached the point, however, where the Scott government could proceed with the ceremonial laying of the cornerstone on Monday, 4 October 1909—what one Regina newspaper called "the greatest day in the history of the province."[39]

The celebration rivalled that of the Saskatchewan inauguration four years earlier. In the early afternoon, while a nineteen-gun viceregal salute boomed in the distance, Earl Grey and his party were escorted by the mounted police in dress uniform along the decorated streets of downtown Regina through a triumphal arch on the bridge over Wascana Creek to the construction site. Here, an estimated six thousand people had gathered at the foot of the main

Boaters on Wascana Lake could watch the new Legislative Building take shape. SASKATCHEWAN ARCHIVES BOARD R-B9442

entrance or in temporary stands around three sides of the grand staircase. The shell of the building was festooned with streamers and flags, while a huge provincial coat of arms, set against coloured bunting in the shape of a sunburst, had been placed above the speakers' platform. Once the official party had taken their seats and the cheering subsided, a group of schoolchildren, holding little flags and waving sheaves of wheat, opened the ceremony with "The Maple Leaf Forever." In recognition of the special occasion, they sang a new verse: "Saskatchewan, Saskatchewan/ Saskatchewan Forever/ God Bless the West and Heaven Bless/ Saskatchewan Forever."[40]

Premier Scott, who served as host for the ceremonies, could hardly contain his excitement. The building "in appearance, stability, and durability ... will appropriately represent the character and ambitions of the people of the province," he triumphantly declared in his opening remarks. "Saskatchewan demands a building of no mean dimensions."[41] The governor general, noting his rare "double privilege" of presiding over the provincial inauguration and now the cornerstone ceremony, was equally effusive about Saskatchewan's destiny. After acknowledging the profound changes the province had undergone since 1905, he boldly predicted, "They are not only a proof of your vigorous growth, but an indication of your future strength."[42] After the provincial attorney general had read aloud the list of items placed in the time capsule, Earl Grey was handed an engraved silver trowel with a special buffalo horn handle; it was the only reminder of the province's Aboriginal past during the ceremony, apart from the attendance of children from the local Indian industrial school. As the band began to play the national anthem, the governor general deftly smoothed the mortar before the block was carefully lowered into place to the thunderous roar of the crowd. Not even a sudden, brief downpour sweeping across the lake could dampen the enthusiasm of the moment. The formal ceremonies concluded with several short speeches of congratulations, including one by Frank Oliver, the minister of the interior, followed by a tour of the building and grounds by the official party. A civic reception at City Hall completed the day's events.

Premier Scott's obvious delight at the cornerstone ceremony was understandable. Just four years earlier he had been handed the demanding job of building a new province and had succeeded probably beyond his own grand expectations. Not only had the new government introduced a wealth of legislation for a rapidly growing Saskatchewan, but had earned a reputation for being a competent administration—a remarkable achievement given the relative inexperience of those at the helm. It also enjoyed almost absolute control over the political agenda. Under Jim Calder, one of Saskatchewan's ablest cabinet ministers, the Liberals used a potent mixture of organization and patronage to broaden and strengthen party support throughout the province.[43] These efforts were especially directed at the sizable immigrant population. Whereas the Provincial Rights opposition took no meaningful steps to secure the foreign vote, the Scott government deliberately sought to woo religious and ethnic minorities to the Liberal fold. In 1907, for example, the premier appointed the first Roman Catholic, W. F. A. Turgeon, to serve in the cabinet; that same year, the Liberal party began publishing a German-language newspaper, *Der Courier*.[44] This kind of accommodation, however, had its limits. Whatever the political gains at stake in immigrant communities, the cultural standards in the province remained British.

The Scott government's dominance was reflected in its electoral success. In 1908, the Liberals won twenty-seven of the forty-one seats in the enlarged Saskatchewan legislature. This majority would become even larger in the July 1912 provincial election, when the Liberals easily took forty-six of fifty-four ridings. The results completely demoralized the fractious opposition, which had only recently decided to throw off the Provincial Rights label in favour of fighting under the Conservative banner. The repackaging, however, made no difference; if anything, things were worse as Conservative strength in the legislature slipped to a mere eight seats.[45] Frederick Haultain chose this moment to step down. After losing three consecutive provincial elections as leader, while trying to keep his 1906 marriage to an emotionally troubled divorcée a secret,[46] he turned his back on a distinguished twenty-five-year career in western politics to become chief justice of the Saskatchewan Supreme Court. Knighted during the Great War, Haultain was also elected chancellor of the University of Saskatchewan in 1917. Upon his death in Montreal in 1942, his ashes were placed at the base of the university's

An interior view of the dome that graces the Legislative Building. SASKATCHEWAN ARCHIVES BOARD R-B2744-3

Memorial Gates. But despite having streets and schools named in his memory, Sir Frederick is Saskatchewan's forgotten father of Confederation.

Walter Scott, by contrast, seemed destined to govern for as long as he wished, as his party won larger majorities each time it went to the polls. The province, meanwhile, appeared well on its way to realizing its destiny. This sense that Saskatchewan was ready to assume its rightful place in Canada was evident at the official opening of the Saskatchewan Legislative Building on 12 October 1912. The guest of honour was the new governor general, Prince Arthur, the third and favourite son of Queen Victoria, who was more popularly known as the Duke of Connaught. Arriving by train late Saturday afternoon, the royal party was whisked along crowded streets to Regina's city hall and then Government House before heading out to the new Legislative Building in the early evening darkness. As they passed under a series of illuminated arches, with such wording as "Saskatchewan Greets You," the building's majestic dome, awash in brilliant light, beckoned them. The duke and duchess, along with their daughter, Princess "Pat," paused for a few minutes at the main entrance to watch a fireworks display on the other side of Wascana Lake, then proceeded into the magnificent rotunda with its marble pillars and arched ceiling under the dome. After being formally welcomed by acting premier Jim Calder on behalf of the people of Saskatchewan, the duke declared the building officially opened. "I do so with the prayer," he solemnly remarked, "that the decisions arrived at ... may, under the blessing of Providence, always be for the lasting benefit of the province of Saskatchewan." At the conclusion of the brief ceremony, Calder presented the governor general with an Indian pipe, formerly owned by Fine Day of the Sweetgrass reserve, as a memento of his visit and a symbol of the old Saskatchewan that had been displaced by "an ever advancing civilization." The royal party then moved into the legislative chamber to receive invited guests before retiring to its private railway car for the night.[47]

The opening of the Saskatchewan Legislative Building, by royalty no less, capped an impressive seven years for the young province. But Walter Scott, the man who had been the driving force behind the building and what it stood for, was not there that day to bask in the glory. Instead, the premier was touring Europe, trying to find a cure for the depression that would haunt him to his final days. The illness may have started during the winter of 1906–07, when he suffered a bout of pneumonia. Thereafter, he fled the province every fall in search of rest in a warmer setting. It might also have been aggravated by the dark secret that he carried with him—that he had been born out of wedlock. Whatever the cause, Scott was not a well man and was away from the province for at least half his tenure as premier. His absences initially delayed government business, but became so lengthy after

1911 that Calder effectively served in his place.[48] Any talk of Scott retiring, however, was quickly dismissed as rumour. Quite simply, he was too important to the party's standing in the province, too closely identified with Saskatchewan's good fortune, to give up the reins of power. That the provincial government was able to perform so effectively under the circumstances was nothing short of remarkable. Perhaps there was some truth to the belief that Saskatchewan was meant for greatness.

CHAPTER SIX

LAND I
CAN OWN

"THERE WAS ONE GOOD THING—we were all in the same boat."[1] That's how Danish immigrant N. K. Neilson nostalgically summed up his homesteading days in the Robsart area in southwestern Saskatchewan in the early twentieth century. He was not alone in his assessment. One of the more popular myths of Saskatchewan history is that the pioneer story was largely a common experience; settlers not only faced the same challenges, but had to contend with similar problems in the struggle to succeed. The actual homesteading record, however, greatly varied from period to period, from region to region, and from settler to settler. Staying on the land and meeting the homestead requirements came at a terrible human cost that many were not willing to pay, especially those without partners or families. Nor was it an egalitarian frontier. Some settlers were clearly better off than others, while most women were deliberately barred from taking up homestead land. What they all shared, though, was the desire to turn dreams into reality, to become something—if not themselves, then their children. "The real divide," one western historian has argued, "was the line that divided past from future—the line of hope, and ... it seemed to stretch into infinity."[2]

If Canadian immigration literature in the early twentieth century was to be believed, Saskatchewan was the land of opportunity. The new province had two things that gave it an edge over other Canadian destinations: good farmland and lots of it. One popular guide even boasted that "all that is needed is a mere scratching of the soil" to bring the virgin prairie under cultivation.[3] This image of Saskatchewan as an agricultural wonderland captured the popular imagination in much the same way as did the Klondike gold discovery only a few years earlier. Tens of thousands of people, many of them with little or no experience in farming, headed to the province to stake their claim to a new beginning. Kristian Askeland left his Ontario home for the same reason: "It was the alluring news of ... the 'new world' to the west ... that moved me to cut the ties with people, home and mother country."[4] English-born Anthony Tyson travelled to Neidpath in 1912 in search of "land I can own,"[5] while nurse Lena Bacon, a Nebraskan widow with a young daughter, was attracted by "the freedom of a great new country with no fences to hold one in. It was a place to give birth to one's own dreams."[6] Maritimer R. W. Sansom, working as a harvester near Souris, Manitoba, in the fall of 1905, was constantly being told by the other hired hands about the homesteads waiting for them in Saskatchewan. "That's all you could hear morning, noon, and night," he reminisced, "and if that old separator stopped for five minutes (which it didn't very often) they would have a sod shack half built ... After working and sleeping with those men for forty days and nights I began to get infected with the disease myself."[7] Sansom applied for land near Rosetown that December.

What enticed these and other settlers to Saskatchewan was the prospect of owning 160 acres of free land. These homesteads were a central feature of the federal government's Dominion Lands policy. Rejecting the traditional river-lot system that the Métis had used along the Red and Assiniboine rivers in present-day Manitoba for over half a century, Ottawa decided in April 1871 to copy the successful American system and adopted a grid pattern based on six-square-mile townships of thirty-six equal sections (640 acres or one square mile). Teams of Dominion Lands surveyors began working that summer and by the end of 1887 had measured an incredible seventy million acres. The survey crews were able to proceed at a steady and accurate pace because the same uniform grid was employed throughout the region, regardless of local soil and climatic conditions. It was simply assumed that most of the land was suited for agriculture. Their work was also less subject to mistake because the system, based on astronomical observation, completely ignored the natural contours of the land in favour of an artificial, standard checkerboard ordering. The only major adjustments were "correction lines," made necessary by the

A crush of prospective homesteaders at the Prince Albert Dominion Lands office. SASKATCHEWAN ARCHIVES BOARD R-A4557-2

gradual northern convergence of meridians. Once the system was in place the location of a homestead anywhere in the North-West proved a relatively straightforward matter.[8]

Dominion Lands policy was designed to satisfy several purposes. Each township contained thirty-six one-square-mile sections, which in turn were subdivided in quarter sections. Most of the even-numbered sections in each township (the numbering commenced in the lower right or southeast corner) were to be used for homesteads. All but two of the odd-numbered sections, on the other hand, were reserved as "railway lands." Sections 11 and 29, designated as school lands, were to support local educational needs, while sections 8 and three-quarters of 26 were turned over to the Hudson's Bay Company as part of the 1869 land transfer agreement that gave Canada control over Rupert's Land. Ottawa intended to use the railway sections to encourage railroad construction in the western interior; railway companies would be offered huge land grants if they built lines to and through the region. But the setting aside of railway reserves in every township served to disperse homestead lands and thereby increase the isolation of the pioneer farmer. Until these land grants were actually taken up by the company, moreover, railway reserves remained closed to settlement. Even though the CPR, for example, signed a deal with the Canadian government in 1881 and

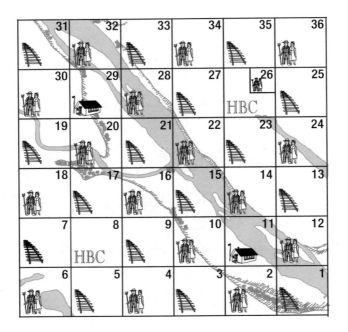

The survey system completely ignored the natural features of the land—most of the surveyed land was set aside for homesteads or railway land grants.

completed the transcontinental line just four years later, it was extremely slow to select the twenty-five million acres specified in its contract with the federal government. Other railway companies and their subsidiaries were equally tardy in choosing their land. This situation rankled Clifford Sifton, especially since the lands would be needed for the expected flood of settlers, and he lost little time after becoming federal minister of the interior in 1896 in seeing that the railways applied for their outstanding land grants. Curiously, Saskatchewan supplied almost half of the twenty-nine million acres claimed by the railways, even though less than 25 per cent of the lines were built in the province. Ontario and British Columbia, by contrast, provided no railway land.[9]

Anyone, excluding Indians, who wanted to file for a homestead in 1905 had to be male, eighteen years old, and prepared to become a British subject, if not one already. Women who were the sole head of a family—in other words, a widow or divorcée with dependants—were also eligible to apply.[10] To secure their land, prospective homesteaders had to visit the nearest Dominion Lands office, choose their 160 acres, or quarter section, and pay a ten-dollar registration fee. This procedure sounds simple but there was no shortage of pandemonium when new areas were opened up to homesteading, especially during the boom years in the early twentieth century. Some even waited outside the office all night to get a particular parcel of land. Settlers could send someone else on their behalf to file for their homestead, but they had to be on their land within six months of application.

To secure title or what was called "patent" to their quarter section, homesteaders had to meet certain basic requirements by the end of three years: they had to live on the land for six months each year, erect a shelter, and cultivate at least fifteen acres. Raising twenty head of cattle and constructing a barn for the animals was an acceptable alternative. These duties might not seem too onerous, but many a settler was defeated by them. Two out of every five homestead applications in the three prairie provinces between 1871 and 1930 were cancelled; the failure rate actually climbed above 50 per cent during the last two decades of the program.[11] Perhaps Englishman W. C. Pollard put it best when he suggested that homesteading was "a gamble in which the entrant bets ten dollars with the Government against 160 acres of land that he can stay on it ... for three years *without starving*."[12] Those who managed to survive and secure their patent could purchase an adjoining quarter section, known as a "preemption," at three dollars per acre; title to the land required an additional three years' residence and another fifteen acres under cultivation.[13] Or they could buy railway land. The railway reserves proved an unexpected blessing by providing successful farmers with the opportunity to expand their land holdings. By 1903, an estimated 50 per cent of the homesteaders in Assiniboia had purchased adjoining railway land.[14]

Prospective homesteaders could expect only minimal assistance from the Canadian government, such as temporary accommodation in immigration sheds or help in locating land. Ottawa generally did no more once people were on their homesteads. Certainly there were exceptions to this policy, such as the terrible winter of 1906–07, when the RNWMP were dispatched with food-laden sleighs to check on settlers in some of the worst-hit areas.[15] Clifford Sifton, however, wanted a population of sturdy, independent homesteaders, who placed individual progress and achievement above everything else. This goal was not simply a matter of saving the government money. The interior minister genuinely believed that the best settlers were those who persevered and succeeded on their own. "I have never known anybody," he once remarked, "that was materially assisted by the Government to amount to anything."[16] An official in his department put it more succinctly: what western Canada needed was "men of good muscle who are willing to hustle."[17]

Timing, location, capital, experience, assistance, endurance—and sheer good luck—were consequently all factors in determining a homesteader's success.[18] Future farm leader and Saskatchewan politician W. R. Motherwell, for example, took up prime land in the Abernethy district in the wake of the

This man sat up all night, waiting to apply for a homestead. LIBRARY AND ARCHIVES CANADA C5093

building of the CPR main line across the prairies. By the time Saskatchewan entered Confederation more than two decades later, he had converted his homestead into Lanark Place, a replica of pastoral Ontario, complete with an ornate, imposing stone farmhouse with separate living quarters for the servants. Although Motherwell's operation was unique—the restored homestead is recognized today as a national historic site—there were other similar fine homes in the area at Balcarres and Sintaluta. Indeed, pioneer days were generally well past in parts of southeastern Saskatchewan by 1905, and settlers moving into the area could expect a range of services and facilities.[19] But unfortunately there were few homesteads available in the region by that time, and only those with enough money could afford to buy land in established districts. Most people who headed to the province in the first decade of the twentieth century had come to make their fortune, enticed by the prospect of 160 acres of free land for a mere ten-dollar entry fee. With little capital, and often even less farming experience, many were forced to apply for land in isolated areas without a rail line or even a nearby town. There was no shortage of takers: in 1905–06 alone, two out of every three homestead applications were in Saskatchewan. Little did this wave of settlers realize, though, that they were not the first occupants of the land in many instances and that many of the homesteads had been abandoned by those who had moved on to another location or had simply given up.[20]

The first crucial decision for homesteaders was choosing their quarter section. Although federal homestead policy was based on the assumption that all the land was equally good throughout the North-West, the quality greatly varied from place to place, even within the same district. Some settlers used local agents to help find good farmland. George Hamilton of Toronto hired a Saskatoon land dealer in the fall of 1904 to take him southwest out along the Old Bone Trail towards Rosetown before making his application. "He had a choice of all the eye surveyed," his daughter Leila recalled, "and selected the best quarter in the district."[21] Others were not so fortunate. Many settlers had no time to inspect their prospective homestead beforehand, made a poor selection because of their inexperience, or were sadly deceived by the government literature, believing that any parcel of land would prove suitable. "We were almost the first people to settle in this part of the country and could have had the best of the land," F. N. Krischke of Baljennie confessed. "Instead we got the worst."[22] A few moved on, unhappy with their original choice. British-born George Shepherd homesteaded first in the Girvin-Stalwart area in 1908 before relocating to Maple Creek five years later.[23]

Upon reaching their quarter section for the first time, homesteaders spent hours tramping over the land, searching for the survey markers and inspecting every acre along the way. It was also when the hard reality of the situation started to sink in, and many had their first doubts about what they were doing. "We reached our homestead at last," recounted one woman. "I'll never forget the desolate feeling that came over me, when, with the contents of the wagon out on the ground, we sat on a box and looked around, not a sign of a human habitation or road leading to one, to be seen, nothing but bluff, water, and grass." She continued, "Then I realized that we were at the end of our journey, that this was to be our home."[24] For many, the prairies were a foreign, if not discomfiting, landscape, completely different from the world they had once known. "Even though I had been told it was prairie land," Helen Shepard of the Consul district remembered, "my first glimpse of the country ... was something of a shock."[25] One Ontario settler regularly walked to two solitary trees more than a mile from his homestead "just to touch them and stand in their shade."[26]

Homesteading was an impoverishing experience for many settlers, especially those living on their own in isolated areas. Not even the favoured British escaped this reality. While the early twentieth century marked the beginning of remarkable technological innovation and steady improvement in Canadian daily life, those in pioneer farm districts seemed to have stepped back in time. Since it often took several years before crops provided a decent income, homesteaders had to become virtually self-sufficient and learn to live a simpler life by making do with little. Hardship and privation were

One family's first home in Saskatchewan. WESTERN DEVELOPMENT MUSEUM 5-A-8

common.[27] "We did not have very much to eat," Dan Thompson described his first year on the family homestead in 1911. "I used to get so hungry I would eat grass."[28] Settlers faced the double challenge of bringing the land under cultivation and trying to survive in the meantime. Survival took valuable time and energy away from other activities, making it difficult for homesteaders to establish themselves, even though they worked incredibly long hours each day. "The ruthless pressure of time ... bears down on the shoulders of every farmer," James Minifie observed of his own father's experience. "There is never enough time on the prairie."[29] Hard work, though, could not guarantee success. Any single calamity during the first few years could prove disastrous, particularly for those with few resources to fall back on. For many, homesteading was a fragile, frustrating existence—a gamble—where many critical factors, such as weather or a rail link, were beyond their control. "In a just world," one historian has noted, "sweat and tears might have counted for something in the rain gauge."[30]

Before breaking a single acre, homesteaders faced three major tasks: finding a reliable source of drinking water, building a shelter, and putting in a garden. Some confidently began to dig a well, only to give up in exasperation after going several feet or starting several times without success. Others pulled water from sloughs, if it was not too brackish, or excavated a pit near the edge of a slough and collected the water that flowed into it. It was not unusual to travel for the better part of a day to retrieve a barrel of water. A couple headed to their homestead in 1906 came across an abandoned, rundown shack on their fourth day on the trail. A poem was faintly scrawled across the weather-beaten door: "I'm twenty miles from water, and forty miles from wood; So I'll leave you now my happy home, I'll leave you now for good."[31]

Homesteaders generally lived in tents until they could erect a more permanent structure. The majority of the first homes were constructed of either milled (dressed) lumber or, more likely, wood from the nearest bush.[32] It could be a daunting assignment for those without any experience. Bob Sansom of Rosetown spent an entire day wandering about his land "trying to figure out how to build the shack."[33] Those on the open, treeless prairie turned to the material at hand and constructed sod homes. But the sod needed adequate root growth to hold together, and the roof would often leak for days after a heavy rain. The Addison sod house, built in 1910–11 in the Oakdale district northeast of Kindersley, and still occupied by Edith (Addison) Gardiner, has recently been designated a national historic site. Most houses were initially one-room, many with earthen floors, and were expanded over time. In 1910, the T. Eaton Company started advertising prefabricated home packages, shipped from British Columbia by rail, in the Winnipeg edition of its catalogue. The blueprints cost $2.50, but the fee was refunded when the house was ordered. Sales were so brisk that the company introduced a separate catalogue of home plans in 1914–15.[34] Shrubs and trees from federal nurseries at Indian Head and Sutherland sheltered the new houses. Almost half of the millions of seedlings distributed were caragana.[35] Today, the shrubs mark the site of former homesteads.

Many homesteaders craved companionship to stave off loneliness. SASKATCHEWAN ARCHIVES BOARD R-A2536

Eaton's sold prefabricated home packages, shipped from British Columbia by rail, starting in 1910.
THE T. EATON COMPANY, 1919

Homesteaders also planted gardens to stave off hunger or add variety to an otherwise monotonous diet. Many did not bring enough provisions, and if they lived in isolated areas or had little money, they often had to make do with what they had—sometimes no more than oatmeal each day. Even a garden was difficult to maintain. "One can hardly grow a garden ... without cats to catch gophers," lamented Lillian Turner, who joined her husband on a homestead west of Saskatoon in 1906. "I hardly know how I shall get on, but will make a desperate effort to manage some way."[36] R. E. Bayles of Glen Adelaide was equally frustrated: "Gophers—it used to be a fight between us who should have the crop."[37] Beginning in 1905, Eaton's shipped canned goods and dried fruit in case lots from its new Winnipeg department store, but these bulk mail orders were generally restricted to settlers who lived near a rail line.[38]

Those best able to meet the homesteading challenge were the thousands of immigrants from the American midwest, provided they secured decent land. Not only were they well equipped, often arriving with household effects, machinery, and animals, but many had homesteaded south of the line and brought practical experience farming the open plains. Continental

Europeans, by contrast, were relatively poor, but no less prepared to create a new livelihood. But they seldom did so on their own, naturally gravitating to areas populated by their own kind, where they found material, as well as spiritual and emotional, support. "We all felt lost," explained Vladimir Wirkowski of Arran. "We wanted to stay together and help one another, just as we did in the Old Country."[39]

By congregating in group settlements, Doukhobors, Mennonites, and Ukrainians settled the land with assistance from their extended family, friends, or the wider community. They were also surrounded by familiar symbols and customs, such as their distinctive homes and traditional village patterns, which served to lessen any feelings of dislocation and isolation.[40] John Letkeman, for example, was one of eight men who investigated the farming potential of the new Mennonite reserve near Swift Current in the late spring of 1904. Before selecting their land, they took turns digging a well to decide where the village, named Schoenfeld, should be located. The group then applied for homesteads in the same area on the understanding that they would work together to establish their farms.[41] These ethnic enclaves, as they were called, intensified the immigrants' sense of separateness from the larger society. They also went against the government ideal of a society of rugged, independent home-steaders, capable of surviving and prospering on their own. But ironically, without this kind of co-operative enterprise, successful settlement of the land would have been difficult at best, if not significantly delayed.

Co-operative activity was not restricted to continental European immigrants. Most homesteaders came to rely on neighbours for help of some kind. One evening in the spring of 1906, Bob Sansom spied a team of oxen waddling along to a small tent about a half mile away from his place and excitedly hurried off to meet Jim McGregor, a moulder by trade, fresh from England. The pair immediately became friends and worked together for the next few months, starting with the building of Bob's house from local poplar. "We managed to get ten acres each broken that summer," Sansom later reported, "built a sod stable, put up some hay, dug a well ... got out a supply of wood for next summer."[42] Some men who were good with a plough did breaking work for neighbours in exchange for other help on their homestead. Often, two homesteaders might simply strike a deal to get supplies; one would go to town, several days' travel away, while the other would remain behind to work on the land so that no time was lost. These partnerships could be rocky, but more often than not proved resilient because of the simple fact that they needed each other. Nor did nationality seem to matter in most instances. Help was help, and a person's ethnic background was less important than their ability to lend a hand when it was needed most. It was only after the land was settled that questions about assimilation and integration became

A new, more substantial home often replaced the first farmhouse. GLENBOW ARCHIVES NA-303-214

more pronounced.[43] There were exceptions, though. Leslie Neatby vividly remembered how his brothers and sisters singlehandedly had to run their Watrous-area homestead because his English parents refused to associate with their "riffraff" neighbours.[44]

Many homesteaders also turned to off-farm work to make some much-needed money. Bob Sansom and Jim McGregor's partnership ended in October 1906, when Bob headed to Minnesota to do logging for the winter, while Jim went to Winnipeg to work at his trade. Come spring, both were back on their homesteads, where Bob had second thoughts about what he was doing and almost gave up twice. "100 miles from civilization, and a little 12x16 shack that you could throw a cat through any place," he looked back on one of his low points. "I got cold feet and the blues so bad that if I had been offered the whole of Saskatchewan you could not have held me here."[45] Homesteaders also found seasonal work with the railways. Art Wheeler, who took up land in the Ladstock district in the fall of 1906, spent the following three summers as a labourer on the Grand Trunk Pacific main line at $1.50 to $1.75 per day, excluding board. Men with their own team of horses earned even more. While based at camp five, east of Punnichy, in June 1907, Wheeler noted, "Probably every homesteader from a wide area was employed ... There were over a hundred teams assembled."[46]

This summer employment, albeit temporary, took settlers away from their land when they could least afford to be away. But in helping to build the railways they were doing their part to end isolation and improve their overall prospects, and the extra cash could ultimately mean the difference between success and failure. Some prospective homesteaders even worked for several years as hired hands, gaining valuable experience and sufficient capital, before they applied for their own quarter section. Sometimes the dream was never realized. Hungarian Martin Bremner came to Indian Head in the early twentieth century intent on securing his own land, but his seasonal jobs, alternating between local farms and the railway, provided little support for his growing family, let alone enough money to homestead.[47]

Women were probably more important than any other factor to a homesteader's survival. Without a spouse, many men would have given up before they secured their patent, and many did. It was common practice for husbands to go ahead alone to get established on their homesteads before sending for their wives and children. Thousands of single men were also attracted to Saskatchewan by the promise of free land and planned to get a start before seeking a partner. What many "bachelor" homesteaders quickly learned, though, was that it was next to impossible to work on the land and maintain a household. There was no one to prepare the all-important noon-time dinner, wash sweat-drenched grimy clothes, or make their first home a little more habitable. Something had to be sacrificed, and it was usually the men's diet and hygiene. Many lived in primitive and isolated conditions during their first few weeks and months on their homestead, which only made things worse. Elizabeth Mitchell, who visited western Canada before the Great War, described bachelors as poor, lonely creatures "who need kindness badly."[48]

Homesick husbands consequently sent for their wives earlier than they had planned, but even then their reunion could be delayed because of the isolation of some districts. In the fall of 1906, Mrs. Margaret McManus and her two little boys spent six anxious weeks in the Saskatoon immigration hall until word reached her husband on his homestead that she had arrived from Scotland.[49] Other men sought wives. Bob Sansom decided to return to his Rosetown-area homestead only because of his pending marriage. Percy Maxwell felt the same way about his engagement to his girlfriend, Mabel. "If it wasn't for her I don't think I would stay on my homestead," he wrote his family. "I am thoroughly sick of baching."[50] Finding partners, however, was difficult in Saskatchewan, where in 1906 the ratio of single men to single women was 1.7 to 1. Nor did the situation for prospective suitors get any better. By 1911, there were 3.5 single men for every single woman in the province. Many bachelors persevered as long as they could, but ultimately the lack of companionship took its toll. According to a sampling of pioneer surveys conducted by the Saskatchewan Archives in 1955 in commemoration of the province's fiftieth birthday, loneliness drove many bachelors from their homesteads. Indeed, where ranchers welcomed isolation, farmers hated it.

Women, like their male partners, were excited about Saskatchewan's

Many prospective homesteaders who started out alone quickly discovered that a partner was essential. SASKATOON PUBLIC LIBRARY LH3348

bright future and joined their husbands on homesteads with a sense of purpose and determination. But it would be a mistake to view them as stoic "helpmates," who simply played a supporting role in wresting a living from the land. Survival on the homestead meant that wives had to learn new skills, do new things that were not normally expected of women at the time. They worked in the fields alongside their husbands, tended animals, ran machinery, and picked up a hammer and nails to repair something. In other words, they did whatever they had to do. At the same time, they were expected to keep their femininity and continue to handle their traditional duties in the home, including the rearing and care of children. This invasion of the so-called male sphere meant that women "hauled a double load" or worked "a second shift" on the homestead. And they performed these never-ending tasks with a flexibility and resourcefulness that seems truly incredible today.[51] Many a man owed his success to his partner's labour and readily acknowledged it. But women were taken for granted far too easily. Nellie McClung, an outspoken advocate of female suffrage, liked to tell the story of Jane, who died three days after giving birth to her seventh child: "The bereaved husband was the most astonished man in the world. He had never known Jane to do a thing like that before, and he could not get over it. In threshing time, too!"[52]

Despite women's many contributions to the homestead, their role and place on the settlement frontier was narrowly proscribed. Although the Laurier government promoted the immigration of women to western Canada as part of the overall plan to boost the population of the region, it regarded farming as a strictly male activity. Ottawa therefore steadfastly refused to extend to women—except in rare circumstances—the right to take up homestead land, even though the United States did so. As Frank Oliver, Sifton's successor as interior minister, informed the House of Commons in 1910, as if it was some well-known fact: "the purpose ... in giving free land to homesteaders is that the land may be made productive ... Our experience is entirely against the idea of women homesteading."[53] The federal government's intransigence provoked a "homesteads for women" movement in the years leading up to the Great War. But the intensive lobbying effort, including letters and a petition, failed to sway Ottawa, and the eligibility rules remained the same until the end of the homesteads program in 1930.

One of the leading figures in the campaign was Georgina Binnie-Clark, who had come to Saskatchewan in 1905 to check up on her brother, Lal, a brewer by trade, homesteading near Fort Qu'Appelle. Shocked to discover that he was failing miserably and ready to quit, Georgina bought a half section of land and with her sister Hilaria ran a successful farm operation for the next few decades. But she deeply resented how a woman farmer was disadvantaged by federal homestead policy. "She may be the best farmer in Canada," Binnie-Clark observed in her prairie classic, *Wheat and Women*, "she may buy land, work it, take prizes for seed and stock, but she is denied the right to claim from the Government the hundred and sixty acres of land held out as a bait to every man."[54]

Women often worked in the fields, in addition to their more traditional duties in the home.
SASKATCHEWAN ARCHIVES BOARD R-A8291

This failure to see women as legitimate homesteaders effectively made their work on the farm "invisible." They may have helped to fulfil homestead requirements in any countless number of ways, but as long as agriculture was deemed a male enterprise, their crucial role was severely discounted or blindly ignored.[55] Nor did women enjoy any dower rights in the three western provinces. Men could dispose of their land as they saw fit without consulting their wives, while women were not guaranteed any share in the property upon their husband's death. "In no country under the sun," explained Isabel Graham, editor of the women's page of the *Grain Growers' Guide*, in calling for provincial dower laws in 1910, "has woman been more responsible for increased land values ... [but] they do not earn anything at home ... their work is valueless."[56] Women readers agreed. One correspondent suggested that "the universal lot of the farmer's wife is one of ceaseless toil without adequate compensation."[57] Men, on the other hand, were strongly opposed to any legislation, even forming a Farmers' Anti-Dower Law Association in the province. "A Saskatchewan Farmer" claimed in a letter to the *Guide* that "nearly all farmers treat wifey generously."[58] Another admitted, "I have a great respect for the ladies—when they know their place."[59] The dower campaign, though, proved more successful than the homestead issue, largely because these rights were recognized in law in other Canadian provinces. In 1915, the Saskatchewan government provided some initial protection for women's interests in the Homestead Act, but it would be another two generations, not until 1979, before women finally secured an equal share in matrimonial property.[60]

Like their husbands, many women found homestead life to be terribly lonely. The isolation and privation weighed heavily upon them because of the lack of female contact and companionship. In fact, historian James Gray half-jokingly quipped that the placement of settlers on individual quarter sections could not have done more "to drive the farm women up the walls of their shacks."[61] Men at least worked with their neighbours or visited town to get supplies or retrieve the mail. Women, meanwhile, were captive to the homestead and its constant demands. It was as if the outside world ceased to exist. "We fared well," remembered a daughter, "but it was hard on mother ... struggling to keep clean and sane in a one-roomed shack. I have heard her say many a time she felt like running out for miles and screaming. Pioneering is hardest on women shut up alone for days and months."[62] Mrs. J. I. Anderson reported she left the homestead so rarely during the first ten years that people in the Gregherd district, except for the local storekeeper, thought her husband was a bachelor.[63] Others had similar stories. Catherine Neil went so long without seeing another woman that when she visited a neighbour with a young baby for the first time, "we ran to each other ... and put our arms around each other's neck and just had a good cry. All the hunger and longing which we had stifled for so long came to the surface."[64]

Some women found the isolation, the primitive conditions, and the constant work to be too much. Barbara Bent remembered being summoned by a neighbour to attend to a homesick woman whose husband was afraid to leave her alone. The couple, no more than in their late teens, had come directly from London, England, to the open Saskatchewan prairie. The woman seemed to be in shock. "Well I stayed with that young couple for three days and nights because I felt so sorry for the little woman," recounted Bent. "I found poor Daisy was just suffering from the intense loneliness ... and I told him [the husband, Charlie] plainly he had better take his little wife to some town and try to work at this trade [watch repair]."[65] In another more desperate case, Mrs. Running, a mother of three children, was being sent home to Ontario for a much-needed visit. But the wait was apparently unbearable, and while visiting friends near Eastend one evening, she politely left the dinner table, put on her hat and coat, and drowned herself in the well behind the house.[66]

Children did much to alleviate the loneliness of the homestead, but pregnancy had its own perils. Expectant women often had to make do without the support and advice of other women; first-time mothers, who knew little about pregnancy and childbirth, were particularly vulnerable, especially if they lived in isolated areas far away from trained medical personnel. Babies were usually delivered at home with the assistance of local women who, by necessity, became midwives. Sometimes only husbands were there to help.

The interior of the Still home in the Lloydminster area, 1905. LIBRARY AND ARCHIVES CANADA PA21186

Mothers and babies often died from complications, especially if a doctor could not be summoned in time. Most infant deaths in Saskatchewan occurred within the first week of birth; in 1914 one-third of all childhood deaths under five were newborns. In fact, it was unusual for a family not to have lost at least one child. In 1910, the Saskatchewan government took steps to deal with infant mortality by introducing a maternity package for new-borns and a maternity grant for mothers in remote areas or in financial need. But the other real need, pre- and post-natal care, was virtually non-existent in pioneer districts. Because of the need for labour on the homestead, women commonly had several children, in some cases over a twenty-year period. They also had little time to recuperate before they were back to work or tending to their other children. Difficulties during pregnancy or childbirth, together with the strain of multiple pregnancies and exhaustion, consequently took their toll. In a contradictory vein, it seemed that "women were indispensable to successful settlement yet treated as dispensable."[67]

Children who grew up on homesteads learned from an early age to per-form any number of chores under all kinds of conditions. Girls in particular came to believe that women's work included seeding and harvesting, espe-cially if there were no boys in the family.[68] Natalie Forness of Maple Creek proudly boasted, "By the time I was fourteen I worked outside like a man."[69] Eldest daughters often served as a second mother to their brothers and sisters. These years clearly left their mark on a generation. "For us children," Leslie Neatby summed up his days on the family homestead, "it meant toil and suf-fering beyond our years. But it toughened us and imparted initiative and a capacity for self-help." They also never forgot the weather. Neatby recalled one dreadful winter when "the unending depression of a chill within doors" forced him and his family to spend time in bed in order to keep warm.[70] Wallace Stegner, describing his adolescent years near Eastend in *Wolf Willow*, spoke of "its wind, which blows all the time in a way to stiffen your hair and rattle the eyes in your head."[71] Sickness, too, left a lasting impression. One of the favourite home remedies was goose grease, which was used so liberally that some children worried that they might grow feathers.[72] Somewhat sadly, Nettie Bellows, the eldest of twelve children, looked back upon her bout with scarlet fever with fondness; it was the only time her mother doted on her, because she feared Nettie was going to die.[73]

Settlers enjoyed simple recreational pursuits. Homesteaders arrived with only a few books and magazines and normally shared them with neighbours, especially during the long winter months. The Aberdeen Association, founded by the wife of Canada's governor general in the 1890s, also sent monthly par-cels of reading material by rail to pioneer districts. One of the most widely read items, apart from the Bible, was Eaton's mail-order catalogue, which

The MacLavertys tending the family garden in the Battlefords area. SASKATCHEWAN ARCHIVES
BOARD S-B1012

boasted, "If you can't find what you want on our pages, it wasn't made or you
didn't need it." Immigrants used the catalogue to learn to read English, while
children would cut out figures and other pictures to make playthings.⁷⁴ Some
districts organized literary societies where participation was more important
than talent. "Everyone had to do something," reported Tom Perry of Watson,
"even if they could only whistle or tell a story—strange to say those were very
enjoyable evenings."⁷⁵ Work bees also doubled as social events. The raising of
a barn, for example, might be followed by a dance to the music of a fiddle,
accordion, harmonica, or spoons. At Leader in 1914, W. T. "Horseshoe" Smith,
a Kentuckian with big ranching plans, built the largest barn in North
America, measuring 400 feet long, 128 feet wide, and 60 feet high. Thousands
attended the opening barn dance. But the astronomical cost of building and
maintaining the immense barn proved too much even for Smith's ambition
and the structure was torn down seven years later and the wood and other
materials sold to local farmers and businesses.⁷⁶

Religion also brought people together. Before churches were erected, services were held in all kinds of places—from a tent, barn, and boxcar to a local
home and district school—and attracted worshippers from all denominations. As one homesteader remarked, "Sunday was the one day and church
the one opportunity in the week to meet neighbours and friends."⁷⁷ Church
and community picnics, with their games for children and adults, proved
extremely popular, as did box socials with men bidding on lunches specially
prepared by local women. The big event of the year, though, was the fair.
Those in pioneer districts were modest, featuring garden produce, baking,
and handicrafts, as well as contests to see who could plough the straightest
line and at the right depth. But in older, more settled areas, fairs highlighted

country life at its best and the competition for prizes was fierce.[78]

In winter, both men and women skated or played hockey on the nearest frozen slough. Curling was also common since it required only a household broom and frozen, water-filled jam or lard cans for the rocks. Cards, dominoes, crokinole, and other games filled the hours when it was too cold to spend much time outdoors. Come the busy months of summer there was little time for sports, but young, single men, whether homesteaders or hired hands, congregated whenever they could for a pick-up game of soccer or baseball; they also played lacrosse and cricket depending on the availability of equipment. The same isolation that drove these men to come together, however, prevented the scheduling of regular games or the formation of local leagues. Instead, they had to be content with the annual sports day, normally held in conjunction with the 24 May or 1 July holidays, when they finally got their chance to play against a visiting team or compete in track events.[79] It was only when transportation and communication improved that sports could flourish. Baseball, for example, followed the CPR main line westward, and teams popped up throughout the province as branch lines were pushed into new areas. The village of Liberty, because of the presence of so many Americans, became known as "The Baseball Town," while Oxbow fielded the U.N. squad—the "useless nine."[80]

Until isolation was ended and distances shrunk, homesteaders scratched out an existence as best they could. Many failed, but many more secured title to their land and stayed for the rest of their lives. Those who homesteaded in Saskatchewan in the new century came looking for a better life in a land where one could "see clear through to half past tomorrow."[81] James Minifie sensed this optimism in his father. He spoke with the "ring of triumph," Minifie declared. "Whatever this great North-West might be, he was proud of it, proud to be part of it."[82] In accepting *and* meeting the government challenge, homesteaders turned abstract plans into reality—turned 160 acres of real estate into a new way of life for themselves and their families. Ronald Jickling realized the larger meaning of what he was doing while hauling a load of wood with his neighbour Stanley Doyle one day. Breaking camp after lunch, Stan said they would likely reach home by sundown. "Then the significance of what Stan said at noon struck me," Ron recounted. "Possibly he didn't realize what he said. He said we would be HOME by sundown. That word HOME was the first time we had, either one of us, used it, and we were coming HOME now ... Well, this place so far is not much of a home, that's for certain, but one has to make a start some place and this is as good a place as any."[83]

CHAPTER SEVEN

A VERY NICE
FAIRY TALE

IT WAS SUPPOSED TO BE A TRIUMPHANT TOUR, and in many respects it was. Five years after Saskatchewan entered Confederation, Prime Minister Sir Wilfrid Laurier embarked on a gruelling, two-month rail tour of western Canada in the summer of 1910 to see first-hand how the region had changed so quickly and dramatically during his term in office. Wherever the sixty-nine-year-old Canadian leader stopped in Saskatchewan—thirteen major speeches in just nineteen days—he was warmly greeted by throngs of well-wishers, including those who had only recently made the country their new home. All wanted to hear, if not see, the man whose administration had been largely responsible for settling the prairie west. But once the formal addresses and presentations were over, Sir Wilfrid was politely but firmly questioned about the Liberal government's agricultural policies. Farmers demanded trans-portation improvements, lower freight rates, better grain-handling facilities— but, most repeatedly and vociferously, the scrapping of the protective tariff. The prime minister fended off the criticism as best he could, especially the pointed reminders about his past support for free trade, but it was evident by the time he returned to Ottawa that the growing ranks of disaffected prairie farmers could be ignored only at the expense of his party's popularity and support. Trying to satisfy Western aspirations would prove equally perilous.[1]

Saskatchewan farmers were a persistent lot. They had to be. Canada expected the virgin North-West soil to produce millions of bushels of wheat for the international export market with minimum effort in only a few years. But growing and harvesting a crop—never mind wheat becoming a trade staple—was anything but certain in the first few decades of western settlement. Although cereal grains and root vegetables had been cultivated at the Red River Settlement and in the shadows of the fur-trade posts for over half a century, farming on a large scale was still largely an experiment in 1870.[2] The western interior also presented challenging climatic problems. Not only is the growing season short—the frost-free period ranges anywhere from 130 to 160 days—but it is also dry because of the semi-arid, continental environment. Even though most rainfall normally comes during the critical months of June and July, drought is an ever-present threat since evaporation exceeds precipitation on an annual basis. What made things worse at the time were several unusually harsh years caused by the spectacular explosion of the Krakatoa volcano in Indonesia in 1883. The spewing of ash into the atmosphere lowered global temperatures for five years.

These peculiar conditions stymied early agricultural efforts. Indian bands, who had just taken treaty and were attempting to farm because of the disappearance of the buffalo, failed to grow even enough to feed themselves. Government authorities liked to believe that Indian idleness had caused this sorry outcome, but these first farming efforts had been doubly handicapped. In choosing reserve land, chiefs had shown a decided preference for rolling, heavily wooded terrain that was better suited for more traditional pursuits such as hunting and gathering than raising crops. The agricultural aid promised in the treaties—the implements, animals, and seeds—was also slow in coming *and* inadequate. Ottawa seemed to expect the Indian adoption of agriculture to be an overnight success on the reserves and was more concerned with saving money than providing the necessary assistance. Even when the federal government introduced a reserve instruction program in 1879, the people hired to teach the Indians how to farm were patronage appointees who had little understanding of western conditions and even less sympathy for the Indians and the dramatic changes they faced. Sadly, by the mid-1880s several bands were reduced to surviving on government rations until their reserves could be successfully cultivated.[3]

White farmers, by contrast, usually had some practical agricultural

Breaking prairie sod with power machinery. WESTERN DEVELOPMENT MUSEUM 1-D(B)-7

experience or at least could get some help. Their harvests, though, were equally dismal in the beginning. Many settlers watched helplessly as their wheat fell victim to frost, drought, smut, and other natural hazards. In August 1887 a correspondent for the *Toronto Mail* reported that crops in the Moosomin district were "a failure, as they always have been, and I fear ever will be, from lack of rain."[4] Unlike the Indians, however, homesteaders could leave, and often did after a few bad years.

This bleak situation prompted Ottawa to set up an experimental farm at Indian Head in 1887 to develop new crop varieties and farming methods better suited to the western environment. Science and technology, not expansionist rhetoric, were needed to remake the prairie wilderness into an agricultural Eden.[5] Over the next decade, Angus MacKay, the first superintendent of the farm, worked tirelessly to improve all aspects of prairie agriculture, from controlling plant diseases, weeds, and insect pests to horticulture and tree propagation to livestock breeding and dairying. The most urgent need, however, was an earlier-maturing wheat. Red Fife, noted for its high yields and superior baking quality, had been the dominant variety for over half a century, but it often ripened too late in western Canada to escape frosts. Starting in 1892, the Saunders brothers, first Percy and then Charles, began crossbreeding experiments with Red Fife at Indian Head and eventually developed the famous Marquis variety that was widely distributed by 1911.[6] Until that time, the experimental farm staff, together with western farmers, worked to find ways to improve wheat production using different techniques and machinery. Indians were not part of this process. Instead, the federal government actively promoted a "peasant farming" policy from 1889 to 1897. Indian Affairs required bands to clear their land and plant and harvest their crops with hand tools, not machinery. Indian agents also regulated off-reserve sales of produce, often denying permits, to prevent competition with white settlers. This form of subsistence agriculture effectively killed any Indian initiative and led to the mistaken conclusion that they were never meant to be farmers.[7]

The most decisive influence on western Canadian agriculture in the late nineteenth century was the experience south of the border. After successfully farming the dry, interior plains of the midwest for two decades, thousands of American settlers brought their equipment and methods north with them when they came looking for homesteads. Their array of implements, ranging from seed drills and disc harrows to binders and separators, befitted an invading army. But their most essential piece of equipment was the popular chilled-steel plough, which sliced cleanly through the tough prairie sod with the precision of a surgeon's scalpel. Equally important, if not more so, were their "dry farming" methods.[8] Faced with the very real problem of being at the

A farmer checking the quality of his grain. LIBRARY AND ARCHIVES CANADA PA21220

mercy of rainfall that was not only limited but variable, American farmers ploughed a portion of their land in late May or early June and then kept it clear of weeds and other vegetation for the rest of the season to conserve moisture for the next year's crop. Angus MacKay at the Indian Head experimental farm promoted this "summerfallowing" technique, in conjunction with crop rotation, as a sure way to produce more bushels of wheat per acre than continuously cropped land. He also maintained that the deep ploughing of fallowed land in the late spring allowed for greater moisture penetration and retention than idle fields with a stubble cover.[9] This practice, sometimes known as "rain follows the plough," would contribute to serious soil erosion, but at the time seemed a plausible solution to the region's precipitation deficit.

With these new methods and machinery—not to mention several years of experimentation and failure—Saskatchewan farmers began to open up large areas of the southern half of the province to wheat production. In the process, they developed a routine that varied only with the season. Before the land dried out in the early spring farmers cleaned their seed grain by hand and soaked it in copper sulphate or bluestone to make it resistant to smut. Once it was possible to get onto the fields, they harrowed or levelled the soil by pulling a rake-like implement over the surface behind a team of heavy horses; if the land had just been ploughed, they first had to disc or break down the furrows before the soil could be harrowed. Seeding came next, initially by hand and then later by the horse-drawn seed drill which deposited seed in neat rows at a pre-set depth. Farmers then harrowed the planted fields again to ensure that no seed was exposed. These various steps took the better part of the spring, even with farmers working incredibly long days, and sometimes went into late June. There was no room for delay. The later the land was seeded, the greater the risk of losing the crop to frost.

The long days of summer brought a new round of activity. Apart from countless maintenance duties, farmers worked their summerfallow, cleared and broke new land, picked rocks from the fields, and cut hay to feed animals. Never far from their thoughts, though, was the looming harvest, and farm families put in extra hours preparing for the busiest time of the year. Once the crop was ready, farmers used a binder to cut the golden stands of grain and tie them into sheaves that were left in rows up and down the fields. A handful of men followed in the heat and the dust, gathering bundles of sheaves and stacking them upright in stooks so that the heads could continue to ripen. Stooking was a back-breaking job that required a deft touch to keep the sheaves from falling over, and many never forgot the experience (including the author's father). The arrival of the threshing crew, numbering as many as two dozen, intensified the pace. Teams of men loaded and hauled the sheaves by bundle wagon to the separator, where another, larger group of

A harvest crew at work near Wauchope in 1914. SASKATCHEWAN ARCHIVES BOARD R-A12371

men constantly fed the sheaves into the machine which separated the heads of grain from the chaff and straw. An engineer and tank or water man, in the meantime, ran the steam engine that powered the threshing machine, constantly keeping an eye on the pressure and the drive belt. It was demanding, constant work, all packed in a few frenzied days. Farm wives were expected to feed the ravenous men and laboured just as hard preparing feasts to be served at cramped tables or consumed in the fields. Children helped in the kitchen and often hauled pails of drinking water to the men. All knew there could be no rest until the season's crop was safely in the bin.[10]

The next task was hauling the grain to market through the fall and into the winter, a much more leisurely job that could take several days, especially if the nearest railhead was any distance away. It was not unusual for farmers in pioneer districts to have to travel as much as forty to sixty miles. How farmers' grain was handled at the shipping point was crucial to their survival, and there was no shortage of complaints in the early days. They felt cheated over how their grain was graded, especially when the elevator agents regularly discounted the quality because of adulteration, shrinkage, discolouration, or chipping. They also resented being at the mercy of large companies when it came to storing and shipping their grain; boxcars, for example, were not always readily available and often unfairly distributed. In 1900, in response to the recommendations of a royal commission, the Laurier government established stringent federal regulations governing such matters as grain inspection, loading, and storage.[11] But the Manitoba Grain Act provisions offered little protection the following year, when the largest western crop to date plugged the system. With the CPR and elevator companies unable to handle the record volume of grain, half the harvest was lost to spoilage.

The grain blockade angered western farmers, especially since they had finally started to produce the kind of crop expected of the region. At Indian Head, where the situation had been particularly bad, several farmers were determined never to see such a calamity happen again and formed the Territorial Grain Growers' Association in 1902 to promote their collective interests. One of the leaders was William Motherwell, the Abernethy-area farmer destined to become Saskatchewan's first minister of agriculture three years later. Another was Edward Alexander (E. A.) Partridge, more popularly known as the "Sage of Sintaluta." Six feet tall and heavy-set, with blue eyes and a handlebar moustache, the imposing Partridge preached the virtues of co-operation as if it were some sacred mantra. Only by coming together and speaking with one voice, he insisted, could farmers stand up to the big companies and begin to exercise control over their economic lives. Some of Partridge's ideas and solutions would prove radical, if not impractical, for the time, but no one could question his commitment or influence. He never tired of taking his message to town hall meetings across the west, often neglecting his own operation for weeks. A restless visionary, he was rarely satisfied with what had been achieved and always thinking of what to do next. Not even the loss of his left foot in a binder accident, the drowning of a daughter in a slough, or the death of two sons in the Great War could shake him from his quest.[12]

One of the first actions of the new grain growers' group was to take the CPR to court over its failure to supply boxcars without discrimination. The local farmers' victory in what was known as the Sintaluta test case, upheld upon appeal to the Supreme Court of Canada, won thousands of converts to the new organization, and it quickly became a force to be reckoned with, especially in the future province of Saskatchewan. The rail system, meanwhile, had to catch up to settlement. Farmers may now have been able to grow a decent crop, but they required ready access to a rail line if they were to make the transition from pioneer homesteader to producer for the international export market. Unless the hauling distance to the nearest shipping point was no more than ten miles, farmers would invariably lose money on every wagonload.[13] "We are in a desperate situation," explained a Hearts Hill farmer. "The elevators pay 18–20 cents for a bushel of oats and it costs 20 cents to take the bushel 40 miles to the elevator ... we must be helped anyhow by a better railroad connection or we have lost everything."[14] Other farmers were equally desperate and complained that they had taken up land in a pioneer

The bumper 1901 crop plugged the grain-handling system at places like Wolseley.
SASKATCHEWAN ARCHIVES BOARD R-A3947

district in the belief that a rail line would soon follow. "We are not going to stand this treatment any longer," wrote an American homesteader. "If we cannot get a railway into this district, we will have to call upon the Government for assistance because it was through them and their representatives that we came into this country."[15]

The CPR, once reluctant to overextend itself, launched an ambitious branch line program in response to the Saskatchewan settlement boom. Vice-President William Whyte confessed, "If someone had told me that the time would come when large shipments of wheat would be made from Swift Current, I would have said that he was a fit subject for the asylum."[16] Now, the company scrambled to improve the railway's carrying capacity. In an effort to consolidate its hold on the southern part of the province, the CPR ran branch lines out from Weyburn, Moose Jaw, and Swift Current. It also extended the Minnedosa line from Yorkton through Saskatoon into central Alberta and constructed a branch from Regina to Saskatoon. And it laid a second track along the Saskatchewan section of the main line from the Lakehead to Calgary.[17]

Central Saskatchewan, at the same time, became the battleground for two new players in the field. In the early twentieth century, both the Manitoba-based Canadian Northern Railway and the eastern-based Grand Trunk (Grand Trunk Pacific) announced their intention to build to the Pacific. It would have made more sense for the two rivals to co-operate in the venture, especially given the cost of building north of Lake Superior and through the Rocky Mountains, but these were not sensible times, and the reckless prosperity of the period seemed to suggest that the country could support two new transcontinental lines. Beginning in 1905, the Grand Trunk Pacific concentrated its energies on building a main line from Winnipeg to Saskatoon and on to Edmonton to the highest possible standard in North America. The Canadian Northern, on the other hand, was more concerned with generating traffic and consequently tried to lay claim to as much territory in central Saskatchewan as possible. Four main trunk lines through the region sprouted a profusion of branch lines in pioneer districts. At one point, the Canadian Northern had more than thirty projects on the go in Saskatchewan, earning the company the nickname "the farmer's friend." But many of the lines were built to service the immediate traffic needs; some were never improved. "In sparsely settled areas," claimed the railway's historian, "the tracks were reported to jump with joy under the weight of every passing freight car."[18] Farmers had no choice but to accept these shortcomings—the alternative was no line at all.

The number of country grain elevators in Saskatchewan grew hand-in-hand with railway mileage. At first, bagged grain was collected and stored in flat warehouses, but by 1900 the elevator, an American invention, became the standard means of storing grain for shipment and the one preferred by railways. It is easy to understand why. Whereas warehouses required enormous manpower and were limited in their function, elevators, with their endless cup-conveyor system, could collect, clean, dry, store, and load grain. The CPR and other railway companies were not interested in going into the business themselves, but provided incentives to persuade companies to build elevators, with a minimum twenty-five-thousand-bushel capacity, along a particular line of track—hence the term line elevators. These arrangements, in turn, allowed a handful of companies to enjoy monopoly control of the storage facilities. In Saskatchewan, three Canadian companies—Lake of the Woods, Ogilvie's, and Northern Elevator—initially held sway across the south. But the massive railway-building program of the first decade of the twentieth century encouraged other investors, including American grain dealers, to enter the trade either by acquiring existing elevators or building along new lines, especially those of the Canadian Northern and Grand Trunk Pacific. By 1912, Saskatchewan could boast 1,007 elevators, more than any other province. Two out of every five of these elevators were American-owned, as was the Canadian Elevator Company, the largest line company in Canada at that time.[19]

As the vast network of branch lines and grain elevators spread over the southern Saskatchewan landscape, the wheat economy took root and flourished. The number of farms in the province jumped from 13,380 in 1900 to 55,971 six years later. Not surprisingly, the number of cultivated acres jumped as well, from 654,931 to 3.3 million acres. Perhaps the most startling figure was the amount of wheat produced. In 1900, Saskatchewan harvested 4.3 million bushels of wheat. Five years later, the total climbed to 31.8 million bushels. Only one year after that, it topped an astounding 50 million bushels (with an average yield of 23.7 bushels per acre). This total, almost half the western wheat production in 1906, would probably have been higher if farmers had not devoted almost a million acres of land to the production of oats, in part to feed their workhorses.[20]

Farmers made a conscious decision to grow wheat because it was "more profitable and practical."[21] Wheat was cheaper to produce and provided a comparatively better return than dairying or raising cattle. It was seen as an easier, quicker route to wealth, despite fluctuations in the wholesale price from year to year. Wheat farmers also got outside help when they needed it most. Every August the railways sponsored what were known as harvest excursions, bringing

THE VOICE FROM THE WEST.

Thousands of harvest excursionists from across the country helped get the western crop to market. *Montreal Daily Star*, 14 August 1907

thousands of migrant workers to the prairies at reduced rates to help bring in the crop. Nearly 17,000 men made the trip west in 1905; a record 27,500 were recruited three years later.[22] Farmers also grew wheat for the simple reason that Saskatchewan's settlement and development had been organized around its production. The homesteads, the railway branch lines, the country eleva-tors—even the harvest excursions—were all part of a grand design to supply wheat to the international export market, supported by the federal govern-ment and investment in the region by large, powerful companies.[23]

It was these very companies, though, that became the focus of the farmers' anger. Granted, the reforms of the Manitoba Grain Act, together with better railway and elevator facilities, had led to improved grain handling. But farmers still chafed at the control enjoyed by large corporations and looked to secure some measure of independence. One such way, they believed, was to build a railway to Hudson Bay and use the old fur-trade outlet to Europe to bypass eastern Canada.[24] They also continued to be dissatisfied with grain prices. Since farmers needed money to pay off their debts, they were forced to sell their grain in the fall to the local elevator agent at the "street" price, the lowest of all possible prices. This small return was discouraging in itself, but even more upsetting when it became apparent that the elevator and milling companies, under the umbrella of the Northwest Grain Dealers' Association, were acting in collusion to prevent any price competition. In January 1905, the Sintaluta branch of the Territorial Grain Growers' Association (soon to be the Saskatchewan Grain Growers' Association) sent E. A. Partridge to investigate the Winnipeg Grain Exchange and how the grain dealers oper-ated. He found a secretive organization—what he described as the "house with closed shutters"—and concluded that farmers would never get a fair deal until they got into the marketing business themselves. It was a bold sug-gestion, pure Partridge, but within a year the farmer-owned Grain Growers' Grain Company had a seat on the exchange, buying and marketing wheat on a commission basis.[25]

One of Partridge's other ideas was the creation of an agrarian newspaper. At the heart of this initiative was the belief that "the root of the farmer's plight was his individualism, his isolation, and his ignorance of matters outside his narrow practical experience."[26] The solution was the June 1908 launching of the *Grain Growers' Guide,* a monthly non-political journal dedicated to edu-cating farmers about the need for co-operative action. The *Guide,* as it became widely known, provided stinging editorial commentary on the enemies of western farmers and was often later accompanied by one of Arch Dale's bril-liant cartoons. It also served as a vehicle for Partridge's most controversial project to date: the public or government ownership of elevators. Called simply the "Partridge Plan," it was nothing less than a revolutionary remaking

Western farmers complained that their profits were not commensurate
with the work they did. *Grain Growers' Guide*, 26 July 1916

of the entire grain-handling system. Farmers and governments would ally to
end the corrupt practices in the grain trade through the nationalization of
the elevator system; the federal government would own and operate terminal
elevators in combination with a system of provincially controlled internal or
country elevators.

Saskatchewan farmers formally adopted Partridge's proposal at the 1908
Saskatchewan Grain Growers' Association (SGGA) convention. This endorsement placed the Liberal government in an extremely awkward position. Since
assuming office in 1905, Premier Walter Scott had governed with one eye on
the interests of the agricultural community, knowing full well that farmers
exercised growing political clout in the province. The annual meetings of the
SGGA, for example, had been nicknamed the "farmers' parliament," largely
because of the organization's considerable influence on government policy.
But Scott had no desire to see the government go into the elevator business,
nor did William Motherwell, the minister of agriculture, who balked at any
form of government ownership. The former farm leader dismissed the Partridge
Plan as "a very nice fairy tale."[27]

The Scott government, however, could not simply ignore the proposal without jeopardizing farmer support. It had to find some alternative to satisfy the demand for action, especially since the Manitoba government had caved in to farmer pressure and embarked on an elevator-buying spree. The premier proposed the appointment of a provincial royal commission to investigate the best way of proceeding. After six months of complaint-riddled hearings about the grain-handling system, the Magill Commission recommended in October 1910 that farmers own and operate a system of elevators with the generous financial backing of the province. Premier Scott welcomed the compromise and introduced a bill to create the Saskatchewan Cooperative Elevator Company in the legislature on 7 February 1911, coincidentally just one day before the annual SGGA convention. Realizing that the government was prepared to go ahead with a co-operative scheme, the SGGA delegates unanimously accepted the elevator commission's report. This change of heart did not mean that the SGGA leadership had been bluffing, using the stick of public ownership to force the Scott government to help them in their battle against the elevator giants. Not all Saskatchewan farm leaders were Partridge disciples. Many, like Yorkton-area homesteader Charles Dunning, a future premier and federal cabinet minister, were prepared to work within the existing system as long as agrarian interests were protected. Still, the debate over the elevator bill was one of the longest in provincial history, thanks to the resistance of opposition leader Frederick Haultain, who maintained that Saskatchewan's farmers were being betrayed by the failure to create a system of government elevators. Scott's skillful manipulation of the issue, though, only strengthened the ties between his party and the province's farmers, and the Saskatchewan Cooperative Elevator Company came into existence on 14 March 1912.[28]

The other popular topic in the pages of the *Guide* was the protective tariff, introduced in 1879 to protect the country's fledgling manufacturing sector from foreign competition. Farmers resented paying more for Canadian machinery and other agricultural necessities, stuffing the pockets of eastern industrialists, when the same American products would have been cheaper if not for the tariff. They also questioned why domestic manufacturers enjoyed special treatment, when they had to sell their grain on an unprotected, competitive international market. Columnist Edward Porritt, who ranted about the many evils of the tariff in the *Guide*, called it the "new feudalism." The implication was unmistakable: as long as the tariff was in place, farmers were little better than latter-day serfs.[29]

Western farmers had great hopes that the tariff would go the way of the dodo when Wilfrid Laurier became prime minister in 1896. After all, the Liberal leader had campaigned on a platform of unrestricted reciprocity or

The Saskatchewan Grain Growers' Association exercised considerable political clout.
SASKATCHEWAN ARCHIVES BOARD R-B4195

free trade with the United States in the general election five years earlier. The new Canadian leader, though, was not about to do anything that might alienate the business community and generally followed the tariff practices of previous Conservative governments. Farmers were naturally disappointed, but it was not until their organizations began to flex their new-found muscle that the issue took on the spirit of a crusade. During the 1906 national hearings of a federal tariff commission, western farmers equated tariff reductions with fairness and justice. Four years later, they got the opportunity to present their case directly to Sir Wilfrid when he embarked on his much-publicized western tour.[30]

Officially, the Laurier tour was intended to give the prime minister the chance to inspect the new west and meet some of its citizens.[31] But the timing was curious. It had been only two years since the last federal election, and it seemed strange that the elderly Liberal leader would put himself through an ambitious campaign-style trip during the hottest months of the year on the prairies. The more likely explanation for the tour was that Sir Wilfrid was genuinely worried about the rumblings coming from the prairie region about the tariff and other related agricultural issues. There was good reason to be concerned. Saskatchewan had grown so fast that the 1911 national census would reveal that the province had become the third most populous in the dominion, behind Ontario and Quebec. Farmers' votes would clearly figure in any future election, and Laurier seemed to want to find out for himself about the nature and strength of the unrest before it turned against him and his government. This desire to soothe western sensibilities probably explains why the minister of the interior, the irascible Frank Oliver, did not accompany the tour.

The prime minister's special five-car train entered Saskatchewan on 19 July 1910, after a series of meetings in neighbouring Manitoba. Over the better part of the next three weeks, Laurier was shuttled about the southern half of the province, exchanging words at brief station stops along the route and speaking at more formal civic receptions in the larger centres. Four thousand turned out to greet the prime minister in Humboldt, another two thousand in Melville. Three hundred stood in the rain at Foam Lake just to shake hands. Laurier used the public meetings to talk about how the province's diverse settlers were building a greater Canada. But no sooner had he concluded his remarks than a delegation from the local SGGA, as if on cue, presented him with a petition about the tariff, government ownership of terminal elevators, the building of the Hudson Bay railway, and freight rates. In Lanigan on 23 July, the meeting took on a chill when David Ross, a farmer delegate, told the prime minister that farmers wanted "straight conversation." "We would like to see a little more being done than you have been doing," he lectured.[32] When another member of the audience declared himself a free trader, Sir Wilfrid shot back, "So am I."[33] It was just as testy in Saskatoon six days later. At a meeting with a grain growers' delegation, John Evans bluntly reminded the prime minister: "In 1896 you promised to skin the Tory bear of protection. Have you done it? If so, I would like to ask what you have done with the hide?"[34] One of the lighter moments was a chance meeting with a local newsboy, John Diefenbaker, outside the Saskatoon train station. After talking for half an hour, the future Progressive Conservative prime minister evidently told Laurier: "I can't waste any more time. I have to deliver my papers."[35]

The demand for reciprocity only intensified with every Saskatchewan stop. In Regina on 1 August, the largest grain growers' delegation to date urged the prime minister to do away with the tariff. Two nights later at a banquet in Weyburn, farmers called protection "wrong" and demanded free trade with the United States.[36] The message was the same at several small towns on the way to Moose Jaw, prompting a seemingly exasperated Laurier to confess at Yellowgrass: "Speaking frankly ... the present tariff is not satisfactory to me."[37] Things seemed to go from bad to worse on 5 August when Laurier's special train collided head-on with a CPR freight west of Pense during a late evening rainstorm. No one was seriously hurt—both train

Prime Minister Laurier toured western Canada in 1910 to see first-hand how the region was booming. LIBRARY AND ARCHIVES CANADA C745

crews jumped just before impact—but Sir Wilfrid was violently tossed about his car.[38] The accident, coming after more than two weeks of protest against the tariff, served as a kind of exclamation point—or perhaps it was an omen. In any event, reporters travelling with the prime minister suggested in their stories that the SGGA, through its constant petitioning, had hijacked the tour. If Laurier felt this way, or was even prepared to do something about the tariff, he gave no indication. All he would say at the end of the tour was that he knew the region better. "I left home a Canadian to the core," he observed in his final speech in Medicine Hat. "I return ten times more Canadian. I have imbibed the air, spirit, and enthusiasm of the West."[39]

The tariff question, however, would not go away. In December 1910, five hundred delegates from the prairie provinces descended on the capital as part of a national effort by the Canadian Council of Agriculture to force the federal government to deal with several festering issues. The group, numbering about eight hundred and representing all provinces except British Columbia and Prince Edward Island, met first in the Ottawa Opera House on 15 December to discuss strategy and draw up what formally became known as the "Farmers' Platform." The next morning, they marched en masse up Parliament Hill and crammed into the House of Commons, filling both the chamber floor and galleries. Delegates sat wherever they could, including the seat of the prime minister. Several cabinet ministers had to perch on the speaker's dais. It remains the only time in Canadian history that a delegation of this size has occupied the House of Commons.[40]

The farm leaders, including Saskatchewan's E. A. Partridge, addressed a number of concerns, but dwelled mostly on the tariff for four hours. As one delegate neatly summed up their purpose, they were there to "talk turkey." But Laurier said little of substance in response, except to remind the group that negotiations were currently underway to secure better trade relations with the United States. The delegates were then shuffled off to see the governor general at a Rideau Hall reception. It was a bitter ending, especially given the distance that many had travelled to take part in the meeting, in several cases at their own expense. One disillusioned delegate told a local newspaper: "We have asked for bread, and you [Laurier] gave us a stone."[41]

The so-called "siege of Ottawa" started a protest tradition that is still part of the Canadian way of life. Whether it helped farmers at the time is questionable. Neither national party at the meeting with the farmer delegation seemed prepared to remove a row of bricks from the tariff wall, let alone take a wrecking ball to it. But then, on 26 January 1911, federal finance minister W. S. Fielding gleefully announced that Canada had reached a broad trade agreement with the United States, starting first with the removal of duties on most natural products. Ironically, the deal had nothing to do with answering western Canadian complaints, but had been initiated by the Americans, who

Harvesting the first crop on a Prince Albert–area farm. SASKATCHEWAN ARCHIVES BOARD R-B1668

had been more than ready at the negotiation table to remove most trade barriers. Farmers were nonetheless elated. Not only did they stand to benefit most from the relaxing of the restrictions on natural products, but they expected the agreement, once formally approved by both governments, to lead eventually to full reciprocity.[42]

Prime Minister Laurier, for his part, believed he had found the issue that would serve as the capstone to his fifteen years in office. Members of the Saskatchewan legislature agreed and unanimously approved a resolution in favour of the deal in early March 1911. The strongest applause during the debate went to opposition leader Frederick Haultain, who passionately championed the trade agreement and what it would do to open American markets to the province's rapidly expanding agricultural industry. The Scott government could not have asked for a better cheerleader.[43] But not everyone was thrilled by the prospect of reciprocity. In Ottawa, federal Conservative leader Robert Borden, once he found his feet on the issue, came out swinging, claiming that the agreement would weaken ties with Great Britain and lead to commercial absorption by the United States.

Laurier met the challenge head-on, calling a general election for September 1911, confident that reciprocity, in combination with his record, would carry the day. But it was a tired Liberal government, bereft of new ideas and directed by an aged leader, that headed to the polls. Borden's linking of reciprocity with Canada's demise, by contrast, tapped into popular fears of American aggression, particularly in older regions. When the votes were tallied, the overwhelming support of Ontario translated into a national Conservative victory. It was a different story in Saskatchewan. Despite Borden's dire warnings about the perils of the trade agreement during a western speaking tour, all but one of the ten federal seats in the province went to the Laurier Liberals. Farmers had come to identify reciprocity with their economic salvation and were not about to abandon the party that had done so much to help build the new west.[44]

Premier Scott hoped that this allegiance would hold true in the July 1912 provincial election, especially since Saskatchewan farmers were still smarting from the defeat of reciprocity at the hands of the Borden Conservatives. But in the emotionally charged aftermath of the 1911 federal election there was also angry talk of forming a new political party. And if farmers took this dramatic step, the Scott government might face a bleak future. The Liberals consequently portrayed themselves during the 1912 election as the party of the province's farmers, the party that had introduced the Saskatchewan Cooperative Elevator Company and a host of other measures to meet the needs of the burgeoning wheat economy. The Saskatchewan Provincial Rights party, meanwhile, had renounced its past support for reciprocity and united with the provincial Conservatives at a convention in Moose Jaw the previous summer. This flip-flop may have aligned the provincial party with its federal counterpart, but it came at the cost of any remaining farmer support.[45] The Liberals won their largest majority to date, a whopping 85 per cent of the seats, and cemented their ties to the agricultural community. Over the next three decades this close relationship between the Saskatchewan government and farmers would shape and influence provincial life almost to the exclusion of other groups, activities, and regions. Wheat was king, and any provincial government knew better than to dispute it.

CHAPTER EIGHT

LIKE VAPOUR
FROM A RIVER

ON A HOT SUNDAY AFTERNOON in late June 1912, the Dominion Day holiday weekend, towering, dark clouds began to build ominously just outside Regina. No one watching the sky that day probably anticipated anything worse than a fierce thunderstorm—until the wind began to howl and a chilling roar could be heard in the distance. The tornado struck Regina from the south, sweeping across Wascana Lake into the centre of the city before ripping through the CPR freight yards and then a residential area. Lasting no more than five minutes, the Regina Cyclone exacted a heavy toll—twenty-eight dead, two hundred injured, twenty-five hundred homeless, and over a million dollars' damage. Some downtown buildings still bear the scars of the powerful wind's onslaught.[1] But the cyclone also had symbolic significance. For the past decade, in response to the settlement boom, Saskatchewan communities had been madly swept up in a reckless race to outdo one another, each obsessed with becoming the leading city in the province, if not on the prairies. The urban population soared at a dizzying rate, faster than all other regions of Canada, as growth became the watchword for success. But a 1912–13 recession, much like the cyclone, burst the real estate and construction bubble, leaving Saskatchewan cities with a legacy of debt, stagnation, and broken dreams.

———

One of the key features of the 1875 North-West Territories Act was the requirement that the head of government reside at a territorial capital. But finding a suitable home for the lieutenant-governor was a challenge. There was not a single major urban centre in the territories at the time. Most communities in what would become Saskatchewan were still closely tied to the fur trade, and many of these settlements—like Cumberland House and Île-à-la-Crosse—were located in the northern boreal forest. The only place that seemed destined to amount to anything was Prince Albert. Founded in 1866 near the forks of the North and South Saskatchewan rivers and named in honour of Queen Victoria's late consort, the Presbyterian mission had become a thriving agricultural centre of some three hundred strong by 1874. Four years later, the frontier town boasted 831 settlers, many of them Ontario farmers, trades- and business people, and professionals drawn to the district in anticipation of the arrival of the CPR.[2] Among them was Hayter Reed, the town's first lawyer and a future deputy superintendent general of Indian Affairs, and Thomas Osborne Davis, a merchant and future Saskatchewan MP and senator. There was also storekeeper Charles Mair, a poet and dramatist who had done much to fan the flames of racial hatred during the 1869–70 Red River Resistance. They were all convinced that the community was destined for greatness.

Prince Albert, however, was passed over as the first capital of the North-West Territories. Instead, that distinction fell to Fort Livingstone,[3] the first western headquarters of the NWMP, at the junction of Swan River and Snake Creek (north of present-day Kamsack just inside the Saskatchewan border). The selection of Livingstone, named for the famous British explorer of Africa, is one of the great mysteries of western Canadian history. The site, located on a small ridge in a heavily timbered area, had few redeeming features, except that it was near Fort Pelly, a Hudson's Bay Company post, and three Treaty 4 Indian reserves (Keeseekoose, the Key, and Cote). It was also on the route of the dominion telegraph line that had been established between Winnipeg and Edmonton by the end of 1876; the transcontinental railway was supposed to follow.[4] Sam Steele, one of the most famous mounties of his era, mockingly described Livingstone as "an extraordinary spot." "How on earth any person in his senses could have selected such a situation," he wondered, "is difficult to imagine." Colonel George French, the first commissioner of the force, reported that a group of local Métis "laughed outright

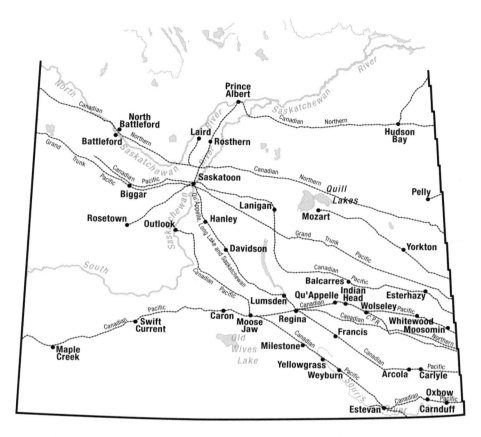

The province's railway network and urban population grew in response to the booming wheat economy in the first decades of the twentieth century.

when I asked opinions as to its suitability."[5] An unexpected bonus was a nearby garter snake hibernaculum. The snakes made drilling on the barracks square an adventure; they also migrated indoors, sometimes crawling into beds. But the mounties got their revenge. A snake-killing competition was held to celebrate Queen Victoria's birthday in May 1875. The winning team was credited with over eleven hundred dead.[6]

David Laird, a former Prince Edward Island journalist and Liberal federal cabinet minister in the government of Alexander Mackenzie, was sworn into office as lieutenant-governor at Fort Livingstone on 27 November 1876. At his side that day, serving as his secretary, was Amédée-Emmanuel Forget, who would become Saskatchewan's first lieutenant-governor in 1905. The first and only session of the North-West Council to be held at Livingstone was convened on 8 March 1877, when Laird read the speech from the throne to his three appointed councillors and anyone else who could be rounded up for the occasion. By this point, most of the mounted police were gone, having gladly fled westward to their new headquarters at Fort Battleford. Over the next two weeks, the council mulled over and unanimously approved twelve bills, in particular a law to try to save the buffalo from extinction; it was Saskatchewan's first piece of environmental legislation. The end of the session provoked another exodus from Fort Livingstone. Laird faithfully remained behind with the snakes, occupying the house originally intended for the NWMP commissioner until that August when he joined the police at the new territorial capital at Battleford.[7] Fort Livingstone had been long abandoned when the ruins were destroyed by a prairie fire in 1884. Fittingly, it is one of the most difficult national historic sites in Saskatchewan to find today.

Battleford's selection as the replacement capital was not as puzzling as the original choice of Fort Livingstone, although it meant that Prince Albert was once again passed over. There was little at the new capital, apart from some crude shacks and huts and a telegraph office where the Battle River flowed into the North Saskatchewan. But federal officials and the NWMP considered the site more centrally located to deal with any possible Indian trouble. Commissioner French also candidly admitted that anything was better than Fort Livingstone. Ottawa agreed, but officially changed the name from the uninspiring Telegraph Flat to the more prestigious Battleford.[8]

Battleford's new status precipitated a mini land rush and building boom in the late 1870s. The transformation, what one author has called the Cinderella days,[9] was nothing short of remarkable. The Battle River flats became an instant town of homes and businesses, including the *Saskatchewan Herald*, the first newspaper to be published between Winnipeg and the Rocky Mountains. The ridge between the two rivers, meanwhile, became the site of a large mounted police barracks; five hundred people would take refuge within the walls of the stockade during the 1885 North-West Rebellion. The most impressive new building was stately Government House, the official seat of government and the new home of Lieutenant-Governor Laird and his family. Built from hewn logs floated down the North Saskatchewan River, the substantial, two-storey mansion proved a construction nightmare because of its location atop the hill overlooking the Battle River. The elaborate interior, featuring a range of woods from oak to butternut to bird's-eye maple, also meant that the project went well over budget. By June 1877, more than thirty-five thousand dollars had already been spent on the structure, and there were several other government buildings yet to be erected.[10] Once completed, Government House not only dominated the Battleford landscape, but endured over the decades, undergoing several renovations and serving several purposes, including a stint as an Indian industrial school.

Government House at Battleford became an Indian industrial school after the capital was relocated to Regina. GLENBOW ARCHIVES NA-299-6

Unfortunately, the building was lost to fire in the summer of 2003. The Battleford skyline will never be the same.

Despite the people and money pouring into the new territorial capital, Battleford's fairy-tale days lasted less than a decade. Most of the federal activity in the region in the mid-1870s—the signing of Treaty 6, the location of the telegraph line, the surveying of homesteads, the placement of the capital, even the construction of Government House—had been based on the assumption that the CPR would be sent through the North Saskatchewan country. Prince Albert consoled itself over the loss of the capital to Fort Livingstone and then Battleford by looking forward to the arrival of the railway and what it promised for the community's future. The town's population grew almost four times between 1878 and 1881—to more than three thousand—making it one of the fastest growing settlements in the North-West.[11] But the transcontinental railway never did arrive. In 1881, the new CPR Syndicate decided to send the main line directly west from Winnipeg across the southern prairies, effectively killing the once-great hopes of Battleford and Prince Albert. Although they would continue to serve as important regional centres, they found themselves two hundred miles north, and not at the heart, of the western settlement frontier. Without a rail link, they could only watch helplessly as development passed them by and their population slipped. Prince Albert's historian called the loss of the CPR "a tragedy," while for Battleford, it was a "time of great disappointment." Poet Charles Mair spoke of "the wronged land."[12]

The CPR's remaking of the map of the North-West prompted the search for yet another new capital. A strong candidate was Fort Qu'Appelle, a HBC post and NWMP divisional headquarters on the river of the same name in southeast Saskatchewan. The Assiniboine, Cree, and Saulteaux had signed Treaty 4 there in 1874, and there were several reserves in the immediate area (Touchwood Hills, File Hills, and Crooked Lakes). In retrospect, the scenic Qu'Appelle Valley, with its deep coulees, rich bottomlands, and wooded hilltops, would have provided a stunning setting for the new capital.[13] But Edgar Dewdney, the new lieutenant-governor for the territories, and William Van Horne, CPR general manager, who had been given the job of choosing an appropriate site, were opposed to running the railway through the valley because of the apparent engineering difficulties. The alternative was about one hundred miles further west, on the open, treeless prairie, where the main line crossed Pile of Bones (Wascana) Creek—what one Englishman derisively called an "exaggerated ditch."[14] Dewdney reserved the site in late June 1882. Less than two months later, when the first CPR train arrived on 23 August, Pile of Bones was officially named Regina in honour of the queen. The following March, the capital was transferred from Battleford.[15]

Like other new communities along the rail line, Regina owed its existence to the CPR. Indeed, the railway often made minor, last-minute changes to the surveyed route to outmanoeuvre speculators who had taken up land at likely townsites. The choice of Regina, at the same time, was not immune from political interference. Lieutenant-Governor Dewdney, a close friend of the prime minister, had been buying up HBC lands along the rail line and just happened to own 640 acres of land immediately next to the original Regina townsite. The CPR responded by placing the train station almost two miles away to the east. Not to be outdone, Dewdney convinced the federal government to locate the new territorial government offices, including the lieutenant-governor's official residence, closer to his section of land. He also used his influence to get NWMP headquarters transferred to Regina; the new barracks were erected along the west side of Wascana Creek, well away from the CPR station. This jostling between Dewdney and the CPR initially led to two rival communities. But even though businesses soon gravitated to the station area and the town evolved from there, the CPR had tired of Dewdney's antics and decided to locate the divisional point, a major source of employment, forty miles down the track at Moose Jaw (where the course of the creek resembled the shape of a jaw bone). Whether the lieutenant-governor realized it or not, ironically, he had a hand in creating two of Saskatchewan's major cities.[16]

The North-West Mounted Police on drill practice near Regina's Wascana Creek. SASKATCHEWAN ARCHIVES BOARD R-B4525

Dewdney justified his selection of Regina as capital by claiming that it lay at the heart of a great agricultural area. What distinguished it, though, was the semi-arid plains environment. Regina would become the only Canadian capital city not located on a major body of water. It was also ridiculed (and still is to this day) for its flatness, its treelessness, its dreary monotony. Harry Graham, who passed through Regina on his way to the Klondike goldfields in 1900, had few kind words for the territorial capital. "It would be almost absurd to go out for a ride," he claimed, "as it is never possible to get out of sight of one's front door. There is no privacy, because your neighbour, even though he be ten miles off, can from his window observe you hanging out the clothes in your garden, or hoeing your turnips, and can almost see what you are having for dinner."[17] Jokes aside, Regina's first few years were not easy ones. The boom that accompanied the designation as capital quickly fizzled out; the town's population that stood at 613 at the beginning of 1884 had slipped by a third six months later. The CPR, the lifeline of the early community, was still a year away from completion, and even more significantly, farmers had failed to flock to the region in the anticipated numbers. The one bright spot was the presence of the mounted police. A steady stream of recruits passed through the training depot, and a large contingent, including the commissioner, was stationed there permanently. In many ways, Regina was as much a garrison town as it was a government one.[18]

Regina's descent into the doldrums in the mid-1880s was mirrored in the towns and villages that had popped up, seemingly overnight, as the CPR main line was laid across southern Saskatchewan. Although places like Moosomin, Broadview, and Swift Current had experienced an initial building frenzy, local expectations were soon dashed once settlers failed to follow.[19] The story was the same, if not bleaker, at communities away from the railway. In 1882, the Temperance Colonization Society of Toronto had founded Saskatoon (from *misaskwatomina*, the Cree word for a local berry) on the east bank of the South Saskatchewan River, almost two-thirds of the way from Regina to Prince Albert. Despite the enthusiasm of the first batch of settlers, the community limped along for almost two decades because of the lack of any significant agricultural settlement in the area. The 1890 arrival of the Qu'Appelle, Long Lake, and Saskatchewan Railway, running from Regina to Prince Albert, only complicated matters. By building along the lower, western side of the river, the railway created a second community that rivalled the original settlement, known locally as Nutana. The experience of the York Farmers' Colonization Company in east-central Saskatchewan was little different. Established in 1883, Yorkton took more than ten years to acquire status as a village and, even then, the population was only 215. The overall urban picture in Saskatchewan was equally dismal. According to the 1891 census, Winnipeg, the capital of Manitoba and so-called gateway to the North-West, dwarfed all other prairie urban centres with a population of more than 25,000. In comparison, no other prairie community tipped the scales beyond the 4,000 mark. Regina could boast only 1,681 residents, while Moose Jaw came next with 1,200, and then Prince Albert with 1,009. It was much the same ten years later during the next national census. Although Winnipeg now topped 42,000, the three largest Saskatchewan communities continued to lag behind. Regina had grown to only 2,249, while Prince Albert (1,785) and Moose Jaw (1,558) had simply switched positions.[20]

The early twentieth-century settlement boom turned this situation on its head. The tens of thousands of prospective farmers who poured into the west after 1900 required the services of villages, towns, and cities if they were going to transform their homesteads into viable commercial operations. They needed a place to handle their grain, secure agricultural equipment and other supplies, buy consumer goods, and get a loan to cover their expenses. This new rural demand fuelled a town-building frenzy; Saskatchewan may have had one of the fastest growing farm populations at the time, but urban areas grew even faster. Between 1901 and 1911, the urban population increased 9.4 times (from 14,000 to 131,000), almost double the rural rate. This change was reflected in the rural/urban breakdown. Whereas 13 per cent of Saskatchewan's population was classified as urban in 1901, the proportion had increased to 27 per cent ten years later. This urban growth, however, was entirely dependent on the wheat economy; Saskatchewan was first and foremost a rural province

The Johnston General Store in Kamsack, 1908. SASKATCHEWAN ARCHIVES BOARD R-A4093

where three out of every four residents lived in the country.[21]

Railways were the main engine of this town-building phenomenon. This role was nothing new. Estevan, for example, was created in 1892 when the CPR built a branch line from Brandon, Manitoba, to access the Souris coal fields in southeastern Saskatchewan. Two years later, when the so-called Soo Line arrived, linking St. Paul–Minneapolis and Moose Jaw, the town's future as a major service centre was assured.[22] But the situation in the early twentieth century was extraordinary, as new communities literally mushroomed from the prairie soil. No less than six hundred towns and villages with a population of at least one hundred found their way onto the map of the three prairie provinces by the start of the Great War in 1914.[23] Even more incredible was how these towns and villages were established. Like the Dominion Lands surveyors measuring the land into homesteads, the railways imposed an entirely functional urban pattern on the landscape. The location and distribution of communities along a rail line were determined not by the natural features of the land, but by the distance that farmers could economically haul their grain to local elevators by horse and wagon. Towns and villages were consequently set at regular intervals, preferably seven to ten miles apart, while larger centres, known as divisional points, where equipment was repaired and crews changed, were established every 110 to 130 miles.[24] One author likened the arrangement of towns to "beads on a string." He continued, "They appear ... as though a giant, armed with a rubber stamp, had marched along the lines impressing townsites at regular intervals upon the prairie."[25] A 1909 news-paper article, headlined "Towns Made to Order," offered a more tongue-in-cheek assessment of this sterile process: "'We'll put a town here,' said the engineer in charge. The man who held the map put a spot on the map. Other men made marks on the ground. There was no ceremony—no one was there to applaud, no residents came out to shout, for there were no residents."[26]

The railways' arbitrary power also extended to the naming of townsites. Names commemorated famous British wars, such as Senlac, the site of the Battle of Hastings in 1066, or national values, such as Imperial or Liberty. People associated with the railway companies were also frequently recognized. Melville was the middle name of Charles Hays, the general manager of the Grand Trunk who would perish on the *Titanic*, while Maymont was named for May Montgomery, the niece of one of the co-founders of the Canadian Northern Railway. Sometimes, the railways were more inventive. The Canadian Northern's literary line, featuring poets like Wordsworth and Browning, ran from Maryfield to Estevan. On other occasions, the companies took a rather prosaic approach. The Grand Trunk Pacific's east-west line through Saskatoon repeated the alphabet not once, but twice: from Atwater to Zelma and then Allan to Zumbro.[27]

The towns themselves reflected this same rigid structure, a degree of sameness more in keeping with a totalitarian society. Since towns essentially

The train station, like this one at Radisson in 1908, was the focus of small-town life. WESTERN DEVELOPMENT MUSEUM 3-A-35

West of Battleford

Bald Butte (centre block), Cypress Hills Provincial Park

Near Dalmeny

Near North Battleford

Near Hudson Bay, Saskatchewan

Cypress Hills Provincial Park (centre block)

Cypress Hills Provincial Park (west block)

Lac La Ronge Provincial Park

Grasslands National Park (east block)

Diefenbaker Lake, Prairie Lake Regional Park, south of Beechy

Churchill River system, east of Stanley Mission

Lac La Ronge Provincial Park

View from Narrow Hills Esker, Narrow Hills Provincial Park

The Great Sand Hills, south of Sceptre

Prince Albert National Park

South of Aberdeen

North of Hafford

Bents

Near Semans

Baljennie (now gone)

Near Vonda

Watrous

Pike Lake

Rotary cloud, east of Saskatoon

Near Yorkton

Summer parade

Craven, Qu'Appelle Valley

Saskatoon

Powwow, Saskatoon

Near Elbow

existed to provide a shipping point for grain and to distribute merchandise, the railway station and freight sheds, together with the elevators and loading platforms, served as the focal point of the communities. The elevators, numbering up to four or five in a row, were indistinguishable except for the company name and colours. All three major railway companies, meanwhile, used standardized designs for their depots. Canadian Pacific Railway stations offered more variety simply because the railroad was older. Those of the Canadian Northern and Grand Trunk Pacific, on the other hand, were virtually identical. The Canadian Northern's most common design, known as "Third Class," was used at over one hundred stations in the province; one of the best examples can be found today at Kelvington.[28]

The main commercial street either fronted on the train station or, more commonly, ran at right angles or perpendicular to the tracks, thereby forming a T. The two choice corners on the street were normally reserved for a hotel and a bank.[29] Other buildings or activities included a general store, hardware store, harness or blacksmith shop and livery stable, lumber yard, implement dealer, church, Eaton's mail-order outlet, post office, café, barber shop and pool hall, bar, and theatre. The railway companies worked in partnership with other large corporations and often gave them preferential treatment along their lines. Many Canadian Northern Railway towns featured a branch of the Bank of Commerce and a lumber yard operated by Canadian West Lumber Company. These businesses, in turn, reinforced the uniform nature of the towns by adopting a generic style for their structures, such as the prefabricated, wooden temple banks adopted by the Bank of Commerce across the prairies.[30] Most of the other commercial buildings along Main Street had false wooden fronts, usually unpainted, that contributed to the sense of repetitiveness. Even some of the churches were based on a ready-made mould. Anglican congregations were encouraged to erect modest buildings, affectionately known as "Canterbury Cathedrals," based on plans provided by the diocese; the specifications included the exact number of shingles and nails.[31] In general, though, places of worship tended to be the most distinctive features of the otherwise nondescript town environment. The onion-domed Ukrainian Catholic church, for example, stood in stark contrast to the ordered townscape and undoubtedly served to accentuate cultural differences among immigrants.

Once established, the new communities became the focus of social activity, whether it was Sunday worship, Saturday night dances, or just getting the mail and supplies or eating at the café. Sporting events were always popular, bringing people together to play and watch. In fact, the proximity of the towns and the regular railway service facilitated the formation of district leagues, and it was not long before fierce rivalries developed. European

The stately Canadian Bank of Commerce stands next to a barn in Canora. LIBRARY AND ARCHIVES CANADA PA21030

immigrants, especially the British, brought their love of soccer, while Ontario settlers were the first people to play hockey in Saskatchewan.[32] But the most popular sport was baseball. The first recorded game in the province was held outside the walls of Fort Battleford in May 1879. Three years later, CPR work gangs were playing pick-up baseball at their camps across southern Saskatchewan. Some of the troops stationed at Fort Qu'Appelle during the 1885 North-West Rebellion also passed the time playing ball.[33] These simple beginnings soon translated into a provincial passion for the game; it seemed a natural fit with the prairie landscape and long summer days. Every small town and village fielded a team, complete with uniforms, and made ambitious plans for a sports day to showcase local talent. There was no shortage of skilled players. Saskatchewan's first premier, Walter Scott, was once a noted pitcher with an all-star squad that barnstormed communities along the CPR main line.[34] Another future premier and gifted Lemberg athlete, Jimmy Gardiner, learned an important lesson during his playing days. "Being a ball player and soccer man taught me one thing," he recalled, "that a politician with common sense will never try to deliver a speech more than five minutes long on a sports day."[35] One of the most hotly contested games was an exhibition match in Melville during Prime Minister Laurier's 1910 western tour.

When the "parliamentarians" defeated the "journalists" before a holiday-like crowd, Sir Wilfrid shouted from the bleachers, "The government has been sustained."[36]

Naturally, larger Saskatchewan communities tended to produce the strongest teams because they had a larger pool of talent to draw upon. This dominance led them to form provincial leagues, such as the Saskatchewan Hockey Association in 1909. But just as it was never certain which team would win the championship in any particular year, so too was it far from clear which Saskatchewan town would emerge as the province's foremost urban centre in the early twentieth century. And that was the other amazing development during this period—the emergence of the large prairie city. Saskatchewan's booming wheat economy demanded central shipping points that doubled as major wholesale and distribution centres for the rapidly growing rural population. There was also a related need for food processing, manufacturing, and light industry, in addition to retail trade, commercial, and financial facilities, which, in turn, required service and professional personnel, as well as construction workers. But agriculture could support only a few major metropolitan centres, and based on the 1901 census figures the winners and losers in this contest for urban supremacy were still anybody's guess. Location was undoubtedly a factor in determining which towns became cities, but what mattered more were the decisions of the three major railway companies and the promotional efforts of local boosters who

The Prince Albert ladies' hockey team. SASKATCHEWAN ARCHIVES BOARD R-B3312

championed the merits and interests of their community to the exclusion of almost anything else.[37]

As the territorial capital and the largest town at the time, Regina seemed the most likely candidate to assume the mantle as Saskatchewan's premier city. But it faced a formidable foe in Moose Jaw, whose residents were not prepared to give any ground to its nearby rival. In fact, the business and civic elite of the two communities understood that there could be only one dominant centre in southern Saskatchewan. Regina and Moose Jaw consequently engaged in a struggle for urban supremacy. They kept tabs on how the other was doing and actively pursued any initiative, offering generous concessions if necessary, to secure a competitive edge.[38] Moose Jaw was first out of the blocks in 1897 when it became the terminus for the CPR Soo line and welcomed thousands of American settlers into the region. Regina had to wait another six years for the arrival of the CPR Arcola branch line from the southeast. Even then, premier-designate Walter Scott tried to use his influence with the Laurier government to secure more lines. The race to official city status was much closer. Regina was incorporated as a city in June 1903; Moose Jaw followed just five months later. What really mattered, though, was population. And here the margin of difference was razor-thin. According to the 1906 special western census, Regina's population had tripled—from 2,249 to 6,169—in the previous five years. Moose Jaw, on the other hand, grew faster to become the largest urban centre in Saskatchewan with 6,249 people.[39]

Moose Jaw's eighty-person advantage over Regina was short-lived. Granted, with its extensive CPR yards, repair shops, and branch lines the city represented a serious challenge, especially given the central role of the railway to the wheat economy. Over the next few years, it also secured a major meat-packing plant (Gordon, Ironside, and Fares), flour-milling facility (Robin Hood Mills), and several large terminal elevators. But Regina's confirmation as the new provincial capital, combined with the concerted efforts of its business community to capture the trade of the burgeoning farm population, won the day for the Queen City. By the time of the next national census in 1911, Regina was a modern city of over thirty thousand—twice the size of Moose Jaw and the fourth largest on the prairies (after Winnipeg, Calgary, and Edmonton). The Saskatchewan capital clearly benefitted from government largesse; the construction of government buildings alone, such as the new Legislative Building, was a boon to the local economy. It also successfully secured several branch lines—twelve ran into the city by 1913—making it the hub for wholesale and retail trade. By the start of the Great War, Regina's metropolitan reach extended to an estimated 250 towns and villages within a trading area of four hundred thousand people. The cityscape reflected this dominance—from bustling freight yards and a sprawling ware-house district to multi-storey office buildings and large department stores.[40] Former Lieutenant-Governor Edgar Dewdney, living in retirement in Victoria, would have been astounded by the transformation. A 1912 news-paper advertisement bragged, "The Eyes Of The World Are Upon Regina ... Whose Growth Can No More Be Stemmed Than The Waters Of The Sea."[41]

Other communities boomed as well during these heady years. Swift Current, the next divisional point on the CPR main line beyond Moose Jaw, leapt from town to city in just three years in response to the steadily growing volume of traffic. By 1907, the CPR yards, with their roundhouse and repair shops, boasted nine miles of track and a seven-hundred-car capacity.[42] Weyburn, on the Soo line between Estevan and Moose Jaw, experienced a similar surge in fortune as the southeast part of the province filled with set-tlers. It emerged as the sixth largest community (2,210) in Saskatchewan by 1911, fewer than one hundred people behind a growing Yorkton (2,309). Further north, Battleford and Prince Albert jockeyed for supremacy in the prairie parkland. It was the railways, though, that ultimately decided their fate. In 1905, the Canadian Northern Railway main line to Edmonton crossed the North Saskatchewan River several miles upstream from Battleford where the valley was not as steep and wide. This unexpected blow was bad enough for

A circus parade through downtown Prince Albert. SASKATCHEWAN ARCHIVES BOARD R-A4384C3

the former territorial capital, but what made things worse was the establishment of a rival townsite and divisional point—North Battleford—on the opposite or north side of the river. Battleford, or "old town" as it came to be called, greatly resented the "theft of its name."[43] It lost much more, though, as it soon found itself eclipsed by the upstart community. By 1911, North Battleford was home to 2,105 people and at the heart of a flourishing agricultural district.

Prince Albert expected the rapid settlement of the North Saskatchewan country to restore the community to its rightful place as the province's northern metropolis and a rival-in-waiting to Regina. But even though the community had achieved city status in 1904 and was ideally positioned on the edge of the great boreal forest, it was bypassed by both main lines of the Canadian Northern and Grand Trunk Pacific railways on their way across the northern prairies. Hopes remained buoyed, though, that Prince Albert would still become a great railway centre once it was named terminus for the Hudson Bay Railway, the gateway to Europe. Until that day arrived, the city looked to the North Saskatchewan River and naively began to promote steamboat traffic as an alternative to shipping by rail. Hand-in-hand with this initiative was the dream of harnessing the hydroelectric potential of La Colle Falls, a series of rapids about twenty-five miles east on the river, and turning Prince Albert into the power-producing or "white coal" capital of western Canada. In April 1912, construction started on a power dam and navigation lock at the staggering cost of $1.2 million. Any doubts about the soundness of the project were eased by the profound belief that cheap power was sure to attract all kinds of businesses and industries to the city.[44]

This excessive optimism paled in comparison to the bullish mood in Saskatoon. A mere sleepy hamlet of 113 in 1901, with no sidewalks, no sewers, no hospital, and no police or fire protection, it skyrocketed to a city of 12,000 in just ten short years—an astounding hundredfold increase. Even then, Saskatoon boosters angrily disputed the 1911 census figures—they believed the population was closer to 17,000—and methodically conducted their own head count, including people staying in hotels or passing through on trains. Saskatoon's phenomenal growth was initially triggered by the arrival of 1,500 Barr Colonists in April 1903, whose temporary presence not only put the town on the map, but ear-to-ear smiles on the face of local merchants. Five years later, thanks to the strenuous efforts of the civic and business elite, all three major railways ran through the city—hence the nickname "Hub City." Then, in 1909, Saskatoon snared the university, making the city the educational centre of the province in addition to its regional trade and distribution role.[45] The community's transformation was so dramatic, so swift, so unbelievable, that it aggressively promoted itself as the "Wonder City." It was even

The Saskatoon ferry with the traffic bridge under construction in the background. WESTERN DEVELOPMENT MUSEUM 4-C-6

suggested by the mayor in 1910 that a population of 100,000 was foreseeable in only "a few years."[46] A writer for the *Toronto Globe* agreed. "At such a rate of speed," he admitted after a visit to the city, "one dare not make any prediction as to what Saskatoon will not have done by a generation from now."[47]

Edinburgh-born Elizabeth Mitchell, who spent a year in western Canada after graduating from Oxford in 1913, did not expect to find such large, bustling communities on the open prairies. "If there is one preeminent character in these western cities," she wrote of her visit to Saskatchewan, "it is the note of change, of rapid and amazing and unpredictable change. Towns rise like vapour from a river." She was particularly struck by the new university taking shape on the east side of the South Saskatchewan River in Saskatoon—Prime Minister Laurier had laid the cornerstone for the Agricultural College Building (now known as the College Building) only three years earlier. "The University of Saskatchewan," she declared, "is the most startling thing I saw in the West ... It is a massive group of fine buildings ... so obviously built to last for five or six hundred years that one's brain reels at the sudden shock of passing from a view of life limited by one generation."[48] Mitchell was also impressed with the emerging cultural life in the province's major cities. In 1906, a natural history museum, now known as the Royal Saskatchewan

Museum, had been established in Regina. Two years later, the Regina Orchestral Society, the forerunner of the Regina Symphony Orchestra, was founded. The following year, the city hosted the first provincial music festival. Theatre also received a boost in 1910 with the opening of impressive new stages in Saskatoon and Regina. The new Regina Theatre, with its thousand-seat capacity, was a vast improvement over the city's first theatre on the second floor of the old town hall above the jail cells; actors often had to compete with the prisoners' singing. Saskatoon and Regina were part of the same North American touring show circuit and offered nightly entertainment in the form of stock company productions and vaudeville bills. Most of the other four hundred halls and theatres in Saskatchewan had to make do with lesser-known performers.[49]

Big city status also meant that some sports went professional. In 1910, the Regina Rugby Club, soon to be known as the Roughriders, began league play. One of the early stars was Piffles Taylor, after whom the Regina stadium was later named.[50] Hockey also moved onto the national scene. Prince Albert became Saskatchewan's first team to challenge for the Stanley Cup in 1911, but lost the series to Port Arthur by a lopsided score. Saskatoon suffered the same fate at the hands of the defending champions the next year.[51] Money was also poured into better sports facilities. J. F. Cairns spent twelve thousand

Yorkton theatre group, 1914. Howard Jackson Collection, CITY OF YORKTON ARCHIVES

dollars on a new baseball park for the Saskatoon Quakers; over six thousand spectators were on hand for the first game there. The Regina Golf Club, meanwhile, joined with tennis and polo enthusiasts to form the Wascana Country Club just outside the city limits; golfers no longer had to contend with the grazing cows and horses that kept the grass down on the fairways at the old site.[52] The city underwent a similar makeover by the planting of thousands of trees—forty thousand in 1912 alone—along streets and boulevards. Wascana Park, bordering the new Legislative Building, received special treatment. Between 1908 and 1912, landscape architect Frederick Todd oversaw the planting of over a hundred different varieties of trees and shrubs, many of them grown for the first time in western Canada. Further development of the grounds was directed by famed British designer Thomas Henry Mawson and his plan to turn Regina into a "garden city."[53] Today, Wascana Centre is the largest urban park in the world. New York's Central Park is one-third the size.

Boosters hailed this kind of growth as a sure sign that their community was well along the road to greatness. Being large was everything in the struggle to achieve urban dominance in Saskatchewan, and the major competitors "super-sized" their cities by pushing out municipal boundaries to unrealistic limits. Regina grew four times in one swoop with the addition of nearly 6,500 acres in 1911; the Queen City's boundaries would not be adjusted again for another four decades.[54] Prince Albert was even larger—on paper. In 1912, it boasted an area of 10,559 acres. At the time, Toronto was 200 acres smaller, but with a population approaching one-third of a million.[55] This appetite for land gave Saskatchewan cities some of the lowest population density ratios among Canadian urban centres. But more importantly for civic leaders, it provided a larger assessment area and tax base to draw upon for local improvements such as roads, sidewalks, water mains, and sewers. During the five-year period from 1909 to 1913, Regina spent twenty million dollars on public buildings alone.[56]

The extended boundaries also fed a real estate mania that Elizabeth Mitchell characterized as "the Great Goddess of the western town."[57] Speculation in city lots was so rife that prices jumped to ridiculous levels. Many properties changed hands several times, sometimes in the same week. Undeveloped areas, no more than gopher-riddled fields, were also put on the market in order to meet the speculative demand of starry-eyed investors.[58] The situation in Saskatoon was perhaps the most spectacular, if only because the city went on a binge that belied its teetotaler beginnings. Between 1910 and 1913, real estate agents, representing 257 firms, sold the equivalent of three Saskatoons of the size of the one that exists today. Over sixty subdivisions, with enticing names such as Highlands, Regal Terrace, and Utopia, were listed during the three-year period. Most were never developed. In all, fifteen thousand acres were surveyed outside the 1911 city limits—enough land to accommodate five hundred thousand people, half the population of Saskatchewan in 2001. One of the shadiest schemes was Factoria, billed as the province's first industrial park, on the northern edge of the city. The promoter, a Chicago businessman, ran full- and half-page ads in the local newspapers every day for six months, claiming that industry was the key to Saskatoon's future growth, that the name, Factoria, meant money. Gullible people lined up to buy undeveloped lots at five hundred dollars each.[59]

This greed had a cost. Because growth was idolized, civic and business leaders ignored or downplayed problems that came with the race to big-city status. The demand for affordable housing, for example, easily outstripped supply. Many workers in Saskatoon took up residence in a semi-permanent tent city on the Nutana side of the river. Communities were also divided: on one level between the Anglo-Canadian majority and the immigrant newcomers, on another between the well-to-do and the labouring class. Germantown in Regina was little more than an ethnic ghetto with deplorable living conditions. Even basic health considerations were ignored. Raw sewage poured into the South Saskatchewan River in Saskatoon, leading to several typhoid deaths and a lucrative market for bottled water.[60] These kinds of problems were largely unavoidable given the kind of rapid urbanization experienced by Saskatchewan's cities, and they would continue to fester in the coming years. A more serious concern was the money that cities were freely spending in a delusional attempt to keep pace with the boom. Not only were cities blithely assuming record debt to provide municipal services and facilities that went well beyond actual need, but they were financing these loans based on highly inflated assessment values.[61] North Battleford was a case in point. The town's first assessment, conducted in 1907, came in at just over a million dollars. By 1912, it was $5.6 million and then almost doubled the next year![62] This fantasy could not last.

That time seemed to have arrived, albeit symbolically, when the tornado, packing winds in excess of three hundred miles an hour, struck Regina in the late afternoon on Sunday, 30 June 1912. Sweeping into the city from the southwest, the cyclone, as it was called at the time, churned up Wascana Lake where a holiday crowd was picnicking, swimming, and boating. It narrowly missed the new Legislative Building, scheduled to be officially opened that fall, but blew out several of the windows. The storm hit the city core with a fury. Buildings surrounding Victoria Park were severely damaged, if not destroyed. An entire residential block of some of Regina's finest homes was completely levelled, while at the telephone exchange a massive switchboard crashed through the floor and into the basement, taking the operators with it. The cyclone widened as it crossed the CPR tracks, smashing through freight yards and warehouses and another residential area. Its path seemed sadistically random. It destroyed some houses and left others—sometimes right next door—untouched. From start to finish, the cyclone lasted no more than five minutes, but its memory would last for years. Katherine Lamont, the daughter of the province's first attorney general, remembered for the rest of her long life hiding under the dining-room table while the upper part of the family's house was blown away.[63] Recent British immigrants Frank and Bertha Blenkhorn were not so lucky. They had denied fate once when they missed their passage on the *Titanic* in April, but died three months later when the tornado picked them up as they crossed Victoria Park that afternoon and threw them against the front of the city library.[64]

One of Regina's newspapers declared that the city would "rise Phoenix-like from its ruins."[65] The prediction seemed to come true; 1912 was a record year for building, most of it reconstruction. The clean-up after the disaster even provided temporary employment for future horror-movie actor Boris Karloff, who had been stranded in the city when the stock company he was touring with went bankrupt the day before the storm.[66] But 1912 gave way to a recession that ate away at the economy until after the outbreak of the Great War. Western Canada was particularly hard hit. Grain prices plummeted. The real estate market, and with it the construction industry, collapsed. And the two uncompleted transcontinental railways sustained mortal blows from which they never recovered. There was even drought in some southern districts. The downturn in the prairie economy immediately led to the loss of twenty-five hundred jobs in Moose Jaw, roughly 15 per cent of the population. In Regina, work on the Chateau Qu'Appelle, a luxury Grand Trunk Pacific hotel near Wascana Park, was suspended. The steel framework stood for more than a decade, a rusting reminder of what might have been, before it was dismantled. Construction also came to an abrupt end on the La Colle Falls hydroelectric project outside Prince Albert, with the dam less than halfway across the North Saskatchewan River. Not only was the city eventually forced to declare bankruptcy in 1918—the first city in Saskatchewan to default on its debt—but it did not finish paying for the project until 1965.[67]

This outcome was tragic but predictable. The very existence and well-being of Saskatchewan's urban centres depended on agriculture and the railroad—something that civic boosters seem to have forgotten in their mad rush for urban dominance. Because of their location, places like Moose Jaw, Regina, and Saskatoon would never achieve metropolitan greatness, but they did become important regional centres serving the booming wheat economy. That role was underscored by the fact that the distribution of seats in the legislature continued to favour rural voters, even though urban dwellers had come to represent a larger percentage of the provincial population during these heady years.[68] By ignoring the fundamental fact that they were there to meet the needs of the farming community, Saskatchewan cities overreached their true potential with disastrous consequences: depressed land values, abandoned property, mounting tax arrears, and crippling debt. They had grown too much, too fast, and now faced an uncertain future of decline and consolidation before they were walloped again by the Great Depression. Saskatchewan cities had enjoyed their "one great spree." The future would be "more sober."[69]

Damaged homes along Smith Street after the 1912 Regina Cyclone. SASKATCHEWAN ARCHIVES BOARD R-B3720

CHAPTER NINE

PAGANISM
IS DYING HARD

WHEN THE OVERHEATED CANADIAN ECONOMY slid into recession in 1912, the great expectations for Saskatchewan were momentarily stalled. The only statistic that continued to climb was the number of new immigrants, and even here, many of these new arrivals would soon swell the ranks of the unemployed. This downturn made little difference to the Aboriginal people of the province, who eked out an existence on the margins of Saskatchewan society. Far from sharing in the largesse of the great Laurier boom, Indians and Métis struggled to preserve their identity, culture, and livelihood in the face of neglect and racism. Not only were they effectively prevented from being part of the emerging wheat economy, but their traditional activities were threatened. They were dismissed as an irrelevant minority, a holdover from another time who were expected to disappear as a distinct people—the sooner the better. David Laird, Indian commissioner for Manitoba and the North-West Territories, confidently predicted in his 1903 annual report that Aboriginal people "must at no distant day become nearly extinct."[1] Few at the time would have disagreed with this assessment.

The first decade of the twentieth century brought more change for Saskatchewan's First Nations. In the 1870s, Cree, Saulteaux, and Assiniboine (Nakota) bands had formally negotiated treaties with the Canadian government that provided federal assistance to help make the transition to agriculture in exchange for the surrender of vast sections of land in the southern half of the future province of Saskatchewan. The signing of Treaties 2 (1871), 4 (1874), and 6 (1876) had come at a time of crisis for Indian peoples. Faced with the impending loss of the buffalo, the mainstay of their economy, they knew that they had to adjust successfully to the changing circumstances or follow their four-legged quarry into possible extinction. They proved persistent negotiators in dealing with the Queen's representatives to ensure that the treaties were not merely land transfer agreements but provided meaningful and ongoing assistance, especially in times of sickness and famine. Even then, Big Bear, a respected Cree leader, doubted whether government support was sufficient and stubbornly remained outside Treaty 6 to see how Ottawa fulfilled its obligations. Only starvation and the heavy hand of Indian officials eventually broke down his resistance, but it took six years. He and other band leaders were strenuously encouraged to settle down on reserves and turn their hand to farming before the region was engulfed with the expected rush of white settlers.[2]

The first few years on the reserves were exceedingly difficult for Indian peoples. The almost overnight disappearance of the once-great buffalo herds, combined with the dismal failure of their first crops and inadequate agricultural assistance, precipitated widespread deprivation and, in many areas, outright starvation. The Canadian government, reluctant to feed what was widely regarded as a dying race and wanting to reduce Indian expenses, grudgingly responded with minimal relief. In contravention of the treaties, many bands were forced to perform menial duties to secure a meagre daily ration of meat and sometimes flour. This hunger crisis was soon eclipsed by the arrival of infectious diseases and other illnesses. The weakened state of many bands, not to mention their wretched living conditions, proved an ideal breeding ground for measles, scarlet fever, smallpox, whooping cough, diphtheria, and tuberculosis. Mortality rates climbed as a deadly mix of malnutrition and infection carried away the aged, the healthy, but mostly the very young. The three Assiniboine bands (Mosquito, Grizzly Bear's Head, and Lean Man) in the Battleford area lost seventy-five members—fifty of them children—out of a population of three hundred in one winter.[3] Father Louis Cochin of the nearby Poundmaker reserve candidly admitted, "The privation made them die."[4]

Cree cemetery at Fort Qu'Appelle, 1885. LIBRARY AND ARCHIVES CANADA PA118766

Despite their impoverished state and stinging sense of disillusionment and betrayal, Indians had made a solemn vow during the treaty negotiations to live in peace and were not prepared to break this pledge and plunge the region into war. Instead, Big Bear and other senior Cree chiefs patiently sought a peaceful resolution to their grievances. This determination to shun violence was made clear when several prominent Cree leaders met with sub-agent Ansdell Macrae at Fort Carlton in July 1884 to discuss the continuing failure of the government to fulfill its "sweet promises." Speaking with the force of years of bitterness and frustration, the chiefs affirmed their allegiance to the Queen, contending it was Ottawa, not the Crown, that had created the current climate of ill will. They also expressed relief that their young men had managed to keep their anger in check.[5] But when the Métis-provoked North-West Rebellion erupted the following year at Duck Lake, violence flared in the North Saskatchewan country at Fort Battleford and Fort Pitt when several warriors took advantage of the unrest to settle personal grudges. Any Indian involvement in the troubles was isolated, sporadic, and limited, certainly not part of a grand alliance with the Métis. Indian Affairs officials, however, deliberately used the apparent Indian support of the rebellion to stamp out any remaining sense of independence, in particular the Indian diplomatic initiative to force the Canadian government to honour its treaty promises. Several leading chiefs, such as Big Bear and Poundmaker, were imprisoned, more than twenty reserves were branded disloyal, and eight warriors were executed at Fort Battleford on 27 November 1885 in the largest mass hanging in Canadian history. The message was brutally clear: Indians were to conform to government directives or feel an iron hand.[6]

Now, in the early 1900s, Indians faced a new crisis that would once again test their resilience. Although Indians remained the responsibility of the federal government (section 91 [24] of the 1867 British North America Act), the creation of Saskatchewan in 1905 meant that they had to contend, albeit indirectly, with another level of government that put its own needs and interests ahead of the Aboriginal population. Indians were identified with the region's territorial past, a link that many newcomers sought to break in building the new Saskatchewan. There were also more direct and immediate challenges. The thousands of homesteaders who poured into the region began to plough and cultivate land that Indians had continued to use for traditional activities after the signing of the treaties. More than ever, Indians were increasingly confined to their reserves and the limited resources found there. Settlers also coveted reserve land in prime agricultural districts and urged the federal government to relocate the occupants to other areas or, at the very least, reduce the size of the reserves. In 1902, for example, the residents of the Broadview district in southeastern Saskatchewan submitted a two-hundred-name petition calling on Ottawa to open up for sale a three-mile strip along the southern boundary of the Crooked Lakes reserves.[7] These pressures undoubtedly heightened the Indian sense that they had become outsiders in their own land and that their future was still as uncertain as it had been a generation earlier.

The situation became even more difficult for Saskatchewan Indians with the death of several treaty-era chiefs in the early twentieth century. The loss of White Bear (1900), Lucky Man (1901), Moosomin (1902), Kahkewistahaw (1906), and Piapot (1908) created a leadership void at a time when leaders were sorely needed.[8] It was probably no coincidence that the death of White Bear coincided with the consolidation of the three Moose Mountain reserves in 1901. Ocean Man (Striped Blanket) and Pheasant's Rump were completely eliminated—freeing up over forty-six thousand acres of fine farmland—and the Assiniboine residents dumped on the other side of the mountain among the Cree and Saulteaux of White Bear, whose reserve was poorly suited for agriculture. Similarly, the Kahkewistahaw reserve "surrendered" more than thirty-three thousand acres, roughly 70 per cent of the original reserve, in January 1907, just months after the death of the chief. When federal Indian Commissioner David Laird, known as Tall White Man, had visited the area only a few years earlier to discuss the question of land surrender, he had met with stiff resistance. The aged Kahkewistahaw remembered that Laird had been present at the signing of Treaty 4 at Qu'Appelle in 1874 and bluntly reminded him, "Did I not tell you a long time ago that you would come

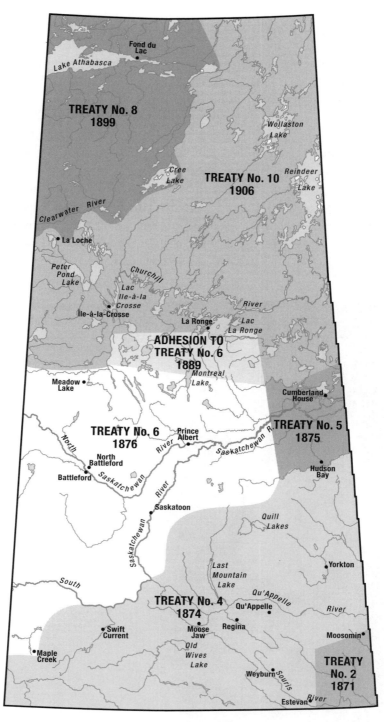

Parts of six treaties fall within Saskatchewan's boundaries. All but one of the treaties predate the creation of the province.

some time, that you would come and ask me to sell you this land back again, but I told you at that time, No."[9]

There were some small victories, though. Cree leader Foremost Man, also known as Front Man or Nekaneet, had entered treaty in 1874, but continued to hunt the few remaining buffalo in the Cypress Hills area. When other bands were forced to leave the region following the closure of Fort Walsh in 1883 and take up reserves to the north and east, he and his followers remained behind and quietly lived in and around the hills without any government assistance. Indian Affairs officials chose to leave them alone for the next few decades, seemingly convinced that their numbers would soon be reduced to a rump of stragglers. But the band remained true to Foremost Man's desire to remain in the hills, even after his death in 1897, and finally secured a reserve (Nekaneet) in the Maple Creek area in 1913. They were the last group of Plains Cree to settle on a reserve in western Canada.[10] About sixty of the

Piapot at the Regina Indian Industrial School, where his granddaughter was a student. SASKATCHEWAN ARCHIVES BOARD R-A21256

Hunkpapa Sioux who had fled north with Sitting Bull following the Battle of the Little Big Horn in 1876 also got a permanent home in Saskatchewan at this time. Although the Sioux were not Canadian treaty Indians, and thus unable to claim land, federal authorities relented in 1912 and established a temporary reserve for them in Wood Mountain near the RNWMP post; it took another eighteen years to be officially confirmed.[11]

These new reserves were the only two in the southwestern part of the province (west of Regina, south of Rosetown) even though First Nations had occupied this territory for centuries. The federal government wanted to keep Indians away from what was widely regarded as some of the best wheat land in the prairie west.[12] But wrangling over Indian land in other parts of the province was unavoidable as agricultural settlement swept northwest across central Saskatchewan after 1905. The existence of a large number of reserves in the area, containing valuable agricultural land, was seen as an impediment to the emerging wheat economy. The number of land surrenders consequently accelerated, reaching a peak in 1909, around the time that Ottawa began to worry that the rate of settlement would soon exhaust the available farmland. Interestingly, many of the buyers of the surrendered Indian land were not from the district, but were speculators who purchased the land by private tender and then resold it for a quick profit, sometimes for at least twice as much as the price per acre paid to the Indians. These speculators included Department of Indian Affairs employees and their families and friends, who used insider information and then hid behind the tender process to conceal their identity. James Smart, deputy minister of the Department of the Interior, and Frank Pedley, deputy superintendent general of Indian Affairs, were among them. A 1915 federal investigation of the land dealings, known as the Ferguson Royal Commission, found Indian officials to be in a conflict of interest, but the censure did not stop the land surrenders, which continued until after the Great War.[13]

One reason given for reducing the size of the reserves was that the Indian population had declined significantly and required less land than originally awarded. Department of Indian Affairs records for the 1880s and 1890s grimly supported this conclusion. For the ten-year period from 1884 to 1894, the Crooked Lakes and File Hills reserves lost 41 and 46 per cent of their population, respectively. Incredibly, the situation on the Battleford reserves was worse. Here, Indian populations declined by more than half during the same period: deaths exceeded births by a two to one ratio. Grizzly Bear's Head, an Assiniboine reserve, had the distinction of having the highest annual mortality rate during the rebellion era: an astounding 305 per 1,000. The next highest was Thunderchild at 233 per 1,000. Quebec City, by comparison, had a death rate of 31 per 1,000 in 1890, the highest among Canadian cities.[14]

A land-surrender meeting in the Pelly Agency in 1908. GLENBOW ARCHIVES NA-5462-10

Federal census data for 1901 and 1906 also lent credence to the notion that Indians in Saskatchewan were a vanishing race. In just five years, the total provincial Indian population slipped from 7,491 to 6,380 or almost 15 per cent. This seemingly steady slide towards extinction, however, had slowed by 1909, when Indian Affairs reported that there were close to 8,000 Indians in the province. This reversal made no impression on the attitude and policies of Indian Affairs officials, who continued to see Indians as a filthy, disease-ridden people. Nor did they believe that their sorry state had anything to do with department policies, but instead attributed the poverty, sickness, and death to the inherent weakness of the race. It was imperative, then, to keep Indians away from the growing white population. "No trespassing" signs were erected at reserve borders, while any hint of a new infection often led to total quarantine for several months, even though most disease originated outside the reserve.[15]

Saskatchewan's other major Aboriginal group, the Métis, was regarded little better during these years. Indeed, they are generally known as "the forgotten people." The 1901 census listed approximately ten thousand "half-breeds" living in the future province of Saskatchewan, but by the time of the special western census in 1906, the category had been dropped. It was as if the Métis, with their distinct dress, rich customs, and "mitchif" language, had disappeared as a separate group, or were not worth counting. This statistical neglect belied their central role in much of the province's early history, first in the Montreal- and London-based fur trade and then in the buffalo-robe trade, freighting, and early farming and ranching. It also completely ignored the ethnic divisions within the group. Whereas people of mixed-blood parentage are collectively called Métis today, those of French and English origin were identified differently in the nineteenth century. The Métis were understood to be of French-Indian descent, French-speaking, and Roman Catholic, while the English half-breeds, also sometimes known as "country born" or "Native English," tended to be of British-Indian ancestry, English-speaking, and Anglican. These distinctions, especially the denominational differences, translated into two separate and distinct groups, whose relationship was often strained, if not at times antagonistic. They may have lived in the same areas, but their interactions were limited.[16]

What brought the two mixed-blood populations together in the late nineteenth century was concern for their future, particularly among the roughly fifteen hundred French and English Métis living along the South Saskatchewan River between Prairie Ronde (Dundurn) on the south and Prince Albert on the north—the so-called South Branch communities. The two groups who had immigrated to the region in steadily increasing numbers in the 1860s and 1870s wanted to participate in the new economy taking shape on the northern plains, but not at the expense of their culture and traditions. When Ottawa repeatedly failed to respond to their petitions, particularly for title to their lands, they collectively decided, along with the white settlers in the district, to ask Louis Riel, the successful Métis leader of the 1869–70 Red River Resistance, to direct their protest. But the Riel who returned to Canada in the summer of 1884, believing himself now to be a religious prophet, began to advocate more forceful measures, including the creation of a provisional government. These activities cost Riel the support of disaffected white settlers, the Roman Catholic clergy, and even large segments of the mixed-blood population. Yet he remained confident about his divine mission, and with the support of only about 250 followers, pushed the peaceful agitation into open rebellion in March 1885. The Canadian government hurriedly responded with an 8,000-strong punitive force, while the Métis, at Riel's urging, made no attempt to conduct a guerilla campaign, except for an ambush at Fish Creek, but calmly prepared to meet the advancing army at a fortified Batoche. The Canadian troops, after a temporary setback, easily overran Métis headquarters on 12 May. Riel initially escaped, but then surrendered in a bid to take his cause to the courts.

Riel appeared in a Regina courtroom later that summer charged with high treason. Although his lawyers claimed their client was insane, the Métis leader's eloquent closing address to the jury was not that of a madman. He was found guilty and sentenced to death. Despite a recommendation for mercy, several appeals, and continuing doubts about his mental fitness, Riel was hanged at Regina on 16 November; his body lies today in the basilica cemetery at St. Boniface, Manitoba. Most of the rank-and-file Métis who had supported Riel were disarmed and sent home after the fall of Batoche. This government strategy of blaming Riel—and Riel alone—for the rebellion deflected attention away from Métis grievances. Nothing was done to address these concerns, even after federal Liberal leader Wilfrid Laurier was elected prime minister in 1896. He had once told a Quebec audience that he too would have shouldered a gun had he lived on the banks of the Saskatchewan in 1885.[17]

Métis communities in the Saskatchewan country did not die in the aftermath of the rebellion, as is commonly assumed. Batoche, for example, was rebuilt and continued to thrive until bypassed by the railway to Prince Albert in favour of nearby Duck Lake. At the same time, a large number of families fled to the United States or sought out other regions where they were less threatened as a people. Many headed to sparsely settled areas north of Battleford (Onion Lake, Meadow Lake) or west and east of Prince Albert (Leask, Marcelin, Birch Hills, and Kinistino) to work as freighters, trappers, and fishermen. Others, such as Norbert Delorme, one of Riel's staunchest supporters, responded to the growing demand for cowboys on southern ranches, especially in Alberta. Those who remained behind turned to subsistence agriculture based on the traditional river-lot system of cultivation. The provision of scrip, in the form of land or money, to those Métis who had been living in the North-West Territories as of 15 July 1870 did little to

Métis prisoners from the 1885 North-West Rebellion. LIBRARY AND ARCHIVES CANADA PA118760

improve their welfare. Many looked upon the scrip as much-needed compensation on the heels of the rebellion and readily sold their money certificates or assigned their land awards to the speculators who openly travelled
with the 1886–87 North-West scrip commissions. But any relief was temporary and they soon went looking for other work, mostly as labourers, to
supplement their marginal farm income. One observer likened the Métis to
"a class of poor people."[18]

This marginalization continued into the twentieth century. As immigration to the region accelerated, the Canadian government reconsidered federal
scrip policy and decided to expand the eligibility rules to include those Métis
born in the territories between 1870 and 1885. This gesture was not designed
to ensure that the Métis finally secured a land base and became a vital part of
the new west. Rather, Ottawa sought to avoid any future dispute over land in
the southern territories and seemed determined to extinguish once and for
all any special land rights the Métis may have enjoyed because of their
Aboriginal heritage. Between 1900 and 1902, scrip commissioners travelled
great distances and held lengthy sittings to ensure that all claimants were
heard, including those who had moved to the northern United States. The
number of communities visited proves how widespread and extensive the
Métis population in Saskatchewan once had been. The 1900 Assiniboia/
Alberta and Saskatchewan commissions took applications across southern
and central areas, including such places as Willow Bunch, Fort Qu'Appelle,
the Touchwood Hills, Swift Current, Maple Creek, Green Lake, Onion
Lake, Battleford, Prince Albert, St. Louis, Duck Lake, Batoche, and Cumberland House. But like earlier scrip commissions, well-funded speculators
scooped up the awards and amassed small real estate empires for their
employers that quickly turned a handsome profit because of the growing settler demand for land.[19]

The 1906 death of Gabriel Dumont, Riel's faithful military commander
and one of the few remaining links to the Métis past, could not have come at
a worse time. The arrival of thousands of immigrants, including a young
John Diefenbaker who claimed to have met Dumont the year before his
death,[20] sparked another internal Métis migration to more remote regions, or
encouraged them to concentrate in a few areas. The sheer numbers of homesteaders, however, effectively swamped the Métis and pushed them to the
fringes of the new society taking shape in the province. They were quickly
made to feel inferior because of their Aboriginal heritage and distinct way of
life, even in their own communities. Prince Albert's origins as the Métis
Isbister settlement, for example, were downplayed, if not forgotten.[21] Many
Métis people in southern Saskatchewan squatted illegally along road allowances, near Indian reserves, or just outside white communities and survived

on casual or seasonal jobs in town, on local farms, or in the bush. The increased contact with other groups soon drove many to assimilate to the dominant anglophone culture and drop their use of mitchif and French if they wanted to fit in and prosper. They also began to lose their identity as a "new nation" and began to identify themselves simply as French or English at census time.[22]

While the Métis in southern Saskatchewan slipped into seeming irrelevance, those in the northern part of the province had to contend with several threats to their livelihood. As settlement swept across the prairies in the early twentieth century, lumber companies responded to the huge demand for building materials and railway ties by pushing the timber frontier steadily northward. By 1909, the Prince Albert Lumber Company employed over two thousand men and harvested an estimated fifty million board feet. Other large mills operated at Prairie River, Crooked River, and Big River, bringing the total Saskatchewan lumber production to twice that of Alberta and Manitoba combined before the start of the Great War. A large-scale commercial fishery also invaded the northern lakes and netted millions of pounds of fish for Canadian and American markets. Government geologists and prospectors, meanwhile, searched for promising ore deposits. There was even greater demand for northern furs because of higher prices and a new rivalry between the HBC and Revillon Frères, a French company that built a series of competing posts through the north in the early twentieth century.[23]

These activities hurt the Aboriginal peoples of the region by placing a severe strain on traditional game and fish resources. At Cumberland House, for example, the NWMP had to distribute relief to destitute Métis.[24] The situation was equally bad for the Indian population. According to the Department of Indian Affairs report for 1908, Indian subsistence hunting and fishing declined by half that year. They not only had to "contend with poor fishing," the annual report stated, but "lacked success in finding fur and game."[25] The federal government seemed more determined to promote the commercial exploitation of the region's resources than live up to the assurances given during Treaty 10 negotiations. The Indians could only complain about the interference with their traditional pursuits at treaty payment time.[26]

First Nations also faced coercion and control from an Indian Affairs bureaucracy that wanted to wipe out their "Indian-ness" and remake them into a people closer to the Anglo-Canadian ideal. To help effect this transformation, government officials sought to supervise early Indian efforts at agriculture and gradually move their charges towards a subsistence level of production that offered no competition to incoming settlers. This federal heavy-handedness initially stymied any Indian initiative at farming and made bands more heavily dependent on government support.[27] But the annual

An elderly Sioux man at Qu'Appelle.
SASKATCHEWAN ARCHIVES BOARD R-A7313

department reports for the period 1897 to 1915 suggest that band economies actually began to grow in step with the overall expansion of farming during the same period. The number of acres devoted to crop production and stock-raising on both Treaty 4 and 6 reserves steadily increased in the years leading up to the Great War, with oats and cattle being the dominant products.[28] What worked against these efforts, though, was the requirement that any off-reserve sale of Indian farm produce had to be approved by the local Indian agent; settlers, on the other hand, could be fined for buying from Indian farmers without a permit. "What kind of policy," Reverend Edward Ahenakew, a native Anglican priest from the Sandy Lake reserve, once asked, "is it that aims at bringing a people to a point of self-respect, and then by the nature of its regulations destroys the very thing for which it works." He continued, "I have seen with my own eyes, Indians wasting a day, even two days, trying to get a permit to sell, when they are short of food."[29]

Indians found other ways to make a living during these years. Besides continuing to hunt, trap, and fish on reserve lands, many sold hay, firewood, and fence posts to new homesteaders. Many of the younger men also found part-time jobs on farms and ranches, especially at harvest or round-up time, did freighting, helped survey gangs, or joined lumber camps. Some of the

Wood Mountain Sioux even worked in Moose Jaw. Women contributed to their family's well-being by selling berries, beadwork, leather items, such as moccasins, but most of all, senega root (also known as snakeroot).[30] Senega, with its reported medicinal powers, enjoyed popular demand among settlers and fetched twenty to twenty-five cents per pound in 1894.[31] These various activities demonstrated what Indians were prepared to do to survive; as the agent for the Fishing Lake band noted in 1913, "They take advantage of any ... opportunity for making money which offers itself."[32] Joseph Dion, a Cree historian from the Onion Lake region, was not so enthusiastic. "We had become," he bitterly observed, "cheap labourers in the eyes of the white man, just an economic commodity."[33]

This assessment was undoubtedly true, but what is also significant is how this part-time labour led to greater interactions with settler society. Indian women were often the only experienced midwives in pioneer districts, and used their traditional knowledge of the healing powers of local plants to treat a wide range of ailments. An immigrant in the Rocanville district described Mrs. Bastien, a local Cree woman who doubled as midwife and doctor, as "the nearest thing to an angel on earth."[34] Indian men, on the other hand, regularly helped recent arrivals get settled on the land. Jim Greyeyes, who raised horses on the Muskeg reserve, provided the new Doukhobor settlement at Petrofka with a team of workhorses to break its fields.[35]

Indians also participated in annual sports days, where those with exceptional athletic ability quickly acquired a reputation and a following. Paul Acoose of the Sakimay reserve was the 1908 five-mile road running champion of western Canada and once beat Tom Longboat, probably one of Canada's most famous Aboriginal athletes, in a much-anticipated head-to-head competition in 1910. His rival at the time was Alex Decoteau from Red Pheasant, who finished sixth in the five-thousand-metre race in the 1912 Olympics in Stockholm.[36] Fair organizers, anxious to feed the public appetite for the "Wild West" days, also regularly invited Indians to perform traditional dances in ceremonial dress as part of the exhibition program. Participation not only carried the promise of cash prizes, but gave Indian families a chance to meet and socialize away from their reserves. Indian officials, however, frowned on these events, believing that their continued practice delayed the pace of assimilation. In 1913, Duncan Campbell Scott, the new deputy superintendent general of Indian Affairs, tried to put an end to what he described as "senseless drumming and dancing" by issuing a circular calling on agents to discourage Indian attendance at white-sponsored fairs.[37]

Scott's edict was part of the general attitude that there was little in Indian culture worth saving and that First Nations needed to be civilized, Christianized, and assimilated before they could take their place in Canadian

Indian women receiving prizes at the 1914 Punnichy fair. WESTERN DEVELOPMENT MUSEUM 3-F-4

society. Education was understood to be one of the keys to this transformation. During the western treaty negotiations in the 1870s, government representatives had promised, at Indian urging, that schools would be established on reserves "whenever the Indians shall desire it."[38] But when it came time to provide education, Ottawa decided to create church-run, usually off-reserve residential schools based on the recommendations of an 1879 fact-finding report by Nicholas Flood Davin, a Regina journalist and lawyer, who had investigated similar schools in the United States.

Both federal officials and missionaries embraced Davin's central argument that Indian children would never be changed for the better unless they were completely isolated from their home environment and the "backward" influences of the family, especially elders.[39] Conservative prime minister John A. Macdonald probably explained this thinking best. "We must, by slow degrees," he told the House of Commons, "educate generation after generation, until the nature of the animal, almost, is changed by the nature of the surroundings."[40] To this end, beginning in 1883, the Canadian government established a system of federally supported denominational schools (boarding and industrial) throughout the southern prairies. Two of the first and most ambitious were the Qu'Appelle Indian Industrial School, located at Lebret (Treaty 4 area) and run by the Catholics, and the Anglican-operated Battleford Industrial School in what was once Government House in the former territorial capital (Treaty 6 area).[41] While boarding schools were nothing new in the North-West and had been run by missionaries in isolated communities like Île-à-la-Crosse in northern Saskatchewan for decades, the new, better-funded

Fathers bringing their children to the first day of school at the Regina Indian Industrial School, 1904. SASKATCHEWAN ARCHIVES BOARD R-B990

industrial schools were designed to teach the children practical trades or occupations, such as carpentry and blacksmithing or sewing and cooking, in addition to the standard academic subjects. This new generation of schools, moreover, was closed to Métis and non-status Indian children; Ottawa would pay for only treaty Indians, the legal wards of the federal government.[42]

Just two decades later, the optimism and enthusiasm behind the residential schools experiment were gone. The federal government not only found that the schools were becoming increasingly expensive, but also began to question their effectiveness. Clifford Sifton, the new minister of the interior, spoke for many when he openly confessed in 1904 that "the attempt to give a highly civilized education to the Indian child ... was practically a failure. I have no hesitation in saying—we may as well be frank—that the Indian ... has not the physical, mental or moral get-up to enable him to compete. He cannot do it."[43] Ottawa responded by dramatically reducing its expectations for the schools, cutting costs, and shifting more responsibility to the churches. Students, in turn, were expected to shoulder a greater share of the day-to-day operations, including tending the fields and working in the kitchen. This manual labour, ironically, was the least of the children's worries. Upon admittance, their individual and cultural identities were erased. Stripped of their clothes and shorn of their braids, they were dressed in a standard uniform, given a Christian name, and forbidden to speak their mother tongue. Those who stepped out of line were publicly humiliated or more often physically punished, sometimes harshly. Runaways from the Crowstand school on the Cote reserve, for example, were brought back, running behind the buggy, with a rope around their arms.[44]

Besides the psychological trauma, many children fell gravely ill. In 1907, Dr. P. H. Bryce, a medical inspector with the Department of the Interior, found health conditions in the prairie residential schools to be truly appalling. The locked, crowded dormitories, inadequate ventilation, poor food, and presence of sickly students promoted the spread of disease, especially tuberculosis, throughout the school population with alarming consequences.[45] The staff, in the words of former Onion Lake student Joe Dion, was "practically helpless"[46]—a fact sadly confirmed by the mortality rate. Deputy Superintendent General Scott callously claimed before the start of the Great War "that fifty per cent of the children who passed through these schools did not live to benefit from the education which they had received therein."[47] It is little wonder, then, that some students ran away at the first opportunity, or that parents refused to hand over their children, even though attendance had been made compulsory. In 1912, Cree headman Star Blanket made an emotional appeal to the governor general during his tour of Saskatchewan following the official opening of the Legislative Building. He argued that residential schools were a violation of treaty rights and insisted that parents

Children tended the garden as part of their training at the Anglican-run Lac La Ronge mission school. LIBRARY AND ARCHIVES CANADA PA45174

should not be forcibly separated from their children, in many instances never to see them again alive.[48] A girl from the Mistawasis reserve had another answer for the loneliness and separation. One day, she told her teacher at the Regina Industrial School that she wanted to commit suicide. He apparently handed her an empty gun and encouraged her to pull the trigger.[49]

Those students who somehow managed to survive residential school faced an unwelcoming world. Graduates were not accepted by white society and could find only menial work. They had also been estranged from their own people. "There he is hanging in the middle of two cultures," John Tootoosis of the Poundmaker reserve once explained his predicament, "and he is not a white man and he is not an Indian."[50] In 1901, William Graham, the agent on the Peepeekisis reserve, attempted to solve the problem of displaced graduates by establishing the File Hills Colony, a place where former pupils from local residential schools would begin anew as farm families in a model setting. Handpicked students were encouraged to marry and then given land, equipment, and other material assistance to help them along the road to eventual independence. By 1907, the File Hills Colony boasted twenty families and was being trumpeted as a showcase for what residential school pupils could achieve with proper guidance and training. It even became a popular attraction for visiting dignitaries. But success was elusive, despite Graham's heavy, if not intrusive, involvement, and the continuing failure of the colony to produce Indian-turned-white farmers ultimately led to its closure in 1949. No other similar ventures were attempted.[51]

The other damning example of government interference in Indian lives during this period was the attempt to stamp out their religious ceremonies. Government and religious officials maintained that Indians would always remain unprogressive and demoralized as long as they adhered to their traditional practices and beliefs. The government solution was to ban the religious dances and ceremonies, in particular those involving self-mutilation, that were at the heart of plains Indian culture.[52] This criminalization of Indian worship soon netted two prominent chiefs. In 1895, Piapot, one of the signatories of Treaty 4, was arrested and imprisoned in Regina for performing a Sun Dance, a solemn undertaking for renewal and thanksgiving, on his reserve. When Assistant Indian Commissioner A. E. Forget attempted to extract a promise from the elderly chief before his release that he would no longer perform the ceremony, Piapot replied through the translator, "Very well, I will agree not to pray to my God in my way, if you will promise not to pray to your God ... in your way."[53] He was jailed a second time in 1901 for participating in a Giveaway Dance and stripped of his chieftainship. His band protested by refusing to elect another chief until after his death in 1908.[54] The other treaty-era chief to run afoul of the dance prohibition was Thunderchild. He was

A Sun-Dance lodge at Onion Lake in the 1890s. GLENBOW ARCHIVES NA-1223-13

charged in 1897 for his involvement in a giveaway ceremony and sentenced to two months. Vindictive officials also took away his treaty medal. Thunderchild would later become a driving force behind a petition to have dancing and other ceremonies confirmed as treaty rights.[55]

Indian officials tried to prevent bands from leaving their reserves to attend dances by means of vagrancy laws and the pass system. Introduced during the 1885 North-West Rebellion, the pass system was intended to regulate and control Indian movement by requiring individuals to obtain approval in writing from the local agent before leaving their reserve. Passes had no legal basis, and the NWMP, who were expected to retrieve violators, soon refused to enforce the system. But Indian Affairs authorities continued to go through the charade of granting passes until the late 1930s in a continuing effort to suppress Indian religious activity and political organizing.[56] The mounties were also regularly called upon by Indian agents to attend communal gatherings in order to intimidate participants and, if necessary, intervene in ceremonies; departmental policy forbade Indians from being on another reserve without permission. Many police were unhappy with this role. Commissioner James Macleod once likened the raid of a Sun Dance by his men "to making an arrest in a church."[57] The Indians themselves resisted, albeit non-violently, attempts to cut them off from their spiritual beliefs. They continued to argue at every opportunity that the performance of sacred ceremonies was a treaty right and that they simply wanted to enjoy the same kind of holiday privileges as white society. The Assiniboine bands at Moose Mountain, for example, repeatedly compared their traditional activities to the celebration of Dominion Day.[58] Some bands also devised ingenious ways to get around the official restrictions. Poundmaker and Little Pine once held dances on the reserve boundary they shared and technically avoided leaving their respective reserves.[59] This kind of persistence, in the face of official repression, prompted one Saskatchewan Indian agent to declare in frustration, "Paganism is dying hard."[60]

In January 1911, a delegation from the Treaty 4 area, travelling with their own translator, took their complaints about federal Indian policy directly to Ottawa. It was a precedent-setting meeting. Not only did the Saskatchewan delegates meet face-to-face with the country's two senior Indian officials, Frank Oliver, the minister responsible for Indian Affairs, and his deputy, Frank Pedley, but the discussions lasted a remarkable five days. Louis O'Soup from Cowesses, who had been present at the signing of the treaty almost forty years earlier, talked about his people's inability to make a living because they had little control over their lives. Other speakers raised a number of related concerns: residential schools, the permit system, the ban on religious ceremonies, and the removal of chiefs. They also demanded to know what had happened to the money secured from the sale of reserve lands.[61] During the daily meetings, the two federal officials repeatedly assured the delegation that Treaty 4 bands were not being cheated; privately, they dismissed the Indian representatives as "a few misguided malcontents."[62] All they agreed to was a personal request for an artificial limb from O'Soup, who had lost his right leg in an accident.

The Saskatchewan delegation that travelled to Ottawa to meet with Indian officials in 1911.
SASKATCHEWAN ARCHIVES BOARD R-B584

Whether Oliver and Pedley realized it at the time, O'Soup's wish had symbolic meaning. Saskatchewan Indians wanted to stand on their own two legs, to live their lives according to the agreements they had entered into with the Canadian government in the 1870s. Nor were they destined to disappear as a distinct people, as their numbers began to rebound from the double onslaught of disease and privation. But federal authorities, convinced that they were right, intensified their efforts to reshape Saskatchewan Indian lives over the next few years. Neither the defeat of the Laurier government in 1911 nor the coming of war three years later diverted Ottawa from this course. As the deputy minister of the Department of Indian Affairs coolly observed in 1920: "I want to get rid of the Indian problem ... Our object is to continue until there is not a single Indian in Canada that has not been absorbed into the body politic, and there is no Indian question, and no Indian Department."[63] Unfortunately, each side considered the other the Indian problem.

CHAPTER TEN

THE BLESSINGS
OF WAR

IT WAS THE SHORTEST LEGISLATIVE SESSION in Saskatchewan's brief political history. On 15 September 1914, just weeks after Canada had been plunged into war, Premier Walter Scott recalled the Saskatchewan legislature to deal with the emergency. "The time is extraordinary, the war is extraordinary," the premier gravely intoned at the opening of the session.[1] He then reported that government members would be contributing 10 per cent of their salaries to the Canadian Patriotic Fund, in addition to fifteen hundred horses that the province was donating to the British cause. The leader of the opposition graciously praised these efforts, while vowing not to stand in the way of the Scott government's prosecution of the war effort. In fact, Liberals and Conservatives solemnly joined together to sing "God Save the King" when the session ended ten days later. This spirit of participation, sacrifice, and co-operation would be severely tested over the next four years. Saskatchewan's large immigrant population found itself the target of vigorous and escalating efforts to confirm and entrench the British character of the province. The reform movement, meanwhile, deliberately used the European conflict and the values of justice, liberty, and democracy associated with it to try to remake Saskatchewan society. The Great War, as it was soon to be called, was supposed to unite the nation. But no one in August 1914 would have surmised at what cost.[2]

When Great Britain went to war against Germany, Austria-Hungary, Turkey, and Bulgaria in early August 1914, Canada was automatically involved in the conflict. The descent into war had come about with amazing speed, and the readiness of Saskatchewan, let alone the country at large, is usually questioned. Yet as one military historian has astutely observed, Canada was probably never better prepared for war, but not for the kind of war that would unfold in the coming weeks and months.[3] Reaction to the news was swift and spontaneous. Crowds gathered in downtown Regina, awaiting the outcome of the British ultimatum, let out a roar, throwing their hats in the air, when the announcement was made. In Saskatoon, an impromptu parade of jubilant, nearly hysterical people marched through the streets waving Union Jacks and singing patriotic songs. So many well-wishers turned out at the railway station ten days later to say goodbye to the first batch of volunteers that the men's departure had to be delayed an hour to give them time to board the train.[4] Military experts concluded that the war would be over by Christmas and that Canadian troops were unlikely to see action. This prediction prompted one enterprising recruit to suggest that a quota be placed on the killing of German soldiers so that there would be enough to go around.[5] In retrospect, many would never have been so blindly enthusiastic if they had known the war was going to last four long years.[6]

Enlistment in the Canadian Expeditionary Force was strong across the prairie west. More than forty thousand, including seventy nursing sisters, eventually volunteered at twenty provincial recruitment centres; nearly half joined in Regina.[7] The vast majority of the first recruits were recent British immigrants, reflecting the numbers that had poured into the province over the previous decade. Sixty-three of the first sixty-eight volunteers from the Swift Current area, for example, were British-born.[8] The story was the same at other recruiting stations. Kent-born Herb Baldwin had been working in Prince Albert for three years as a plumber's assistant when he enlisted at the start of the war at seventeen.[9] Gus Lambert, a nineteen-year-old London artist, had followed his twin brother, Tony, to a farming district outside Saskatoon in 1913 and then followed him into service a year later. Harold Baldwin from the English Midlands left his Rosetown homestead, with the crop still in the field, as soon as he heard about the war and walked into the Saskatoon armouries with a scruffy face and ragged harvest clothes, ready to

The men of the 27th Light Horse, cheered in Moose Jaw as they head to war. MOOSE JAW ARCHIVES 71-82

sign up. Not even the fact that he was two inches below the regulation height could turn him away. "Here was an opportunity," he recalled in his book about his experiences, *Holding the Line*, "to kill two birds with the same stone—gratify my love of adventure and serve the Empire at one and the same time."[10] This idea of helping the home country in its time of need was echoed by other Britons at the time. The tug of patriotism, however, was often cited to mask their failure at homesteading or inability to find steady work, particularly during the stubborn recession that crippled the western Canadian economy before the war. It has been estimated that one-fifth of the Canadian Expeditionary Force fled long-term unemployment.[11]

Saskatchewan youth were attracted by the idealism of the war and the opportunity to strike a blow against the evil Hun. This sentiment was best expressed, albeit in purple prose, in the University of Saskatchewan student newspaper, *The Sheaf*. The November 1914 edition spoke of the need "to help hurl back ... the iron-toothed menace of a pseudo-civilization, founded on brute philosophy."[12] The war could not have come at a worse time for the university, for it had just occupied its new facilities and was starting to enlarge its program. The siren call of the war, however, proved too much for the students; 330 enlisted, as did several faculty, including Irish-born Reginald Bateman, the first professor of English to be hired by the university. "We hear much, perhaps too much, at the present time of the horrors of war," an eager Bateman lectured a Saskatoon audience on the eve of his departure. "I wish today to speak of its blessings ... the climax of human endeavour ... the only adequate test of a nation's spiritual quality ... a purifier which purges the corruption of a too-long-continued peace."[13] Almost half (seventy-two) of the male graduates of the university also served.[14] Some volunteers were given a nudge. The mother of an agriculture student complained to university president Walter Murray that her son had enlisted under duress. "They make you feel like two cents at the U if you don't enlist," he had told his mum.[15] At first, the university continued to offer its programs, but was forced to close the College of Engineering for the 1916–17 academic year when the student body enlisted en masse. The universities of Alberta, Saskatchewan, and Manitoba eventually decided to form a special Western Universities Battalion, the 196th. One of its driving forces was Chaplain E. H. Oliver, Saskatchewan's first professor of history and creator of the University of Vimy Ridge, the first battlefield university in France.[16]

A much smaller, but no less noteworthy, group to enlist were Saskatchewan First Nations. Initially, the Canadian government did not see the need to seek Indian recruits and it is not known how many volunteered during the first months of the conflict. But as the war deteriorated into a prolonged, bloody stalemate, Indians were actively encouraged to enlist. This call to arms contradicted decades of federal Indian policy aimed at persuading Indians to put down their weapons and abandon their warrior past. Their reputation as fighters now interested Canada's military commanders, and there was even talk of a separate Indian unit. Recruitment agents shamelessly appealed to the Indian warrior spirit, even presenting a magic-lantern show of war scenes on the Red Pheasant reserve in February 1915. Some Indian agents also used their influence to rid themselves of supposed troublemakers. Those who volunteered generally did so because of their continuing affection for their treaty partner, the British Crown, although many were also driven overseas by reserve poverty or sought escape from residential schools. John Anderson and John Fisher, two seventeen-year-olds, ran away from the school on Gordon's reserve and enlisted in Regina in November 1916. Fifteen-year-old Moses Lavallee of the File Hills Colony, on the other hand, seemed happy at school, but wanted to use his training in the brass band to become a bugler. He secretly enlisted in Yorkton in December 1916 and told the agent of his whereabouts only after he reached England. He never got his wish, though, to become a bugler. Because of his skills with a rifle, Lavallee would become one of several Indian snipers at the front. The exact number of Saskatchewan Indian volunteers is uncertain because of incomplete Indian agency records, but a recent study suggests that as many as 137 of the approximately 400 western Canadian Aboriginal enlistees were from the province.[17] Determining the names of Métis soldiers is even more difficult because they were never identified as a distinct group.

Large sporting events, like this baseball game at the new Cairns Field in Saskatoon, were discontinued during the Great War. SASKATOON PUBLIC LIBRARY LH2558

British-born Saskatchewan recruits who had some previous training were immediately funnelled into the Princess Patricia's Canadian Light Infantry and joined the front lines in January 1915. The Regina Pats junior hockey club, founded in 1917, was named in honour of the regiment.[18] Other infantry units raised in Saskatchewan were either merged with larger groups or broken up overseas to provide replacements. The 52nd Regiment, more popularly known as the Prince Albert Volunteers, enlisted almost to a man during the first week of the war, but sailed from Canada as part of the 11th Battalion. Similarly, the Moose Jaw–based 60th Rifle Company was supposed to be mobilized as part of the 3rd Canadian contingent, but the men were added to other units. The same fate awaited the Saskatoon Fusiliers when they reached England. The most famous and distinctly Saskatchewan group was the 46th Infantry Battalion, raised and headquartered in Moose Jaw beginning in February 1915. The battalion drew recruits from throughout southern Saskatchewan, including the university, but more than half were from the Moose Jaw area. It remained intact until the end of the war as part of the Canadian 4th Division, absorbing Saskatchewan reinforcements from other dismantled battalions.[19] Some volunteers also served in Canada's fledgling navy, such as seaman Edward Lavallee from the File Hills Colony. There were also Saskatchewan men in the British Royal Flying Corps. Lieutenant Harold Hartney, a Saskatoon lawyer, transferred to the air force the same day his platoon was sent to the front and annihilation in its first battle. Hartney rose to flight commander and was credited with six kills before being shot down by Baron von Richtofen, the famous Red Baron. Fortunately, he was able to ditch his plane safely behind Allied lines.[20]

The popular conception of the war in Saskatchewan showed little understanding of the reality at the front. There was nothing romantic about trench
warfare, and if the men were on a crusade, it was against the perennially wet
feet, the never-ending mud, and the rats. "We are powerless to describe our
continual conflict with that mud," recounted Harold Baldwin. "It was everywhere—in our eyes, our hair, our tents, our clothes, our grub; we often had
to swallow it as well as wallow in it."[21] Saskatchewan soldiers distinguished
themselves in all the major battles of the Great War, but their success came at
a terrible cost. Baldwin and his new pal, Bill Moore, who signed up at the
same time, lost their left legs in the same battle. The other Baldwin from
Prince Albert, Herb, came close to death after being buried alive by an
exploding shell; he died in Toronto in 2003 at 105, one of the last survivors of
the war.

Gus Lambert found himself posted near his twin brother, Tony, in France
and visited him at least once during the summer of 1916. He entered the
battle to take Vimy Ridge the following spring, knowing that his brother was
recovering in an English hospital after being wounded at the Somme. Gus
was not so lucky. Stopping to assist a wounded officer, he was shot in the
head by a sniper on 10 April 1917. He had written his family three days earlier,
eerily predicting his own death: "France à la mud, Dear People, In case ole
Fritz gets my number don't worry. After all I've had a good run out here—
more than most of the boys. Anyway, you're [sic] Tony here still and he'll get
a fair exchange! This note may read a bit straight—but when one has been so
near the finis so many times he gets hardened. All luck and love, Your loving
son."[22] In 1969, when Tony's son contacted the Saskatchewan farm family
that Gus had worked for before the war, John Jaspar fondly wrote, "I can
remember crowding around him at the table, with my brothers and sisters, to
watch him sketch."[23]

Gus was one of nearly forty-four hundred Saskatchewan deaths on the
battlefield.[24] Alex Decoteau, the Canadian Olympian from Red Pheasant
reserve and an Edmonton policeman at the time of his enlistment, was killed
at Passchendaele in October 1917. Several other Indian soldiers, described as
medically unfit, were sent home with burnt lungs from gas attacks or suffering from tuberculosis picked up in the trenches; they died within a few
years of returning to their reserves.[25] Lyman (Hick) Abbott, a right winger for
the Regina Vics, was widely regarded as one of the best hockey players in
western Canada at the time of his enlistment. He spent four years in France,
receiving the Military Cross twice, before being killed by a sniper's bullet
while leading his men into action. In 1919, Regina established the Abbott
Memorial Cup for the best junior hockey team.

The toll among university recruits was sixty-six dead, including Professor

Recent British immigrants, Gus (left) and Tony Lambert, were among the first to enlist. Gus sketched the Jaspars while working for the family before the war. LAMBERT FAMILY

Bateman, who served three tours overseas, even taking a reduction in rank the last time to fulfil his overwhelming sense of duty. Jean Murray, the daughter of the university president, remembered sitting on Bateman's lap as he was driven in a crowded car to the train station to go back to the front. She had sensed his "tension and fear."[26] Bateman, as did many university soldiers, fought as a member of Saskatchewan's own 46th Infantry, which quickly earned a reputation as the "suicide battalion" because of its involvement in some of the bloodiest battles of the war. During twenty-seven months on the battlefield, the battalion sustained 4,917 casualties (1,433 dead, 3,484 wounded). This number is astounding since only 5,374 men served in the unit. Fewer than 500 escaped without injury.[27]

One of the most famous members of the 46th was Hugh Cairns, a British immigrant and soccer enthusiast who was working as an eighteen-year-old plumber's assistant in Saskatoon at the start of the war. Cairns went overseas with the 65th Battalion but transferred to the 46th, perhaps to be with his brother. The Saskatoon soldier first came to the attention of his superiors at Vimy Ridge in April 1917 when he captured two German machine-gun emplacements and repelled repeated counterattacks despite being wounded by shrapnel. His "conspicuous bravery" earned him the Distinguished Conduct Medal. Then, on 1 November 1918, a little more than a week before the armistice, Cairns and his unit encountered heavy fighting at Valenciennes. It is not known what propelled him that day; it might have been the loss of his brother only days earlier. General Arthur Currie, the Canadian commander who was leading Canadian troops towards nearby Mons, described his actions as "superhuman." At the first sign of resistance, Cairns, now a sergeant, grabbed a Lewis gun and ran firing recklessly towards the enemy position. He charged two other machine-gun nests in the same ferocious fashion, killing several Germans and taking prisoners. Later that same day, while reconnoitering ahead at Marly, a wounded Cairns and three others chanced upon sixty enemy soldiers in a yard. When the Canadians called on them to surrender, a German officer shot Cairns in the stomach. In the melee that followed, Cairns was wounded again and carried away, clinging to life, on a door used as a stretcher. He died the next day. Cairns was posthumously awarded the Victoria Cross, the sixth Saskatchewan and last Canadian soldier to receive the British Empire's highest military honour during the war. At the unveiling of the Canadian Vimy Memorial in France in 1936, the French government awarded him the Legion of Honour, while the town of Valenciennes renamed a street in his memory, the only such tribute ever accorded a non-commissioned officer of a foreign army. In Saskatoon, Cairns was remembered in the name of a new school and the local armouries. His soccer buddies also erected a statue of Cairns in Kiwanis Park to honour local athletes killed in action.[28]

On the home front, community associations and organizations sought patriotic work from the first days of the war. Indeed, for many women, raising funds or donating materials provided a chance to prove their patriotism and do their part to help win the war. It also kept them busy while waiting for news about loved ones overseas. There was no shortage of charities requiring funds—from the Canadian Patriotic Fund, which supported soldiers' families, to the Canadian Red Cross to the Belgian Relief Fund.[29] Women throughout the province, including those on reserves,[30] got together on a regular basis for knitting and sewing bees or held social functions to raise money, often under the umbrella of Homemakers' Clubs, which grew from 90 to 190 in the province because of the demands of the war.[31] The other

Sergeant Hugh Cairns of the 46th Battalion was awarded the Victoria Cross posthumously. LIBRARY AND ARCHIVES CANADA PA6735

group that became dominant in domestic war work was the Imperial Order Daughters of the Empire. With over fifty chapters in Saskatchewan, IODE members literally headed into battle on the home front. They had no qualms about publicly challenging a man's failure to enlist and have been called "the government's best recruiting agents."[32] They also raised vast sums of money for the Red Cross and other patriotic funds through such creative events as birthday teas where women were required to donate a penny for every year of their age. And they opened and furnished soldiers' clubs where men in training or on leave could enjoy some recreation and camaraderie. Where these women excelled, though, was in the production of large quantities of much-needed soldiers' comforts and first aid supplies. The Admiral Sturdee Chapter in Weyburn, for example, made 727 pairs of socks, 11 sweaters, 8 mufflers, 300 shirts, and 6 dozen pairs of pajamas in 1918.[33]

During the early months of the war, the Saskatchewan IODE, like many provincial residents, turned against the German population. After all, they were the enemy. Besides, in attacking things German, IODE women could feel that they were participating directly in the war. "From this day until my death," they vowed as part of a national boycott campaign, "I pledge myself never willingly nor knowingly to buy an article made by the bloody hands that killed our boys."[34] This harassment of Germans marked a significant departure from the popular attitude towards them in early twentieth century Saskatchewan, when they were valued immigrants to the new province. In fact, most overt discrimination before the war was directed at visible minorities, people like Indians, Blacks, and Asians. The Chinese were especially persecuted. Moving east from British Columbia along the railway across the prairies, they settled in places such as Swift Current, Moose Jaw, and Regina, where they generally lived in segregated areas and ran laundries, restaurants, and grocery stores. The Saskatchewan Chinese population numbered less than one thousand in 1911,[35] but they were still reviled as a "yellow peril," a threat to the moral fibre of white Canada and the sanctity of white women in particular. Any white woman caught up in the clutches of a "Chink," it was imagined, would surely become a prostitute or opium addict. In 1908, Saskatchewan took the vote away from the Chinese. Four years later, in response to mounting public prejudice, the Scott government introduced "An Act to Prevent the Employment of Female Labour in Certain Capacities," which essentially forbade white women from working for an Oriental employer or visiting, except as a customer, any building owned or operated by an Oriental person. It was an unprecedented piece of racial legislation in Canada, one that was soon challenged by Quong Wing, a Moose Jaw restaurateur and naturalized Canadian who was fined for employing two white waitresses. Quong Wing decided to fight the legislation, first before the Saskatchewan Court of Appeal in 1913 and then before the Supreme Court of Canada the following year, but his conviction was upheld. According to the courts, the two races should be kept separate.[36]

The coming of the Great War added a new menace to Saskatchewan society—the enemy alien. According to the 1911 census, Germans and Austro-Hungarians constituted, after the British, the second (68,628) and third (41,651) largest immigrant groups, respectively, in the province; taken together, they made up nearly one-quarter of the population and were heavily represented in several farming districts and the city of Regina.[37] While the Germans were generally favoured as some of Saskatchewan's finest new citizens before the war, there had always been doubts about the suitability of immigrants from the Austro-Hungarian Empire, particularly Ukrainians, and their ability and willingness to assimilate to the British-Canadian way of life. Elizabeth Mitchell, who toured the prairies in 1913, expressed this unease when she asked, "Can Canada ... afford to base herself on an ignorant, non-English-speaking peasantry, winning a bare living by unceasing labour? ... The immigration of the last few years has been really overwhelming and cannot be met with a careless 'Everything will come right.' The need for the moment is for a pause and time to think and rearrange."[38] Those who had been worried that groups like Ukrainians would drag down Saskatchewan society and destroy forever the British character of the province now used the war as the justification to do something about them. As the *Swift Current Sun* smugly observed, "This has been brewing for a long time, but the war has brought it to a head, and Anglo-Saxons to their senses."[39]

The day the war started, Premier Scott called for public calm and restraint, reminding Saskatchewan citizens that Germans and Ukrainians were their neighbours. Undoubtedly, he was motivated in part by the fact that his government depended upon the immigrant vote for electoral support.[40] But Scott's assessment of the situation was supported by RNWMP surveillance reports which found that western Canadians had absolutely nothing to fear from these immigrants. Such assurances, however, did little to ease public hysteria. M. Donaldson, the Winnipeg-based general manager of the Grand Trunk Pacific Railway, for example, believed that the "foreign element" might rise up along the rail line in east-central Saskatchewan, in places like Melville, and called for the imposition of martial law before it was too late. What fuelled this paranoia was the massing of unskilled Ukrainian workers in western urban centres in the fall of 1914. Many of these men, in most cases recent immigrants, had been laid off from the railways and construction projects during the pre-war recession and drifted into towns and cities in search of work and relief. They were soon joined by hundreds more who had been fired from their jobs for patriotic reasons. The presence of these destitute

Men at the front catch up with news from home. SASKATOON PUBLIC LIBRARY LH5515

men in such large numbers alarmed the western public and made the need for action all the more imperative.[41]

The Robert Borden Conservative government initially resisted implementing any restrictive measures, but quickly realized that the growing number of impoverished immigrant workers pouring into cities had to be stopped or it could very well face civil unrest. Arthur Meighen, one of Borden's ablest ministers and a future Canadian prime minister, bluntly summed up the problem: "The aliens were out of work and in that state were a menace to the community."[42] Ottawa consequently responded to the crisis in late October 1914 with an enemy alien registration and internment policy proclaimed under the provisions of the new War Measures Act. Germans and Ukrainians living in cities or their immediate vicinity were required by law to register and report monthly; those in rural areas were excluded because they were not regarded as a problem. Failure to report, or any other breach of the regulations, such as trying to leave Canada without permission, resulted in internment. Within weeks of the cabinet order, one of the first acts of a new interventionist state, several hundred unemployed workers had been detained by local registrars or rounded up by the police and sent to distant work camps. Eventually over eight thousand individuals, including a handful of women and children, would be held in some two dozen camps across the country.

In implementing its internment policy, the federal government made a clear distinction between enemy aliens from Germany and the Austro-Hungarian Empire. It regarded German nationals as a genuine security threat and tried to ensure that they were separately confined in jail-like settings. Otherwise, German immigrants who had become naturalized Canadians were generally left alone. It did not mean, though, that they were immune to condemnation or abuse, especially after the stories of so-called German atrocities in Belgium became front-page news. The German torpedoing of the ocean liner *Lusitania* in May 1915 only intensified the calls for stiffer measures. The *Swift Current Sun* claimed that "the German race has gone blood mad," while Reverend A. E. Haydon told his Saskatoon congregation that the struggle had now become a "Holy-War."[43] Hostile gangs twice attacked the offices of *Der Courier*, Regina's German newspaper.[44]

Most German immigrants in Saskatchewan, including the German-speaking Mennonites, quietly went about their lives, contributing to the war effort to prove their loyalty. But the strain often proved too much for many, and they deliberately exchanged one nationality for another. According to census data for the years 1911 and 1921, the number of people in the three prairie provinces who gave their birthplace as Germany fell from 18,696 to 13,343 during the ten-year period. Those born in Sweden, Norway, and

Holland, on the other hand, increased from 33,826 to 38,925, or roughly by the same amount as the German decline during the same period.[45] Several Saskatchewan communities also changed their names in response to the war. Prussia, for example, was dropped in favour of Leader, while Kaiser became Peebles and Schultz was renamed Prelate.[46]

Ukrainians not only constituted the majority of the internees, but were treated much differently. These men had tackled heavy, manual jobs under primitive, at times appalling, conditions for resource industries and the railways before the war. It made perfect sense, from the Borden government's point of view, to call upon them to perform the same kind of demanding work during their detention. Frank Oliver, the former minister of the interior and no fan of Ukrainian immigration in the past, objected to this policy, insisting that the internees had committed no crime against the state. His views were shared by William Martin, a Saskatchewan MP and future premier of the province, who reminded the House of Commons, "I am ... inclined to look upon these people ... as being entitled to a certain amount of consideration."[47] But the Borden Conservatives were not going to pass up the chance to put the men to work in isolated regions of the country.

Many of the Ukrainian internees from Saskatchewan, plucked from major communities along the province's rail lines, were sent to Banff, Jasper, Mount Revelstoke, and Yoho national parks to build roads and other tourist facilities. It was a bitter experience. Not only did the men resent their captivity—many could not understand why they were being treated as traitors—but they recoiled at the forced labour and resisted in whatever ways they could, even risking being shot for attempting to escape. Release, if it could be called that, came in 1916 when Canadian military commitments overseas translated into a serious labour shortage at home. Internees began to be paroled to various western Canadian companies, including several that had dismissed immigrant workers only two years earlier, on the understanding that they had to accept their job placement and report regularly to the local police office. The nightmare may have been over, but the Canadian Ukrainian community would be forever scarred by its wartime treatment.[48]

The handling of the enemy alien question was only one example of how attitudes towards non-British immigrants had hardened because of the war. Before 1914, it was confidently assumed in Saskatchewan that the assimilation and integration of foreigners would proceed apace. But any generosity of spirit, any patience with the newcomers as they adjusted to their adopted home, eroded with the coming of the war. As one historian has aptly observed, an "angry atmosphere" had come to dominate public life.[49] This tension was nowhere more evident than in the emotionally charged issues of language and schools. In early 1913, Premier Scott, who also doubled as minister of

Walter Scott (right) and his successor, William Martin, who would take over as premier in 1916. SASKATCHEWAN ARCHIVES BOARD R-A12113

education, sought to end an ambiguity in the province's school act by requiring the religious minority ratepayers to support the separate school in their district.[50] It was a straightforward amendment, designed to deal with a funding problem, but it provoked a vicious backlash from Reverend Murdoch Mackinnon of Regina's Knox Presbyterian Church, Premier Scott's own minister. Mackinnon steadfastly maintained that any measure that strengthened the financial status of separate schools was inherently bad and only served to increase the nefarious influence of the Roman Catholic Church in Saskatchewan society. That influence, the preacher insisted, had to end if the province was to become a bastion of British civilization; the alternative was a backward, unprogressive people.[51]

Mackinnon was not alone in believing in the need for Anglo-conformity in Saskatchewan society at the time. Nativists like Mackinnon could not comprehend, let alone appreciate, how immigrants could hold multiple loyalties, keeping their language, religion, and culture, while developing into Canadian citizens.[52] The coming of the war fanned these passions glowing below the surface of Saskatchewan society and ignited an all-out assault on the province's ethnic minorities. The attack on separate schools soon became an attack on teaching children in any language other than English in Saskatchewan schools. Under existing educational regulations, French instruction was allowed in the primary grades, while French or another language other than English could also be used for an hour at the end of the school day. But according to a provincially commissioned study of rural education, tabled in the legislature in early 1918, more than three hundred schools in immigrant districts used a language other than English for the better part of the school day. Students, moreover, completed only a few grades before leaving school or never attended a full term because schools were regularly closed.[53] These findings suggested that the province's schools were not fulfilling their Canadianization role, something that had become even more important during these days of war.

Tapping into this growing public anxiety over Saskatchewan's assimilation challenge, the provincial Conservative opposition, led by W. B Willoughby, called for an end to foreign language or bilingual instruction in schools. So too did the influential Saskatchewan Grain Growers' Association (SGGA), the Saskatchewan Association of Rural Municipalities, and the ultra-Protestant Orange Lodge. Several of the province's newspapers joined the chorus, such as the *Regina Daily Post*, which urged the Liberal government to bring about English-only schools "by whatever means are found possible and most

"The Door Steadily Opens." *Grain Growers' Guide*, 21 September 1910

expeditious."[54] What minorities regrettably discovered is that the campaign for school reform was not just about educational standards. The use of English alone in the province's schools was now seen as essential to the survival of democracy, the empire, and the nation.[55]

The language crusade presented a serious challenge to the governing Liberals, especially since the party was so closely associated with the immigrant community. But the ugly mood of the Anglo-Protestant majority could be ignored only at the party's electoral expense; the war had made toleration impossible and endangered diversity. It was also apparent that the quality of immigrant education was far from satisfactory and that, at the very least, fully qualified English-speaking teachers should be placed in schools in foreign districts. The Saskatchewan government responded by first passing a School Attendance Act in 1917, making attendance compulsory for children between seven and fourteen. Late the following year, it took the next step and amended the School Act to forbid the use of languages other than English as of 1 May 1919. As a compromise, French could be used as a language of instruction in grade one and taught as a subject of study for one hour only in subsequent years. This concession prevented the resignation of Attorney General Alphonse Turgeon, the French Catholic representative in the provincial cabinet.[56] But the government lost long-time agriculture minister W. R. Motherwell, who was not opposed to educating immigrants in English, but questioned "the lionizing process of squeezing their mother tongue out of them all at once."[57] Reverend Mackinnon, now serving as a military chaplain in Calgary, was even less pleased with the amendment, but for the opposite reason. "French must go," he roared. "We do not want Quebec reproduced in Saskatchewan. Let all enlightened citizens speak, write and wire until French goes with German."[58] He would have to wait for more than a decade to get his wish.

The emotions unleashed by the war would also bring about prohibition and women's suffrage in Saskatchewan. But, like the treatment of ethnic minorities, banning booze and giving women the vote did not suddenly appear on the reform agenda when war was declared. Protestant denominations, women's groups, and other organizations had been actively pushing for these kinds of reforms since the early twentieth century. The Great War now made them achievable. Reverend Haydon of Saskatoon had called the European conflict a "Holy-War." Other religious and spiritual leaders used similar terms. The implication was quite clear; the members of the Canadian Expeditionary Force were soldiers of Christ, and those who had fallen were saviours.[59] And a war of righteousness required, indeed demanded, change at home as well. What also helped the reform movement was the beginning of a new role for government in the everyday lives of Canadians. The war

The bar in the Imperial Hotel, Langenburg. SASKATCHEWAN ARCHIVES BOARD R-A2497

necessitated an activist state to ensure that the country's military machine ran efficiently and effectively. Governments were no longer reluctant to tread in areas that had previously been considered out of bounds.

Some of the first reform legislation in Saskatchewan was actually passed before the war. In 1908, the Scott government introduced the Children's Protection Act, which provided for the care of neglected and dependent children.[60] Five years later, in response to the arrival of moving pictures in the province, it appointed the first board of film censors to prevent the supposed corrupting influence of the new medium.[61] But the major reform thrust of these years, the "banish the bar" movement, made little headway, even though drinking was a particularly persistent social problem at the time. Because the first wave of immigrants during the settlement boom was overwhelmingly single young men, the consumption of alcohol became a popular recreational activity. Lonesome bachelors, away from home and family and friends, often sought escape for a few hours inside a bottle. The preponderance of unattached men also encouraged the establishment of brothels, especially near major railway centres. One of the most notorious red-light districts in western Canada was River Street in Moose Jaw, which also served Regina clientele because of the heavy mountie presence in the provincial capital. Even Saskatoon, which began its days as a temperance colony, was not immune to the sins of the flesh. The first prostitutes set up shop near the bridge that the Grand Trunk Pacific Railway was building across the South Saskatchewan River. Patrons were apparently comforted by women of different races.[62]

The first concerted effort to end the liquor traffic in the province, and thereby smash the booze-brothel syndrome, began with the formation of the Social and Moral Reform Council of Saskatchewan in Regina in 1907. Just as the elimination of foreign languages was supposed to solve the problem of rural schools, prohibitionists believed that booze was at the root of most of society's problems and that its elimination would work miracles. Within a year, the council had successfully lobbied the provincial government to introduce legislation that allowed communities and rural municipalities the option of voting to go "dry." But when a delegation called on the premier to introduce Saskatchewan-wide prohibition in 1911, Scott had no political appetite for it, knowing full well that the measure did not have sufficient public backing. Two years later, prohibition advocates reorganized themselves under a broader, better-financed "Banish the Bar" movement, headed by the province's leading religious and temperance leaders, known as the Committee of One Hundred. The new association, however, encountered only disappointment as the Scott government continued to refuse to lend its legislative powers to smite the province's saloons.[63]

The women's suffrage movement encountered similar problems before the war. Unlike the pitched battles in Great Britain, the United States, and even neighbouring Manitoba, the struggle for voting rights for Saskatchewan women was not a battle at all, but "good-natured," even "unspectacular."[64] At the same time, it was no less frustrating for those involved. Women in the province first began demanding the vote as the logical extension to their prohibition work. Members of the Women's Christian Temperance Union soon realized that they could not bring about the changes in society that they were seeking until they exercised some electoral muscle. They genuinely believed that women had a special contribution to make to public life, that the hand that rocked the cradle, to paraphrase suffragist Nellie McClung, should rule the world. This maternal feminism, as it has been called, was matched by a pronounced call for equality rights. Single women resented their inability to apply for homesteads because of archaic federal rules, while married women chafed at the prospect of having no claim to the assets of their farms, farms that they helped build alongside their husbands, because of the lack of dower rights. Securing the vote was seen as the only way to eliminate these inequalities.[65]

The question of women's suffrage was first raised in the Saskatchewan legislature in December 1912 by J. E. Bradshaw, the Conservative member for Prince Albert. Those who attended the debate expected a chauvinistic parade of platitudes about the weaknesses of the fairer sex, but except for one dissenting voice, members of both sides of the legislature warmly supported the idea in principle. Government members insisted, though, that woman's suffrage was premature. "The vote is undeniably hers," observed a sanctimonious W. R. Motherwell, "but does she want it?"[66] This official line—that women would secure the franchise once they had demonstrated that they wanted it—led to one of the most memorable political cartoons in Saskatchewan history: Premier Scott imploring a woman, on her haunches like a dog, to speak. It was also a brilliant, perhaps disingenuous strategy. The Scott government never specified how women were to prove that they wanted the vote, nor did it say exactly how much support was needed to give them the keys to the legislature. The premier could and did delay action on the question with impunity on the pretext that women had not shown enough interest. Not even the wholehearted support of the powerful SGGA, which realized that the farm women's vote could strengthen the agrarian voice, made any difference.[67]

The war made the Saskatchewan government's position on both prohibition and women's suffrage untenable. Temperance advocates now drew on the rhetoric of the war to argue that the production of alcohol was not only a waste of resources, but that its consumption impaired the fighting ability of Canada's soldiers. They even suggested that bars were "meeting places for our Empire's enemies and breeding places for sedition."[68] This equation of prohibition with patriotism quickly wore down the Scott government's resistance and in March 1915, just eight months into the war, the premier announced during a speech at Oxbow that all drinking establishments in the province would be closed 1 July for the duration of the war and replaced with government-run liquor stores. "To stand still any longer," Scott confessed to a close friend, "meant suicide for this government."[69]

The dispensary system seemed a reasonable solution to the evils associated with the bar and was widely applauded. But no sooner had government stores opened in Saskatchewan than both Alberta and Manitoba moved to total prohibition. These developments placed the province at the rear of the prairie reform movement and effectively forced the Saskatchewan government, if it wanted to retain its reputation as a progressive administration, to hold a prohibition referendum in December 1916. Temperance supporters made the vote a loyalty test—with the expected results. A whopping 80 per cent, four of every five respondents, voted to shut down the new government dispensaries. "As the war against Germany became longer and more bitter," one historian has noted, "the war against booze enlisted more and more recruits."[70] Unfortunately, the referendum further strained relations with the

SPEAK!

VOTES FOR WOMEN

The Scott government insisted that women would secure the vote once they had demonstrated that they wanted it. SASKATCHEWAN ARCHIVES BOARD R-B6493

province's ethnic minorities, including the French-Catholic community, who were made to feel that a vote for liquor was somehow a vote for the Kaiser.

Women enjoyed similar success in securing the provincial franchise that same year. The premier's 1912 challenge that women had to prove they wanted the vote led to the sending of hundreds of letters and petitions, mostly from rural areas, to the Saskatchewan legislature. But when Scott was pressed on the matter in early 1914, he lamely responded that the government had no mandate from the people "to bring about so radical a change."[71] Women redoubled their efforts once war broke out. They rightly pointed to the many roles they were performing to backstop the Canadian war effort, including the sending of their sons, husbands, and brothers to the front. They also questioned why the foreigner enjoyed the vote while they struggled and sacrificed to help build the province without any formal say in government and the laws that affected them. Representatives from various feminist organizations, meanwhile, came together in Regina in February 1915 to form the Provincial Equal Franchise Board of Saskatchewan, a central agency to coordinate and broaden the suffrage campaign.

These efforts, including the sending of a delegation to ask for the franchise "not as a favour but because it is just,"[72] again failed to sway the premier. But when Scott learned in late 1915 that Manitoba intended to give women the vote early in the new year, the provincial government scrambled to ensure that Saskatchewan followed suit. The bill to revise the franchise, introduced on Valentine's Day, made Saskatchewan the second province to adopt female suffrage. Before the approval of the legislation, the premier lectured women watching from the legislature gallery that "government is a serious business ... keep in mind the supreme importance ... of these responsibilities."[73] But as his own behaviour sadly demonstrated, he moved on the issue only because further delay would have hurt the provincial government and, more importantly, the fortunes of the provincial Liberal party. Far from being about noble principles like equality, it was political opportunism at its worst.[74]

Saskatchewan women first voted in the prohibition referendum in December 1916 and hoped to usher in a new day on the road to a better world. Three years later, history was made again when Sarah Ramsland, a thirty-seven-year-old mother of three, became the first woman to sit in the Saskatchewan legislature when she won a by-election to replace her deceased husband, the former Liberal member for Pelly. "If for one moment," she personally assured her parents after her election, "I thought I could not be the same lady I had always tried to be I would never have entered politics. And I am sure my own good judgment will be used in every instance ... my vote ... can *never be bought*."[75] Ramsland's high hopes and even higher ideals were reflective of the Great War years in Saskatchewan when the province's citizens fought at home and abroad in the name of democracy. There was never any doubt about the righteousness of the struggle or the sanctity of participation. If there was any criticism, it was the need to fight harder, make greater sacrifices, if Canada was going to help win this war to end all wars and take its place among the leading nations of the world. That time seemed to have arrived in the fall of 1917 when the Borden Conservatives in Ottawa called for the formation of a coalition government and the introduction of conscription for overseas service. Saskatchewan would rally to this cause, but ironically it would only further divide the province.[76]

CHAPTER ELEVEN

LITTLE SHORT
OF MADNESS

ONE OF SASKATCHEWAN'S GREAT HOPES in 1914 was that the Great War would lift the province out of its economic doldrums and set it on the road to recovery. And for the agricultural sector, the war did just that. The feeding of Allied armies created a seemingly insatiable demand for wheat and other farm items at record-high prices. Saskatchewan producers responded by expanding their holdings in the search for larger harvests and even larger profits; pioneer homesteads in many instances completed the transition to viable commercial operations. Farmers also set aside their complaints about the protective tariff and other federal agricultural policies in the greater interests of Canadian unity, unwavering in their support of the dominion's war effort. This willingness to back the war, whatever the cost, would unfortunately come back to haunt the province. In growing as much wheat as possible, Saskatchewan became more than ever dependent on one crop, gambling its future well-being on the vagaries of an international market over which it had no control. The creation of a national or union government in Ottawa, meanwhile, challenged the close relationship between Saskatchewan farmers and the provincial Liberal party and ultimately intensified the call for independent political action. The Great War may have forged a new Canadian nation, but at the same time it amplified the distinctiveness of Saskatchewan.

War could not come soon enough for Saskatchewan's cities. Badly staggered by the 1912–13 recession, places like Moose Jaw, Prince Albert, Regina, and Saskatoon looked to the war to stop the slide into financial ruin. The most urgent problem was mounting debt, a legacy of the boom years when cities had not only recklessly spent millions of dollars on facilities and infrastructure they would not need for the foreseeable future, but had blithely borrowed the money to fund this development based on unrealistic local assessment values. The collapse of the boom left cities scrambling to avoid default. Regina's debenture debt in 1913 was over $4 million. The ever-ambitious Saskatoon was on the hook for nearly twice that much—an incredible $7.6 million.

Cities tried to salvage the situation by hiking property taxes. But lots and buildings were grossly overvalued, and many ratepayers defaulted on their taxes. Arrears in Regina alone in 1916 were over $800,000. Other people simply walked away from their property. In Prince Albert, abandoned houses and businesses, taken over by the city, dotted the urban landscape. Another solution was to limit municipal services and reduce civic salaries and then funnel any savings towards the retirement of the debt. Saskatoon cut its annual expenditures by over 50 per cent in just two years. These measures, however, barely dented the debt charges and left western cities literally stuck in their development. They also did little to appease angry investors, especially when Battleford and then Prince Albert were forced to suspend interest payments on their bonds.[1]

The Great War was supposed to turn this sorry situation around. Moose Jaw, at the heart of several major railway branch lines, wanted to become the province's mobilization centre in the expectation that the presence of hundreds of troops would have significant economic spinoffs. Other Saskatchewan cities anticipated recovery through war orders. But even though the federal Militia Department spent almost five million dollars between August 1914 and February 1915 outfitting the Canadian Expeditionary Force, Saskatchewan was not offered any of this work.

The province fared little better when it came to munitions production, securing less than 1 per cent of the available contracts. This lack of industrial and manufacturing work hurt Saskatchewan businesses and encouraged many urban dwellers, already looking for jobs because of the recession, to go where

Women provided harvest help during the war. MOOSE JAW ARCHIVES 76-116

their skills were needed or answer the call of King and country and enlist.[2] Several cities saw their population, once the bellwether of a community's success, actually shrink. Between 1911 and 1916, Regina and Prince Albert lost four thousand and six thousand people, respectively, while Saskatoon replaced Moose Jaw as the second largest city in the province. Those who stayed faced a future of retrenchment, stagnation, and chronic unemployment compounded by the sacrifices demanded by the war. Saskatoon grocer Charles Woodside's one wish in 1916 was that "someone would be foolish enough to come along and buy me out."[3] Until that time, he and others like him had to survive on business mostly generated by the agricultural sector.

Farming was also hurting before the war. A recession-induced drop in grain prices caused the first ever decline in major crop acreage in 1914.[4] A severe drought in the southwestern part of the province only aggravated the already dismal outlook. This region, with its light soils and scanty precipitation, had always been considered too arid for cultivation. But during the frenzied years of the great settlement boom, the federal government had amended the Dominion Lands Act in 1908 to allow homesteading in ranching country; prospective settlers could file for 160 acres of homestead land and buy an adjoining preemption of the same size at three dollars per acre. These larger farms were supposed to make up for the soil deficiencies, and land-hungry immigrants, mostly from the United States, poured in by the thousands. By 1910, there were elevators, towns, and wheat fields where there had been none only two years earlier. The "magician's wand never produced [a] more striking effect," boasted a Department of the Interior pamphlet.[5] But doubts began to set in when the broken land started to drift in the drying winds. In January 1913, Ottawa appointed a special ranching and grazing commission, known as the Pope Commission after its chairman, to investigate whether certain districts should be closed forever to homestead entry and set aside for grazing.[6] Indeed, the need to rethink land policy in the area was driven home during the summer of 1914 when crops failed, in some places for the third consecutive year. The situation was so desperate that the provincial government had to provide relief to destitute farmers. Premier Walter Scott even floated the idea of a temporary debt moratorium until producers could get back on their feet.[7]

Saskatchewan's agricultural community was also still smarting over the rejection of reciprocity in the 1911 general election. The record of the new Borden government on several key farm issues held out little hope for any meaningful change. The federal Conservatives maintained the high tariff policy of its predecessors, while allowing concerns about freight rates and elevators to continue to fester. The solution to this ongoing neglect, insisted the widely read *Grain Growers' Guide* in the spring of 1914, was for the west to break free from the constraints of the traditional two-party system and send its own representatives to Ottawa. This kind of talk alarmed both national parties, given the region's rapidly growing political clout, and prompted Prime Minister Borden and Liberal opposition leader Sir Wilfrid Laurier to plan to tour the prairies late that summer to try to head off any move toward independent political action.[8] But then the war intervened. The cancellation of the leaders' visits did not mean, though, that western Canada was not to play a fundamental role in the national war effort. Ottawa not only expected Saskatchewan to provide soldiers, but encouraged the province to grow wheat, and lots of it, for the Allied cause.

The response to this challenge was nothing short of phenomenal. Equating patriotism with production, Saskatchewan farmers seeded over ten-and-a-half million acres in the spring of 1915. Growing conditions were never better. The wheat harvest, the largest in the province's history, topped 224.3 million bushels—half the production for the entire country. The yield, at 25.1 bushels per acre, also broke a provincial record going back to 1905. Farmers were naturally pleased, but even more so because of an accompanying rise in wheat prices because of wartime demand—from only 66 cents per bushel in 1913 to $2.40 in 1916. These prices, together with the belief that it would be a short war, encouraged farmers to grow as much wheat as possible. Cropped acreage consequently increased by roughly two million acres in both 1916 and 1917 and then by another million acres in 1918.[9] The story was particularly spectacular in southwestern Saskatchewan which produced ninety-six million bushels of wheat in 1915, almost twice the total provincial production in 1905. The mammoth harvest removed any doubts about the region's agricultural potential and easily convinced more settlers to take up land or expand their holdings.[10] By 1916, the population in the district had reached 178,200 (from 46,450 ten years earlier), while the number of farms increased almost five-fold (8,750 to 38,000) and the area of crop land grew nine times (.5 million acres to 4.5 million) since the 1906 special census. "This was a land rush," observed a grasslands historian, "to equal the best of them."[11]

The provincial government introduced various wartime measures to facilitate rural enlistment and promote crop production. It amended the Rural Municipalities Act to exempt from taxation farmland of men who volunteered for overseas service. It also passed a Farm Implements Act, which required machinery dealers to explain in clear language the contractual obligations of purchasers, and established a Farm Loan Board to provide low-cost government loans for farm operation and expansion.[12] The provincial Bureau of Labour, in the meantime, in cooperation with the Department of Education, pulled boys in their early teens from schools to handle farm work, especially at harvest time, without academic penalty. Any student who completed three months' service was formally recognized with a bronze badge as a "Soldier of the Soil."[13] The Department of Agriculture also recruited children to kill gophers, which reportedly destroyed a quarter million acres of crop each year. On 1 May 1917, tens of thousands of kids from 980 schools in the province competed in Saskatchewan's first official Gopher Day. Armed with poison, snares, traps, and guns, they were sent into the fields by their teachers to wage battle with the "enemy of production." By sundown, more than half a million of the pesky rodents had been exterminated, with the Charlottenberg School District Number 1755 winning the revered Gopher Shield for the most tails.[14]

Ottawa also did its part to push settlement of the land by easing homestead regulations so that farm employment as a hired hand could be counted towards the annual six-month residency requirement on the home quarter. At first glance, the success of this provision appears doubtful. The annual number of homestead entries in the province steeply declined after 1914 and never recovered to the settlement boom levels. Still, several thousand homesteads were occupied in Saskatchewan during the war even though immigration had been suspended.[15]

The Borden government also sought to increase production by temporarily seizing "underutilized" Indian reserve land in western Canada. Known as the Greater Production Campaign, the sweeping initiative empowered the Indian commissioner to either lease reserve land to non-Aboriginal farmers for a fixed term or turn it over to government operators who would work it using non-Aboriginal labour. Since the program violated treaty provisions, it required an amendment to the Indian Act.[16] During the 1918 debate on the proposed changes, Frank Cahill, a Liberal MP from Quebec and former Saskatoon resident, lectured the government, "I think if we are going to do any confiscating of land for the benefit of the whiteman, you should take the

The Gopher Shield was awarded to the school whose students killed the most gophers in one day. SASKATCHEWAN ARCHIVES BOARD R-A20630

whiteman's land." Arthur Meighen, the minister responsible for Indian Affairs, coolly replied that there was no need to "waste any time in sympathy for the Indian," that using reserve land to grow wheat was "a lot better than a few squirrels caught by the Indian."[17] What was particularly sad about this episode was the two-faced attitude of the Conservative government. At the same time it was suggesting that Indians stood in the way of greater production, it was featuring Moo-chew-eines, a nearly blind Cree from Onion Lake, and his self-less contribution of $150 to the Canadian Patriotic Fund on a poster distributed across the country to raise money for the war effort. "Pale Face, my skin is dark," the poster read, "but my heart is white: for I also give to the Canadian Patriotic Fund."[18]

The immense 1915 wheat harvest was not simply a consequence of good weather. By the beginning of the war, Saskatchewan producers had developed a better understanding of growing conditions on the prairies and had readily embraced dry farming practices. None were more skilled at this process than Seager Wheeler, more popularly known as the Wheat King. Born on the Isle of Wight, Wheeler dreamed of joining the British navy. But when he was turned away by the minimum height requirement, the seventeen-year-old headed for the North-West Territories in 1885 and the promise of adventure on the sealike prairies. He first took a homestead north of Saskatoon in the Clark's Crossing area and then bought a better parcel of CPR land outside Rosthern in 1897.

Unlike other successful farmers who wanted to enlarge their holdings, Wheeler concentrated on improving the quality of his wheat. He would carefully inspect and select the heaviest grain heads in his crop and then spend hours each night by lantern sorting through the seed by hand for the best kernels. He also worked at perfecting his dry farming practices. "What is wanted," he later advised, "is not more acres in crop, but better producing acres." Wheeler's experimentation and perseverance were rewarded in 1911 when he won first prize, a thousand dollars in gold coins, at an international competition in New York for the best spring wheat grown on the continent. Wheeler was crowned world wheat king again for three consecutive years from 1914 to 1916 and then won an unprecedented fifth title in 1918. This rare accomplishment served to confirm what governments, railways, and their promotional literature had been claiming for years: that Saskatchewan had the best wheat-growing land in the world. His achievement continues to be recognized today by the designation of the Wheeler farm as a national historic site.[19]

Seager Wheeler, Saskatchewan's wheat king, with his many trophies.
SASKATOON PUBLIC LIBRARY
LH1089

The University of Saskatchewan, in co-operation with the provincial government, was also instrumental in the widespread adoption of dry farming techniques. At the cornerstone ceremony for the new agriculture building in July 1910, Premier Walter Scott talked about the fundamental link between education and agriculture in Saskatchewan. "Farming is the foundation of civilization," he maintained. "It is in keeping with the character of our province that the main part of the highest institution of learning in the province shall be an agricultural college."[20] University President Walter Murray shared these sentiments and reached into the provincial Department of Agriculture to recruit people who had worked closely with W. R. Motherwell, Saskatchewan's first minister of agriculture. The first dean of the new College of Agriculture, W. J. Rutherford, had served as deputy minister of the department. F. H. Auld, the new director of agricultural extension, had been Motherwell's chief statistician. And John Bracken, formerly provincial superintendent of fairs and exhibitions, was named the first professor of field husbandry.

The trio, sometimes joined by Motherwell and Wheeler, lost little time organizing two-to-three-day short courses throughout southern Saskatchewan on the principles of dry farming. In 1914, more than fifteen thousand people attended one of the twenty-one courses. By 1918, the program was offered in no less than fifty-seven centres.[21] The agricultural specialists were also regular guests on the fair circuit, sometimes serving as judges in the seed, produce, and field competitions when not lecturing about the best farming methods. Much of this material was brought together by John Bracken in his two books, *Crop Production in Western Canada* (1920) and *Dry Farming in Western Canada* (1921), both published by the *Grain Growers' Guide*. Seager Wheeler also offered practical, first-hand advice in his popular *Seager Wheeler's Book on Profitable Grain Growing* (1919).

This agricultural extension work became more sophisticated in 1915 with the launch of the Better Farming Train, a federally funded initiative to provide the Saskatchewan farming community with the latest information on agricultural and domestic developments. Each year for five weeks, starting in early June, a specially equipped train, divided into six sections (livestock, field crops, poultry, dairy, farm mechanics, and household science) and staffed by university instructors, toured the province, stopping in one community in the morning and another in the afternoon. By the time the train returned to Saskatoon, more than thirty thousand visitors had walked through the display, stopping to examine the exhibits and ask questions or attend a talk in one of the lecture cars. Women spent most of their time in the household science section, fascinated with the latest labour-saving devices, such as the wringer washing machine or the pumping system that would bring water into the farmhouse. There was even a nursery car for babies

Children watching a movie during a visit of the Better Farming Train.
SASKATCHEWAN ARCHIVES BOARD R-A136-6

and toddlers, while older children enjoyed movies in the lantern car.[22]

The response to the Better Farming Train and university short courses demonstrated how Saskatchewan farmers and their families were anxious to improve their agricultural practices and living conditions and put their pioneer days behind them. This desire was part of an overall transition to large-scale commercial agriculture which had been accelerated by the war. If Saskatchewan farmers were going to meet the great demand for food, then they had to work larger parcels of land, employing the best dry farming techniques. Farm acreage statistics document this transformation. In 1911, 95,000 farms had on average 125 acres in field crops. Ten years later, there were not only more farms (120,000), but they averaged more land in crop (209 acres).[23] The increasing rural population and the steadily growing importance of agriculture made farmers an even more dominant force in provincial life. The 1916 Saskatchewan electoral riding redistribution, for example, continued to favour rural areas at the expense of urban centres. Moose Jaw, Regina, and Saskatoon had only one representative each in the enlarged fifty-nine-seat legislature even though they collectively represented 10 per cent of the provincial population.[24]

Farm women also came to play a more active role in public life during this period. The 1913 formation of a women's section within the SGGA signalled a collective effort by women to look beyond their own personal circumstances to begin to address some of the larger problems of rural society. Certainly, suffrage was a key concern, but it was only one element in the overall quest to improve the quality of life in rural Saskatchewan. Zoa Haight, a widely respected leader of the movement, regularly spoke of the need to organize and co-operate to bring about the betterment of the rural community, not just for women, but for everyone. "We are all Grain Growers, first, last, and all the time," she maintained. "Their interests are our own."[25] The women who were most active in the organization came from comfortable British or American backgrounds, usually married to members of the SGGA or the Saskatchewan Cooperative Elevator Company. They had a definite plan of action: the establishment of libraries, the building of community halls, the

The executive of the Women's Section of the Saskatchewan Grain Growers' Association, 1918.
SASKATCHEWAN ARCHIVES BOARD R-B4481

improvement of medical services and schools, and the co-operative purchase of staple commodities.[26]

Homemakers' Clubs, on the other hand, were non-political, more diverse in membership, and more concerned with ending the loneliness and isolation of farm women. Organized in early 1911 by F. H. Auld, director of agricultural extension for the University of Saskatchewan, and modelled after the Women's Institutes of Ontario, the clubs brought local women together to share practical information on a wide range of topics from housework and food preservation to gardening, decorating, and raising poultry.[27] Although directed by the university, which also made available guest speakers and a travelling library, Homemakers' Clubs thrived on local initiative and soon evolved into an integral feature of the rural landscape. The coming of the war provided a new purpose and a new focus. While clubs knitted or sewed for the troops at the front, the conversation often turned to prohibition, suffrage, and other reform causes.[28] It was the companionship, however, that women cherished above everything else. "It isn't altogether what I learned," explained one member about her club experiences, "it is the other women I have come to know through our meetings ... it has brightened my life and given me new courage, and I don't any longer feel a shut-in."[29] For many women, attending club meetings was the first time they left their farm on a regular basis.

Saskatchewan's movement away from pioneer operations to commercial agriculture also had a downside. The provincial economy became more vulnerable, more susceptible to pendulum-like swings in fortune. Before the war, people like Dean Rutherford of the College of Agriculture had been actively extolling the benefits of mixed farming—raising animals, not just field crops—and how it would provide greater stability in the long term. He even predicted in 1914 that "extensive wheat farming is only a passing stage."[30] His boss, Walter Murray, agreed and once warned, "This province cannot afford to put all its eggs into one basket."[31] But the wartime demand for wheat and the high prices that went along with it proved too seductive for prairie farmers, especially when it was understood to be patriotic. Wheat acreage in the three prairie provinces consequently shot up from 9.3 million acres in 1914 to 16.1 million at the end of the war and accounted for two-thirds of the entire prairie field crop by 1919.[32] Most of this crop was grown in Saskatchewan; the province boasted almost two-thirds of the prairie wheat acreage and produced on average at least 60 per cent of the wheat grown in western Canada during the war.[33]

Other sectors of the provincial agricultural economy, such as ranching, thrived as well during the Great War years, but their success still lagged behind that of wheat.[34] After the killing winter of 1906–07, many large American companies in southwestern Saskatchewan sold their remaining cattle and withdrew from Canada. Those that remained behind were big enough, like the Matador or 76 ranches, to sustain the losses or, in the case of the T Bar Down, switched to horse breeding because of the steadily growing demand for work animals.[35] This decline in stock numbers soon reversed itself in response to rising beef prices through the war and the securing of duty-free access to the large Chicago market in October 1913. The federal government also moved on the findings of the Pope Commission and introduced new grazing regulations that provided for leases of up to twelve thousand acres of dominion land, deemed unsuitable for farming, for a ten-year period at an annual rate of two cents per acre.[36]

The buoyant beef market immediately led to an increase in stocked land in the province, especially in the southwest. The number of cattle in the region tripled from 82,000 head in 1901 to 249,000 by 1916, an incredible turnaround from the setback of 1906–07. This increase was reflected in live exports to Winnipeg during the war: from 54,010 in 1914 to 166,856 in 1918.[37] Six long-time ranchers, meanwhile, helped form the Saskatchewan Stock Growers' Association in Moose Jaw in July 1913 to act as a lobby group on behalf of cattle producers. Two of the new association's first acts were the establishment of its own newspaper, *The Saskatchewan Farmer*, and the hosting of an annual stampede to help raise funds for the organization.[38] But even though the fortunes of the ranching industry seemed to parallel those of farming during the war years, growing wheat remained more popular than mixed farming. It not only offered the potential for greater, more immediate profit, but did not require spending money on buildings, forage, and year-round help. By 1919, earned income from wheat was twice that earned from livestock.[39]

In their blind rush to cash in on higher wheat prices, Saskatchewan farmers also neglected their stewardship of the land. Although schooled in dry farming techniques, many could not resist the temptation to seed fields that should have been rested or summerfallowed. Some even burned off the stubble after the crop had been harvested in the fall, further compromising the health of the soil. This negligence was justified and even encouraged by federal authorities in the interests of greater production, but for Saskatchewan's agriculture minister, it was "little short of madness."[40] It also had a cost. In 1916, a serious stem rust infestation reduced the provincial wheat crop to 147.6 million bushels, down from 224.3 million the previous year, even though nearly two million additional acres were being cultivated. The size of the harvest slipped again the next year, but higher prices made up for the reduced yields. The 1918 crop was even smaller, slightly more than 92.5 million bushels, thanks to the unfortunate combination of drought and poor farming practices. The harvest in southwestern Saskatchewan was particularly bad, with yields aver-

The 1916 Moose Jaw Stampede. MOOSE JAW ARCHIVES 72-60

aging less than five bushels per acre where they had been eighteen only two years earlier. Once again, the provincial government had to provide relief to hard-pressed settlers, as well as ship in hay to help sustain cattle and horse herds.[41] New farmers were particularly hard hit. In 1916, there were 5,722 homestead cancellations, just slightly less than the 6,247 homestead entries for that year. This trend continued for the next two years with the number of homestead entries exceeding cancellations by only about 500.[42]

Farm production costs—and farm debt—also soared during the war. Spurred on by higher wheat prices, farmers expanded their holdings by buying a second quarter section or sometimes even a third. Some also rented land from farmers who had gone to war. This demand for land was so strong that the CPR sold 600,000 acres in railway grants in 1918, dramatically up from the 160,000 the company sold two years earlier.[43] Farmers assumed this debt in the expectation that it would soon be erased by wheat profits. But they also had to contend with spiralling wage costs because of the scarcity of farm labour. Official harvest wages in Saskatchewan almost doubled during the war: from $2.50 per day in 1914 to $4.50 in 1918. Some farmers were apparently willing to pay more, in some cases as much as ten dollars. Canadian soldiers, by comparison, were paid only $1.10 per day.[44] These inflated wages often meant that hired hands went to the highest bidder, leaving other producers scrambling at harvest time.

The Saskatchewan government tried to deal with the crisis in 1916 by

One of the greatest needs of Saskatchewan farmers during the war was hired help.
The Farmer's Advocate, 25 February 1915

appealing for rural residents, including boys and girls and the elderly, to join harvest gangs; the agriculture minister even asked for volunteers from his own department. Ottawa also temporarily released soldiers to help with seeding and harvesting in 1917 and 1918, and called on Indian workers.[45] The continuing labour shortage, however, forced many farmers to acquire machinery, even though wartime inflation had increased implement prices. Now that they were working larger acreages to reap larger profits, farmers saw no alternative but to purchase separators, cultivators, and the like, thereby going deeper into debt. Prairie machinery dealers reported record sales in 1917. But the movement to smaller, gas-powered tractors, away from the cumbersome, dangerous, steam-driven behemoths of the past, was gradual and would not take off until the late 1920s. Most farmers continued to use horses, as evidenced by the doubling of the number of work animals in the three prairie provinces during this decade. It was a different story, though, for the automobile, such as the Ford Model T, which was readily acquired in an effort to ease the problems of distance and rural isolation.[46]

Saskatchewan farmers might be faulted for becoming wheat specialists, but Ottawa should shoulder some of the blame. The Canadian government promoted the cultivation of wheat during the war at the expense of more balanced agricultural development. Farmers, moreover, were not simply obsessed with making a quick profit, but saw themselves as helping the overall war effort by feeding Allied armies. Their assistance also extended to various funds and activities, including the unique Patriotic Acre Fund. Sponsored and promoted by the SGGA, the program called on farmers to set aside harvested wheat from one or more acres as a gift to Great Britain. The donated grain was milled and shipped in special sacks bearing the SGGA emblem. In 1915, five thousand acres were pledged, enough to fill forty rail cars each carrying eighty thousand pounds of flour.[47] This kind of support never slipped, even as the Great War's toll mounted and more and more Saskatchewan farm families lost loved ones. The hand of the war could be seen everywhere, from the weekly memorial services in rural churches to the rag-tag harvest crews to the suspension of local sporting leagues because athletes were fighting overseas. But when Ottawa launched its first Victory Loan bond drive in 1917, dominion organizers were staggered when the Saskatchewan campaign raised nearly twice as much as expected—roughly twenty-four million dollars.[48]

This commitment to the Great War would be sorely tested in 1917 when Prime Minister Borden announced his intention to form a coalition or union government and introduce conscription for overseas. As casualties mounted

Boy Scouts promoted the sale of Victory Loan bonds. SASKATCHEWAN ARCHIVES BOARD R-B8132(18)

and recruitment sagged, Borden concluded that Canada could only continue to meet its obligations and secure victory with conscripted soldiers and that such a controversial measure required the creation of a national government. The prime minister hoped for the support of the Laurier Liberals, but Sir Wilfrid balked at the proposal, questioning the need for conscription. Laurier also feared that any Liberal involvement in a coalition government would alienate Quebec, already seething over the prospect of compulsory military service. Not to be deterred, the Conservative government turned to leading western Liberals for support. It also moved to undermine the influence of anti-conscriptionists by ramming the Wartime Elections Act through Parliament in September 1917. Unabashedly partisan in design, the legislation sought to improve the chances for a coalition victory and conscription by extending the vote to the mothers, wives, sisters, and daughters of men who had served or were serving overseas, while taking it away from immigrants from enemy countries who had been naturalized since 1902. All Doukhobor and Mennonite conscientious objectors were also disenfranchised.[49]

The conscription/coalition conundrum came at an already difficult time for Saskatchewan, which had just come through an emotionally charged election in June 1917. In that contest, the Liberals had won their forth consecutive victory at the polls, but had done so with a new leader, William Melville Martin. The change at the top had been precipitated by former premier Scott's continuing and deepening bouts of depression and his uncharacteristic outburst in the Saskatchewan legislature against Reverend Murdoch Mackinnon over provincial education policy.[50] The government had also been tarred with the brush of scandal. In February 1916, J. E. Bradshaw, the Conservative member for Prince Albert, stood up in the legislature and alleged that members of the government and provincial civil service had personally benefitted from highway work, liquor kickbacks, and public building contracts. The charges were eventually investigated by three provincial royal commissions, and the guilty, including several Liberal backbenchers, speedily brought to justice.[51] But the damage had been done, especially when reform was the watchword of the moment. With some gentle prodding, Scott quietly stepped down on 16 October 1916, ending his distinguished, eleven-year career as the province's first premier at the age of forty-nine. "For at least four years," Liberal journalist J. W. Dafoe privately noted, "Walter has been neither physically nor mentally capable of carrying the premiership."[52] His natural successor was Jim Calder, who had served at Scott's side since 1905 and run the Liberal organization in the province. Calder, however, argued that the circumstances called for someone who had not been part of the previous administration.

That someone was the lanky, innocent-looking Billy Martin, who had come to Regina from Ontario to practise law in 1903 and had sat in Parliament as the Liberal representative for the city since 1908. It was once claimed the new premier had been raised on "porridge, progress, and predestination."[53] Emmett Hall, a contemporary of Martin and future Supreme Court of Canada judge from Saskatchewan, believed that he could easily have replaced Wilfrid Laurier as national Liberal leader.[54] The forty-year-old Martin quickly put the stamp of integrity on the new government by purging from the party those who had been implicated by the Bradshaw charges. He also signalled that agriculture would remain the top priority by naming Charles Avery Dunning, the accomplished general manager of the Saskatchewan Cooperative Elevator Company, the new provincial treasurer. Dunning's appointment was clearly calculated to bolster the tarnished public image of the provincial Liberal party and demonstrate that the new government would be pro-farmer and forward-looking. One of Martin's major new initiatives was the request that federally controlled lands and resources be transferred to the province, something that he had championed during his days in Ottawa.[55]

Premier Martin went to the Saskatchewan electorate to secure a mandate in June 1917. The war itself was never an issue. Instead, the opposition Conservatives played upon anti-immigrant feeling in the province and claimed that the Liberals were too cozy with people from enemy countries. A Conservative campaign ad in the *Prince Albert Herald* attacked the Liberals as "a party that considers one Alien in Saskatchewan of more value than seven soldiers in the trenches."[56] This strategy cost the Conservatives the large immigrant vote, while making the Liberals appear tolerant and fair-minded. The electoral waters were also muddied by the entry of the Non-Partisan League into Saskatchewan after its smashing success in neighbouring North Dakota. The new party appealed to farmers to act as a group and elect their own government. But the SGGA, which had worked closely with the Liberal government for years and eschewed independent political action, refused to endorse the new party. The ensuing spat between the two groups drove the SGGA closer to the Liberals, who portrayed themselves as a "farmers' government."[57] The Non-Partisan League, in turn, fielded only a handful of candidates, including Zoa Haight, the first woman to run for a seat in the Saskatchewan legislature. In the end, the Liberals won fifty-one of fifty-nine seats, their largest majority to date, and sent another opposition leader into retirement.[58] Women, who participated for the first time in a provincial election, tended to vote for the party that had extended the franchise to them.[59]

The provincial Liberals' elation was cut short by developments in Ottawa. Prime Minister Borden's call for conscription was popular in Saskatchewan, which had remained steadfast in its support of the war effort. "Why not make everyone available go and do their bit," wrote a Gull Lake soldier's wife to the prime minister, "and there would not be half the hard feelings in the country."[60] The sticking point, however, was the unpopularity—in some quarters, hatred—of Borden's party and its identification with the 1911 defeat of reciprocity. Westerners who wanted conscription did not want to vote for the high-tariff Conservatives. The proposal to create a union government removed this roadblock by directly appealing to the growing western desire for a non-partisan administration that would put winning the war above everything else. Saskatchewan's Jim Calder explained the popular attraction of this notion in an unvarnished letter to Wilfrid Laurier. "To put the whole situation in a nutshell," he wrote, "the people ... are growing weary of governments and politics as they existed in the past ... We need a strong central authority that will set about a thorough house cleaning and get action along sane lines."[61] Calder and other leading western Liberals consequently abandoned their national leader and accepted Borden's invitation to help form a national government to contest the next federal election. It is more than likely that the new Wartime Elections Act encouraged them to make this leap by disenfranchising a large block of traditionally Liberal, immigrant voters from the prairies. The draconian measure certainly appealed to westerners with a British background, who resented the prosperity of enemy alien farmers while Anglo-Saxon blood was being spilled on the battlefield.[62]

The December 1917 federal election held out the hope of ending the federal two-party system and partisan politics and bringing about the reforms that farmers and other westerners had talked about for at least the last decade. Sensing this groundswell, Premier Martin deliberately distanced himself from Laurier and publicly supported the Unionist cause. He also made it clear, in an attempt to limit the damage to the provincial party, that his own views did not necessarily reflect those of other government members.[63] Sir Wilfrid, for his part, remained personally popular in the province. Not only had he brought Saskatchewan into Confederation, but he had tried to secure reciprocity and went down fighting. His refusal to support conscription and coalition, however, made him an easy target for his opponents. The *Prince Albert Herald*, in an angry editorial that suggested that Laurier would pull Canada out of the war, bluntly asked its readers, "Do we want German rule?"[64] Jim Calder, now federal minister of immigration and colonization, used the Liberal electoral machine that he formerly managed in the province to orchestrate a sweeping victory. All sixteen federal constituencies in Saskatchewan went Unionist, a complete reversal from the previous federal election when Laurier took all but one of the seats. The very success of the campaign, though, precipitated divisions within Liberal ranks in the province. It also created high expectations of the new national government, the feeling that the old days of doing things at the expense of the west were now over.[65]

H.R.H. The Prince of Wales

Entering the Legislative Assembly Hall
Regina, Sask   Oct. 4, 1919.

Kilroe.
Regina.

Premier Martin stands on a lower step to avoid drawing attention to the Prince of Wales' height during his visit to the Saskatchewan legislature. SASKATCHEWAN ARCHIVES BOARD R-B3730

By 1918, any remaining Canadian enthusiasm for the Great War had been replaced by a grim determination to see the struggle through to the end. Even the great promise of Union government, in office for only a few months, had begun to fade. In late March, the Germans launched a punishing offensive that inflicted heavy casualties on Allied forces and put the outcome of the war, let alone its end, in doubt. Prime Minister Borden responded by summarily cancelling military exemptions for young agriculturalists, including farmers' sons, that had been promised in the conscription bill. Those called up in Saskatchewan tended to accept their fate with little protest, seeing conscription as a necessary cost of winning the struggle. As one father poignantly told Charles Dunning as his last son faced conscription, "None of us wants anybody else to fight our battles for us."[66]

There were other disappointments. Much-anticipated federal tariff reductions on farm machinery never materialized. Nor did the new Union government have much to do with Parliament, preferring to operate by cabinet directive. Some initiatives were applauded in western Canada, such as the introduction of prohibition, the extension of the federal franchise to women, and the eventual banning of newspapers in enemy alien languages, but the

Union government did not give the region a stronger voice in Ottawa, nor did it seem prepared to act on western concerns. Residents of the prairie west, however, were not about to abandon the national government experiment, but temporarily set aside their aspirations for reform until victory in Europe had been secured.[67]

The end of the Great War came suddenly, almost unexpectedly. In early August 1918, the Canadian Corps, now an experienced fighting machine, broke through the German line at Amiens and began the slow, costly push towards Cambrai and Valenciennes. By 10 November, after days of fierce German resistance, the Canadians and British were outside the Belgian border city of Mons, where the first fighting of the war had taken place.[68] Early the next morning, an armistice was signed and word quickly spread that all shooting was to end at 11 A.M. Twenty-six-year-old Private George Price of the 28th Northwest Battalion was on patrol that day. As he was crossing a bridge at 10:58 A.M., a German sniper mortally wounded him in the chest. The Nova-Scotia-born Price had gone west before the war and worked as a CPR section man in Moose Jaw. In late 1917, he had been found guilty of robbing his landlady and sentenced to one month of hard labour in the Regina jail. He tried to avoid incarceration by promising to join the army, but the judge turned him down. Upon his release, Price was conscripted and sent overseas. He was the only Canadian killed that day and the last Allied soldier to die during the Great War.[69]

News of the war's end sparked celebrations across Saskatchewan. In Regina, over eight thousand people gathered at Wascana Park to pay tribute to the fallen, while nearby farmers set haystacks ablaze, lighting up the sky around the city. The Saskatoon fire department led a nighttime parade, with bells ringing, under a canopy of northern lights.[70] But the jubilation was tempered by a new, deadlier, invisible enemy—the Spanish flu. Soldiers brought the virus from Europe to Canada, spreading it across the country as they returned to their homes by rail. Highly contagious, the flu struck with amazing speed, often killing its victims within twenty-four hours. Unlike other strains, this new virus also targeted healthy young adults in their twenties and thirties.

The first reported flu death in Regina was 6 October 1918; less than two weeks later, it had claimed victims in Saskatoon and Prince Albert. In the first month of the epidemic in Moose Jaw, there were 253 deaths. Cities responded by closing schools and banning public gatherings to try to restrict the contagion. The twentieth of October 1918 was the first "churchless" Sunday in the history of the province. In Saskatoon, one observer likened the empty streets to "a city of the dead." One of the safest places during the epidemic was the University of Saskatchewan. President Murray had placed the entire campus under quarantine, except for Emmanuel College, which became an emer-

The end of the war was punctuated by the arrival of the Spanish flu epidemic. MOOSE JAW
ARCHIVES 83-169

gency treatment centre staffed mostly by women volunteers. The story was
different in other parts of the city and the wider province. The impromptu
celebrations at the end of the war exposed more people to the virus and the
number of deaths escalated. More than twenty-five hundred people—half
the total provincial casualities—died in November 1918. Not even the dispensing of vast amounts of so-called medicinal alcohol, available only by
prescription because of prohibition, made any difference.[71]

Rural Saskatchewan was hit hardest. The RNWMP immediately placed
stricken reserves under quarantine. This measure may have limited the spread
of the virus, but did little to help the resident Indian population, whose
health was already compromised by inadequate medical care and poor living
conditions. The death rate in the Battleford agency alone was four times the
provincial rate during the epidemic.[72] Further west at the Onion Lake reserve,
trader Sydney Keighley reported that as many as seventy-five Indians had
died and that "the church was piled high with bodies."[73] The situation at residential schools was little better. At the Onion Lake Catholic boarding school,
nine Indian children died in November 1918 even though the building had

been under quarantine since mid-October.[74] Several bands planned to hold Sun Dances during the summer of 1919, because of the great sickness that had befallen them, but the Department of Indian Affairs turned down each request and sent in the mounties to suppress any attempt to hold a ceremony.

In farming districts, meanwhile, the natural inclination of many people was to head to the nearest town or village to face the epidemic with friends and be closer to medical aid. The crowding together, however, only facilitated the spread of the virus, and many communities, especially along major rail lines, adopted quarantines. Ironically, isolated homesteads offered the best protection, unless someone brought the disease to the farm.[75] Shirley Keyes Thompson recalled how her husband Lowell returned from the annual grain growers' meeting in Regina with the flu. "We felt not unlike sheaves being dropped by the binder," wrote the Biggar-area farm wife. "We were in a state of siege and the enemy was within our door."[76] Care for the sick mostly fell to selfless women, who made the rounds and provided comfort in whatever way they could. One such person was twenty-four-year-old Eleanor Beaubier, a schoolteacher at Sonnenfeldt, a Norwegian settlement south of Weyburn near the border. During the epidemic, she organized local sickrooms and went from home to home until she fell gravely ill herself and died. When a CPR branch line reached the area in 1927, the village was renamed in her honour.[77]

After the flu had subsided, Canada officially marked the end of the war with a national Peace Day on 19 July 1919. The event triggered a new round of victory celebrations, including a two-mile parade of veterans, children, and local service clubs through the streets of Saskatoon, followed by the release of doves. Communities also commemorated the dead and the sacrifices of the war by erecting statues, cairns, and cenotaphs in public places in the years that followed. Two unique Saskatchewan memorials were the tree-lined Road of Remembrance in Saskatoon's Woodlawn Cemetery, with a small plaque on every elm bearing the name of a fallen soldier, and an art collection by Nutana High School, with each work dedicated to a former student who had been killed overseas. Regina's Carmichael United Church installed a memorial stained-glass window, the "Great Sacrifice," which featured a rising dawn behind the main figures.[78]

This imagery, the idea that the European conflict marked a new beginning, was particularly apt for Saskatchewan. The war did more than provide what future premier Charles Dunning called the "economic salvation" of the province. It expanded and entrenched the growing of wheat as the single most important economic activity in the province. It also exacerbated ethnic tensions and divisions within the region, while at the same time intensifying the prairie west's sense of distinctiveness from other parts of the country. And it ushered in an era of reform that sought to bring about a better society. But for many, a more immediate concern was to put their lives back together now that the war to end all wars was finally over. Captain E. H. Oliver of the University of Saskatchewan captured this sentiment in a letter home in which he expressed his simple "hope there will be no next war." What many never realized at the time was that the world they had set out to save was gone, never to return.

CHAPTER TWELVE

ABSOLUTE PERFECTION

PREMIER WILLIAM MARTIN welcomed the end of the war with a mixture of relief and uneasiness. Just one day after the armistice, the Saskatchewan leader had privately observed that "for the next few years we will have problems and conditions to face in this country ... which will perhaps be more serious than even those which we have had to deal with over the past five years."[1] It was an accurate prediction. Post-war Saskatchewan was a much different place from the province that went to war in 1914. Indeed, the coming of peace had released a new set of "problems and conditions" that had festered during the Great War. Saskatchewan workers were upset about the hardship and deprivation caused by skyrocketing inflation during the war years, while farmers wanted greater attention paid to the agricultural community's needs and interests. There was also renewed debate about the merits of prohibition. One of the most troubling issues, though, was the cultural makeup of the province. Whereas the British-Canadian majority had once grudgingly tolerated such non-traditional immigrants as Doukhobors, Mennonites, and Ukrainians, expecting that they would eventually embrace the Anglo-Canadian way of life, any patience with the pace of assimilation had dissipated with the Great War. By the 1920s, many residents of British origin regarded the persistence of ethnic identities as a blight on the province's future. Some even questioned whether the integration of continental European immigrants into the larger society was desirable, let alone possible, and called for an end to the kind of immigration that had helped make the province one of the fastest growing in the dominion. Saskatchewan may have had the most ethnically diverse population in Canada at the time, but it stubbornly resisted becoming a multicultural society.

Saskatchewan's first post-war challenge—if it could be called that—came from organized labour. The trade-union movement in the early days of the province had been relatively weak because of the lack of industrial development and was consequently confined to a few thousand skilled or what were known as "craft" workers in male-dominated railway, construction, and printing shops. Little effort was made to organize women in the paid workforce, since their numbers were small and they generally held low-paid, service sector jobs, such as domestic work. Working women, in the words of one author, were essentially "invisible." Union activity was also conservative and deliberately avoided radical ideas or tactics in favour of pursuing so-called bread-and-butter issues like wage rates, working hours and conditions, and the employment of non-union workers. Most strikes in Saskatchewan in the years immediately before the war were over wage demands and lasted no more than a few weeks.[2] One of the few exceptions was a rowdy, two-month strike in Moose Jaw in 1908. The climax came when a gang of hot-headed railway men kicked and stoned some Scottish labourers who had been hired by the CPR as replacement workers.[3]

The Great War soured the mood and outlook of Saskatchewan labour. It was not that workers refused to support the war effort. What distressed them, though, was that their wages did not keep pace with the rampant inflation that ate away at their pay packets. A Saskatchewan worker who spent $6.49 on groceries in June 1914 was charged $11.11 for the same food basket in December 1916. Other expenses, such as clothing, fuel, and rent, rose just as dramatically. According to provincial Department of Labour statistics, the annual cost of living for an average family of five jumped 50 per cent from 1913 to 1918 (from $1,180.50 to $1,772.09). The situation was particularly bleak for women, who entered the war already working for lower wages. A female clerk at Saskatoon's Woolworth's store, for example, started at five dollars per week in 1914, seven dollars per week less than a common labourer's earnings.

The Moose Jaw train station, 1923. WESTERN DEVELOPMENT MUSEUM 7-D-19

The spiralling wartime inflation drove many workers into overcrowded housing districts on the edge of cities, where there were often no sidewalks, sewers, or running water, but plenty of poverty. The Department of Health reported in 1916 that it was not unusual to find several families living under one roof and sharing a single stove. What made things worse was that many workers, especially those on construction jobs, were laid off each winter and had to survive somehow without a regular paycheque.[4] When a federal royal commission investigating the state of industrial relations in Canada visited Saskatchewan in early 1919, a member of the Saskatoon Trades and Labour Council testified that any government that failed to deal with the growing labour unrest "unmistakably courts disaster."[5] Mrs. Resina Asals of the Regina Women's Labour League issued a similar warning. "There is only one thing that the workers have to thank the capitalists for," she told the commission. "They have tightened the screw up so much that they are awakening the worker."[6]

The Saskatchewan government, after years of sidestepping the matter, responded to labour's increasingly angry complaints by introducing a minimum wage act in 1919. But it balked at provincial legislation that would force employers to recognize unions and engage in collective bargaining.[7] Workers across the west, in the meantime, remained disgruntled and tried to make up for their losses during the war years by demanding better settlements with their employers. These efforts to secure some control over their industrial lives, however, met with stiff resistance, and at a western labour conference in Calgary in the spring of 1919, delegates resoundingly endorsed the proposal to bring both skilled and unskilled workers together in larger unions along industrial lines (what was known as the One Big Union movement) and to employ radical tactics, such as the general strike, to force employers to accede to their demands.

Only a few weeks later, the building and metal trades in Winnipeg struck over the issues of collective bargaining and higher wages. The walkout soon escalated into a general strike when tens of thousands left their jobs in sympathy on 15 May and effectively paralyzed western Canada's largest city for more than a month. Although it would later be determined that the disaffected workers had legitimate grievances and reasonable demands, Ottawa saw things much differently. In the wake of the 1917 Russian Revolution, the federal government feared that the export of Communism to the shores of North America would imperil a society made vulnerable by the sacrifices of the war years. And by adopting the weapon of a mass shutdown, the striking workers in Winnipeg, albeit unintentionally, gave substance to public fears of an international Bolshevik conspiracy set on destroying Canada. It is little wonder, then, that the federal government, with the blessing of the Canadian business community, crushed the strike.

The Winnipeg General Strike spilled over into Saskatchewan when labour leaders called on workers across the country to stage sympathy walkouts. The provincial attorney general, W. F. A. Turgeon, expected little trouble, but Ottawa was concerned enough to promise the Martin government the use of the militia if needed. There was even speculation that foreign agitators might cut the telegraph lines leading to the provincial capital. Labour's initial enthusiasm for supporting the Winnipeg showdown quickly dissipated when it came time for action. In Regina, the majority of union members overwhelmingly voted against strike action. About two hundred workers ignored the decision and left their jobs, but most straggled back after only a few days. The story was much the same in Moose Jaw, home to the largest concentration of union members in the province. Here, only about 20 per cent of the city's twenty-five hundred unionists provided qualified support for a sympathy strike. The railway workers in Prince Albert and several towns along the Canadian Northern main line staged walkouts, but the strikes were little more than an inconvenience.[8]

It was only in Saskatoon that anything resembling a general strike took place. On 27 May, more than one thousand workers, including postal employees, teamsters, steam engineers, plumbers, painters, machinists, and streetcar operators, went out and stayed out for almost a full month until the situation in Winnipeg had been resolved. But because essential services in the city were soon restored and maintained, the strike did not adversely affect most citizens. It also ended without incident. H. J. Baillie, one of the leaders of the strike, claimed that the experience had politicized Saskatoon workers, that they now saw themselves as part of a larger class struggle. He probably was inspired by the fact that the Saskatoon walkout was one of the strongest sympathy strikes in the country, but it is debatable whether the Saskatoon workers were motivated by a sense of solidarity, since One Big Union organizers subsequently enjoyed only limited success in the province. It is more likely that the Saskatoon labour community bore the brunt of the city's too-rapid growth before the war and supported the sympathy strike out of a frustration that bred a sense of class-based injustice. It is also apparent from the 1919 experience that the concept of industrial unionism did not fit the Saskatchewan situation where union membership was relatively small, physically isolated in a few major urban centres, and rigidly organized along craft lines. This inherent conservatism explains why the reaction to the Winnipeg General Strike was "half-hearted" at best and why the organized labour movement in the province over the next decade was subdued.[9]

Operators at the Saskatoon telegraph office, 1923. SASKATCHEWAN ARCHIVES BOARD R-B2237

The other major protest in the immediate post-war period came from farmers. Despite many grievances dating back to the early twentieth century, they had faithfully supported the Canadian war effort and rallied behind the adoption of conscription and Union government in 1917. But once the Great War was over, many western farm leaders resumed their critique of federal agricultural policies, this time advocating independent political action as the answer to their economic woes. The idea of sending their own representatives to Ottawa was not a naked grab for power. Farmers had realized for some time that neither national party would seriously act on any of their problems as long as the Liberals and Conservatives were dominated by big-money interests: the banks, railways, and manufacturers. It was only by electing their own representatives that they could expect to receive fair and just treatment. Farmers also genuinely believed that they answered to a higher moral standard. They were convinced that it was their sacred duty in the wake of the war to bring about the regeneration of Canadian society. The many virtues associated with rural life—energy, thrift, efficiency, sobriety, equality, and independence—could not only improve democracy, but make for a better Canada. The creation of a new party was also a logical development in light of political developments over the past decade. Farmers were still nursing wounds from the 1911 defeat of reciprocity at the hands of the Robert Borden Conservatives. They had also been effectively divorced from the Liberals when former prime minister Wilfrid Laurier ran against coalition and conscription in the 1917 election. Many farmers felt betrayed by the Union government's failure to provide truly non-partisan government. Less than a year after the war, several western members of the House of Commons left the Union government and formed the National Progressive Party, a western-based, farmers' protest group intent on contesting the next federal election. The decision would send shock-waves through the Canadian political system.[10]

The "agrarian revolt," as it was popularly known, swept through the prairie west like a grass fire and by 1921 had toppled the provincial governments in both Manitoba and Alberta. The long-serving Saskatchewan Liberals, however, managed to weather the storm. Their survival, although remarkable for the time, was not that surprising. After all, the Liberal party had been cozy with farmers since the formation of the province. Premiers Scott and then Martin had also invited prominent members of the agricultural community, like Charles Dunning, to join the cabinet. Dunning, who had assumed the treasury portfolio in 1916, was followed into the cabinet in 1921 by J. A. Maharg, who had been president of the SGGA for the past eleven years. This recruitment strategy meant that farmers had powerful representatives at the cabinet table and that the government, in turn, was in a kind of partnership with major agricultural bodies, like the twenty-one-thousand-member Saskatchewan Cooperative Elevator Company and the thirty-five-thousand-strong SGGA.[11] But the relationship threatened to come undone in the euphoria that accompanied the creation of the Progressive party. At the 1920 annual SGGA convention, several members, caught up in the reforming zeal of the agrarian crusade, urged the organization to enter politics. The meeting proved "a very hot time,"[12] but in the end, most delegates realized that nothing could be gained by taking on the Martin government. "There was no need to upset a Liberal government of farmers," one historian concluded about the episode, "simply to put in a farmers' government."[13]

The decision of the powerful SGGA to remain out of provincial politics buoyed the Martin government, although the premier remained wary of the Progressive threat, especially since several farm leaders had formed a provincial wing of the new party. Martin responded by publicly disassociating the provincial Liberal party from its national counterpart, now led by William Lyon Mackenzie King. He then called an election for June 1921, knowing full well that the Progressive forces were still getting organized in the province. "When you have your guns and ammunition ready," a civil servant observed at the time, "you are a fool to wait until the other fellow has his ready."[14] During the campaign, Martin deliberately played down the party identity in favour of portraying the administration as a farmers' government in all but name. His opponents were a loose collection of mostly Progressives and Conservatives, many running as independents in keeping with the spirit of democratic reform that animated the new movement. Come voting day, the Liberals were handily returned to office for the fifth consecutive time, capturing forty-six of sixty-three seats in the legislature. The Conservatives, leaderless going into the election, were reduced to two members, while the other opposition seats were filled by an assortment of independents, including the province's first labour representative, CPR conductor W. G. Baker from Moose Jaw.[15]

Martin's handling of the Progressive challenge at the provincial level seemed brilliant, all the more so when the Progressives grabbed fifteen of Saskatchewan's sixteen seats in the December 1921 federal election. The three-way contest also produced Canada's first minority government, with the Progressives holding the balance of power in the House of Commons. Ironically, the Saskatchewan premier was one of the first casualties in the fallout from the election. During the federal campaign, perhaps emboldened by his provincial victory, Martin not only publicly questioned Progressive policies, but campaigned on behalf of former provincial agriculture minister W. R. Motherwell, who was running as a Liberal candidate in Regina. The premier's actions now made him a liability in a province dominated by farmers; as one commentator wryly noted, "He had cooked his goose."[16] The search immediately began for a successor who could repair the damage to the government's relationship with the agricultural community while keeping the Progressives at bay. There was really only one choice: the highly capable, practical-minded Charles Dunning, who at thirty-seven gave up his job of keeping the province's books in order to become Saskatchewan's third premier in April 1922. Martin, meanwhile, was named to the Saskatchewan Court of Appeal and began a long judicial career that lasted almost forty years until his retirement in 1961 at eighty-four.[17]

Premier Dunning moved quickly to ensure that Saskatchewan farmers remained in the Liberal fold. He promised efficient, honest government, dedicated to agricultural matters, while distancing himself from the federal Liberal party. The message was simple: Ottawa, not Regina, was to blame for agrarian unrest. He also took dead aim at the Progressive threat by attacking the need for farmers to enter politics at the provincial level when a sympathetic government was already in place. Such directness would not have been possible had Dunning not been a former farmer and agricultural leader. He was also careful not to criticize provincial farm organizations, just the idea of political action. His strategy was amply rewarded in June 1925 when the Liberals won re-election with an even larger majority (fifty-two seats) than four years earlier and with 51.5 per cent of the popular vote—an amazing record for a government that had been in office for two decades. Many attributed the Liberal success to party organization, but equally important was Dunning's skilled leadership in running the affairs of the province.[18] Prime Minister Mackenzie King was certainly impressed and would soon invite the Saskatchewan premier to Ottawa to join the Liberal cabinet as his western lieutenant.

Saskatchewan was also revisited in the 1920s by problems that many believed had been resolved during the war. One of the most vexing was prohibition. On 1 January 1917, the day after government-run liquor dispensaries were closed, the RNWMP turned over policing duties in the province to the new Saskatchewan Provincial Police. The Martin government had created the police force ostensibly to enforce prohibition.[19] It was a formidable, at times frustrating, task. Despite the force's best efforts and a good deal of manpower, it made little headway stamping out the illegal production and consumption of booze in the province, in large part because people refused to co-operate with police investigations. Although there had been sixteen hundred convictions under the Saskatchewan Temperance Act by 1919, prohibitionists still complained that the Martin government was not doing enough to enforce the law. The provincial attorney general admitted in frustration, "How can we expect absolute perfection when so great a majority think it is perfectly

The Saskatchewan Provincial Police, including this detachment at Robsart, were disbanded in 1928. SASKATCHEWAN ARCHIVES BOARD R-A7537

right and legitimate to take a drink? ... That is the real problem."[20]

Two resourceful brothers who exploited the situation to their financial gain were Harry and Sam Bronfman, whose parents had fled the pogroms in Russia in 1889 and initially settled at Wapella. Encouraged by the settlement boom in the early twentieth century, the brothers embarked on a thriving hotel business, headquartered at the Balmoral Hotel in Yorkton. When prohibition threatened their profits, they entered the lucrative mail-order liquor business, something that was allowed at the time. When that loophole was closed by the federal government, they found another one: liquor could be prescribed for medicinal purposes. In 1919, Harry secured a wholesale drug-gist's licence and established the Canada Pure Drug Company. Soon, tens of thousands of cases of whisky were being shipped by rail to the Bronfmans' bonded warehouses in Yorkton to be distributed across Saskatchewan as medicinal spirits. The real bonanza came when the United States adopted prohibition. With a ready supply of liquor at hand, the Bronfmans established a series of heavily guarded export houses in small towns near the Canadian-American border and began peddling booze, much of it now blended in Yorkton, to "rum runners" from the United States. The brothers, as the major players in the cross-border trade, made a handsome profit. But things turned ugly one night in October 1922 when their brother-in-law was murdered at the Bienfait railway station. Harry and Sam, horrified by the brutal killing, soon left the province after winding up their affairs. But their Saskatchewan experience served them well when they later established the Seagrams distillery empire in Montreal.[21]

The departure of the Bronfmans coincided with the federal closure of export houses. But booze continued to be readily available in the province in the form of home brew. A 1923 police estimate suggested that Saskatchewan had more stills than all the other provinces combined.[22] Although the new Dunning government initially pledged itself to uphold provincial temperance legislation, citing the reduction in public drunkenness and petty crime, it soon became apparent that the public preferred a more moderate course of action. But before formulating new liquor legislation, the provincial government decided to hold a plebiscite; just as voters had been asked in 1916 to give their opinion on the adoption of prohibition, they were now to be consulted on whether prohibition should continue. The result of the July 1924 vote was an overwhelming no. The government responded by establishing a provincial liquor board which would control the sale of alcohol in government-run stores. It refused, however, to allow the sale of beer by the glass in licensed premises. That change was still considered too controversial in 1925 and would have to wait another decade.[23]

The other major issue from the war years that continued to bedevil provincial life was the place of non-British immigrants. But unlike prohibition, which had become generally unpopular by the early 1920s, there would be no backing away from the assimilationist demands of the Great War years. The anti-foreigner sentiment in Saskatchewan actually became more strident in the months following the war. Returning troops reacted angrily when they had to compete with ethnic workers for jobs or grew resentful of immigrant farmers who had prospered and expanded their holdings during their absence. The turmoil behind the 1919 Winnipeg General Strike, at the same time, suggested that radical aliens were at work in Canada, and it did not take much to reach the larger conclusion that people from eastern and central Europe carried the communist virus and would infect their host society unless checked. Even immigrant children were singled out. Ethel MacLachlan, the first Juvenile Court judge in the province and Saskatchewan's first female judge, linked juvenile delinquency and ethnicity and argued that assimilation of the new Canadian was one sure way to reduce the number of young offenders.[24] For many, it seemed as if the province had reached an important fork in the road: one way led to greatness as an Anglo-Canadian society, the other to certain ruin as a polyglot catch-all.

This obsession with the cultural makeup of Saskatchewan was nothing new to visible minorities, who had always been coolly received, if not shunted to the margins like unwanted refuse. In fact, the Great War and its lofty

Saskatoon's "Chinatown" in the early 1920s. SASKATOON PUBLIC LIBRARY LH4148

ideals had failed to break down the barriers that separated people of colour from society at large. One person who learned this sad truth was Yee Clun, a Chinese immigrant who had settled in Regina around 1901 and operated the extremely popular Exchange Grill restaurant. In 1924, he decided to test a recent amendment to the provincial Female Labour Act, which gave municipalities the authority to license restaurants and laundries where white women were employed, and asked Regina City Council for permission to hire white female help because of the shortage of Asian labour. Although Yee Clun was the respected leader of the Chinese community and supported by several prominent white Regina citizens, his application was vociferously opposed, especially by several local women's organizations that feared close contact between the two races. When the issue was discussed at council in July 1924, Mrs. W. M. Eddy of the Regina Women's Labour League insisted that approval of the application was "not in the best interests of white women or the community in general" and would turn the Queen City into the "Queer City of the West."[25] The council later voted to deny the licence to Yee Clun, but this decision was overturned by Judge Phillip Mackenzie of the Court of King's Bench; the mayor admitted at the trial that the application was turned down on racial grounds. Astounded by the court decision, which clearly went against the veiled intent of the law, the Saskatchewan legislature amended the act again in 1926 without weakening its discriminatory provisions. It remained on the books until 1969.[26]

There also continued to be little place in post-war Saskatchewan for Aboriginal peoples. According to census data, instead of disappearing as a distinct group as predicted, the number of Indians grew steadily from 12,914 in 1921 to 15,268 ten years later.[27] Although these statistics indicated that Indians were still a small minority in the province, they had come to expect more equal treatment thanks to their contributions to the war effort. Edward Ahenakew, a Cree Anglican priest from the Sandy Lake reserve, declared, "The part that we took in the war proved that we had reached a stage of development that should allow us some freedom in the management of our own affairs."[28] Duncan Campbell Scott, the deputy minister of Indian Affairs, agreed. "Each of them [veterans] will be a missionary of the spirit of progress," he enthused at the end of the war, "and their people cannot long fail to respond to their vigorous influence."[29] But Scott's "progress" was simply another word for assimilation. The Canadian government was not about to stop interfering in and controlling Indian lives; instead, federal assimilationist policies had to be accelerated if First Nations peoples were to take their place in the new, post-war Canada.

The Métis, on the other hand, were to be deliberately ignored; it was as if they were supposed to just fade away. They were not counted as a distinct group in the census, nor did Ottawa or Regina want to assume any responsibility for them. Left to fend for themselves, some congregated on the outskirts of towns and villages and tried to integrate as best they could. Others headed for remote areas, where there was always hope of engaging in some of their traditional activities. Many more squatted in makeshift shacks along grid roads or on Crown lands—hence the name, "the road allowance people." Whatever their circumstances, they were united by neglect, poverty, and misery, all of which further contributed to their sense of identity.[30]

Saskatchewan Indians during the 1920s were an administered people, no closer to the rights they had valiantly fought to uphold during the war. Indian Affairs redoubled its efforts to stamp out traditional religious practices by turning down all requests to hold dances and instructing its agents to limit visiting between reserves through the strict use of passes. The mounted police were also regularly called upon to break up ceremonial gatherings, especially when off-reserve residents were involved. In 1922, in response to a rash of religious activity in the Battlefords area, the local Indian agent threatened Thunderchild with the loss of his gold braid, the symbol of his chieftainship, if the practices did not stop.[31] Indian economic initiative also continued to be handcuffed by the permit system, which forbade individual band members from selling their produce or acquiring livestock or farm implements without the written permission of the local agent. The sorry consequences were explained in the House of Commons in July 1924 by M. N. Campbell, a Saskatchewan Progressive who farmed in the Pelly area. "I remember, about twenty years ago, when I first visited the Cote Indian reserve near Kamsack, that most of the Indians there were prosperous ... self-supporting," he reported. "I regret that ... the Indians have become poverty-stricken ... degenerating, losing out in every conceivable way ... their individual efforts are controlled ... they are not allowed to ... do anything on their own behalf."[32]

This control extended to Indian children, who continued to be sent away to a growing number of residential schools in the province. Parents who kept their children at home faced new penalties added to the Indian Act in 1920. The schools by this time had become a key instrument of assimilation. Indian officials reasoned that children educated in the white culture were more likely than their parents to abandon their "primitive" past and integrate into the larger society.[33] But the learning environment was greatly compromised by limited funding, poor facilities, and abusive teachers. A nurse visiting the Muscowequan school in 1922 found the "floor thick with mud, could hardly tell it from the outside."[34] The following year, an Ottawa press-gallery reporter was slipped a damning letter that Edward B. at the Onion Lake school had written to his parents. "I am always hungry," the boy starkly recounted. "I am going to hit the teacher if she is cruel to me again. We are treated like pigs."[35] These kinds of reports were all too common, but nothing compared to the horrific news from Beauval on 19 September 1927, when a late-night fire engulfed the boys' wooden dormitory, killing nineteen young students, aged seven to twelve, and their supervisor, Sister Lea.[36]

The Indian reaction to their marginal status was disillusionment and frustration. Many leaders were struck by the glaring contradictions between the authoritarian policies of the Department of Indian Affairs and the promises of the treaties. And much like western farmers, they turned to political organization to try to reverse decades of mistreatment. Shortly after the war, three reserves (Piapot, Pasqua, and Moscowpetung) in the Qu'Appelle Valley organized themselves into "allied bands" and formed what was known as the Protective Association for Indians and their Treaties. The group, as suggested by its name, initially concentrated on safeguarding treaty rights, but in 1928

Indians working as stonepickers in the Davidson area. SASKATCHEWAN ARCHIVES BOARD S-B2010

it sent a delegation to Ottawa to demand that a royal commission investigate the Department of Indian Affairs.[37] The other, larger Indian organization was inspired by Fred Loft, a Mohawk Great War veteran and outspoken critic of federal Indian policy. "Not in vain did our young men die in a strange land," he declared. "We will take our place side by side with the white people ... in this, our country."[38] Indian Affairs tried to intimidate Loft by denouncing him as a troublemaker, even a Bolshevik, but he convened the first congress of the League of Indians of Canada in northern Ontario in 1919. Two years later, the League held its first Saskatchewan meeting on the Thunderchild reserve, where delegates complained about the lack of Indian participation in decisions affecting their daily lives. Saskatchewan Indians embraced the League and made up a good portion of its prairie membership, but they had nothing to show for their efforts by the time of the fiftieth anniversary of the signing of Treaty 6 in 1926.[39]

What really distinguished Saskatchewan in the 1920s was how non-British immigrants were perceived and treated. Gone were the days of toleration. One of the first casualties of this new public mood were "Old Colony" or traditional Mennonites, who had come directly to Saskatchewan from Russia or from Manitoba with the federal assurance that there would be no interference with their religious beliefs, including their schools. But the province's new education legislation, forged in the heat of wartime passion, required Mennonite children to attend public schools and be instructed in English. The Old Colony leaders in both the Swift Current and Hague-Osler areas stubbornly refused to abide by the new regulations, seeing them as a betrayal of the agreement that had brought them to Canada, and threatened to leave. A determined Premier Martin was equally prepared not to compromise. Although several public schools were built and staffed by the provincial government in the Old Colony settlements, the parents would not send their children and were fined. Eventually about two thousand Mennonites fled the province for Mexico and Paraguay in the early 1920s, while the premier was congratulated for his firm handling of the Mennonite problem. But there were no winners in the episode. The Old Colony Mennonites, after the Doukhobors some fifteen years earlier, became the second disaffected group of immigrants to leave Saskatchewan.[40]

This emphasis on the need for conformity was shared by many Protestant church leaders in the province. E. H. Oliver, principal of the Presbyterian Theological College in Saskatoon, for example, steadfastly maintained that foreigners had to be Canadianized if the region was to remain solidly British in outlook and values. And the best way to bring this about was for the church to become actively involved in the daily lives of the immigrant population.[41] Forget about service in Africa or Asia for the time being—the Saskatchewan

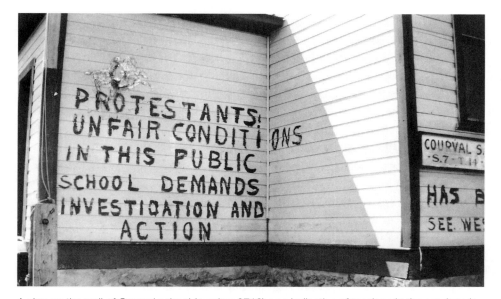

A sign on the wall of Courval school (number 2710) was indicative of tensions in the province in the late 1920s. SASKATCHEWAN ARCHIVES BOARD R-A4819(4)

frontier had become more important. This home missionary activity was carried out in such places as Wakaw, Canora, or Insinger, known for their large concentrations of continental European immigrants. It also took several forms: mission hospitals, where medical personnel were also ordained in the ministry and attended to patients' spiritual needs as well as their physical ailments; settlement homes or social settlements, where a couple offered night classes and generally served as role models of the Anglo-Canadian way of life; and home-schools, where immigrant children would be remade into good little Canadians. All of these church-run institutions expected the immigrant to meet and adhere to "appropriate" standards of Canadian citizenship and Christian behaviour. At the same time, people working in the area readily believed that the changes they were demanding of immigrants were achievable. This optimism was captured in the rephrasing of the Lord's Prayer at one of the mission facilities: "Thy Kingdom come, Thy will be done, in Calder as it is in heaven."[42]

The Martin government also took steps to speed up the assimilation of non-British immigrants by appointing Dr. J. T. M. Anderson as provincial director of education among new Canadians in 1918. Anderson, who had come west from Ontario in 1908 to be a schoolteacher, had been taken aback by the ethnic makeup of his classroom. His subsequent work as a school inspector in the Yorkton district convinced him that the "deficient" or culturally inferior "foreign element" represented the greatest threat to Canada's future well-being. It was therefore the special role of the English-only public school to serve as the training ground for Canadian norms, values, and institutions, to break the children's attachment to their home cultures and traditions, and offer them a better, brighter future as Canadian citizens loyal to the British flag and the British empire.[43] In his 1918 book on the subject, *The Education of the New Canadian*, Anderson bluntly argued that Saskatchewan had reached "a critical period" in its history and that its destiny would be determined by how it responded to the great educational problem it faced. "They [foreigners] are endangering our national existence ... making us the laughing stock of all enlightened peoples," he gravely warned. "Let us insist upon the state exercising its right to see that everyone of these New Canadians obtains what in free Canada should surely be one's birthright—a public school education!"[44] To this end, Anderson arranged to have fully qualified, English-speaking teachers paid a three-hundred-dollar annual scholarship, essentially a bonus, to work in pioneer immigrant districts.[45]

One of Anderson's great successes was the Slawa school (number 3030), located between Hafford and Radisson in a district where more than two-thirds of the population were Ukrainian. The school boasted one of the

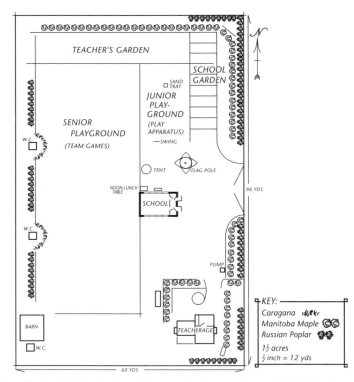

Teacher Robert England's sketch of the Slawa school grounds near Hafford in the early 1920s.

province's best teachers in the person of Robert England, who looked upon his posting as a herculean challenge. In his confidential school report for July 1922, he voiced many of the stereotypes associated with foreigners at the time: they lacked "the sense of honour;" they could be deceitful, superstitious, and childish; they were lethargic; and they did too much singing, drinking, and dancing, especially at weddings. What turned this pathetic situation around, according to England, was how he made the school "a much talked-of force in the community." In addition to teaching Canadian values and standards as an essential part of the curriculum, he and his wife offered night school, held weekly Boy Scout and Girl Guide meetings, put on plays, planted a school garden, supervised organized games, undertook home visits, and arranged field trips. The glue that held all these activities together was the speaking of English. England insisted that English not only be used in the classroom, but be the language of the playground, the lunch break, and all other school-related and community events. And it seemed to be taking hold. At the time of England's report, he had been at the Slawa school for only two years, but was pleased with the improvement in the attitude of the children and their parents. He candidly admitted, though, that "immigration from non-English-speaking countries should be restricted until our present population is assimilated."[46]

This questioning of Canada's immigration policy would become strident when prospective settlers began pouring into the province again in the mid-1920s. After the war, Ottawa initially concentrated on securing immigrants from Great Britain, the United States, and northwestern Europe. But the expected numbers never materialized, and the federal government, with the encouragement of the railways, once again turned to central and eastern Europe to fill the remaining vacant lands of western Canada. The number of immigrants remained well below the record levels of the early twentieth century. Only 8,186 headed to Saskatchewan in 1923. What was different from the pre-war period, however, was the preponderance of immigrants from "non-preferred" countries. Only 31 per cent of the immigrants in 1923–24 were British, whereas those from continental Europe represented 56 per cent.[47] This influx of non-British immigrants accelerated under the September 1925 Railways Agreement, which empowered the Canadian Pacific and Canadian National railways to recruit agricultural immigrants from central and eastern Europe. The agreement was supposed to last two years, but was extended until 1930 at the urging of the railways, which successfully argued that continental Europeans were best suited to the back-breaking work of clearing new farmland. Few, though, were actually turned away, even if they had no intention of staying on the land. Over the five-year period of the agreement, more than a third of a million continental European immigrants

Schools were expected to instill Anglo-Canadian values in immigrant children. LIBRARY AND ARCHIVES CANADA PA127070

entered Canada. The impact on Saskatchewan was reflected in the census figures for 1911 and 1931. The percentage of people of British origin in the province dropped from 54.7 to 47.5 per cent over the twenty-year period. The continental European population, on the other hand, grew to 20 per cent in 1931, an increase of more than 5 per cent. The non-British population was also younger than its British counterpart and predominantly rural.[48] Yet, despite being the most ethnically diverse province in Canada, Saskatchewan was still an Anglo-Canadian stronghold, whose political, economic, and social life was dominated by people from British backgrounds.

The new Saskatchewan premier, James Garfield (Jimmy) Gardiner, who had succeeded Dunning in February 1926, had a keen appreciation of the province's cultural pluralism. Reflecting back on his school-teaching days in the Lemberg district before the Great War, he had once observed that in the classroom "one could learn first-hand the characteristics of almost every European nationality." As provincial Liberal leader, he openly valued the contribution of continental Europeans and their role in building Saskatchewan. "In the most cosmopolitan province in the Dominion," he told the Canadian Chamber of Commerce in 1927, "we recognize men of worth, no matter where they come from."[49] Others vehemently disagreed. New immigrants were accused of taking jobs from British labourers by working for lower wages and taking land away from better-qualified settlers. They were also blamed for the increase in crime and for spreading communism. Their greatest sin, though, was destroying the Anglo-Saxon character of the province.[50] By the end of the 1920s Saskatchewan was the third most populous province (921,000) in Canada, but for many this growth came at too heavy a cost. Non-British immigration had to be severely curtailed, if not completely halted, or the province and its once great future would be lost.

One of the most outspoken critics of federal immigration policy was George Exton Lloyd, the heralded saviour of the Barr Colony and by 1922 the Anglican bishop for Saskatchewan. Known as the "fighting bishop," Lloyd believed in a British west and was prepared to do whatever was necessary to realize this vision. At first, he focused his energies on Canadianizing the foreigner. He helped bring five hundred teachers to western Canada, under the auspices of the Fellowship of the Maple Leaf, to assimilate immigrant children to British principles and traditions. He soon decided that the bigger problem was the number of non-British immigrants entering the country under the Railways Agreement and formed the appropriately named National Association of Canada to lobby the federal government for a more exclusionist policy. Lloyd publicly claimed that he was not against foreigners as long as their numbers remained manageable, but he feared that the current flood of "dirty, ignorant, garlic-smelling continentals" posed a real danger. He also maintained that too many races were being mixed in Canada and that the country was becoming a "mongrel nation." As part of his anti-immigrant crusade, Lloyd reportedly cranked out an astounding seventy thousand letters in 1928, many published by local papers, and engaged in an extensive speaking tour. "The real question at stake," he declared, "is not whether these people can grow potatoes, but whether you would like your daughter or granddaughter to marry them, that is, will they develop into good loyal citizens of Canada and the Empire?"[51]

Bishop Lloyd's anti-immigrant tirade was backstopped by a new organization in the province, the Ku Klux Klan. Reinventing itself as a British, Protestant patriotic organization, the fabled Klan entered Saskatchewan from the United States in the fall of 1926 when two organizers began selling thirteen-dollar memberships. They had no difficulty finding customers. Part of the Klan's appeal was its spirited attack on continental European immigration. It accused Ottawa of subverting the British character of the province by opening the doors to people who could never be assimilated. As one hate-mongering Klansman told a Saskatoon audience, "I am not loyal to a Canada composed of men who jabber all the tongues ... men who crowd out our own people ... by offering to work for ten cents an hour, men who come to Canada with tags on them telling you their destination. God deliver Canada from men of this character ... let us see that the slag and scum ... is skimmed off and thrown away."⁵² What made the Klan's message even more seductive, though, was its rabid anti-Catholicism. It attributed all the problems of post-war Saskatchewan—from immigration to education to immorality—to the Roman Catholic "menace" and warned that Catholics could not be trusted because they owed their allegiance to Rome. It even charged that the federal Liberal government was a mere puppet of the Catholic hierarchy which sought to create a second Quebec in the west.⁵³ One of the first Klan organizers later admitted that he "fed the people 'antis' ... whatever they could be taught to fear."⁵⁴

The Ku Klux Klan ideology found a receptive audience in Saskatchewan by exploiting existing prejudices and anxieties.⁵⁵ The Anglo-Protestant majority had always been uneasy about the settlement of "non-preferred" immigrants in the province, and the recent influx under the Railways Agreement only made the situation more worrisome. Many were distressed by the changes that Saskatchewan society was undergoing and wanted comforting answers. Anti-Catholicism also had a long history in Canada and was one of the reasons for the acrimonious debate over the 1905 autonomy bills creating Saskatchewan and Alberta. It was also a fact of daily life in the province. Francis Leddy, a future dean of arts and science at the University of Saskatchewan, recalled walking with his Catholic school chums in Saskatoon in 1919 to the Protestant chorus of "Catlickers, Catlickers."⁵⁶ The Klan's arrival in Saskatchewan, then,

Ku Klux Klan rallies in Saskatchewan, like this one at Regina in 1928, featured cross burnings. SASKATCHEWAN ARCHIVES BOARD R-A16411

could not have come at a more opportune time. By aggressively articulating the grievances of those who believed that the British character of the province was under attack, it became a force in the province—even though the first organizers absconded with the membership fees.

By 1929, the Klan boasted 25,000 members in some 125 locals or klaverns; by comparison, the SGGA never numbered more than 35,000 at the peak of its popularity in the early 1920s. Members of all three political parties in the province belonged to the Klan, as did Protestant clergymen and civic officials, including the mayor of Moose Jaw. Some prominent figures were certainly suspected of being members, but would never say. Klaverns were generally restricted to the southern half of the province in areas with a Protestant majority. One of the hotbeds of Klan activity was Moose Jaw, where organizers promised to clean up the city's notorious River Street. On 7 June 1927, Moose Jaw hosted the Klan's first major rally in the province, culminating in the nighttime burning of a giant cross before a crowd of several thousand.[57]

The temptation to capitalize on the racial and religious animosity aroused by the Saskatchewan Klan proved too much for the new provincial Conservative leader, Dr. Anderson. One year after his term as director of education among new Canadians had ended in 1923, he was selected, in the words of one Conservative delegate, as "the modern Moses ... to lead us out of the political wilderness which we have been wandering in for the last twenty years."[58] He would not disappoint the party. Anderson lashed out at federal immigration policy, insisting that Saskatchewan should have a greater say in the number and kind of immigrants that came to the province. He also derided the Gardiner government for abusing its power and influence and ignoring the rampant corruption within the administration. It was his criticism of the education system, however, that proved most effective, especially since he seemed to be speaking from experience. Anderson reported that French continued to be used beyond grade one in some of the province's public schools at the expense of English instruction. Even worse, the Protestant minority in a few districts were forced to attend Catholic-run schools with nuns serving as teachers and with crucifixes and other religious symbols on the walls.[59] This kind of sectarian influence, Anderson maintained, was abhorrent. It had to end, along with the government's odious pandering to the Catholic and non-British population of the province. He did not bother to mention that these complaints applied to only about a dozen of the province's 4,776 schools.

Premier Jimmy Gardiner, never one to back down from a good political fight despite his diminutive size, met Dr. Anderson's accusations head on. With statistics at hand, he contended that the charges about the public school system were simply not true. Nor did the new immigrants, given their numbers, constitute any threat to the province's British institutions. He also vigorously attacked the Klan as an alien growth on Saskatchewan soil, the work of extremists spewing bigotry and misinformation. Gardiner's stand was laudable, even courageous, but for one who was supposed to be so in tune with the public mood, given his adroit handling of the party's electoral machinery, he underestimated the situation his government faced. The Klan, together with nativists like Bishop Lloyd and Dr. Anderson, had broken down traditional Liberal alliances in the province and polarized Saskatchewan politics.[60] By opposing these forces, Gardiner appeared unsympathetic and unresponsive. Lloyd said as much in 1929 when he announced that the Saskatchewan government's policy on immigration "is non-British, if not anti-British ... Mr. Gardiner ... has deliberately thrown dust into the eyes of the public on this question."[61] The Gardiner government was also hurt by the fact that the Liberal party had been in office for nearly a quarter century and its appeal was slipping. Not even the 1928 disbanding of the Saskatchewan Provincial Police, whose independence had come to be questioned, and its replacement by the RCMP could end the allegations that the government had things to hide. The premier also did not help his position by refusing to co-operate with the Progressive forces in the province. Described by his biographers as a "relentless Liberal,"[62] he had no patience with third parties. Unlike his three predecessors, he invited no prominent members of the agricultural community to sit at his cabinet table.[63]

Gardiner called a provincial election for June 1929. A bitter contest, the results were mixed. The Liberals and Conservatives won twenty-eight and twenty-four seats, respectively, in the sixty-three-seat legislature, not enough for either party to form a majority government. It fell to a smattering of Progressives and independents, eleven in total, to decide the government's fate. The ever-combative Gardiner decided not to step down, but advised the lieutenant-governor to recall the legislature for early September. There, the Liberals were easily defeated on a non-confidence motion, making Gardiner the only sitting Saskatchewan premier up to that time to be defeated in office.[64] Dr. Anderson immediately formed what he termed a "Co-operative Government" in recognition of the three groups in the coalition. Gardiner considered the title fraudulent—it was really a Tory regime in disguise—and attacked the credibility of the new government at every opportunity. But his partisan theatrics could not deny the fact that the Anderson coalition had ended an era in Saskatchewan political history.

The new Co-operative government lost little time fixing the supposed educational shortcomings that had been the subject of so much controversy. As of July 1930, the wearing of religious garb and the displaying of religious symbols were banned in the province's public schools. Less than a year later, the School Act was further amended to forbid the teaching of French in the first grade; it could be taught only as a language of study for one hour each day.[65] Premier Anderson also tackled the immigration question by appointing a provincial royal commission in January 1930 to examine past federal policies and recommend a strategy for the future. After six months of testimony, the commission recommended that immigration policy be more selective by giving British settlers preferential treatment.[66] The school legislation and immigration hearings were a response to the very real concerns that helped put Anderson in office, but did nothing to resolve the larger issue that the province faced at the end of the 1920s—namely, the place of non-British immigrants. These people had come to Saskatchewan, just like Anglo-Canadian settlers, to start a new life in a new province. They also had dreams of a better future and knew they had to adjust to survive and prosper. But their cultural distinctiveness was not something that could be checked at the provincial boundaries as if it were baggage. Saskatchewan had to find a way to accommodate the new immigrants, a way of accepting them as valued citizens. That would be a true test of the province's character.

The Konias family, which settled at Henribourg, was part of a new wave of continental European immigrants in the mid-1920s. SASKATCHEWAN ARCHIVES BOARD R94-390, P. 29

CHAPTER THIRTEEN

WHERE WE LEFT OFF

ONE OF THE CASUALTIES OF THE GREAT WAR was Canada's fiftieth birthday party. With the outcome of the European conflict still in doubt in 1917, the celebration of Dominion Day was a subdued affair. That made the next major anniversary, the 1927 diamond jubilee, all the more special. Regina, like many other communities across the country, hosted an afternoon parade through the downtown streets, led by serge-clad RCMP on horseback. At Wascana Park, two thousand singing schoolchildren opened the official program, followed by several short messages of congratulations and a reading of some of the speeches by the political leaders who helped bring about Confederation in 1867. Although the official theme was Canada's achievements over the past sixty years, Premier Jimmy Gardiner was clearly thinking of the future. At his fulsome best, he alluded to the Saskatchewan success story, noting how Canada's founders had made possible "this great Province, already the third Province of the Canadian Confederation."[1] Gardiner's remarks were backed up by a full-page government ad in a special edition of the *Regina Leader*. An impressive list of statistics confirmed Saskatchewan's place as the third wealthiest province and the granary of the world. There was no mistaking the undercurrent. The day may have belonged to Canada, but Saskatchewan owned the future.

⟿

When the guns finally fell silent in Europe, Saskatchewan optimistically looked forward to a return of the heady days of the early twentieth century. In fact, the war years, with their seemingly insatiable demand for wheat, had only strengthened the province's conviction that it held a central place in Canada's future. The sense of self-importance had never been stronger. In November 1918, Premier William Martin confidently predicted "the beginning of our development again at the point where we left off when the war began."[2] But the end of the fighting in Europe was followed in 1920 by a stubborn recession that the country was unable to shake for the next three years. As the shrinking economy tried to adjust to peacetime conditions, demobilized soldiers and laid-off workers swelled the ranks of the unemployed, while hundreds of businesses, including the western-based Home Bank, failed. Canada's gross national product, the indicator of the country's economic health, declined by one-fifth in 1921 and continued its slide the following year. Exports decreased as well, falling in value from $1.24 billion in 1920 to just $740 million two years later.[3]

The prairies were particularly hard hit by the post-war recession. Wheat prices tumbled more than 75 per cent from a high of $2.63 per bushel in 1919 to a mere 65 cents in 1923. This collapse was a cruel blow to farmers whose production costs and debt loads had steadily escalated in response to the wartime appetite for wheat. And they blamed the Union government for their troubles. During the last year of the war, Ottawa had temporarily suspended the open-market system for buying and selling Canadian wheat and assumed monopoly control under a Board of Grain Supervisors, later renamed the Wheat Board. Instead of being paid the price of wheat at the time of delivery, producers received an initial payment and then subsequent payments based on the average price for that year's crop. This arrangement brought much-needed stability and rewarded farmers with the same price for their wheat, and generally a high one at that. The federal government, however, was anxious to remove itself from the economy at war's end and restored the private grain trade for the 1920 crop year. Farmers naturally attributed the subsequent drop in wheat prices to the killing of the Wheat Board, when in fact the depressed prices were largely a consequence of several countries, in particular Argentina and Australia, dumping huge surpluses of wheat on the world market after the war.[4] Indeed, the situation could have been worse for the western farmer had the Union government not rescued the bankrupt

The rapid growth of the four western provinces translated into more seats
in the federal House of Commons. *Montreal Star*, 15 February 1923

Grand Trunk Pacific and Canadian Northern railways by forming Canadian
National Railways (CNR) in 1919. The loss of the two railways would have
seriously disrupted the movement of grain and been catastrophic for settlers
in the northern prairies. As it was, less than a hundred miles of track were
added to the province's rail network in the early 1920s.[5]

Farmers had survived lower crop yields during the last years of the war
because of record-high wheat prices. But the collapse in prices spelled the end
for small, marginal operations. Between 1921 and 1926, for the first time in
provincial history, the number of farms actually declined—from 119,451 to
117,781. Many abandoned farms were in southwestern Saskatchewan, where
there had not been a decent crop since 1916 because of an unrelenting
drought. The poor harvests, combined with mounting farm debts, prompted
a mass exodus from the region, even before the post-war recession. The Maple
Creek district lost a quarter of its original homesteaders between 1911 and 1921
and even more during the early 1920s.[6] It has been estimated that as many as
two-thirds of the Americans who immigrated to southern Saskatchewan

before the war had returned to the United States by the mid-1920s.[7] Poor hay crops also decimated the local ranching industry. Horses were evacuated en masse, while cattle shipments from the region had never been higher since the brutal winter of 1906–07.[8]

W. R. Motherwell, the provincial minister of agriculture, ascribed the repeated crop failures to the settlers, claiming in 1918 that "success or non-success is chiefly ... due to straight good or bad farming."[9] Wheat King Seager Wheeler also insisted that it was "possible to grow a very satisfactory crop in any season."[10] But the dry farming techniques heralded by the two agricultural experts only made the situation worse in the south country. By constantly keeping summerfallow free of weeds by regular ploughing, the soil began to drift and was soon out of control in several areas. Mixed farming was also not the answer, since feed crops suffered during the drought. Some even began to wonder whether the region should ever have been opened to homesteading in 1908. "After the land is broken up," a surveyor working along the international border lamented, "it is fit for nothing."[11]

The provincial government, inundated with demands for relief, convened a Better Farming Conference in Swift Current in early July 1920 to discuss how best to deal with the crisis. John Bracken, formerly of the University of Saskatchewan College of Agriculture and soon to be Manitoba premier, touted the merits of scientific agriculture. "We have been farming too much on faith and have not had enough facts," he declared.[12] Those facts were soon forthcoming when the province established a royal commission to investigate farming conditions in the region. The committee toured the region and held public hearings in twelve communities in October 1920, handing out questionnaires to farmers and ranchers. One man expressed the frustration of many when he asked: "If we go, how can we go? If we stay, how can we stay?"[13] The commission's 1921 report recommended the creation of local agricultural research stations, a comprehensive soil survey, and the development of community grazing tracts. But nowhere did it question the suitability of the land for farming or ranching. The report suggested that the region "probably" had less precipitation than other parts of the province, but added that southwestern Saskatchewan was "undoubtedly ... capable of sustaining a large number of people."[14]

This faith in the potential of the land was an integral part of the 1917 Soldier Settlement Act, a plan by the federal government to reward Great War veterans and help them make the transition to civilian life by placing them on western homesteads. All unoccupied dominion lands within fifteen miles of a railway were to be set aside in 320-acre parcels (160 acres of soldier settlement land and 160 acres of homestead land). Loans were also provided for buildings, equipment, and stock. Because of heavy settlement over the past two decades, the Saskatchewan contribution to the scheme was largely confined to the so-called forest fringe or northern edge of the parkland, from Hudson Bay Junction on the east to the region north of Prince Albert and around Turtle and Brightsand lakes on the west. Although the provincial government readily admitted that it was not the best agricultural land, it still believed that it might provide as many as 100,000 homesteads. The Soldier Settlement Board also withdrew 200,000 acres from the Porcupine Forest reserve in east-central Saskatchewan, despite the fact that this tract had been closed to settlement before the war because of the rolling, heavily timbered terrain and gravelly or sandy soils.[15]

Ottawa expected tens of thousands of veterans to apply for Soldier Settlement land, given the money to be made from agriculture—and they did. But picking land and getting settled was another matter. As late as November 1920, only five thousand veterans had taken up farms in Saskatchewan under the plan.[16] The Soldier Settlement Board decided that the problem was the quality of the land along the southern edge of the boreal forest and began to cast about for something more fertile and accessible. The search quickly zeroed in on Indian reserves. Not surprisingly, the Department of Indian Affairs agreed to co-operate with this patriotic initiative and readily identified "surplus" or "underutilized" Indian lands to be sold, by compulsion if necessary, to the Soldier Settlement Board.

The first batch of surrenders was officially announced in July 1919. Six Saskatchewan reserves turned over a total of 72,620 acres, well above the 2,500 and 6,000 acres secured in Manitoba and Alberta, respectively. The Wood Mountain Sioux, having finally secured a reserve only seven years earlier, lost half their land (5,760 acres), while the Ochapowace reserve, which had strenuously resisted all surrender efforts before the war, gave up over 18,000 acres.[17] Given agricultural prices at the time, the reserves might have expected to enjoy a small windfall, but the Soldier Settlement Board was able to acquire some of the best agricultural land in the province at bargain rates.[18] What made this process especially tragic was that Indian veterans, unlike their white counterparts, were not eligible for Soldier Settlement land. The few that qualified for a grant—less than 1 per cent of the approved applicants—were given small parcels cleaved from their home reserve.[19]

All Soldier Settlement grant applicants were supposed to have some practical agricultural experience, but local officials were not prepared "to deny a returned man a chance to try his hand at farming."[20] Efforts were made, however, to try to lessen the pioneering challenge by providing some basic services in more remote areas. The first Red Cross Outpost Hospital in the British Empire, for example, opened in October 1920 at Paddockwood, north of Prince Albert. But the real problem for many soldier settlers proved to be

the marginal land they were expected to transform into viable farm operations. It took several back-breaking months, especially in the Porcupine
settlement, to clear trees and pick stones. One Smoking Tent pioneer near
the Etomani River jokingly recalled, "When I removed one of my stumps I
had a huge hole, large enough for a good size[d] cellar."[21] Another grumbled
about his homestead "sitting in water ... surrounded by mosquitoes."[22] What
made things worse was that veterans embarked on their new farming career
just as agricultural prices started to drop in 1920. They stubbornly held out
for as long as they could, but the failure rate steadily increased each passing
year. Those who remained on their plots survived at a subsistence level, rarely
marketing a crop.[23]

Established farmers had problems of their own. In 1920, they harvested
113 million bushels of wheat, considerably less than the 1915 provincial record
but still more than Manitoba and Alberta combined. Three years later, they
brought in the largest crop in Saskatchewan history: 271.6 million bushels.
These returns should have pleased farmers—and their creditors—but not
when wheat prices were below a dollar. Despite the record harvest, farm
income still dropped by sixty million dollars in 1923.[24] Farmers also had to
contend with higher freight rates. In 1918, while the Union government was
moving to nationalize the Grand Trunk Pacific and Canadian Northern railways, western rates were advanced 15 per cent and then another 25 per cent
because of wartime inflation. A further, larger rate increase was introduced
two years later, just before wheat prices swooned. Where it had cost twenty-
four cents to ship a hundred pounds of wheat from Saskatoon to the
Lakehead at the start of the war, the freight bill stood at thirty-eight cents in
September 1920. These higher grain-handling charges aggravated the situation of Saskatchewan farmers, who were more than a thousand miles from
the shipping ports.[25] It seemed as if their old grievances about the grain-handling and marketing system were getting worse.

Premier Martin tried to deal with the slumping wheat prices by consulting with local farm leaders about the possibility of creating a provincial pool,
similar to the one that had been run by the Union government.[26] His successor, Charles Dunning, then held a special legislative session in June 1922
to formally endorse a scheme to re-establish a compulsory national wheat
board. When that solution failed, Dunning tried to work with the other two
prairie provinces to create a regional wheat board, but had nothing to show
for his efforts after two years of fruitless negotiations. It consequently fell to
the farmers to come up with their own solution. In December 1921, the
Farmers' Union of Canada (FUC), a more militant farmers' organization, was
organized in Ituna and actively began to pursue economic solutions to
farmers' long-standing problems. One of its first initiatives was the creation

In 1924, Premier Charles Dunning visited the British foundry where he had worked as a boy before coming to Canada. SASKATCHEWAN ARCHIVES BOARD R-B29

of a voluntary provincial wheat pool, where members would be contractually committed to deliver their crop for a five-year period. The larger SGGA initially refused to cooperate with its new rival and pursued an alternative pooling scheme until Premier Dunning used his influence to convince the two organizations to work together.

The organizational drive to get farmers to sign up for the Saskatchewan Wheat Pool was launched in the summer of 1923. Those behind the campaign realized that at least 50 per cent of the province's wheat acreage had to be under contract for the pool to succeed. To help achieve this goal, the SGGA began publication of its own newspaper, *The Progressive* (renamed *The Western Producer* the following year), to extol the merits of the scheme. The premier also issued an official statement calling on interested farmers to take out contracts.[27] The person who turned the membership drive into an evangelical crusade, however, was Aaron Sapiro, a California lawyer and produce pool organizer, who had been invited to western Canada to help get wheat pools off the ground in the three provinces. Sapiro spoke with fervour and commitment. At the Third Avenue Methodist Church in Saskatoon he made co-operative marketing sound like God's plan of salvation. "Get wise! Organize!" he thundered. "Organize rightly, and if you do it now, you will not only be doing the greatest thing you have ever done for yourselves … but you will be contributing the finest thing you have ever done … towards the citizenship of your whole province."[28] Frank Underhill, a University of

Saskatchewan history professor at the time, remembered almost half a century later that "his speech was the most magnificent to which I have ever listened."[29] Sadly, though, Sapiro's spirit of harmony ran smack into the rising nativism of the period. When Ukrainian-Canadian John Stratychuck spoke at pool rallies, he was treated to shouts of "bohunk" and "goddamn foreigner."[30]

By June 1924, the Saskatchewan Co-operative Wheat Producers had signed up enough members to begin pooling. The new organization initially used the storage space of existing grain elevator systems in the province. But within two years, the more radical FUC had successfully spearheaded a drive by the wheat pool to purchase the facilities of the Saskatchewan Cooperative Elevator Company. The momentum generated by this union of the two largest provincial grain-handling and marketing bodies led to the amalgamation of the province's two farmers' organization later that same year. Putting aside their rivalry in the interests of the agrarian community, the SGGA and the FUC formed the United Farmers of Canada (Saskatchewan Section) (UFC). Despite the optimism behind the title, there would be no other provincial sections. The new Saskatchewan Wheat Pool also joined with its counterparts in the other two prairie provinces to form a central selling agency in Winnipeg. Offices were soon opened in several Canadian ports, as

"Getting into a Comfortable Place." *Grain Growers' Guide*, 1 August 1923

well as in New York and fifteen wheat-importing countries. There was much at stake. Collectively, the three pools controlled 60 per cent of the prairie wheat crop.[31]

The emergence of the Saskatchewan Wheat Pool did not mean the end of the open market system. Instead, it offered producers an alternative way to sell their wheat. Farmers no longer had to play the perennial guessing game of when to market their crop; they got the same price as all other pool members, no matter when they fulfilled their delivery contract. The pool also did not shield farmers from fluctuating wheat prices; members may have received a better price for their wheat than some of their non-pool neighbours, but they were still at the mercy of international markets. In order to reduce this vulnerability, some Saskatchewan agricultural leaders argued that the pool should be made compulsory. By controlling the entire Canadian wheat crop, they insisted, farmers could not be pushed around and would collectively fare better in the world marketplace. Opponents, on the other hand, maintained that a 100 per cent pool would weaken the voluntary, co-operative spirit behind the movement and incur the resentment of more traditional, independently minded farmers. Although the issue was never resolved, the debate over co-operative activity encouraged the growth of pooling in other areas, such as dairying and egg production. Consumer co-operatives were also placed on a sounder footing during these years.[32] By the 1920s, there were three hundred co-operative buying clubs in the province, which purchased products in bulk, such as a boxcar of sugar, for distribution to members at lower prices. There were also several local Co-op retail stores, created under the auspices of the SGGA Trading Department, which carried hardware and other farm supplies, groceries, and even petroleum. In 1929, the UFC turned control of the wholesale business over to the consumer co-operatives through the creation of the new Saskatchewan Co-operative Wholesale Society. It would go on to become the largest co-operative wholesaling operation in the country.[33]

The creation of the Saskatchewan Wheat Pool coincided with western freight rate relief. When the federal Progressive party swept the prairie west and rural Ontario in the 1921 general election to become the second largest group in the House of Commons, many expected a profound shift in Canadian politics. The Progressives and their reform mandate now held the balance of power, and neither the Liberals nor Conservatives could govern without their support. But the Progressives, in keeping with their independent spirit, refused to enter into a formal agreement with the Mackenzie King Liberals, who held the largest block of seats in the new Parliament. Nor did they want to directly challenge the Liberals and form the official opposition, even though they had more representatives than the Conservative party,

The front entrance to the Sherwood Building in Regina, 1926. SASKATCHEWAN ARCHIVES BOARD R-A15020

now led by Arthur Meighen. Instead, the Progressives decided to support the minority Liberals on a conditional basis. This strategy effectively neutered the new party and left it with little flexibility. When the Liberals introduced piddling reductions to the tariff in the 1922 budget, the Progressives were forced to support the government, even though free trade had been a key plank in the party's election platform. The alternative was to side with the tariff-happy Conservatives, who were opposed to any change in policy. This dismal turn of events fuelled western disillusionment with the Progressive experiment and sent many supporters off in search of economic solutions.

The Progressives showed more backbone when it came to the restoration of the Crow's Nest Pass freight rate. In 1897, the Laurier government had struck a deal with the CPR to help finance a new line through the Crow's Nest Pass from Lethbridge to Nelson to access the promising mineral deposits of southwestern British Columbia. In exchange for a federal cash subsidy, the CPR agreed, *in perpetuity,* to lower rates on flour and grain moving east to the Lakehead and on certain settlers' items moving west. The new rates, written right into the legislation, were a transportation bargain for prairie farmers. It cost half a cent to move a ton of grain a mile.[34]

But in 1918, the Union government temporarily suspended the statutory rates because of wartime needs. Four years later when the rates were scheduled to come into force again, Prime Minister King wanted to refer the matter to a select committee in order to dodge opposition from the railways.

The Progressives, however, rallied in support of the Crow and threatened to bring the government down unless this major western demand was acted upon. King was cornered, and after protracted negotiations with the CPR, agreed to introduce legislation that would restore the rates on a partial basis. As of 1925, the Crow would apply to all railway lines in western Canada, but be restricted to grain and unprocessed products.[35] It proved to be "the most notable legislative achievement" of the Progressives.[36]

Canada finally managed to climb out of the recession by 1924. Wheat prices also began to rebound and reached $1.21, almost twice as high as a year earlier. But in a cruel twist of fate, drought gripped much of the southern half of the province that summer. Even though more acres were devoted to wheat than any other previous crop year, the 1924 harvest was less than half the previous year. The average yield was only 10.2 bushels per acre, a new low for the decade. Many experienced farmers looked upon the harvest stoically. Israel Hoffer, a Jewish homesteader in the Alameda area with an unshakeable faith in the land, had a habit of saying, "Next year ... things will be different."[37] It was a much different story for farmers in southwestern Saskatchewan. Writer Wallace Stegner remembered his father, George, growing "furious" with the failure of his Eastend-area farm and sometimes getting in the way of that fury.[38]

George Stegner's anger was understandable. In July 1922, Anton Huelskamp, the postmaster at Masonville along the eastern edge of the Great Sand Hills, wrote Premier Dunning requesting government assistance to

The booming western economy in the late 1920s was reflected in the volume of traffic in the Moose Jaw rail yards. MOOSE JAW ARCHIVES 94-328

move his young family out of the district. It was one of the last letters that he handled in his official capacity. The town that had been founded in 1914 simply disappeared that fall, as if swallowed up, and cannot be found today on any map or in any gazetteer. The plight of the region's farmers became so desperate that Ottawa approved an amendment to the Dominion Lands Act in May 1923 to fund their removal. Hundreds were evacuated.[39] Thousands more simply left on their own. The provincial government wanted nothing to do with the relocation. Department of Agriculture officials claimed that any provincial involvement was as "unreasonable as it is unnecessary" since the federal government had coaxed homesteaders into the region.[40] They also blamed farmers for not diversifying. The premier, not wanting the evacuation to become an exodus, callously accused the people of giving up. Those who were leaving the land "are the least competent of our settlers," he coldly told the minister of the interior in May 1924, "and are not entitled to further assistance."[41]

Good weather returned in 1925, and with the Saskatchewan Wheat Pool now in place, the Crow rate restored to its historic low level, and international wheat prices holding steady, the province's farmers sowed as much wheat as possible. Almost two-and-a-half million *more* acres were devoted to wheat that year. From 1925 to 1927, total production averaged 236 million bushels, but the bumper year was 1928, when an astounding 321.2 million bushels of wheat—almost a third of a billion—were harvested, with an average yield of 23.3 bushels per acre. The crop was the largest ever produced by any province or state in the world.[42]

These kinds of harvests, together with better prices, only encouraged more farms to grow more wheat. They also gave farmers another reason not to diversify their operations. Many had already been dissuaded from raising cattle by a new American tariff on cattle imports and a drastic decline in British demand. Beef prices in 1924 reached their lowest point since the killing winter of 1906–07. Advocates of mixed farming could not have been pushing animal husbandry at a worse time. Growing wheat was also seen to be less demanding. A municipal official once explained "that mixed farming is too much work and as long as they can get by with wheat farming they will."[43]

The return of good harvests and good prices coincided with the arrival under the Railways Agreement of tens of thousands of new immigrants taking up farms in the provincial parkland. The buoyant mood also kick-started new branch-line construction reminiscent of the pre-war boom. The CPR and CNR, in a fierce battle for traffic, added another two thousand miles of track to the provincial rail network during the decade. Settlers in the southwest, meanwhile, seemed to develop amnesia about past drought conditions. Wetter growing conditions produced larger yields that encouraged more farmers to take up land in the region or bring more acreage into production. Between 1921 and 1931, more than a third of a million acres were broken by the plough, most of it during the latter part of the decade.[44] The CPR also overcame its reluctance to build in the region and laid track from Assiniboia to Mankota, from Rockglen to Killdeer, and from Consul east along the international border to Val Marie, formerly 70 Mile Crossing. Until the construction of these branch lines, southwestern Saskatchewan had been one of the most isolated agricultural regions in the province, with some homesteaders more than fifty miles away from the railway.[45] The real sign of the changing face of the region was the federal government's decision not to renew the Sand Lake lease of the 76 Ranch, the last great ranch from the late nineteenth century. Once the company learned of the decision, it moved its operations to Montana in 1926 rather than fight Ottawa's ruling. The 76's departure opened up seventy-seven thousand acres to homesteading. Dozens stood in line overnight at the new Val Marie Dominion Lands office for their chance at the land. But Phillip Long, the son of the ranch foreman, knew what awaited them, how their "dreams [would] dry up and blow away."[46]

This obsession with growing as much wheat as possible came at the expense of a more diversified provincial economy. In 1920, the Martin government had created a Bureau of Labour and Industries to encourage exploitation of Saskatchewan's natural resources and lessen the dependence on agriculture. Most of the bureau's energies were initially devoted to commercial development of large lignite coal deposits in the Estevan-Bienfait area. The bureau also sent exploration parties north in the early 1920s to examine mineral deposits in the Lac La Ronge district.[47] But these activities were hampered by the post-war recession and generally took a back seat to wheat production, especially once prices recovered. Large corporations also investigated the resource potential of the province. An Imperial Oil geological party, for example, conducted a brief survey in 1919, but left without drilling a single test hole. The return of prosperity in the mid-1920s sparked new exploration, especially in the Unity-Vera area, but all wells came in dry.[48]

Mining showed more promise. As early as 1914, prospectors working out of Prince Albert found gold on Amisk (Beaver) Lake along Saskatchewan's northeastern boundary. The small boom was eclipsed the following year when Tom Creighton discovered copper, silver, and gold on the Manitoba side of the border at Flin Flon.[49] Teams of prospectors swarmed the region, using airplanes and outboard motors to investigate a greater range of territory. The *Regina Leader* even predicted that northern Saskatchewan was "on the eve of great development."[50] But the drop in base metal prices in 1920 put a damper on what companies were willing to spend in the region to bring mines into operation.

Gold prospectors with their gear setting across frozen Lake Athabasca in 1919. SASKATCHEWAN ARCHIVES BOARD R-A9257(3)

The lumber industry limped into the new decade as well. Wartime demand had hinted at a different fate. In 1916, the Prince Albert Lumber Company confidently reported that it was "cleaned out of every stick of lumber as fast as it runs through the mill."[51] In fact, during the winter of 1917–18, the company hauled over half a million logs from the forest south of Red Deer (Waskesiu) Lake in present-day Prince Albert National Park. This intensive cutting quickly exhausted trees in its southern timber berths, and the more northerly berths set aside by the federal government were too distant from Prince Albert. The company consequently announced in October 1918 that it was suspending operations in Prince Albert in favour of establishing a smaller mill closer to the timber stands at some future date. Then, disaster struck. A fire, fed by the brush of old logging slashes, burned a large stretch of the forest south of Red Deer Lake in the spring of 1919. The roar of the blaze was heard as far away as Montreal Lake and left the region covered in ash. Estimates of the damage varied: government cruisers reported that 50 per cent of the timber had been fire-killed, whereas company representatives put the figure at 90 to 100 per cent. Although federal forestry officials were anxious that the remaining good timber be culled as soon as possible, the Prince Albert Lumber Company decided to relocate its operations to northern Manitoba. It instructed the federal forestry branch to cancel its remaining timber berths and do what it pleased with thousands of logs that had been left behind in the bush or along the Spruce River. That left the Big

River Lumber Company as the only major player in the region, but it too soon closed its mill and forfeited its timber berths. Smaller companies with portable sawmills continued to cut trees through the 1920s, but provincial production was one-seventh of what it had been in 1912.[52]

The commercial fishery was the only northern resource activity that really thrived during the period. Moving steadily north, companies like the Northern Saskatchewan Fish Company, Waite Fisheries, Johnson Fisheries, and the McInnis Fish Company claimed the best lakes in the region and heavily fished them each winter. There was no catch limit. In 1921, sixty-nine men working for Waite Fisheries of Big River netted over four hundred thousand pounds of fish (mostly whitefish) on Red Deer, Little Trout, and Big Trout Lakes. The annual catch fluctuated over the next few years, but production was nonetheless staggering: over two million pounds of fish were pulled from the three lakes and hauled to Big River over five seasons.[53] This insatiable demand took its toll on northern lakes, especially since fish grow slowly in cold water. Waste was common; in one instance, Johnson Fisheries left over one hundred thousand pounds of fish to rot along the shores of Peter Pond and Churchill lakes when spring came early in 1924.

Commercial fishing also led to considerable hardship for the Cree and Dene population when traditional fishing sites were exhausted. In 1929, Father Riou at Stony Rapids in the northwest corner of the province pleaded with the federal government to prevent commercial companies from working nearby Black Lake. The local RNWMP corporal countered that the Fond du Lac Dene band did mostly hunting and trapping, and that the commercial fishery should have a free hand in the area. This dismissal of Indian interests, despite the provisions of Treaty 10, was not the first time that Aboriginal access to a traditional source of food was compromised. In 1917, Ottawa had explicitly forbidden Indians from splitting and drying fish for the winter to ensure that there was no competition with commercial operations. The federal government also later assigned Indians a few protected lakes, including Bittern south of Montreal, while reserving the majority of the northern lakes for commercial purposes.[54]

Indian trapping and hunting were also increasingly threatened by non-Native competition. High fur prices at the end of the war enticed hundreds of white trappers to the region, first along the Churchill River and then as far north as Cree, Wollaston, Reindeer, and Athabasca lakes. Buyers for Revillon Frères, the Hudson's Bay Company's major competitor in the region, were ready to pay cash for quality furs. These newcomers disrupted Indian trapping activities, but as long as prices were high, most prospered. One local trapper, Tommy Clarke, arrived at a HBC post with four thousand dollars' worth of furs after only two months on his trapline south of Wollaston in the fall of 1919.[55] The collapse of prices in 1920, however, staggered the fur industry. Revillon Frères began a retreat from the region that ended in bankruptcy, while more than half the HBC posts in the Saskatchewan district reported losses for 1922. The downturn led to overtrapping and overhunting as Indians, Métis, and whites scrambled to earn a living. The HBC, meanwhile, reduced employment opportunities at posts in order to trim operating expenses. It also balked at providing relief to its loyal Aboriginal customers as it had done in the past.[56]

Northern Indians sustained another blow in 1919 when the Saskatchewan government, with the concurrence of the federal Department of Indian Affairs, started to apply provincial game laws to the Cree and Dene of the Treaty 10 area. By the early 1920s, there were more game guardians and Saskatchewan Provincial Police constables in northern Saskatchewan than in any other part of the province. Managing the province's wildlife resources was apparently more important than the Indian need for food and resulted in widespread destitution. Commercial fishing, lumbering, and mining, on the other hand, seemed to be immune from the conservation regulations.[57]

The uneven health of the northern economy greatly troubled the city of Prince Albert. Like other Saskatchewan cities in the early 1920s, it faced a long, slow recovery after the Great War. It anxiously looked to its favoured position as the gateway to the provincial north to shield it from the worst effects of the post-war agricultural recession. But when the lumber industry shut down, Prince Albert cast an envious glance at Banff and Jasper national parks in Alberta and decided that it too would try to get involved in the lucrative tourist industry. The opportunity to cash in on the scenery of northern Saskatchewan came unexpectedly in October 1925 when William Lyon Mackenzie King, who would become Canada's longest-serving prime minister, lost his seat in the federal election. Within a few weeks of the defeat, Jimmy Gardiner, the new Liberal premier of Saskatchewan, telegraphed King that the MP for Prince Albert was willing to step aside.[58] Not one to question destiny—King's mentor, Wilfrid Laurier, had won election in the district of Saskatchewan (which included Prince Albert) in 1896—the prime minister gladly accepted the invitation. What he did not realize, though, was that the offer of a safe Liberal seat came at a price: a national park north of the city in the Sturgeon River Forest reserve. King agreed to the deal, and in March 1927, his government created the fourteen-hundred-square-mile Prince Albert National Park over strenuous objections by federal park authorities who resented the political interference. At the official opening ceremonies the following August, the organizing committee presented the prime minister with a cottage on the shores of Lake Waskesiu as a gift for his role in securing the park.[59]

The establishment of Prince Albert National Park demonstrated the lengths to which the city was prepared to go to turn its fortunes around. Other Saskatchewan urban centres were just as desperate. The return of thousands of soldiers only added to the chronic unemployment that was a defining feature of western cities during this period. So too were their debt loads, a hangover from the pre-1913 building spree that showed no signs of abating. In 1925, Saskatchewan cities spent on average 43 per cent of their budgets on debt charges. Tax arrears also continued to be a serious problem. Hundreds of lots were forfeited to cities because of the non-payment of taxes. The situation in Saskatoon was particularly acute. The value of tax arrears and acquired land stood at $1,860,000 in 1926, up by almost half a million dollars from 1921. The city responded by jacking up assessment rates and introducing new municipal taxes.[60] Regina, although much better off, would spend the 1920s trying to consolidate the urban landscape. There were a few major building projects during the decade, most notably the Hotel Saskatchewan (1927), but the downtown core saw little significant change. Vacant lots served as a reminder of what might have been. Even more symbolic was the transfer of national police headquarters to Ottawa to coincide with the 1919 creation of the RCMP. This loss was tempered, however, by the fact that Regina remained the training depot for the new force—no small concession when the barracks were the city's number-one tourist attraction throughout the 1920s.[61]

By the end of the 1920s, more and more farmers were adding combines to their arsenal of machinery. SASKATCHEWAN ARCHIVES BOARD R-A15122-1

Saskatchewan cities might have fared better during this period had their economic base not been so narrow, but manufacturing was limited at best, in part a consequence of wartime demand for food. Remarkably, the province had less than sixty-two hundred industrial workers at a time when urbanization and industrialization were transforming the face of Canada, especially Ontario and Quebec. What kept cities and towns going was what had always kept them going—serving the province's agricultural community. When wheat prices began to recover from the post-war slump, there was a corresponding sharp rise in retail and wholesale trade in the province. In Regina, for example, Eaton's greeted the return of prosperity with a new department store, while construction companies had never been busier since 1913. The city also emerged by the end of the decade as Canada's largest distributor of farm machinery, surpassing long-time rival Winnipeg. In 1928, the year of the record provincial wheat harvest, Regina dealers sold thirty-eight million dollars' worth of equipment. Local car dealerships did almost as well, which might have been a deciding factor in convincing General Motors to build a large car-assembly plant in the city. Imperial Oil was already poised to take advantage of the growing regional demand for petroleum products and had built a refinery on the north side of Regina just before the end of the war.[62]

The mechanization of agriculture was one of the most far-reaching developments of the 1920s. This process had started before the Great War, but roared into the new decade with the improvement of the internal combustion engine, the introduction of new power machinery, and stronger commodity prices. The number of tractors on Saskatchewan farms more than doubled from 19,243 in 1921 to 43,308 ten years later. Truck registrations also climbed dramatically during the latter part of the decade, from 8,688 in 1926 to 18,861 by 1929. When truck and car registrations are combined (76,032 in 1932), Saskatchewan had the highest ratio of vehicles per one thousand people in the country. Farmers running larger operations also began to buy the new combine-harvester, normally on credit. At the beginning of the decade, the technology was relatively new and sales were modest, but in 1928, Saskatchewan farmers purchased 2,356 combines, a sixfold increase from the previous year. Sales were even stronger in 1929, reaching almost 2,500, or 70 per cent of the machines sold on the prairies. The widespread adoption of the combine, however, was still several decades away. By 1931, less than 5 per cent (6,019) of the province's 136,472 farms used one of the new machines. Indeed, conditions among soldier settlers and new immigrants in the parkland were still more in keeping with the nineteenth century. Nor had Saskatchewan farmers ceased to use draught animals. In 1926, the horse population peaked at 1.1 million. In other words, there were more horses than people in the province.[63]

The heavy trucks, tractors, and other new agricultural implements began a revolution in Saskatchewan farming whose repercussions are still being experienced today. The labour-saving machinery enabled the province's farmers to get crops planted and harvested in a shorter period of time and thereby lessened the threat of frost damage. It also strengthened the trend towards larger farm size. Individual farmers could not only handle bigger farms, but found it more economical to operate the machinery on more fields. As a consequence, average farm size grew to 390 acres by 1926 and then 407.8 acres five years later. At least 70 per cent of the province's farmers held more than 200 acres of land.[64] These new conditions did not end the need for hired help, but altered the nature of the relationship. Whereas hired hands in the past usually aspired to become farmers themselves, that kind of opportunity was now rare. Instead, because of the large pool of available workers, farmers tended to treat hired help as little better than a "proletariat," expecting them to handle the dirty or physically demanding jobs and then move on.[65] Indians and Métis labourers sometimes filled this role. They also continued to supply firewood, hay, and fence pickets, often neglecting their own attempts at farming in the process.[66]

Farm mechanization was seldom accompanied by labour-saving devices in the farm home. Women and children were still expected to perform monotonous labour in and around the house, when not helping in the fields. Leaders of the Women's Grain Growers' Association and later the Women's Section of the UFC repeatedly called for an end to this drudgery, insisting that an efficient home was essential to an efficient farm. Why should the barn, they asked, be better equipped than the house? Violet McNaughton, editor

Farm Girls' Week at the University of Saskatchewan. UNIVERSITY OF SASKATCHEWAN ARCHIVES A-1326

of the women's pages of *The Western Producer*, even launched "The Running Water Club" to promote the installation of indoor water systems and eliminate the hauling of water from wells in all kinds of weather. But when it came to spending money on the new labour-savers, the operation of the farm came first. And since farm machinery did not require electricity, the rural household went without a number of domestic appliances, such as a washing machine, that were considered necessities by urban women.[67]

Other technology, however, was readily incorporated, especially if it helped end the loneliness and isolation of the farm. By the 1920s, many rural homes had a telephone, an innovation that led to a popular new hobby: listening in to conversations on the party line. Fewer families had cars, but those that did were able to go to town on a more regular basis. Come winter, though, the vehicles were often put away for several months. The most memorable addition to the home was the wireless radio. People recall nostalgically how the wireless opened a new world to them. They would lie on the floor, propped up by their arms before the radio's speaker, and listen for hours to shows from stations whose call signs were memorized like the ABCs.[68] Harlo Jones of Dinsmore was one of them: "Just as today's children would find it difficult to imagine a world without television, I would have difficulty trying to envision our world ... without radio. We children didn't find the news a great matter of import at that age, but Sunday dinner without Jack Benny or Charlie McCarthy was unthinkable. And it was dangerous for anyone to utter a sound during the broadcast of the grain quotations."[69] Every family member had their favourite program, but Saturday night hockey proved the most enduring and the most memorable for at least two generations. Regina's CKCK, Saskatchewan's first commercial station, made broadcasting history when Pete Parker called the play-by-play between the Capitals and the visiting Edmonton Eskimos on 14 March 1923. Foster Hewitt made his radio debut from Toronto's Maple Leaf Gardens nine days later.[70]

Because airwaves were relatively uncluttered at the time, Saskatchewan radio listeners were able to pick up American broadcasts from as far away as Denver and Chicago. But the medium was also used to showcase local talent. In 1923, Horace Stovin of Unity began broadcasting under the signal 10AT (later CHSC) from the dispensary at the back of "Our Drug Store."[71] That same year, CFQC went on the air in Saskatoon. One of the regular guests was the "Famous Farmer Fiddlers." Even the Saskatchewan Wheat Pool opened a Regina station in 1927 to convince farmers to renew their delivery contracts. Most of the local radio announcers were British and regularly mispronounced the name of the province, when not mangling local terms and names such as slough (called "sluff").[72] Martha Bowes, the province's first woman announcer for Saskatoon's CJWC and one of three in Canada at the time, had no such

Frank and Jim Bentley listening
to a Westinghouse radio in
1926. SASKATCHEWAN ARCHIVES
BOARD S78-102

trouble, often assuming several different roles during a day's broadcast.[73] Under an agreement with the CNR, local radio programming was also fed into transcontinental trains as they crossed the province during the 1920s. CFQC radio participated in this service using the call sign CNRS. One Sunday morning, passengers in the observation car listened to a church service being held in Saskatoon, more than a hundred miles away. When the train pulled into the station later that day, the on-board radio operator turned over a collection of almost thirty dollars.[74]

Radio enjoyed a wide following in Saskatchewan because of the novelty of the medium. But there were other forms of popular entertainment, such as the touring Chautauqua, which offered educational lectures, musical performances, and plays.[75] The end of the decade also marked the arrival of talking pictures. In 1929, the Capitol Theatre in Saskatoon began showing movies with sound.[76] It was sport, however, that helped shape and define the image of the province in the 1920s. People in the province loved to play games, perhaps a reflection of the relative youthfulness of the population. Curling attracted a large number of participants at all levels, especially after 1928 when Saskatchewan began sending teams to the Brier, the new Canadian national men's championship.[77] But it was baseball and hockey that dominated the provincial sports scene. Every school and community had a ball team, and towns would vie with one another to put on the best money tournament. Many of the visiting teams from the midwestern United States featured black players who were barred from American leagues despite their talent. Girls and women also played, but quickly switched to softball after it was introduced to the province after the war.[78]

The other provincial passion was hockey. By the early 1920s, Saskatchewan was producing some of the best hockey talent in the country. Many a farm or small-town boy went on to star in the new, four-team Western Canadian Hockey League. But in 1927, the National Hockey League became the premier professional league in North America and raided the western teams for their players. The New York Rangers secured Bill and Fred Cook of the Saskatoon Sheiks, while Toronto and Montreal fought over the rights to Sheiks' goalie, George Hainsworth. The real prize was Eddie Shore of Fort Qu'Appelle, the franchise player for the Boston Bruins. Known as the "Iceman" because of his aloofness, Shore personified the rough-and-tumble rushing defenceman and was selected the league's most valuable player four times.[79]

The most remarkable sports achievement of the 1920s belonged to Ethel Catherwood, who literally jumped to prominence on the international stage. Although born in North Dakota in 1908, Ethel was raised on a homestead near Scott before moving with her family to Saskatoon in her late teens. In 1926, while representing Bedford Road Collegiate, she easily won the high jump in the city track-and-field championships with a jump of five feet. Two

Saskatoon high jumper Ethel Catherwood is the only Canadian woman to win a gold medal in a track and field event at the Olympics.
LIBRARY AND ARCHIVES CANADA PA126728

years later, the Saskatoon Lily, as she was nicknamed, headed to the ninth Olympic Games in Amsterdam after setting a new world record at the Canadian qualifying meet. On the last day of the games, Ethel won the gold medal by outjumping an elite field of competitors. She returned home a national hero. Saskatoon even declared a civic holiday in her honour. But at the height of her fame, unable to regain her earlier form before the next Olympics, a bitter Ethel turned her back on Canada and lived her remaining days in obscurity in the United States. To this day, she remains the only Canadian woman to win a gold medal in an individual track-and-field event at the Olympic Games.[80]

Catherwood's feat was one sure sign that Saskatchewan was well along the road to greatness. Another was the resolution of the long-standing natural resources question. In 1905, when Saskatchewan and Alberta were carved out of the old North-West Territories, they were denied control of their public lands and resources—just as Manitoba had been in 1870—even though it was a right enjoyed by all other Canadian provinces. At first, not wanting to lock horns with the friendly Laurier administration in Ottawa, Saskatchewan quietly pocketed the generous federal subsidy it received in lieu of its lands. But when the new Conservative government extended Manitoba's northern boundary to the 60th parallel and Hudson Bay in 1912, the Saskatchewan government began demanding control of the province's resources. Repeated attempts to hammer out an agreement foundered over the question of compensation for lands that had already been sold. Finally, in 1927, Premier Gardiner successfully convinced Prime Minister King of the justice of the western case. In the ensuing negotiations, Gardiner proved a tough bargainer, claiming that Saskatchewan's right to compensation should date back to 1870, when Canada secured control of the western interior. He also proposed that the province's northern boundary be pushed to the Arctic Ocean in order to give Saskatchewan its own ocean port. These stiff demands delayed settlement of the matter before Gardiner was defeated in the 1929 provincial election. It consequently fell to the new Anderson government to accept the transfer of the resources to provincial control in 1930. It took another sixteen years, including a Supreme Court decision and a royal commission investigation, before the amount of compensation was finally sorted out.[81]

Although Jimmy Gardiner did not enjoy the satisfaction of formally receiving control of the province's resources—he had to watch over Anderson's shoulder as the new premier signed the transfer agreement—his remarks at the diamond jubilee celebrations about Saskatchewan's special place in Canada had been borne out during the 1920s. By the end of the decade, the province was rapidly closing in on a million residents. There was also no disputing Saskatchewan's claim as the "wheat province." In fact, farmland had been settled at such a pace that the Anderson government decided to discontinue homesteading following the natural resources transfer. The triumph of wheat, however, had made the province something of an anomaly. While Canada was increasingly becoming an urbanized, industrialized country, more than two-thirds of Saskatchewan's population lived on the land and at least 85 per cent of the provincial workforce was dependent on agriculture. The singular devotion to the production of wheat was also shortsighted, even reckless, in the world that Saskatchewan farmers woke up to after the Great War. Any significant drop in prices, as experienced during the nasty post-war recession, could have devastating consequences for producers and the provincial economy, no matter how much wheat was harvested. The warning signs were already there when the price of wheat slipped below a dollar in 1927 and dropped even lower the following year. What was not apparent at the time, though, was the size of the economic calamity that awaited the province in the 1930s.

Premier Anderson (lower left) signs the 1930 land transfer agreement while former territorial premier Frederick Haultain (standing, left) and former premier Jimmy Gardiner (standing, right) look on.
SASKATOON PUBLIC LIBRARY LH3605

CHAPTER FOURTEEN

NOTHING
OF EVERYTHING

"**M**ORE LIES HAVE PROBABLY BEEN TOLD** about the weather of the Dirty Thirties than about any other subject except sex," quipped James Gray in *Men Against the Desert*, "yet most of the lies could have been true."[1] Gray's remark aptly captures the dreadful conditions people faced in southern Saskatchewan during the 1930s. Every conceivable calamity—from unrelenting drought and scorching temperatures to blinding dust storms to insect plagues and crop diseases—descended on the region and its people. One popular legend was that children reached school age before knowing what rain was or came running home in fright when they felt a drop of rain for the first time. Another was that parents decided whether to send their children outside by throwing a gopher up in the air; if the animal dug a burrow, then there was too much dust swirling around. Or there was the young baseball player who lost his direction while rounding the bases during a dust storm and was later found several miles out on the prairie.[2] These stories, no matter how exaggerated, help explain why the Great Depression left such an imprint on Saskatchewan society, why no one who lived through those "ten lost years" was left untouched. But the ecological problems of the decade only compounded the real source of the disaster—record-low commodity prices and international demand. Stalled export sales and plummeting prices sent shockwaves through the entire provincial economy, pounding the agricultural sector before washing over retail, service, and transportation industries. In the face of this deluge, Saskatchewan, having gambled its future on wheat, was helpless.

They were the poster family of the Dirty Thirties. In late June 1934, Abram and Elizabeth Fehr and their seven children, one of them a three-month-old baby in his mother's arms, were stranded in Edmonton's Market Square, barefoot, hungry, and broke, when a newspaper photographer captured their utter desperation in what would become one of the most enduring images of the Depression. Just two years earlier, the Fehrs, Mennonites from the Nuenlage Colony north of Saskatoon, had sold everything they owned, bought an old car, and headed for a new start in Alberta's Peace River country. But life in northern Alberta was little better. Their first crop was hit by frost. The following year, the Peace River flooded. Anxious to return to Saskatchewan, the Fehrs started for home one month after baby Peter was born. For the next eight weeks, they battled mud, breakdowns, and constant hunger. Abram worked at local farms along the way to earn a few pennies to feed his starving family and buy gas for the car. By the time they reached Edmonton in late June, Elizabeth was too weak to nurse her baby. Two city police constables found the family and took them to the station, where the Salvation Army gave them food and clothing. The next day, before the Fehrs continued on to Saskatoon, a photographer for the *Edmonton Journal* snapped a picture of the family standing in front of their car and trailer. The accompanying article described them as "a pitiful spectacle of depression dereliction."[3]

The Fehrs epitomized the desperate plight of prairie families in Saskatchewan during the Depression, victims of forces largely beyond their control. In the 1920s, while Great Britain and the rest of Europe were recovering from the destruction and dislocations of the Great War, North America soared to unprecedented heights of growth and prosperity. The international demand for North American products, however, collapsed in the late 1920s under the weight of rebounding European economies. Worldwide overproduction led to lower prices. The famous stock market crash of 1929 was a symptom, not the cause, of this instability in the world economy. The situation went from bad to worse when countries tried to shore up their sagging economies by erecting high tariff walls at the expense of other equally vulnerable economies. What

Saskatchewan's Fehr family photographed in Edmonton in 1934 after their car broke down.
GLENBOW ARCHIVES ND-3-6742

might have been a short-term emergency turned into a long-term crisis because of Canada's growing economic integration with the United States. Most of the development and expansion in the 1920s had been financed with American dollars, and when the United States began experiencing its own economic woes, this investment evaporated—with painful consequences. The Canadian economy would remain in poor health until the ailing United States was on the mend.[4]

Saskatchewan was one of the first casualties of the Depression. Much of its prosperity in the 1920s had been fuelled by the sale of wheat, which represented one-quarter of Canada's total export trade. Now, on the eve of the new decade, not only did international demand for wheat collapse, but the price went into a free fall. Beginning in 1930, at a time when Saskatchewan farmers derived approximately 80 per cent of their cash income from wheat, its price tumbled to forty-seven cents a bushel and remained well below a dollar for the rest of the decade. The repercussions were catastrophic. The 1932 harvest, for example, was not only the largest since 1928, but graded higher than any crop in the previous twenty years. Yet it sold for only thirty-five cents a bushel, the lowest price for wheat in centuries! These meagre returns were compounded by the fact that the price of wheat fell more than the price of most other items—in some cases, it dropped more than twice as much. Farmers consequently found themselves getting considerably less for their wheat, but paying relatively more for everyday items for their home and farm operations. With expenses outstripping cash receipts, and already carrying a heavy debt load from the expansion of the 1920s, many simply could not stay afloat. When they went down, they took with them other sectors of the provincial economy, like the vortex created by a sinking ship. Few were spared, if only because nearly seven of every ten people in Saskatchewan, according to the 1931 census, lived and worked in rural areas. But large urban centres also suffered. Because cities and towns acted primarily as agricultural service centres, businesses floundered, unemployment soared, and tax arrears mounted as the price of wheat went into a tailspin. Saskatchewan's retail trade shrank almost 50 per cent from 1930 to 1933, the greatest contraction in any province. Per capita income, meanwhile, declined a humbling 72 per cent between 1928 and 1933. Saskatchewan became the most heavily indebted province by the end of the 1930s, an almost complete reversal of the financial situation at the beginning of the decade.[5]

The other complicating factor for Saskatchewan was fluctuating wheat yields. The 1928 record crop was followed by a disappointing harvest, less than half the size of the previous year. These poor yields would become the norm during the 1930s, when severe drought placed a stranglehold on the short-grass prairie district. Hot, drying winds scooped up loose topsoil and whipped it into towering dust storms that made outside activity nearly impossible. Darkness at noon was not uncommon, while churning soil piled up in deep drifts along buildings, fence lines, or ridges. At the peak of the storms, an estimated quarter of a million acres of land was blowing out of control, while some three to six million acres had been sucked dry of any moisture. Even in areas where erosion was not a serious problem, the withering heat stunted the wheat crop, preventing the heads from filling out. Some fields were so patchy that harvesting seemed a terrible joke. Total wheat production dropped by a third during the decade even though the area devoted to wheat increased by more than a million acres during the same period. The years 1931, 1933, and 1934 were particularly bad, with average yields of just under nine bushels per acre. The 1937 harvest was even worse. Wheat production dropped to a stunning thirty-five million bushels, a paltry 2.5 bushels per acre. It was the smallest harvest in thirty years, the major difference being that the 1908 crop had been grown on less than 20 per cent of the 1937 acreage.[6]

Since Canada had experienced severe recessions before, as recently as the early 1920s, most expected the worst to be over in a year, maybe two, and that traditional practices, like reducing expenditures and laying off employees, would tide the country over until the recovery kicked in. No one realized that the downswing would last until 1933 when the unemployment rate hit a lofty 30 per cent, which translated into 1.5 million Canadians out of work. Some regions of the country, like Saskatchewan, would not see a rebound in fortunes until the latter part of the decade.

Unemployment had long been a persistent feature of Canadian life. Prior to the 1930s, unskilled workers rarely enjoyed a regular pay packet. They provided raw muscle for agriculture, forestry, construction, and shipping, and whenever international prices went flat, they were dismissed in large numbers. Unskilled workers also had to compete with thousands of new immigrants each year, while employers had the luxury of a large pool of labour at their disposal, which kept wages down. Work was also seasonal. Jobs in several sectors of the economy, such as construction and shipping, ended with the onset of winter.[7]

Despite Canada's long experience with unemployment, it was widely believed before the Depression that a healthy person without a job was lazy. Work could always be found by accepting a position at a lower wage or by turning to the land. Indeed, one of the constant refrains during this period was that there was always work to be had on the farm. There was also no unemployment insurance. Employers in the 1920s, especially farmers who depended on temporary harvesters, argued that if an individual was provided with any kind of income support, then the person would not only stop looking for a job, but others would be discouraged from seeking work as well. Those in need of help were grudgingly given relief, which was deliberately kept to the minimum required to keep someone alive. Under such a system, people were effectively forced to keep working, no matter how wretched or distasteful the job, and turned to relief only as a last resort. Even then, accepting relief carried the psychological stigma of failure and disgrace. The needy had to solemnly vouch that they had no other resources to fall back on and that they were completely destitute. Many were too ashamed to ask for help. Mrs. P. E. Bottle of Craven screwed up her courage to write Prime Minister R. B. Bennett in February 1935, but was still worried about her reputation in the community. "Please don't think I'm crazy for writing you," she confessed, "but I've got three little children, and they are all in need of shoes as well as underwear ... I don't know what to do. I hate to ask for help ... but if you don't want to do this please don't mention it over radios as every one knows me around here and I'm well liked, so I beg of you not to mention my name. I've never asked anyone around here for help or cloths [sic] as I know them to [sic] well."[8] The prime minister sent five dollars.

Under the terms of the 1867 British North America Act, provinces and municipalities were solely responsible for the distribution of relief. The federal government had no obligation to step in, and the new Conservative prime

The prolonged drought, portrayed here as a wolf at the door,
forced many farmers to abandon their land. *Montreal Star*, 17 September 1934

minister was not about to do so. During a special Parliamentary session convened in September 1930 to deal with the worsening crisis, the Bennett government provided twenty million dollars in emergency relief assistance to the provinces on the understanding that the aid was a temporary measure and did not represent any new commitment on the part of Ottawa.

The only Saskatchewan group that the federal government was legally bound to look after during these dark days was the Indian population. Even here, though, the Department of Indian Affairs was more interested in economy and generally did as little as possible to help bands in need. Relief rations, distributed mostly to the elderly, were modest at best. The monthly allotment usually consisted of flour, lard, tea, bacon, sugar, shotgun shells, and snare wire—remarkably, the same kind of items dispensed half a century earlier. Many reserve farmers, like their white counterparts, were unable to produce a crop or feed their cattle. There was also little demand for part-time Indian labour. Families were consequently forced to rely on traditional resources, limited at the best of times, for their survival. Some even sent their children to residential schools to ensure that they got fed. Elders today refer to the decade as "the hungry thirties."[9]

Ottawa's rigid adherence to the idea of local responsibility put Saskatchewan communities on the front line in dealing with the growing jobless problem. The challenge was particularly daunting for the province's major cities, already hobbled by debt from the reckless overexpansion before the Great War.[10] Indeed, the 1930s snuffed out any lingering hope that Regina might still emerge as the pre-eminent centre in western Canada. The collapse in agriculture inevitably spilled over into retail and construction, and as sales dried up like much of Saskatchewan's farmland, Regina businesses cut staff in a desperate bid to stem the hemorrhaging. A sign of the hard days ahead was the closure of the General Motors plant and the loss of nearly one thousand jobs. The Hudson's Bay Company also reneged on its promise to build a department store. By July 1931, almost one in four adult male workers in the Queen City had lost his job.

It was much the same story elsewhere. In Prince Albert, the CPR abandoned its plans to extend the Debden–Meadow Lake line to Lac la Biche, therein providing a direct rail link to the northland; work also ceased on Union Station and would not resume for almost a quarter century. Local opposition successfully prevented closure of the train station in Moose Jaw, but the city bled jobs when the Saskatchewan government went looking for ways to reduce expenditures through consolidation of provincial services in the capital. Moose Jaw College also closed its doors in 1931, forfeiting the field to the rival school in Regina. Saskatoon, the province's second largest city in the 1920s, also saw its fortunes put on hold. In late 1928, the CNR decided to build a luxurious, chateau-style hotel on the banks of the South Saskatchewan River. The steel skeleton was put up over the winter of 1930–31. By the next fall, the grand brick-and-stone exterior was complete. Then, Saskatoon's castle on the river sat empty and silent, while the company waited for the return of better times before finishing the interior. It would be another four years before the Bessborough finally opened on 10 December 1935—an early Christmas present for the city.[11]

The exact number of Saskatchewan urban unemployed during the early 1930s is difficult to determine. Statistics from the period provide only the number of families and individuals assisted in any given year and fail to capture those who refused, or were denied, a helping hand. Cities insisted that relief applicants meet a residency requirement of at least six months, which was later expanded to a full year as the weekly tallies of the unemployed soon reached the thousands for Saskatchewan's larger cities. To ensure that relief was uniformly administered in urban centres—and to keep expenditures down since the province was providing a large share of the funds—the Saskatchewan government issued guidelines. The head of a family had to register for relief, which would be granted only after an investigation had confirmed that the applicant was without any means of support; in other words, applicants were to be screened to ensure that they were genuinely deserving of help. If a child was working, the earnings were deducted from the family's relief allowance. The suggested monthly food quota was $6 per adult and $2.50 for each child, redeemable as a voucher from a standard, though rather limited, list of grocery items; substitutions were not permitted. A fixed amount for water and light and a portion of rent were also to be paid, but only after the account had fallen into several months' arrears or the tenants faced eviction. A monthly quota of fuel, normally Saskatchewan lignite coal, was also provided. Cities and towns adhered to these recommended schedules as best they could, depending on the parsimony of local officials, but were sometimes pushed to the wall by financial exigencies.

One of the key relief assumptions was that men mattered more than women—what one commentator has called a "gendered" policy.[12] Men, especially those with families, were given priority for relief assistance and relief work, because they were seen by society as breadwinners. There were no similar programs for women in Saskatchewan, even if they had once been part of the labour force and lost their jobs. The care of the unemployed female was understood to be a family duty, the responsibility of husbands, fathers, brothers, even uncles or male cousins, certainly not the state. In fact, in the early 1930s, there was a backlash against women in the workplace. They were collectively blamed for exacerbating the employment crisis, accused of being "bread snatchers and home wreckers."[13] Women, it was argued, should be forced to do the right thing and give up their jobs to men and go home where they belonged.

This emphasis on traditional gender roles was ironically at odds with what women actually did to mitigate the impact of the Depression. Many families survived these bleak years because women publicly complained about relief policies, challenging authorities to provide more adequate assistance or resisting attempts to make the process even more demeaning than it already was. Women also had to use their ingenuity in running the household. Relief supplies, for example, tested a woman's creative skills in the kitchen. One person used to think that her mother was not a good cook, but then later realized, "How could she be a good cook when she had nothing to work with?"[14] Women also canned and pickled vegetables grown in makeshift gardens in vacant lots and kept chickens, ducks, or pigs in backyard pens to supplement the otherwise monotonous relief diet. Some deliberately went without food or chose to eat after the other family members. "I don't actually remember seeing my mother eat" was one of the most common refrains among Depression children.[15]

Those who administered urban relief were genuinely concerned that people would become hooked, as if it was some highly addictive drug that would undermine the moral underpinnings of Canadian society. They saw it as their duty to preserve the work ethic, seemingly at any cost. "We distribute nothing without work," explained the Saskatoon city clerk in January 1931, "as we feel otherwise we would be creating paupers and there is no doubt in my mind that this is the greatest danger at this time."[16] Many men initially welcomed the prospect of a job, especially if it meant they could walk with their heads up. But there were not enough municipal projects to keep the unemployed busy, even if the work was restricted to those on city relief rolls.[17] Many cities consequently invented make-work activities, known at the time as boondoggling, that required no money and no machinery but would keep relief recipients busy. Men were called upon to shovel snow, pull weeds, sweep sidewalks, cut wood, and collect litter—tasks that carried with them a certain degree of public humiliation. A. C. MacNeil, a Saskatoon salesman who had lost his job, actually preferred working in the filth and stench at the city dump in order to keep his pride intact. "I would not want any of my friends to know or even suspect that I was forced into this corner," he admitted.[18]

Saskatchewan cities were able to offer more meaningful relief work under special federal public works funding in 1930 and 1931. Regina undertook a major overhaul and expansion of the waterworks system, reconstructed the Albert Street bridge, dredged Wascana Lake, and constructed an exhibition hall for the 1932 World Grain Exhibition and Conference. Moose Jaw decided to take advantage of the geothermal water that flowed beneath the city and built an enclosed pool on the Crescent Park grounds; over three thousand people attended the official opening of the Natatorium on Thanksgiving Day 1932. Perhaps the most interesting project, in terms of how the work was apportioned, was Saskatoon's Broadway Bridge, linking the old Nutana neighbourhood with the downtown core. Work on the $850,000 bridge commenced in December 1931 and continued around the clock into the new year, even during the most brutally cold winter days. Three daily shifts were drawn from the city's unemployment register, but with an important qualification. Married men with a larger number of dependents were awarded more days of work on the project than those without families. Supervisors also tried to ensure that as much construction as possible was done by pick and shovel in order to employ more labourers at the basic wage of forty-five cents per hour. These special provisions were considered necessary because twenty-four hundred married men had registered

Regina's Albert Street bridge was a relief project. SASKATCHEWAN ARCHIVES BOARD R-B3078

for relief as of September 1931, and Saskatoon officials were determined to ensure that hundreds found temporary employment on the project by the time it opened the following November.[19]

In the spring of 1932, worried about the country's financial rating, Prime Minister Bennett announced that Canada could no longer afford the federal public works program. Instead, he adopted the cheaper course of direct relief or "the dole," with the federal government paying one-third of the costs and covering provincial obligations where necessary. This decision could not have come at a worse time for Saskatchewan since the falling economy had yet to reach bottom. Soon, there were far too many needy people calling on the limited resources that municipalities had to offer. Almost one in five persons living in the province's cities depended on direct assistance in 1932, a situation that remained fairly constant until the end of the decade. In Regina alone, the amount spent on direct relief soared from around fourteen thousand dollars in 1929 to nearly a half million dollars in 1934. By the fall of 1938, the city's total relief tab reached ten million dollars. Relief payments were supposed to be funded in the first instance from civic revenues, but ratepayers were generally in no position to settle their outstanding tax bills. Saskatchewan cities consequently had to borrow money through debentures to meet their obligations, thereby adding to their debt load and mortgaging their future. They also came to depend heavily on the province to bail them out and avoid certain bankruptcy.[20]

This new emphasis on direct relief was based on the naive hope that recovery was just over the horizon. But the nadir of the Depression in Saskatchewan was 1937, a time when other parts of the country were already recuperating. Both Prince Albert and the Battlefords reported that local demand for relief was never greater than during the winter of 1937–38.[21] Swift Current rebelled against the unfair municipal burden and announced the suspension of direct relief in August 1932; local families were given only one-half the monthly allowance to tide them over until the city secured more help from senior governments.[22] Saskatoon, on the other hand, became mean-spirited and punitive in dispensing direct relief. In mid-November 1932, the city introduced a new relief application form that gave officials the right to enter homes at any time, day or night, to ensure that recipients were truly destitute and not hiding luxury items such as a radio. The form also required relief disbursements to be repaid in full, by the confiscation of personal effects and property if necessary! One Saskatoon woman remembered seeing her father cry for the first time when he was compelled to accept the city's terms before he got food for his hungry children. He cried again at the loss of his self-respect, believing he had signed away his manhood. Several Saskatoon families angrily refused to accept what a *Star-Phoenix* editorial called "blackmail." And when they were unceremoniously cut off relief, thirty women and children occupied city council chambers for two days in Saskatoon's first sit-down strike, while the local police tussled with supporters outside the building. The episode ended peacefully when the protestors secured minor changes to the new relief policy, but it underscored what women were willing to do to see that the basic necessities of life did not come at the cost of their families' dignity.[23]

The official opening of Moose Jaw's Natatorium, another Depression project. MOOSE JAW PUBLIC LIBRARY ARCHIVES 68-686(3)

Unemployed married men, especially those with children, were given preference on Saskatoon's Broadway Bridge project. SASKATOON PUBLIC LIBRARY LHA202

The Depression was also accompanied by a severe housing crisis in both Regina and Prince Albert. Unlike Moose Jaw and Saskatoon, which lost citizens during the first half of the 1930s, Regina's and Prince Albert's populations continued to grow as people from rural areas either migrated to the provincial capital in search of work, if not help, or tried to escape to a region less afflicted by the punishing drought. Prince Albert was the fastest-growing city in western Canada in 1936 and would continue to attract new residents during the latter half of the decade. But the growth created new headaches. With construction largely at a standstill, people in Regina rented empty offices or basements in downtown stores, making the Queen City one of the most overcrowded cities in Canada by the end of the decade. According to a 1938 survey, 7.4 per cent of all Regina families lived in one room; the national average was 2.5 per cent. The situation in Prince Albert was little better. The same survey found almost half the houses in the city without indoor plumbing; one in eight homes was considered unsanitary.[24]

Among Prince Albert's newest residents were Métis families from the surrounding area. They would move into Prince Albert, support themselves as best they could for a year, and then apply for relief. By 1936, the city's relief officer claimed that nearly half of Batoche had relocated in this way.[25] This survival strategy was a natural response for a people who had known only poverty since the early twentieth century. Relief, in many instances, was better than their isolated existence on the margins of Saskatchewan society. But some resented the presence of the Métis, insisting that they had no right to relief since they were not normally residents of the city and would never become ratepayers. Charlotte Whitton, a widely respected Canadian social worker and future mayor of Ottawa, was one of these critics. In May 1932, Prime Minister Bennett hired Whitton to examine the distribution of relief in some of the worst hit areas of western Canada. In her report that fall, Whitton complained about "the breed," a shiftless, gypsylike people who were "a problem and a menace both to the Indian and white races with whom they mingle." She was adamant that the Métis were to blame for their deplorable condition (it had nothing to do with the inherent racism of Saskatchewan society) and found it "hardly justifiable" that they qualified for the same levels of relief as "the ordinary population." The solution, Whitton maintained, was to restrict "the breed" to special areas, similar to Indian reserves, where they would receive limited assistance. At the very least, they should be ineligible for federal aid, including any emergency relief spending.[26]

One of Whitton's other worries was that relief would sap people of their hope and initiative. But the Depression certainly did not dull the Saskatchewan public's enthusiasm for cultural and sporting activities. In 1933, Prince Albert hosted the first northern festival of the Saskatchewan Music Association. That same year, the Regina Little Theatre held the province's first drama festival. The Saskatchewan art community also received a welcome boost when landscape painter Gus Kenderdine opened a summer school at Emma Lake in 1936; he was also named director of the School of Fine Arts at Regina College and curator of the art collection that Regina lawyer Norman MacKenzie willed to the University of Saskatchewan.[27]

Football, in the meantime, acquired quite a following in Regina when the city's professional team, renamed the Roughriders in 1924, emerged as the perennial western representative in the national championship in the late 1920s and early 1930s. They were also perennial losers—despite winning the western title fourteen times between 1914 and 1935. Fans in Regina were first treated to radio coverage of the Grey Cup game by CKCK in 1930, when the Riders lost 11-6 in the mud in Toronto's Varsity Stadium. Great things were expected in 1936, when Regina upset the Winnipeg Blue Bombers, the defending champions, in the playoffs. But the Roughriders were declared ineligible to play for the Grey Cup that year because of the American players on their roster.[28] Hockey was even more popular, especially when the exploits of homegrown players could be heard on national radio. Ken Doraty, formerly of the Moose Jaw Canucks, went into the NHL record book when, playing for the Toronto Maple Leafs in 1933, he ended a scoreless tie in the sixth overtime period of the last game in a Stanley Cup semi-final series.[29]

Perhaps the greatest Saskatchewan sports story to come out of the Depression involved future hockey great Gordie Howe. Born in Floral in 1928, Gordie was just nine days old when his family moved to Saskatoon. Like other Depression families, Albert and Katherine Howe were struggling to raise their eight children as best they could. One night in 1933, a despondent woman pounded on the Howe door at 413 Avenue L North. Needing money to buy food for her children, she sold Katherine the sack she was carrying. When the contents were dumped out on the floor before the Howe children, out fell an old pair of large hockey skates. Gordie, then just six years old, grabbed one, his older sister Edna the other. For the next few days, the pair attempted to skate on one foot on the frozen slough near their home. Edna eventually gave up and Gordie claimed the other skate. He stuffed the toes with paper, laced them up, and went skating for the very first time. He never looked back.[30]

Howe's future career owed much to his mother's generosity, a willingness to help others in times of distress. That's certainly something that rural southern Saskatchewan needed in the early 1930s. The twin scourge of record-low wheat prices and prolonged drought walloped the province's agricultural community. Total farm cash income nosedived from $273 million in 1928 to just $66 million in 1931, where it roughly remained for the better part

Kids made their own fun during the Depression. WESTERN DEVELOPMENT MUSEUM 5-F-18

of the decade. The average net cash income for a Saskatchewan farmer went from $1,614 in 1928 to a mere $66 by 1933; by 1937, this annual income had crept up to $141.[31] The dramatic decline in farm income meant that producers did not have the money they needed to run their operations let alone pay off any outstanding loans for land and machinery. What made the outlook even bleaker was that ninety-five, roughly one-third, of the province's rural munici- palities suffered their third consecutive crop failure in 1931. Conservative Premier J. T. M. Anderson, who had knocked the long-reigning Liberals from office on the eve of the Depression and had bravely tried to weather the storm during the first two years of his mandate, was reduced to vowing in a Yorkton speech in July 1931 that "no one in Saskatchewan would be allowed to starve."[32] One month later, he established a non-partisan agency to oversee the distribution of emergency assistance to the province's farm families.

The Saskatchewan Relief Commission provided direct relief (food, fuel, clothing, and medical aid) and agricultural support (such as seed, feed, and fodder) to try to keep families on the land and producing a crop in the event that international wheat prices bounced back. It was an expensive rescue operation. During what was supposed to be the commission's only year of activity, total expenditures amounted to $18.7 million, almost evenly shared between the provincial and federal governments. Nearly 50 per cent of Saskatchewan's rural population, or approximately three hundred thousand people, were assisted in one way or another. In fact, conditions in several districts were so terrible that the commission dispensed relief for another two years, on the understanding that strict economy would be observed and that any advances would technically have to be repaid. This aid was supplemented by the Saskatchewan Voluntary Relief Committee, an umbrella group of church and other charitable organizations that solicited donations of fruit, vegetables, and other foodstuffs from other provinces and then arranged for carloads—249 in 1931—to be shipped to distressed areas by the railways free of charge.[33] One of the unexpected bonuses was dried salt cod from the Maritimes. "When I first saw the codfish," remembered Gordon McLeod of Elfros, who went to town with his father when the relief train arrived, "I wasn't too sure what it was." Nor did most Saskatchewan residents know what to make of it. They tried boiling it, frying it, even toasting it—and most absolutely hated it. Stories went around that people used the dried fish for shingles on their barns, saltlicks for their cattle, or even as snowshoes. "You'd put it on a slab of poplar," McLeod half-jokingly recalled years later, "and some celery and carrots on it and then you'd cook it. And then throw the cod away and eat the board."[34]

Two newspaper reporters at the time, D. B. McRae and R. M. Scott, claimed that people in southern Saskatchewan needed a sense of humour and an oversupply of hope to cope with the many problems they faced. It was not editorial posturing. In September 1934, the pair toured the "burnt out" area, as it was being called, and filed stories along the way. Their articles contrast the conditions they found and the faith of the local farmers in the land. Between Cadillac, Kincaid, and Gravelbourg, in southwestern Saskatchewan, they found that six years of drought had reduced life "to the lowest common denominator." From Tribune, south of Weyburn, they reported, "Today many of the stores and shops are vacant, windows nailed up, people gone. There is scarcely a scrap of crop in the country." The Chinese cook at the Fillmore restaurant provided a more sweeping assessment of how bad things were. "No crop," he bluntly asserted. "No garden, no oats, no potatoes, no feed. Nothing of everything." But at the same time, no matter where the reporters went, they were constantly being assured by farmers that "the land is still all right. All it needs is rain."[35] This continued determination to plant wheat every spring, as if by instinct, helps explain why crop acreage actually increased during the Depression. After all, this was "next year country." But the real challenge throughout the 1930s was not trying to grow enough wheat, but getting a decent price for it.

Until prices recovered, the more immediate challenge for the residents of southern Saskatchewan was trying to endure ecological problems of Biblical proportions. Droughts had always been a persistent feature of the prairies, occurring on average every twenty years or so. The 1930s, however, were notorious for the number of consecutive dry years. The drought also extended to the North Saskatchewan country in 1937, whereas before then it had been largely confined to the so-called Palliser's Triangle south of Saskatoon. No one in the southern half of the province escaped from the almost complete lack of rain that year. It was also a time of extremes. The winter of 1935–36 was one of the coldest on record, followed the next summer by one of the longest heat waves in Canadian history. One year later, on 5 July 1937, Midale and Yellowgrass reached 113°F (45°C), the hottest temperature ever recorded in Canada.[36]

It did not take long for the abnormally dry conditions to spawn dust storms across southern Saskatchewan. The first struck in January 1931. Shocked residents of Moose Jaw reported that it was impossible to see across the street during the "black" blizzard. The next major storm coincided with seeding that spring and blanketed roads with drifting soil that sometimes formed impassable dunes. By the summer of 1934, town fairs had to be cancelled because of the dirt in the air. In his classic novel, *As For Me and My House*, Sinclair Ross wrote, "The sun through the dust looks big and red and close. Bigger, redder, closer every day. You begin to glance at it with a doomed feeling, that there's no escape."[37]

Dust storms brought life to a standstill in rural Saskatchewan. PROVINCIAL ARCHIVES OF ALBERTA A3742

The swirling dust was an unfortunate fact of life for much of the decade, an unwelcome visitor that appeared at the worst possible time, such as Moose Jaw's annual spring clean-up day in 1939. During the storms, mothers were known to put lamps by windows so that children could find their way home from school. They also fought a frustrating battle to keep the dust out of their houses, setting wet rags on window sills and hanging wet sheets over door-ways. But it still managed to seep through.[38] The memory of the drought and the dust-laden winds would haunt people for years to come. "It is a despairing thing," remarked Etha Munro four decades later, "to watch your farm and pastureland die a slow death over a period of several years, each year getting drier and more hopeless than the year before."[39] Another dust-bowl survivor painfully recalled, "The wind had a moaning sound, sometimes a high pier-cing sound, it made my head ache. The wind blew day and night for, I am sure, five years."[40]

The other major problem was insect infestations. Tens of millions of pale western cutworms, often mistakenly identified as army worms, munched their way across the land, devouring crops, stripping shrubs and trees, and laying waste to gardens. Then there was the wheat stem sawfly, which chewed through the lower stem of the stalk, causing the grain to fall over.[41] The undis-puted champion insect pests, however, were the grasshoppers, which flew in with the winds "in numbers beyond all calculation, even beyond the exag-gerative genius of the yarn spinners of the prairies."[42] The hot, dry weather provided ideal breeding conditions and by 1934 it was estimated that one hundred thousand square miles in Saskatchewan were infested. There was no shortage of amazing stories about the hoppers—how their swarms darkened the sky, how they ate the clothes on lines, even how the guts from their squished bodies stopped trains. They made the drought conditions worse by destroying any plant cover, including the hated Russian thistle. Beginning in 1933, Saskatchewan mounted an aggressive campaign against the grasshoppers using a simple mixture of sawdust, bran, and liquid sodium arsenate, perfected by entomologist Norman Criddle of Manitoba. Thousands of farmers, under provincial government supervision, mixed and spread the poison bait, sometimes by spoon and ladle, over millions of acres to bring the plague under control.[43]

The once-vibrant rural society buckled under these conditions. Houses, barns, and equipment fell into disrepair, while small-town businesses either collapsed or limped along on the relief trade.[44] One of the first victims was the thirty-year-old Weyburn Security Bank. Rural municipalities severely reduced their activities, since few residents were able to pay their taxes. Schools also suffered from the lack of educational materials and supplies, while teachers not only had their salaries slashed or held back, but often had to depend on the generosity of local residents to help tide them over. Curiously, the total number of teachers in Saskatchewan declined by only twenty-one between 1929 and 1935, but more than six hundred women were replaced by men during the same period.[45] Rural residents tried to see that life went on as normally as possible under the circumstances. Towns continued to hold sports days, especially baseball tournaments. Even though the prize money was smaller, the competition was reportedly fiercer. In winter, according to Harlo Jones of Dinsmore, "the biggest event ... was the annual adult bonspiel ... it seemed that everybody moved into the rink."[46]

Women seemed to bear the brunt of these years more heavily than their partners. Since hired help was now beyond the reach of most operations, they worked alongside their husbands, all the while providing encouragement and support. Women also had to run the farm household with fewer store-bought supplies; like their mothers a generation before, they made more things at home, whether it be soap or clothing.[47] Mending and darning was an art, while any kind of spare material was saved and converted into something useful. "I hated one dress," reminisced a young girl at the time. "Sometimes the stamp didn't wash out very well and even though my mother had dyed the bags, I still had 'Quaker Flour' and a circle across my back."[48] In retrospect, she was lucky. Two sisters in the Bengough area apparently took turns going to school on alternate days because they had only one dress to wear between them.[49]

Some women sought solace in their garden—if it survived the drought. It was one of the few places where they could find pleasure and fulfilment in a world seemingly turned upside down.[50] But poverty took its toll, as did the isolation, since many farm homes could no longer afford a radio, telephone, or newspaper. "There is a feeling that one has been shoved out of life," mused "The Forgotten Woman" to the "Mainly for Women" pages of *The Western Producer* in 1934. "Some call it a living death."[51] Author Max Braithwaite, a Saskatchewan rural schoolteacher, saw in the faces of his students' mothers "the same tired look of resignation ... drought and cold and worry and child-bearing had cast them in the same sad mould."[52] It is probably not surprising that there were 129 recorded maternal deaths from abortions and self-induced abortions during the 1930s.[53]

For children, the Depression was a time of making do with what little they had and learning to wait for better times. One of the most popular pas-times—and a rewarding one at that—was killing gophers, whose rapidly multiplying numbers threatened to take over parts of southern Saskatchewan. At a penny per tail, a successful hunting trip provided money for candy and some fresh meat for the stew pot.[54] It would be a mistake, however, to believe that kids did not suffer during these years. One of the most poignant letters written to the premier in 1934 was sent by young Margaret Bichel of Cactus Lake in west-central Saskatchewan. Margaret had learned that the children living in dried-out areas had received twenty-five cents from the government for Christmas and, with her best penmanship, asked for the same amount for her brothers and sisters.[55]

The health of children in relief areas was a particular concern of the provincial Department of Health. Of the 34,564 students examined in 1931, 4,754 (13.75 per cent) were underweight, 14,524 (42 per cent) required dental work, 6,701 (19.4 per cent) had an unhealthy throat (probably from inhaling dust), and 179 (5.2 per cent) had nervous disorders.[56] There was at least one known death from lack of food. In November 1932, three children suffering from typhoid fever were admitted to Hafford General Hospital, where the eldest died shortly thereafter. "The truth," Dr. A. O. Rose candidly reported, "is that the state of malnutrition of the whole family was such that ... their resistance to disease was markedly diminished ... this child died of starvation."[57]

Some people resorted to desperate acts. Tom Sukanen, a Finnish immi-grant who had homesteaded near Macrorie, spent the decade building an ocean-going ship that he intended to sail all the way home. He suffered a breakdown while hauling the vessel to the Saskatchewan River and later died in the Battleford asylum. Today, Sukanen's ship is on display at a small museum outside Moose Jaw.[58] Edna Weber, meanwhile, was only sixteen in September 1937 when her parents sold her into marriage to a farmer thirty years older. Her father reportedly told the dust-bowl bride, "If you do this thing, it will help all of us ... they'll be one less mouth to feed here."[59]

Mary and John Reimer and their son, George, were dust-bowl refugees who sought a new start in the Park Valley district. SASKATCHEWAN ARCHIVES BOARD R-A17268

This desire not to be a burden lay at the heart of the Bates tragedy. In 1932, Ted Bates was forced to close his butcher shop in Glidden and headed to Vancouver with his wife, Rose, and only child, Jackie, to try his luck there. But the new business failed after only a year, and when the Bates applied for relief they were told that they had to return to Saskatchewan. In November 1933, thanks to assistance from the Salvation Army, they arrived in Saskatoon. Once again, they were turned down for relief. Too proud to go home to Glidden, the couple rented a car and headed west on 4 December. That night, they pulled into the isolated Avalon schoolyard near Biggar and left the vehicle running, expecting the carbon monoxide to kill them in their sleep. But in the morning when they were found, only eight-year-old Jackie was dead. The RCMP charged Ted and Rose with murdering their son. The people of Glidden rallied around them and hired a Saskatoon lawyer who secured an acquittal at their March 1934 trial in Wilkie.[60]

Thousands of others sought a new beginning by moving out of the dried-out areas into other parts of the province. Beginning as early as 1930, the news of normal rainfall in the districts north of the North Saskatchewan River encouraged farmers to abandon their land in favour of starting over again in areas where there was at least the chance of growing a decent crop. This trickle became a flood once it became apparent that the drought had a stranglehold on southern Saskatchewan. But leaving was never easy. Mrs. A. W. Bailey, who traded the family farm south of Regina for a new home in the Bjorkdale district, recalled asking her husband to stop the truck before her former house passed out of sight. "In those few moments," she wrote, "I got a lasting mental picture of the little home where my first babies were born. The house that had sheltered us from the snow and wind and dust storms would stand lonely and silent now, with the mice playing in the rooms and the frost cracking the flowered wallpaper ... I closed my eyes and said a silent little prayer."[61] The refugees headed north with their worldly possessions in all kinds of conveyances. Heavily loaded trucks and horse-drawn Bennett buggies (cars with the motors removed) pulled small trailers, converted hay racks, and specially built cabooses, often trailing a few cows. At night, there would be a string of campfires along the highways heading north, as families prepared meals and talked about their new homes and the future.

In 1930, the provincial Royal Commission on Immigration and Settlement had concluded that the probable limit of northern agricultural settlement ran from Amisk Lake on the eastern side of the province to Île-à-la-Crosse on the west. It was a wildly optimistic assessment, based on the slow, orderly occupation of the land, not an invasion by anxious people intent on settling almost anywhere as long as they got land. Forty-five thousand refugees— roughly the equivalent of the Saskatoon population at that time—moved into the forest fringe of central Saskatchewan between 1930 and 1936; two-thirds arrived in 1933 and 1934, some even coming from southeastern Alberta. By the time of the 1941 census, there were approximately eighty thousand

This family, with all their belongings in tow, were headed to the Carrot River district in 1934.
SASKATCHEWAN ARCHIVES BOARD R-A4287

people in the province's north, more than at any other time in the past.[62] The Saskatchewan government scrambled to deal with the influx and passed the Land Settlement Act in 1931 to provide limited financial assistance to qualified persons settling on unoccupied lands deemed suitable for agriculture. But any attempt to control northern settlement was quickly overwhelmed by people pushing into new areas and squatting on any available land. "We just kept going along the highways and the trail," explained A. Vaadeland of Lake Four village, just outside the southwest corner of Prince Albert National Park, "and then, at what looked like the last house, we just asked if the next quarter was empty. We felt certain we could make a go of this land."[63] By 1932, the province was forced to withdraw large sections of the Big River, Pasqua, and Porcupine forest reserves to accommodate the migrants, and opened for settlement the land that was to form part of the proposed Candle Lake Indian reserve.[64] It also entered into an ambitious agreement with the Bennett government, known as the Relief Settlement Plan, which provided federal funding to get the urban unemployed back on the land. This new scheme, based on the romantic notion that working hands and backs would never be idle in a rural setting, was little more than a thinly disguised attempt to reduce the number on direct relief.[65]

Those who arrived in the middle north in the early years of the decade usually secured the best land near the railway branch lines in the Meadow Lake, Big River, Paddockwood, Nipawin, Carrot River, Arborfield, and Hudson Bay districts. But like the soldier settlers who moved into the same general areas a decade earlier, many of the new settlers survived on non-farm income and, ironically, continued relief assistance. At the end of five years, few had cleared more than twenty-five acres of land, and any crop they produced, such as oats, was usually bartered for fuel, lumber, and food.[66] The situation was equally precarious among former residents of Saskatoon, Regina, Moose Jaw, and Swift Current, who had jumped at the government offer to establish their families on pioneer farms in the Loon Lake area.[67]

Reverend A. R. Taylor, who visited the Little Saskatoon and Tamarack settlements in 1932, was struck by the suffering he found among the inexperienced settlers, hinting that some were one step away from the asylum.[68] His findings were supported by the scores of letters sent to the provincial government by people who had not found the promised land in the north. "I am very poor. The crops have all frozen. I cannot sell anything. I have tried so hard to do well," a farmer from Aneroid in southwestern Saskatchewan pleaded in 1934. "My family have had no new clothes for long time. Please help me to make it through the winter. I am in very bad shape."[69] Such conditions eventually turned the migration north into an exodus. Beginning in 1937, after two bitterly cold winters, hundreds began to flee the region,

Tens of thousands of dust-bowl refugees headed north in the 1930s to begin anew along the southern edge of the boreal forest.

returning to their former communities or trying their luck in another province. Others hung on as best they could, often realizing that they had made a bad initial choice and moving to another location. Betty Fawcett, who was five years old when her family headed north in 1934, lived in two different places, Swan Plain and Gronlid, before finally settling at Carrot River.[70] Still, it was a marginal existence at best. A 1939 survey found fewer than six hundred viable farms in the middle north.[71]

The other unexpected consequence of the great trek north was the hardship it brought the local Aboriginal population. At first, the Depression precipitated a slump in fur, fish, and lumber prices, forcing businesses like the Hudson's Bay Company to reduce and retrench their operations, but the supplying of thousands of new settlers soon revived the sluggish northern economy. Several small, portable sawmills were kept busy providing wood for new homes.[72] Many newcomers also lived on a steady diet of fish and big game, while trying their hand at trapping to supplement their meagre income. Brothers Arthur and Ab Karras, who moved north from Yellow Grass in 1932 intending to become full-time trappers in the Big River region, had to push on to remote Cree Lake because of the depletion of fur-bearing animals.[73]

This strain on local resources came at the expense of the Indian and Métis populations and their traditional livelihood. Clifford Dunfield, a reporter for *The Western Producer*, found that Aboriginal peoples in the Île-à-la-Crosse area had been reduced to subsisting on roots, fish, and the generosity of the local post and mission.[74] The situation was little better further north, where itinerant white trappers not only overran Indian traplines, but prospectors deliberately started fires to clear the country to facilitate their work. In 1937, it was estimated that 80 per cent of the northern forest was on fire because of the abnormally dry weather and the carelessness of settlers in clearing their land. This burning precipitated a shift in the migration pattern of the barren ground caribou away from northeastern Saskatchewan.[75] The result for the Dene of the region, in Arthur Karras' words, was "a grim, lifeless desolation."[76]

These same words could have applied to hundreds of thousands of people who lived through some of the worst years in the province's young history. The Great Depression hit Saskatchewan harder than any other region of the country. But remarkably, despite the broken dreams, the cruel setbacks, and the misery and deprivation, people never lost faith in the land and its ability to provide a good living. Even many of those who left the dried-out areas were not prepared to abandon farming, but simply sought a better life in another part of the province. This stubborn persistence was reflected in the population trends for the decade. Saskatchewan's total and rural populations reached their highest levels several years into the Depression (931,547 and 753,004, respectively, in 1936) and began to decline only after the horrendous summer of 1937. Most Saskatchewan residents stayed and accepted their fate, but what they craved were meaningful solutions to the province's woes, solutions that would bring stability and restore the province's great promise. As a Kincaid farmer summed up the situation, they were not interested in "patching up old clothes ... only to find that the garment had given away somewhere else."[77]

CHAPTER FIFTEEN

SWAPPING HORSES

THE 1930S have been called Canada's "ten lost years,"[1] the decade when the country seemed to have been shunted to a forgotten railroad siding and not put back on the main track until the start of the Second World War. It is a popular assessment. The first chapter of a classic work on the period is evocatively titled, "Our world stopped and we got off." The last line of the book is equally revealing: "Few of us who survived the ordeal can help looking back over our shoulders now and then—and perhaps shuddering a little as we look."[2] But even though many who lived through the bleak years saw few good things coming out of the experience, the Great Depression had a profound impact on Saskatchewan political attitudes and the party system. The record-low commodity prices and prolonged drought did more than expose the inherent vulnerability of the provincial wheat economy. They also revealed the inadequacy, if not the bankruptcy, of traditional measures in resolving Saskatchewan's agricultural woes. Some maintained that minor tinkering and adjustments would be enough to set things right, while others insisted that only far-reaching, even radical, solutions would get the province back on track. Whatever the answer, the 1930s were an intensely political decade in Saskatchewan history.

When Conservative leader J. T. M. Anderson defeated the seemingly entrenched Liberal government in the 1929 provincial election, it was nothing less than a singular achievement. By pandering to the latent racial and religious prejudices of the Anglo-Saxon majority, while bringing together the diverse opposition forces into a workable coalition, Anderson was able to win office, something that no other Conservative politician, including the capable Frederick Haultain, had been able to do in a quarter century. His victory, however, was bittersweet. By the time the new Co-operative government recalled the Saskatchewan legislature for its first session in February 1930, the shadow of the Depression already darkened the province. The deepening economic crisis effectively pushed the emotionally charged issues that had brought Anderson to office to the sidelines, replacing them with a host of new problems, the likes of which had never bedeviled any previous government. The new premier was doubly cursed. The Depression not only robbed him of the source of his electoral support, but dictated his legislative agenda for the next five years. The new government, according to a political commentator, "could only hope for a miracle to save it."[3]

Premier Anderson, despite his Conservative leanings, was guided by the idea of co-operation in running the province. And he was remarkably successful in keeping the loose collection of Progressives and independents onside; not once did either group threaten the stability of the minority government. One of the conditions for this support was civil-service reform and an end to the blatant patronage that had been a hallmark of past Liberal administrations. The Anderson government delivered on this demand by passing a new Public Service Act in 1930, based largely on the recommendations of a provincial commission.[4] The following year it established the Saskatchewan Relief Commission, a government agency that dispensed rural assistance for three years without a whiff of political interference or insider profiteering.[5] The government also tackled the growing problem of rural debt—both in the form of outstanding bank loans for farmland and machinery and mounting tax arrears. In 1931, it introduced the first of several bills in this area, the Debt Adjustment Act, which offered debtors the opportunity to work out new arrangements with their creditors through the mediation efforts of a debt commissioner or, alternatively, to apply for a debt moratorium. Other legislation tried to deal with tax arrears by providing for more favourable repayment schedules for defaulters. These measures barely dented the problem—total agricultural debt was a staggering $525 million by the end of 1936—but at least farmers and businesses were one step closer to keeping their property.[6]

A clown tries to get a smile from visitors at the 1931 Regina fair. SASKATCHEWAN ARCHIVES BOARD R-B11262

The Anderson government also extended a lifeline to the Saskatchewan Wheat Pool. For the 1929–30 crop year, the three prairie pools had set the initial delivery payment at a dollar per bushel on the assumption that the final price for wheat would be at least in the $1.50 range. But then the international price began its downward slide and the pools found to their horror that the grain on hand was not even worth the initial price; they had overpaid producers by twenty-three million dollars. Banks, which had loaned the money for the initial payment, understandably started to panic. The three prairie governments, recognizing the importance of the pooling network to the regional economy, promised to back the pools' loans at a meeting in Regina in December 1929. The reprieve from certain bankruptcy, however, was short-lived, particularly since the initial payment for 1930–31 (only seventy cents) was still too high, and the financial crisis only worsened. At this point, Ottawa agreed to bail out the pools, but on federal terms. Prime Minister R. B. Bennett insisted that pools stop selling wheat; they could continue as co-operative elevator companies. He also appointed a respected former private grain dealer, John I. McFarland, to assume responsibility for marketing the pools' wheat; one of his first acts was to close the pools' central selling agency.[7] These setbacks for the prairie pools proved extremely disheartening and re-ignited the heated debate over whether there should be a national, compulsory pool. The Anderson government was not immune to this sentiment and passed enabling legislation in early 1931 to create a 100 per cent provincial pool. But it backed away from the idea when the Saskatchewan Court of Appeal ruled that such action infringed on federal marketing powers.[8]

As the provincial situation grew bleaker, Premier Anderson decided in the fall of 1932 to reach out to former premier Jimmy Gardiner, coldly staring across from the opposition benches, and invite the Liberals to enter a formal coalition to do battle with the Depression. One government member even dangled the presidency of the University of Saskatchewan before Gardiner if he would quietly retire from provincial politics and allow other Liberals to join the cabinet. Anderson was lucky not to lose his hand in the offer. Gardiner had the dubious distinction of being the only Saskatchewan premier to be defeated while in office. He was worried that his 1929 electoral defeat might have cost him the coveted mantle as federal Liberal leader Mackenzie King's prairie lieutenant and was determined, for the sake of his political future, to deliver Saskatchewan to the Liberal fold once again. Gardiner consequently showed no pity for his successor. Indeed, Anderson was confronted with the largest opposition in Saskatchewan history. To compound matters, the members on the Liberal benches "knew more about the management of government than did the government itself." The opposition strategy was to highlight government extravagance. Having led the province at a time of relative prosperity and balanced budgets, the Gardiner Liberals charged that Saskatchewan was on the road to ruin thanks to the huge deficits that the Co-operative government was racking up. When an irritated Anderson pleaded for helpful suggestions from the opposition instead of constant criticism, Gardiner encouraged the government to resign.[9]

Premier Anderson's co-operative efforts did not extend to the Communist Party of Canada. Founded in 1921 and taking its direction from Soviet Russia, the moribund party seemed headed for extinction before the Depression imbued the movement with a vigour and relevance unparalleled in its short history. Taking advantage of the massive layoffs and accompanying hardships of the early 1930s, the Communists went on the offensive in the critical battle for the hearts and minds of the Canadian working class. Under its umbrella organization, the Workers' Unity League, the party tried to sign up labourers in traditionally non-unionized sectors of the economy and force recognition strikes. In another bold move, it was the first and only group to attempt to organize the country's unemployed, under the banner of the National Unemployed Workers' Association, in a common fight against the bastions of power and wealth. These proselytizing efforts attracted followers for the simple reason that the Communists held out hope in place of growing despair. Joblessness was not the consequence of personal failing, but the collapse of the capitalist system.[10]

The Communists were particularly active in the province's larger cities, where they organized the jobless to march on relief offices, hold street-corner demonstrations, or circulate petitions. In Saskatoon, labour radical Steve Forkin proved such a thorn in the side of local authorities that the mayor and city commissioner refused to meet with any delegation that included him. In Regina, meanwhile, a branch of the National Unemployed Workers' Association tried to have the relief officer removed apparently for his tight-fisted behaviour.[11] The Communists also appealed to disillusioned agriculturalists by forming the Farmers' Unity League (FUL) in Saskatoon in December 1930. In its newspaper, *The Furrow,* the FUL scorned the capitalist system while extolling the merits of a workers' and farmers' socialist government, achieved by revolutionary means if necessary. Regina citizens got a chance to pronounce on these activities on May Day 1931, when the Communists held a Friday night rally in the city's Market Square that drew a reported ten thousand people. Trouble erupted when several onlookers, incensed by the unfurling of the red flag, attacked paraders as they attempted to march along downtown streets. While both sides jeered and taunted one another, faces were bloodied and banners torn down. It took city police almost three hours and several arrests before the fighting was finally halted.[12]

This clash was only a warm-up to what happened on the streets of Estevan less than six months later. Deep-seam coal mining had been a seasonal industry in southeastern Saskatchewan since the early 1900s. The mines were extremely busy in the winter, producing soft lignite coal for local consumption, and then shut down in the summer, when the laid-off workers, mostly continental European immigrants, were expected to find temporary employment on local farms. But by 1930 there were few opportunities to work on the land, and mine families became entirely dependent on the coal industry for their survival. Falling prices led to smaller profits for mine owners, who passed these losses on to the workforce by drastically cutting wages. Miners also worked long hours without breaks under extremely hazardous conditions; safety provisions in the provincial Mines Act were never fully enforced and repairs were rarely carried out. The housing situation was just as bad. The sixteen-year-old daughter of a miner, one of nine children, described waking up in a company house in winter: "When the weather is frosty ... you cannot walk on the floor because it is all full of snow, right around the room."[13] Miners were forced to accept these conditions if they wanted to keep their jobs, a situation that soon pushed them to seek outside help. In early 1931, they contacted traditional labour unions, but were turned down. They even approached the provincial mines inspector, but were rebuffed. Desperate, they looked to the Communist-led Mine Worker's Union of Canada, which gladly signed them up at an organizational meeting in Estevan in late August 1931.

Predictably, the owners of the six major mines in the Estevan-Bienfait fields refused to recognize the new union; it is debatable whether they would have accepted *any* union. Six hundred miners voted to strike on 7 September and vowed to stay off the job until the union recognition question was resolved. Over the next few weeks, while the striking miners remained peaceful, the employers attacked the Communist nature of the new union, claiming that violence against mine property was inevitable. The Anderson government, in the meantime, with the active co-operation of the federal government, bolstered the local RCMP detachment in anticipation of trouble. When the mine owners and operators started using scab labour, the union organizers decided to hold a sympathy parade in Estevan on 29 September, henceforth known locally as Black Tuesday. As the motorcade reached the city, the striking miners, along with their wives and families, were confronted with an armed cordon of mounted police blocking Fourth Street. The fire department had also been called out in the event hoses were needed to disperse the crowd. Refusing to turn back, one of the miners jumped on the fire truck and started hitting it with a crowbar. He was killed by a police bullet. A vicious battle ensued. The miners, wielding clubs and bricks, never had a chance against the mounties and their revolvers.

When the fighting was over, three were dead, while several others, including local citizens, were wounded. Both the provincial government and the police blamed the trouble in the coal fields, including the riot, on foreigners intent

The clash between mounties and striking coal miners and their families left three dead in Estevan in September 1931. SASKATCHEWAN ARCHIVES BOARD R-A8806-1

on overthrowing constituted authority and proceeded to arrest and convict a handful of union organizers and miners. Members of the RCMP, on the other hand, escaped any reprimand. At the trials, the police insisted that they had not drawn their weapons until attacked. But a photograph in the *Estevan Mercury* clearly shows the Mounties, with guns in hand, lined across the parade route.[14] This discrepancy did not bother Premier Anderson, who was the guest speaker at the founding meeting for a Canadian Legion branch at Bienfait, hurriedly organized a mere two weeks after the riot. "There are people who are trying to take advantage of these present conditions to sow seeds of discontent," he warned. "I will ... combat with all proper means any attempt to destroy the fundamental principles of our British citizenship."[15] The defeated miners responded with their own message. The headstone of the three dead men—Julian Gryshko, Peter Markunas, and Nick Nargan—buried together in the Bienfait cemetery reads, "Lest We Forget. Murdered in Estevan, Sep 29 1931 by RCMP."[16]

Estevan would not be the only place where the mounted police would be used to deal with a difficult situation. Nor was it the only time that the provincial government would dismiss legitimate grievances as the work of a few radicals and reds. One of the major problems of the 1930s was what to do with the single homeless unemployed. By the fall of 1932 and the failure of yet another prairie harvest, there were more than one hundred thousand homeless souls wandering the country, atop boxcars, on the backs of trucks, or on foot, trying to survive by their wits. Many were single men, including Great War veterans, who until the Depression had eked out a living in Canada's resource industries, moving from job to job and from region to region, depending on the season and the demand for their services. There were also several thousand young people, fresh-faced teenagers who had quit school to help support their parents and then left home so that they would not be a burden.

Most transients gravitated to larger cities and towns in their quest for work and, more importantly, relief. But the strict residency requirements adopted by municipalities made them ineligible for assistance, and they had to keep on the move. Ottawa steadfastly refused to assume any responsibility for the growing jobless army, even though the federal minister of labour, after a June 1931 tour of western Canada, cautioned, "Young men can hardly be expected to starve quietly."[17] All Prime Minister R. B. Bennett would do was provide emergency funds under the 1931 relief act, so that western provinces could run their own relief camps for the homeless. He also tried to reduce the number seeking relief by instructing the federal Department of Immigration and Colonization to deport any non-naturalized immigrant who had been convicted of vagrancy or had become a public charge by applying for assistance. Sadly, many of these same people had been brought to Saskatchewan only a few years earlier under the Railways Agreement and were now being shovelled out because they had become destitute.[18]

The Anderson government used the federal relief funds to run camps outside major cities, in provincial parks, and in Prince Albert National Park. One of the largest, opened in early November 1932, was located on the Saskatoon exhibition grounds. It was also one of the most volatile. About two hundred of the city's single unemployed had openly brawled with city police over their refusal to enter what they regarded as a "slave camp."[19] By the following spring, relief administrators had become worried about the simmering tension within the crowded camp and identified some fifty "troublemakers" for transfer to Regina on 8 May 1933. But when the group to be relocated took refuge in the dining hall, surrounded by their supporters, two mounted RCMP troops galloped into the camp to disperse the angry crowd and help the city police remove the men. In the ensuing melee, Inspector L. J. Sampson, who commanded the mounties, fell from his saddle. With his feet caught in the stirrups, he struck his head on a telephone pole while being dragged by his horse. "That poor young man died right in front of our eyes," recalled Bill Hunter, a future Saskatchewan sports promoter, who watched the riot with some childhood friends. "The police told us to get the hell home, and we sure did."[20]

Reeling from Sampson's tragic death, the RCMP attributed the trouble to outside agitators. They also refused to accept any role in inciting the riot, insisting that the use of force was not only unavoidable, but would become increasingly necessary as long as the scourge of Communism was at the door. Premier Anderson felt much the same way. Two days after the relief camp riot, he publicly declared Saskatoon the headquarters of Communism in Saskatchewan and personally pledged, "As long as I live in public life I shall do all in my power to drive those disciples of the Red Flag out of Saskatoon and out of the province."[21]

Anderson's anti-Communist stance was a popular one. Most people looked upon Communism as an alien growth on Saskatchewan soil, something sinister that threatened to destroy Anglo-Canadian values and undermine the state, the church, and the family. Certainly, things were bad, but Communism was not the kind of political doctrine that good, loyal citizens would knowingly embrace or advocate. What worried Anderson and others, though, was not just the Communist organization of aggrieved miners or the jobless. Their greater fear was that Communism would take hold among the province's large continental European population. In fact, because of the assumed link between ethnicity and radicalism, it was widely believed that many new immigrants, especially Ukrainians and Doukhobors, were either infected with

Bolshevism or more susceptible to it than other groups. The mounted police consequently conducted surveillance work among immigrant communities, particularly in east-central Saskatchewan. They also collected information on troublesome individuals who had been in Canada for less than five years and hence subject to deportation.[22] The RCMP commissioner even went so far as to suggest in 1932 that "if we were rid of them [foreigners] there would be no unemployment or unrest in Canada."[23]

The more serious challenge to the Co-operative government and the Liberal opposition, however, came from a new, distinctly Saskatchewan party. During the first few years of the Depression, the United Farmers of Canada (Saskatchewan Section) provided some of the most stinging criticism of the Anderson government's handling of the crisis. They openly feuded with the premier over rural relief and the extent of the suffering, dismissed debt legislation as simple tinkering, and generally complained that any new policy initiatives were stunted and ill-considered. This belief that the provincial government was not doing enough, combined with their emasculation at the hands of the Depression, convinced Saskatchewan farmers that the time had arrived for direct political action. At its February 1931 annual convention, the UFC formally voted to enter politics. But it would be no ordinary or traditional party. The UFC not only embraced a socialist agenda, but actively pursued co-operation with the Independent Labour Party, which had been formed by urban-based Progressives and other like-minded people in Regina

A member of the Independent Labour Party speaking in Regina in 1930. SASKATCHEWAN ARCHIVES BOARD R-B2518

in 1925 and organized on a province-wide basis in October 1931. In July 1932, the two groups decided to come together and fight the next provincial election as the Farmer-Labour Party (FLP).[24]

The formation of such a new, radical party might seem strange in the Saskatchewan setting, but those farmers who desperately wanted to do something about their plight and regain some of their lost dignity in the process had no other choice. The Anderson government, despite its Co-operative label, had not a single farmer representative at the cabinet table. Liberal leader Jimmy Gardiner's record was little better. While premier, he had alienated the province's farmers by fighting the Progressives at every opportunity. And even if he was sympathetic to the agricultural community, Gardiner was in no position to help from the opposition benches. Nor did his party seem to be in touch with the problems of rural Saskatchewan. Throughout the early 1930s, the Liberals continually pushed tariff reform as a panacea for the current economic crisis. The adoption of a socialist platform was also not surprising. Since the early twentieth century, Saskatchewan farmers had been advocating all kinds of reforms—from co-operative grain handling to free trade to a national, compulsory grain-marketing board. E. A. Partridge, the revered farm leader who had spearheaded the early agrarian movement, once called for a total recasting of prairie society along totalitarian lines in his 1926 book, *A War on Poverty*.

It was the Depression, however, that pushed a growing number of angry farmers in the direction of socialist reform. Losing money on every bushel of wheat they tried to harvest and facing the loss of the family farm to creditors, they began to see such initiatives as a planned national economy, government ownership of utilities and natural resources, a national bank, and a public health system as the only way out of the mess they found themselves in. These ideas found a natural home in the UFC, which had always been on the radical edge of farmer organizations. The really big, controversial step, though, was the decision to enter politics at the 1931 convention—something that not all delegates supported. Those who did argued that farmers had to act like a partisan party if they were going to avoid the failures of the Progressive party in the 1920s. They also recognized the need to work with the other socialist group in Saskatchewan, the Independent Labour Party, to broaden their appeal and attract as many people as possible to their cause.[25]

There has been considerable debate, even to this day, about the true nature of the FLP. Some have suggested that Saskatchewan was not a radical hotbed in the 1930s and that the new party actually sailed a rather moderate course on the winds of pragmatic reform. Others have dismissed such an interpretation as sheer nonsense and pointed to the revolutionary colours flown on the new party's mast.[26] What is apparent is that the FLP represented a radical alternative at the time: farmers and labourers were not only joining together to deal with the disruption and dislocations of the Depression, but doing so as socialists. One of the most-cited examples of the new party's socialist agenda was the use-lease system of land tenure, under which the government would control all land and lease it to farmers. This policy smacked of the land collectivization underway in Soviet Russia in the 1930s and was often held up to substantiate the claim that the FLP was a Marxist group. But in reality, the kind of socialism advocated by the new party had more to do with Jesus Christ than some obsessed German political philosopher. Outraged by the poverty, deprivation, and hopelessness wrought by the Depression, the FLP turned to the Bible and applied its teachings to the everyday problems of Saskatchewan society.[27] Louise Lucas, one of the party's organizers, once confessed how "she was trying to view the situation from the standpoint of a mother and a Christian."[28] What they came up with was a Christian socialism, which combined a practical Christianity with British Fabianism and its emphasis on gradual, social democratic reform. The party, for example, was not necessarily against private ownership, but rather the evils of monopoly capitalism which allowed mortgage companies to seize land from struggling farmers. George Williams, one of the founders of the new party, tried to explain this distinction in a 1932 pamphlet, *What is this Socialism?*: "Socialism does not mean … that if you have two shirts you must give one to your friend … It does mean that no one will be obliged to go without a shirt."[29] Another early party supporter, J. H. Sturdy, stressed that the FLP stood for equality of opportunity.

The person chosen to lead the new party to the promised land was Major James Coldwell (his first name was not a military title). Born in England in 1888, he immigrated to Canada before the Great War and served as a school principal in Saskatchewan, first in a rural district and then in several Regina schools. A Conservative turned Progressive, Coldwell moved steadily leftward through the 1920s, in response to the problems of the working-class neighbourhoods in which he worked, while serving as an extremely popular alderman. By 1931, he headed the Independent Labour Party, and his reputation and integrity made him an ideal candidate to head the fledgling FLP; both the Conservatives and Liberals had previously courted him.[30] Coldwell's moderate reform socialism helped ease public fears about the new party. He once said that "socialism meant simply putting into practice the principles of Christian brotherhood."[31] He also established the party tradition of education and organization through personal example, making a determined effort to speak to political gatherings throughout the province on evenings and weekends, while holding down his day job as a Regina principal. "I drove back to Moosomin after the Rocanville meeting on Saturday night," he informed

The cover of a CCF brochure featuring Saskatchewan leader M. J. Coldwell.
UNIVERSITY OF SASKATCHEWAN ARCHIVES
MG224

party headquarters in December 1932, "catching the train at 4 a.m., 28 below zero, twenty five miles, and no heat in the car, I was pretty well frozen."[32] He sometimes hired a plane to get around, but not without mishap. When returning by air from a meeting in Prince Albert in the spring of 1934, the engine failed and his plane was forced to make a dramatic forced landing at Govan. "One thing, quite unintentionally, it is giving us tremendous publicity," Coldwell remarked. "Well, I prefer less publicity at this price."[33]

In August 1932, delegates from the FLP represented Saskatchewan at a Calgary meeting to bring together the diverse farmer and labour groups across the country into a new national party, the Co-operative Commonwealth Federation (Farmer, Labourer, Socialist). The CCF held its first convention in Regina the following summer. James Shaver Woodsworth, former Methodist preacher and Winnipeg Labour MP, was selected as leader, and the party's official platform, known as the Regina Manifesto, was vigorously debated and adopted. Although the FLP was formally affiliated with the CCF, it was decided to keep the original party label until after the next Saskatchewan election. Both parties, however, became victims of a smear campaign. It was bad enough the federal party's constitution was called a manifesto, but the last sentence had the ring of revolution: "No CCF Government will rest content until it has eradicated capitalism and put into operation the full programme of socialized planning which will lead to the establishment in Canada of the Co-operative Commonwealth."[34]

Prime Minister Bennett lumped the new party in with the nefarious Communists, the same group he had vowed to crush with "the iron heel of ruthlessness."[35] Federal Liberal leader Mackenzie King, on the other hand, was slighted by the emergence of the CCF after all the Liberals had done for the west and dismissed it as the "plaything ... of pseudo-intellectuals, monetary cranks, advocates of 'Socialism in our time,' and faddists."[36] Back in Saskatchewan, Premier Anderson accused the FLP of advancing ideas more popular in Russia, while opposition leader Gardiner, no fan of third parties, treated his new foe "with suspicion but also with derision."[37] What was ironic about these attacks is that the Farmers' Unity League, the true Communist organization in Saskatchewan, resented any association with the new party and denounced it as fascist. The tendency to confuse the two groups, however, alarmed FLP organizers, and they worked hard to promote their message that they aimed to bring about "a new economic order by peaceful constitutional means."[38]

Saskatchewan Indians, numbering more than fifteen thousand in 1931, also resumed their organizational efforts during the decade. After languishing during the late 1920s, the League of Indians of Canada found new life as a strictly western group dedicated to securing redress for treaty grievances made worse by the Depression. The key player in the rejuvenated organization was

John B. Tootoosis worked tirelessly to organize Saskatchewan Indians. N. Sluman and J. Goodwill, *John Tootoosis*

John Baptiste Tootoosis, League secretary for Saskatchewan and the grand-nephew of the revered Chief Poundmaker. Once described as a "walking encyclopedia" because of his intimate knowledge of Indian issues, Tootoosis stormed the back roads of western Canada promoting the League, while trying to evade local Indian Affairs officials and the mounted police because he was away from his home reserve without a permit.[39] In 1936, the sixtieth anniversary of the signing of Treaty 6, he travelled to Ottawa to find out what had happened to the resolutions that had been passed at the annual League meetings and faithfully forwarded to the Department of Indian Affairs for consideration. When he asked the secretary of the department for answers then and there, the official rolled up the documents that Tootoosis had carried with him and threw them to the side of his desk. The action provoked an angry outburst from the Saskatchewan leader, and the pair would have come to blows if not for the intervention of another bureaucrat.[40] Tootoosis' hostile reception led to a large League gathering the following year at North Battleford. Chiefs and headmen also used the annual treaty payment meetings to complain bitterly about Ottawa's indifference.[41] But the frustration would only continue to grow and fester as long as the Indians had no voice in running their own affairs and no opportunity to participate in the larger provincial society.

The other group that continued to feel neglected, despite having the vote, was the Métis. Not even the League of Indians of Western Canada wanted to include them; Tootoosis consistently argued that the goals and interests of the two groups were fundamentally different.[42] In 1935, Joseph Ross, a Regina labourer, began to call for a Métis organization to lobby the provincial and federal governments for much-needed assistance and the settlement of their traditional land claims. With the help of fellow Métis Henry McKenzie, Ross founded the Half-breeds of Saskatchewan. But despite its title, the group was largely a Regina body and focused its energies on urban issues. Two years later, the organization was reconstituted as the Saskatchewan Métis Society and set its sights on becoming a provincewide network. Ross, who had secured a pass upon his retirement from the railway, toured the province, promoting the SMS and trying to organize locals. It was a difficult task, given that most Métis were just trying to survive the Depression. Ross also learned that the needs of northern and southern Métis often differed and that any new provincial organization had to find room for these competing interests. Until that time, many Métis continued to look to the province or the federal government for assistance.[43]

Premier Anderson sought a new mandate in July 1934. Although the Co-operative government had become identified with the Depression, campaign literature urged Saskatchewan voters, "Don't Swap Horses When

Grey Owl was one of the big attractions in Prince Albert National Park during the depression. LIBRARY AND ARCHIVES CANADA C036186

Crossing a Stream."[44] It was a naive wish. While Anderson had been preoccupied with solving the province's woes, he had neglected Conservative party organization. His emphasis on co-operation had also come undone with the emergence of the FLP and the accompanying shift in electoral alignments.[45] The Anderson government was further handicapped by its direct political links to the widely unpopular federal Conservative government. The depth of the loathing for Prime Minister Bennett was perhaps best illustrated by the behaviour of a Ukrainian woman in the St. Benedict area; she would cut out photographs of Bennett from the newspaper and then poke out the eyes with her scissors before gluing the pictures in her scrapbook.[46]

The Liberals under Gardiner reached back in time to portray themselves as the practical, reform alternative to the Anderson government. They advocated less spending, claiming that the province had "already experienced five years of extravagance" and that good government held the solution.[47] The former premier also realized that the FLP represented the real roadblock to returning to power and told the electorate that the choice was between Liberalism and socialism. He was helped in this cause by the Roman Catholic Church in Saskatchewan, which publicly opposed the new party because of its godless socialism. In May 1934, two Catholic students who had joined a CCF Young People's Club in Wilcox were given an ultimatum by Athol Murray, head of Notre Dame College: either leave the club or leave the college.

"Roman Catholic discipline must be maintained," Father Murray defended his action. "A Catholic cannot be a CCF if a CCF means Socialism."[48] The FLP was distressed by the Church's position, especially given Saskatchewan's large Catholic population, and tried to educate the public about its particular brand of socialism and how it differed from Communism. Coldwell, however, still expected a good showing in the election and even predicted a landslide victory at one point.[49]

Saskatchewan voters delivered a landslide in the 1934 election—but not for the FLP. In one of the most lopsided victories in the province's electoral history, the Liberals won fifty of the fifty-five seats in the legislature. The Conservatives were denied a single seat, even though they polled one-quarter of the popular vote, slightly more than the FLP. They would not send another member to the legislature for another thirty years.[50] What the overwhelming Liberal victory tended to obscure, though, was the FLP's ascent to official opposition, thanks to the election of five candidates, thereafter known as "the quints." This outcome was small consolation to a "bitterly disappointed" Coldwell, who was personally defeated in Regina in his bid to enter the legislature. But the two-party system was still intact in Saskatchewan, albeit with different players, and those who opposed the Liberals had to find comfort with the FLP, which had assumed the reform mantle of the Liberals. This fundamental revolution in Saskatchewan politics was not understood, let alone appreciated, at the time. Even the political veteran Jimmy Gardiner missed the significance of the results. But it would become readily apparent by the next election that the province had entered into a decades-long political struggle where the battle lines were clearly drawn and surrender was not an option.[51]

Anderson stayed on as provincial Conservative leader until October 1936, when he stepped aside in favour of Prince Albert lawyer and future prime minister, John G. Diefenbaker. He tried to keep his hand in the political game, but failed to win a seat at the federal or provincial level despite repeated attempts. He also went without reward for his years of service to the province until 1944, when he was made superintendent of the Saskatoon School for the Deaf two years before his death. Anderson's legacy of co-operation and coalition lives on today, though, in the Saskatchewan Party, an alliance of Conservatives and Liberals.[52] Gardiner, meanwhile, immediately turned to the task of restoring the financial health of the province, assuming the treasurer's portfolio in addition to his job as premier. Less than two weeks after his election victory, Gardiner headed to Ottawa to receive the blessing of Mackenzie King and claim his crown as prairie kingpin. King, sensing his own victory at the polls was only months away, encouraged the Saskatchewan premier to leave provincial politics to run in the next federal election. But

Gardiner demurred, asking for time to get his new government up and running. It was as if he was still smarting from his 1929 defeat and wanted to prove to the province that he could do a better job than Anderson in wrestling the Depression into submission.[53]

Premier Gardiner's decision put him on a collision course with Prime Minister Bennett over the federal government's handling of the transient problem. In October 1932, Ottawa had finally established relief camps for the single homeless unemployed under the auspices of the Department of National Defence; the men were fed, clothed, sheltered, and paid twenty cents per day in exchange for labour on various make-work projects. Although the scheme was universally applauded at the beginning, it did not take long for the camps to become the focus of discontent and disillusionment. In April 1935, hundreds of disgruntled men walked out of camps throughout British Columbia and descended on Vancouver in a bold attempt to reverse their dead-end lives and secure some meaningful employment. But no level of government wanted to help the men, least of all the Bennett government, which believed that the Communists had orchestrated the protest. Eventually, the relief-camp strikers decided to go to Ottawa and present their grievances directly to the prime minister.

An estimated one thousand On-to-Ottawa trekkers left Vancouver by freight train in early June 1935. No one expected the trek to survive the trip through the mountains. But the same kind of organizing zeal that had kept the strike going in Vancouver gave the trek a seemingly unstoppable momentum as it headed across the prairies. After the trek had left Calgary,

The On-to-Ottawa trekkers were stopped by the RCMP in Regina in June 1935. SASKATCHEWAN ARCHIVES BOARD R-B3485(1)

picking up more recruits, the Bennett government publicly branded it a Communist plot and announced that the RCMP would stop the unlawful movement in Regina. Premier Gardiner was infuriated by the federal order to dump the men on the doorsteps of the provincial capital, like unwanted waifs, and insisted that the railways were obligated to take the men out of Saskatchewan. He also predicted that the massing of the mounted police could lead to only one outcome—a riot. But Gardiner's ranting and hand-wringing were dismissed as partisan theatrics, and all the Saskatchewan government could do was prepare for the arrival of the trek, now numbering an estimated two thousand men, in the early morning hours of 14 June.

The much-anticipated Regina showdown turned into a two-week stale-mate between the trekkers and the police. On 17 June, two federal cabinet ministers met with trek leaders in Regina and, after failing to reach any kind of agreement, invited them to send a delegation to Ottawa to deal directly with the prime minister. But instead of resolving the standoff, the Ottawa meeting degenerated into a shouting match between Bennett and trek leader Arthur "Slim" Evans. The trekkers refused to give up, though, and tried to send a group of men eastward by car and truck on 27 June, only to have the convoy intercepted by the mounted police. With no way out of Regina, and with their own funds exhausted, the trekkers decided to end the trek and return to the west coast. Ottawa insisted, however, that the men had to dis-band on federal terms—namely, go to a nearby holding facility at Lumsden where they would be processed.

Sensing the Lumsden camp was a trap, the trek leadership turned to the Gardiner government for assistance on the afternoon of 1 July, the Dominion Day holiday. Later that evening, while the provincial cabinet was meeting to discuss the trekker request, the RCMP, with the support of the Regina City Police, decided to execute arrest warrants for the trek leaders at a public rally at Market Square. The mounted police could easily have made the arrests at any time during the day, but with clubs and tear gas at the ready, chose to pluck the men from a peaceful fundraising meeting—with the expected results. The raid quickly degenerated into a pitched battle between the police and trekkers and citizens, which spilled over into the streets of downtown Regina. Order was not restored until early the next day, but only after the city police had fired directly into a crowd of rioters. The toll was two dead—not one as usually reported—hundreds injured, and tens of thousands of dollars of damage to downtown Regina. A provincial commission, which included former premier William Martin, would later blame the trekkers for the riot, while completely exonerating the police.[54]

Prime Minister Bennett's rough handling of the trek was another unpop-ular measure that voters had to chew on in the October 1935 general election.

It was widely conceded that the Conservatives would go down to defeat. Many looked to Mackenzie King to propose new programs or talk about new ideas during the campaign, but the wily federal leader remained noncommittal. Not wanting to give his opponents anything to attack, he believed it best to hammer away at Bennett's mismanagement of the unemployment crisis, while portraying the Liberals as the only viable and trustworthy alternative. The strategy worked, and the Liberals stormed back into office with the largest general election victory to date. Jimmy Gardiner resigned as premier and leader of the Saskatchewan Liberal party on 1 November and was named to the federal cabinet as minister of agriculture three days later. Attorney-General Tommy Davis, the most famous Tommy in Saskatchewan until the Douglas fellow came along, could have succeeded Gardiner, but did not want the premiership. Instead, he supported William J. Patterson as the new leader. The forty-nine-year-old Patterson, formerly a banker, was the first Saskatchewan premier to be born in the province. He was also a veteran, having been wounded in France while serving as a lieutenant in the Canadian Light Horse Infantry. Perhaps providentially, he had been a delegate at the convention that had selected Walter Scott as Liberal leader in 1905.[55]

By the fall of 1935, it seemed that the stars were finally in alignment for Saskatchewan, with both the prime minister and the minister of agriculture representing the province. But whereas King had once regarded the west as the future of the country, he now saw it as a troubled region, mired in debt and home to third-party protest. He consequently gave the prairies less attention—or at least tried to.[56] One example was the Prairie Farm Rehabilitation Administration (PFRA), a temporary initiative introduced by the Bennett government in April 1935 to arrest soil drifting and promote water conservation in the drought-stricken short-grass prairie district. Although the emergency program was intended as a co-operative measure with the three prairie provinces, the federal government was effectively assuming control, committing almost five million dollars over five years. It fell to the new King government, however, to continue to fulfill the legislation, and the prime minister was not keen. "It is part of U.S. desert area," he noted in his diary. "I doubt if it will be of any real use again."[57] But Gardiner, whose department was responsible for administering the program, embraced the PFRA as the only realistic solution to the mistake of opening the area to farming in 1908. In fact, in 1937, as the situation in southern Saskatchewan worsened, Gardiner pushed through an amendment that empowered Ottawa to take land out of cultivation and create community pastures. Two years later, the act was made permanent, a recognition that ongoing management was necessary to ensure the ecological integrity of the region.[58]

Another Conservative policy that Prime Minister King wanted to end was

Premier Patterson (right) was the first premier born in what would become Saskatchewan.
SASKATCHEWAN ARCHIVES BOARD R-A10420

the Canadian Wheat Board. Under intense western pressure to create a national marketing agency, Prime Minister Bennett had established a voluntary wheat board in the dying days of his administration. As of 1935, farmers had the option of selling their wheat through a federal agency for a maximum fixed price. King wanted to limit government intervention and was prepared to kill the Canadian Wheat Board at the first opportunity. But the board controlled the bulk of the 1935 crop, over two hundred million bushels, and could not be dissolved until the wheat was sold. This reprieve allowed prairie farmers to argue for the continuation of the Wheat Board, and in the face of possible western unrest over the issue, King shelved the idea.[59]

Prime Minister King also returned to power determined to improve the financial position of the federal treasury after years of what he regarded as extravagance by the Bennett government in helping to cover the relief responsibilities of the three prairie provinces.[60] When Saskatchewan and Manitoba warned Ottawa in 1936 that they might default on their loans, the prime minister was unsympathetic, arguing that federal support had become a crutch and that the sickly provinces should be forced to stand on their own. But on second thought, the new Liberal government decided to appoint a sweeping royal commission in August 1937 to investigate the division of powers and financial responsibilities between the federal and provincial governments. In preparing its brief to the Rowell-Sirois Commission, the Patterson government worked closely with its Manitoba counterpart to present a united western response.[61] The report provided a detailed snapshot of how the Depression had ravaged the prairie region and explained how the fiscal arrangements underlying Confederation made no sense in the current circumstances. Until the commission made its recommendations, though, Saskatchewan continued to seek help from Ottawa in meeting its relief obligations. Fortunately for the province, the King government provided temporary aid—no small concession when the relief bill from September 1937 to March 1938 exceeded six million dollars.[62]

Although Saskatchewan had just come through the worst winter of the Depression, Premier Patterson decided to secure his own mandate and go to the polls in June 1938. His record as Gardiner's successor had followed the traditional Liberal script. Observing that "the administration of the public business of a Province is fundamentally a business proposition,"[63] Patterson had offered prudent, practical government that tried to meet the needs of the Saskatchewan public in an even-handed and responsible manner. He was not averse, though, to adopting controversial measures, such as introducing the province's first sales tax to help underwrite rural education. He was also prepared to help people to help themselves by passing legislation allowing for the creation of credit unions. He even tried to assist dust-bowl refugees who had traded one meagre existence for another by establishing a Northern Settlers' Re-establishment Branch. The premier was not prepared, however, to go as far as the CCF (formerly the FLP), whose program he viewed as the antithesis to his more individualistic political philosophy. Comments were made during the campaign about CCF dictatorship, but nothing approaching the vicious partisan attacks on the party in later years.[64]

The CCF was ready to do battle with the Patterson Liberals with a new leader, new strategy, and new organization. When M. J. Coldwell was elected to the House of Commons for Rosetown-Biggar in the 1935 federal election, he was replaced as provincial leader by George Williams, who had entered the Saskatchewan legislature in 1934 as one of the five FLP members and had served as opposition leader. Under Williams' stewardship, the CCF abandoned its contentious use-lease land policy at its 1936 convention in favour of placing greater emphasis on a planned economy. The party also tried to emulate the Liberals by making party organization, especially in non-Anglo-Saxon districts, a priority. It recruited and equipped a volunteer army of dedicated workers who exceeded even Liberal practices by "ma[king] politics an all-day, every-day, occupation." Their most potent argument was that Saskatchewan was no better off with the Patterson Liberals and that the government wanted to "keep everything rigid, stationary, and unchanging." In fact, the intensity of the CCF attack prompted a somewhat beleaguered Tommy Davis to privately wish for the return of the Conservatives.[65]

The wild card in the 1938 provincial election was the Social Credit party. Fresh from its overwhelming victory in the 1935 Alberta election and its impressive success in the 1935 federal election, the party moved into Saskatchewan with its seductive monetary theory, portraying itself as a force that would liberate the province from the shackles of the Depression. Both the Liberals and CCF responded by characterizing Alberta premier William Aberhart as a despot intent on ruling the province from Edmonton; Coldwell, for one, claimed that Saskatchewan voters were being treated to the Canadian version of Italian dictator Mussolini invading Ethiopia.[66] This strategy repulsed the Social Credit challenge and allowed the Liberals to return to office with thirty-eight of fifty-two seats. But the results also confirmed the CCF as a legitimate contender for power in the province. The Liberals had assumed that the appeal of the new protest party would dissipate with the return of better prices and better crops. The majority of the ten CCF seats in 1938, however, were secured in areas where farmers were generally better off, while the Liberals garnered votes in districts where the people were still largely dependent on government relief.[67] The obvious conclusion, according to George Williams, was that "the CCF is here to stay, that it is the alternative to the Liberal party."[68] This reading of the situation was only more bad news for the Conservatives, who had once again failed to win a seat in the legislature and seemed condemned to wander in Saskatchewan's political wilderness for decades. That certainly appeared to be the fate of party leader John Diefenbaker, who despite his insatiable political ambition, had now lost every election he had contested at every level.

Once returned to power, the Patterson government began making preparations for the event of the decade—the visit of King George VI and Queen Elizabeth in the spring of 1939. It was the first time that a reigning British monarch had toured Canada, and nothing was going to prevent Saskatchewan's citizens from seeing the royal couple. Indians were especially excited about the visit because of their historic ties to the Crown through the treaties. At each stop on the westward leg of the tour across the southern prairies, even at small towns along the Canadian Pacific line where the royal train was not expected to stop, huge crowds gathered to catch a passing glimpse of the king and queen. More than one hundred thousand waited through light drizzle in Regina on 25 May; another forty thousand braved a heavy downpour in Moose Jaw. The rain did not deter the royals either. They insisted that activities continue as planned, even asking that the top be left down on their car as they made their way through the streets in each city. The

King George VI and Queen Elizabeth, followed by Prime Minister King (far left) and Premier Gardiner, during a stop at Biggar during the 1939 royal tour. SASKATCHEWAN ARCHIVES BOARD R-A6064

long-awaited break in the drought, coupled with the arrival of the king and queen, seemed a sign of good things to come.

On the return trip across the country, the royal train travelled across the prairie parkland on the Canadian National line with stops in Saskatoon and Melville on 3 June. Melville was one of the last western stops on the tour, and one of the last chances for people to see the couple. Farm families reportedly came from as far as two hundred miles away. Cars and trucks rolled in all day from all directions, including Manitoba and the northern United States. Special trains, meanwhile, brought groups from nearby towns. The towns of Yorkton, Esterhazy, and Canora simply closed for the day. By the early evening, several hours before the royal couple was scheduled to arrive, hundreds, then thousands of people began to gather at the Melville train station, where a huge sign proclaiming, "Welcome to Their Majesties," had been painted on the side of the Pool elevator.

Shortly after 10 P.M., the royal train pulled into Melville to the deafening roar of the crowd. Moments later, King George and Queen Elizabeth stepped into a blue spotlight to another thunderous cheer. Smiling and waving, but unable to see much beyond the platform because of the darkness, Queen Elizabeth, better known today as the late Queen Mum, asked that the spotlight

The Melville Pool elevator decorated for the 1939 visit of the King and Queen.
SASKATCHEWAN ARCHIVES BOARD R-A15061

be passed over the audience. She and the king were stunned by the size of the crowd: there were an estimated sixty thousand people on hand. In one day, Melville, with a usual population of four thousand, had become Saskatchewan's largest city. The couple briefly mingled with the crowd before returning to their train just twenty minutes after their arrival. As they waved from the back of the last car before disappearing inside, fireworks were set off.

Melville's extraordinary welcome made headlines across North America. Reporters were particularly struck by how the region's immigrant population, mostly from central and eastern Europe, had so eagerly embraced the visiting couple. The reception also left a lasting impression on the royals. In a telegram to town officials the next day, King George confessed, "The Queen and I will not easily forget the scene which greeted us at Melville."[69] More than anything else, though, the Melville celebrations reassured British officials of Canadian loyalty to the Crown. Throughout the royal tour, there were regular dispatches about the deteriorating situation in Europe and the looming threat of another war. Naturally, British officials travelling with the royal couple wondered how Canadians would respond. The brief Melville stop left no doubt.

CHAPTER SIXTEEN

GETTING THINGS DONE

SASKATCHEWAN WAS MORE PREPARED for the 1939 royal tour than it was for another world war.[1] But even though the province, like the rest of the country, had been caught flat-footed by the march to war against Nazi Germany, more than seventy-five thousand Saskatchewan men and women served in the armed forces during the six-year conflict. Those left at home rallied to support the war effort in whatever way they could. In fact, the past decade of hardship and deprivation—of going without and making do—actually served the Saskatchewan public well in meeting the heavy demands of the Second World War. In making these sacrifices, though, people looked forward to a new and better post-war world, full of promise and the return of prosperity. The Great Depression may have humbled the province, but citizens refused to accept any limitations on Saskatchewan's future. By the mid-1940s, they were ready for change, especially if it offered the prospect of long-term stability. The 1944 Saskatchewan election consequently completed the political revolution initiated by the Depression by bringing to power the CCF, the first socialist party to form a government in North America. The CCF promised a new vision of the future fuelled by renewed confidence in the province's potential. It seemed like 1905 all over again.

Canada went to war in September 1939 out of a sense of duty to Great Britain. Unlike the buoyant mood at the outbreak of the Great War, there was no great enthusiasm for what lay ahead, no bold talk of committing every man and every dollar to guarantee victory. Instead, the Mackenzie King government steadfastly pursued a "limited liability" policy in the interests of maintaining national unity. There would be no conscription for overseas service, nor would there be any large military commitments. This policy perfectly suited the "phony war" phase in late 1939. The German offensive in the spring of 1940, however, changed the entire complexion of the conflict, and with the fall of France and the Nazi occupation of western Europe, Canada emerged as Great Britain's foremost military ally.

The King government responded to the crisis by introducing the concept of conscription for home defence. All men and women over sixteen years of age could now be called upon for home-guard duty or other essential war service, while volunteer members of the armed forces would be sent overseas. It also committed more troops to the war as soon as new divisions could be organized. But Ottawa never wavered from its limited liability approach, thanks largely to the entry of the United States into the war following the Japanese bombing of Pearl Harbor in December 1941. By then, hostilities reached not only across the Pacific, but into Africa, the Middle East, and Asia. The growing number of Canadian casualties from this "total war," especially after the successful Normandy invasion in June 1944, eventually forced a reluctant King government to introduce conscription for overseas service in November. But, because the decision had been delicately handled by the governing Liberals as a measure of last resort, it never precipitated the kind of national crisis that had scarred the country in 1917.

At the beginning of the war, only two Saskatchewan militia units were mobilized. The Saskatoon Light Infantry (machine gun) was part of the First Canadian Division that was sent to England in the late fall of 1939 under the command of Moosomin-born General Andy McNaughton. The other Saskatchewan infantry unit, the Weyburn-based South Saskatchewan Regiment, was held back until the bleak summer of 1940. It was soon joined by the Regina Rifles, which were hurriedly brought to full strength in June 1940 with the addition of companies from Prince Albert and North Battleford.[2] Saskatchewan men also served in several other units during the course of the war. Provincial historian Dr. John Archer, for example, was an instructor with the Royal Canadian Artillery. An estimated one thousand Aboriginal recruits, about half of them Indians, also enlisted, including all ten sons of the Arcand family from the Muskeg Lake reserve.[3] Volunteers had any number of personal reasons for joining, but many sought to escape the lingering effects of the Depression. "Things were pretty tough; there wasn't much work around," confessed Métis veteran Joseph Fayant. "I thought, 'What else am I going to do? Where am I going to make a living?'"[4]

Soldiers from Saskatchewan distinguished themselves in battle. David Greyeyes of Muskeg Lake earned the Greek Military Cross for selflessly supporting the Greek Mountain Brigade during the Italian campaign, while Joseph McGillivray, a Métis trapper from Cumberland House, helped capture the notorious Kurt Meyer, the German general who had ordered the execution of captured Canadian servicemen during the Falaise campaign in the summer of 1944.[5] In May 1943, twenty-three-year-old Ken Brown, a Lancaster bomber pilot from Moose Jaw, required eight passes at low level through a mist-shrouded valley before scoring a direct hit on the huge dam at Sorpe and going down in military history as one of the famed "Dambusters."[6] Another soldier from Moose Jaw, Major David Currie, won the Victoria Cross in August 1944 for routing a large German force from the village of St. Lambert-sur-Dives in France and then repulsing repeated counterattacks over the next few days. He is the only Saskatchewan-born recipient of the award. The French town of Les Martres-de-Veyre, meanwhile, is twinned with Wynyard in memory of rear gunner Peter Dmytruk, who was shot down in 1942 and worked for the French Resistance in the Auvergne region before being mortally wounded trying to run a German roadblock.[7] One of the most amazing Saskatchewan war stories was not about fighting, but survival. At the urging of the local priest, the francophone community of Debden placed pictures of the men who had volunteered around the church altar and prayed daily for their safety. Forty-six went to war, many of them seeing combat, and yet all forty-six returned home. People said it was a miracle.[8] Today, the names of Saskatchewan's war dead live on in northern lakes, bays, islands, and other geographical features named in their memory.[9]

Beginning in 1941, Saskatchewan women were also given the opportunity to enlist in the army (Canadian Women's Army Corps or CWAC) and air force (Women's Division, RCAF). The following year, the navy welcomed female recruits (Women's Royal Canadian Naval Service or Wrens). Although none of the women had combat roles, they performed essential duties, becoming wireless operators, mechanics, parachute riggers, drivers, and clerks. They also came under enemy fire at times.[10] Mollie Hough of Saskatoon made an unexpected contribution to the war effort. In June 1943, while training as a Wren, Mollie was photographed in a bathing suit reclining on a diving board

Men enlisting at Prince Albert. GLENBOW ARCHIVES PA-3250-1C

at a swimming pool. The picture was published in the *Maple Leaf*, the newspaper for Canadian troops, and distributed to hundreds of thousands of fighting men. Something about the photo hit home, especially for the Canadian units battling their way north through Italy, and the pin-up of Mollie, the gal next door, became more popular than those of Hollywood stars. Mollie herself had no idea that she had become such a celebrity until she started receiving letters from Canadian servicemen overseas, to the chagrin of her new husband.[11]

Another Saskatchewan woman played a more direct role in the war. In the late 1930s, Gladys Arnold from Macoun was the Canadian Press representative in Europe and filed several stories warning about German rearmament. The day before Paris fell to the Nazis, Arnold escaped during the night and eventually reached London, where she interviewed General Charles de Gaulle and took up the Free French cause. This work took her to Washington where she met American president Franklin Roosevelt; she also had dealings with British leader Winston Churchill. In 1971, the French government named her a Chevalier of the Legion of Honour, a rare award for a foreigner, especially a woman.[12]

In Saskatchewan, the war touched all aspects of daily life. Because of the demand for food and materials, ration coupons were introduced for certain products, such as coffee, tea, sugar, butter, and gasoline. Fashion was also affected, as clothing styles were simplified in order to save material; men's suit jackets were no longer double-breasted, while pants became pleatless and cuffless. This spirit of sacrifice in the name of the war was reinforced by volunteer work, whether it be the annual Victory Loan drives and "Back the Attack" community rallies, which encouraged the purchase of war savings stamps, or the collecting of scrap iron and other salvageable materials in door-in-door canvassing blitzes. Some Saskatchewan families took in young boys and girls, known as "guest children," who had been evacuated from Great Britain to the safety of Canada in 1940.[13]

Sports were put on hold because of the number of men away fighting the war. In 1942, the Canadian Football League cancelled play indefinitely. The Brier, the national men's curling championship, was also suspended in 1943, the year that Saskatoon was scheduled to host the event. When competition resumed three years later, the prizes included war bonds. People could still listen to NHL games on the radio, but many local stars put aside their professional hockey careers to serve King and country. Max Bentley, popularly known as the "Dipsy Doodle Dandy from Delisle," missed two seasons with the Chicago Blackhawks. When he returned from the war in 1946, he became part of the famed Pony Line, with brother Doug and Bill Mosienko, and won two consecutive scoring titles before being traded to the Toronto Maple Leafs. About two dozen Saskatchewan women played in the All-American Girls' Professional Baseball League, established by chewing gum tycoon Phil Wrigley in 1943 to fill the void left by male players serving in the war. Regina-born Mary "Bonnie" Baker was an all-star catcher for the South Bend Blue Sox and likely served as the inspiration for the Geena Davis character in the feature film *A League of Their Own*.[14]

The war also permeated popular forms of mass entertainment. Radio brought the war into Saskatchewan homes through Canadian Broadcasting Corporation (CBC) announcer Lorne Green, the "voice of doom," and correspondent Matthew Halton. American movies took on explicit war themes after the bombing of Pearl Harbor. And the sound of the war came to be identified with the big dance bands from the United States and their infectious swing music.[15]

Another consequence of war was the large number of young people leaving the province to take up war-related jobs. Men too young to fight or turned down for medical reasons found employment in factories in central Canada or on the west coast. Women were also recruited under a national campaign, "Roll Up Your Sleeves for Victory!," to fill tens of thousands of positions in war industries. In October 1942, for example, an employment officer came to Regina to hire five hundred women for an Ontario munitions plant. The work, and the money that went along with it, was a sharp contrast to the Depression years. Many would never return to the province.[16]

The war also revived old concerns about the loyalty of Saskatchewan's

Downtown Saskatoon, with the Bessborough Hotel in the distance, in the early 1940s.
SASKATCHEWAN ARCHIVES BOARD R-B7873

large ethnic population. According to the 1931 census, the mother tongue of two out of every five people in the province was neither French nor English. In fact, the population of German descent numbered around 130,000, or about 15 per cent. Most of these people had lived in the province for one or two generations and were an integral part of the provincial fabric. But what alarmed some Saskatchewan citizens were the activities of the Deutscher Bund, an organization founded in 1934 to unify Germans across Canada and cultivate and promote National Socialism. By 1939, more than half of the country's seventy-one Bund cells were located in the province, mostly among recent, young German immigrants who had been pauperized by the Depression and looked back nostalgically to their homeland. As the prospect of war drew closer, members of the Loon River Bund decided to return to Germany; ironically, Sudeten refugees fleeing Nazi oppression later acquired their land. Once war did come, the RCMP moved quickly to quash the Bund, rounding up several prominent Nazi sympathizers and interning them under the Defence of Canada regulations.[17] The provincial government, however, was not satisfied with the measures and created a Saskatchewan Veterans Civil Security Corps in 1940, ostensibly to monitor immigrants of enemy origin.[18] Premier William Patterson even counselled Jimmy Gardiner to be wary of Germans. This behaviour, bordering on alarm, was not restricted to the premier. One long-time Liberal worker in Regina reported in June 1940 that "every member of the Government is going goofy right now."[19] The same comment could have applied to about one hundred Regina citizens and soldiers who went on a two-night rampage in the east end of the city and damaged several ethnic businesses.[20]

A more vexing problem was what to do with hundreds of conscientious objectors who were still required to undertake basic military training under the 1940 National War Services Regulations. The University of Saskatchewan had a simple solution. When seven students, most of them from St. Andrew's College, refused to take compulsory training because of their pacifist beliefs, J. S. Thomson, the new president and a Great War veteran, expelled them.[21] A more deft touch was needed in dealing with Mennonites and Doukhobors, who had been promised, as a condition of their immigration to Canada, that they would never have to bear arms. Ottawa eventually decided in December 1940 that conscientious objectors, defined as members of any religious organization, be required to provide some form of "alternate service" labour for the same period of military training. The following June, Mennonite men in their early twenties began receiving their call-ups, and after confirming their status at a hearing before a War Services Board, were sent to Prince Albert National Park for four months. Away from their tightly knit communities for the first time and anxious to fulfil their term of service, the men proved hardened workers. They did maintenance duties that would otherwise have been neglected because of the war and built a large breakwater on Waskesiu Lake.[22] Doukhobor men, on the other hand, were called upon to complete the new road from Montreal Lake north to La Ronge. The construction of the highway through the boreal forest proved something of a nightmare because of muskeg, but the eighty Doukhobor workers were equal to the challenge and completed about twenty-five miles of road during the summer of 1941. The highway confirmed Prince Albert's historic position as gateway to the provincial north; the business it generated, however, did little to solve the community's serious financial problems.[23]

Saskatchewan cities looked to the war to get them out from under the huge debts they were carrying from the Depression years. They were convinced that the securing of war contracts would provide a much-needed economic shot in the arm and thereby reduce the number still on urban relief rolls. They also saw war work as a way to revive the service and construction industries and renew an urban landscape that had not changed significantly since 1912. But despite intense lobbying by civic governments and local boards of trade, Regina was awarded the only major government order—the production of anti-tank gun carriages by the old General Motors plant, renamed Regina Industries Limited.[24] The other, more promising possibility for Saskatchewan communities was securing a training school as part of the new British Commonwealth Air Training Plan (BCATP). In December 1939, after weeks of often-difficult negotiation, Canada agreed to serve as home for an empire-wide program to train fighter and bomber crews for the war. It was a hugely ambitious undertaking that aimed to produce fifty thousand graduates. Indeed, at Prime Minister King's insistence, the official announcement called the scheme Canada's "most effective contribution to the war effort."[25] American president Franklin Roosevelt, who always seemed to find the right phrase, claimed that the plan would make the dominion "the aerodrome of democracy."[26]

Saskatchewan, with its clear skies, wide open spaces, and sparse population, seemed a likely candidate for several of the schools. It also had had some unusual training experience twenty years earlier. In May 1919, the same month as the first flight between Regina and Saskatoon, "Keng Wah Aviation" of Saskatoon began instructing young Chinese pilots at the request of Dr. Sun Yat-sen of the Chinese Nationalist League.[27] The province's urban centres were aware that air-training facilities promised all kinds of economic spin-offs for the nearest community and were determined to be at the head of the queue when it came time to select BCATP sites. Towns and cities from Big River to Shaunavon to Melville consequently did their best to promote their advantages, while insisting that they deserved special consideration. Both Weyburn and Estevan claimed that they were owed a base because of the rav-

Aircraft from Moose Jaw on a training flight. SASKATCHEWAN ARCHIVES BOARD S-RM-B391

ages of the drought. Mossbank maintained that the presence of air force personnel would "weld together the various races in our midst into one united Canada and strong Commonwealth."[28] A recent study contends that partisan politics played no part in the selection of the western Canadian training sites, but those charged with making the decisions must have known that Prince Albert was the prime minister's home constituency, and that the plan was the key feature of his government's war policy. In the end, fourteen training sites, some including several types of schools, were awarded to Saskatchewan. This figure represented 40 per cent of the BCATP facilities on the prairies. What is more impressive, however, was the fact that half the pilots and one-third of some other aircrew categories Canada-wide were trained in the province.[29]

Although the first facility in Saskatchewan, the Elementary Flying Training School at Prince Albert, began operating in July 1940, it sometimes took more than a year to ready the bases for occupation. The construction boom was a portent of what the arrival of thousands of trainees would mean to the communities. Weyburn was so thrilled about the turnaround in its fortunes that it ordered nameplates for its streets.[30] The *Yorkton Enterprise* predicted nothing but good things for the city. "This [base] will help all lines of business," it reported. "Airmen have clothing to buy, suits to be cleaned, shoes to be purchased, and yes, shoes to be shined."[31] These kinds of benefits naturally promoted ties between the schools and the host communities, even if it was just a taxi ride into town or a meal in a favourite restaurant. And given the numbers involved, interaction was unavoidable. The North Battleford base housed thirteen hundred men at a time when the city had a population of forty-seven hundred.[32] Local people also felt a tug of pride for the trainees and the program, a fact driven home almost every day as the yellow Harvards flew overhead. It was the closest that many would come to the war, and they showed a lively interest in base life and the "boys'" progress. No less than eleven thousand people, more than twice the population of Yorkton, turned out for the open house at the Service Flying Training School in June 1941. Less than a week later, when an Australian pilot was killed in a flying accident, it "seemed as though all Yorkton ... had suffered the loss of a personal friend."[33]

For many of the foreign trainees, life on the open prairies was quite a shock. But apart from the occasional condescending British attitude about the lack of culture, the men quickly adjusted to their new environment. Vernon Peters, a British instructor at the Caron Elementary Flying School, told his wife in December 1941 that the "streets are full of teddy bears" because of the people wearing fur hats and coats. "I like their accent & their racy slang & their air of zest & vitality."[34] Local people did their best to make

336 | SASKATCHEWAN: A NEW HISTORY

the men feel at home. On Christmas Day, they would come by the base to pick up one or two trainees for a few hours. School administrators reciprocated by inviting the community to special events. Four thousand people attended the last graduation ceremonies at North Battleford in March 1945. Several of the trainees also played for the Yorkton Terriers hockey team, rechristened the Flyers, for the duration of the war.[35]

These good relations were marred by an ugly incident involving the Moose Jaw base, one of the largest training sites in the country. Many of the British airmen stationed there struck up romances with local girls, a situation that bred jealousy and resentment among the city's young men. The simmering rivalry finally boiled over at a Saturday night dance in September 1944 when a fight between a member of the Royal Air Force (RAF) and a local boy escalated into a brawl in the alley outside. But the worst was yet to come. Only days later, eight British trainees were ambushed and knocked unconscious in Crescent Park by a large gang of teenagers. Word of the attack reached the Temple Gardens dance hall, where 350 RAF members immediately poured into the streets for their long anticipated showdown with the local youth. By the time the RCMP had broken up the fighting, dozens had been bloodied and bruised.[36]

The Moose Jaw riot, although an isolated incident, underscored the tensions at play in a society at war. These were dark, stressful days that left an imprint on the people and the province, as had the Depression. Alexandrina Miller of Weyburn reflected on what the presence of the BCATP trainees meant to their young lives. "We learnt a lot from the fraternization with the British RAF," she recalled. "We were basically Country bred kids that had not travelled far from home, while these boys and men ... had experienced War and the effects of War, whereas for us, War was a word that meant Ration Books and watching for names on the 'Missing in Action' lists."[37] Some, like Alexandrina, married and moved to England or some other Commonwealth country, only to return with their husbands after the war. Other local women joined the Royal Canadian Air Force (RCAF).

Male and female enlistment rates in the air force were high in Saskatchewan relative to other provinces and often included volunteers from the same family. When seventeen-year-old David Ferguson of Fort Qu'Appelle graduated as an air gunner in September 1944, his older brother, Robert, a squadron leader, pinned his wings on him.[38] This kind of bond helped make the BCATP an overwhelming Canadian success story; more than 130,000 pilots and aircrew were contributed to the war effort. The plan also left a legacy of co-operation in the province, of working together to defeat a common enemy. Such was the case in the fall of 1942 when the province appealed for harvesters. About fifty RAF men from the Swift Current school, on a forty-

"Going to be a Hornet's Nest for Somebody." *Toronto Daily Star*, 11 October 1939

eight-hour leave, offered to go to local farms. "They had never seen a farm, never seen wheat," remembered a fellow trainee, "and were out stooking."[39]

This farm help was needed because of the rebound in agricultural production by the start of the war. The return of normal precipitation levels, together with better cultivation practices, often pioneered by the farmers themselves in consultation with university and federal scientists, produced a decent harvest in 1938. The director of the PFRA bravely concluded that "'the Dust Bowl' no longer exists."[40] This confidence was rewarded. The 271 million bushels harvested the following year had been surpassed only by the 1928 provincial wheat crop. But the better harvests, although welcome, could not protect producers from the vagaries of prairie agriculture. It fell to Jimmy Gardiner, the federal agriculture minister, to champion a solution. The 1939 Prairie Farm Assistance Act (PFAA) guaranteed federal payments to farmers who suffered total or partial crop failures. It was landmark legislation, grounded in the notion that Ottawa had a role in stabilizing western agriculture.[41]

Armed with better weather and PFAA support, Saskatchewan farmers expected the demand for wheat to skyrocket with the outbreak of war, taking prices as high as three dollars per bushel. Gardiner encouraged this belief. "Wheat is the outstanding Canadian produce," he told the House of Commons in August 1940, "the one material resource that is of greater importance than any other."[42] Farmers responded by seeding more wheat than ever before and harvesting 500 million bushels, more than half in Saskatchewan. But the Nazi occupation of western Europe cost Canada its traditional wheat customers. Great Britain, meanwhile, was in no position to absorb the surplus; it was more interested in buying meat and other agricultural products, such as butter and cheese. The need for a new agricultural strategy was driven home by the fact that Canada had over 700 million bushels of unsold wheat in January 1941, and that the price per bushel was just slightly more than half a dollar.[43]

The answer, according to the federal Department of Agriculture, was diversification. Adopting the slogan "Less Wheat in 1941 Will help Win the War," Ottawa encouraged western farmers to grow more feed crops and increase their livestock production. This conversion was not easy for a group whose lives had been largely organized around the production of wheat. The livestock industry had also gone into a steep decline during the 1930s because of the drought and the accompanying lack of feed. To force producers to reduce the growing of wheat, the federal government introduced elevator delivery quotas. It also paid farmers an acreage bonus to plant oats and barley or nothing at all. This appeal to farmers' pocketbooks led to a three-million-acre reduction in wheat acreage in Saskatchewan in 1941 and a much smaller wheat harvest. Ideal conditions in 1942, however, produced over 300 million bushels, grown on only 12.3 million acres, the smallest provincial wheat acreage since 1922. But the transition to other crops was making headway. Saskatchewan's wheat acreage in 1943 had declined by 40 per cent since 1940, mostly in the parkland. That same year, for the first time in the twentieth century, more coarse grains had been grown in western Canada than wheat. Some of the new crops included sunflower seeds and rapeseed.[44]

The increased cultivation of feed grains allowed for greater livestock production. Because of the strong British demand for pork, especially bacon, hog production on the prairies soared 400 per cent from 1939 to 1943. The growth in beef production, although not as dramatic, was still steady because of the home market. Milk production also increased, leading to larger dairies and more cheese and butter factories. The raising of chickens, normally a sideline, was also commercialized, largely in response to the British demand for dried eggs, derisively known as "Canadian sawdust."[45] These changes were not made without complaint. Farmers chafed at federal wartime price controls,

Douglas Murray getting a haircut on the farm south of Leross. WAGNER FAMILY

arguing that they were not getting adequate compensation for their products, especially in light of the prices they had been paid in the late 1920s.[46] But the transformation of prairie agriculture in the early 1940s generally went smoothly because of federal controls. New debt was limited because land prices did not rise as they had done during the Great War. Machinery was rationed, going to those farmers who could make best use of the equipment, and farm labour was regulated to ensure that there were enough field workers, especially in the fall. Some of these harvesters included Indians, relocated Japanese Canadians, and German prisoners of war, in addition to women and adolescents.[47] Perhaps the best example of federal intervention, however, was the decision of the King government to make the Canadian Wheat Board a compulsory body—something that farmers had wanted for over two decades. Effective September 1943, it became the monopoly agent for the marketing of wheat.[48] Farmers accepted this government planning in the belief that it would help transform their livelihood from "an uncertain gamble to a business with some foundation and future to it."[49]

As an Allied victory in the war seemed likely in late 1944, Canadians worried that the coming of peace would bring with it another recession, as had happened after the Great War. It was not only the farmers who looked to government to provide stability, security, and prosperity in a post-Depression, post-war world. People wanted to build on the sacrifices and successes of the war years to capture the promise of the future and realize a better life.[50] These demands made the national CCF, with its emphasis on government planning and economic intervention, the most popular party in Canada according to a fall 1943 Gallup poll. Prime Minister King, who had a nose for detecting changing political winds, responded by moving the federal government slightly leftward and assuming responsibility for economic stability through such measures as the 1944 Family Allowances Act (the baby bonus). Whether the Patterson government could do the same thing in Saskatchewan, however, appeared doubtful. Despite a record of sound fiscal management during the Depression and war years, the Liberal government seemed incapable of providing any imaginative new policies that would satisfy the public appetite for change. Instead, the Patterson government was increasingly identified with preserving the status quo, especially after it took the highly unusual step in 1943 of extending the life of the legislature an extra year because of the war.[51]

The CCF, by contrast, was ready with a broad reform plan for post-war Saskatchewan. Since the last provincial election in 1938, the party had further distanced itself from its radical beginnings in favour of a moderate—some have argued, pragmatic—program, more in keeping with the needs and interests of Saskatchewan residents.[52] What made these policies particularly attractive, however, was their comprehensiveness and interconnectedness. The CCF did not just talk about saving the family farm, but emphasized the need to put rural life on a sounder footing. It also spoke of using the state to bring about reform in education, health, and social welfare services so that every citizen enjoyed access to certain minimum standards. And it advocated diversifying the Saskatchewan economy, by state direction and management if necessary, to avoid another Depression.[53] The CCF continued to court successful farmers who were concerned about maintaining their wartime gains, but also aggressively went after the ethnic, urban, and worker vote. Party membership, meanwhile, which had temporarily stalled at around four thousand after the start of the war, grew six times by 1944. The delay in calling the election had only given the CCF more time to prepare, all the while righteously claiming that the Liberals were desperately clinging to office.[54] The CCF's greatest asset, however, was Thomas Clement (Tommy) Douglas, who had been selected provincial leader in 1941 when George Williams enlisted in the army and went overseas. Whereas Patterson, in Prime Minister King's assessment, appeared "heavy, lethargic," his new opponent was a "man of high ideals ... a better leader."[55] It is doubtful that the CCF would have enjoyed the same degree of success without the charismatic Douglas at the helm.

Born outside Glasgow, Scotland, in 1904, Tommy was seven when his working-class family immigrated to Canada and the promise of a better life in

CCF leader Tommy Douglas visiting Canadian troops. LIBRARY AND ARCHIVES CANADA PA138035

booming Winnipeg. He spent the Great War years back in Scotland, while his father fought on the continent, and returned to Canada just in time to witness the 1919 Winnipeg General Strike. Douglas wandered about the crowd of strikers, listened to the impassioned speeches, and then watched the RCMP gun down two men on Bloody Saturday. The experience would imbue his Baptist faith with a sharp reformist edge. Douglas entered Brandon College in the mid-1920s to complete his schooling and eventually become a minister dedicated to bringing about the Kingdom of God on earth. Although short and slight in build, the young Tommy exuded confidence, a sureness rooted in his faith and his unfailing conviction about the oneness of humanity. His first full-time posting was Calvary Baptist Church in Weyburn in 1929, where he worked tirelessly to ease the suffering and privation wrought by depression and drought. A visit with the striking miners in the Estevan coalfields in 1931 confirmed his growing belief that government was failing society at the time of its greatest need. The move to politics was "a relatively logical and painless one" for Douglas.[56] Attracted to the new FLP, he ran unsuccessfully in the 1934 provincial election, but was elected the following year to the House of Commons. Douglas would serve nine years in Ottawa, a fact that is often overlooked due to his close identification with provincial politics. His time there as one of only a handful of CCF representatives honed his already impressive speaking skills, and made him acutely aware of the formidable challenges he faced as a social democrat. It was perfect training for the rough-and-tumble Saskatchewan arena.

Tommy Douglas, by the sheer force of his personality, had an immediate impact on the fortunes of the provincial CCF party. He maintained that the electorate needed a clear, consistent understanding of what to expect from a CCF government and campaigned, seemingly effortlessly, to communicate that message in town halls, on the streets, and at kitchen tables. "He had a smile," recalled a college friend, "and a way of dealing with people."[57] He was sharp-witted and always had a quip, no matter what the occasion. When his chair collapsed at a Fir Mountain meeting, spilling him on the platform, he dragged himself up and, rubbing his butt, announced, "Mr. Chairman, that is just where Mr. Gardiner's Liberals give me a pain."[58] But what made Tommy truly unique, according to Al Johnson, former president of the CBC and one-time senior Saskatchewan bureaucrat, was his mixture of trust and optimism. "[T]he essence of Douglas lay in his idealism," Johnson reflected on his first dealings with the CCF leader sixty years earlier, "and in his capacity to inspire others with his sense of mission." He continued, "Douglas believed in the best of everyone—even those who differed with him ... This belief in the goodness of human nature is important to an understanding of [Douglas]."[59]

The Saskatchewan electorate finally went to the polls on 15 June 1944, just nine days after the Normandy invasion and the beginning of the end of the war. The Liberals, poorly organized and bereft of any inspirational policies, launched a vicious attack on the CCF, deliberately playing upon public fears of communism and fascism. The *Regina Leader-Post* even warned that a socialist victory "may start Canada on the road to strife and devastation."[60] Such tactics only sullied the Liberal image, especially when the CCF leader was a Baptist preacher and CCF candidates and their supporters now represented a broad segment of the population. Besides, people wanted meaningful change, not defensive posturing, and when the votes were tallied, the thirty-nine-year-old Douglas stormed into office. The CCF won forty-seven of fifty-two seats and 53 per cent of the popular vote. Patterson, who retained his seat by just six votes, was one of only five Liberals in the new legislature, while the Conservatives were once again shut out.[61] Douglas was sworn into office on 10 July by another former premier, Saskatchewan chief justice William Martin.

The 1944 election results confirmed—yet again—that the CCF was no temporary phenomenon. They also sent shockwaves through the federal Liberal establishment: if the party could not withstand the CCF onslaught in Jimmy Gardiner's own fiefdom, then what might happen in other parts of

Near Dundurn

Near Weyburn

A berry farm

Near MacDowall

Aberdeen

Near Blaine Lake

Allan Hills, east of Kenaston

Near Foam Lake

Near Unity

Qu'Appelle Valley

Livestock farm

Indoor rodeo, Saskatoon

Blackstrap Lake

There are close to 100,000 lakes in Saskatchewan.

Sulphide Lake, Lac La Ronge Provincial Park

Wakaw

Swathe of canola, near Wakaw

Saskatoon

Saskatoon Exhibition

Green machine

Mule deer near Swift Current

Redberry Lake National Migratory Bird Sanctuary

Old buildings near St. Denis

Near Quill Lake

Quiet winter months

St. Michael's Church at Lepine celebrates its 100th year in 2005.

Innovation Place, Saskatoon, University of Saskatchewan

Fort Battleford

Regina

Regina newsboy George Baker with paper declaring the end of the war in Europe. SASKATCHEWAN ARCHIVES BOARD S78-114

EXTRA THE LEADER·POST EXTRA

VICTORY!

SURRENDER IS UNCONDITIONAL

the country? Gardiner blamed the Saskatchewan fiasco on the Patterson government, contending that it was "worse than useless as an ally" in the fight against the socialist threat.[62] But the former premier, fearing rivals, had left the Liberal party vulnerable when he went to Ottawa in 1935.[63] Patterson, on the other hand, was more concerned about the future of the province. Speaking to a Young Liberal convention barely one month after the election, he likened the CCF victory to an alien invasion by "an organization of a nature and a kind never seen before in Saskatchewan."[64] Patterson stepped down as provincial Liberal leader in 1946 and resigned his seat three years later. But in 1951, he was coaxed from retirement in Ottawa to return to his home province as lieutenant-governor, becoming the only person in Saskatchewan history to serve as viceregal representative and premier. Despite the distinction, he remains one of the province's least known leaders.

The CCF was elated about the decisiveness of its victory. "Saskatchewan is now all set to make history," boasted the *Saskatchewan Commonwealth*, the party's weekly newspaper. "The people in the province ... are ready for a new kind of government—and a new kind of government is undoubtedly what they are going to get."[65] As the war was finally coming to an end in Europe and the Pacific, the government introduced the most ambitious legislative agenda since the first Scott government almost four decades earlier. In its first sixteen months in office, the Douglas government approved 192 bills and created several new departments (Co-operation, Labour, and Social Welfare) and Crown corporations. It approved, for example, a new Trade Union Act, which created a provincial Labour Relations Board and gave civil servants the right to organize, established a compulsory automobile insurance plan (one of several Canadian firsts), and enacted a new Public Service Act. It also incorporated rural and municipal telephone companies into Saskatchewan Government Telephones, acquired private power companies to create an integrated provincial power grid under the auspices of the Saskatchewan Power Commission, and launched a provincial bus company. A former government official reported that the "cabinet as a whole groaned with overwork, but the individual ministers unquestionably were initiating this activity themselves."[66] Premier Douglas compared his role to that of a ringmaster, where the circus performers all wanted the spotlight.[67]

One of the unpredictable stars of the new CCF cabinet was Joe Phelps, a Wilkie-area farmer and minister of natural resources. A *Leader-Post* legislative reporter once described the Phelps style: "indignant, hands waving, arms flying, at times so vehement that one expected him to take off like a whip-lashed aeroplane."[68] Douglas called him "a steam engine in pants."[69] Phelps, who represented the more radical wing of the party, operated in "an environment of ferment, change and uncertainty" in his blind rush to "get things done."[70] In the foreword to the first major policy statement issued by his department, he vowed "to establish complete social ownership and management of key industries in the development of our resources."[71] Phelps then went on a shopping spree and secured a Regina shoe factory/tannery, Moose Jaw woollen mill, and Prince Albert box factory—with little or no consultation. When the cabinet, after a prolonged debate, voted against the purchase of a defunct brick plant in Estevan, the natural resources minister exclaimed, "But my gosh fellows. I've already bought it."[72] Phelps believed, perhaps naively, that these enterprises would wean the province from its overdependence on agriculture and help bring about a more diversified economy. But the new manufacturing ventures (known as Import Substitute Industrialization) were undertaken without much analysis, and it was not long before they began to lose money, largely because of the small Saskatchewan market and the availability of cheaper out-of-province imports. Their eventual closure not only demonstrated the potential perils of public ownership, but were a source of embarrassment to the Douglas government for years to come.[73]

The other major figure in the early Douglas government, often regarded as the premier's alter ego, was provincial treasurer Clarence Fines, a former Regina alderman, veteran party member, and fundraiser extraordinaire. Fines faced a monumental task. Despite the Patterson government's fiscal

CCF cabinet minister Joe Phelps pursued a number of ill-fated manufacturing ventures.
SASKATCHEWAN ARCHIVES BOARD R-A2892-2

conservatism, Saskatchewan was carrying the largest per capita debt of any province. Fines concluded that the new government's ambitious reform program would be compromised unless the province's financial situation was dramatically improved. He delivered a remarkable string of sixteen consecutive balanced budgets, a feat that earned him the reputation of being "a dedicated socialist with the acumen of a tycoon."[74] Fines' other challenge was to fulfill the CCF's campaign promise of long-term, coordinated planning. Towards the end of the war, it appeared that the federal government was prepared to take the lead in reforming government management practices. Prime Minister King invited Canada's premiers to Ottawa in April 1945 to consider a set of "Green Book" proposals. In exchange for provincial taxing powers, Ottawa was prepared to assume responsibility for full employment and a comprehensive social welfare package. Premier Douglas was delighted with the proposals, but vehement opposition from several premiers scuttled the talks. With the Green Book promises on hold, Saskatchewan went ahead with its own governance revolution. The budgeting system and cabinet functions were integrated, while a professional public service was developed. Many of the new government officials came from across North America, attracted to the province by the opportunity to be a part of the bold Saskatchewan experiment.[75]

The key planning agency in the early Douglas government was the Economic Advisory and Planning Board (EAPB), which began operations in January 1946. The board was headed by George Cadbury, a British Fabian socialist of the chocolate family fame, who had been personally recruited by the premier. Douglas wanted Cadbury to advise the cabinet on how best to direct future economic policy "in the interests of the population with a view to ... the economic and social problems with which the government has to deal."[76] His appointment, together with that of other expert advisors, elicited a stern rebuke from the opposition Liberals, who charged that such practices were foreign to Saskatchewan. Patterson told a Regina radio audience in 1947 that the control of the government had been assumed by "a shadowy group."[77] In his first major report to cabinet in the fall of 1946, Cadbury proposed a mixed economy for the province. The Saskatchewan government should still strive to create new businesses, but in areas that offered greater promise of success, such as non-agricultural staples. He also argued that government's economic blueprint should include the active encouragement of private investment. This EAPB recommendation was clearly at odds with the founding philosophy of the party and likely upset some CCF disciples, but it reflected the reality of the situation—and the reality of staying in power for the CCF, which had already moved miles beyond its 1930s beginnings.[78]

Despite the EAPB's emphasis on diversification, Cadbury—and Premier Douglas—recognized that agriculture remained the backbone of the Saskatchewan economy. One of the new government's first bills was a Farm Security Act, which was designed to protect farmers from foreclosure, in particular the loss of the home quarter. There was also a debate in the legislature about limiting the size of holdings in the interests of preserving the family farm. One of the most controversial initiatives, undertaken by the new Department of Co-operation and Co-operative Development, was the establishment of co-operative farms. Young veterans and their families would be encouraged to pool their resources—land, buildings, and machinery—and farm the land collectively, thereby taking advantage of economies of scale. The opposition assailed the idea as communism in disguise. But several hundred people, inspired by the possibilities of the scheme, signed on, especially when start-up money was available through the federal Veterans' Land Act. The first co-operative farm was incorporated near Sturgis in 1945. By 1949, there were seventeen such ventures in the province, including the Matador operation on the South Saskatchewan River, which specialized in cattle. The farms ran much like businesses, with the work being apportioned and both men and women receiving wages. Within a decade, though, the initial enthusiasm had dissipated, and the members began to disband the farms and divide the assets. Other ventures fell victim to the environment. In

1947, convinced that the new agricultural technology could be used success-fully in marginal regions, the provincial government began clearing wet, forested land in the Carrot River district for Riverbend, the first of ten co-operative farms. But the poor soil and cool, wet climate undermined the project, and the farms were dissolved after only a few frustrating years.[79]

Cadbury's economic recommendations also led to strict guidelines for the creation of any new government businesses—thus clipping Phelps' wings. As the premier himself admitted years later, "We did too much ... unsettled a lot of people by trying to bring about a social revolution in almost every aspect of human life, instead of tackling two or three fields."[80] But the natural resources minister continued to exercise a free hand in the provincial north, where his social experimentation did not face the same kind of constraints or scrutiny. Phelps regarded the northern situation as "pretty grim,"[81] believing that the Hudson's Bay Company and the Catholic and Anglican churches were largely responsible for the sorry state of the Indians and Métis. His reformist zeal blinded him to the fact that the large influx of whites during the Depression had seriously eroded Aboriginal activities in the region. Phelps' solution, in the words of a government insider at the time, was to "change the habits of the native in the North to accord more perfectly with their own [CCF] theories of social justice."[82] What this approach meant was that the Indians and Métis were rounded up, beginning in the late 1940s, and placed in settlements where they were to be assimilated into a more modern society.

A train struggles to break through snow dumped during a blizzard in 1948. SASKATCHEWAN ARCHIVES BOARD R-A27895

But it was to be a society still segregated from the northern white community. Phelps and his cohort of planners expected Aboriginal peoples to continue to engage in their traditional pursuits, such as trapping and fishing, even though they had been removed from the land. This time, though, the province would control and regulate these activities through new compulsory agencies, the Saskatchewan Fur Marketing Service and the Saskatchewan Fish Marketing Board. The CCF was convinced that it knew what was best for the north and did not bother to secure input from those most affected.[83]

The Douglas government had a much different relationship with Indian peoples in the settled agricultural south. In 1944, Joseph Dreaver, chief of the Mistawasis band and a Great War veteran, tapped into the political activism generated by Indian participation in the war to establish the Association of Indians of Saskatchewan. The new organization, made up of Indian veterans and so-called "progressive" farmers from southeastern reserves, wanted better health and educational services and an end to the restrictive pass and permit systems. It was also prepared to work through Premier Douglas, who had been made an honorary chief (Red Eagle) shortly after assuming office, and asked him in late 1945 to use his influence to convene a meeting of Saskatchewan Indian delegates. The Regina conference, held in the legislature cafeteria, endorsed the idea of a single provincial body, but it took another two meetings before the Union of Saskatchewan Indians (USI) was formally created in Saskatoon in 1946.

Chief Dreaver and others appreciated Douglas' efforts to help bring the province's Indians together, but there was some resentment when the CCF tried to influence their agenda. It was even suggested that the USI was a pawn of the premier, especially since the government had financed the meetings. From the beginning, however, the first president, the feisty John Tootoosis, asserted the union's independence by making the treaties its foremost concern.[84] He also crossed swords with the federal government, which continued to administer its constitutional responsibilities with a heavy hand. Federal policy was not even blunted by the sad contradiction that Indian soldiers had fought overseas to defeat Nazi racism, only to return home to the sting of discrimination in Canada. The new Saskatchewan Indian organization learned this sorry truth first-hand. Indian agents from throughout the province were meeting with Ottawa officials in Saskatoon the day after the founding USI convention. When Tootoosis, fresh from his election as president, asked to join the discussions, he and several chiefs were shooed away with the brusque warning that there would be no talking with Indians.[85]

The province's Métis, on the other hand, continued to experience organizational problems, largely because of the differences between those on the land in the north and those living in southern urban centres. In 1943, the northern

Métis, seeing the Saskatchewan Métis Society as essentially a Regina-based body, formed the rival Saskatchewan Métis Association (SMA). After the war, Joe Phelps hired Jim Brady and Malcolm Norris, co-founders of the Métis Association of Alberta, to work for the Department of Natural Resources and serve as liaison between the government and Aboriginal peoples in northern Saskatchewan. The pair did some organizational work for the SMA, but preferred more radical solutions and eventually joined the communist Labour Progressive Party. The Douglas government, meanwhile, took steps to deal with destitute Métis living on relief in shantytowns on the edge of small communities, such as Lestock. It forcibly moved large numbers of families to Green Lake, a fur-trade community northwest of Prince Albert, where each family was given a lease to forty acres of Crown land and expected to practice subsistence-level farming. Fittingly, the new settlement was known as the Green Lake experiment.[86]

The Liberal opposition slammed this kind of social engineering by "outside" planners for turning Saskatchewan into "a police state."[87] Under its new leader, Walter Tucker, a lawyer who served in both world wars and had represented the federal riding of Rosthern since 1935, the party abandoned the pragmatic politics of the past and fervently took up the banner of "free enterprise." This strategy attempted to divide Saskatchewan politics along strict ideological lines by appealing to Cold War fears and the threat posed by Soviet Russia. For the Liberals, CCF socialism was just one step away from

In 1948, electricity was generally available only to larger Saskatchewan centres, like Rosetown.
UNIVERSITY OF SASKATCHEWAN SPECIAL COLLECTIONS LXY-1710

Communism, Regina just one edict from becoming another Moscow. Sometimes the claims made against the Douglas government strained credulity. Former premier Patterson insisted during the 1947 throne speech debate that the Department of Education was secretly compiling files on every person in the province, while Tucker charged during a leaders' debate that same year that the Reds were behind the Douglas government, even funding it.[88] Nor was the virulent attack restricted to the Liberals. The provincial Conservative leader once decried the CCF as "the greatest hoax and denial of democracy and freedom which ever existed in Canada."[89]

The June 1948 provincial election was fought along these battle lines. Running on the slogan "Tucker or Tyranny," the Liberal leader made little mention of his party's platform, preferring to hammer away at CCF dictatorship. Douglas managed to fend off the attacks, without being cornered, because of his superb speaking skills. The election results pleased neither party. Although Liberal strength in the Saskatchewan legislature increased to nineteen seats, from a historical low of five in 1944, the party's share of the popular vote actually declined. There had been no dramatic shift in vote away from the CCF, as many in the party had predicted, and the once-mighty Liberals faced another term on the opposition benches.[90] If there was any good news for the Liberals, it was that the two-party system was healthy and intact in Saskatchewan. The CCF's huge 1944 majority plunged from forty-seven to thirty-one seats in the legislature; most of its continuing support was in urban centres, a trend that persists to this day under its successor, the New Democratic Party. The party's share of the popular vote slipped as well, because of Conservative and third-party candidates. Douglas initially attributed the results to poor party organization and overconfidence,[91] but there was no denying that the government's policies had alienated people. A University of Toronto social scientist even told the premier there was no reason to be disappointed. "The miracle is not that you lost seats," he counselled, "but that you were re-elected at all ... with the extensive reforms that you've introduced in the last four years."[92]

One of the casualties of the 1948 election was Joe Phelps. His defeat prompted calls to Douglas to find him another seat in the legislature or at least make use of his talents somewhere else in the government. The premier sensed, however, that Phelps' sweeping experiments in social ownership had severely tested the limits of what Saskatchewan residents were willing to accept. The time had come to slow down, or the party would suffer the consequences at the next election. This change of pace, beginning in 1948, has been interpreted as an abandonment, if not a betrayal, of the CCF reform agenda.[93] But from its first days, the CCF learned that it had to be flexible if it was going to achieve electoral success. The post-war search for stability and long-term growth, and the accompanying demands for government planning and intervention, had created conditions that were ideal for the CCF in Saskatchewan, but any policies and initiatives, no matter how innovative or well meaning, still had to take place within the existing provincial framework. By the late 1940s, then, there had been no radical remaking of Saskatchewan, no new social order on the prairies, despite the lofty expectations of party stalwarts and the dire predictions of CCF opponents.[94] In fact, the province, after surviving the Depression and the war, faced a new conundrum: it was a largely rural, agricultural province out of step with much of the rest of post-war Canada. Dealing with this challenge would occupy, at times confound, successive provincial governments for decades.

CHAPTER SEVENTEEN

MAKING DREAMS COME TRUE

I T WAS CALLED THE BRIDGE to the future. For decades, residents of south-western Saskatchewan had been demanding a bridge to replace the old ferry crossing at Saskatchewan Landing and provide a year-round road link between the Battlefords and Swift Current along historic Highway 4. And when Premier Tommy Douglas officially opened the bridge in June 1951, more than ten thousand appreciative people were on hand to witness the ribbon-cutting ceremony with an even larger number listening to the event on CHAB radio. In a sense, the bridge over the South Saskatchewan River marked the government's determination in the 1950s to take the province down the road to modernity. Douglas said as much when he claimed that the project should "remind us not to forget our dreams and also remind us to take off our coats and make these dreams come true."[1] But the following April, a huge ice jam ripped the steel spans from the concrete piers and dragged the twisted wreckage into the river. The bridge was quickly rebuilt and opened for traffic again in June 1953. This time, though, there was no special celebration to mark the event.[2] In fact, the future no longer seemed as bright or promising. The most recent census confirmed that the province continued to bleed people—a loss of one hundred thousand, or 10 per cent, in the fifteen years since 1936. Agriculture, meanwhile, was beset with instability and had been displaced from its favoured position in the national economy by other resource industries. The most troubling development, however, was the shuffling of rural society to the margins of post-war Canada. Saskatchewan, the most rural of Canada's western provinces, had to find its way in a new world where rural life was seen as backward, lacking in opportunity, but worst of all, in decline.

Premier Douglas opens the new bridge at Saskatchewan Landing in 1951. SASKATCHEWAN ARCHIVES BOARD STAR-PHOENIX COLLECTION S-SP-734-6

If anything defined "the fifties" in Canada, it was babies—and lots of them. By the early 1950s, the national birth rate topped four hundred thousand babies per year (including the author) and never dropped below that rate over the decade. The baby boom represented a new beginning for Canadians, anxious to put behind them the deprivation and dislocations of the Great Depression and the Second World War. Indeed, the first fifteen years after the war were a period of unprecedented growth for Canada, the likes of which had not been seen since the creation of the province of Saskatchewan in the early twentieth century. The gross national product quadrupled between

1945 and 1960, while the demand for workers in industry and manufacturing had never been stronger. Canada's population also soared, from 11.5 million in 1941 to 18.2 million in 1961; this number included almost two million immigrants. The symbol of this new post-war Canada was the white, middle-class, two-parent family, living in a new housing division in the suburbs, where the husband was the breadwinner and his wife stayed at home and raised their children. It was also a consumer-driven society, bent on reaping the rewards of prosperity, whether it be a new home or car, a television set, or more leisure time with the family. There was also greater opportunity, made possible largely because of improved access to better education and training, especially at the post-secondary level.[3]

Saskatchewan, by contrast, was a much different place. Whereas the province, with its tens of thousands of wheat farmers, had once been considered Canada's future, those days were past. Unlike half a century earlier when the "last, best West" captured the imagination of prospective settlers, few post-war immigrants chose to make Saskatchewan their home, heading instead to the country's larger cities. This negligible immigration rate, combined with out-migration from the province beginning in the mid-1930s, changed the demographic character of Saskatchewan. The percentage of the population born within the province steadily increased, giving Saskatchewan a strong local identity and a distinctly regional outlook. Gesiorowksi, Hounjet, Pasqualotto, and Syroteuk were just as much Saskatchewan family names as Barnhart and Brennan. Those in their prime working years, meanwhile, once a distinguishing feature of the prairie labour force, were outnumbered by 1960 by those under nineteen or over sixty-five; many of the elderly retired poor because of the Depression.[4]

Western Canada also reached a watershed in the 1950s when the rural population slipped to a minority. As of 1961, rural residents represented only 42.2 per cent of the total regional population. Saskatchewan joined this trend. During the ten-year period from 1941 to 1951, when the total provincial population sagged 7.2 per cent (minus 64,000), the rural farm population fell an astonishing 22.4 per cent (minus 115,000).[5] In other words, the province's cities grew at the expense of the countryside, but these gains came at a cost. The loss of farms cut into the wholesale trade of urban centres. Those who headed to the cities also faced a severe housing shortage, a legacy of depression and war. Regina was one of the most overcrowded cities on the prairies at the end of the 1940s, and it was not uncommon to see large houses converted into apartments or people living in garages. But despite the departure of over one hundred thousand rural people in the 1940s, the province remained essentially a rural place until the end of the 1960s. Seven of every ten Saskatchewan citizens still lived in a rural setting in 1951.[6]

The Douglas government was committed to providing electricity to fifty thousand Saskatchewan farms by the end of the 1950s. HUGH MCPHAIL

The decrease in Saskatchewan's rural population was directly linked to widespread mechanization and the consequent movement to larger farms. Once wartime restraints were lifted, farmers rushed to take advantage of the availability of new machinery. While the total number of Saskatchewan farms declined from 138,713 in 1941 to 93,924 twenty years later, the average size of the remaining farms increased by almost 60 per cent (432 to 685 acres) during the same period.[7] These larger holdings did not mean, however, that Saskatchewan agriculture continued to enjoy its dominant place in the export economy. In the post-war world, Canadian trade fortunes increasingly depended on other raw and processed materials at the expense of wheat. Mining, not agriculture, would come to drive the new western economy.

Large-scale mechanization also failed to improve the popular image of farming and rural life in general. Long regarded as the backbone of society and the source of its core values, rural Canada had been pulled from its central role on stage and relegated to a spectator's seat in a rear balcony. The new Canada of the 1950s was an urban, modern, affluent place, not some unsophisticated backwater where people went around with dirt or something worse on their shoes. As comedian Groucho Marx mockingly asked in a spoof of a favourite song, "How're you gonna keep 'em down on the farm ... after they've seen the farm?"[8]

Measured against the new standards of the 1950s, Saskatchewan must have seemed something of an anachronism, a province more in keeping with an older Canada. But there was nothing outdated or out-of-step with the program that the CCF government devised for Saskatchewan in the late 1940s and 1950s. If anything, the Douglas administration encapsulated the spirit of the post-war period, when democracies sought to use their influence and intervention to bring about a better world. Having run on the motto of "Humanity First," the CCF government was committed to providing the province's citizens with equal access to the highest possible levels of education, health care, and welfare. It was also resolved to diversify the Saskatchewan economy to help finance its programs, while taking whatever steps were within its power to bring about farm security and place agriculture on a more stable footing. The goal of this reform program, the so-called "beacon" for the CCF party, according to a senior government mandarin, was to create the "conditions under which individual freedom and human well-being might flourish."[9]

One of the first tests of the Douglas government was the place of the province's Aboriginal population in the new Saskatchewan. "It has been said that the measure of any society is what it does for the least fortunate group," the premier observed in March 1946. "It is not enough ... to raise the standard of living if there continues to remain ... a small, underprivileged, diseased, illiterate minority in society."[10] Douglas had put these words into action earlier in 1946 when he used his position as premier to facilitate the establishment of the Union of Saskatchewan Indians. He hoped that the new province wide organization would serve as a springboard for Indians to promote their collective interests. Indeed, it appeared that the time had arrived for meaningful change when the Canadian government appointed a Special Joint Committee of the Senate and House of Commons that same year to review the Indian Act and its administration.

The creation of the Joint Committee was essentially an admission that federal Indian policy had failed and that there was a desperate need for a workable solution.[11] Finding that answer, though, did not initially involve Indian input. It was only after hearings had commenced in 1947 that Indian delegates were permitted to make presentations to the committee. Almost all of the Indian briefs commented on education shortcomings, made worse by severe cutbacks during the Depression and then the war. The representatives wanted an end to the religious basis of the schools and the cultural remaking of Indian students. "Our greatest need to-day is proper education," explained Chief Joseph Dreaver of the Mistawasis band.[12] Ottawa, however, was not about to lessen its grip on its Indian wards, despite the telling criticism at the Joint Committee hearings, and approved an amended Indian Act in 1951, which maintained the basic assimilative thrust of Canadian Indian policy. Schools continued to be part of that process. The only major concessions were the lifting of the federal ban on Indian dancing and fundraising for claims purposes.

The Douglas government had become increasingly uneasy with the Indian situation in the province. In 1947, the Saskatchewan legislature had passed the first Bill of Rights in Canada, which prohibited discrimination on racial and religious grounds. But any euphoria associated with the landmark bill was dampened by reality. Indians, segregated and living in poverty, had few prospects of work and faced a hopeless future. W. J. Berezowsky, the CCF member of Cumberland and himself a victim of discrimination because of his Ukrainian heritage, was appalled by conditions on Saskatchewan's reserves and introduced two private member's bills in the mid-1950s, calling for Indian access to the same level of services enjoyed by other provincial citizens. The premier felt much the same way, largely because he could not countenance one segment of the Saskatchewan population living apart from the rest of provincial society. It was just not the CCF way. "We don't settle all the Chinese people out in ... some corner of the province," he once observed.[13]

The Douglas cabinet finally moved on the matter in 1956 and established a new Committee on Indian Affairs, which immediately produced a report with three specific recommendations: the extension of the provincial franchise to Indians, the removal of liquor restrictions for Indians, and the transfer of responsibility for Indians to provincial jurisdiction.[14] These initiatives formed the basis of the CCF government's Indian policy in the late 1950s. At their heart, according to Douglas, was the principle that "Indians ... integrate into white society."[15] But what the premier failed to do, like other well-meaning politicians both in the past and future, was consult with the people who were the object of these policies. And what worried John Tootoosis and many other Indian leaders was that voting and liquor privileges might adversely affect their treaty rights. When the provincial government subsequently held a conference with the new Federation of Saskatchewan Indians at Fort Qu'Appelle in October 1958, confidently assuming that its plans would be warmly embraced, Douglas had to back down and publicly agree not to do anything without Indian approval. Two years later, though, the premier reneged on his promise and introduced legislation giving Indians the right to vote and drink. He justified his decision by insisting that treaty rights would remain secure, while Indians would be taken more seriously as full and equal partners of Saskatchewan society.[16] Unfortunately, other citizens did not share this view. Beginning in the late 1940s, more and more Indians moved off-reserve and into towns and cities in search of better opportunities. But they were shunned as if they carried some dreaded disease

Dene children at Stony Rapids, 1955. HUGH MCPHAIL

and found that they had traded one poverty for another.

The situation for Aboriginal peoples in northern Saskatchewan was not much better, even though the CCF government looked upon the long-neglected region as a kind of giant laboratory for its reform program, where they could do things that they would not have attempted in the more settled southern half of the province. CCF policy for the region was riddled with contradictions. When Joe Phelps, the maverick minister of natural resources, went down to defeat in the 1948 election, he was replaced by J. H. "Brock" Brockelbank, a practical-minded cabinet minister who had served as CCF leader of the opposition in the Saskatchewan legislature in the early 1940s. Brockelbank lacked Phelps' fervour for innovation, but was not about to undo the policies of his predecessor, especially when he was convinced that "the long-term solution" for northern Saskatchewan was "cultural assimilation."[17]

The nucleation of Indians and Métis into settlements continued through the 1950s in the expectation that they would become "productive" participants in state-owned or co-operative enterprises. Traditional activities such as fishing and trapping, however, provided minimal income at a time when the Aboriginal birth rate also started to climb. In times of distress in the recent past, impoverished Indians and Métis would have turned to the churches or the Hudson's Bay Company for relief, but the CCF government blamed these institutions and their paternalism for many of the problems of northern society. It was far better, the government maintained, for Aboriginal peoples in the new communities to try to fend for themselves, or if necessary, secure minimal social assistance by working on special projects; dependency was to be avoided at all costs. Nor was the Douglas government prepared to spend much on infrastructure in northern Aboriginal settlements, whether it be roads, telephones, or sanitation facilities.[18] In the end, the CCF northern policy proved a recipe for disaster. Yet instead of acknowledging its short-comings or taking corrective steps, the Douglas government tended to blame Aboriginal peoples for their misfortunes. A 1958 provincial report found that northern government employees considered the Métis a "shiftless lot" who could not be trusted.[19] Even more disturbing was the statistic that three out of every five northern Aboriginal men between the ages of sixteen and thirty had served time in prison.[20]

The CCF government also had a direct hand in creating two northern soci-eties—one white and well off, the other Aboriginal and poor. In the mid-1940s, in response to the growing American demand for uranium for its nuclear program during the Cold War, Eldorado Mining and Refining Limited, a federal Crown corporation, began prospecting in northwestern Saskatchewan and soon staked several promising claims in the Lake Athabasca area. The company initially used Goldfields, an abandoned mining commun-ity in the area, for its operations, but in 1952 the Douglas government started building Uranium City on the north shore of Lake Athabasca to service the Beaverlodge Mine and other smaller operations.[21] Within a year, the com-munity boasted over fifteen hundred people, a school and hospital, and regularly scheduled flights from Prince Albert and Edmonton. Predictions that the population might grow five times by the end of the decade led to the construction of a sewage and water system at provincial government expense. The nearby mines, in the meantime, hired no Aboriginal workers. The Department of Natural Resources claimed that their "pre-industrial way of life" made them unsuitable employees. Nor were Indians and Métis to be part of the new community. In 1953, the Douglas government relocated Aboriginal squatters outside town limits and forbade them from living any closer than one mile to Uranium City.[22]

The story was much worse at Island Falls and Sandy Bay, two very dif-ferent settlements that grew up near the Churchill River dam that supplied hydroelectric power to the Hudson Bay Mining and Smelting Company operations just across the border at Flin Flon, Manitoba. Those white workers who lived with their families in the company town at Island Falls enjoyed modern housing and a wide range of recreational facilities. Aboriginal workers who performed menial jobs for the company, on the other hand, lived in relative squalor at Sandy Bay, going without electricity even though

Uranium City was built by the provincial government to service the uranium industry in northwestern Saskatchewan. UNIVERSITY OF SASKATCHEWAN ARCHIVES MG146D.7

the plant was only about a mile away. Although the CCF government knew about the situation—two studies in the late 1950s claimed it was perhaps the most shameful example of northern discrimination—nothing was done.[23]

The Douglas government had a more enviable record in the field of education, but its actions were not without controversy. When Saskatchewan's population peaked in the mid-1930s, there were an estimated five thousand school districts in the province. Most were rural, one-room schools where the teacher juggled eight grades while sometimes supervising older students who were taking high school courses by correspondence. During the Depression, the buildings, never known for their comfort, were allowed to deteriorate. Then the war took away hundreds of qualified teachers who volunteered for duty. Scrambling to keep their schools open, some district boards turned to teenaged women who had limited training and no experience. Many of these young, courageous teachers were not much older than their pupils. Eighteen-year-old Freda Damon, who instructed thirty-one students at Happy Centre School near Willowbrook, had one student older than her and another the same age.[24] The CCF government, a firm believer in the power of an educated society, was determined to reverse this situation by bringing about a higher level of education and providing better access to that education. It also had to get children back in the schools. Dozens of rural schools were closing because they were rundown, lacked teachers, or lost students as farms were being abandoned.

The minister in charge of revitalizing the province's education system was Woodrow Stanley Lloyd, the youngest member of the 1944 Douglas cabinet and the only one born in Saskatchewan (in Antelope). Lloyd was a natural choice; he started teaching at nineteen in a one-room school at Swan Lake in 1932 and through hard work and determination worked his way up to president of the Saskatchewan Teachers' Federation in 1940. Lloyd was not a political animal—he liked politics if not for the elections—but had been attracted to the CCF party from its early days and found comfort in the principles underlying the Regina Manifesto.[25] Douglas considered him the finest mind in his government. Resolute and unflinching, especially when he believed he was right, Lloyd promoted the movement to Larger School Units, or LSUs as they were called, as the *only* way to deliver a quality education to the sparsely settled Saskatchewan population. "Educational progress," he bluntly advised the premier, "will not be clear until the whole province is in larger units."[26]

Lloyd's educational reforms, first raised in the legislature in November 1944, elicited a stern rebuke from the opposition and a tidal wave of protest from rural residents, who regarded the schools as an integral part of their communities, especially since the buildings served as the meeting place for other local activities. Parents not only opposed the prospect of their children spending hours riding school buses, but feared the loss of local schools would weaken their already faltering battle against rural decay. The Douglas government tried to soften the blow by making available equalization grants to ensure minimum provincial education standards, as well as providing a mechanism to hold a formal local vote on amalgamation if demanded by 20 per cent of the district ratepayers. It was not prepared, however, to withdraw the contentious legislation and went ahead with the most revolutionary revision to the province's education system since the creation of the province.[27] At the start of the 1950s, one in five one-room schools was being closed annually; by the end of the decade, the rate was two out of every five. Attendance, in the meantime, increased for all age groups.[28]

The loss of the one-room rural school was yet another sign that Saskatchewan was undergoing a fundamental transformation. The Douglas government recognized the significance of this change and in 1945 passed the Saskatchewan Archives Act, which created an agency to collect and preserve material about the province's past. The new Saskatchewan Archives Board opened two offices, one in Regina, the other in Saskatoon, and launched what is now one of the oldest provincial historical journals in the country, *Saskatchewan History*.

The disappearance of old farm machinery for scrap metal during the war also persuaded a group of citizens in the Battlefords area to establish an agricultural museum in an old British Commonwealth Air Training Plan hangar in 1948. Saskatoon followed suit the next year. At the urging of former cabinet minister Joe Phelps, the provincial government gave this movement its formal blessing and financial support with the passage of the Western Development Museum Act in 1949. Two other branches were later added at Yorkton and Moose Jaw in 1951 and 1972, respectively. Today, the collection features over sixty-five thousand artifacts, mostly from the province's settlement period, while the old quarters have been replaced by modern facilities, including Saskatoon's "Boom Town," a replica 1910 streetscape.

There was also a cultural renaissance during this period. In 1950, Yorkton hosted its first International Documentary Film Festival (now known as the Short Film Festival), the longest-running event of its kind in Canada. Two years later, the University of Saskatchewan scored a musical coup when it wooed Toronto-born composer Murray Adaskin to Saskatoon to head the music department. Not to be outdone, Regina countered in 1953 with the opening of the Norman MacKenzie Art Gallery, thanks to a generous bequest from the late lawyer. Education Minister Lloyd did his part by setting up the first of several regional libraries in Prince Albert in 1950. A 1947 survey had found that farm families spent less than ten dollars per year on magazines, newspapers, and books.[29] "It's not a question of whether we can afford this library," explained a Nipawin woman. "We can't afford to be without it."[30]

The CCF government's most heralded cultural initiative was the 1948 creation of the Saskatchewan Arts Board, the first agency of its kind in North America. Modelled after the British Arts Council, the Arts Board was designed to provide provincial residents with more opportunity to participate in "creative activities in the fields of drama, visual arts, music, literature, and handicrafts ... and to establish and improve the standards for such activities in the province."[31] If artists, authors, and the like had a chance to realize their potential at home, it was hoped that they would not leave the province, never to return, as others had done before them. Those who left included twenty-one-year-old Shaunavon-born actress Francis Hyland who headed to Ottawa in 1948 to audition for a place at London's Royal Academy of Dramatic Art and went on to become one of Canada's greatest Shakespeareans. True to her prairie roots, she also starred in the 1963 National Film Board of Canada classic, *The Drylanders*, about the struggles of a farm family.

With Arts Board support, the first Emma Lake Artists' Workshop was held in 1955, giving local individuals a chance to meet and work with established artists. These sessions led directly to the successful 1960 national tour of the "Regina Five" (Ron Bloore, Kenneth Lochhead, Arthur McKay,

Women examine the latest batch of books available through the provincial travelling library.
SASKATCHEWAN ARCHIVES BOARD R-A5376(4)

Douglas Morton, and Ted Godwin). The literary counterpart, at the Qu'Appelle Valley Centre, often featured Weyburn-born W. O. Mitchell, author of *Who Has Seen the Wind* (1947) and the popular weekly CBC radio series *Jake and the Kid*. Ironically, Mitchell's compelling, albeit fictional, portrayal of life in rural Saskatchewan helped to fix in Canadian minds the impression that the province and the Depression were synonymous.

The powerful government Economic and Advisory Planning Board believed that these cultural initiatives should occupy "a lowly place" relative to other, more urgent funding priorities—and for good reason.[32] Education spending alone climbed almost 40 per cent during the first half of the 1950s as Saskatchewan moved to LSUs and larger school grants. By 1957–58, education constituted about a third of the provincial budget.[33] After its sobering 1948 election victory, the Douglas government chose to finance these expenditures by increasingly relying on private enterprise and encouraging investment in industrial and resource development. This change of direction—some condemned it as a graceless retreat—smacked of heresy to party disciples; it was akin to saying that the CCF party had been wrong in the past to rail against large corporations and the evils of capitalism. But Phelps' misadventures in social ownership had made the Douglas cabinet extremely wary of investing more public funds in risky projects. It made more sense to concentrate on public ownership of utilities and leave other, potentially cost-lier development to private companies. The CCF government also realized that its ambitious reform agenda would certainly be delayed, and perhaps jeopardized, unless there was a stable investment climate and the province's productive capacity improved.[34] "We have now gone as far as we can go in terms of social security," the premier candidly admitted in the legislature at the beginning of the 1950s, "until we put a better economic base under [it]."[35] To that end, the government created a new Industrial Development Office to advertise Saskatchewan's investment potential and facilitate and promote industrial and resource development.

In putting out the welcome sign for private capital, the premier publicly announced that no steps would be taken to expropriate or nationalize any new ventures. At the same time, he made it clear that he had a responsibility to protect the interests of the Saskatchewan public and ensure that the province received a fair return for its resources.[36] The way that the CCF government chose to balance these competing interests—private development, yet public benefit—was through the traditional use of royalties. This strategy, coming from the same party that had campaigned in 1944 for the social ownership of natural resources, was part of the pragmatic evolution of the CCF government as it matured in office. It also proved somewhat aggravating to the Liberal opposition. "This government cannot make up his mind," an exasperated Walter Tucker lamented, "whether it is socialist or free enterprise."[37] Another Liberal insider derisively described the Douglas government as "a Socialist administration, which does not believe in socialism."[38] Those closer to the CCF were more generous in their assessment. Tommy McLeod, one-time secretary to the EAPB, suggested that the government became "activist rather than overtly socialist."[39] Whatever the interpretation, private enterprise came to play a much larger role in the Saskatchewan economy than had been anticipated when the CCF assumed office in 1944.[40]

Oil was the darling resource of post-war Saskatchewan. The first significant oil and natural gas finds in the province were made at Lloydminster in 1934 and then at Kamsack three years later. But it was not until 1945 that the first commercial oil field, consisting of thick or "heavy" crude, came into production in the Lloydminster area. By then, however, the major players in the industry had been spooked by talk of CCF expropriation and began to shut down their operations and move their rigs across the border. The exodus became a stampede in 1947 with news of the Leduc gusher in Alberta, and it took a personal plea from Premier Douglas—and the promise of favourable concessions—to get Imperial Oil and other multinationals to resume their exploratory work in the province.

By the end of the 1940s, all of the area from Saskatoon to the 49th parallel had been reserved by the major oil companies, anxious to repeat the Leduc discovery in Saskatchewan. But more than seventy unsuccessful wells were drilled before medium crude was found at Fosterton in January 1952. This strike marked the turning point in the industry's fortunes and a series of producing wells were drilled across the southern half of the province over the next few years. By 1954, Saskatchewan's annual production reached 5.4 million barrels of oil and 4.8 billion cubic feet of natural gas. These volumes did not match the output from the Alberta oil patch, whose reserves dwarfed those of Saskatchewan, but the oil boom was still a welcome bonanza. The preferred light crude in the Williston basin in southeastern Saskatchewan found a ready market in the United States, pushing production up to 100,000 barrels per day by 1957. That same year, the province boasted more oil and gas wells than grain elevators.[41]

Revenues from oil and natural gas, along with increased mineral production, especially uranium, filled provincial coffers during the 1950s, giving the Douglas government a string of consecutive surpluses. The new resource developments also helped diversify the Saskatchewan economy. By the end of the decade, the non-agricultural sector accounted for almost two-thirds of the province's commodity production; fifteen years earlier, it had represented only one-fifth.[42] This swing had as much to do with the troubled times that farming had experienced since the end of the war as it did with the booming resource industries. Agricultural production costs had risen at the war's end when farmers readily acquired new, more powerful trucks, tractors, and combines. But the full-scale mechanization of the industry was not matched by rising commodity prices. A twelve-foot self-propelled combine in 1946, for example, cost the equivalent of 1,983 bushels of wheat (at $1.62 per bushel). Twelve years later, that same combine sold for 5,593 bushels because of inflation and a much lower price for wheat (only $1.29 per bushel).[43] Farmers could not also resist returning to their favourite cash crop, spring wheat, and although the diversification gains during the war were not completely undone, wheat acreage climbed to over sixteen million acres by the start of the 1950s. The larger seeded area and good weather produced huge crops, including a mammoth harvest of 449 million bushels in 1952, the largest in provincial history. But international wheat prices remained below those of the late 1940s and continued to erode through the latter part of the decade. Even worse, Canada could not sell all of the wheat, and it began to pile up in elevators, storage bins, and farmyards, while farmers went unpaid.[44]

It was equally bad for the livestock industry. The first recorded case of foot-and-mouth disease in Canada struck a McLean farm in November 1951. It would be four months, however, before it was officially diagnosed. By

Checking the quality of the crop. SASKATCHEWAN ARCHIVES BOARD S-RM-B1765

then, some of the diseased livestock had been shipped to a Regina meat-packing plant, whose sewage contaminated farms along Wascana Creek. The United States slapped an embargo on cattle imports and meat products, while rifle-toting mounties were dispatched to quarantined farms to cull entire herds. Some four thousand animals had to be destroyed, including the goat "Ruffle," the former mascot of the Regina Roughriders football club. By 1954, the losses amounted to almost seventy million dollars.[45]

Producers looked to the federal government to sell their wheat and provide temporary income assistance or compensation. The new Liberal government of Louis St. Laurent, however, did little to resolve the wheat glut and accompanying cash shortfall, despite the strenuous efforts of minister of agriculture and former Saskatchewan premier Jimmy Gardiner, who had unsuccessfully contested the federal Liberal leadership in 1948. Gardiner's distant, second-place finish at the convention seemed a sure sign of agriculture's crumbling support at the federal level. Further proof was forthcoming in 1952 when Prime Minister St. Laurent refused to approve the building of the South Saskatchewan River Dam. Talked about for decades and endorsed by the PFRA, the dam was designed to provide enough water to irrigate half a million acres of land, as well as generate hydroelectric power. It had the unqualified support of both Gardiner and Douglas, who remembered all too well the prolonged drought of the 1930s. But the prime minister did not consider the project to be in the national interest, like the St. Lawrence Seaway, and repeatedly turned down provincial entreaties to proceed with the dam.[46] Gardiner privately blamed St. Laurent's intransigence on his lack of "understanding of western needs."[47] The Saskatchewan Wheat Pool was more scathing. In its annual report for 1957, it argued with some bitterness that "the federal government does not seriously pay much attention to the problems of any province except the ones who, by the power of their votes, can make or break a government."[48]

The problems faced by farmers in the 1950s hastened the depopulation of rural districts, as did the new resource industries and the new jobs they created. From 1956 to 1961, while Saskatchewan's rural farm population declined 16 per cent, the urban population jumped by almost 24 per cent. Communities located close to the oil and natural gas fields enjoyed exponential growth rates. Lloydminster's population grew an astounding 438 per cent between 1941 and 1961 (1,052 to 5,667). Kindersley's increase was almost as spectacular, shooting from 990 to 2,990 people during the same period.[49]

Regina, located along the route of the interprovincial pipeline, also benefitted from the oil boom. The city's refineries not only increased their capacity, making the provincial capital the second largest oil-refining centre on the prairies after Edmonton, but the regional demand for pipe to transport oil and natural gas led to the construction of the Interprovincial Steel and Pipe Corporation plant (IPSCO) with financial assistance from the province.[50] Regina and other Saskatchewan cities also reported stronger retail sales during this period thanks to their growing populations. These internal markets made up for some of the lost wholesale trade to the diminishing farm community, but cities continued to seek out some special advantage as they had done when jostling for supremacy at the beginning of the century. Regina jealously defended its role as home to the large provincial civil service and several Crown corporations. Prince Albert was headquarters for government operations in the provincial north, while Moose Jaw secured a RCAF training facility (15 Wing) when the old BCATP base was reopened in 1952. The Battlefords, meanwhile, looked to tourism, especially after the old NWMP fort was designated a national historic site.

Securing the future of rural Saskatchewan, on the other hand, was a much more difficult matter—and one that troubled Premier Douglas personally. As Al Johnson, the former deputy finance minister, commented years later, the premier regarded all the past studies of farm problems as "parts of a single puzzle, and he wished to see them put together."[51] To secure this broad perspective, the CCF government established a Royal Commission on Agriculture and Rural Life in October 1952. For the next year, the commission, headed by W. B. Baker, director of the School of Agriculture at the University of Saskatchewan, sponsored eighty community forums and nearly sixty public hearings, as well as surveyed hundreds of rural residents. It is little wonder that it was known as the "people's commission." Most of the discussion revolved around the twin issues of distance and isolation and the related problem of rural depopulation. Presenters offered all kinds of solutions, such as directing immigrants to rural areas, limiting the amount of land that farmers could own, and bringing together all the farmsteads in a district in a villagelike setting.

The commission issued a series of fourteen reports between March 1955 and April 1957. Some of its findings proved controversial, such as the recommendation that the family farm be redefined to reflect the new realities of post-war agriculture, or that the nine-township rural municipalities be replaced by a county system. Many were also beyond the powers of the provincial government, especially those dealing with the marketing of wheat and farm income. But what made the commission so important to the province's history—and its future—was that it provided a comprehensive snapshot of a society undergoing fundamental change and the many problems and challenges associated with that change.[52] Further research in this area was subsequently pursued by a new Centre for Community Studies established at the University of Saskatchewan in 1957 in co-operation with the provincial government. The university also expanded its coverage of the social sciences in direct response to the commission's work.[53]

Although the royal commission was supposed to provide a blueprint for action, the Douglas government could not wait and went ahead with its own plans to improve rural services and provide a degree of stability. One of the first major initiatives was the rebuilding of the province's road system. Saskatchewan had over one hundred thousand miles of roads, more miles per capita than the other three western provinces combined. But the roads had badly deteriorated during the Depression; by the start of the 1950s the province had less than one thousand miles of paved highway. The government set itself the goal of constructing a provincewide system of all-weather grid roads and by 1964 had chalked up more than thirteen thousand miles. It also finished the Saskatchewan section of the Trans-Canada Highway in 1957, the first province to complete its share of the national road.[54] Millions of travellers have since identified Saskatchewan with that stretch of highway, through the flat—many would say monotonous—southern prairie landscape. Saskatchewan Government Telephones, in the meantime, expanded and upgraded the provincial system through the 1950s and started work on a

A rural swimming hole. SHFS BAKER COLLECTION 3116

microwave system to be tied into the national network. These efforts may not have dispelled rural isolation, but farm families could at least take comfort from the thought that help was just a phone call away. Television, on the other hand, was strictly an urban novelty. The first stations began broadcasting in the province in 1954, but reception was largely restricted to the immediate Regina, Moose Jaw, and Saskatoon areas.[55]

The CCF government's most ambitious revitalization program, as set out in the Rural Electrification Act of 1949, was to provide electricity to fifty thousand farms and all towns and villages by 1960. Indian reserves, a federal responsibility, were excluded from the program. Many observers scoffed at the idea because of the immensity of the task. The problem was not the small number of farms that already had electricity—less than 5 per cent—but that the potential customers were so sparsely settled, a consequence of the federal homestead policy decades earlier. It was estimated that there would be only 1.18 farms per mile of power line and that long tap-offs, the distance from the line to the farmstead, would be required. The other potential difficulty was that wheat farmers were not large consumers of electricity and that their unstable incomes might make them reluctant to sign up for power, especially when they had to pay for the line and the posts to their farms.

The Saskatchewan Power Corporation (SPC) overcame these problems through a slick promotional campaign, featuring "Penny Powers" (Lillian McConnell), who extolled the benefits of electricity in columns and letters and toured the province giving practical demonstrations of the uses of electricity. Penny's efforts secured her several unsolicited marriage proposals. More importantly, she won over rural homemakers who cajoled their husbands into getting a power line run to the farmhouse; it was no coincidence that 90 per cent of the electricity initially consumed in rural districts was for domestic purposes. By 1956, all towns and villages in southern Saskatchewan were served with power. Two years later, SPC reached its target of fifty thousand farms.[56] Some people were uneasy about electricity. One girl, left at home alone for the first time, remembered her parents turning off the power at the pole before they headed to town. "Power hadn't been there that long," she recalled, "and I think there was a fear that maybe we were safer with the power off."[57] Another farm family had only one light bulb and would move it from room to room wherever a light was needed.[58]

The Douglas government also laid the groundwork for natural gas use throughout the province when it assigned responsibility for distribution to SPC. By 1953, natural gas pipelines from the Brock-Colville fields had reached Swift Current and Saskatoon. Two years later, with the discovery of more reserves, SPC launched an aggressive expansion program and was soon piping gas to all of Saskatchewan's major urban centres. Distribution to farms was several decades away.[59] Under the 1960 Family Farm Improvement Program, the government also provided financial assistance to farm families and towns and villages to install sewage and water systems. These kinds of improvements were long overdue. At the start of the 1950s, only one in five farm homes had running water, let alone a bathroom. The situation in smaller communities was just as bad. As late as 1966, more Saskatchewan households had a television set than indoor plumbing or flush toilets.[60]

Rural leaders pushed back, however, when it came to the reorganization of rural municipalities (RMs) into larger units. In 1956, when Douglas reported that the government was actively pursuing a new form of local government on the advice of the Royal Commission on Agriculture and Rural Life, the president of the Saskatchewan Association of Rural Municipalities accused the premier of secretly plotting to do away with RMs since his first days in office. The vehemence of the attack owed much to lingering anger over the closure of rural schools. Local officials fiercely resented how the educational changes had been forced on them and were not about to give up any more control without a spirited fight. The government tried to defuse the issue by appointing a special committee to find some acceptable compromise, but despite years of study, it shelved the idea in 1962 in the face of continuing local opposition.[61]

Measured against all that the Douglas government had done to improve the quality of life in rural Saskatchewan, the inability to replace the RMs

MOUSELAND

It's the story of a place called Mouseland. Mouseland was a place where all the little mice lived and played, were born and died. And they lived much the same as you and I do. They even had a Parliament. And every four years they had an election. Used to walk to the polls and cast their ballots. Some of them even got a ride to the polls. And got a ride for the next four years afterwards too. Just like you and me. And every time on election day, all the little mice used to go to the ballot box and they used to elect a government. A government made up of big, fat, black cats.

Now if you think it's strange that mice should elect a government made up of cats, you just look at the history of Canada for the last 90 years and maybe you'll see that they weren't any stupider than we are.

Now I'm not saying anything against the cats. They were nice fellows. They conducted their government with dignity. They passed good laws ... that is, laws that were good for cats. But the laws that were good for cats, weren't very good for mice. One of the laws said that mouseholes had to be big enough so a cat could get his paw in. Another law said that mice could only travel at certain speeds, so that a cat could get his breakfast without too much effort.

All the laws were good laws. For cats. But, oh, they were hard on the mice. And life was getting harder and harder. And when the mice couldn't put up with it any more, they decided something had to be done about it. So they went en masse to the polls. They voted the black cats out. They put in the white cats.

Now the white cats had put up a terrific campaign. They said: "All that Mouseland needs is more vision." They said: "The trouble with Mouseland is those round mouseholes we got. If you put us in ... we'll establish square mouseholes." And they did. And the square mouseholes were twice as big as the round mouseholes, and now the cat could get both his paws in. And life was tougher than ever.

And when they couldn't take that any more, they voted the white cats out and put the black ones in again. Then they went back to the white cats. Then to the black cats. They even tried half black cats and half white cats. And they called that coalition. They even got one government made up of cats with spots on them—they were cats that tried to make a noise like a mouse ... but ate like a cat.

You see my friends, the trouble wasn't with the colour of the cats. The trouble was that they were cats ... they naturally looked after cats instead of mice.

Presently there came along one little mouse with an idea. My friends, watch out for the little fellow with an idea. And he said to the other mice: "Look fellows, why do we keep on electing a government made up of cats? Why don't we elect a government made up of mice?" "Oh," they said. " ... he's a Communist. Lock him up!" So they put him in jail.

But I want to remind you, that you can lock up a mouse or a man ... but you can't lock up an idea.

Mouseland, as told by Tommy Douglas.

might not appear to have been much of a failure. But the anguish over the issue underscored how rural Saskatchewan was starting to hurt in the 1950s. Better services could not restore the once vibrant rural society, nor did the government's modernization efforts halt rural decline. The rate of rural population loss in the 1950s might not have been as great as during the 1940s, but people were still leaving the farm, especially adolescents. High school, radio, movies, even all-weather roads, introduced young people to another world beyond the farm. A woman who grew up in the Marsden area in the 1950s found "the isolation ... incredible. I just couldn't wait to get away from that lifestyle."[62] Keeping these sons and daughters on the land was one of the purposes behind a new farmers' organization. At its 1949 annual convention, the United Farmers of Canada (Saskatchewan Section) decided to distance itself from the provincial CCF party and plot a more independent course as the new Saskatchewan Farmers' Union (SFU). Led by former cabinet minister Joe Phelps, the SFU argued that greater agricultural security would help solve many of rural Saskatchewan's problems, especially depopulation.[63]

The CCF government's commitment to rural Saskatchewan and its sound management of the economy earned Tommy Douglas a third consecutive mandate, something that had been achieved only by former Liberal premier Walter Scott during the first years of the province. The size of the 1952 election victory—forty-two of fifty-three seats and 54 per cent of the popular vote—seemed to validate the course that had been charted since the late 1940s. The ever-popular Douglas, at just forty-eight years of age, was at the height of his power and appeared destined to lead his party and govern the province for as long as he wanted. The Liberals, by contrast, had reached their lowest point in party history and faced a bleak future below the political radar. Perhaps Douglas best captured the different trajectories in the two parties' fortunes during a lopsided debate with the hapless Liberal leader. "Mr. Tucker is big enough to swallow me," he responded to a disparaging comment about his size, "but if he did he would be the strangest man in the world. He would have more brains in his stomach than he does in his head."[64]

Despite such cheekiness, the premier remained an extremely accessible leader, whose door was always open to the people of Saskatchewan and who insisted on personally answering the many letters he received. There was also nothing fancy about him. If he was working in the legislature, he invariably took his lunch in the basement cafeteria and always had the same standing order: poached eggs, tomato juice, and prunes. Official visitors sometimes joined him in line and dined on trays at the arborite tables.[65]

During the 1950s, CCF success was matched by the prosperity enjoyed by the province. The booming economy, fuelled largely by petroleum and mineral developments, ushered in an age of affluence that seemed light years

Gordie Howe, nicknamed Mr. Hockey, was a superstar for the Detroit Red Wings in the 1950s. SASKATOON PUBLIC LIBRARY LHQC205-1

away from the Saskatchewan of the 1930s. The provincial per capita income was above the Canadian national average four out of ten years during the 1950s.[66] The population, in turn, began to rebound, and for the first time since the Depression there was an increase in the number of people calling Saskatchewan home; by 1956, the provincial population stood at 880,665 or an increase of almost 50,000 in five years.

These buoyant times seemed to be played out in the sports arena. In 1951, led by legendary quarterback Glenn Dobbs, or the "Dobber" as he was known, the Roughriders returned to the Grey Cup for the first time since 1934. Despite a name change—they officially became the Saskatchewan Roughriders in 1948—and new green and white team colours, they failed in their eighth attempt to win the national football championship. On the ice, Saskatoon's Gordie Howe joined with Ted Lindsay and another Saskatchewan native, Sid Abel from Melville, to form the Detroit Red Wings' "Production Line," the most successful scoring trio in the NHL in the early 1950s. They would have played against Chicago Black Hawks centre Fred Sasakamoose of the Ahtahkakoop band, the first Saskatchewan treaty Indian in the NHL. The Red Wings' 1955 Stanley Cup victory, their fourth in the past six seasons, was overshadowed by another championship event that spring, and a Saskatchewan first. The Garnet Campbell rink of Avonlea won the province's first Brier at Regina's Exhibition Stadium with a perfect 10–0 record.[67]

The Regina Brier was part of Saskatchewan's golden jubilee celebrations. Unlike similar events in the past, like the opening of the new legislature in 1912, which tended to look to what the future held for the province, the fiftieth anniversary committee chose to commemorate the achievements of the province's pioneers. It was as if the current generation was reaching back in time to shake hands with those who had settled the land and thank them for their efforts in building Saskatchewan. There was a spate of community histories, the designation of over fifty historical sites, and a history of the province by award-winning author Jim Wright. In keeping with the official theme, the Douglas government built a one-million-dollar Museum of Natural History in Regina in honour of past pioneers. At the building's dedication in May 1955, Governor General Vincent Massey quoted a passage from the Bible to suggest that the jubilee was "a period when time stood still."[68] That certainly was the message conveyed by a frieze near the building's north entrance. Carved in Tyndall stone in bold relief was a skyward-looking farmer, clutching sheaves of wheat, along with his wife and child. The accompanying text spoke of "their vision, toil, and courage which gave so much to Saskatchewan." The irony was that the world the pioneers had built was now

Governor General Vincent Massey opens the new Museum of Natural History in Regina during the province's 1955 jubilee celebrations. SASKATCHEWAN ARCHIVES BOARD R-PS55-057-13

under siege. Nor did the distinct cultural pluralism of Saskatchewan society receive much attention, while the Aboriginal past was rarely mentioned—Louis Riel's name was left off a commemorative historical map.[69] It fell to Hollywood to tell the story of Sitting Bull's Sioux seeking refuge in Canada in a movie called *Saskatchewan*, starring Alan Ladd as a mounted policeman. At the world premiere of the film in Regina, the audience was treated to bad acting set against the backdrop of the Canadian Rockies![70]

Premier Douglas revelled in the jubilee celebrations and was a featured guest throughout the province. He attempted to cash in on this goodwill the following year when he went back to the electorate for a fresh mandate, promising more of the same policies. This time, he faced a new Liberal opponent in A. H. "Hammy" McDonald, who had succeeded Walter Tucker in 1954 and advocated "a middle of the road" policy, in keeping with his diffident personality. The change in leaders, however, made no difference to party fortunes, and the Liberals emerged with just fourteen seats in the 1956 contest. Nor was the CCF particularly happy, even though it won a fourth consecutive term. Douglas not only had to govern with fewer seats—only thirty-six—but the Social Credit party had run a full slate of candidates and elected three members. The premier tried to put a positive spin on the results, insisting that Social Credit success was a protest vote against liberalism and not socialism; after all, the three new Social Credit seats had formerly been held by the Liberals. But such an explanation did not account for the obvious decline in CCF support.[71]

Douglas' aura of invincibility also suffered a serious blow when he debated W. Ross Thatcher, the Liberal candidate for Assiniboia in the 1957 federal election, in Mossbank that spring. To the CCF, Thatcher was nothing more than a traitor. Born in Neville in 1917 and educated in commerce at Queen's University, Thatcher ran the family hardware business in Moose Jaw before winning a seat in the House of Commons as a CCF candidate in 1945. Although never comfortable within the party, he spent ten years in the federal CCF caucus before crossing the floor to sit first as an independent and then a Liberal backbencher. Thatcher's desertion might have become a parliamentary footnote if not for his blistering denunciation of Saskatchewan's Crown corporations as "a tragedy ... a very costly fiasco ... a dismal failure" during a Commons debate.[72]

These incendiary remarks were a red flag to Douglas, who immediately challenged the former CCFer to a public debate on the issue. Thatcher gamely accepted, and the showdown was set for the Mossbank community hall on 20 May 1957, the Victoria Day holiday. Despite the cold, wet weather, nearly twenty-five hundred people turned out to watch Tommy, in his own words, "drive Ross Thatcher out of the province."[73] But the Mossbank massacre was

A smiling Premier Douglas stands next to a grim Ross Thatcher before taking the stage for their famous debate at Mossbank in 1957. SASKATCHEWAN ARCHIVES BOARD R-LP1230

at best a draw, maybe even a victory for the Liberal newcomer. Whereas Douglas felt obliged to provide a detailed accounting of the government's record on public ownership, at the expense of his famous oratorical flare, Thatcher calmly held his own and presented an equally convincing case. According to one reporter who scored the match, Thatcher emerged "as a new power in Saskatchewan politics—not because he won but because he did not lose."[74] Two years later when the provincial Liberals sought a new leader to replace the ineffectual McDonald, they did not have to look far to find their saviour.

The Douglas government's more immediate concern was the revival of Conservatism on the prairies. In the 1957 general election, John Diefenbaker, the former leader of the Saskatchewan Conservative party and federal Progressive Conservative leader since 1956, ended twenty-two years of uninterrupted Liberal rule by winning a narrow minority government. Diefenbaker's victory was a testament to the persistence and endurance of one of Canada's most enigmatic leaders—whom one biographer has dubbed a "rogue Tory." Born in Ontario in 1895, he was raised and educated in

Saskatchewan, where he earned a popular reputation as an uncompromising criminal lawyer. But his true interest was politics, not law, and he was convinced that he would be prime minister one day. That seemed unlikely, though, as he lost every election he contested until 1940 when he was finally sent to the House of Commons as the representative for Lake Centre; he successfully switched to the Prince Albert constituency in 1953. Diefenbaker liked to joke that Conservatives on the prairies were an endangered species, but Liberal neglect of western Canada after the war helped undermine the once-close ties between the region and the party. Diefenbaker also spoke the language of the west, promising to make agriculture a federal priority and ensure that rural Canada had a central place on the national agenda. This call for a new Canada, together with Diefenbaker's populist appeal, turned his tenuous hold on power into a majority of record proportions in the 1958 election. All but one of the forty-eight seats on the prairies went Conservative.[75]

Diefenbaker lost no time addressing Saskatchewan concerns. The new government signed an agreement with the province to proceed with the long-delayed South Saskatchewan River Dam. It also approved two pieces of legislation designed to deal with farmer grievances that had festered since the early 1950s. The Agricultural Stabilization Act provided price supports for several agricultural products, while the Prairie Grain Advance Payments Act gave farmers much-needed cash advances on stored grain until the massive backlog could be cleared. These steps signalled the beginning of a new deal for the province at the federal level. They also likely encouraged, if not pushed, the Douglas government to take new action of its own. Ever since the disappointing 1956 election results, the premier and his cabinet evidently believed that "people wanted something more, or perhaps something different" and that "somewhere they had gone wrong."[76] That something, Douglas concluded, was medicare. The CCF government had been committed to introducing a universal health insurance plan since 1944, but had been held back by the province's financial position. Now that Saskatchewan's fiscal picture had dramatically improved, the premier decided that days of caution were over. The time had arrived to take the party back to its social gospel roots and fulfill a long-standing promise.[77]

CHAPTER EIGHTEEN

BOTH SIDES NOW

"**I**'VE LOOKED AT LIFE FROM BOTH SIDES NOW, From win and lose, And
still, somehow, It's life's illusions I recall: I really don't know life at
all." It's become her signature song. Originally released by Saskatoon's
Joni Mitchell in the late 1960s, "Both Sides Now" was reprised on a retro-
spective album three decades later to critical acclaim. Few songs and even
fewer musical artists have enjoyed such enduring popularity. What Mitchell
and her millions of fans never realized, though, is that the song's title, even
some of the lyrics, applied to Saskatchewan during the 1960s. At the beginning of the decade, with the province never more prosperous, the Tommy
Douglas government was finally poised to realize the long-term goal of universal, state-supported medical care. For the CCF party, it was a time, in
Mitchell's words, "When every fairy-tale comes real." Four years later, Ross
Thatcher, leading a rejuvenated Liberal party back to power, brashly set out
to remake the province along free-enterprise lines and end two decades of
CCF socialism. As Mitchell's song explained, "But now old friends are acting
strange, They shake their heads, They say I've changed, For something's lost
and something's gained, In living every day." This "Both Sides Now" theme

defined Saskatchewan in the 1960s, especially for Premier Thatcher, who tried to reduce the debate about the province's future to a simple choice between capitalism or socialism. He was to learn, however, that the promise of the "New Saskatchewan" largely depended on outside forces over which the province had little control. "So many things I would have done," mused Mitchell, "But clouds got in my way."

Joni Mitchell is one of the most influential artists of her generation. CANADIAN PRESS

When Tommy Douglas took office in Saskatchewan in 1944, he also took on the health portfolio. This double duty underscored the importance of health care to the new CCF government. "We believe ... we can ultimately give our people a completely socialized system of health services, irrespective of ... individual ability to pay,"[1] Douglas had pledged in a radio address the year before the provincial election. It was also a response to the premier's personal experiences with the health care system in Canada. Shortly after his immigration to Winnipeg before the Great War, the young Douglas had been hospitalized with osteomyelitis, an acute bone infection, and faced the likely amputation of his leg if a specialist had not taken him on as a charity case.[2]

As Saskatchewan premier, he was determined to ensure that no one, because of lack of resources, found themselves in a similar predicament. Nor did he ever want to see a repeat of his 1930s experience, when as a young Weyburn preacher he performed funerals for people who might have lived if not for the Depression. "I buried a young man at Griffin, and another one at Pangman," he sadly recounted years later, "both young men in their thirties with small young families, who died because there was no doctor readily available, and they hadn't the money to get proper care. They were buried in coffins made by the local people out of ordinary wood."[3]

By the time of the CCF victory, Saskatchewan already had pioneered a number of health care firsts. Beginning in 1916, the provincial government allowed rural municipalities to hire doctors and pay them a grant or stipend to retain their services for the local community. That same year, it enabled towns, villages, and RMs to come together to establish and maintain "union hospitals." Over time, while traditional fee-for-service medicine held sway in Saskatchewan cities, a form of socialized medicine took root and flourished in the countryside; rural districts set and collected health taxes, built and managed hospitals, and hired and paid medical personnel. The province also tackled the scourge of tuberculosis, one of the leading causes of Canadian deaths in the early twentieth century (including former Liberal prime minister Wilfrid Laurier), by becoming in 1929 the first jurisdiction in North America to provide free diagnosis and treatment of the disease. A 1921 screening program had found that 57 per cent of Saskatchewan schoolchildren were infected. By the start of the Second World War, the province had brought the disease under control and boasted the lowest mortality rate in the country.[4]

Premier Douglas, as health minister, wanted to take medical care in the province to another level and immediately commissioned a health services survey by renowned physician Dr. Henry Sigerist of Johns Hopkins University. The new government then used the Sigerist report to fashion a number of health initiatives in the first few years of its mandate. In November 1944, it established a Health Services Planning Commission to oversee the creation of a system of regional health boards for managing and providing local care.[5] The first of these health districts, established in Swift Current in December 1945, provided the sprawling region's inhabitants with a tax-supported medical insurance program—another first in Canada—and served as a testing ground for the eventual adoption of provincewide medicare.[6] The Douglas government also acted on a number of specific recommendations: free cancer treatment (1944); comprehensive health care for those on social assistance, including pensioners and spouses (1945); and an air ambulance service (1946). The crowning achievement, the introduction of Canada's first universal hospital insurance program in 1947, offered a complete range of hospital benefits to Saskatchewan's residents for an annual premium.[7]

These measures made a medical college at the University of Saskatchewan an absolute necessity if the province was going to meet its growing health care commitments, and the new school began admitting students in 1953. The Douglas government also generously funded hospital construction and expansion in the southern half of the province, while increasing the number of nursing stations across the north. It was at the new University Hospital in November 1951 that the first calibrated application of cobalt-60, also known as the cobalt bomb, successfully treated a cancer patient.[8] Saskatchewan was also at the forefront in the experimental use of LSD (d-lysergic diethylamide) as a possible cure for schizophrenia. Dr. Humphry Osmond, superintendent of the Weyburn Mental Hospital in the early 1950s, coined the term "psychedelic," well before it became synonymous with 1960s counterculture.[9]

Douglas relinquished the health portfolio in 1949 after a period of intense activity quite in keeping with his personality. But the cost of providing a full medical care insurance plan was still prohibitive, as the government struggled to find the right economic elixir to get the province back on its feet after the Depression and war. That all changed in the late 1950s, thanks to buoyant oil

W. O. Mitchell leads a Saskatchewan Arts Board Writers' Workshop in 1963. Riddell, *Cornerstone of Culture*

and mineral revenues and a decision by the new federal government of John Diefenbaker to fund almost half the cost of the Saskatchewan Hospital Services Plan. The premier, who had repeatedly promised to introduce medicare as soon as the province could afford it, jumped at the opportunity to implement this cherished CCF goal and, in doing so, demonstrate to the province and the country that the party could still do imaginative things after a decade and a half in office.[10] He glowingly outlined the rationale for medicare to a radio audience in December 1959: "If we can do this—and I feel sure we can ... Saskatchewan [will] lead the way. Let us therefore have the vision and courage to take this step ... toward a more just and humane society."[11]

The CCF medical care insurance program was to be based on five principles: prepayment of costs, universal coverage, high quality service, public administration, and a form of service acceptable to both providers and recipients. On this last point, Douglas believed, perhaps naively, that the government and the province's doctors could reach an amicable agreement. "We have no intention of shoving some preconceived plan down doctors' throats," he had vowed. "We want their co-operation ... I am convinced we will get it."[12] But the College of Physicians and Surgeons bristled over the lack of consultation before the premier announced the policy and declared that it was adamantly opposed to any compulsory scheme that threatened to put the medical profession under government control. It also refused to work with a special advisory committee to oversee the introduction of medicare and did everything possible to obstruct the government's plans.[13]

The other stumbling block was the new leader of the provincial Liberals, Ross Thatcher. Winning on the first ballot at the September 1959 convention, he was the party's fourth leader since 1944. But unlike his predecessors, Thatcher seemed more than capable of toppling Douglas as evidenced by his gutsy performance at Mossbank in 1957. He also gave the party a purpose that had been missing since it had been chased from office in 1944. In fact, Thatcher told the leadership convention that he was a Liberal "by conviction," driven there by CCF waste and mismanagement.[14] This message was repeated over and over again in the coming months and years as he trashed socialism for ruining the province's great post-war promise. The Douglas government, he once ridiculed, "usually takes some teacher or preacher or someone who knows nothing about business and puts him in charge of an enterprise ... the CCF can't sell nuts to chimps."[15] At other times, he could be deadly serious. "It is our job to emerge from the dark cloud of CCF government," Thatcher gravely reminded the party. "CCF socialism was born here. It should be buried here."[16] His ascension to the Liberal leadership meant that Saskatchewan, the land of Douglas and Diefenbaker, was more than ever the home of the "politics of personalities."[17]

Thatcher's response to the medical care plan was to call for a plebiscite. "Why should a move," he asked rhetorically, "with such far-reaching consequences and involving such huge expenditures be made by a few socialist planners without direct consultation with all citizens?"[18] Douglas countered that the Saskatchewan people would be given the chance to pronounce on the plan in the June 1960 election. This decision to turn the election into a medicare referendum was designed to blunt the doctors' opposition and force them to accept the program once the CCF party was returned to office. But the medical college raised a war chest from member contributions and launched an ambitious publicity campaign against the plan. It soon became apparent, though, that the doctors were not politicians. Their information package was offensive at best, even suggesting that women experiencing menopause might be forced by the scheme to see a psychiatrist or be admitted to a mental asylum. The mishandling of the issue eroded public sympathy for the doctors, while allowing the CCF to profit from every gaffe. Douglas was easily returned to office for the fifth consecutive time with thirty-eight of fifty-four seats, a slightly larger majority. What the premier's medicare victory obscured, though, was Thatcher's growing influence after less than a year in provincial politics. Not only did the Liberals capture all of the other seats at the expense of Conservative and Social Credit candidates, but the party increased its share of the popular vote by almost the same amount as the CCF percentage decline. Much of this success was the direct consequence of better organization, something that Thatcher owed to his days with the CCF.[19]

Premier Douglas interpreted his election victory as a mandate to proceed with medicare. The College of Physicians and Surgeons, meanwhile, remained "unalterably opposed" to the plan and did its best to delay the report of the special advisory committee charged with recommending how to proceed. The depth of their anger was revealed when the committee sought individual input from the province's doctors. "This socialist garbage," wrote a group of Regina medical practitioners, "is an insult to any normal human being. Yours in bitter hatred."[20] The introduction of the legislation was also complicated by the imminent departure of Tommy Douglas from provincial politics. The national CCF was about to join with organized labour to form the New Democratic Party (NDP), and the premier was being courted to lead the new federal party. But Douglas was reluctant to abandon his Saskatchewan career until medicare was in place. "I have started a big job here," he said during a newspaper interview, "and I would like to finish it if the people will let me."[21]

That seemed unlikely, though, as the advisory committee had still not reported by the time Douglas won the NDP leadership in August 1961. It was another two months—and only days before Douglas was officially scheduled

"Frankenstein." Ed Sebestyen, *Saskatoon StarPhoenix*

to leave provincial politics—before the CCF government finally introduced the Saskatchewan Medical Care Insurance bill, which essentially mirrored the majority report of the advisory committee, except for the exclusion of utilization fees. The Liberal opposition attacked the government's decision to push ahead with the plan, claiming that it was more interested in boosting Douglas' federal career than dealing with hard questions, such as the "staggering costs involved."[22] The doctors also warned that trouble lay ahead by overwhelmingly voting against co-operation. The premier, however, was not prepared to back down and advised his successor, Woodrow Lloyd, then serving as provincial treasurer, to proceed with the legislation.

Douglas resigned in early November 1961 after a remarkable seventeen years as premier. His departure was deeply regretted by many in Saskatchewan, not only for his contributions to the province, but because his political skills and personal integrity would likely be needed to defuse the potentially explosive medicare issue. But Lloyd was ready to step out from his predecessor's shadow. The unshakeable resolve that had carried him through far-reaching educational reforms in the face of angry opposition, and his profound confidence in the merits of medicare, would bear him through this new crisis. Once the legislation was approved, Lloyd personally tried to bring the medical college on side, even delaying the introduction of the plan three months to 1 July 1962 so that negotiations could proceed. The discussions foundered, however, over the continuing fear that the medical profession would come under government control. By the late spring of 1962, a strike seemed a real possibility, as a majority of the province's doctors threatened to withdraw their services unless the legislation was rescinded. Lloyd was unmoved. "We are at war," he confided to one of his daughters, "and will be for some time."[23] One of the unexpected casualties was the former premier. In his first federal election as national NDP leader in June 1962, Douglas suffered a humiliating defeat in Regina. "I'll lay me down and bleed a while," he quoted an old ballad during his concession speech on television, "and then I'll rise and fight again."[24] He would enter the House of Commons later that fall after winning a by-election in British Columbia and serve there until 1979.

True to their warning, doctors suspended their services on 1 July, except for limited emergency care at certain hospitals. Into their place stepped British physicians who had been recruited by the Lloyd government. Saskatchewan doctors willing to abide by the plan also organized community clinics. In the first days of the strike, there was considerable public unease, even dread, fed by the uncertainty of what was going to happen. Some citizens had formed "Keep Our Doctors" (KOD) committees in June and initially talked of forcing the Lloyd government to withdraw the medicare act. But once the strike was underway, these grassroots organizations became politicized and seemed more intent on driving the CCF from office.[25] Ross Thatcher naturally used the unrest to his advantage. At a four-to-five-thousand-strong KOD rally in front of the Saskatchewan legislature on 11 July, at which both Lloyd and Douglas were hanged in effigy, the Liberal opposition leader, surrounded by most of his caucus, went to the legislature chamber and demanded that the legislature be recalled to deal with the crisis. For added effect, Thatcher was photographed kicking the locked door of the chamber.[26] These antics were matched by KOD rhetoric. "Tell those bloody Commies to go to hell when it comes to Canada," Father Athol Murray of Notre Dame College told a Saskatoon KOD meeting. "I loathe the welfare state and I love the free-swinging freedoms."[27] The vice-president of the provincial KOD, a Dutch refugee after the war, declared at the Regina rally, "I could have just as well migrated to East Berlin."[28] The Weyburn KOD even sent an urgent telegram to the secretary-general of the United Nations with the plaintive message, "Our freedom is at stake."[29]

Despite the vilification, Premier Lloyd was resolved to calmly ride out the medicare storm, believing that the doctors' demands could not override the larger interests of Saskatchewan society. His stand was largely supported by the media, which rebuked the medical profession for putting itself above the law. But the bitter strike also divided provincial society, as Citizens for Medical Care groups were organized to counteract the KOD committees. In the third week of the strike, at Lloyd's invitation, Stephen Taylor, a British doctor and member of the House of Lords, arrived in Saskatoon on 17 July, ostensibly to act as special advisor to the premier on medicare. But Lord Taylor quickly assumed the role of mediator and spent the next week bringing the politicians and doctors together and finding common ground. By 23 July, the two warring parties had signed the Saskatoon Agreement, which preserved the principle of universality while removing those sections of the legislation that implied government control of doctors.[30] "This province has been sick," Taylor told the press in announcing the settlement. "I prescribe for it absolute rest."[31]

The CCF government immediately reconvened the legislature and, in one of the shortest sessions in Saskatchewan history, amended the medicare act in accordance with the agreement. In 1963, Lloyd was named an "outstanding citizen" by *Maclean's* magazine, while Douglas' prediction that medicare would be adopted nationwide was realized three years later when the federal government approved the Medical Care Act. Lord Taylor's prescription, however, did little to heal the rifts created by the nasty dispute. As one observer at the time perceptively commented, "To some it was a truce; to others, a peace."[32]

Although medicare dominated Saskatchewan life for several years, there were other noteworthy developments during the period. In 1962, the Lloyd government, working closely with the City of Regina and the University of Saskatchewan, created Wascana Centre, a one-thousand-acre development surrounding Wascana Lake. Designed by celebrated architect Minoru Yamasaki, later known for his work on New York's World Trade Center, the inner-city park tied together the Saskatchewan legislature and the new Museum of Natural History with other cultural, educational, and recreational activities. One of Wascana Centre's first occupants was the new Regina Campus of the University of Saskatchewan. In 1959, in response to growing enrolment at the post-secondary level, Regina College had been given full degree-granting status; two years later, it became a branch of the provincial university and selected a new site to the south of Wascana Lake.[33]

An even bigger story—at least by Saskatchewan standards—was the unparalleled success of the Richardson rink, originally from Stoughton but curling out of Regina clubs. These lions in winter, skipped by the tall, lanky Ernie, won four Briers and four international (Scotch Cup) championships

Premier Douglas with the four-time Brier champion Richardson rink. SASKATCHEWAN ARCHIVES
BOARD R-A11522

in five years (1959, 1960, 1962, and 1963). Their record is still untouched. Saskatchewan women also curled their way to prominence. In 1960, the Joyce McKee foursome totally dominated the first unofficial national championship. She repeated the feat the following year at an official competition and then three more times as a member of the Vera Pezer rink (1971–73), the first women's team to roll off three consecutive national titles.[34]

The gloom that hung over agriculture also lifted in the early 1960s. By 1961, there were slightly fewer farms in Saskatchewan (93,924) than there had been half a century earlier (95,013), but these modern commercial operations were on average more than twice as large as the farms in 1911 (686 to 296 acres) and capable of producing at least twice as much grain, depending on growing conditions.[35] Wheat sales, however, had been static for several years, especially since the United States, through trade practices and subsidies, had replaced Canada as the world's largest exporter. By 1960, the country's wheat surplus stood at 510 million bushels, with nearly 20 per cent stored in bins and fields on Saskatchewan farms. "I can't go on like this," complained a Regina-area farmer, who watched helplessly as the province's farm net income slipped to one-quarter of what it had been five years earlier.[36]

Prime Minister Diefenbaker initially balked at providing subsidies, but with his popularity in western Canada starting to slip, he announced in

August 1960 acreage payments of a dollar an acre up to a maximum of two hundred acres. The proposed two-hundred-dollar payout was regarded by farmers as more of an insult than a solution, and the frustrated prime minister handed the federal agriculture portfolio to his friend and colleague Alvin Hamilton. The affable Hamilton, like Diefenbaker, had earned his political spurs losing repeatedly as a Conservative candidate in Saskatchewan until he was finally elected for Qu'Appelle in 1957. He now went looking for a customer for Canada's wheat and found one in Communist China, whose recent harvests had been poor. In December 1960, the Diefenbaker government sold an initial twenty-eight million bushels of wheat to China. Less than six months later, it concluded another deal for 187 million bushels. An ecstatic Hamilton told farmers he could sell as much grain as they could grow.[37] Saskatchewan producers took him at his word and harvested a record half a billion bushels of wheat in 1963.

Other sectors of the provincial economy thrived as well. By 1961, the oil and gas industry had created four thousand direct jobs and hundreds of others servicing the sites and the workers.[38] Almost every major economic indicator was up in 1962 and again in 1963, prompting the *Saskatoon Star-Phoenix* to dub Saskatchewan the "Cinderella province."[39] Nor did the Lloyd government simply sit back and bask in the benefits of a booming economy. In 1963, it created the Saskatchewan Economic Development Corporation to facilitate private industrial expansion and research. The Liberal opposition decried the new agency as a peculiar move by a supposedly socialist government—"a step in the right direction by the wrong people"—but supported the bill nonetheless.[40] In fact, it seemed as though the CCF government had successfully put the medicare crisis behind it, and could confidently set its sights on winning a sixth consecutive election.

Standing in the way, however, was Ross Thatcher. "There's nothing wrong with socialism," he sarcastically said about the Saskatchewan experience, "except it doesn't work."[41] What bothered Thatcher about the CCF economic performance was that it really was not much of a success story compared to the other two prairie provinces. Between 1951 and 1966, while Manitoba and Alberta grew 24 and 56 per cent, respectively, Saskatchewan lagged behind at just 14 per cent.[42] This third-place status, combined with high taxes and continuing rural decline, was denounced by Thatcher as the price that the province was paying for CCF waste, inefficiency, and mismanagement. What was needed, he insisted, was a united free-enterprise vote to rid Saskatchewan of the pesky socialists.[43]

Premier Lloyd called an election for April 1964. Most pundits predicted an easy CCF victory, as did overly complacent party workers. What many failed to sense was the mood for change. After all, the CCF had been in power for two decades and made its share of enemies, especially during the doctors' strike. One political commentator has suggested that medicare served the same role as the Ku Klux Klan did in the 1929 election in bringing together anti-government forces.[44] What many also discounted was Thatcher's organizational abilities and how he revitalized the Liberal party in a way that would have impressed the old master, former Liberal premier Jimmy Gardiner, who died in 1962. Thatcher worked hard to woo traditional Progressive Conservative supporters, and tried to limit head-to-head battles with other free-enterprise candidates. He also went after young voters, who had no memory of the Depression and hence were not necessarily inclined to support the CCF. Indeed, he presented the provincial Liberal party as a distinctly Saskatchewan organization by distancing himself from the federal Liberals and portraying the CCF as under the thumb of Tommy Douglas and the new labour-dominated NDP.

What was particularly remarkable about the Liberal campaign was Thatcher's relative silence about medicare and the socialism–free-enterprise paradigm that had been his mantra since 1959. He evidently realized that medicare was here to stay and that socialism was not such a scary word after twenty years of CCF rule. Instead, the Liberal platform focused on the economy, promising to take the province to new heights of development.[45] "Saskatchewan Missed the Boat Once," one Liberal ad warned the electorate, "We Can't Afford To Miss the Boat Again."[46]

The Regina Five outside the Norman MacKenzie Art Gallery in 1964. UNIVERSITY OF REGINA ARCHIVES AND SPECIAL COLLECTIONS, ACC. 80-20, 847

Polling day brought confusion and shock. Since the CCF and Liberals both secured about 40 per cent of the popular vote, the margin of victory in several ridings was extremely slim. It was only after several recounts that Lloyd stepped aside for Thatcher, whose party had won a stunning thirty-two seats to the CCF's twenty-six. The other surprise was the election of Martin Pederson, the Progressive Conservative leader, in the Arm River riding; the victory was the first for a Tory candidate in thirty-five years. Several explanations were put forward to make sense of the CCF defeat, the most common being that Woodrow Lloyd was not Tommy Douglas. Perhaps the simplest answer, in the words of someone who had been there in 1944, was that the government "died, above all, of old age."[47]

At forty-seven, Ross Thatcher became Saskatchewan's ninth premier and one of its most aloof. He was a ruthless, demanding leader, the epitome of the party boss with the trademark cigar, who ruled the Liberal caucus with an iron fist and expected absolute devotion and support.[48] Thatcher was respected and even feared, but unlike Douglas, who also dominated his party, he was never loved. His smile always seemed forced, as if his face was meant to be set in its stern countenance. The new premier immediately announced a civil-service hiring freeze, convinced that the bureaucracy was bloated and in need of downsizing. He also believed, as did many other Liberals, that the civil service was a nest of CCF sympathizers, but refrained from the massive dismissals that many expected.[49] Many bureaucrats, however, chose to leave Saskatchewan to find work in other provinces or join the federal civil service at the very time the Lester Pearson government was putting in place the welfare state. Their influence in government circles across the country would earn them the sobriquet "the Saskatchewan mafia."[50] Those who remained behind had to get used to a radically different style of administration. Whereas the CCF under Douglas and Lloyd had given the province two decades of activist government, a constant refrain of policies and initiatives, Thatcher did relatively little even in comparison to premiers before 1944. The Liberal leader was most interested in slashing government expenditures—at least 10 per cent of the budget in his first year—and gladly refused to replace some of the departing civil servants to save the province money.[51]

Once Thatcher was in office, he resumed his attacks on the CCF, always referring to the opposition as "the socialists," and forever talking about the need to make the province "a haven for free enterprise." The influential *Wall Street Journal* aptly described his purpose as "slowing down socialism."[52] In practice, though, despite its huffing and puffing about the perils of state intervention in the lives of Saskatchewan citizens, the Thatcher government made no attempt to dismantle medicare or other popular CCF social welfare initiatives, prompting one observer to claim that the difference between the two parties was "more in outlook and in intent than in actual policies."[53]

The Liberals also maintained that a robust, free-enterprise economy was the cure for two decades of CCF inefficiency and stagnation. But even here, Thatcher was hard-pressed to do much better, since the province had never been more prosperous. The premier, however, devoted his energies to the economy to the exclusion of almost everything else, insisting that free enterprise was going to break the socialist stranglehold and liberate business in the province.[54] To this end, one of the government's first actions was a royalty holiday for deep oil-well drilling. "If the oil industry—or any other industry—is to flourish and expand, there must be a proper political and economic climate," Thatcher told oil executives gathered in Regina in September 1964. "Our administration will endeavour to provide such a climate."[55]

The resource that promised even bigger gains than oil was potash or sylvinite, potassium-rich compounds used in fertilizers. Discovered by accident during drilling for oil in 1942, the province's potash reserves run northwesterly-southeasterly in a wide belt across southern Saskatchewan at a depth ranging from three to seven thousand feet. Current estimates place the amount of recoverable potash at 120 billion tons or roughly 40 per cent of world reserves—enough to keep the industry going for hundreds of years using conventional methods. Because of the costs involved in bringing a mine into production, the Douglas government tried to interest private capital in developing the industry. But it was not until 1953 that it reached a long-term, low-royalty deal with the Potash Corporation of America, which began producing Saskatchewan's first potash at its Patience Lake mine, just east of Saskatoon, five years later. The province's second and largest mine came on stream in 1962, when International Minerals and Chemicals Corporation, another American firm, successfully completed a shaft through the Blairmore formation near Esterhazy. By the end of the decade, ten mines were in operation with a total capacity in excess of five million tons per year.[56]

Although the potash industry owed its beginnings to the CCF, Thatcher extolled the success of the new mines as an example of what was possible under free enterprise. It was a view shared by the mining companies. At the Saskatchewan Potash Show in Saskatoon in October 1965, the president of International Minerals and Chemicals confidently predicted that hundreds of millions of dollars would be invested in potash development. "Nothing but growth lies ahead," he enthused. "What an extraordinary opportunity exists for this Province!"[57] In fact, it seemed that potash would do for Saskatchewan what oil had done for Alberta. A University of Saskatchewan study suggested that the wealth being generated by the new industry would likely exceed the value of all other mineral production by 1970.[58]

It was certainly changing the urban face of the province. Saskatoon's population jumped 20 per cent (from 95,526 to 115,247) in the first half of the 1960s in response to the city's new role as industrial hub to six district mines. It was the fastest growing city in Canada and proudly laid claim to the title of potash capital of the world. Similarly, towns outside mines, like Colonsay and Lanigan, became front-line service communities, with the resultant population increase. It is no exaggeration to suggest that the potash boom accelerated the urbanization of the province and helped push the urban population ahead of that of rural Saskatchewan by the end of the decade.[59]

Although Regina and Saskatoon remained essentially "British" cities at the end of the 1950s, ethnic differences increasingly became less pronounced as the children of European immigrants integrated into society at large. Historian Gerry Friesen, who came to Saskatoon from Prince Albert in 1961, assumed that heritage mattered little during his undergraduate days at the University of Saskatchewan. In fact, Saskatoon's distinctiveness, like that of other Canadian cities at the time, was encountering changes introduced by American mass culture. The outlook, tastes, and styles of a new generation were being influenced by trends south of the border—from juke-box music to television programs to the food consumed at drive-in restaurants like A&W. Even student protest was more concerned with the Cold War, Blacks, and the

University of Saskatchewan students snake dancing through Saskatoon traffic. UNIVERSITY OF SASKATCHEWAN ARCHIVES A6267

American military-industrial complex than problems in Canada's own backyard. The new liberalized atmosphere of the 1960s, however, did find expression in the avant-garde work of Saskatchewan visual artists, such as Otto Rogers and Warren Petersen. Saskatoon's new Mendel Art Gallery, established in 1964 on the banks of the South Saskatchewan thanks to a generous bequest from meat packer Fred Mendel, also hosted the controversial theatre, Circle in the Centre, where local stars, including Eric Peterson and Janet and Susan Wright, made their semi-professional debut.[60]

The Thatcher government's other triumph, heralded as a further step towards greater diversification of the provincial economy, was the successful negotiation of a contract to build a pulp mill near Prince Albert. For years, the CCF had tried unsuccessfully to bring the pulp-and-paper industry to northern Saskatchewan. The CCF record in encouraging the lumber industry was no better. The net value of forestry was less than 1 per cent of the province's total commodity production in 1958.[61] Thatcher's open invitation to private capital seemed to be the answer. In August 1964, Karl Landegger of the New York–based Parsons and Whittemore Inc. contacted the premier to ask whether the Saskatchewan government was willing to support a pulp mill in the Prince Albert region. In the ensuing negotiations, the province became a partner in the project, but the relationship was an unequal one. Thatcher agreed to guarantee a fifty-million-dollar bond issue, assuming 80 per cent of the risk in return for only 30 per cent of the equity. Opposition leader Woodrow Lloyd welcomed the creation of the mill, but questioned the generous concessions awarded Parsons and Whittemore.[62] The premier waved aside the concerns, insisting that "unless the need for profits is recognized ... no progress is possible in industrial development."[63] He could also brag that he had succeeded where the CCF had failed and looked to reap the political rewards in the north when construction of the pulp mill started in the summer of 1966.[64]

In announcing the mill, Thatcher promised that the project would "bring a better life to many northern residents of Saskatchewan of Indian ancestry."[65] In fact, in keeping with his grudge with socialism, he was determined to do a better job than the previous CCF government in improving the lives of Aboriginal peoples and their place in provincial society. It would be no easy task. At the beginning of the decade, the Saskatchewan Indian population stood at twenty-three thousand and was growing at a rate of more than 20 per cent per year on reserves. They also remained an impoverished group. The average per capita income for Indians in 1958 was slightly over two hundred dollars—less than one-sixth the provincial average income.[66] This limited income was partly attributable to the large-scale mechanization of farming. Bigger farms meant fewer field jobs for Indian labourers.[67]

Premier Thatcher welcoming Aboriginal children to his office. SASKATCHEWAN ARCHIVES BOARD
R-B7277

For the CCF government, movement off-reserve and into urban jobs had been regarded as the only realistic solution to the overcrowding, low standard of living, and general lack of opportunity. And by the early 1960s, more and more Indians were heading to the city in search of employment. In the ten-year period between 1961 and 1971, the Aboriginal population of Regina climbed from 539 to 2,860, while that of Saskatoon went from 207 to 1,070.[68] City residents were uneasy with their arrival, seeing their presence as "problematic" and "out of place." Policy-makers, on the other hand, mistakenly assumed that Indian migration to cities signalled their decision to abandon their Aboriginal identity and integrate into mainstream society.[69]

Indians were also not welcome in small-town Saskatchewan. In the spring of 1963, *Maclean's* journalist Peter Gzowski travelled to the North Battleford area to investigate the murder of a young Saulteaux Indian by nine white men from Glaslyn. What he found was "Canada's Alabama." While the local Indians "live[d] in conditions that would appall most civilized Canadians," the nearby white communities were determined to keep them at arm's length: off their streets, out of their businesses, and away from their children. Gzowski even suggested that "our problems may be worse" than the southern United States because "the truly frightening thing here" was the pervasive, subtle undercurrent of discrimination, what he called "the race prejudice of gentle, friendly people." Nor did the article hold out much hope for the future. Gzowski argued that if the Indian really wanted to join the twentieth century North American way of life, then he had to accept his fate and cast off his values, language, and religion. But "*our* acceptance of *him*," he warned, "could well be an even more difficult decision."[70]

The situation in northern Saskatchewan was perhaps even worse. By the early 1960s, the CCF vision for the region was in tatters. Trapping and fishing could not adequately sustain the rapidly growing Aboriginal population, and many families endured a bleak existence on social assistance. Indians and Métis had traded their traditional life in the bush, where they had intimately known the land and its rhythms, for a supposedly new beginning as displaced paupers in isolated communities with overcrowded, substandard housing.[71]

Several researchers at the Center for Community Studies at the University of Saskatchewan concluded that the new settlements in the region could support only a fraction of their population and recommended large-scale relocation to the south. They also took issue with the government view that northern Aboriginals were ill-suited for wage employment and advocated improved education and training. These findings were deliberately suppressed by the center in favour of a more flattering assessment of the CCF record in northern Saskatchewan. But just before the Lloyd government stepped down in 1964, the premier approved the publication of the damning report, suitably titled *A Northern Dilemma*.[72]

Premier Thatcher saw no such dilemma in dealing with Saskatchewan's Indian and Métis communities. Like Douglas before him, he was genuinely distressed by the deplorable conditions on reserves and ashamed of Métis destitution at a time of unprecedented provincial prosperity. He also feared that a failure to do something about the situation would lead to more serious problems in the near future.[73] Thatcher consequently created a new Indian and Métis Branch within the Department of Natural Resources, whose primary purpose was to find jobs for Aboriginal people, and in doing so, "accelerate the process by which these people become an integral part of Canadian society."[74] If the province's Indians and Métis were going to escape from poverty, the premier reasoned, they needed work, not handouts, and the chance to support themselves. Much like Douglas and his integration policy, Thatcher was essentially calling for assimilation. He had no patience with talk of Indian customs, traditions, and treaty rights. "What is their culture?" he once remarked. "Living in tents or dirty filthy shacks on a reserve? Culture is fine, but we've got to be realistic and bring them to where the jobs are."[75]

In October 1964, the Thatcher government convened a conference in

An Aboriginal family in the Co-op Store at Frobisher. SASKATCHEWAN ARCHIVES BOARD R-B5613

Saskatoon for Indian and Métis representatives and encouraged them to work together. The Federation of Saskatchewan Indians, however, regarded its interests as distinct from those of the Métis and resented the implication that special status and treaty rights were somehow expendable.[76] The northern Métis, meanwhile, used the meeting as a springboard to launch a new organization, the Métis Association of Saskatchewan, in Prince Albert in April 1965. Headed by leftist Malcolm Norris, the association sought to cultivate Métis political consciousness and promote self-determination. But it faced competition from the Saskatchewan Métis Society, an older Regina-based organization now supported by the premier. With government funding, the Métis Society, led by Joe Amyotte, neutralized Norris and absorbed the rival association at a joint convention in Regina in May 1967.[77] Thatcher expected the society to co-operate with his efforts, especially when the government was providing new housing in the north, funding various economic development projects, and making hundreds of job placements. He even introduced a Native hiring quota, insisting that the public service reflect the Aboriginal proportion of the provincial population.[78]

The place of women in Saskatchewan society was an entirely different matter. After the Second World War, women from many backgrounds began to question their subordinate status in a male-dominated world, as well as challenge commonly held sexual stereotypes. Those who worked in the home, or in the home and on the farm, found that their many contributions were downplayed or little recognized, while those in the labour force had to contend with lower pay, few opportunities for advancement, and, if they had children, limited outside help.

In February 1967, the federal government established a royal commission to investigate the status of women in Canada; it served as a forum for women across the country to express their needs and voice their frustrations, as well as listen to the experience of others. The Regina and Saskatoon hearings drew record audiences, mostly women from white, middle-class backgrounds. But the written submissions and oral presentations, described by the chair as "no nonsense," covered a range of topics, from marital property rights and household duties to daycare and poverty.[79] Eleanor Hitchings of Saskatoon talked about her double duty as a working mother. "Bitter?" she asked. "A little, I suppose, but that's the way it was."[80] The Saskatchewan Farmers' Union Women even admitted that their "constitution says women have equal status, but this is questionable."[81]

Some of the reaction to the commission and its mandate was predictably negative. One male Regina letter-writer suggested that participants needed "a good psychiatrist or some tranquilizer pills."[82] But the hearings and subsequent report helped forge women's networks and provided a much-needed agenda for action. Since women were first given the right to vote in Saskatchewan elections during the Great War, only six had sat in the legislature by 1964.[83] Three of those six represented the CCF, which despite its emphasis on equality of opportunity, had put forward only five women candidates for election in the thirty-year period, and eight elections, since 1934.[84] One of the two women in the legislature in 1964 was Liberal Sally Merchant, a popular Saskatoon radio and television personality (the host of CFQC's *Hello Sally*) who had the credentials to be cabinet material. But she was passed over by Thatcher, apparently because of her gender.[85]

The bigger picture, meanwhile, could not have been brighter. In 1966, Saskatchewan farmers seeded 19.4 million acres, the largest wheat crop in provincial history, and harvested a record 537 million bushels. That same fall at Vancouver's Empire Stadium, the Saskatchewan Roughriders ended the longest drought in Grey Cup history by drubbing Ottawa 29-14 behind the playmaking of the little field general, quarterback Ronnie Lancaster, and the punishing running of George Reed. The post-game interviews had to be held in the Ottawa dressing room because the CBC, convinced that Saskatchewan would lose, had set up its cameras there before the final whistle.

The long-delayed South Saskatchewan River Dam was also completed. At the opening ceremonies on 21 July 1967, Prime Minister Lester Pearson paid

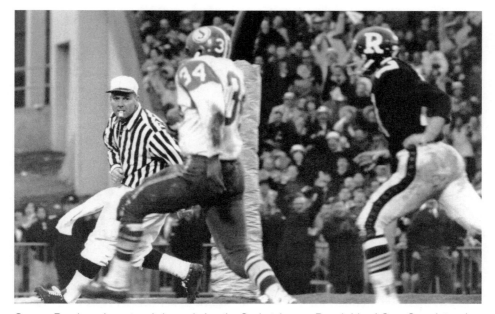

George Reed scoring a touchdown during the Saskatchewan Roughriders' Grey Cup victory in 1966. CANADIAN PRESS

tribute to the three provincial personalities behind the project through the naming of the Gardiner Dam, Lake Diefenbaker, and Douglas Park. It seemed as if Saskatchewan had finally regained its step after the Depression and was once again marching down the road to greatness. Why else would Cabri-born Bobby Gimby, with his jewelled trumpet and cape, be leading in pied-piper style a group of children singing his centennial birthday tune, "CA-NA-DA, One little, two little, three Canadians, WE LOVE THEE."[86]

Premier Thatcher, perhaps wanting to take advantage of the upbeat mood during the centennial, called an election for early October 1967. It was an unusual time for a provincial election, what with harvest winding down, even more so since the Liberals had completed only three years of their mandate. But Thatcher maintained that he needed to solidify the Liberal hold on power and reassure the wider world that "socialism was safely behind Saskatchewan."[87] The Liberals portrayed themselves as common-sense managers, capable of making difficult decisions in the best interests of the province. In 1966, for example, the government put an end to several decades of time-zone confusion and adopted Central Standard Time year-round.

The opposition, now known as the CCF-NDP, attacked the government's sellout of the province's resources, while promising several new social welfare programs, such as denticare for those under seventeen. The campaign, however, failed to arouse the electorate and the Liberals were returned to office with only a slightly increased majority—thirty-five seats to the CCF-NDP's twenty-four—even though both major parties polled almost the same percentage of the popular vote. None of the winning candidates were women. The Progressive Conservatives also lost their only seat in the legislature, a cruel blow to defeated candidate and leader Martin Pederson, since the federal party under Diefenbaker had swept all seventeen federal seats in the province in the 1963 and 1965 general elections.[88]

Ross Thatcher had always been a volatile leader, who overruled his ministers and ran what many regarded as a one-person government. Few could have predicted, however, how the premier would become inexplicably more tough-minded and erratic after winning the 1967 election. Whereas he had been bullish on the province's economic prospects heading into the campaign, he announced an immediate austerity program, fearing that a recession was imminent, and slashed government spending, including several election promises involving money. Thatcher also seemed to want to pick fights. In 1966, during a strike by Saskatchewan Power Corporation employees, the Liberals had alienated labour by introducing the Essential Services Emergency Act, which sanctioned government intervention, including possible decertification, if union action affected the province's economic well-being or interfered with the provision of necessary services. Now, after the election, he attacked academic freedom when he announced that University of Saskatchewan spending would be brought under direct government control. But what angered people more than anything was the introduction of health utilization fees in the March 1968 provincial budget. Thatcher found that the growing demand for health services under medicare was placing a severe strain on the provincial budget and hoped to cover the rising costs by imposing a flat fee for each doctor visit and hospital stay. To the public, though, they were deterrent fees, or in the words of the opposition, a tax on the sick, and they made the Liberal government extremely unpopular.[89]

Thatcher's relationship with the Métis and Indians also turned sour. Dr. Howard Adams, a St. Louis–born Métis educated at the University of California at Berkeley and nurtured by the Black Power movement, brought a militancy to the Métis Society of Saskatchewan as its new president.[90] A fiery spokesperson for Métis nationalism, he directly challenged the government's integration policy by insisting that the Métis were a distinct Aboriginal group with outstanding claims. He also dismissed Thatcher's job placement program as mere "window dressing and a waste of time" when the real problems of the Métis were being ignored.[91] To back up his charge, Adams claimed to have the names of nine hundred Métis who were close to starvation in the north. A subsequent investigation found no hard evidence, but a journalist reported from Meadow Lake in February 1970, "Starvation may be in doubt—privation is not."[92]

Indians also became increasingly estranged from the Thatcher government. Those given jobs rarely stayed for long because of the culture shock; some complained that they were expected to give up their Indian identity. At the political level, Thatcher's all-consuming concern with the economic salvation of Indian people, the sense that he knew what was best, smacked of paternalism and went against the Federation of Saskatchewan Indians' push for self-government.[93] Perhaps the breakdown in relations was best exemplified by the fate of the Mistaseni rock. The huge boulder, a sacred Cree shrine, was destined to be submerged by the new man-made Lake Diefenbaker. When engineers working on the project were unable to find a way to move the rock to higher ground along the South Saskatchewan River valley, it was blown up.[94]

The other major problem for the Thatcher government was the cooling down of the provincial resource sector. The demand for uranium stalled, forcing Eldorado Ltd. to curtail operations at its Beaverlodge mine by the end of the decade. Oil production reached a peak of 93.2 million barrels in 1966 and then began a gradual decline; several of the province's refineries would close in the next decade as the processing of crude was centralized in Alberta. Potash also fell in price from $37.53 a ton in 1965 to $19.87 four years later, largely because of market saturation and reduced world demand.[95] By 1970, the province's mines were capable of producing twice as much potash as North America consumed. The oversupply led to charges by United States producers that Saskatchewan was dumping cheap potash on the American market. In order to avoid possible punitive measures, such as tariffs, Thatcher flew to New Mexico, home to the American potash industry, in the fall of 1969 and struck an arrangement with the governor to establish a minimum price for potash and cap production. When the pro-rationing regulations went into effect at the start of the new year, Saskatchewan mines operated on average at half capacity. The premier defended the "conservation" measures for bringing stability to the potash market and raising prices, but reduced production meant reduced royalties for the provincial treasury. The episode also confirmed the vagaries of selling unfinished or raw products on the international market, something the Saskatchewan government should have known from the province's experience with wheat since the beginning of the century. Potash may have diversified the economy, but it was an unstable foundation on which to build the "New Saskatchewan."[96]

The province's traditional economic activity, growing wheat for the international market, suffered from too much success during the latter half of the 1960s. The record crop in 1966 plugged the grain-handling system at the same time that world demand and prices began to fall. Farmers, however, never reduced their production because of their dependence on the crop,

John Diefenbaker dominated federal politics in western Canada in the 1960s.
Ed Franklin, *Globe and Mail*

which constituted two-thirds of total farm sales in the province, and seeded an even larger acreage to wheat the following year. By 1969 and the harvest of the third largest wheat crop in Saskatchewan history, the province's farms were swimming in unsold wheat. It was estimated that there were four hundred million bushels in storage in all kinds of makeshift bins, including former one-room schools.

To alleviate the distress, the Thatcher government introduced the unique Grain for Fees Program, which enabled students to pay part of their university fees in grain. Beyond that, it fell largely to federal authorities to deal with the crisis. The new Pierre Trudeau government responded with cash advances, interest-free loans, and a wheat acreage reduction program, known as LIFT (Lower Inventories For Tomorrow), whereby farmers were paid to leave their land fallow. Frustrated producers generally disliked the plan, believing it was their job to grow grain and that the real problem was the federal Liberal government's failure to sell their crop, as the Diefenbaker government had done in the early 1960s. Thatcher, for his part, readily exploited the anger, even adjourning proceedings in the legislature in early April 1970 to meet with several thousand members of the Saskatchewan-based National Farmers' Union gathered on the steps outside. But even though the premier distanced himself from the despised Trudeau, he refused to countenance talk of western separation.[97]

Thatcher sought a third consecutive Liberal mandate in June 1971. This time, he would square off against a new challenger in Allan Blakeney, who had succeeded Woodrow Lloyd as provincial NDP leader in July 1970. (CCF was dropped from the party name in 1968.) Born and raised in Nova Scotia and educated at Oxford University on a Rhodes Scholarship, Blakeney came to Saskatchewan in 1950 to work in the provincial civil service. Ten years later, he entered the legislature as a CCF member for Regina and held various cabinet posts before being sent to the opposition benches by the Thatcher victory in 1964. In retrospect, it was probably a good thing that the CCF was out of power during this period, because of the internal divisions precipitated by the Waffle movement, a call for an independent, socialist Canada by younger, more radical members of the federal party. Lloyd, who was distressed by the growing foreign ownership of Canadian resources, supported the Waffle at the 1969 NDP national convention. His decision alienated more moderate members of the Saskatchewan party, and he resigned, with some prompting, the following year.[98] Blakeney's hard-fought leadership victory over Roy Romanow, who had first been elected in 1967, was symptomatic of the polarization within the party, and he had to work hard to restore unity and bring about some semblance of harmony.

The Liberals fought the 1971 campaign on whether a private enterprise or socialist government was best for Saskatchewan, pointing to a new deal with Parsons and Whittemore to build a second pulp mill at Meadow Lake. They also continued to attack the socialists for their spendthrift ways, citing their long list of costly election promises, while mocking Blakeney as "little Allan" because of his height.[99] The NDP, by contrast, offered an attractive, comprehensive program provocatively called "A New Deal for People." It also ran an effective campaign. While Thatcher toured the province at a frenetic pace by airplane, the Blakeney Bus bumped along the rural roads of southern Saskatchewan, giving the new leader every chance to be seen and heard.[100]

The election results were anti-climatic. Saskatchewan voters repudiated the Thatcher Liberals, sending only fifteen members to the legislature to the NDP's forty-five. Davey Steuart, a Liberal stalwart from Prince Albert, half-jokingly offered an explanation: "If there was someone or some group in the province we hadn't alienated by the election of 1971, it was because we hadn't met them yet."[101] An exhausted Thatcher, weakened by diabetes, was devastated by the people's verdict, but took full responsibility for the disaster. He travelled to NDP headquarters in downtown Regina and offered his sincere congratulations, biting back on his bitterness. "But now it's just another show," wrote Joni Mitchell. "You leave them laughing when you go, And if you care, don't let them know: Don't give yourself away." It was Thatcher's last public appearance. Three weeks later, he was dead.

CHAPTER NINETEEN

NEXT YEAR COUNTRY

I N 1975, SEVENTEEN-YEAR-OLD CHARLENE GRUENDING was one of sixty graduates from St. Ursuline Academy in Bruno. Her father bought her a three-piece, sand-coloured set of Samsonite leather luggage. Three years later, Sheila Bean graduated from Rouleau High School with seven classmates—all girls. As a gift, her parents gave her a huge, white, hard-sided Samsonite suitcase; she also received a smaller matching train case from her aunt and uncle. In 1979, Lucille LeGatt was a member of the graduating class at St. Brieux High School. Her sister Irene followed the next year. Both got identical three-piece, wine-coloured Impala luggage. What all four women have in common—besides the luggage (which they still own)—is that they are children of Saskatchewan farmers. Two now live and work in Calgary, while the LeGatt sisters make Saskatoon their home. Their departure from the family farm, maybe even from the province, was expected in the 1970s. In fact, their stories are part of the larger phenomenon of rural depopulation which NDP leader Allan Blakeney assailed in the Saskatchewan legislature as "the continued erosion of our way of life."[1] Doing something about the problem would test the new provincial government. Not only were there no easy answers, but the trend seemed unstoppable.

The man sworn in as Saskatchewan's new premier in June 1971 seemed an unlikely politician. Forty-six-year-old Allan Blakeney was shy and somewhat reserved—a "process man" in the words of his biographer[2]—more comfortable providing a detailed, scholarly analysis of public policy than leading a political party or doing the obligatory "glad-handing." But Blakeney, who described himself as a "pragmatic socialist,"[3] had been a keen student of comprehensive, integrated planning during his days with the Government Finance Office in the 1950s and wanted to revive that legacy under his own premiership. He also firmly believed that any government was duty bound "to reduce the sense of isolation and of economic insecurity which permeated Saskatchewan life and to encourage and strengthen the sense of neighbourliness and community."[4] The NDP would attempt to fulfil these twin goals by implementing the most ambitious agenda since Tommy Douglas had come to power almost three decades earlier—what the party confidently called its "blueprint for the 70s." There was to be a clear break from the former Liberal government's way of doing things under Ross Thatcher. Blakeney once criticized his predecessor for "delegat[ing] far too little of his decision making."[5] By contrast, the new NDP government would depend heavily on the professional expertise and competence of public servants whose duty was to grapple with problems and suggest policy options. Cabinet ministers, for their part, were expected to determine whether the recommendations were publicly acceptable and how to proceed with their implementation.[6]

One of the first problems tackled by the new government was the continuing disappearance of the family farm. According to the 1971 census, Saskatchewan had lost 29,102 people over the past five years, dropping from 955,344 to 926,242 residents. The population was now smaller than it had been in the middle of the Great Depression, while the Saskatchewan share of the total prairie population had slid from almost 40 per cent in 1931 to less than 25 per cent. The rural numbers were even bleaker. More than 50,000 had left the countryside since 1966 and for the first time in provincial history Saskatchewan now had more people living in urban centres (defined as having a population of 1,000 or more). Most of the rural refugees were farmers and their families or the children of farmers—with their luggage as high school graduation presents! The number of farms in the province dropped to 76,924 in 1971, almost less than half the number at the start of the Second World War. The decline since 1966 was particularly precipitous. In the five-year period to 1971, the farm population fell a staggering 17 per cent. Despite this exodus, Saskatchewan still had the largest farm sector in Canada, at a little more than one-fifth of the provincial population.

The family farm became an endangered Canadian icon during the early 1970s. CANADIAN PRESS

But it was an aging group. No more than 4 per cent of farmers in 1971 were under twenty-five, a dramatic reversal from the homesteading days at the beginning of the century when the province had one of the youngest populations in the country.[7]

Rural depopulation was not a new problem for Saskatchewan, but it was not until after the Second World War, when the trickle became a flood, that rural decline became *the* defining feature of provincial life and part of the popular image of Saskatchewan. In the fifteen years after the war, agriculture was completely mechanized, doing away with the heavy workhorse and the hired hand, as well as the need for harvesters. Although the number of people working in agriculture had declined to only 27.4 per cent of the provincial labour force by 1971, farmers were harvesting twice as much as they did half a century earlier. The size of farms, meanwhile, steadily grew in response to the introduction of more powerful, more efficient machinery. Whereas the average size of a Saskatchewan farm in 1941 was 432 acres, by 1971 it had doubled to 845 acres—more than five times the size of a homestead. As one researcher coldly noted, "The farmer ... who regards farming as a way of life rather than a business, is sure to be eliminated in time."[8]

These improvements dramatically increased the capital value of prairie farms, from an average of $6,565 in 1941 to $72,805 four decades later. But they did not make the operations any less vulnerable. Rising machinery costs were not matched by higher wheat prices during this period; hence, many producers were even more debt-ridden than their pioneer counterparts. Indeed, farmers faced what was called a "cost-price squeeze." They had to contend with spiralling prices for machinery, fuel, fertilizer, or land, at the very time when the international demand for wheat was sluggish and prices were consistently low. What made this predicament particularly painful for Saskatchewan producers was their continuing overreliance on wheat. Farmers stubbornly refused to relinquish the title of Canada's wheat province. In several districts in southern Saskatchewan in the mid-1960s, wheat still accounted for as much as 75 per cent of the total value of farm sales. One of the popular jokes at the time was about a Saskatchewan wheat farmer who won the lottery. Asked what he planned to do with the unexpected windfall, he vowed to keep farming until the money ran out.[9]

Since Saskatchewan farmers had no control over the demand for grain or the price and could do little about increases in production costs because of inflation, their annual income went on a wild, roller-coaster ride. These fluctuations, combined with the inherent instability of the business, forced people off the land in growing numbers. The wheat glut of the late 1960s precipitated one of the largest mass migrations from the land in provincial history, as reflected in the 1971 census figures. Those who remained behind to work increasingly larger operations led a stressful existence because of the pressures and uncertainties of modern agriculture. Gone were the days when farming was regarded as a simple, idyllic occupation. Nor were the changes restricted to the field and farmstead. The loss of thousands of farmers and their families, together with the change in agriculture from a labour-intensive to a capital-intensive industry, undercut the foundations of rural life. Businesses soon closed their doors, local organizations limped along as best they could or ceased to meet at all, and villages and smaller towns began a slow, certain decay. Hope for the return of better times became a scarce commodity, all the more so since young people were discouraged from entering farming because of the capital resources now required.[10] At least most prospective settlers at the turn of the century could afford the ten-dollar fee for 160 acres, even if they eventually failed to prove up their homestead.

This sense that rural Saskatchewan was undergoing a fundamental transformation accounted for the bittersweet public response to the play *Paper Wheat*, by Saskatoon's 25th Street Theatre, established in 1972. A nostalgic look at the struggles of the pioneer farmer, alternating between tragedy, satire, and humour, *Paper Wheat* played to critical acclaim throughout the province in 1977 before embarking on a successful national tour. "I was among the first men to break this soil for cultivation," mused the sodbuster at the end of the play as he movingly recounts all the changes he had witnessed. "I threshed the bumper crop of 1915 and I knew the desolation of '37. I've seen the coming of the railroad, radio, telephone, television ... I'd give it all to be young again and feel that I could change the world."[11] One of the themes running through *Paper Wheat* was that the common challenge of bringing the land under cultivation created a shared identity among immigrant farmers during the homesteading days. But Ken Mitchell's *The Shipbuilder*, a 1970s play based loosely on the true story of Tom Sukanen, who went mad building an ocean-going vessel to return to his native Finland, suggested that ethnic tensions had been a divisive and persistent force in Saskatchewan rural society and that conformity came at the price of personal identity. These plays, with their quite different interpretations, were part of a growing trend in prairie theatre to examine the region and look back at its history. As Andras Tahn, creator of *Paper Wheat*, reminded his audience, "And when you come to see our plays and we talk about a crocus, it's your own bloody crocus. So what if it's not a cut flower imported from somewhere else."[12] One of the most successful homegrown products was *Year of the Moose*, an ambitious musical extravaganza co-written by Mitchell, Geoffrey Ursell, and Barbara Sapergia to commemorate Moose Jaw's one-hundredth birthday. The play featured the classic Saskatchewan song "Is There Anybody Here from Moose Jaw?"

One of the popular activities threatened by rural depopulation was organized sports. Just as distance and isolation had made regular play difficult at the beginning of the century, the loss of thousands of farm families now hurt community teams. If rural kids wanted to play in a league, they had to spend more time on the road travelling to games. Many wore the team colours of larger centres. It made little difference, though, to the success of Saskatchewan athletes. The Emily Farnham rink won the women's national curling championship in 1974; it was the fourth consecutive title for Saskatchewan. On the men's side, Harvey Mazinke ended a long Saskatchewan drought at the Brier in 1973. Rick Folk would repeat the feat in 1980. The province also continued to serve as the cradle for future NHL stars. Bryan Trottier of Val Marie and Clark Gillies from Moose Jaw helped lead the expansion New York Islanders to four consecutive Stanley Cups beginning in 1980. Two of the most remarkable stories, however, were on the baseball diamond. Pitcher Reggie Cleveland of Moose Jaw became the first Canadian to start a World Series game in 1975, while Terry Puhl of Melville, who played for more than a decade in the majors for the Houston Astros, was named a National League all-star in 1978. Closer to home, Saskatchewan's first Indian summer games were held on the Cote Reserve in 1974 as part of the celebrations commemorating the hundredth anniversary of the signing of Treaty 4.

The flip side of rural depopulation was increased urbanization and the growing dominance of a few metropolitan centres. At one time, Saskatchewan had over nine hundred communities to serve the needs of the wheat economy, but many of these small villages were bypassed by railway branch lines or quickly became superfluous once farmers began to expand their holdings.[13] "I think a lot of these places started dying the day they were born," observed

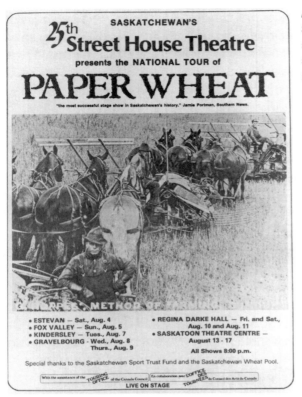

Paper Wheat was one of Saskatchewan's most popular and successful plays. UNIVERSITY OF SASKATCHEWAN SPECIAL COLLECTIONS 25TH STREET THEATRE II.III

one old-timer in a collection of reminiscences.[14] Reorganization and consolidation were temporarily held back by the Depression and then the war, but the centralization process could not be avoided, just delayed. By 1980, 2,750 rural schools, 390 rural post offices, and 322 local telephone exchanges had been closed, while dozens of communities simply faded away as if they never existed. The process was accelerated by the building of paved intercity and all-weather grid roads in the 1950s and 1960s. In the first years of settlement, it might have taken a farmer as much as an hour to go to town. By the 1960s, because of better cars and better roads, that same farmer could now travel to the nearest city in about as much time, where he often did his business, including shopping, at the expense of local stores.[15]

Those families who abandoned farming, or children who left the farm, usually moved to one of the major urban centres—if they stayed in the province. "Saskatchewan," wrote Nipawin-born writer Sharon Butala, "was only a holding area where one waited impatiently till one was old enough to leave in order to enter the excitement of the real world."[16] A 1966 study of rural migrants to Saskatoon found that they had turned their back on the land for a higher standard of living, better opportunities, reduced anxiety about their future, and less isolation.[17] Long-time rivals Regina and Saskatoon were the clear beneficiaries of this internal migration. While the provincial capital almost doubled in size between 1951 and 1971 (71,319 to 138,956), the city of bridges grew by an astonishing 135 per cent in the same period (53,268 to 125,079) and finally emerged as a legitimate equal. Collectively, the two cities were home to almost 30 per cent of the provincial population. But they were still dwarfed by the other three dominant regional centres: Winnipeg, Edmonton, and Calgary.[18]

Regina and Saskatoon, despite their size, still retained a few vestiges of small-town Saskatchewan, such as store closings on Wednesday afternoons. They were the rich cousins, though, when it came to buying a special new dress, watching a first-run movie, catching an airplane, going to university, or seeing an international star perform. By 1970, both cities were home to first-rate entertainment and convention facilities: the Saskatchewan Centre of the Arts and the Centennial Auditorium (Prince Albert's E. A. Rawlinson Centre for the Arts did not open until 2003). The big size also brought big problems, such as crimes that were supposed to happen elsewhere. In the late 1960s, Saskatoon's innocence was shattered by the sexual assault and murder of Gail Miller on her way to work one cold winter morning, and Alexandra Wiwcharuk, who had been last seen alive sitting by the river. Nothing,

Ski champion Nancy Greene officially opens Mount Blackstrap in anticipation of the 1971 Canada Winter Games. SASKATCHEWAN ARCHIVES BOARD STAR-PHOENIX COLLECTION S-SP-B6302-4

though, prepared the city for the summer of fear when four young children, two in June 1975 and two more in July, simply vanished. For the next few weeks, the streets of Saskatoon were strangely silent as watchful parents kept their kids inside. Pedophile David Threinen was eventually picked up for questioning and admitted to abducting and murdering the children.

The 1971 provincial election had been fought against the backdrop of the worsening farm crisis and the changes that many feared would accompany it. Unable to sell their wheat because of depressed markets in the latter half of the 1960s, farmers looked to the federal government, which had assumed responsibility for the marketing of grain through the Canadian Wheat Board, for some kind of assistance. The production of wheat for the international market, however, was not as important in the post-war economy as it once was. In fact, agriculture did not seem to matter to the Liberal governments of Lester Pearson and Pierre Trudeau, which had increasingly come to depend on urban support for their political well-being. A flippant Trudeau had once rhetorically asked, "Well, why should I sell the Canadian farmers' wheat?"[19]

Nor did there continue to be a powerful provincial spokesperson within the federal government to look after the interests of wheat farmers. That role had once been filled by Jimmy Gardiner, who had given up the Saskatchewan Liberal premiership to serve as federal minister of agriculture for twenty-two uninterrupted years, and then by John Diefenbaker, Prince Albert's favourite son, during his rocky, six-year reign as prime minister. Even the once strong Saskatchewan-Ottawa connection that had characterized the Laurier and early King years had come undone, largely because of Premier Ross Thatcher's ruthless determination to be Liberal kingpin in the province and his utter disdain for his federal counterparts.[20]

The Trudeau government's prescription for agriculture's melancholy was a heavy dose of Liberal rationality in the form of a 1969 task force report, *Canadian Agriculture in the Seventies.* Choosing modernization and consolidation over intervention and subsidization, the report insisted that agriculture be forced to stand on its own, that the number of inefficient farms be reduced, and that wheat acreage be drastically cut back. Organizations such as the National Famers' Union angrily dismissed the recommendations as an attack on the family farm and the place and importance of agriculture in the national fabric.[21] The Saskatchewan NDP, in the meantime, could not have asked for better ammunition in the 1971 provincial election and readily linked the federal report to the Thatcher government. One television commercial featured a hand sweeping away a toy farmstead, while the voice-over claimed that two-thirds of Saskatchewan farms would be wiped out by the federal Liberals by 1990. Another ad reduced the population drain to a simple, startling statistic. "Last year 3 people every hour left our province," it read. "And never returned."[22]

During the election campaign, Blakeney had extolled the family farm as something special, even sacred, to Saskatchewan. The problem was how to save it. In devising a solution, the NDP sought inspiration from the early days of the CCF party and its controversial, Depression-era use-lease policy. Under a new program approved in the spring of 1972, the provincial government established a Land Bank Commission to buy land from retiring farmers and then lease it to young farmers with the option to purchase it at the end of five years. The scheme was intended to facilitate the intergenerational transfer of farmland by making it possible for prospective farmers to get into agriculture without having to put up the necessary capital.[23] But the Liberal opposition, now headed by Thatcher's faithful lieutenant and the party's first Roman Catholic leader, Davey Steuart, decried the plan as nothing more than a "hoax and a fraud" by a socialist government intent on nationalization. One Liberal MLA even suggested, in a calculated attempt to create unease among descendants of eastern European immigrants, that the Land Bank would "make a man a serf of the Government for the rest of his life."[24]

The Blakeney NDP coolly ignored the criticism and went ahead in 1973 with FarmStart, a Crown corporation that provided funding to begin or expand livestock operations, such as feeding hogs. The following year, the government limited the amount of farmland that could be owned by non-Saskatchewan residents, either individuals or corporations. It refrained, however, from placing any restrictions on farm size, as was being advocated by the National Farmers' Union, which feared the emergence of a "land owning elite" and the shutting out of young farmers if the trend to larger holdings continued. It also refused to reopen the touchy subject of rural municipal amalgamation until the Saskatchewan Association of Rural Municipalities began to show interest in exploring alternatives to the current form of local government.[25]

Premier Blakeney promoted the government's various agricultural initiatives as the "Saskatchewan option," whereby the family farm would continue to serve as the backbone of provincial life. "The Saskatchewan option is clean air and small communities," he announced during his annual bus tour of the province in August 1974, "being close to nature and the land."[26] But the most recent statistics told a much different story. In the first five years of the NDP government, the province lost close to two thousand farms. In fact, the rate of rural farm depopulation between 1971 and 1976 was nearly 18 per cent, making it the worst five-year period in twenty-five years.[27]

The culprit was the unexpected return of better prices and stronger international demand, triggered by a major crop failure in Russia. By 1972, the price of wheat reached a post-war high of $2.15 per bushel and farmers reaped record incomes. They became even giddier the next season in what became reverently known in farm circles as "the year of $5 wheat." Producers who had taken advantage of provincial assistance to diversify their operations found that it now cost more to feed their animals and switched back to wheat to share in the bonanza. Many more expanded their land base, since the amount of wheat that farmers could deliver for marketing, known as their quota, was based on the number of acres in production. The average farm size consequently increased almost 10 per cent from 1971–76 (845 to 923 acres), which in turn displaced more people from the land and threatened the existence of more rural businesses and communities. The Blakeney government, which had made so much of rural revival, was helpless to stop the trend. Nor did the good times last; beginning in 1976, prices started to fall, dragged down by slumping markets in the wake of yet another worldwide grain surplus. That was the same year that Saskatchewan farmers harvested 830 million bushels of wheat, the largest crop in provincial history. It made no difference, though, as their annual net income began to slide once again—by as much as one-third in 1977! There seemed to be no escape from the vicious cycle and little reprieve for the family farm.[28]

The Blakeney government also believed that it could do better than its Liberal predecessor in dealing with Aboriginal issues. There certainly was room for improvement. Former premier Thatcher's well-meaning but intrusive actions had alienated the province's Indian and Métis population, who were frustrated by his unwillingness to understand their concerns. This failure to listen also lay at the heart of the Trudeau government's controversial 1969 "White Paper on Indian Policy," which essentially blamed all Indian problems on their failure to integrate into mainstream society and called for the revoking of Indian status, the elimination of the Department of Indian Affairs, the withdrawal from treaty obligations, and the transfer of federal Indian responsibility to the provinces. Appalled by Ottawa's so-called solution, especially since they had been led to believe that there would be full consultation, First Nations leaders forced the Trudeau government to retreat from its assimilationist approach in favour of one that eventually recognized Aboriginal title and rights.[29] In Saskatchewan, Thatcher applauded the federal white paper, while the NDP, at the urging of former premier Woodrow Lloyd, called instead for a new relationship with the province's Aboriginal community. Integration, Blakeney acknowledged shortly after assuming the party leadership, was not necessarily the answer to discrimination. The NDP election program reflected this change of attitude by promising to fund treaty research and provide money for Indian- and Métis-initiated and administered programs.[30]

A young student
interviews Premier
Allan Blakeney.
SASKATCHEWAN ARCHIVES
BOARD 79-2740-06

By the early 1970s, the Federation of Saskatchewan Indians (FSI) was moving in a direction quite opposite to that of the federal white paper. Under the able leadership of Chief Walter Deiter and then David Ahenakew, the FSI had emerged as a strong, effective organization bent on securing Indians greater control over their lives. Ahenakew actually called what was happening in Saskatchewan "a quiet revolution."[31] In 1969, the FSI appointed an education task force and then used the two-volume report to help secure Indian control over their education in the province. This change was facilitated by the establishment in 1972 of the Saskatchewan Indian Cultural College (now Saskatchewan Indian Cultural Centre), which aimed to promote cultural research, including the arts, music, and languages, and assist with educational programming. At the local level, beginning with the James Smith reserve in 1973, bands started to assume control of their own schools. This activity coincided with the takeover of former federal residential schools at Lebret, Duck Lake, Prince Albert, and Beauval. Some of the instructors were trained in the new Saskatchewan Indian Teacher Education Program (ITEP) at the University of Saskatchewan.[32] The NDP government co-operated with these initiatives wherever possible. In 1975, for example, it worked with the FSI to create the Saskatchewan Indian Federated College (now First Nations University of Canada), the first Indian-controlled educational institution in Canada.[33]

The FSI also increasingly promoted the collective identity of the Indian population and became even more determined to resolve outstanding land claims and realize self-government. An FSI report on Indians living off-reserve (27.4 per cent of the 1976 registered Saskatchewan Indian population) forcefully argued that these people were "not urban Indians" who had "reject[ed] their Indian culture and traditions, their home reserves or their fellow band members."[34] Chief Ahenakew also used the 1973 provincial visit of Queen Elizabeth to raise unexpectedly the matter of broken treaty promises. But the most forthright statement of the Indian position was provided by former FSI president, John Tootoosis, at the end of the decade. "I come from the Poundmaker Reserve," he asserted. "That Poundmaker Reserve is neither Saskatchewan nor Canada. It is my nation."[35]

The NDP government's relationship with the Métis, on the other hand, was rocky at best. When the Métis Society of Saskatchewan (MSS) blocked the road out of Buffalo Narrows during Blakeney's 1971 campaign bus tour through the province's north, the NDP leader responded by promising to create a special government department for the north.[36] Exactly how that department would function was never discussed in any detail during the election. It was not a new idea—both the Douglas and Thatcher governments had considered creating a separate ministry of northern affairs—but it fell to the new NDP government to give it life with the 1972 creation of the Department of Northern Saskatchewan (DNS), the first provincial department of its kind in Canada.[37]

The role of DNS was to coordinate and deliver all government services in the region through a single ministry. Such a total approach to the north, it was argued, would result in a better standard of living for the otherwise neglected region—and in doing so, help fulfill the NDP's "New Deal for People" pledge made during the recent election campaign. It would be a major test for the new government. Not only was the northern population of 21,820 largely Aboriginal (6,000 Indians and 7,000 Métis), but it was also divided along racial lines, with non-white society facing a host of problems, starting with poverty and chronic underemployment.

By the fall of 1972, government officials and money were pouring into La Ronge, the unofficial new capital of the provincial north. The NDP government expected the new department, through the provision of improved northern services, to create the kind of conditions that would lead to meaningful local government. The MSS and its scrappy new leader, Jim Sinclair, saw things differently. Sinclair wanted a form of Métis self-government in the north, not the imposition of an outside, white-dominated bureaucracy whose objectives might differ from those of northerners. He seemed worried that an all-powerful DNS would overwhelm local initiative and be little better than the last attempt at remaking the north under former CCF natural resources minister Joe Phelps twenty-five years earlier.

It was not long, then, before the Blakeney government and the MSS were at loggerheads. In December 1973, the MSS sent about one hundred shouting demonstrators, some with chainsaws, into the Saskatchewan legislature to complain about the lack of jobs in forestry. The sit-in ended after two tense days following an acrimonious meeting with the premier and the DNS minister. June 1974 brought more trouble when Blakeney and several cabinet ministers held an open meeting about government policy in Kitsaki Hall in La Ronge. While DNS minister Bowerman was greeted with a chorus of boos, Blakeney was repeatedly peppered with demands from MSS officials to redress their grievances. At one point, the premier attempted to explain why it was necessary to employ southern bureaucrats in DNS operations. When he suggested that the pace of government and development would likely be delayed if only untrained northerners were involved, one heckler asked, "Are you calling us retarded?" When Blakeney responded that he doubted whether anyone wanted all the skilled people from the south to leave, another person

The creation of the University of Regina did not go over well in Saskatoon.
Ed Sebestyen, *Saskatoon StarPhoenix*

shot back, "At least it would be better than imperialism." Jim Sinclair used the comments to point to the frustration at the heart of the MSS position and bluntly told the premier that southern experts should serve only as consultants.[38]

Sinclair's confrontational tactics only hardened Blakeney's resolve to stand by the DNS experiment. But this support was severely tested by more damaging developments. Some DNS field employees publicly complained about the failure to involve northerners in department policies and called for Bowerman's resignation—giving substance to the MSS complaint that DNS was just another form of colonialism. Their dismissal did little to quell the mounting questions about how the department was being run and for whom. In April 1974, the Liberal opposition tried unsuccessfully to have the legislature appoint an independent inquiry into government activities in the north. The next month, the Public Accounts Committee reported that DNS spending was riddled with irregularities. When an accounting team went north to La Ronge to examine the books, they found an unrecorded half million dollars in cheques and money indiscriminately stashed throughout the main office.[39] The Blakeney government tried to limit the damage by sending in a new deputy minister to bring some order to what one critic described as a "vast and bewildering" DNS bureaucracy.[40] It was not clear, however, how the government was going to repair the growing northern disillusionment and discontent.

One of the frequent Métis complaints was that DNS had done little to end economic stagnation in the region. This need for jobs was not restricted to the provincial north. The changing wheat economy no longer provided high levels of agricultural employment, and those leaving the farm could hardly be expected to remain in Saskatchewan unless there was the prospect of work in other areas. But what would keep the economy thriving—and people in the province—with the family farm limping along from one crisis to another? Like governments before them, the NDP believed that future stability and prosperity largely depended on the exploitation of non-renewable natural resources. But the Blakeney government wanted to approach this development differently; it was determined to end the continued sell-out of resources to private capital, especially when the province seemed to lose out in the deal. One of its first acts was the cancellation of the proposed Meadow Lake pulp mill that Premier Thatcher had negotiated, seemingly in desperation, with the same American firm behind the Prince Albert plant. The NDP had also rethought its past reliance on private industry to develop provincial resources and concluded that multinational corporations could hardly be expected to address the greater interests of the province. Instead, the Blakeney government intended to use Crown corporations as the centrepiece of its economic development strategy, something that the Douglas government had retreated from by the late 1940s. "At the outset let me make it clear," the premier told the legislature in March 1972, "that this government ... will develop our resources for the benefit of Saskatchewan people. Where appropriate, this will be done through Crown corporations."[41]

The Blakeney government lost little time pursuing this new policy. In March 1973, it created the Saskatchewan Oil and Gas Corporation (Sask Oil) with a mandate to enter into all aspects of the petroleum industry. It also slapped a new royalty surcharge on all oil production. The rationale for these moves, as explained in an internal planning document, was a desire for the province "to take its own development into its own hands, in its own interest ... to be distinctive."[42] But apart from the new tax, the province did not embark on any major entrepreneurial role in the oil industry. That did not mean, though, that the oil industry was pleased with the Blakeney government. Claiming that new taxes were severely reducing profits, the oil industry slowed down production and cut exploration activities, throwing hundreds out of work in the province's oil service sector. It also decided to challenge the constitutional validity of the new tax. In February 1974, Canadian Industrial Gas and Oil Limited (CIGOL), an independent Calgary-based producer, initiated an action contending that the royalty surcharge was an indirect tax and hence beyond the powers of any province. It was anticipated by both sides that the case would likely go as far as the Supreme Court of Canada. What particularly irked the Blakeney government, however, was the intervention of the federal government in support of the company position. It seemed as if Ottawa wanted the field of resource taxation to itself at the expense of Saskatchewan's aspirations, that the so-called national interest trumped the province's desire to maximize resource rents and build a more diversified and stable economy.[43]

The more promising resource industry for the NDP's development strategy was potash, largely because of Saskatchewan's giant share of the world's known reserves. But like oil, it was the source of legal and constitutional wrangling. In December 1972, Central Canada Potash launched an action challenging the constitutionality of the pro-rationing system introduced by the Thatcher government to regulate provincial mine output in the depressed world market; it also demanded compensation for lost sales under the quota scheme. Since the case hinged on whether pro-rationing violated federal trade and commerce powers, Ottawa lined up against the province as a co-plaintiff. This action stunned the Blakeney government. Not only had pro-rationing been initiated at industry request, but the federal government had not moved against the Thatcher government when the quota system had first been instituted.[44] The premier angrily vowed to "use all weapons open to us to defend the people of Saskatchewan and their resources."[45]

Government-industry relations continued to deteriorate through 1974. As the price for potash rebounded in response to world demand, the Blakeney government wanted a share of these profits, in the tens of millions of dollars, for the provincial treasury. But past governments, anxious to see the potash industry get off the ground, had locked the province into fixed royalty rates until 1981. The NDP stickhandled around this problem by introducing a new potash reserve tax in October 1974, which only further alienated the province's potash producers.[46] Premier Blakeney, however, was not about to be diverted from his goal of ensuring that Saskatchewan benefitted from its new-found resource wealth while reducing its past heavy dependence on agriculture. "Resource development potential ... finally offers us a chance to diversify our economic base," he once explained. "But like any farmer, we're a bit cautious. Saskatchewan isn't called Next Year Country for nothing ... we [need to] ask ourselves the question: how can we manage this promised development ... so that we move closer to our number one goal: economic stability?"[47]

This seeming obsession with the management of the province's oil and potash resources might mistakenly suggest that nothing else was going on in Saskatchewan at the time. But the Blakeney government had also taken steps on the social welfare side of the ledger, introducing a free dental care program for children and a prescription drug plan, while eliminating Thatcher's unpopular medicare user fee. It also established a provincial legal aid plan and the Saskatchewan Human Rights Commission. And it tackled the thorny question of what to do with the Regina campus of the University of Saskatchewan. Acting on the advice of an advisory commission headed by former Supreme Court judge Emmett Hall, the government created a separate university in the Queen City; that decision is subject to debate to this day in Saskatoon.[48]

To help support cultural activities, as well as sports and recreation, the government used profits from lottery sales to establish the Saskatchewan Lotteries Trust Fund. The timing could not have been better. In 1973, Rudy Wiebe, born to Mennonite parents in the Speedwell-Jackpine region north of the Battlefords, won a Governor General's Literary Award for his novel *The Temptations of Big Bear*. Three years later, another immigrant son, Andrew Suknaski, introduced a new style of prairie poetry with the release of *Wood Mountain Poems*. Saskatchewan sculptors Joe Fafard and Victor Cicansky, along with several other artists, meanwhile garnered national recognition for their collaborative work "The Grain Bin" at the 1976 Montreal Olympic Games. So too did Saskatoon-based Humphrey and the Dumptrucks, who toured the country with their unique bluegrass-folk

Digging the shaft of a potash mine. SASKATCHEWAN ARCHIVES BOARD S-SP-267-2

sound. These achievements, though, were no match for the international success of Buffy Sainte-Marie from the Piapot reserve. She wrote several hit singles, which were covered by other artists, including Elvis Presley, appeared as a regular on the American children's television program *Sesame Street* and then won the 1981 Academy Award for the best motion picture song "Up Where We Belong."

Premier Blakeney was vying for his own "Oscar" for best actor in a continuing role when he called an election for June 1975. Making resources *the* issue of the campaign, Blakeney called on the electorate to give him a strong mandate to make it "crystal clear to Ottawa that we are serious in our determination to defend our provincial rights and to get a fair deal for Saskatchewan and the West."[49] This attack on outside forces had a strong echo in the provincial past, a reminder of earlier struggles against the banks, railways, and elevator companies. It also spoke to Saskatchewan's continuing sensitivity over control of its public lands and resources, a constitutional right that the province had been denied for twenty-five years. But the NDP election strategy had more to do with practicality than principle. Thanks to the higher provincial taxes on booming oil and potash sales, revenues had steadily rolled in, making for four consecutive surplus budgets, reduced taxes, and the lowest unemployment rate in the country. If the Blakeney government was going to lose this resource income, it was going to go down fighting.

The opposition Liberals found themselves in an awkward position during the campaign. Although the NDP was gunning for the federal Liberal government, the provincial party was caught in the crosshairs. Blakeney insisted that a vote for the provincial Liberals would be read "as support for a federal government takeover of our resources."[50] Davey Steuart, contesting his first election as leader, had done a remarkable job getting the Liberal party afloat again. "The boat is sunk," he had quipped upon taking over after Thatcher's death, "and we are trying to rebuild it."[51] But the party's policies, emphasizing the virtues of free enterprise, were essentially the same as those offered during the 1960s, and it was difficult to reconcile Steuart's comments about the "deadening hand of socialism" with the prosperous Saskatchewan under the NDP.[52]

The Liberals also had unexpected competition on the free-enterprise side of the political spectrum. In 1973, thirty-seven-year-old Dick Collver, a Saskatoon accountant and investment advisor, became leader of the moribund Progressive Conservative party. Collver's task was a monumental one. The party had elected only one candidate for only one term since 1929, had secured only 2 per cent of the popular vote in the 1971 election, and had been leaderless for almost a year after an aborted merger with the Social Credit party. The plain-spoken, at times gruff, Collver worked tirelessly to rebuild party organization and finances, while fashioning himself as a populist leader intent on restoring power to the people. This message, however vague, resonated with voters who resented NDP big government and centralization and considered the Liberals an ineffective alternative. In a way, the Conservatives had transformed themselves into the latest provincial protest party, performing much the same function as the CCF in the early 1930s.[53]

The NDP was returned to office in 1975 with a slightly reduced majority (thirty-nine of sixty-one seats), but with a 14 per cent drop in popular vote (54 to 40 per cent). The Liberals collected fifteen seats and remained the official opposition. The big winners were the Conservatives, with a remarkable seven seats and 28 per cent of the popular vote. It was only the second time in Saskatchewan political history, the first being 1929, that there were three major parties with sizable representation in the legislature. It would not last; Steuart uncannily foretold what the future held for the Liberals when he admitted, "It was a wonder we weren't wiped out."[54] Blakeney accepted the results as an endorsement of NDP programs and policies, but it was also apparent that the party faced a new contender in the Collver-led Conservatives, whose recent showing in the political ring had the makings of a title fight in the future.

Nine days after the provincial election, the potash producers initiated a new court action, claiming that the 1974 reserve tax was unconstitutional.

Premier Blakeney tries to get Ottawa to listen to Saskatchewan concerns about resource taxation. Ed Franklin, *Globe and Mail*

This growing legal entanglement was certainly exasperating, if not a little overwhelming. It also left the Blakeney government with few options. It could back down and seek an understanding with the industry, but the court challenges raised serious doubts about how much negotiation room the province might have in the sensitive area of taxation. Recent experience with the producers had also suggested that Saskatchewan had little effective control over the development of the industry, especially when several companies shelved their expansion plans because of their dispute with the government. The other key factor was the sheer size of the potash reserves and their potential significance to the provincial economy for decades to come. Potash might not appear as sexy as oil and gas in the late-twentieth-century world economy, but it would always be needed for food production.[55]

In November 1975, the Blakeney government boldly announced in the speech from the throne that it planned to nationalize part, if not all, of the provincial potash industry. It was not a course of action that the NDP had originally contemplated. But once it was forced to decide what was in the best interests of Saskatchewan, it chose to assume control of the industry rather than compromise with the recalcitrant companies.[56] The takeover would be implemented through the Potash Corporation of Saskatchewan, a

Crown corporation that the government had earlier established to work in partnership with private potash companies to expand existing mines or establish new ones. Now, it had a much more ambitious mandate. Premier Blakeney insisted the decision made good business sense; the province, and not the industry, would now determine the nature and pace of development, while reaping the long-time benefits through the Crown corporation. He also maintained that the government could handle the nationalization costs, estimated at anywhere from five hundred million to a billion dollars, without resorting to higher taxes or jeopardizing other programs.[57]

Both opposition parties condemned the proposal, claiming that it would drive private capital out of the province and keep it away for years to come. They also chastised the government for threatening the financial well-being of the province by spending potentially billions of dollars on potash develop-ment when it was subject to the same market fluctuations as the wheat economy. "This is the greatest risk," Liberal leader Steuart gravely warned, "that has ever been launched by any provincial government."[58] The opposi-tion decided to delay passage of the bill for as long as it could and organized a filibuster that froze the government's legislative agenda for twenty-eight consecutive sitting days. Outside the legislature, the potash industry teamed up with private business, including the Saskatoon Board of Trade, to launch a media campaign against the legislation. "Can a government that failed at the shoe business learn the potash business?" asked a full-page ad in the *Saskatoon Star-Phoenix*, reminding readers of CCF minister Joe Phelps' earlier misadventures in public ownership.[59]

The government shook off the criticism and passed the potash legislation in late January 1976. It then entered into secret negotiations and by offering an attractive compensation package snagged its first mine that summer. By the spring of 1978, the province owned 40 per cent of Saskatchewan's produc-tion capacity. The news was not all good though. The Supreme Court of Canada determined in 1976 that the province could not keep the revenue if taxes were subsequently ruled unconstitutional. This judgment had the potential to force the government to repay millions of resource dollars that had been collected over the past few years—millions of dollars that were needed to finance potash nationalization.[60] The United States Senate also passed a motion that same year linking Saskatchewan with the Organization of Petroleum Exporting Countries because of its potash policies.[61] The real low point, though, was the 1976 Grey Cup, which ironically pitted the Saskatchewan Roughriders against the pretenders from Ottawa. In the dying seconds of the game, Tony Gabriel grabbed a pass deep in the Saskatchewan end zone to complete a 23–20 comeback victory for Ottawa. A profound silence fell over the province after the catch. It's remembered as "the darkest day in the history of Saskatchewan sports."[62]

While the potash wars tended to dominate Saskatchewan news in the mid-1970s, the Blakeney government was also heavily committed to developing another resource: uranium. In 1968, Gulf Minerals announced a major find at Rabbit Lake (near Wollaston Lake) on the northeast side of the province. One year later, the French firm Amok reported another discovery south of Lake Athabasca at Cluff Lake. These deposits were not only large and near the surface, but some of the highest grade in the world. Those involved in the industry confidently predicted that northern Saskatchewan was poised to become the Saudi Arabia of uranium. "It's not a flash in the pan," assured a member of the Saskatchewan Mining Association. "In the long term, it could have almost as much impact on Saskatchewan ... as oil ... on Alberta."[63] Only a few years earlier the same praise was being showered on potash.

The Blakeney government was anxious to be involved in all aspects of the uranium industry, from getting new mines operational to benefitting from the production and sale of the ore. In keeping with its new emphasis on public enterprise, the government created the Saskatchewan Mining Development Corporation (SMDC) in 1974, ostensibly to ensure that the province had a role in the exploitation of its minerals. But the principal purpose of the new Crown corporation was to join with private companies in

The Cluff Lake Mine, south of Lake Athabasca, was part of the expansion of the provincial uranium industry in the late 1970s. SASKATCHEWAN ARCHIVES BOARD STAR-PHOENIX COLLECTION S-SP 12988-24

pursuing the great uranium potential of the north—at considerable public investment.[64] The government also committed the province to accelerating uranium production without stopping to consider whether Saskatchewan should continue to be involved in the mining of such a controversial product. It was not until the 1976 NDP convention that the party agreed to a resolution that stipulated that a public inquiry should be held into each new mine. There would be no general investigation into the merits of uranium mining and no moratorium on exploration and development, as originally proposed.[65] Coincidentally, just a year earlier, SMDC was part of a joint venture that found one of the largest uranium deposits in the world at Key Lake in north-central Saskatchewan.

In the fall of 1975, Rabbit Lake became the second operating uranium mine in northern Saskatchewan, the first being Beaverlodge near Lake Athabasca. Amok also wanted to bring the Cluff Lake find into production; in keeping with the new NDP policy, the government appointed a board of inquiry, headed by Justice E. D. Bayda, to recommend if and how to proceed. Although the hearings elicited dozens of presentations in opposition to the project, from church, peace, and women's associations to anti-nuclear and Aboriginal groups, the commission recommended in June 1978 that the project proceed with caution. Two years later, the province went through a similar exercise—with the same results—when another environmental assessment panel approved the construction of a new mine at Key Lake. The Blakeney government justified this expansion of uranium mining on the grounds that Saskatchewan was meeting the growing needs of an energy-hungry world.[66] But there were limits to what was acceptable. Eldorado Nuclear, which had been expanding its operations in the late 1970s, wanted to build a uranium refinery at Warman, just north of Saskatoon. In August 1980, after weeks of emotionally charged hearings, a federal environmental advisory panel turned down the proposal because of its uncertain social impact on the largely Mennonite community in the area.[67] Curiously, these same kinds of concerns had not prevented the construction of the new northern mines.

Uranium, like oil and potash, was expected to contribute to the provincial treasury and thereby lessen Saskatchewan's dependence on agriculture. The Key Lake mine alone, according to a *Saskatoon Star-Phoenix* 1978 report, was supposed to generate three to five billion dollars, in large part because of the province's direct participation in the project through SMDC.[68] Although this kind of wealth had to wait until the mine started production, revenues from all non-renewable resources reached the hundreds of millions of dollars by the late 1970s. And they were expected to keep growing as millions more were being invested in resource development and exploration.

This decade of prosperity seemed to be threatened, however, by two Supreme Court decisions affecting the taxation of Saskatchewan resources. In November 1977, the court ruled that the oil royalty surcharge tax was unconstitutional and ordered the province to repay all the monies collected from CIGOL, estimated at five hundred million dollars. The Blakeney government scrambled to pass legislation to keep the revenues that had been collected over the past four years, while successfully negotiating a compromise taxation agreement with the oil industry that cleared the way for increased production. But the normally dispassionate premier was not about to let Ottawa's role in the CIGOL case pass without comment. "I have become convinced," he told the Canadian Club in Toronto in a blistering speech, "that their unrelenting attack on our resource policies is prompted ... by a desire to extend the central powers of the federal government at the expense of provincial powers."[69]

The second Supreme Court ruling came during the October 1978 provincial election campaign. Once again, the NDP wanted to make control of the province's resources the major issue of the campaign. The party also highlighted Blakeney's leadership in a deliberate attempt to raise doubts about the abilities of Conservative leader Dick Collver, generally regarded as a threat to a third consecutive term. This strategy could have been derailed in the middle of the campaign when the Supreme Court upheld the Central Canada Potash suit that pro-rationing was illegal.[70] After all, it was the Blakeney government that had got the province into such a mess—and there were more decisions forthcoming. Had not the provincial opposition insisted for years that the socialists were bad managers? But the NDP effectively used the judgment to once again pound Ottawa and its use of the Supreme Court, in Blakeney's words, "to wrest control of our natural resources away from us." The NDP campaign slogan was more subtle but equally effective: "Who do you trust to best manage our resources?"[71] The answer was Allan Blakeney, and he was returned to office with a larger majority, forty-four of sixty-one seats, heavily based in the urban areas of the province. The Conservatives became the official opposition with seventeen seats. The real shocker, though, was the fate of the Liberals under new leader Ted Malone. For the first time in the province's history, the party was shut out of the Saskatchewan legislature. Malone predicted that the Liberals would come back from "the election wreckage," but he frankly conceded, "Obviously, I will not be leading you for too much longer."[72]

Blakeney's election triumph seemed to herald another long period of NDP dominance, one that might even rival that of Douglas. Neither opposition party seemed much of a threat. The Liberals, dumbstruck by the recent debacle, would likely take several elections to become a force again. Dick

Queen Elizabeth II waves from the back of a train during a visit to Fort Qu'Appelle in 1978.
CANADIAN PRESS

Collver, meanwhile, resigned the Conservative leadership under a cloud of controversy to sit as an independent. Shortly thereafter he announced the creation of the "Unionest Party" to try to convince western Canada to join the United States (the name was a contraction of "best union"). Collver and his smiling sidekick, Dennis Ham, another former Tory MLA, claimed to be giving a much-needed outlet to western alienation, but the response to the new party was generally one of derision. One long-time MLA draped a large Canadian flag over his desk in the legislature, while others suggested that the pair should forfeit their seats because of their separatist views.[73]

Despite such distractions, the province approached its seventy-fifth anniversary with renewed confidence and vigour. Inspired by the slogan "Celebrate Saskatchewan," the Blakeney government passed the Heritage Property Act to formalize and guide the designation of heritage properties in the province. It also unveiled two major heritage projects of its own. The Administration Building, part of a three-building complex that had once housed the old territorial government in Regina, was restored and reopened, as was Government House, the former residence of the lieutenant-governor. The Douglas government had unceremoniously closed Government House in 1945, banishing the viceregal representative to the Hotel Saskatchewan, while selling the furnishings at discount prices at public auction; it consequently took considerable effort to locate and retrieve the artifacts.[74]

The NDP government also initiated the creation of a new provincial honour, the Saskatchewan Award of Merit (later renamed the Saskatchewan Order of Merit), which was first presented by the lieutenant-governor in 1985; one of the first recipients was former premier Tommy Douglas, who would be voted "The Greatest Canadian" in a CBC poll in 2004. There were also two new anniversary books, published under the auspices of the Saskatchewan Archives Board: John Archer's *Saskatchewan: A History* and Doug Bocking's *Saskatchewan: A Pictorial History*. In the final few lines of his monograph, Archer could not help but reflect on the province's new-found wealth and what it meant for the future. "Will the old virtues withstand the erosion of luxury?" he asked. "Who knows? One can only hope ... that the great heritage of the past will not be wantonly dissipated by the sons and daughters who grew up in the radiance of the western dream."[75]

Premier Blakeney, for his part, could be proud of where he had taken the province over the past decade. "We were forced," he acknowledged at the

The Saskatchewan Legislative Building decorated for the province's seventy-fifth anniversary celebrations. SASKATCHEWAN ARCHIVES CELEBRATE SASKATCHEWAN ALBUM

reopening of Government House, "to survive many things including the cauldron of the Depression."[76] Those days now seemed well past. Not only was the oil industry back in full swing, especially in the Lloydminster area, but the government had reached a new taxation agreement with the potash producers on the understanding that all remaining litigation would be dropped. This deal sent a sigh of relief through the industry, which did its own celebrating by recording higher profits and increased production by both the Potash Corporation of Saskatchewan and private companies. A sure sign of how well the province was doing at the end of the decade was the one-billion-dollar balance in the Heritage Fund, a special "rainy day" account that the Blakeney government had established using resource revenues. "Our entire history has been characterized by a search for economic stability—a search which earned us the name, 'next year country,'" resources minister Jack Messer confidently declared. "The creation of the fund signals that 'next year' is here."[77] It remained to be seen whether this prediction would ring hollow in the coming years, whether even more students would receive luggage as graduation presents.

CHAPTER TWENTY

IN A
MUDHOLE

N AUGUST 1979, JOHN DIEFENBAKER made his last trip home to
Saskatchewan. The eighty-six-year-old former Progressive Conservative
national leader and prime minister had died alone in his Ottawa home
just months after winning his thirteenth consecutive federal election.
Diefenbaker's body lay in state on Parliament Hill before being taken by
special train across the country to Prince Albert and then Saskatoon.
Thousands of Canadians lined the route to say farewell. At the grave site
overlooking the South Saskatchewan River, next to the Diefenbaker Centre
on the University of Saskatchewan campus, Prime Minister Joe Clark eulo-
gized his former mentor as "the great populist of Canadian politics," a man
of "frontier strength ... who went on to change the very nature of this country
and to change it permanently."[1] Diefenbaker's burial that day in "the prairie
soil he loved"[2] ironically coincided with the dramatic turnaround in the ill-
starred fortunes of the provincial Conservatives. Ever since the party had
been resoundingly bounced from office during the Great Depression, it had
wandered the Saskatchewan political wilderness. Not even Diefenbaker's
magic could break the provincial hex, although Saskatchewan voters had

consistently sent Conservative representatives to Ottawa since the late 1950s. But in 1982, political newcomer Grant Devine led the Conservatives to the largest electoral victory in Saskatchewan history. He was determined to change the very nature of the province and change it permanently.

John Diefenbaker will always be fondly remembered as the western farmers' friend, especially for his government's unparalleled success in selling their wheat. But these large international sales did little to solve the problems facing prairie agriculture. In fact, the situation on the family farm went from bad to worse in the early 1980s when the federal government repealed the cherished Crow's Nest Pass freight rates. These statutory rates, based on an agreement between Ottawa and the CPR in 1897 and confirmed in perpetuity in 1925, have been called "the best transportation bargain on the continent."[3] By keeping the price of shipping grain and unprocessed grain products frozen, the Crow enabled western Canadian producers to compete in world markets even though they grew their crops inland. The low rates also served as an incentive for prairie farmers to grow wheat and other grains by providing some much-needed financial relief when other production costs were steadily on the rise. It is little wonder, then, that Saskatchewan with its millions of acres of farmland became one of the largest grain exporters in the world.

People wave goodbye to former prime minister John Diefenbaker as his funeral train heads to Prince Albert. CANADIAN PRESS

But the Crow benefits also had a downside. The rates not only discouraged agricultural diversification since it was more expensive to ship other products such as livestock to market, but limited the processing of foodstuffs because it was cheaper to send the raw product out of the region. The two national railways also complained that the Crow rates had become unrealistic since they were being paid only about a third of the true cost of hauling grain. And without this revenue, or the "Crow gap" as it was called, both Canadian Pacific and Canadian National were extremely reluctant to invest in new grain hopper cars or upgrade existing rail lines to carry heavier, faster rolling stock.[4]

In the early 1960s, the railways tried to get around the Crow rates by seeking Ottawa's permission to abandon deteriorating, unprofitable branch lines—more than one thousand miles of track in Saskatchewan alone. The federal government decided instead to pay an annual subsidy to the railways to continue to operate branch lines until a royal commission, headed by Justice Emmett Hall, could determine what should be done with thousands of miles of tracks. Hall's 1977 report on branch-line retention and abandonment was heralded for its wide consultation and served as a benchmark for subsequent investigations of the issue. But it still left unresolved the matter of how a rationalized system was to be rehabilitated and upgraded, especially when the railways were unwilling to embark on a modernization program as long as the Crow rates remained in place.[5]

The Trudeau government's answer came on a wintry day in Winnipeg in February 1982, when federal transport minister Jean-Luc Pepin boldly announced that the statutory Crow freight rates were to be abolished. Saskatchewan wheat producers reacted with disbelief and then anger. Getting rid of the Crow might make cold, economic sense, especially if it was necessary to secure a better grain-handling system, but it came at a time of profound change in rural Saskatchewan. Not only were antiquated branch lines being abandoned, but the number of operating country elevators had been reduced in favour of larger, more efficient inland terminals that could clean grain to export standards. Between 1951 and 1974, 506 elevators at 248 communities had been closed.[6] Farmers were forced to truck their grain longer distances to new delivery points. These costs were at least tolerable under the Crow, but higher freight bills threatened to put more family farms out of business and precipitate a new round of rural decline. It was a fate that many in rural Saskatchewan bitterly refused to accept, especially when the Crow rates were supposed to last forever. "A deal is a deal" was the common sentiment on coffee row. Perhaps most galling, though, was that the Crow was being scrapped by a Quebec-dominated Liberal government which had not elected a single member west of Winnipeg in the 1980 federal election.

The NDP government of Allan Blakeney pounced on Pepin's announcement as the basis for a spring 1982 election call and a fourth straight mandate. The premier had repeatedly opposed any tampering with the Crow and now quickly mobilized the party as the defender of the province's agriculture industry. He could also boast ten consecutive surplus budgets and a thriving group of Crown corporations, collectively the largest employers in the province with over five billion dollars in assets in 1981.[7] The province seemed to have greater control over its economic destiny than at any other time in the past.

The Blakeney government had also taken concerted steps to answer those critics who complained that potash came before people. In 1979, it passed the Matrimonial Property Act to provide guidelines on the division of farm property on marriage breakdown. What prompted the legislation was a January 1978 Supreme Court of Canada decision in a case involving a divorced Saskatchewan farm couple (*Rathwell v. Rathwell*); the court used the idea of "remedial constructive trust" to rule that the spouse's contribution to the purchase of the land should be recognized even though the husband held sole title.[8] The NDP also established the Meewasin Valley Authority to regulate development along the South Saskatchewan River corridor in Saskatoon.[9] It even set aside its differences with the Métis to help found the Gabriel Dumont Institute, the only Métis educational institution of its kind in Canada. Roy Romanow, the province's point man on intergovernmental relations, meanwhile, had distinguished himself and Saskatchewan on the national stage by brokering a new constitutional accord. All in all, it was an enviable record for any provincial government—or so it seemed.

What no one anticipated was the impact of Grant Devine in his first election as Progressive Conservative leader. Widely dismissed as a political nobody, he had failed in two attempts to win a seat in the legislature, had never even held elected office. But the Regina-born farmer and professor in the College of Agriculture at the University of Saskatchewan inherited a revitalized party when he took over from Dick Collver in late 1979. A good part of this resurgence had to do with Collver's appeal to the anti-socialist forces in the province. Indeed, he sounded much like former Liberal premier Ross Thatcher when he declared that Saskatchewan was "a sleeping giant ... chained by the dogmatic idiots in the NDP."[10] The Blakeney government had also inadvertently given the party credibility by focusing its attack on Collver during the 1978 provincial election. Defeated Liberal leader Ted Malone even went so far as to declare that "the NDP created the Tory monster."[11] The province's battles with Ottawa, moreover, had cultivated a certain amount of disenchantment with governments and their priorities, and when disaffected voters wanted to cast a protest vote in the name of change, they turned to the Conservatives.

Premier Grant Devine (second from left) was a staunch defender of the province's agricultural community. SASKATCHEWAN ARCHIVES BOARD 84-1494-R16-30A

Despite his political inexperience, the thirty-seven-year-old Devine was an irrepressible performer on the hustings, whose contagious enthusiasm knew no limits except perhaps the boundaries of the province. "Had he been cruise director of the Titanic," remarked a legislature reporter, "he would have spent his final hours bragging about how many good swimmers there were aboard."[12] Devine, often dressed in blue jeans and cowboy hat, projected a folksy, down-home image, someone who understood the province, its people, their values—but most of all their needs. Describing himself as "just a farmer who happened to get a Ph.D degree," he conducted an extremely aggressive, popu-list campaign based on the theme "There's so much more that we can be." He berated the bloated Blakeney government for its waste and mismanagement, ridiculing the NDP campaign slogan of "tested and trusted" as "rusted and busted." He also charged that the premier was too preoccupied with the well-being of his "family" of Crown corporations to see that real Saskatchewan families were struggling with the double yoke of inflation and taxation. "If things are so good," Devine continually asked, "where's the prosperity ... and where are the children?"[13] This attack caught the NDP flat-footed and put Blakeney on the defensive for most of the campaign, looking desperate, out-of-touch or just plain bewildered at times. The Crow rate was rarely mentioned.[14]

Election day delivered a Tory avalanche, or more appropriately, a Devine victory. The party that had polled only 2 per cent of the popular vote in the 1971 election was swept into office with fifty-five of sixty-four seats and 54 per cent of the popular vote—the largest number of seats ever won by a party since 1905. The truly astounding surprise was the Conservative strength in the province's two major cities, traditional NDP strongholds: Tory candidates won all ten seats in Saskatoon and eight of ten Regina seats. "The good old province of Saskatchewan is not going to be the same any more," an exuberant Devine thundered to seven hundred ecstatic supporters at the Estevan curling rink on election night. "We're going to be number one."[15]

The NDP loss was staggering. Not only was the former government reduced to a mere nine seats, but most cabinet ministers were defeated. Roy Romanow, who at one time suggested that potash would do for the NDP what medicare had done for the CCF, was defeated by a gas station cashier. If there was any consolation, it was that the party's share of the popular vote had sagged to only 37.6 per cent. The Liberals, meanwhile, once again failed to elect a single member and polled just 4.5 per cent of the vote, a new low for the party that had ruled Saskatchewan before the Second World War like its own fiefdom. Ralph Goodale, the new leader and a former Liberal MP, had been carefully rebuilding the Liberals as a party of moderation and consensus. But Senator Sid Buckwold of Saskatoon, one of the senior Liberals in the province, had rightly predicted that a middle-of-the-road alternative would lose in an increasingly polarized Saskatchewan political atmosphere.[16]

The new Conservative government lost little time in taking over from the shell-shocked Blakeney troops. In an unprecedented outdoor ceremony in front of the Legislature Building in early May, Premier Devine and his new cabinet, including Joan Duncan and Patricia Smith, the first two women to hold ministerial posts in Saskatchewan, were sworn into office. Not a single member had any government experience. "We have started the new beginning," Devine roared to the crowd's approval. "People all across Canada are watching Saskatchewan and will continue to watch us."[17] The premier then delivered on one of his key election promises and announced the removal of the 20 per cent provincial tax on gasoline—a move that cancelled more than $125 million in provincial revenue. He implemented his second major promise, mortgage interest relief, during a short legislative session in June. Devine had little trouble making the transition from the visitors' gallery to the premier's chair, and his almost constant campaign-style of governing created the impression that anything was possible; his critics simply lacked vision. This bullish mood was reflected in the far-fetched scheme of hockey promoter and local sports hero "Wild Bill" Hunter to purchase the St. Louis Blues franchise of the National Hockey League and transfer the club to Saskatoon where it would play in a yet-to-be-built eighteen-thousand-seat arena.

The pervasive theme of the Conservative election campaign was that the Blakeney government had become too involved in the province's economy at the expense of private initiative. "Profit has become a dirty word in Saskatchewan," the premier admonished. "We have to become proud of profit."[18] This overriding concern with free enterprise did not mean, however, that the Devine government was going to swing the province radically to the right and simply dismantle all twenty-three Crown corporations that it had inherited. Instead, a new Crown Corporation Review Commission, known as the Wolff Commission after its chairman, was created to investigate the operation and necessity of every member of the so-called Saskatchewan family of Crown corporations. At the same time, the government took immediate steps to end any further government intervention in the provincial economy, particularly in the resource sector. Devine was convinced that the Saskatchewan economy would perform at a higher level, even rival that of neighbouring Alberta, once the constricting, socialist barriers to growth had been removed so that a favourable business climate could flourish. This

Saskatoon tried unsuccessfully to secure a NHL franchise in the early 1980s. PHILLIP MALLETTE

message—that private enterprise was once again welcome in Saskatchewan—
was the theme at a government-sponsored "Open for Business" conference
in Regina that November. In one of his most memorable remarks, the premier declared that the province had decided not to participate in the current
recession.[19]

Someone should have told the Saskatchewan economy. Soft international
markets bedeviled the potash industry in the first half of the 1980s, leading to
high inventories and reduced production. The year of Devine's victory coincided with the layoff of twelve hundred Potash Corporation of Saskatchewan
workers. The uranium industry was even worse off. The price of yellow cake
(uranium concentrate) began to slump at the start of the decade, prompting
Eldorado Nuclear to announce in December 1981 the pending closure of
Beaverlodge, the oldest mine in the province. Eldorado's decision delivered a
mortal blow to Uranium City, since almost one-third of the community's
three thousand people worked for the mine.[20] By June 1983, the population
had shrunk to six hundred, while the Devine government scrambled to find
a way to keep the town on the north shore of Lake Athabasca alive. This task
was probably made more difficult by the shutting down of the Department
of Northern Saskatchewan (DNS) the year before. The Conservatives had long
considered DNS to be an NDP boondoggle and transferred many of its functions to other departments upon assuming office.[21]

Despite weak demand and low prices in the early 1980s, two new uranium
mines began production. Cluff Lake opened in 1981. Two years later, Key
Lake came on stream, effectively tripling provincial output. Key Lake was
heralded as a state-of-the-art facility, but on 5 January 1984, just four months
after the official opening, a break in the reservoir released one hundred million litres of radioactive water.[22] The provincial Department of Environment
downplayed the seriousness of the leak by telling the media that from "a
technical standpoint, all that's happened is that the surface area of the reservoir had been increased."[23] There had also been a number of smaller spills at
the Rabbit Lake/Collins Bay mine complex on Wollaston Lake. Aboriginal
people living in the area, increasingly frustrated by the threat to their way of
life, blockaded the road to the mine in mid-June 1985. It was the first coordinated act of northern civil disobedience against uranium mining. The barrier
was lifted after eighty hours, while the chief of the Hatchet Lake band met
with company and government officials in Saskatoon. The two sides agreed
to explore ways to improve relations, including possible Native employment
opportunities.[24] Four years later, when a faulty pipeline valve sent a million
litres of radioactive waste into a stream feeding Wollaston Lake, the mine
failed to notify the band, even though radium levels in the spilled water were
ten times higher than the allowable provincial limit.[25]

The Saskatchewan oil industry experienced ups and downs in the 1980s. By 1982, production and exploration had slid 50 per cent from their 1980 levels, while the entire southwest field was shut down because the American refinery that processed the sour crude cancelled its Saskatchewan orders. Colin Thatcher, the new mineral resources minister and millionaire son of Saskatchewan's last Liberal premier, set out to turn this dismal situation around by introducing tax and royalty holidays, especially for new wells. The incentives touched off a drilling frenzy with the revenue from the sale of oil exploration rights setting records for three consecutive years. In 1984 alone, 2,970 new wells, an all-time provincial high, were drilled. One American oilman called Saskatchewan "the best drilling risk in North America."[26] The boom encouraged the Devine government to become heavily involved in the financing of two heavy-oil upgraders, one in Regina attached to the Consumers' Co-operative Refinery and the other near Lloydminster. Construction of the government-subsidized Regina plant, popularly known as the Co-op Upgrader, started in 1984, but the Lloydminster project was continually put on hold while Saskatchewan sought a partner with deep pockets. This search was compromised by tumbling oil prices in 1986 and the loss of five thousand jobs in the oil patch.[27]

Agriculture turned in a poor performance in the 1980s, even though Premier Devine, like Blakeney before him, touted himself as the latest saviour of the family farm. To help promote greater farm ownership, the government immediately abolished the NDP Land Bank in favour of a Farm Purchase Program, which provided interest rebates on loans for land acquisitions. But the nearly six thousand Saskatchewan farmers who took advantage of the government-subsidized loans did not count on a farm economy that rivalled that of the Great Depression for bleakness. Part of the problem was poor growing conditions, but farmers were also paying more to ship their grain to market. Over the protests of several agricultural organizations and all three provincial political parties, the Western Grain Transportation Act replaced the Crow in late 1983 with government subsidies to the railways and steadily increasing freight rates for producers.

The most grievous problem, though, was the collapse of commodity prices. At the beginning of the decade, many of Canada's customers stopped buying grain. Customers in the developing world did so for financial reasons, while China and Russia desired to become self-sufficient. Yet even though export sales declined, farmers continued to increase their output in a quixotic effort to sustain their income in the face of rising production costs. Then, at mid-decade, the United States and the European Economic Community entered into a cutthroat subsidy war to capture a larger share of the international market for their domestic producers. International prices went into a

A fire destroyed several elevators at Kyle in 1981. UNIVERSITY OF SASKATCHEWAN ARCHIVES MG247
SERIES 10

tailspin, leaving Saskatchewan farmers with millions of bushels of unwanted
grain. Those who had purchased land or expanded their holdings in the early
1980s were unable to meet their loan payments and found themselves helplessly sliding down the slippery slope of debt. Even the value of farmland
depreciated during the period, creating a larger financial headache since
loans had been secured against overvalued property. "Everything that could
go wrong," summed up an agricultural reporter, "did."[28]

The Devine government responded by offering a universal, low-interest
farm loan program just months before spring seeding. It seemed that no cost
was too high if it meant keeping people engaged in agriculture. Any producer, regardless of his or her financial situation, was eligible for a one-time
twenty-five-dollar per acre production loan at 6 per cent interest. An estimated 90 per cent of Saskatchewan's farmers, including many who were
well-off, took part in the generous program at a cost of one billion dollars to
the provincial treasury.[29] The money, though, failed to rescue those producers
who were already overstretched and failing, and their bills continued to pile
up at an alarming rate. Total farm indebtedness climbed from $3.5 billion in
1981 to $6.12 billion in 1986. Other statistics for the same five-year period
went in the opposite direction. The number of farms in the province fell

from 67,318 to 63,341, a decline of 5.8 per cent, while the total farm population dropped from 187,163 to 168,505, less than a third of what it had been
half a century earlier. Even the number of country elevators was halved—
from 1,805 to 898. The most dramatic decline, however, was in total net
income. Whereas it had stood at $614.1 million in 1981, it was only $168.2
million in 1986.[30] The sense that rural life would never be the same again was
reflected in the applications under the new provincial Heritage Property Act.
By December 1983, three years after the passage of the act, 171 of the 208
heritage designations were in small towns—from churches, schools, and
railway stations to homesteads, trails, and cemeteries.[31]

The drastically reduced income forced a growing number of families to
find off-farm work if they wanted to remain on the land. This phenomenon
had parallels with the early days of the province when homesteaders hired
themselves out to more prosperous farmers or worked in the bush or on
railway gangs and road crews until they could get established. Spouses stayed
on the homestead, doing whatever was required of them in the yard, the
barn, or the fields, when not tending to their children. Many women earned
much-needed "pin" money through the sale of eggs, butter, and other farm
products.

Fast forward to the 1980s, and farm couples were once again working side-
by-side in an attempt to earn a livelihood from farming. During the heyday
of the wheat economy, hired hands had often helped with seeding and harvest, but now women were operating the new farm machinery or driving the
grain truck until their children could help with these tasks. And it was now
mostly women who held down full-time day jobs in their home community
or the nearest city.[32] Indeed, what often gets overlooked about the farm crisis
of the 1980s is how much extra responsibility women were assuming. In 1987,
off-farm earnings accounted for more than half of the total net farm income
for that year.[33] Nettie Wiebe, a farm activist and first female president of the
National Farmers' Union, termed women's increased responsibilities a "triple
load": farm work, family duties, and paid employment.[34]

Participating in the labour market was especially difficult for farm women
during this period because of the lack of daycare for children; less than 5 per
cent of licensed spaces were located in rural Saskatchewan. The lack of adequate care may have directly contributed to the almost one hundred farm
kids, four and under, who suffered accidents and had to be hospitalized
between 1979 and 1984.[35] Working mothers also continued to come up
against traditional values which maintained that a woman's place was in the
home. They even had to deal with sexism at the highest level. In May 1987,
social services minister Grant Schmidt, who was also responsible for women's
issues, warned his audience at the National Council of Women's banquet

that his speech would be "braless." It "had a point here, a point there, but was shaky in the middle."[36]

Farmers were not the only ones shouldering a growing debt load. In November 1982, finance minister Bob Andrew tabled a revised budget for 1982–83 that contained the largest deficit in provincial history: $220 million. In fact, it was only the third budgeted deficit in Saskatchewan history![37] Andrew argued that the shortfall had been caused by the previous government's overly optimistic projections of resource revenues. "Saskatchewan is recession-resistant," he corrected the premier, "not recession-proof."[38] The following March, in what would become a spring ritual for Conservative finance ministers during the 1980s, Andrew was back before the House tabling a second straight deficit budget—this time $317 million. Allan Blakeney, who had initially seemed out of place as opposition leader, took advantage of the coming of television to the legislature to illustrate vividly the financial mess that the province was in. Waving a stack of bank notes for the cameras, he claimed that the Tory debt equalled a string of ten-dollar bills placed end-to-end from the Atlantic to the Pacific. "Four thousand, seven hundred miles of bills," he asserted, "that's your deficit."[39] Blakeney's theatrics made no impression on the government's spending. By 1985–86, the budget deficit had ballooned to $579 million for a total provincial debt of $1.5 billion.

Premier Devine, for his part, seemed unfazed by the financial incompetence of his government. Nor was he apparently bothered by the contradiction between words and action. The Conservative government had talked about downsizing the provincial bureaucracy and lowering taxes as if it was some sacred mantra, and yet it was continuously spending more than it took in, like a losing gambler who did not know when to quit. Devine liked to attribute the province's fiscal woes to three decades of socialist rule and insisted that the damage could be undone by spending money to cultivate a pro-business environment. Fulfilling the Conservative election promises, however, had put the province into deficit and kept it there trying to pay the interest on a steadily increasing debt. Other initiatives, such as the farm loan program, only compounded the problem by committing the province to expenditures that exceeded total revenues.[40] Always the optimist, Devine was convinced that the situation would turn itself around. "Don't say whoa in a mudhole," he fondly counselled. This unbridled faith in the province's future was plainly evident when the population reached the million mark for the first time in December 1983. "We now have over one million citizens," an elated Devine told the legislature, "that are capable of reaching for the stars, of making Saskatchewan a magical place to be envied world-wide. They just require the tools and the opportunities to succeed."[41]

Devine's "reaching for the stars" metaphor unfortunately did not extend

Debt hobbled Saskatchewan farm operations in the 1980s. BRIAN GABLE, *GLOBE AND MAIL*

to the province's Aboriginal peoples. In April 1982, several months of intense lobbying across the country had finally succeeded in getting "the existing aboriginal and treaty rights of the aboriginal peoples of Canada" recognized in the new Constitution Act. This achievement represented a milestone in Aboriginal-government relations, in that "aboriginal peoples" were formally defined as Indians, Métis, and Inuit and that their rights, as they existed in 1982, were enshrined in law and beyond the reach of the federal and provincial governments. But the new constitution never defined these rights, leaving it instead to a series of first ministers' conferences to come up with a definition agreeable to all parties.

Premier Devine represented Saskatchewan at all four conferences. Despite Prime Minister Trudeau's impassioned plea in 1984 to accept Aboriginal self-government in principle, Devine and the other western premiers steadfastly refused to give their consent until the full implications of such a concept were understood.[42] He made the same argument three years later at the final meeting to try to hammer out an agreement. "I could take you through the towns and villages of Saskatchewan; they wouldn't understand these proposals," Devine explained. "If we do it wrong, we'll set things back 100 years."[43]

These words elicited a stern rebuke from Regina's Jim Sinclair, representing the Métis National Council. "I think it's unfair of you to accuse all of Saskatchewan of racism," he denounced the premier before a national television audience, "when you're advancing it at this table."[44] Devine shrugged off Sinclair's outburst as no more than frustration over the collapse of the talks. But it seemed strange that similar uncertainty about the Free Trade Agreement and the Meech Lake Constitutional Accord did not prevent the premier from being an unabashed cheerleader for these national initiatives.[45] It was also clear, as *Saskatoon Star-Phoenix* columnist Verne Clemence later argued, that Devine was worried about "a backlash from some in the non-native community who want no part of any movement to extend rights to Indian and Métis citizens."[46]

It was this same fear that prompted the Devine government to freeze ongoing negotiations over long-standing treaty land claims in the province. At the time of treaty in the 1870s, Indian bands were entitled to reserves based on the formula of 128 acres of land per person. But some bands never received their full allotment or, in a few cases, never secured a reserve at all. Others had been stripped of land through forced or fraudulent surrenders during the settlement boom in the early twentieth century. The matter was further complicated when Saskatchewan was finally given control over its public lands and resources in 1930. Under the terms of the Natural Resources Transfer Agreement, the federal government was still primarily responsible for settling claims, but unoccupied provincial land could now be used to cover shortfalls.

The Blakeney government did not shrink from this duty and in 1976, coincidentally the hundredth anniversary of the signing of Treaty 6, reached a compensation agreement with federal claims negotiators in consultation with the Federation of Saskatchewan Indians (FSI). Known as the Saskatchewan formula, it proposed that entitlements be based on the band population as of 31 December 1976, not at the time the treaty was signed. The agreement, however, quickly bogged down in bickering between Regina and Ottawa over land and money, prompting a few bands to pursue their claims through the courts. But instead of trying to resolve these differences, the Devine government ordered a policy review, choosing to appease rural residents who were alarmed about the implications of treaty land entitlement. A handful of claims, however, did proceed, perhaps the most notable being that of the Lucky Man band, which finally received a reserve in the Battlefords area 110 years after it had entered treaty in 1879.[47]

The other groundbreaking development was the creation of urban reserves in several Saskatchewan communities. After the Second World War, a steadily increasing number of Indians had migrated to urban centres to escape reserve poverty and unemployment. It was not long before band councils also looked to the province's cities for business opportunities not available in rural districts, as well as for ways to deliver services to band members. In 1979, the

Peter Ballantyne Cree Nation decided to take advantage of the Trudeau government's commitment to settle outstanding claims and asked for forty-one acres of unoccupied federal land in a residential area in Prince Albert. It was the band's hope that the site, to be used for educational purposes, would become an extension of the parent reserve.

The Prince Albert city council reacted with alarm, predicting a host of jurisdictional problems, especially if municipal laws did not apply to the proposed reserve.[48] "We cannot have an island of self government in the middle of Prince Albert," declared Mayor Dick Spencer. "There must be one set of bylaws for all citizens regardless of race or colour."[49] But the band council, with the support of the FSI, refused to be governed by municipal regulations because of the precedent it might set. Nor was the federal government willing to withhold reserve status, and by order-in-council in August 1982, it created the Opawakoscikan Reserve, the first urban reserve in Saskatchewan. Other similar requests quickly followed. The Flying Dust band claimed federal property in Meadow Lake, while the Star Blanket band selected surplus federal land in Fort Qu'Appelle. Because federal land was involved, the provincial government could not stop these reserve designations and simply grumbled that municipal agreement should be secured beforehand. Carol Lafond of the Muskeg Lake band offered a more positive assessment of the urban reserve movement, suggesting that the band's acquisition of a federal lot on the eastern outskirts of Saskatoon for commercial purposes would enable her people to "quit being dependent on handouts."[50]

Handouts were exactly what the two major political parties promised the Saskatchewan electorate in the October 1986 provincial election. The Devine Conservatives offered matching home improvement grants, home improvement loans, subsidized mortgage rates on new homes, and grants for first-time home buyers. It was no wonder that the Tory campaign slogan was "Keep on Building Saskatchewan." Even hot tubs, landscaping, and swimming pools qualified for funding. Not to be outdone, the NDP announced a similar package of grants and mortgage relief. Party strategists even dressed Allan Blakeney in plaid shirts and sent him out mainstreeting in an effort to emulate the folksy Devine.[51] Only the Liberals sounded a note of warning, claiming that the Conservative/NDP giveaways were sullying the province. "We'll keep them honest," declared leader Ralph Goodale in the naive belief that voters would be disgusted by the blatant attempts to bribe them.[52]

The Conservatives pinned their re-election hopes on once again winning rural Saskatchewan. In the months before the campaign, Devine named himself agriculture minister to send a signal about the importance of the province's farmers to the Tory government. He also played up his party's empathy for ordinary people, suggesting during a fanciful moment that even

By 1991, two of every five provincial residents lived in Regina (shown here) or Saskatoon.
REGINA LEADER-POST

long-time CCF premier Tommy Douglas, who had died in Ottawa in February, would have supported the Conservatives in the forthcoming election.[53] The big-ticket item, though, was Devine's resolute promise of a major federal deficiency payment to make up for low grain prices. Just how important this money was to Conservative fortunes was demonstrated early in the morning of 3 October, when a sleeping reporter at the Kelvington motel was awakened by Devine's plaintive telephone conversation in the room next door. "If I lose this," the premier pleaded, "it's going to be damned tough for Mulroney next time around."[54] Within hours, the new Conservative prime minister announced a billion-dollar aid package. This close relationship between the Saskatchewan and Canadian governments had not been seen since the early twentieth century when the Liberals were in power in Regina and Ottawa.

The election results represented a moral victory for the Liberals and NDP. Goodale became the first—and only—Liberal elected to the legislature since the 1978 election bloodbath. The NDP won 45.1 per cent of the popular vote, narrowly outdistancing the Tories who earned 44.8 per cent. But when it came to seats in the legislature, the Conservatives were returned to office with a comfortable majority of thirty-eight to the NDP twenty-five. The real story of the election, however, was how the federal bailout had given the Devine forces a boost at the expense of a divided province.[55] While the Conservatives captured all but three rural seats, the NDP won twenty of twenty-four urban seats, including eighteen of the twenty seats in Regina and Saskatoon. A somewhat chastened Devine vowed to win back urban support. Blakeney, on the other hand, indicated that he would be stepping down after twenty-six years in the legislature. Goodale would wait two years before resigning to run in a federal riding. He would be replaced by political novice Lynda Haverstock, a clinical psychologist who had worked in rural communities helping families deal with the problems of farm stress. She was the first woman leader of a political party in Saskatchewan.

After the 1986 election, it was as if a different party, even more right-wing, had taken over the levers of power. No longer would the Devine government lack ideological clarity, as it would soon bulldoze ahead with a new privatization agenda in a determined effort to wipe out the CCF/NDP legacy. Nor would it continue to ignore or downplay the mounting fiscal crisis, but desperately try to bring the debt monster to heel through cutbacks, firings, and taxes.[56] The outrage over the extent and nature of the cutbacks, from social assistance to aid for the mentally ill or handicapped, precipitated one of the largest demonstrations in Regina history, when seven thousand protestors marched on the legislature in June 1987. Even the breezy bravado was noticeably absent as Devine asked for more time to deal with the worsening economic situation, readily admitting at one point that he was a premier "in some trouble."[57]

One group that needed Devine's continuing help was the province's farmers. In 1986, perfect growing conditions produced a record harvest, but prices remained low because of the American government's decision to subsidize its producers. Two years later, a prolonged drought cut the harvest in half and cost fourteen thousand workers their jobs in the agricultural sector. Continuing dry conditions, combined with lower grain prices, meant that the average producer did not make enough money from the sale of the 1989 crop to cover 1990 operating expenses. No less than a third of the province's farmers were in serious financial trouble.[58] Even Devine's farm operation was hurting.

What kept many producers on the land were payouts from the Western Grain Stabilization Fund and special government aid packages, such as the 1986 Special Canadian Grains Program (Mulroney's one-billion-dollar pledge) and the 1989 Canadian Drought Crop Assistance Program. One study of 1986 federal and provincial subsidies pegged the amount awarded at thirty-three thousand dollars per Saskatchewan farmer; the Devine government's own calculations said it was closer to thirty-six thousand.[59] This emergency assistance may have provided immediate relief to cash-strapped farmers, but it did not resolve the more fundamental problem—their debt load. It also encouraged the move to even larger farms and the continued cultivation of marginal lands since the level of aid was based on the number of acres farmed.[60] Agriculture, meanwhile, accounted for an increasingly smaller segment of Saskatchewan's domestic product, dropping to 12 per cent in 1988.[61] But this fundamental change seemed to be lost on Devine who "virtually spoke of nothing else" but agriculture.[62]

The Conservative government's fixation on rural Saskatchewan alienated the urban population. While most city dwellers sympathized with the farming crisis, they were bothered by the universality of the province's aid programs, even though roughly a third of Saskatchewan farmers were relatively prosperous and did not need the money. They also resented the fact that they were paying for these generous subsidies at a time when they faced drastic budget cuts, higher taxes, and a provincial debt headed into the stratosphere. "It's become a common topic of conversation. You hear it all over," remarked a union official. "I don't remember it ever like this before."[63] There were even anti-farmer jokes making the rounds in the larger cities: "Why was the farmer buried only one foot underground? So he could keep his hand out."

The growing chasm between the city and the country was also a reflection of the changing economic base of the province's major urban centres. Cities and larger towns were no longer wedded to the agricultural sector. Post-war diversification into non-renewable natural resources had created a more broadly based Saskatchewan economy with new demands for different kinds of services. Many of these jobs were located in the larger cities.[64] While the populations of Moose Jaw, North Battleford, Swift Current, Weyburn, and Yorkton remained fairly constant between 1981 and 1991, Prince Albert, Regina, and Saskatoon grew 8.9, 9.8 and 20.7 per cent, respectively. Estevan and Lloydminster also enjoyed modest growth because of activity in the oil industry. The numerical dominance of Regina and Saskatoon was particularly hard to ignore. By 1991, two out of every five Saskatchewan citizens lived in the two cities. The former temperance colony on the South Saskatchewan River (186,058) had also passed the Queen City (179,178) for boasting rights as the largest centre.

Many of these urban residents had no direct connection to agriculture, had never even visited a farm. Those who had left rural Saskatchewan, meanwhile, still visited their home communities, especially during seeding and harvest, but increasingly identified themselves with the city, their new jobs, and their new friends, and would never go back to the farm. The landscape and its rhythms, however, continued to exert a powerful influence on people and provided inspiration to the arts, especially literature. This renaissance was reflected in the establishment of new presses, such as Coteau, Fifth House, and Thistledown, and the success of a new generation of authors. "I think writers in this province have committed themselves to the region," reflected Esterhazy-born author Guy Vanderhaeghe, winner of two Governor General's Literary Awards for fiction. "They write about the Saskatchewan experience."[65]

The cultural makeup of the province's larger urban centres also differed substantially from rural areas. Immigrants had once been attracted to Saskatchewan by the promise of homestead land, but now most newcomers moved to the city. A growing number of these new citizens were visible minorities, such as the "boat people" refugees from southeast Asia. Faced with adjusting to a new language, climate, and way of life, their integration into Saskatchewan society was perhaps made easier by the new provincial Human Rights Code. The province's gay and lesbian community, though, enjoyed no such protection. When asked to comment in 1988 on Burnaby MP Svend Robinson's announcement that he was homosexual, Devine, a devout Catholic, stated, "I feel the same way about bank robbers ... in my view immoral."[66] Ironically, J. T. M. Anderson, the leader of the Conservative party, had said much the same thing about Catholics six decades earlier.

Esterhazy-born Guy Vanderhaeghe won the first of two Governor General's Literary Awards for fiction in 1982.
FIFTH HOUSE LTD.

Discrimination on the basis of sexual orientation was added to the Human Rights Code in 1993.[67]

Until agriculture could get back on its feet, the Devine government redoubled its efforts to build the Saskatchewan economy. But the success of these projects was more miss than hit and cost the provincial treasury hundreds of millions of dollars. In 1988, the Conservative government finally struck a deal with the Alberta and federal governments and Husky Oil of Calgary to build the Lloydminster upgrader. The terms, however, proved onerous for the province, especially since the new Co-op Upgrader in Regina was already a financial drain.[68] The government also sold the Prince Albert Pulp Mill to the American conglomerate Weyerhaeuser on the understanding that the new owner would build a fine-paper mill; not only did the plant go for a bargain price, but Regina was to help finance the second mill. Other initiatives failed miserably—from producing barbecue briquettes in the premier's Estevan riding to making Regina the plastic shopping cart manufacturing capital of the world.[69] Devine seemed oblivious to these costly flops. "I'm going to give it all I've got to make the changes I believe people want to see," the premier once promised. "I'm not going to do it at half-speed."[70]

This bold change came in mid-January 1988 when Premier Devine called a news conference to announce the creation of a new Department of Public Participation with responsibility for the sale of Crown corporations and government services to the private sector. Just how far the Conservatives were willing to go was revealed when the government introduced a Public Participation bill in the legislature in early June. Described by the minister as simple enabling legislation, the bill gave the new department sweeping powers to do whatever was necessary to promote and pursue public participation initiatives. Roy Romanow, the former NDP attorney general and the only candidate to replace Blakeney at the November 1987 leadership convention, compared the legislation to a blank cheque and pointed out—as he would do repeatedly in the ensuing months—that the government had no mandate to undertake privatization. The real danger for the Tories, however, was that the public participation thrust not only went against the traditional Saskatchewan emphasis on state-directed development but was being implemented during a period of economic stagnation.[71]

The following March, Lieutenant-Governor Sylvia Fedoruk, the first woman to hold the viceregal post, announced in the speech from the throne that the government was preparing share offerings for SaskEnergy (the natural gas side of SaskPower), the Potash Corporation of Saskatchewan (PCS), and the general commercial insurance side of Saskatchewan Government Insurance. A feisty Devine predicted that these privatization plans would

Four past and future CCF-NDP premiers at the 1970 party convention (from left, Woodrow Lloyd, Allan Blakeney, Tommy Douglas, and Roy Romanow). ELEANORE AND ROY ROMANOW

spell the demise of the NDP. "This is their Alamo, their Waterloo," he chortled. "This is the end of the line for them."[72] Romanow was not intimidated. To a chorus of backbench shouts of "pirate-ization," the NDP leader likened the government's plans to a scorched-earth policy and warned that the face of Saskatchewan would never be the same again.[73]

These verbal exchanges took on a new dimension on 21 April 1989 when the opposition called for a standing vote on the introduction of government legislation to offer a public share offering in SaskEnergy and then walked out as the division bells rang. With the business of the legislature effectively frozen, a defiant Romanow told a news conference that the heritage of the people of Saskatchewan was at stake and that his party was prepared to keep the bells ringing until the government either called an election or withdrew the legislation. "It's SOS, Save our Saskatchewan," he said.[74] An Angus Reid poll released in early May bolstered the opposition's position—67 per cent of the province's residents (including one-third of the Tories' own supporters) were opposed to the government's SaskEnergy policy and 58 per cent of the respondents rejected privatization in general.[75] The stand-off finally ended on 9 May—after a seventeen-day hiatus—when the NDP MLAs returned to the legislature and the bill was formally adjourned while a commission investigated the matter. Devine would later decide to shelve the idea.

Although the Conservative government had been temporarily thrown off course by the SaskEnergy dispute, it pushed ahead with a bill to provide for the privatization of PCS through the sale of shares. But the New Democrats were equally determined to thwart passage of the legislation—PCS was the shining symbol of the Blakeney years—and held the floor of the legislature for endless hours, talking about matters at times only remotely related to potash. After trying longer sitting hours to move the bill along, the Conservative house leader gave notice that the government planned to limit debate. A sanctimonious Romanow called the decision an "unprecedented attack on freedom in the province of Saskatchewan," conveniently forgetting that his own party had hijacked the legislature when it walked out over SaskEnergy.[76] On 7 August, for the first time since 1905, the government invoked closure and the longest single debate in provincial history (120 hours) came to an end one week later. In his first and only speech before the passage of the bill, Premier Devine argued that privatization of PCS would reduce the taxpayers' burden, while allowing for the diversification of the economy and debt reduction. The session, lasting a brutal 105 days, probably did more to polarize provincial politics than any other event in recent history and its bitterness lingers to this day.[77]

At the Conservative convention that fall, Devine lambasted the NDP as a moribund party intent on "a rush into the past." Declaring the Blakeney era in politics dead, he boasted, "The Berlin Wall is falling and it's not going to be rebuilt in Saskatchewan."[78] Bravado aside, it was the Conservatives who were in deep political trouble with an election expected in 1990, while their heralded "open for business" development strategy, what one critic called "credit card politics,"[79] translated into four billion dollars in debt. The province's poor economic performance, meanwhile, was taking its toll—and not just in the countryside. According to *Poverty Profile 1988*, a report by the National Council of Welfare, Saskatchewan had the second highest poverty rate in Canada (after Newfoundland); almost 20 per cent of the population (one-third of them children) was living in poverty. A subsequent inquiry into hunger in Regina, released in October 1989, reported that one in every four city residents was poor and in many cases malnourished.[80] It was no coincidence that food banks had opened in the larger cities in the province.

Understandably, many chose not to stay, but began to leave the province in numbers that had not been experienced since the late 1960s. For each of the three years between 1988 and 1990, Saskatchewan lost from eight to ten thousand people per year. In fact, the population came close to dropping below the magic million mark in 1991. Those wanting to leave southern Saskatchewan by train were out of luck. In October 1989, Ottawa announced the cancellation of VIA Rail's passenger service along the CPR line. This route had been in operation for more than a century and had created most of the small towns and hamlets along the line.

Cree artist Allen Sapp accepts his Order of Canada from Governor General Adrienne Clarkson. CANADIAN PRESS

The news was not all cheerless though. In 1989, the government created SaskFilm, a successful, non-profit agency to promote employment and development opportunities in film, video, and related media. That same year, the Allen Sapp gallery, featuring the work of the Red Pheasant Cree, opened in North Battleford. There was also a "local boy makes good" story. Former Saskatoon Conservative MP and cabinet minister Ray Hnatyshyn was installed as Canada's twenty-fourth governor general. He succeeded Jeanne Sauvé, the first woman and the first person from Saskatchewan (originally from Prudhomme) to hold the position. Impending job losses also sparked an innovative development in the brewing industry. When the Carling plant in Saskatoon faced closure following the merger of Carling O'Keefe and Molson breweries, the employees formed the Great Western Brewing Company and introduced a new, award-winning product line. Then, there was the miracle of 1989. After finishing third in regular-season play, the beloved Saskatchewan Roughriders defeated the Hamilton Tiger-Cats 43–40 in Toronto's Skydome in the greatest Grey Cup game in Canadian Football League history.

Saskatchewan also got two new special places. In June 1989, the Devine government created the province's first park reserve when it set aside two thousand square kilometres to protect the Athabasca sand dunes in north-western Saskatchewan. The federal and provincial governments also reached an agreement—after thirty years of lobbying—to establish Grasslands National Park in the Saskatchewan badlands, the same region that had fool-ishly been opened to homesteading in 1908. A senior advisor to the federal minister of the environment later revealed that Grasslands had been part of a political trade-off in exchange for a federal licence to proceed with the Rafferty-Alameda project in Devine's home riding.[81] Two dams in south-eastern Saskatchewan, one across the Souris River, the other across Moose Mountain Creek, were to provide flood control, as well as water for irrigation and for cooling the huge turbines of the Shand generating station that was being constructed near Estevan. The project suffered a setback in the spring of 1989, when the Federal Court of Canada, acting on a challenge from the Canadian Wildlife Federation, ruled that the environmental assessment pro-cess had been circumvented by the Devine-Ottawa deal and lifted the licence. But the province, citing safety concerns, pushed ahead with construction over the objections of a federal review panel which eventually resigned in frustration. By 1991, both dams had been completed, while the environ-mental assessment process had been steamrollered.[82]

So too seemed the Devine government when the premier asked for televi-sion time the night of 5 March 1990 to make a major announcement. Claiming that "the world [had] declar[ed] economic war on Saskatchewan and our way of life," a grim Devine told the provincial audience that the home improvement program, mortgage reduction plan, and gas tax rebate would be cancelled to free up money for agriculture.[83] One year later, the government announced Fair Share Saskatchewan, a scheme to transfer gov-ernment departments and agencies, along with hundreds of civil-service jobs, to smaller communities throughout the province. In his typical salesmanlike hype, Devine claimed that it was "time to share the assets of government business."[84] Opponents mockingly described the program, in a word play on a popular Hollywood film at the time, as "Dances with Gophers."

The Conservatives were shoring up support in rural Saskatchewan in anticipation of the election that was finally called for October 1991. They would need it. The Tories were reduced to ten rural seats with only 25 per cent of the popular vote. The NDP took all but one of the other seats—fifty-five in total—as Roy Romanow cruised to a landslide victory. Not all disgruntled voters, though, swung back to the NDP. The Liberals polled a surprising 24 per cent of the popular vote and seemed poised to replace the discredited Conservatives. But it would be difficult with only one seat in the new legislature, that of leader Lynda Haverstock.

The postscript to the election was even uglier for the Conservative party.

While the election was underway, the RCMP began investigating the alleged misuse of communication allowances for Conservative party purposes. Known as "Project Fiddle," several party officials and MLAs concocted a scam whereby false invoices were submitted for work that was never done, the money was paid to one of three bogus advertising agencies, and then the funds were transferred to the Conservative caucus account to be used for various purposes, including personal gain. The Legislative Assembly Office, responsible for paying the invoices, was bilked of nearly one million dollars. Twelve Conservative MLAs, eleven of them former cabinet ministers, including former deputy premier Eric Bernston, were found guilty of various fraud offences and given sentences ranging from jail time to paying restitution and/or performing community service. "Whatever else the government did," observed David Smith, a respected political scientist, "those scandals put all else into the shadows."[85]

Like the scandals, the Devine years were an aberration in Saskatchewan history. Even though there had been premiers who shared Devine's faith in the land and its people, no one had been a bigger, more vocal cheerleader for the province on the national stage. Previous governments had also wanted Saskatchewan to grow and prosper, but the Conservatives seemed impatient with the pace of development and desperately pursued success all at once and at any cost; being pragmatic and recognizing limits signified a lack of courage,

Ray Hnatyshyn's appointment as governor general was a popular one. CAM CARDOW

a lack of confidence in the province and its potential. Yet Devine's breezy bravado about Saskatchewan's rightful destiny diverted attention away from the fundamental changes that the province was undergoing in the closing decades of the twentieth century. Saskatchewan was indeed a different place after nine years of Tory rule, but not in the way that Devine had boldly predicted. Dealing with the changes would be difficult for the province. The Conservatives' spendthrift ways only made it more painful.

CHAPTER TWENTY-ONE

OUR SHARED DESTINY

THERE COULD HAVE BEEN NO BETTER SETTING for the landmark agreement. On 22 September 1992, a perfect fall day in Saskatoon, seven hundred invited guests and dignitaries gathered at the new Wanuskewin Heritage Park just north of the city to witness the most important land deal in provincial history. For several millennia, Indians had been coming to this traditional gathering place along the South Saskatchewan River, where they sought shelter from winter's biting winds in the deep coulees and drove buffalo over the steep cliffs to be butchered below. Their ancestors had now returned to the sacred spot to sign a Treaty Land Entitlement (TLE) Agreement between the federal and provincial governments and the Federation of Saskatchewan Indian Nations (FSIN). The deal provided twenty-five bands with $455 million to buy approximately 1.57 million acres, land that had been promised in the treaties more than a century earlier but never awarded. "These agreements represent Canadians saying yes to you, acknowledging historical errors and making amends for them," earnestly remarked Prime Minister Brian Mulroney at the outdoor ceremony. "And they are a way for Aboriginals to say yes to Canada." An immensely pleased FSIN Chief Roland Crowe responded that the settlements would help achieve the dream of Aboriginal self-government: "We know this is going to make a different life for all of us." Just how different no one could predict at the time. Premier Roy Romanow readily admitted, though, that Saskatchewan had to embrace its Aboriginal people or the province's future would be compromised, if not lost. "We have great reason to be proud— great reason to celebrate," he told the audience that day. "We're acknowledging our shared destiny."[1]

One of the last things that the new Romanow government needed upon assuming office in November 1991 was new spending commitments, like the provincial share of Treaty Land Entitlement. The NDP had won the recent election by making no major promises, except that a Romanow government could be counted upon to repair the damage wrought by nine years of Tory rule. "Let the word go forth from every corner of our province tonight," a triumphant Romanow had declared the night of his massive victory at the polls, "that Saskatchewan is back."[2] A more fitting diagnosis of the situation was provided by former finance minister Janice MacKinnon when she observed that the new government had "inherited a province on its knees."[3] According to a special Financial Management Review (or Gass) Commission, the Devine government had run up provincial debt from zero in the spring of 1982 to a staggering $8.865 billion by October 1991. In addition, bad investments and bad loans brought the debt load to $14.8 billion, giving Saskatchewan the dubious distinction of having the highest per capita debt in the country. Standard and Poor's, the New York–based credit-rating agency, put the crisis into perspective when it reported that the galloping debt represented 180 per cent of the province's annual revenue. The response was the immediate downgrading of Saskatchewan's credit rating.[4] More bad news followed in the months ahead. "Ours was not a known script with a known ending," MacKinnon would later admit. "It was a drama that unfolded as the demands of the situation quickly forced us to choose and act."[5]

Premier Romanow made the slaying of the debt his government's top priority and appointed a small war cabinet to come up with a plan of attack. Gone was the optimism that had animated the province since the end of the Second World War, replaced by a cheerless sense of duty to try to restore fiscal credibility for the sake of future generations. In his 1993 New Year's address to the Saskatoon Chamber of Commerce, Romanow warned, "We've got to beat this inherited monster ... threatening to devour our programs and our objectives."[6] This message, and the tax increases, program reviews, and

NDP leader Roy Romanow does some shadow boxing at a 1991 election rally. CANADIAN PRESS

service reductions that went along with it, disappointed many left-wing NDP supporters who expected a return to the largesse of the 1970s. Many wondered why the Romanow government was so obsessed with the debt when it was the legacy of the Devine years. Others suggested that the premier was turning his back on the party's heritage and traditions.

The fifty-two-year-old Romanow, however, had served a long political apprenticeship since entering the legislature in 1967 and knew that a return to the Blakeney "big government" ways was no longer possible in the new economic climate. He also drew inspiration from the practices of past CCF governments under Douglas and Lloyd, which had placed balancing the books ahead of new programs.[7] Romanow's resolve to clean up Saskatchewan's financial mess and restore confidence in government was at no time more apparent than at a NDP cabinet meeting in early 1993 when finance minister MacKinnon, nicknamed "Combat Barbie" because of her steely toughness, revealed that the new budget would contain even deeper spending cuts. When some frustrated ministers argued that the province should default on its debt, an angry premier stormed out of the meeting threatening to call an election to put in place a government willing to deal with the fiscal crisis. The next day, Romanow visited Lieutenant-Governor Sylvia Fedoruk to brief her on the situation, a move that brought dissident members of the caucus scurrying

Roy Romanow's decision to focus on the provincial debt disappointed
some left-wing party members. ALAN KING

back into line.[8] This unity of purpose meant that the NDP could focus its energies on grappling with the debt for as long as necessary—just as the Douglas
government had patiently waited years before introducing medicare.

Going hand-in-hand with deficit reduction was the government's plan to
stimulate the economy. Its "Partnership for Renewal" policy statement
marked a distinct break from the Blakeney period when the government
encouraged economic activity through Crown corporations and imposed
hefty royalties on the resource sector. In fact, Premier Romanow conceded
that some elements of the Devine revolution were here to stay when he indicated that the new government had no plans to reverse the privatization of
the Potash Corporation of Saskatchewan or raise royalty rates on oil and gas
production. Nor would the NDP be embarking on any more risky megapro-
jects, but would do its best to reduce the province's liability in the Regina and
Lloydminster heavy oil upgraders, even ending its financial involvement.
What the Romanow government proposed instead, seemingly taking a page
from the Thatcher era, was to work with the small business community. The
private sector would create the jobs, while the government would facilitate
the enterprises by providing infrastructure support, training a skilled workforce, introducing special tax incentives, or seeking out other potential investors. This partnership initiative was certainly modest when measured against

government ambitions in the 1970s and 1980s, but it resulted in some impressive economic growth. The deficit monster, at the same time, was wrestled to the ground faster than anticipated because of a booming national economy, and by 1995 the government tabled a balanced budget.[9]

Dealing with the red ink took a toll on Saskatchewan. The population slide that had begun during the final years of Conservative rule had eased somewhat by the mid-1990s, but the province was never able to move beyond the one million threshold. Some sarcastically suggested that the province's number one export was people, not wheat, and that rural residents should be classified as an endangered species.[10] Saskatchewan's focus on its debt problems did not mean, however, that it ceased to play a role in national life. Drawing on his constitution-building experience in the early 1980s, Premier Romanow actively campaigned for the "no" side during the 1995 Quebec independence referendum, as well as fervently pushing the idea of a "social union" contract when the federal government made deep cuts to social program transfers to the provinces. He would later go on to head a royal commission investigation into health care.[11]

Saskatchewan's cultural contributions also made national, sometimes international, news. The Saskatoon-based Northern Pikes topped the pop music charts in 1990 with their double-platinum "Snow in June" album, while Regina rocker Colin James won two Juno awards the following year. In 1995, Buffy Sainte-Marie was inducted into the Juno Hall of Fame, joining Joni Mitchell who had been installed fourteen years earlier. Poet Anne Szumigalski, regarded by many as the matriarch of Saskatchewan writing, was also recognized. The British-born Szumigalski immigrated to Saskatoon in 1951 and served as mentor to generations of aspiring writers over tea in her home while helping to found the Saskatchewan Writers' Guild and *Grain* magazine. In 1995, after two previous nominations, she won the Governor General's Literary Award for poetry for *Voice*. Following her 1999 death, one friend observed that Szumigalski's life and work demonstrated "that our stories are as good as those from anywhere, and that home-grown talent is as worthy of attention as that from anywhere else."[12]

The province also continued to send promising hockey talent to the pro leagues. One of the most famous local stars was Kelvington's Wendel Clark, who was captain of the Toronto Maple Leafs during the early 1990s. Upon his retirement, he held the Leaf record for playoff goals, but failed to help secure for Toronto that elusive Stanley Cup. The Saskatchewan Roughriders were equally unlucky and were trounced during one of their rare appearances in the Grey Cup final in 1997. Interestingly, the football club has never won the national championship when the NDP has been in office. Saskatoon-born speed skater Catriona LeMay Doan, who carried the Canadian flag into the opening ceremonies at the 2002 Winter Olympics, had no such problem. When Catriona skated to victory in the five-hundred-metre event at Salt Lake City, she became the first and only Canadian to defend a gold medal at any Olympic Games.

The NDP government's adept handling of the debt crisis, ahead of other provincial governments struggling with similar predicaments, prompted one commentator to joke, "News that Saskatchewan might still have a future was welcome indeed."[13] That future, though, was to be profoundly different from the comfortable image of the province. In the national consciousness, sleepy Saskatchewan was frozen in time, a land of wheat fields, grid roads, and country elevators, where nothing important ever happened and anybody with talent or ambition left to make their mark elsewhere. Journalist Peter Gzowski, who got his start in Moose Jaw, called it the most Canadian of provinces. The reality was an increasingly urbanized society with a diverse economic base and a rich cultural life, trying to come to terms with its agricultural past and Aboriginal population. Indeed, on the eve of the new century, the province was grappling with the twin challenges of meeting the needs of its growing Aboriginal community and maintaining a decaying rural Saskatchewan.[14]

It had been initially assumed in 1905, if not quietly hoped, that Indians would disappear from the Saskatchewan landscape and become little more

Saskatoon's Catriona LeMay Doan was the first Canadian woman to defend her gold-medal victory at consecutive Olympic Games. CANADIAN PRESS

than a historical footnote. But the projected growth and age profile for the Indian population at the end of the twentieth century made such racist attitudes unrealistic, if not untenable. According to the 1991 census, Indians constituted 8 per cent of the provincial population, the largest proportion for any Canadian province. And their numbers were projected to climb exponentially. One federal study predicted that the Indian population in Saskatchewan could double in just twenty-five years, from 78,000 to 154,000, bringing its share of the provincial population up to almost 14 per cent. It would also be a significantly younger group than the dominant white society. Almost one in three Indians in 2015 was expected to be under eighteen, while some 60 per cent would be in their working years (eighteen to sixty-four).[15] This demographic profile had parallels with the early twentieth century when hundreds of thousands of land-hungry settlers invaded the province, swamping the Indian population. Now the First Nations population was in the ascendancy.

Tommy Douglas was the first of several successive premiers to confront the so-called "Indian problem" in the province. The record was one of mixed success. In reflecting on his term in office from 1971 to 1982, Allan Blakeney confessed that his "greatest disappointment" was his government's failure to advance Aboriginal/non-Aboriginal relations in the province. "I early reached the conclusion that white society was not going to solve the problems of native people," he wrote in 1997. "Our job, as a government, was to give them the tools and let them finish the job."[16]

Giving them the tools now fell to Roy Romanow. The new premier had known prejudice first-hand as an immigrant kid from the working-class district of Saskatoon. Romanow's Ukrainian father, Michael, had immigrated to the city in 1927, and it was not until he was secure in his job as a section man for the CPR that he sent for his family in 1938. Roy was born the following year. Although educated as a lawyer at the University of Saskatchewan and working part-time for CKOM radio and CFQC television, he felt like an outsider whenever he left the familiar confines of the west side.[17] Romanow would draw on this experience, knowing full well that Indians could not be treated the same way as continental Europeans had been in the past. In his view, politics was about co-operation and community, and it was the duty of the government to work out a practical relationship with the Indian community, whereby they would be given the opportunity to participate as full partners in all aspects of Saskatchewan life.[18] Treaty Land Entitlement was an integral part of this process and was consequently supported by the Romanow government even though the province was responsible for 30 per cent of settlement costs at a time when it was cutting back in other areas. In 1989, wanting to avoid expensive claim-by-claim litigation because of the failed

Saskatchewan formula, the Mulroney government and the FSIN had sought a comprehensive agreement by establishing the Office of the Treaty Commissioner. Former Saskatoon mayor Cliff Wright was handed the delicate job of settling the claims of more than two dozen bands, mostly from the Battleford and Qu'Appelle areas, and devised a new compensation formula that formed the basis of three-way negotiations between the FSIN and the Canadian and Saskatchewan governments.

The framework agreement, signed at Wanuskewin three years later, provided participating bands with money to buy land of their own choosing in rural or urban areas, including privately held property, on a willing-buyer/ willing-seller basis. It was estimated that the deal could effectively double the land base held by First Nations. Reserves made up only 1.5 per cent of the province's total area at the time. Treaty Land Entitlement offered the prospect of bands playing a more direct, meaningful role in the province—to the benefit of themselves and society at large—by providing them with an array of potential economic opportunities.[19] "We want to work with other groups," observed Chief Denton George of the Ochapowace band near Broadview. "That was always our intention from the time the treaties were signed."[20]

Many in Saskatchewan society, however, did not share the sentiments

Prime Minister Brian Mulroney and Premier Roy Romanow watch as Chief Roland Crowe of the Saskatchewan Federation of Indian Nations signs the Treaty Land Entitlement Agreement at Wanuskewin in September 1992. SASKATCHEWAN ARCHIVES BOARD STAR-PHOENIX COLLECTION S-SP-3644C.6-6A

spoken at the Wanuskewin ceremonies. Rural municipal officials expressed alarm about the potential loss of tax revenue on band-owned property. Others simply did not want Indians living next to them or taking over local businesses.[21] There was also a strong belief that Indians were asking for more than originally agreed to in the treaties and that the province should not be obliged to pay for past wrongs.[22] The FSIN tried to defuse this misunderstanding by encouraging TLE bands to hold town-hall-style meetings to educate the general public about the agreements. In fact, it took two years before the first TLE purchase of private rural land—a symbolic 129 hectares in the Spiritwood area—was made by the Witchekan Lake band in October 1994.[23]

What ultimately helped dissipate some of the resistance was the promise of millions of dollars pouring into communities. The Neekaneet band near Maple Creek, for example, gave the local beef industry a boost when it bought twenty-eight thousand acres in the Cypress Hills in 1995 and stocked the land with several hundred head of cattle.[24] A far less ambitious but no less significant venture was the entry of Muskoday First Nation into market gardening to take advantage of the highway traffic near Prince Albert. "We sat and we watched economic opportunity go through one side of the reserve and out the other," admitted a member of the band, "without capturing any of those dollars."[25]

This shared destiny that Premier Romanow had talked about at Wanuskewin did not include gambling. Just three days after the TLE ceremonies, the NDP government warned the White Bear band not to proceed with its plan to open a casino on its reserve southeast of Regina. But Chief Bernard Shepherd was not prepared to back down, insisting that First Nations had the right to set up casinos on their reserves without government approval and that gambling revenue would be used to improve reserve life, starting with jobs. "The issue is not about gaming, it is about jurisdiction," he fired back at the government. "White Bear Band wants to ... create employment not ... conflict."[26] The white community at nearby Carlyle publicly stood by the Indians because of the economic spinoffs at stake.

The Bear Claw Casino opened at the end of February 1993, only to be raided by the RCMP, who carried away the gaming machines and closed its doors. But the issue would not go away since bands believed that they had the right under self-government to operate casinos without a provincial permit. By November 1995, the Romanow government and the FSIN had hammered out an agreement that would enable a new Saskatchewan Indian Gaming Authority to establish four casinos anywhere in the province. One year later, Bear Claw Casino officially became the first casino in Canada on reserve land. The premier was circumspect about his government's backtracking on gambling. "My job is to try to build bridges," he stated when the deal was announced. "What we have to do is seek accommodation and compromise."[27] Unfortunately, the jobs and revenue came at the cost of hundreds of addicted gamblers and thousands of ruined lives, not to mention government dependence on the windfall profits.

The government was not so accommodating when it came to Indian access to game resources. In mid-September 1994, while a Canadian Forces helicopter hovered over a hunting camp on Watapi Lake in northwestern Saskatchewan, two military policemen and two provincial conservation officers rappelled to the ground and charged a surprised James Sylvester and Henry Catarat with shooting a moose inside the Primrose Lake Air Weapons Range. The two Dene men from the Buffalo River reserve at Dillon were exercising their Treaty 10 right to hunt—a right seemingly confirmed in the 1930 Natural Resources Transfer Agreement when Saskatchewan finally secured control of its provincial lands and resources from the federal government.[28] Provincial Court Judge Jeremy Nightingale agreed, quashing the charges in August 1998 and ordering restitution for the confiscated moose. Two years later, however, the Saskatchewan Court of Appeal summarily overturned the acquittal on the grounds that the Dene had no right of access to the region, even though the range had been part of their traditional territory for generations. The Supreme Court of Canada later refused to hear the case. In this instance, neither Regina nor Ottawa was interested in negotiation but preferred a legal precedent for keeping the Dene from hunting on provincial lands leased by the federal government.[29]

The Métis, numbering around eighty thousand at the beginning of the 1990s, had even more difficulty securing recognition of what they regarded as their traditional rights. Although the Métis had been formally recognized in the 1982 Constitution Act as one of Canada's three Aboriginal peoples, the federal government consistently maintained that any Métis claim to land had been forever extinguished through scrip disbursements in the late nineteenth and early twentieth centuries. And without a land base, the Métis argued, it was difficult to pursue self-government. In 1993, in a concerted effort to make some headway, the Métis Society of Saskatchewan renamed itself the Métis Nation of Saskatchewan (MNS) and adopted a constitution that declared the right to self-government. That same year, it reached a framework agreement with the provincial and federal governments aimed at devolving programs and services to the Métis, as well as providing for greater Métis control over certain institutions and communities.[30] A Saskatchewan judge, for example, set a precedent in June 1993 when he used a sentencing circle made up of members of the Saskatoon Métis community to determine the fate of a Métis man who had been convicted of robbing a gas station attendant.[31]

But there were limits to what was possible because of the continuing debate

Lieutenant-Governor Sylvia Fedoruk visits a classroom in La Ronge. S. FEDORUK

over which level of government had jurisdiction over the Métis. This uncertainty prompted the frustrated Métis to turn to the courts to secure their rights. In Beauval in March 1994, the MNS filed a statement of claim to much of the land in the northwestern part of the province, a Métis traditional area dating back to the early days of the fur trade. The MNS contended that the 1906–07 scrip commissions did not negate Métis title to this territory and that the Métis presence in the area had been deliberately ignored when the air weapons range was established in 1953. "Why are we excluded once again?" asked Métis leader Clem Chartier. "It does not feel good to be on the outside looking in."[32] The civil suit remains bogged down in a protracted research phase.

Finding answers to the problems of rural Saskatchewan was equally demanding, even though successive governments had valiantly tried since the end of the Second World War to slow the pace of depopulation and preserve the family farm. The latest census continued to document how the province's agriculture industry was taking on a new, barely recognizable form. Between 1986 and 1991, nearly twenty-five thousand people left rural Saskatchewan; most, in fact, left the province entirely, making Saskatchewan one of the few provinces in the country to lose people. Fewer than 50 per cent of those born in Saskatchewan still lived here by 2001, another provincial distinction.

Not unexpectedly, the number of farms also declined between 1986 and 1991—by more than 2,500 to 60,840. This Saskatchewan farm crisis, as a

Regina sociologist has rightly pointed out, was really "a crisis in *family* farming."[33] Those who quit farming during these years were usually middle-aged couples, often with children, who found the odds of making a decent living unbeatable. Getting out, though, proved painful. "Quitting farming is not just a case of losing a job," one recent study has observed, "it is a lost way of life ... the place you live, the life you lead, your family heritage."[34] Those who managed to hang on were weighed down with doubt and anxiety, leading to family violence, marital breakups, substance abuse, and suicide. The NDP government responded by establishing a Farm Stress Line so that people could get anonymous, over-the-phone counselling. One of the hardest things for families was coping with the shame of losing their farm to the creditors. "Everybody knows," related a woman who wanted to keep her identity confidential, "everybody finds out that *you* are the ones that are in trouble with the bank. And it's devastating."[35] Another informant likened the process to a slow, painful death. In the end, the anger usually turned to despair and then resignation. "There was no point in trying to keep it going," recounted Gail Forbes who farmed with her husband, Murray, near Senlac. "The government wants to see big business take over farming. It's really very sad, but they don't care about the family farm."[36]

Forbes was right. Farming had become "agribusiness." The average farm size in 1991 was 1,091 acres or just under seven quarter sections, almost three times larger than the average farm at the start of the Depression when there were twice as many farms. Even more significant, though, was the emergence of superproducers. Whereas the top 5 per cent of the province's farmers controlled 16.7 per cent of the acreage in production in 1976, they cropped 19.8 per cent twenty years later. Even greater concentrations were underway in cattle, chicken, and hog production, reducing more farms each year to marginal status.[37] Indeed, it was rare to find a farm in the 1990s that produced enough income to support a family. Nor were the federal and provincial governments willing to make up the shortfall by providing Saskatchewan farmers with the same generous subsidy support enjoyed by their American and European competitors. One in three farm men and two of every three farm women consequently spent more than 50 per cent of their work hours on off-farm employment. More men would have likely worked at other jobs but they lacked the skills and education for the new job market. Age was also a factor. Farmers on average were in their late fifties and were not expected to retire because many had used up all their savings to keep the farm going. This same persistence had kept their ancestors on their homestead; now, it meant that Saskatchewan producers constituted one of the oldest farm populations in Canada.[38]

Agriculture was also more diversified, driven by farmers as much as by the markets. In 1994, for the first time in provincial history, canola dethroned wheat as the leading cash crop in Saskatchewan. A more telling sign of the change, though, was the selection of Gary and Bonnie Meier of Ridgedale as the 1993 Outstanding Young Farmer Award recipients. Having once specialized in large volume commodity crops, the couple now grew oilseeds, pedigreed grain, and pulse and forage crops, as well as raising leaf-cutter bees for alfalfa production. "If we are going to continue in a farming operation we are going to have to figure out how to do it on our own," Gary observed at the award ceremony. "Those who don't figure it out won't be here and will be doing something else in five years."[39] It would be a mistake, however, to suggest that diversification became the rule in the 1990s. Farmers began to alternate legume and cereal crops on their fields, but the greatest change was in improved varieties of traditional grains and oilseeds. There were only about one thousand certified organic producers in Saskatchewan, out of fifty thousand farmers, and the number going into niche markets, like mustard and other spices, also remained small.[40] Many continued to practice large-scale, high-input farming, taking advantage of genetically modified crops, especially canola.

Off-farm employment, along with new agricultural practices and products, kept families on the land, but it allowed little time for other activities, such as volunteer work, especially when couples had to juggle jobs with running the farm. The loss of people also invariably reduced the number of services, such as banks, and threatened to close schools, elevators, churches, and hospitals. It was a simple truism that rural communities largely owed their existence to the wheat economy, and as agriculture rapidly changed, small towns and villages atrophied. Social structures broke down, as did the sense of community.[41]

Country residents, however, refused to accept quietly any retrenchment in provincial rural services and expenditures, as if their needs were less important. As part of cost-cutting in the 1992–93 budget, the Romanow government was prepared to let one thousand kilometres of paved roads revert to gravel but sheepishly withdrew the proposal in the face of stiff rural opposition. The NDP also backed away from a provincial task force report to change the structure of local government when the Saskatchewan Association of Rural Municipalities blasted the idea. Unlike its handling of the debt, it seemed as if the Romanow government lacked the courage to stick with tough decisions affecting rural Saskatchewan. But as one observer pointedly asked at the time: "If services had to be cut, where and how would this be done?"[42]

One thing the provincial government would not do was pay the full costs of the new Gross Revenue Insurance Plan (GRIP) that had been introduced by the Mulroney government to help Canadian farmers at the insistence of

More than one thousand farmers demanded help from the NDP government during a protest at the Saskatchewan legislature in 1999. CANADIAN PRESS

former premier Grant Devine. The NDP found the program too costly and changed the coverage provisions retroactively—after the official notification deadline and after Saskatchewan producers had already made their seeding plans. In protest, irate farmers hanged an effigy of the agriculture minister, Bernie Wiens, outside the legislature the opening day of the spring 1992 session. The blunder cost the NDP support in rural Saskatchewan.[43]

The government tried to do a better job defending the province's farmers when it came to the Crow benefit. Under the 1984 federal revisions to the historic Crow's Nest Pass freight rates, prairie farmers had been paid a transportation subsidy. But in 1995, the Liberal government of Jean Chrétien, struggling with the federal debt and wanting to meet its obligations under new international trade agreements, moved to kill the benefit entirely. Saskatchewan farmers stood to lose $300 million annually in freight-rate subsidies. The Romanow government complained loudly about how higher freight rates would bring about another round of farm bankruptcies, but it made no difference. Farming was just another Canadian business to Ottawa policy-makers, and producers had to adjust to the new conditions, and quickly, or become another casualty.[44]

The other controversial initiative during the early 1990s—this time, a provincial measure—was health care reform. Upon taking office, the Romanow government talked about completing the Douglas medicare legacy: Saskatchewan residents would not only enjoy universal access to medical care, but be encouraged to live healthy lifestyles in order to reduce the incidence of sickness and disease.[45] This "wellness model," as it was called, was expected to lead to a more "rationalized" health care system. But the proposed changes went beyond mere tinkering. Hospital expansion under the Blakeney and Devine governments had given the province more hospital beds per capita than any other country in the world—77.9 beds per thousand compared to the Canadian average of 30.7 beds. Saskatchewan even had more hospitals than any other province except Ontario.[46] Servicing the debt now took precedence over operating these facilities, and the convenient rationale was the continuing decline in rural numbers and the fact that the most serious cases were sent to Regina or Saskatoon anyway.

In March 1993, the government introduced the revolutionary Health Districts Act, which replaced the more than one hundred hospital boards with some thirty health care regions. It also announced shortly thereafter the closure of twelve hundred hospital beds over the next three years, followed by the bombshell that more than fifty acute-care hospitals in rural areas would shut their doors by the end of the year. Outraged rural residents staged a thousand-strong protest rally on the steps of the legislature, directing their anger at health minister Louise Simard, the "Queen of Mediscare." But even though Saskatchewan prided itself as the birthplace of medicare, there would be no turning back, as the government introduced closure to speed passage of the health reform package.[47]

The Progressive Conservatives condemned these policies as "Romanow's rural revenge." This championing of rural Saskatchewan was the same strategy shamelessly employed by Grant Devine during the last few years of his premiership, and it continued to resonate with farmers and townspeople, especially wherever the local hospital was slated for closure. It also saved the Tories from complete collapse after the devastating 1991 election and enabled them to limp along even after Devine had stepped down at the end of 1993 and the leadership remained vacant for almost two years. In November 1994, Bill Boyd was elected the new leader by telephone ballot, a first for a provincial party, and faced a provincial election the following June. It was expected that the fraud convictions of several senior members of the former government would deliver the Tories into political oblivion, but they managed to hold onto five seats with almost 18 per cent of the popular vote. "It's been a great night," confessed a beaming Boyd, "because really, we're not supposed to be here."[48] All of the seats were in rural ridings.

The other surprise in the 1995 election was the relatively poor showing of the Liberals. No one doubted that the NDP would secure another large majority, given its impressive record in restoring the province's finances, but the Liberals had been touted as successors to the demoralized Conservatives and were expected to win as many as a third of the seats in the legislature. Yet even though the Liberals were the only party to enjoy an increase in popular support (35 per cent of the popular vote in 1995), they captured just eleven ridings out of a possible fifty-eight. These results made the once mighty Liberals the official opposition for the first time since the mid-1970s and held out the possibility of continued party renewal. But many Liberal insiders had expected much more and turned on leader Lynda Haverstock. The maneuvering came to a climax at the November 1995 convention, where several caucus members threatened to sit as independents unless the leader stepped aside. When only 52 per cent of the delegates voted in favour of her leadership, Haverstock resigned rather than deal with the constant backroom scheming against her. "Now they're going to have to do something with all that destructive energy," she lashed out at her critics.[49] Five years later, Haverstock was a popular appointment as the province's second female lieutenant-governor.

It was a new provincial party that benefitted from the implosion of the

Lynda Haverstock is sworn in as lieutenant-governor. CANADIAN PRESS

Liberals. In August 1997, four Conservative and four Liberal members formed a coalition in the legislature, known as the Saskatchewan Party (SP). The seven men and one woman, all representing rural Saskatchewan, had concluded that a new political alliance offered the best hope of defeating the NDP. So too did the Progressive Conservatives. Treading water and in desperate need of a life preserver, the party had become synonymous with corruption and might never form another government again. Their federal counterpart had also been crushed in the 1993 general election and seemed headed for extinction at the hands of the western-based Reform Party. It made sense, then, when the Conservative executive decided in November 1997 to put the party into hibernation, a kind of Rip van Winkle sleep, to be possibly revived a decade later. The Saskatchewan Party option not only promised a fresh start for the Tories, but immediate status as the official opposition since it controlled more seats than the Liberals in the legislature.[50] But the new coalition and new name made no difference to the NDP. One of Romanow's favourite sports was trashing the Conservatives for leaving the province in a financial quagmire in 1991. He now took great delight in reminding the public at every opportunity that a Tory was a Tory and even feigned difficulty remembering the new party's name in the legislature.

The creation of the Saskatchewan Party and the elections of 1999 and 2003 completed a fundamental shift in provincial politics that had started during the latter part of Grant Devine's premiership. For almost six decades, the political debate had raged back and forth over whether private enterprise or socialism could best meet the needs of the province and its people. But in the late 1980s and early 1990s, Devine staked his political future on rural Saskatchewan and its way of life, a position that came naturally for the premier given his background and populist style. This approach to Saskatchewan politics exacerbated the cleavage between cities and the countryside, as evidenced in the 1995 election results. The NDP handily secured a second term, but most seats—forty-two—were in urban ridings, including twenty-two of the twenty-three seats in Regina and Saskatoon.

The Saskatchewan Party, under its first leader Elwin Hermanson, a Beechy farmer, lay preacher, and former federal Reform MP, moved to capitalize on this phenomenon by speaking out for rural Saskatchewan and giving voice to its needs, its hopes, and most of all, its deep sense of alienation after a quarter century of profound and painful change. In the September 1999 election, the new party campaigned on who could best represent the interests of agriculture, an Achilles heel for the NDP which seemed unable to deal effectively with the most recent farming crisis.[51] This deliberate targeting of rural Saskatchewan produced the province's second coalition government since 1929. Although the Saskatchewan Party received 40 per cent of the popular vote to the NDP's 39 per cent, Romanow held onto power by bringing three Liberals, including leader Jim Melenchuk, into his government. The October 2003 election was little different. This time, the two parties came down to a photo finish, with the NDP, now led by Lorne Calvert, a former Moose Jaw United Church minister, prevailing by a mere two seats (thirty to twenty-eight). Once again, though, rural voters largely embraced the Saskatchewan Party as the group most able to represent them in Regina.[52]

The 2003 election marked the first time in provincial history that neither of Canada's two original parties, the Liberals and Conservatives, held a seat in the Saskatchewan legislature. In fact, politics in the province were dominated by two distinctly homegrown parties—a throwback to the first years of the province when Frederick Haultain, the former territorial premier and first opposition leader, argued that his Provincial Rights party could best defend the interests of Saskatchewan. What differed from the last century was the inability of a party to form the government despite capturing most of the rural seats. For the better part of the twentieth century, the party that represented the province's farming community unfailingly assumed office. The dramatic decline of agriculture, combined with the steady growth of the big city, however, turned this situation on its head and kept the Saskatchewan Party from office. The province's four largest cities (Regina, Saskatoon, Moose Jaw, and Prince Albert) had twenty-seven of the fifty-eight seats in the legislature. And as the countryside continued to lose people, the importance and influence of the urban vote would only grow.[53]

What had not changed, though, was the predominantly male makeup of the legislature. Saskatchewan women were still underrepresented in the province's political life. Janice MacKinnon has recounted how Roy Romanow boasted about appointing the first female finance minister in Canada, even joking that the best men in his cabinet were women.[54] But by the beginning of the new century, only twelve women, representing 21 per cent of the members, sat in the legislature. One wonders whether the shabby treatment of Lynda Haverstock was a factor.

Aboriginal representation was even worse. In 1999, only two Aboriginals, Keith Goulet and Buckley Belanger, both representing the province's north, were elected for the NDP. Not only were few Aboriginal candidates recruited by the three provincial parties (6 of the 206), but they were restricted to ridings with large Aboriginal populations. Joan Beatty, an Aboriginal woman and NDP cabinet minister, has since replaced Goulet following his retirement from provincial politics in 2003, while Denis Allchurch represents the Rosthern-Shellbrook constituency for the Saskatchewan Party. Representation by other visible minorities has been non-existent. Maybe the province's political leaders need to look to the Saskatchewan Roughriders for inspira-

CBC journalist Peter Gzowski broadcast his last *Morningside* show from Moose Jaw.
CANADIAN PRESS

tion. Roy Shivers and Danny Barrett are the only Black general manager and coach in professional football—anywhere at anytime. Two researchers have suggested that the lack of diversity in the legislature makes a mockery of the provincial motto, "From many peoples, strength."[55]

In 1993, Tory Rick Swenson derided the adjustment of the province's constituency boundaries to reflect the new political might of urban centres as "rural cleansing."[56] But it was hard to dispute the new reality. By 2001, two out of every three people lived in an urban setting, a complete reversal of the situation only half a century earlier. Regina (178,225) and Saskatoon (196,811) had achieved complete metropolitan supremacy. They were five times larger than their nearest urban challengers, Prince Albert (34,291) and Moose Jaw (32,131), and continued to grow at the expense of smaller centres. The dominance of the two cities was reflected in provincial workforce statistics; there were four people employed in service industries for every one person in agriculture. It was also apparent in the downtown skylines, large modern facilities, and number of new subdivisions—in some cases, occupying areas that had been slated for development during the pre-Great War boom.

Regina, as provincial capital and headquarters for several Crown corporations, had a more built-up downtown core featuring several large office towers. Saskatoon, on the other hand, was not only numerically larger, but prided itself as the more attractive—the "Paris of the prairies" according to the lyrics of a Tragically Hip song. Most recently, Saskatoon has also begun to sell itself as "science city" in recognition of Canada's greatest post-war science project, the country's first synchrotron on the University of Saskatchewan campus. These labels, however, could not disguise the fact that larger Saskatchewan urban centres, like cities elsewhere, had taken on a sameness as American multinational chain stores forced the closure of local, often family-run, businesses and placed their distinctive advertising footprint on the urban landscape. Today, there is little to distinguish Regina's Albert Street from Saskatoon's Eighth Street or Prince Albert's Second Avenue and the shopping malls are virtual carbon copies.

What many Saskatchewan urban centres also had in common was a sizable and growing Aboriginal contingent. Indian and Métis people had been moving into cities since the end of the Second World War and by 2001 constituted about 10 per cent of the population in Regina and Saskatoon, and as much as 20 per cent in North Battleford and 30 per cent in Prince Albert. It was also a young population: the 1996 census found that 41 per cent of the Aboriginal population in the province's two largest cities was under the age of fifteen. Such a large Aboriginal presence was hard to ignore, but theirs was a world that was largely separate from mainstream urban society. At the public hearings before the Royal Commission on Aboriginal Peoples, Robin Bellamy of the Saskatoon Friendship Inn described "an inner city culture for Aboriginal peoples ... a culture of prostitution, substance abuse, physical abuse, verbal abuse, and poverty."[57] Sadly, though, the hand-wringing over the rural-urban split tended to obscure the festering Aboriginal/non-Aboriginal divide in the province's cities.

Prince Albert, as one of Saskatchewan's oldest communities with a long historical relationship with the Indian and Métis of the area, might have been expected to have been more open to its large Aboriginal population. But in January 1991, white supremacist Carney Nerland, who ran a gun shop on River Street, shot Leo Lachance, a Cree trapper from the nearby Big River reserve. Lachance's murder and the lenient treatment of the accused, a police informer, led to a public inquiry which reported in November 1993 that it did not find any evidence of organized racism in Prince Albert. The inquiry did conclude, though, that "we are still a long way from being a tolerant society."[58]

The situation in sophisticated Saskatoon was no better. The discovery of the frozen bodies of three Aboriginal men on the outskirts of the city was largely ignored until a poorly-clothed Darrell Night, who had been abandoned by two police officers near the local power station in January 2000, survived to talk about his ordeal. The national attention generated by the "starlight tours," not to mention the sullied reputation of the Saskatoon police force, prompted the provincial government to appoint a Commission on First Nations and Métis Peoples and Justice Reform in November 2002. It remains to be seen, though, how the $2.8-million, two-volume report will be translated into action to help secure Aboriginal justice. Those pushing for greater understanding include Harvard-educated Mary Ellen Turpel-Lafond, who became in 1998 the first Treaty Indian to be appointed to the provincial court of Saskatchewan, and who has drawn attention to the impact of fetal alcohol syndrome.

Dealing with the new provincial landscape proved difficult, sometimes frustrating, for Saskatchewan's two homegrown political parties in the first years of the new century. The Saskatchewan Party's appeal to rural Saskatchewan ignored other areas of provincial society. A return to the old left-right political divide was also not the answer. The party had to learn, just as Thatcher did over medicare and Devine over the privatization of SaskEnergy, that the Saskatchewan electorate had come to identify the province with the principles and programs put in place by the CCF and the NDP.[59] Nor could the new Calvert government be smug, even though it carried the

Premier Lorne Calvert takes part in the blanket toss during a break in the Western Premiers' Conference in Inuvik in July 2004. CANADIAN PRESS

mantle of the CCF legacy and portrayed itself as the only party that could be trusted to do the right thing in adjusting policies to meet changing circumstances. Instead of offering positive, pragmatic change, the NDP refrained from engaging in any meaningful debate about the issues confronting the province, seeming more content with preserving the status quo.[60]

This political jockeying did not mean that solutions could not be found; there were just no easy answers. Saskatchewan could also not expect outside help. The close connection between the province and the governing federal Liberals in the first half of the twentieth century had gone sour since the end of the Second World War and worsened under Liberal leader Jean Chrétien, whose neglect of the region seemed intentional. In the end, then, the people of the province would have to look to themselves and their innovative spirit, as they had repeatedly done in the past, particularly since the Great Depression. Saskatchewan has a history of dealing creatively with challenges, disadvantages, and obstacles. That is what has made the province so special—a gritty resolve to focus on local issues, while maintaining a clear sense of the wider world, and coming up with new strategies in keeping with the irrepressible Saskatchewan spirit.

A ROAD MAP
TO THE FUTURE

FREDERICK HAULTAIN THOUGHT BIG. When the territorial premier debated the future of the North-West Territories at Indian Head in December 1901, he attacked the federal plan to "cut this country up into little provinces" and called instead for one large province. "Are you afraid of the proposal?" he toyed with his audience that day. "Are you afraid to be part of a province exceeding all others in area, in population, and in resources? Are you staggered at the realization of your splendid prospects?"[1] Haultain never got his wish in 1905, but the new province of Saskatchewan was no less confident about its destiny. Indeed, if galloping population growth and wheat production in the early twentieth century were any indication, then Saskatchewan seemed well on its way to greatness. The future would just have to catch up.

A century later, Saskatchewan faces a much different, more difficult future, thanks to the peculiar provincial situation where there is both a growing young Aboriginal population and a declining, aging non-Aboriginal population.[2] These circumstances, certain to become even more pronounced over the next few decades, threaten to push and pull the province in different directions. At the very least, they offer interesting challenges, all the more so when the loss of the family farm and rural depopulation are factored into the equation. This time, though, it is the province that will have to catch up, since the future will not wait. Nor are there any ready answers. As Terry Mountjoy, Regina's manager of social development, philosophically commented in direct contrast to Haultain's earlier bravado, "There is no clear road map to the future. The path will not be *found*. It must be *created*."[3]

One of the big challenges for the province will be retaining people. At one time, Saskatchewan was the third most populous province after Ontario and Quebec. But those days are long past; Saskatchewan has slipped below the one-million population mark since October 2001 and seems unable to reverse the downward trend.[4] Regina, Saskatoon, and other large provincial cities will continue to grow, but at the expense of rural areas which seem to lose people like passengers from a sinking ship. Distance, in the meantime, has once again become a factor in rural lives as the low population density and low demand mean that many services are now available only in larger centres. Indeed, there is a concerted push these days for more school consolidations and some form of regional government to replace the century-old rural municipality system.[5] The limited tax base, on the other hand, prevents local facilities, including roads, from being properly maintained.[6]

The precipitous decline of rural Saskatchewan is a reflection of the changed provincial economy. Over the past century, geography and climate were two constant concerns as farmers grew and marketed crops to feed the world's population. The problem today, though, is that agriculture, what Roy Romanow once called the "heart and soul of this country, the way it was built up,"[7] now makes only a marginal contribution to the provincial economy.[8] Nor does the federal government seem to care about the plight of producers or the place of agriculture in the national economy, and has severely limited assistance. "How many years can you get kicked in the shins before you fall down?" poignantly asked farmer Lilliane Sabiston of Kelliher in a *Globe and Mail* interview about the state of western agriculture during the 2004 harvest.[9]

The environment, not markets, will probably be Saskatchewan farmers' biggest worry in the new century. Global warming, also known as the greenhouse effect, is expected to raise mean temperatures over the western interior by as much as five celsius degrees by 2100, generating more intense weather, in particular increasing the severity of drought.[10] A more immediate problem is the chemically dependent farming that has evolved since the Second World War. Producers now plant herbicide-resistant crops, such as Roundup Ready canola by Monsanto, and spray broad-spectrum, non-selective herbicides to control weeds. Since these chemicals have to be applied throughout the growing season, farmers may be creating a new generation of herbicide-resistant weeds, as well as causing unknown damage to the ecosystem.[11] European customers have also begun to challenge the safety of the genetically modified (GM) products and forced the shelving of the introduction of GM wheat in 2004.

The decline in the relative importance of agriculture does not mean that the provincial economy is any less vulnerable. Next to Ontario, Saskatchewan is the second most dependent province on international trade (about 38 per cent of the provincial GDP), with the United States accounting for a little more than 50 per cent of foreign sales. But even though the range of trade resources is diverse, from potash and energy to grain and beef, and trade is carried on with several countries, the province has no control over international price and demand.[12] In the late 1990s, for example, commodities prices were all down—what is sometimes referred to as "Blakeney's nightmare." Even the loss of a foreign market, such as the prolonged closure of the American border to Canadian beef because of the bovine spongiform encephalopathy (BSE) or "mad cow" crisis in 2003, can have catastrophic consequences for Saskatchewan producers.

Some maintain that the best hope for the province's economic future continues to be greater diversification through provincial incentives. But no amount of forced growth can overcome the natural disadvantages of Saskatchewan's location and market size. Crown corporations have also recently started to operate outside provincial boundaries. These ventures, however, raise justifiable questions about whether the investments would be better made at home, especially when the Crowns have lost money. Another alternative, more in keeping with the new globalized economy, is for the government to facilitate development in co-operation with both private and public enterprises, but not take the lead. A good example is Innovation Place in Saskatoon, a research development park that is making the province one of the world leaders in agricultural biotechnology.

Any new economic development must involve northern Saskatchewan residents and end decades of marginalization during which time the region was treated as little more than a colony by imperial Regina. Had not Frederick Haultain demanded provincehood for similar reasons more than a century earlier? This neglect also extends to the contaminated northern environment; there are at present forty-two abandoned uranium mines and mill sites awaiting decommissioning.[13] Ironically, members of the Clearwater River Dene Nation put up a barricade on Highway 955 in late August 2004 to demand jobs at the $34-million decommissioning of the former Cluff Lake mine to help ease the high unemployment rate at nearby La Loche. "We're wanting a portion of that," explained Chief Roy Cheecham about the importance of the contract to his people. "Not all of it, but a portion of that."[14]

Interior view of the rings at the Canadian Light Source (synchrotron) on the University of Saskatchewan campus. CANADIAN LIGHT SOURCE, UNIVERSITY OF SASKATCHEWAN

The integration of the provincial north will mean jobs. In fact, new jobs must be created throughout Saskatchewan to replace those being lost in agriculture. It is estimated that only 5 per cent of the population now works in agriculture, where it had once employed hundreds of thousands.[15] This quest for new jobs means addressing the fact that Saskatchewan has the least-educated population in Canada. According to the 2001 census, more than one-third of the province's residents had not graduated from high school, while the number of adults twenty-five and older with a university degree was below the national average.[16] Education and training will be needed if the provincial workforce is to participate in the new knowledge-based economy. Otherwise, Saskatchewan might be doomed to become, in the words of University of Saskatchewan economist Eric Howe, the "Mississippi of the North."[17]

By far, though, the most critical issue for Saskatchewan in the new century will be the role and place of the growing Aboriginal population—something that many citizens would rather not think about, let alone deal with. "It is open to question," one expert on the province's political history has observed, "whether the non-Aboriginal people of Saskatchewan fully appreciate the magnitude of the change taking place."[18] As of 2001, Aboriginal people— Indians and Métis—made up almost one in eight of Saskatchewan residents

(13.5 per cent). By 2045, just four decades away, they are projected to account for one in three people. Saskatchewan cannot afford to discount its Aboriginal population, particularly given their lowly place in provincial society, or there will be bigger, more serious problems in the future.[19]

The people of Saskatchewan have started to respond to these many challenges in their typical resourceful fashion, starting with innovative schemes at the community level. Foxford, for example, sponsors an annual snowmobile "poker derby" to support the community hall. In the spring of 2002, Bellegarde held a lottery to predict when a battered car would sink through the melting ice of a local slough; the proceeds were to keep the rink open for another season. Further south at Moosomin, forty men played hockey for twenty-four hours in November 2001 to raise money for a nursing home. That same fall, Arcola lost its rink to a fire and launched an ambitious fund-raising campaign that included the sale of two homemade apple pies for $500 at auction. "The thing is," reasoned Darcy Singleton, president of the rink board, "if you don't rebuild the rink, it's just one more nail in our coffin."[20]

Despite the relentless population decline over the decades, Saskatchewan remains the most rural of the three prairie provinces: 36.7 per cent of the population still resided in rural areas in 1996 compared to only 28.2 and 22.3 per cent for Manitoba and Alberta, respectively. Nor is rural society any less complex, any less vibrant than its urban counterpart—it is certainly not static or one dimensional. What has changed in the new century, however, is that rural and urban residents probably share more in common than at any other time in the province's history because of new technology, such as the Internet and email, and mass consumer culture.[21]

One Alberta political scientist has asked that if rural communities are no longer truly distinctive, then why are they worth protecting?[22] But rural Saskatchewan remains an integral part of the provincial identity and the people there deserve a certain minimum standard of living and basic services. "Keeping small-town Saskatchewan alive," insists Wynyard's mayor Sharon Armstrong, "is critical to everybody's Main Street."[23] Small communities, however, need to find something beyond special fundraising events or there will be winners and losers as the consolidation continues. Educated children need a reason to stay or return.

Co-operative or community-owned initiatives have provided a solution in several instances. Wilkie's Western Grain Pelleting has been such a success that a seed-cleaning facility and inland terminal were opened in the area, while Pound-Maker Agventures operates a large feedlot and ethanol plant in Lanigan. An account of these new rural businesses is appropriately titled *Don't turn out the lights*.[24] Serendipity can also make the difference. Rouleau has found new life as the mythical Saskatchewan town "Dog River" in the new

CTV hit comedy *Corner Gas*, starring Brent Butt of Tisdale. Eastend features Scottie, the remains of a *Tyrannosaurus rex* uncovered in 1994 and now one of the star attractions of the new T.rex Discovery Centre. Predictably, one newspaper reported that Scottie died of boredom. Larger communities have also sought ways to hold onto their dreams. Moose Jaw, forever in the shadow of Regina, has worked hard to revitalize the downtown core through such attractions as the Temple Gardens Mineral Spa, the "Tunnels of Little Chicago," the annual Festival of Words, and the famed Snowbirds at 15 Wing.

There are also promising success stories in northern Saskatchewan. The forestry giant Weyerhaeuser has recently struck a partnership arrangement with three northern Indian bands, the first anywhere in the world for the American multinational. This joint venture replicates the success of the Kitsaki Development Corporation, created by the Lac La Ronge band to work with established companies in mining and transportation or on its own in traditional resource areas, such as the harvesting and marketing of wild rice.[25] Other communities, meanwhile, have taken the "green revolution" to heart. As part of its Sustainable Living Project, Craik has been attracting national attention with its Eco-Centre, a multi-purpose facility built from recycled materials and heated with solar energy. Headlines were also made with the creation of the Old Man on His Back Prairie and Heritage Conservation Area, the former ranch of Peter and Sharon Butala in southwestern Saskatchewan. A herd of buffalo was released in the refuge in 2004, marking their return to the area after over a century. One of the most surprising success stories, though, is that of SaskFilm, whose promotion of the local movie industry is making Saskatchewan the new Hollywood North.[26]

The province is also moving, albeit in a piecemeal fashion, towards a form of Aboriginal self-government. In May 2001, in consultation with Aboriginal organizations, the NDP government released a policy statement, "A Framework for Cooperation," which seeks to address the needs and priorities of urban Aboriginal peoples in four key areas: education and training, workforce development, employment and economic development, and individual and community well-being (such as social services, justice, and housing). The Calvert government also announced in September 2004 the future creation of a separate Department of First Nations and Métis Relations—a move applauded by the Saskatchewan Party. Some have attacked these kinds of initiatives as "race-based inequality" and indicated that everyone should be treated the same. But Aboriginal people in the province have never been treated the same as the non-Aboriginals and the consequences are painfully evident today.

First Nations leaders have also not been helpful at times. During the gambling controversy in 1994, the chief of the Federation of Saskatchewan Indian

The popular television show *Corner Gas* is filmed on location in Rouleau (the mythical town of Dog River). CANADIAN PRESS

Nations charged that casino opponents were "enemies" of Indian people.[27] There have also been instances where Aboriginal accountability, especially concerning the spending of public funds, has been sadly lacking. What ultimately matters, however, is the recognition—*by both sides*—of the urgent need to remove barriers and find common solutions. There needs to be a return to the days of the nineteenth century when white and Aboriginal communities interacted with one another and had something of a shared past.[28] "We need to know what their expectations are," confessed Donna Coleman of Wadena in a May 2001 interview about the town's relationship with the nearby Fishing Lake reserve, "and what we can do to enhance the partnership ... That's where it has to start ... an understanding of ... how we would be able to work together."[29]

This path has been a bumpy one in rural Saskatchewan. Some non-Aboriginal residents, already hurting because of changes wrought by depopulation and consolidation, seem resentful of their Indian neighbours and the "handouts" they enjoy. A good example is the recent compensation awarded victims of sexual abuse at the Gordon Indian Residential School. Although administrator William Starr has admitted that he preyed upon young boys for more than a decade, some in the Punnichy area have questioned the legitimacy of the claims. What they may not understand is that the shattered lives have reached across generations and contribute to Aboriginal poverty and unemployment today.[30]

Treaty Land Entitlement has been another flashpoint. White farmers soon discovered, however, that Indian buyers were willing to offer good prices for land despite the problems in agriculture and have kept values from plummeting. In the Indian Head area, the Carry-the-Kettle band bought thirty-four thousand acres and then leased it back to local farmers.[31] Such initiatives are helping to revive the fortunes of rural Saskatchewan and even greater benefits can be expected if the two sides increasingly try to find new ways of working together.

Cities present another thorny nest of challenges, if only because the Aboriginal population is not considered really part of the urban community. It could even be argued that the situation has parallels with the immigrant experience. In a paper read before the Royal Society of Canada in May 1926, E. H. Oliver, the first historian appointed at the University of Saskatchewan,

Aboriginal architect Harold Cardinal designed the new First Nations University of Canada building in Regina. CARLEEN SHEPHERD, FIRST NATIONS UNIVERSITY OF CANADA

reviewed the contribution of continental Europeans to Saskatchewan society. "We need the artist, the poet, the thinker, the musician, and composer quite as much as the sewer-digger and the track-layer," he concluded. "It is high time we encouraged these people to bring their best to us. Some of them possess rare genius."[32]

What Oliver did not seem to appreciate was that there were poets, thinkers, and musicians among the people who had decided to make the new province their home, but that they faced outright prejudice and heated calls for assimilation from respected people just like him. Indeed, he was speaking just before the anti-immigrant, anti-Catholic Ku Klux Klan stormed through the province. It was not until after the Second World War, after the province had survived the crucible of depression and then war, that "foreigners" with strange-sounding names were widely accepted as part of society and had the opportunity to make the kinds of contributions that Oliver had been talking about. The 1970 appointment of surgeon and decorated war hero Stephen Worobetz as lieutenant-governor was something that Premier Ross Thatcher claimed was long overdue in a province with a large Ukrainian population.[33]

It is unknown when Saskatchewan will have its first viceregal representative of Aboriginal descent. But what must be realized is that Aboriginal people are not only an integral part of the provincial fabric, but can be expected to make a contribution to society in any number of ways—just like Oliver's poets, thinkers, and musicians. Many already are. In 2004 the Canada Council recognized the work of Métis author Maria Campbell with a prestigious Molson Prize for her contribution to Canada's cultural heritage. Educational authorities have also been working with Aboriginal partners to ensure that Aboriginal students secure the training and qualifications to enable them to compete successfully for jobs in the Saskatchewan of the future. The unparalleled success of the First Nations University of Canada is a good beginning. Significant steps have also been taken to ensure that Aboriginal peoples and their history are an integral part of education at all levels.[34]

It has been suggested that the change already underway in the province "offers a new opportunity for Saskatchewan to lead Canada once more."[35] These words might seem overly ambitious, if not unrealistic, given the complex challenges facing the province in the new century. It will take vast amounts of time and energy—but most of all, commitment—to try to find the answers, if there are any. But Saskatchewan has never been a province to think small, never one for believing that things were out of its reach and settling for second place.

One only has to look at the story of the Sandra Schmirler curling rink, four self-described "little girls from Saskatchewan" who dreamed big and

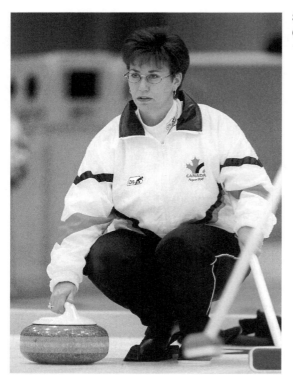

Sandra Schmirler skipped her rink to Olympic gold at the Nagano games in 1998. CANADIAN PRESS

dominated the sport in the 1990s by capturing three Canadian and world championships and Olympic gold at Nagano in 1998.[36] Two years later, the country was rocked with the news of Sandra's death from cancer at age thirty-six. The 6 March funeral was carried live across Canada on CBC Newsworld and CBC national radio, while the afternoon draw of the Brier was delayed in Saskatoon so that the Regina service could be beamed into Saskatchewan Place.

In his eulogy, Brian McCusker, husband of one of Schmirler's teammates, talked about how Sandra never forgot her small-town roots and had to overcome many obstacles even though she made things look easy. He also joked about how the feisty skip would have been impatient with the delay of the Brier, not wanting to miss the first stone. "So Sandra, if you're still listening and haven't switched over to that Brier game," he said, "I want you to know it's that positive outlook on life, that thumbs-up attitude that has touched so many of us." Second Joan McCusker, who had been part of a special tribute to Schmirler at the Brier opening ceremonies, mused about the future and what Sandra's life meant to her. "I think it's safe to say," she told a reporter, "that we can't quit."[37] Neither will Saskatchewan.

Appendix

Politics in Saskatchewan

Premier	Party	Term
Walter Scott	Liberal	1905–1916
William M. Martin	Liberal	1916–1922
Charles A. Dunning	Liberal	1922–1926
James G. Gardiner	Liberal	1926–1929
James T. M. Anderson	Conservative-Progressive Coalition	1929–1934
James G. Gardiner	Liberal	1934–1935
William John Patterson	Liberal	1935–1944
Tommy Douglas	CCF	1944–1961
Woodrow S. Lloyd	NDP	1961–1964
W. Ross Thatcher	Liberal	1964–1971
Allan Blakeney	NDP	1971–1982
Grant Devine	Progressive Conservative	1982–1991
Roy Romanow	NDP (coalition with Libs. from 1999)	1991–2001
Lorne Calvert	NDP (coalition with Libs. to 2003)	2001–present

Lieutenant-Governor	Term
Hon. Amedee E. Forget	1905–1910
Hon. George W. Brown	1910–1915
Hon. Sir Richard Lake	1915–1921
Hon. Henry W. Newlands	1921–1931
Hon. Hugh E. Munroe	1931–1936
Hon. Archibald Peter McNab	1936–1945
Hon. Thomas Miller	1945 (02–04)
Hon. Reginald J.M. Parker	1945–1948
Hon. John Michael Uhrich	1948–1951
Hon. William J. Patterson	1951–1958
Hon. Frank Lindsay Bastedo	1958–1963
Hon. Rober L. Hanbidge	1963–1970
Hon. Stephen Worobetz	1970–1976
Hon. George Porteous	1976–1977
Hon. C. Irwin McIntosh	1978–1983
Hon. Frederick W. Johnson	1983–1988
Hon. Dr. Sylvia O. Fedoruk	1988–1994
Hon. John E. N. Wiebe	1994–2000
Hon. Dr. Lynda M. Haverstock	2000–present

GEOGRAPHY

Canada West Facts

	Alberta	Saskatchewan	Manitoba
Total area (km²)	661,190	652,330	649,950
Forested area (km²)	376,878	234,839	353,481
Fresh water (km²)	19,836	19,570	103,992
Farm land (km²)	204,969	267,455	77,994
Other (km²)	59,507	103,466	220,983
Largest lake (km²)	Lake Claire 1,436	Lake Athabasca 7,935	Lake Winnipeg 24,387

1 km²=.386 m²

Saskatchewan Lakes

Fifteen lakes in Saskatchewan are larger than 400 square kilometres (154.44 square miles)

Lake	km²
Lake Athabasca	7,935
Reindeer Lake	6,650
Wollaston Lake	2,681
Cree Lake	1,434
Lac La Ronge	1,413
Peter Pond Lake	778
Dore Lake	640
Churchill Lake	559
Deschambault Lake	542
Frobisher Lake	516
Black Lake	464
Montreal Lake	454
Primrose Lake	448
Amisk Lake	430
Pinehouse Lake	404

1 km²=.386 m²

Area of Canadian Provinces and Territories as % of Total

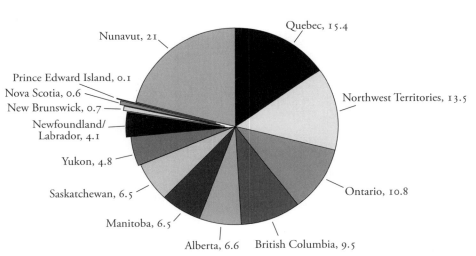

Nunavut, 21

Prince Edward Island, 0.1
Nova Scotia, 0.6
New Brunswick, 0.7
Newfoundland/
Labrador, 4.1

Yukon, 4.8

Saskatchewan, 6.5

Manitoba, 6.5

Alberta, 6.6   British Columbia, 9.5

Quebec, 15.4

Northwest Territories, 13.5

Ontario, 10.8

AGRICULTURE

Number of New Homesteads in the Prairie Provinces, 1895 to 1931

Year	Saskatchewan	Alberta	Manitoba
1895	461	1,000	866
1896	362	411	993
1897	301	230	609
1898	960	1,049	1,426
1899	2,159	1,745	2,124
1900	2,703	2,470	2,154
1901	2,332	3,806	1,933
1902	6,612	5,681	2,263
1903	19,941	8,069	3,253
1904	15,659	8,201	2,005
1905	19,787	9,138	1,707
1906	27,692	12,263	1,806
1907	13,501	6,843	1,231
1908	18,825	9,614	1,748
1909	21,120	13,771	3,761
1910	21,575	17,187	2,529
1911	25,227	15,964	3,082
1912	20,484	15,184	3,158
1913	17,556	12,942	2,826
1914	14,504	12,208	3,186
1915	8,790	10,076	4,420
1916	6,247	6,410	3,960
1917	4,105	4,550	2,276
1918	2,741	3,808	1,593
1919	1,191	2,169	813
1920	1,918	3,448	1,232
1921	1,670	2,874	725
1922	2,733	2,928	1,488
1923	2,104	2,207	879
1924	1,699	1,326	632
1925	1,804	1,192	464
1926	2,363	1,556	616
1927	2,702	2,145	797
1928	2,961	3,411	688
1929	5,808	8,933	643
1930	6,089	9,795	727
1931	2,834	7,122	454

Number of Farms in the Prairie Provinces, 1901 to 1931

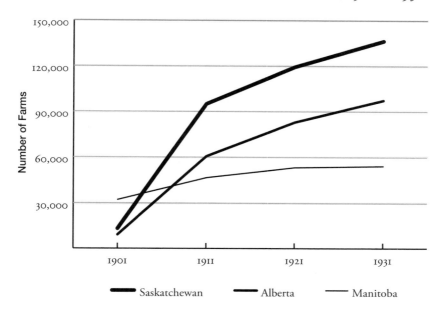

Saskatchewan — Alberta — Manitoba

Number of Farms in Saskatchewan

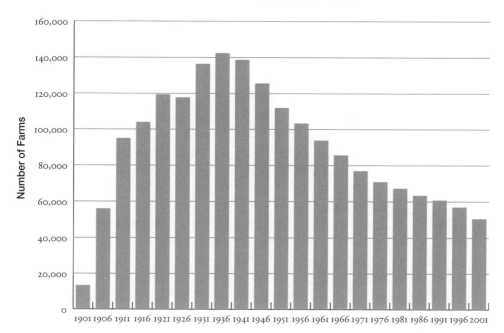

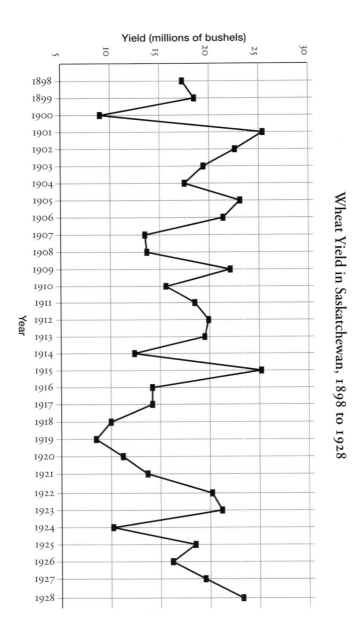

Wheat Yield in Saskatchewan, 1898 to 1928

POPULATION DEMOGRAPHICS

Cities and Places in Saskatchewan

Place	Pop. 2001	Pop. 2004	Latitude	Longitude
Assiniboia	2 500	2 400	49.62°N	105.98°W
Biggar	2 200	2 100	52.05°N	107.98°W
Canora	2 200	2 100	51.63°N	102.43°W
Carlyle	1 300	1 200	49.63°N	102.27°W
Carnduff	1 000	970	49.17°N	101.78°W
Caronport	1 000	970	50.45°N	105.82°W
Carrot River	1 000	970	53.28°N	103.58°W
Dalmeny	1 600	1 500	52.33°N	106.78°W
Davidson	1 000	987	51.27°N	105.97°W
Esterhazy	2 300	2 200	50.65°N	102.08°W
Estevan	10 200	9 900	49.14°N	103.01°W
Eston	1 000	1 000	51.15°N	108.75°W
Foam Lake	1 200	1 200	51.65°N	103.53°W
Fort Qu'Appelle	2 200	2 100	50.77°N	103.78°W
Gravelbourg	1 200	1 100	49.88°N	106.55°W
Grenfell	1 100	1 000	50.42°N	102.92°W
Gull Lake	1 000	969	50.10°N	108.48°W
Hudson Bay	1 800	1 700	52.85°N	102.38°W
Humboldt	5 200	4 900	52.20°N	105.12°W
Indian Head	1 800	1 700	50.53°N	103.67°W
Kamsack	2 000	1 900	51.57°N	101.90°W
Kelvington	1 000	960	52.17°N	103.52°W
Kerrobert	1 100	1 100	51.92°N	109.13°W
Kindersley	4 500	4 300	51.47°N	109.13°W
Kipling	1 000	989	50.10°N	102.63°W
Langenburg	1 100	1 100	50.83°N	101.70°W
Langham	1 100	1 100	52.37°N	106.97°W
Lanigan	1 300	1 200	51.85°N	105.03°W
La Ronge	3 300	3 100	55.10°N	105.30°W
Lumsden	1 600	1 500	50.65°N	104.87°W
Macklin	1 300	1 300	52.33°N	109.95°W

Place	Pop. 2001	Pop. 2004	Latitude	Longitude
Maple Creek	2 300	2 200	49.92°N	109.47°W
Martensville	4 400	4 200	52.29°N	106.68°W
Meadow Lake	4 600	4 400	54.13°N	108.43°W
Melfort	5 600	5 400	52.86°N	104.61°W
Melville	4 500	4 300	50.94°N	102.81°W
Moose Jaw	32 600	32 000	50.39°N	105.54°W
Moosomin	2 400	2 300	50.15°N	101.67°W
Nipawin	4 300	4 100	53.37°N	104.02°W
North Battleford	17 100	18 100	52.79°N	108.29°W
Outlook	2 100	2 000	51.50°N	107.05°W
Oxbow	1 100	1 100	49.22°N	102.17°W
Pilot Butte	1 900	1 800	50.47°N	104.42°W
Preeceville	1 100	1 000	51.95°N	102.67°W
Prince Albert	34 800	34 200	53.20°N	105.75°W
Regina	178 200	174 600	50.45°N	104.61°W
Rosetown	2 500	2 400	51.55°N	107.98°W
Rosthern	1 500	1 400	52.65°N	106.33°W
Saskatoon	196 800	195 000	52.15°N	106.66°W
Shaunavon	1 800	1 700	49.65°N	108.42°W
Shellbrook	1 300	1 200	53.22°N	106.40°W
Swift Current	14 800	14 600	50.30°N	107.80°W
Tisdale	3 100	2 900	52.82°N	104.05°W
Unity	2 200	2 100	52.43°N	109.17°W
Wadena	1 400	1 300	51.95°N	103.80°W
Warman	3 500	3 300	52.32°N	106.57°W
Watrous	1 800	1 700	51.67°N	105.47°W
Weyburn	9 500	9 300	49.67°N	103.86°W
White City	1 900	1 900	50.44°N	104.35°W
Wilkie	1 300	1 200	52.42°N	108.70°W
Wynyard	1 900	1 800	51.77°N	104.18°W
Yorkton	15 200	15 000	51.21°N	102.47°W

Urban and Rural Population of Saskatchewan

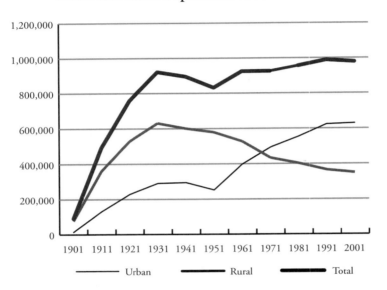

Urban and Rural Population of Saskatchewan

Year	Urban	% Urban	Rural	% Rural	Total
1901	14,266	16%	77,013	84%	91,279
1911	131,395	27%	361,037	73%	492,432
1921	228,958	30%	528,552	70%	757,510
1931	290,905	32%	630,880	68%	921,785
1941	295,146	33%	600,846	67%	895,992
1951	252,470	30%	579,258	70%	831,728
1961	398,091	43%	527,090	57%	925,181
1971	492,445	53%	433,790	47%	926,235
1981	553,575	58%	402,865	42%	956,440
1991	623,397	63%	365,531	37%	988,928
2001	629,036	64%	349,897	36%	978,933

Population of Saskatchewan Cities

	Prince Albert	Moose Jaw	North Battleford	Swift Current	Yorkton	Weyburn
1901	1,785	1,158		121	700	113
1911	6,254	13,823	2,105	1,852	2,309	2,210
1921	7,558	19,285	4,108	3,518	5,151	3,193
1931	9,905	21,299	5,986	5,296	5,027	5,002
1941	12,508	20,753	4,745	5,594	5,577	6,179
1951	17,149	24,355	7,473	7,458	7,074	7,148
1961	24,168	33,206	11,230	12,186	9,995	9,101
1971	28,464	28,464	12,698	15,415	13,430	8,815
1981	31,380	33,941	14,030	14,747	15,339	9,523
1991	34,181	33,593	14,350	14,815	15,319	9,673
2001	34,291	32,131	13,692	14,821	15,107	9,534

Population of Saskatoon and Regina, 1901 to 2001

Date	Saskatoon	Regina	Saskatchewan	% in two cities
1901	113	2,249	91,000	3%
1911	12,004	30,213	492,000	9%
1921	25,739	34,432	758,000	8%
1931	43,291	54,209	922,000	11%
1941	43,027	58,245	896,000	11%
1951	53,268	71,319	832,000	15%
1961	95,526	112,141	925,000	23%
1971	126,449	140,734	926,000	29%
1981	154,210	162,613	968,000	33%
1991	212,800	193,900	989,000	41%
2001	225,927	192,800	978,933	43%

Population of Canada, Provinces, and Territories, 1901 to 2001

Population given in thousands

Date	Canada	Nfld.	P.E.I.	N.S.	N.B.	Que.	Ont.	Man.	Sask.	%Can.pop.	Alta.	B.C.	Yuk.	N.W.T.	Nun.
1901	5,371		103	460	331	1,649	2,183	255	91	1.7%	73	179	27	20	
1911	7,207		94	492	352	2,006	2,527	461	492	6.8%	374	392	9	7	
1921	8,787		89	524	388	2,361	2,934	610	758	8.6%	588	525	8	8	
1931	10,377		88	513	408	2,875	3,432	700	922	8.9%	732	694	4	9	
1941	11,507		95	578	457	3,332	3,788	730	896	7.8%	796	818	5	12	
1951	14,409	361	98	643	516	4,056	4,598	777	832	5.8%	940	1,165	9	16	
1961	18,238	458	105	737	598	5,259	6,236	922	925	5.1%	1,332	1,629	15	23	
1971	21,568	522	112	789	635	6,028	7,703	988	926	4.3%	1,628	2,185	18	35	
1981	24,343	568	123	847	696	6,438	8,625	1,026	968	4.0%	2,238	2,744	23	46	
1991	27,927	568	130	900	724	6,896	10,085	1,092	989	3.5%	2,546	3,282	28	36	21
2001	30,007	513	135	908	729	7,237	11,410	1,120	979	3.3%	2,975	3,908	29	37	27

Note: Nunavut is included in the Northwest Territories up to 1981

PopulationReporting Aboriginal Ancestry (origin) Canada 1901 to 2001

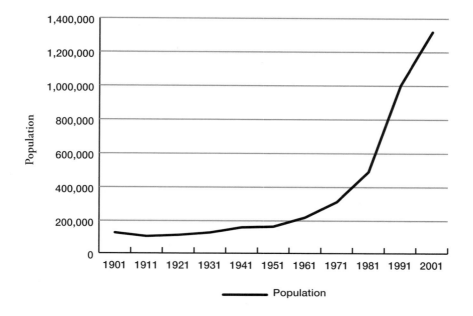

Aboriginal Population of Canada 2001 Census

	Total population	Aboriginal population	North American Indian	Métis	Inuit	Non- Aboriginal population
Canada	29,639,030	976,305	608,850	292,305	45,070	28,662,725
Newfoundland and Labrador	508,080	18,775	7,040	5,480	4,560	489,300
Prince Edward Island	133,385	1,345	1,035	220	20	132,040
Nova Scotia	897,565	17,010	12,920	3,135	350	880,560
New Brunswick	719,710	16,990	11,495	4,290	155	702,725
Quebec	7,125,580	79,400	51,125	15,855	9,530	7,046,180
Ontario	11,285,545	188,315	131,560	48,340	1,375	11,097,235
Manitoba	1,103,700	150,045	90,340	56,800	340	953,655
Saskatchewan	978,933	130,185	83,745	43,695	235	848,748
Alberta	2,941,150	156,225	84,995	66,060	1,090	2,784,925
British Columbia	3,868,875	170,025	118,295	44,265	800	3,698,850
Yukon Territory	28,520	6,540	5,600	535	140	21,975
Northwest Territories	37,100	18,730	10,615	3,580	3,910	18,370
Nunavut	26,665	22,720	95	55	22,560	3,945

Ethnic Composition of Saskatchewan's Population, 1881–1971*

Year	Total Population	British	%	German	%	French	%	Scandi-navian	%	Russian & Ukrainian	%	Other East European	%	Native Indian	%	Other	%
1881	19,114	2,052	10.7	21	0.1	2,079	10.9	17	0.1	0	0	n/a	n/a	14,914	78.0	31	0.2
1885	32,097	16,208	50.5	299	0.9	663	2.1	73	0.2	15	0.1	n/a	n/a	14,288	44.5	551	1.7
1901	91,279	40,094	43.9	11,743	12.9	2,634	2.9	1,452	1.6	11,675	12.8	4,791	5.2	17,734	19.4	1,156	1.3
1911	492,432	251,010	51.0	68,628	13.9	23,251	4.7	33,991	6.9	18,413	3.7	47,742	9.7	11,718	2.4	37,649	7.6
1916	647,835	353,098	54.5	77,109	11.9	32,066	5.0	49,708	7.7	33,662	5.2	68,536	10.6	10,902	1.7	22,754	3.5
1921	757,510	400,416	52.9	68,202	9.0	42,152	5.6	58,382	7.7	73,440	9.7	65,978	8.7	12,914	1.7	36,026	4.8
1926	820,738	416,721	50.8	96,498	11.8	47,030	5.7	63,370	7.7	87,682	10.7	57,682	7.0	13,001	1.6	38,754	4.7
1931	921,785	437,836	47.5	129,232	14.0	50,700	5.5	72,684	7.9	98,821	10.7	72,783	7.9	15,268	1.7	44,461	4.8
1936	931,547	427,088	45.8	165,549	17.8	50,295	5.4	72,028	7.7	98,117	10.5	60,517	6.5	21,394	2.3	36,559	3.9
1941	895,992	397,905	44.4	130,258	14.5	50,530	5.6	68,806	7.7	105,710	11.8	67,169	7.5	22,548	2.5	53,066	5.9
1951	831,728	351,862	42.3	135,584	16.3	51,930	6.2	62,439	7.5	97,852	11.8	58,298	7.0	22,253	2.7	51,510	6.2
1961	925,181	373,482	40.4	158,209	17.1	59,824	6.5	67,553	7.3	101,332	11.0	79,395	8.6	30,630	3.3	54,756	5.9
1971	926,245	390,190	42.1	180,095	19.4	56,200	6.1	59,105	6.4	95,995	10.4	57,160	6.2	46,550	4.4	46,950	5.1

*Note: Some respondents after 1971 reported multiple identities and hence the data is not included.

Birthplaces of Saskatchewan Residents

Year	Born in Sask.	Total Sask. Population
1911	101,854 20.7%	492,432
1921	287,652 38.0%	757,510
1931	442,258 48.0%	921,785
1941	531,905 59.4%	895,992
1951	548,903 66.0%	831,728
1961	664,820 71.9%	925,181
1971	709,850 76.6%	926,245
1981	746,000 78.1%	955,440
1991	790,870 81.4%	971,160

Residence in Western Canada of Persons Born in Saskatchewan

Year	Total Reporting Born in Sask.	Living in Sask.	Living in Alta.	Living in BC
1911	108,140	101,854 94.2%	1,743 1.6%	1,993 1.8%
1921	314,830	287,652 91.4%	6,997 2.2%	8,389 2.7%
1931	502,165	442,2585 88.1%	16,991 3.4%	18,484 3.7%
1941	667,832	531,905 80.0%	27,836 4.2%	46,407 7.0%
1951	817,404	548,903 67.2%	59,047 7.2%	107,570 13.2%
1961	1,030,750	664,820 64.5%	102,197 9.9%	136,180 13.2%
1971	1,183,525	709,850 60.0%	145,040 12.3%	178,400 15.1%
1981	1,280,830	746,000 58.2%	195,290 15.3%	210,780 16.5%
1991	1,343,225	790,870 58.9%	—— ——	204,350 15.2%

Notes

CHAPTER ONE:
THE BANNER PROVINCE

1. *Regina Leader*, 9 August 1905, 30 August 1905, 6 September 1905.
2. Quoted in N. Ward, "Rt. Hon. J. G. Gardiner and 1905," *Saskatchewan History* 28, no. 3 (autumn 1975): 117.
3. *Regina Leader*, 30 August 1905, 6 September 1905.
4. J. Duffy, *Fights of our Lives: Elections, Leadership, and the Making of Canada* (Toronto: Harper Collins, 2002), 30.
5. On 15 July 1870, Canada officially acquired Rupert's Land and the Northwestern Territory from the Hudson's Bay Company; the area was collectively designated the North-West Territories. The spelling was changed to Northwest Territories following the creation of Saskatchewan and Alberta in 1905. The region was called the North-West because of its location relative to Montreal, Toronto, and Ottawa.
6. G. MacEwan, *Frederick Haultain: Frontier Statesman of the Canadian Northwest* (Saskatoon: Western Producer Prairie Books, 1985), 4.
7. Quoted in D. Owram, ed., *The Formation of Alberta: A Documentary History* (Calgary: Alberta Records Publication Board, 1979), 115.
8. E. Eager, "The Constitution of Saskatchewan," *Saskatchewan History* 15, no. 2 (spring 1962): 42.
9. Quoted in P. A. Russell, "Rhetorics of Identity: The Debate over Division of the North-West Territories, 1890–1905," *Journal of Canadian Studies* 20, no. 4 (winter 1985–86): 104.
10. N. L. Nicholson, *The Boundaries of Canadian Confederation* (Toronto: MacMillan, 1979), 130–34.
11. J. W. Brennan, "A Political History of Saskatchewan, 1905-1929" (unpublished Ph.D. diss., University of Alberta, 1976), 28–32.
12. Ibid., 27.
13. Brennan, "Political History," 40; J. A. Bovey, "The Attitudes and Policies of the Federal Government towards Canada's northern territories, 1870–1930" (unpublished M.A. thesis, University of British Columbia, 1967), 108.
14. Nicholson, *Boundaries*, 135–37; D. E. Smith, ed., *Building a Province: A History of Saskatchewan in Documents* (Saskatoon: Fifth House, 1992), 7.
15. Nicholson, *Boundaries*, 137–40.
16. Quoted in Eager, "Constitution of Saskatchewan," 48. In the United States, every state enjoyed the same rights and privileges upon admission to the union.
17. Brennan, "Political History," 46; C. C. Lingard, *Territorial Government in Canada: the autonomy question in the old North-West Territories* (Toronto: University of Toronto, 1946), 221.

18. D. J. Hall, "A Divergence of Principle: Clifford Sifton, Sir Wilfrid Laurier, and the North-West Autonomy Bills, 1905," *Laurentian University Review* 7, no. 1 (November 1974): 11, 19.
19. R. C. Brown and R. Cook, *Canada, 1896–1921: A Nation Transformed* (Toronto: McClelland and Stewart, 1974), 78–79.
20. E. Eager, "Separate Schools and the Cabinet Crisis of 1905," *Lakehead University Review* 2, no. 2 (fall 1969): 114.
21. Smith, ed., *Building a Province*, 8.
22. D. E. Smith, *Prairie Liberalism: The Liberal Party in Saskatchewan, 1905–71* (Toronto: University of Toronto Press, 1976), 6–8, 19.
23. L. G. Thomas, *The Liberal Party in Alberta: a history of politics in the province of Alberta 1905–1921* (Toronto: University of Toronto Press, 1959), 3.
24. Brennan, "Political History," 51–53; G. L. Barnhart, *Peace, Progress and Prosperity: A Biography of Saskatchewan's First Premier, T. Walter Scott* (Regina: Canadian Plains Research Center, 2000), 41–46.
25. *Regina Leader*, 23 August 1905.
26. Eager, "Constitution of Saskatchewan," 42.
27. *Regina Leader*, 6 September 1905.
28. *Winnipeg Free Press*, 5 September 1905; *Edmonton Journal*, 8 September 1905; *Regina Leader*, 6 September 1905.
29. *Regina Leader*, 6 September 1905.
30. *Regina Leader-Post*, 1 September 1995.
31. *Regina Leader*, 6 September 1905, 13 September 1905.
32. *Regina Leader*, 6 September 1905.
33. Ibid.
34. *Moose Jaw Times*, 8 September 1905; *Saskatoon Phoenix*, 8 September 1905, 29 September 1905; *Winnipeg Tribune*, 5 September 1905; *Edmonton Evening Journal*, 8 September 1905; *Toronto Globe*, 5 September 1905; *Montreal Gazette*, 5 September 1905.
35. Smith, ed., *Building a Province*, 5–6.
36. *Regina Leader*, 6 September 1905; *Moose Jaw Times*, 8 September 1905.

CHAPTER TWO:
ANOTHER COUNTRY ALTOGETHER

1. *Moose Jaw Times*, 8 September 1905.
2. Quoted in D. Owram, ed., *The Formation of Alberta: a documentary history* (Calgary: Alberta Records Publication Board, 1979), 183.
3. Quoted in D. Quiring, "Battling Parish Priests, Bootleggers, and Fur Sharks: CCF Colonialism in northern Saskatchewan" (unpublished Ph.D. diss., University of Saskatchewan, 2002), 17.

4. Jennifer Brown, "A Colony of Very Useful Hands," *The Beaver* 57, no. 4 (spring 1977): 39–45.

5. Fr. G. Carrière, "The Early Efforts of the Oblate Missionaries in Western Canada," *Prairie Forum* 4, no. 1 (spring 1979): 5–9; P. Duchaussois, *Mid Snow and Ice: The Apostles of the North-West* (London: Burns, Oates, and Washbourne, 1923), 91.

6. M. Zaslow, *The Opening of the Canadian North: 1870–1914* (Toronto: McClelland and Stewart, 1971).

7. B. Waiser, *Saskatchewan's Playground: A History of Prince Albert National Park* (Saskatoon: Fifth House, 1989), 11–14; H. J. Moberly, *When Fur was King* (Toronto: Dent, 1929), 174–76; A. J. Ray, *The Canadian Fur Trade in the Industrial Age* (Toronto: University of Toronto Press, 1990), 50.

8. Quoted in K. S. Coates and W. R. Morrison, "Treaty Ten (1906)," Treaties and Historical Research Centre, Indian and Northern Affairs, 1986, 14.

9. A. J. Ray et al., *Bounty and Benevolence: A History of Saskatchewan Treaties* (Montreal: McGill-Queen's University Press, 2000), 171.

10. B. Stonechild and B. Waiser, *Loyal till Death: Indians and the North-West Rebellion* (Calgary: Fifth House, 1997), 51–52.

11. Ray et al., *Bounty and Benevolence*, 141–46, 148–69.

12. Quoted in ibid., 171.

13. J. S. Murray, "A Guide to the Records of the Métis Scrip Commission in the National Archives of Canada" (Ottawa: Queen's Printer, 1998); L. Goyette, "The X Files," *Canadian Geographic* 123, no. 2 (March/April 2003): 72.

14. Quoted in Ray et al., *Bounty and Benevolence*, 172.

15. Ibid., 172–75; A. Gulig, "Yesterday's Promises: The Negotiation of Treaty Ten," *Saskatchewan History* 50, no. 1 (spring 1998): 26, 29.

16. Ray et al., *Bounty and Benevolence*, 175–77; Coates and Morrison, "Treaty Ten," 29–31; *Treaty No. 10 and Reports of Commissioners* (Ottawa: Queen's Printer, 1966), 13.

17. Gulig, "Yesterday's Promises," 29; Ray et al., *Bounty and Benevolence*, 177–78; *Treaty No. 10*, 9; Goyette, "The X Files," 76.

18. *Treaty No. 10*, 5.

19. Ibid., 5–6.

20. Ibid., 7–8.

21. Ibid., 7, 11.

22. Coates and Morrison, "Treaty Ten," 45–52.

23. Goyette, "The X Files," 76.

24. *Treaty No. 10*, 6.

25. Ibid., 14; Ray et al, *Bounty and Benevolence*, 179.

26. *Treaty No. 10*, 14; J. S. Murray, "A Guide to the Records of the Métis Scrip Commission in the National Archives of Canada;" Goyette, "The X Files," 77–78.

27. Gulig, "Yesterday's Promises," 33; Ray et al., *Bounty and Benevolence*, 184–5.

28. *Treaty No. 10*, 14; Gulig, "Yesterday's Promises," 33; Ray et al., *Bounty and Benevolence*, 183–84.

29. Ray et al., *Bounty and Benevolence*, 184–85.

30. *Treaty No. 10*, 15–16.

31. Gulig, "Yesterday's Promises," 39 n. 43; Canada, *Seventh Census of Canada, 1931, v. 2: Population by areas* (Ottawa: King's Printer, 1933), 98.

32. L. Sanders, "How Many Northern Residents were Cheated in 1906?" *Next Year Country* 3, no. 1 (August-September 1975): 18.

33. Gulig, "Yesterday's Promises," 29.

34. R. Fumoleau, *As Long As This Land Shall Last* (Toronto: McClelland and Stewart, 1973), 18.

35. Quiring, "Battling Parish Priests," 17.

36. Canada, House of Commons, *Debates*, 30 March 1906, 950.

CHAPTER THREE: DEAD COWS HANGING

1. Quoted in S. M. Evans, "The End of the Open Range Era in Western Canada," *Prairie Forum* 8, no. 1 (spring 1983): 71.

2. D. Breen, *The Canadian Prairie West and the Ranching Frontier, 1874–1924* (Toronto: University of Toronto Press, 1983), 236–37.

3. W. A. Waiser, *The Field Naturalist: John Macoun, the Geological Survey, and Natural Science* (Toronto: University of Toronto Press, 1989), 17–18.

4. Ibid., 34–48.

5. W. A. Waiser, "A Willing Scapegoat: John Macoun and the Route of the CPR," *Prairie Forum* 10, no. 1 (spring 1985): 65–81.

6. B. Potyondi, *In Palliser's Triangle: Living in the Grasslands, 1850–1930* (Saskatoon: Purich Publishing, 1995), 56.

7. For a discussion of the relationship between the grasslands, the buffalo, and Aboriginal peoples, see T. Binnema, *Common and Contested Ground: A Human and Environmental History of the Northwestern Plains* (Norman, OK: University of Oklahoma Press, 2001), 17–54.

8. G. Ens, *Homeland to Hinterland: The Changing Worlds of the Red River Métis in the Nineteenth Century* (Toronto: University of Toronto Press, 1996), 77–80; T. Poirier, ed., *Wood Mountain Uplands: From the Big Muddy to the Frenchman River* (Wood Mountain, SK: Wood Mountain Historical Society, 2000), 20–24; Potyondi, *In Palliser's Triangle*, 29.

9. B. Stonechild and B. Waiser, *Loyal till Death: Indians and the North-West Rebellion* (Calgary: Fifth House, 1997), 27–45.

10. G. Pannanen, "Sitting Bull: Indian without a Country," *Canadian Historical Review* 51, no. 2 (June 1970): 123–40.

11. Stonechild and Waiser, *Loyal till Death*, 47–49, 62.

12. Poirier, ed., *Wood Mountain Uplands*, 20–31.

13. Légaré's descendants are seeking $46,891 from Ottawa and $8,412 from Washington. *National Post*, 2 August 1999; *Regina Leader-Post*, 10 January 2001.

14. Potyondi, *In Palliser's Triangle*, 46–50. The Nikaneet reserve (Cree) was set aside in the Cypress Hills in 1913, the Wood Mountain reserve (Sioux) in 1917.

15. See Breen, *The Canadian Prairie West and the Ranching Frontier*.

16. D. C. McGowan, *Grassland Settlers: The Swift Current Region during the Era of the Ranching Frontier* (Regina: Canadian Plains Research Center, 1975), 11.

17. Potyondi, *In Palliser's Triangle*.

18. Ibid., 65; McGowan, *Grassland Settlers*, 84.

19. S. M. Evans, "American Cattlemen on the Canadian Range, 1874–1914," *Prairie Forum* 4, no. 1 (spring 1979): 128–30; Potyondi, *In Palliser's Triangle*, 53–55.

20. McGowan, *Grassland Settlers*, 86–87; Evans, "American Cattlemen," 130–31; Potyondi, *In Palliser's Triangle*, 55–56.

21. T. B. Long, *Seventy Years a Cowboy* (Saskatoon: Freeman Publishing, 1965), 36.

22. Potyondi, *In Palliser's Triangle*, 65; S. M. Evans, "The Origin of Ranching in Western Canada: American Diffusion or Victorian Transplant?" *Great Plains Quarterly* 3, no. 2 (spring 1983): 87.

23. H. Otterson, "Thirty Years Ago on the Whitemud River," Glenbow Archives, 4.

24. Ibid., 10–12.

25. Winnifred Hancock diary, 1906–07, Southwest Saskatchewan Oldtimers Museum.

26. W. M. Elofson, *Cowboys, Gentlemen, and Cattle Thieves: Ranching on the Western Frontier* (Montreal and Kingston: McGill-Queen's University Press, 2000), 66–70.

27. P. Dederick and B. Waiser, *Looking Back: True Tales from Saskatchewan's Past* (Calgary: Fifth House, 2003), 74–76.

28. R. Millar, "Will James a.k.a. Ernest Dufault," *Saskatchewan History* 53, no. 1 (spring 2001): 39–44.

29. Quoted in S. M. Evans, "The Origin of Ranching," 87.

30. E. Gossner, "Wanted: Joseph Erving Kelley," *Western People*, 3 September 1998, 6–7.

31. B. LaDow, *The Medicine Line: Life and Death on a North American Borderland* (New York: Routledge, 2001), 115.

32. Poirier, ed., *Wood Mountain Uplands*, 63–64.

33. Otterson, "Thirty Years Ago," 12.

34. J. Cherwinski, "Cold Comfort: The Brutal Winter of 1906–07 and the Defining of the Prairie Regional Identity" (unpublished paper presented before Canadian Historical Association, Toronto, 2002), 6.

35. Otterson, "Thirty Years Ago," 16–17.

36. Ibid., 19.

37. R. D. Symons, *Where the Wagon Led* (Toronto: Doubleday, 1973), xxviii.

38. W. Stegner, *Wolf Willow: A History, A Story, and a Memory of the Last Plains Frontier* (New York: Viking, 1962), 220.

39. Symons, *Where the Wagon Led*, xxvii.

40. Otterson, "Thirty Years Ago," 21–22.

41. Potyondi, *In Palliser's Triangle*, 58.

42. Otterson, "Thirty Years Ago," 21.

43. Potyondi, *In Palliser's Triangle*, 84.

44. Breen, *The Canadian Prairie West and the Ranching Frontier*, 142, 149; LaDow, *The Medicine Line*, 154.

CHAPTER FOUR:
THE GRAND ROUND-UP

1. C. Martin, *Dominion Lands Policy* (Toronto: McClelland and Stewart, 1938), 171, 396–430.

2. J. H. Archer, *Saskatchewan: A History* (Saskatoon: Western Producer Prairie Books, 1980), 103–104.

3. E. H. Oliver, "The Settlement of Saskatchewan to 1914," *Transactions of the Royal Society of Canada* 20, series 3, section 2 (1926): 65.

4. B. Waiser, "William Bell," in *Dictionary of Canadian Biography, v. XIV*, ed. R. Cook (Toronto: University of Toronto Press, 1998), 56–58.

5. A. J. Arnold, "The Jewish Farm Settlements of Saskatchewan: From 'New Jerusalem' to Edenbridge," *Canadian Jewish Historical Society Journal* 4, no. 1 (spring 1980): 25–43; A. Feldman, "Were Jewish Farmers Failures?" *Saskatchewan History* 55, no. 1 (spring 2003): 21–30.

6. Archer, *Saskatchewan*, 73–75; M. Guitard, "La Rolanderie," *Saskatchewan History* 30, no. 3 (autumn 1977): 110–14.

7. W. P. Ward, "Population Growth in Western Canada, 1901–71," in *The Developing West*, ed. J. Foster (Edmonton: University of Alberta Press, 1983), 158.

8. D. J. Hall, "Clifford Sifton: Immigration and Settlement Policy, 1896–1905," in *The Settlement of the West*, ed. H. Palmer (Calgary: University of Calgary, 1977), 60–85.

9. Quoted in ibid., 81.

10. Canada, *Census of Population and Agriculture of the Northwest Provinces: Manitoba, Saskatchewan, Alberta* (Ottawa: King's Printer, 1907), xix.

11. Ibid., xi–xviii, 81–85; Ward, "Population Growth," 174–75.

12. Hall, "Clifford Sifton," 77.

13. Quoted in ibid, 76.

14. Quoted in Arnold, "Jewish Farm Settlements," 39.

15. Hall, "Clifford Sifton," 79.

16. Quoted in ibid., 77.

17. Ibid., 78–81.

18. The 1906 aggregate census data does not provide a population breakdown according to racial origin. Canada, *Census of Population and Agriculture*, 86; Hall, "Clifford Sifton," 71.

19. Oliver, "Settlement of Saskatchewan," 73;
M. Cottrell, "The Irish in Saskatchewan, 1850–1930,"
Prairie Forum 24, no. 2 (fall 1999): 188–89;
A. Lalonde and R. Lapointe, "The Peoples of
Saskatchewan in Pictures: the Francophones,"
Saskatchewan History 52, no. 1 (spring 2000): 17–19;
R. Lapointe and L. Tessier, *The Francophones of
Saskatchewan: A History* (Regina: Campion
College, 1988), 101, 107.

20. L. H. Thomas, "From the Pampas to the Prairies:
The Welsh Migration of 1902," *Saskatchewan
History* 24, no. 1 (spring 1971): 1–12.

21. P. Dederick and B. Waiser, *Looking Back: True
Tales from Saskatchewan's Past* (Calgary: Fifth
House, 2003), 68–70.

22. L. Bowen, *Muddling Through: The Remarkable
Story of the Barr Colonists* (Vancouver: Douglas
and McIntyre, 1992), 10–11, 15, 152, 166–67.

23. K. D. Bicha, *The American Farmer and the Canadian
West, 1896–1914* (Lawrence, KS: Coronado Press,
1968), 11. In 1901, almost two-thirds of the American-
born population in Canada lived east of Manitoba;
a decade later, two-thirds lived west of Ontario. R.
Widdis, *With Scarcely a Ripple: Anglo-Canadian
Migration into the United States and Western
Canada, 1880–1920* (Montreal and Kingston:
McGill-Queen's University Press, 1998), 292.

24. Quoted in Hall, "Clifford Sifton," 70.

25. Oliver, "Settlement of Saskatchewan," 70–71;
Bicha, *The American Farmer*, 100–106; K. O. Bjork,
"Scandinavian Migration to the Canadian Prairie
Provinces, 1893–1914," *Norwegian American Studies*
26, no. 1 (1974): 3–30.

26. F. Stambrook and S. Hryniuk, "Who Were They
Really?: Reflections on East European Immigrants
to Manitoba before 1914," *Prairie Forum* 25, no. 2
(fall 2000): 218–19; O. Martynowych, *Ukrainians
in Canada: The Formative Period, 1891–1924*
(Edmonton: Canadian Institute of Ukrainian
Studies, 1991), 3–24.

27. J. C. Lehr, "Governmental Coercion in the
Settlement of Ukrainian Immigrants in Western
Canada," *Prairie Forum* 8, no. 2 (fall 1983): 179–94.

28. Quoted in J. C. Lehr, "Peopling the Prairies with
Ukrainians," in *Canada's Ukrainians: Negotiating
an Identity*, ed. L. Luciuk and J. Hryniuk
(Toronto: University of Toronto Press, 1991), 405
n. 41. See also J. C. Lehr, "Government
Perceptions of Ukrainian Immigrants to Western
Canada, 1896–1902," *Canadian Ethnic Studies* 19,
no. 2 (summer 1987): 1–12.

29. G. Friesen, *The Canadian Prairies: A History*
(Toronto: University of Toronto Press, 1984), 267–69.

30. F. H. Epp, *The Mennonites in Canada, 1786–1920*
(Toronto: Macmillan, 1974), 311–18.

31. C. J. Tracie, *Toil and Peaceful Life: Doukhobor
Village Settlement in Saskatchewan, 1899–1918*
(Regina: Canadian Plains Research Center, 1996).

32. Quoted in P. Berton, *The Promised Land: Settling
the West, 1896–1914* (Toronto: McClelland and
Stewart, 1984), 57–58.

33. Tracie, *Toil and Peaceful Life*, 123, 212–13;
K. Szalasznyj, "The Doukhobor Homestead
Crisis, 1898–1907" (unpublished M.A. thesis,
University of Saskatchewan, 1977), 239.

34. Quoted in C. Betke, "The Mounted Police and
the Doukhobors in Saskatchewan, 1899–1909,"
Saskatchewan History 27, no. 1 (winter 1974): 10.

35. R. B. Shepard, *Deemed Unsuitable* (Toronto:
Umbrella Press, 1996), 76–85.

36. Ibid., 3.

37. Ibid., 100.

38. W. A. Mackintosh, *Prairie Settlement: the
Geographical Setting* (Toronto: Macmillan, 1934),
53, 69.

39. B. Potyondi, *In Palliser's Triangle: Living in the
Grasslands, 1850–1930* (Saskatoon: Purich
Publishing, 1995), 57–58; Bjork, "Scandinavian
Migration to the Canadian Prairie Provinces,
1893–1914," 24; B. LaDow, *The Medicine Line: Life
and Death on a North American Borderland* (New
York: Routledge, 2001), 154; W. M. Elofson,
*Cowboys, Gentlemen, and Cattle Thieves: Ranching
on the Western Frontier* (Montreal and Kingston:
McGill-Queen's University Press, 2000), 20.

40. B. Waiser, *The New Northwest: The Photographs of
the Frank Crean Expeditions, 1908–09* (Saskatoon:
Fifth House, 1993).

41. S. Carter, *Lost Harvests: Prairie Indian Reserve
Farmers and Government Policy* (Montreal and
Kingston: McGill-Queen's University Press, 1990),
244–46.

42. P. Martin-McGuire, *First Nation Land Surrenders
on the Prairies, 1896–1911* (Ottawa: Indian Claims
Commission, 1998), xxi–xxiii.

43. See M. K. Lux, *Medicine That Walks: disease,
medicine, and Canadian plains native peoples, 1880–
1940* (Toronto: University of Toronto Press, 2001).

44. Martin-McGuire, *First Nation Land Surrenders*,
xxviii–xxxviii. See also S. Raby, "Indian Land
Surrenders in Southern Saskatchewan," *The
Canadian Geographer* 17, no. 1 (spring 1973): 36–52.

45. J. Funk, *Outside, the Women Cried* (Battleford, SK:
TC Publications, 1989).

46. Martin-McGuire, *First Nation Land Surrenders*,
xxix.

47. Widdis, *With Scarcely a Ripple*, 297.

48. The admission of these foreign navvies translated
into an increase in the number of single men in
western Canada. But unlike male immigrants
before them, they were a transient population,
moving from job to job from season to season,
who did not intend to settle in the country.
D. Avery, "Canadian Immigration Policy and the
'Foreign' Navvy, 1896–1914," *Canadian Historical
Association Historical Papers*, 1972, 144–45.

49. Quoted in D. E. Smith, "Instilling British Values in the Prairie Provinces," *Prairie Forum* 6, no. 2 (fall 1981): 139.

50. P. F. Sharp, "The Northern Great Plains: A Study in Canadian-American Regionalism," *Mississippi Valley Historical Review* 39, no. 1 (June 1952): 76.

51. Oliver, "Settlement of Saskatchewan," 86–87; Friesen, *The Canadian Prairies*, 244.

52. J. S. Woodsworth, *Strangers within our Gates* (Toronto: F. C. Stephenson, 1909), 234.

53. J. H. Thompson, *Forging the Prairie West* (Toronto: Oxford University Press, 1998), 77.

CHAPTER FIVE:
SASKATCHEWAN FOREVER

1. D. E. Smith, ed., *Building a Province: A History of Saskatchewan in Documents* (Saskatoon: Fifth House, 1992), 5–6.

2. *Regina Leader*, 5 October 1909.

3. *The West*, 6 September 1905.

4. J. W. Brennan, "A Political History of Saskatchewan, 1905–1929" (unpublished Ph.D. diss., University of Alberta, 1976), 49, 56; J. T. Saywell, "Liberal Politics, Federal Policies, and the Lieutenant-Governor: Saskatchewan and Alberta 1905," *Saskatchewan History* 8, no. 3 (autumn 1955): 84, 87–88; J. Courtney and D. E. Smith, "Saskatchewan," in *Canadian Provincial Politics*, ed. M. Robin (Toronto: Prentice-Hall, 1978), 285; J. Archer, *Saskatchewan: A History* (Saskatoon: Western Producer Prairie Books, 1980), 136.

5. G. L. Barnhart, *Peace, Progress and Prosperity: A Biography of Saskatchewan's First Premier, T. Walter Scott* (Regina: Canadian Plains Research Center, 2000), 49–50.

6. Brennan, "A Political History of Saskatchewan," 62; E. Eager, *Saskatchewan Government: Politics and Pragmatism* (Saskatoon: Western Producer Prairie Books, 1980), 5–6.

7. Brennan, "A Political History of Saskatchewan," 35, 55, 71; Eager, *Saskatchewan Government*, 207; Courtney and Smith, "Saskatchewan," 286.

8. Archer, *Saskatchewan*, 138.

9. Barnhart, *Peace, Progress and Prosperity*, 65; Smith, ed., *Building a Province*, 9–10.

10. Brennan, "A Political History of Saskatchewan," 86; D. E. Smith, *Prairie Liberalism: The Liberal Party in Saskatchewan, 1905–71* (Toronto: University of Toronto Press, 1975), 48–49.

11. Quoted in J. E. Murray, "The Provincial Capital Controversy in Saskatchewan," *Saskatchewan History* 5, no. 3 (autumn 1952): 88.

12. Ibid., 81–105.

13. Barnhart, *Peace, Progress and Prosperity*, 65.

14. J. W. Brennan, *Regina: An Illustrated History* (Toronto: Lorimer, 1989), 73–74; G. L. Barnhart, *Building for the Future: a photo journal of Saskatchewan's Legislative Building* (Regina: Canadian Plains Research Center, 2002), 8–9.

15. Barnhart, *Building for the Future*, 10–13.

16. W. Carlyle, "The Changing Geography of Administrative Units for Rural Schooling and Local Government on the Canadian Prairies," *Prairie Forum* 12, no. 1 (spring 1987): 18–21; Smith, ed., *Building a Province*, 15, 132–33.

17. A. R. Turner, ed., "Reminiscences of the Hon. J. A. Calder," *Saskatchewan History* 25, no. 2 (spring 1972): 67.

18. R. Love, *SaskTel: the Biography of a Crown Corporation and the Development of Telecommunications in Saskatchewan* (Regina: SaskTel, 2003), 69–90.

19. T. Barris, *Fire Canoe: Prairie Steamboat Days Revisited* (Toronto: McClelland and Stewart, 1977), 191, 253; B. Peel, *Steamboats on the Saskatchewan* (Saskatoon: Western Producer Prairie Books, 1972), 5, 225–28; D. Polachic, "Last Steamer on the Saskatchewan," *Western People*, 6 September 1990, 10–11.

20. Archer, *Saskatchewan*, 147; P. L. McCormick, "Transportation and Settlement: Problems in the Expansion of the Frontier of Saskatchewan and Assiniboia in 1904," *Prairie Forum* 5, no. 1 (spring 1980): 3–4.

21. Archer, *Saskatchewan*, 155; T. D. Regehr, *The Canadian Northern Railway: Pioneer Road of the Northern Prairies, 1895–1918* (Toronto: Macmillan, 1976), 198–201. Regehr claims that the Canadian Northern used the provincial bond guarantees to build branch lines that would give the company control of the northern prairies.

22. Archer, *Saskatchewan*, 144–45; G. Friesen, *The Canadian Prairies: A History* (Toronto: University of Toronto Press, 1984), 347; I. A. Poelzer, "Local Problems of Early Saskatchewan Education," *Saskatchewan History* 32, no. 1 (winter 1979): 1–15.

23. Smith, ed., *Building a Province*, 15.

24. J. E. Murray, "The Contest for the University of Saskatchewan," *Saskatchewan History* 12, no. 1 (winter 1959): 1.

25. G. Abrams, *Prince Albert: The First Century, 1866–1966* (Saskatoon: Modern Press, 1966), 24, 39–41, 84; Murray, "The Contest," 3.

26. M. J. Hayden, *Seeking a Balance: the University of Saskatchewan, 1907–1982* (Vancouver: University of British Columbia Press, 1983), 1–25.

27. Quoted in Smith, ed., *Building a Province*, 137.

28. Murray, "The Contest," 17.

29. Hayden, *Seeking a Balance*, 32–43.

30. There is considerable ongoing debate over the breakdown of the vote. See, for example, J. M. Pitsula, "Higher Education Policy in Saskatchewan and the Legacy of the Myth," Public Policy Paper 12, Saskatchewan Institute of Public Policy, February 2003.

31. Photographic reproduction of telegram, 7 April 1909, in Hayden, *Seeking a Balance*, opposite 44.
32. Quoted in Barnhart, *Peace, Progress and Prosperity*, 72.
33. Quoted in D. Kerr and S. D. Hanson, *Saskatoon: The First Half Century* (Edmonton: NeWest Publishers, 1982), 83.
34. Hayden, *Seeking a Balance*, 44–45. Thirteen hundred acres were eventually purchased for the site of the university at a cost close to $150,000.
35. P. S. Nishida, "The Establishment of Saskatchewan's Mental Hospitals, 1912–1940" (unpublished M.A. thesis, University of Regina, 1988); H. D. Dickinson, *The Two Psychiatries: The Transformation of Psychiatric Work in Saskatchewan, 1905–1984* (Regina: Canadian Plains Research Center, 1989), 20–22.
36. S. Skinner et al., *Corrections: An Historical Perspective of the Saskatchewan Experience* (Regina: Canadian Plains Research Center, 1981).
37. Barnhart, *Peace, Progress and Prosperity*, 75.
38. Barnhart, *Building for the Future*, 18–23. There were eventually ninety-one design changes to the original building specifications.
39. *Regina Leader*, 5 October 1909.
40. Ibid.
41. Quoted in Barnhart, *Building for the Future*, 27.
42. *Regina Leader*, 5 October 1909.
43. Smith, *Prairie Liberalism*, 25–51.
44. J. W. Brennan, "Wooing the 'Foreign Vote': Saskatchewan Politics and the Immigrant 1905–1919," *Prairie Forum* 3, no. 1 (spring 1978): 61–78.
45. Brennan, "A Political History of Saskatchewan," 172–97.
46. L. H. Thomas, "The Political and Private Life of F. W. G. Haultain," *Saskatchewan History* 23, no. 2 (spring 1970): 56–58. Premier Scott believed that Haultain was "hobbled by some handicap."
47. *Regina Leader*, 14 October 1912.
48. Barnhart, *Peace, Progress and Prosperity*, 105–24.

CHAPTER SIX:
LAND I CAN OWN
1. *Robsart Pioneers Review the Years* (Robsart, SK: 1957), 49.
2. B. LaDow, *The Medicine Line: Life and Death on a North American Borderland* (New York: Routledge, 2001), 191.
3. Quoted in W. A. Waiser, *The Field Naturalist: John Macoun, the Geological Survey and Natural Science* (Toronto: University of Toronto Press, 1989), 53.
4. *Range riders and sodbusters* (Eastend, SK: Eastend History Society, 1984), 251.
5. E. T. Parson, *Land I can own* (Ottawa: E. T. Parson, 1981).
6. L. K. Bacon, "Four Years in Saskatchewan," provided by S. Haid (n.d.).
7. R. W. Sansom typescript, provided by D. McKercher (n.d.)

8. W. A. Waiser, "The Government Explorer in Canada, 1870–1914," in *North American Exploration, v. 3: A Continent Comprehended*, ed. J. L. Allen (Lincoln, NB: University of Nebraska Press, 1997), 426–34.
9. B. Waiser, *The New Northwest: The Photographs of the Frank Crean Expeditions, 1908–1909* (Saskatoon: Fifth House, 1993), 6 n. 13; C. Martin, *Dominion Lands Policy* (Toronto: McClelland and Stewart, 1973), 47.
10. The entry application, the first document to be filed, listed the location of the land and the age, place of birth, nationality, citizenship status, previous place of residence, and previous occupation of the homesteader.
11. Martin, *Dominion Lands Policy*, 172–74.
12. W. C. Pollard, *Pioneering in the Prairie West* (London: A. H. Stockwell, n.d.), 51 [emphasis added].
13. Ottawa discontinued the preemption option in 1890, but reintroduced it in 1908.
14. R. Widdis, *With Scarcely a Ripple: Anglo-Canadian Migration into the United States and Western Canada, 1880–1920* (Montreal and Kingston: McGill-Queen's University Press, 1998), 326.
15. See J. Cherwinski, "The Rise and Incomplete Fall of a Contemporary Legend: Frozen Englishmen in the Canadian Prairies During the Winter of 1906–07," *Canadian Ethnic Studies* 31, no. 3 (fall 1999): 20–43.
16. Quoted in D. J. Hall, "Clifford Sifton: Immigration and Settlement Policy, 1896–1905," in *The Settlement of the West*, ed. H. Palmer (Calgary: University of Calgary Press, 1977), 75.
17. Quoted in ibid., 71.
18. See L. Dick, "Estimates of Farm-Making Costs in Saskatchewan, 1882–1914," *Prairie Forum* 6, no. 2 (fall 1981): 183–201.
19. S. Carter, *A Materials History of the Motherwell Home*, Canada Parks Service manuscript report, no. 320, 1979, 278.
20. Widdis, *With Scarcely a Ripple*, 257, 329.
21. L. Reed, "Pioneer Courage on the Prairie," *Saskatchewan History* 39, no. 3 (autumn 1986): 108.
22. A. R. Turner, "Pioneer Farming Experiences," *Saskatchewan History* 8, no. 2 (spring 1955): 44.
23. G. Shepherd, *West of Yesterday* (Toronto: McClelland and Stewart, 1965).
24. "Simple Experiences of Pioneer Days," Women's Canadian Club competition, 1924, A. S. Morton manuscript collection, c555/1/2.29, University of Saskatchewan Libraries Special Collections.
25. Quoted in J. W. Bennett and S. B. Kohl, *Settling the Canadian-American West 1890–1915: pioneer adaptation and community building* (Lincoln: University of Nebraska Press, 1995), 57.
26. R. Rees, *New and Naked Land: Making the Prairies Home* (Saskatoon: Western Producer Prairie Books, 1988), 107.

27. Bennett and Kohl, *Settling*, 64.

28. *Robsart Pioneers*, 38.

29. J. Minifie, *Homesteader: A Prairie Boyhood Recalled* (Toronto: Macmillan, 1972), 52.

30. LaDow, *The Medicine Line*, 87.

31. "A Reminiscence of a Bigone Day," 1924, Morton manuscript collection, MSDS C555/2.1.

32. K. M. Taggart, "The First Shelter of Early Pioneers," *Saskatchewan History* 11, no. 3 (autumn 1958): 81.

33. Sansom typescript.

34. L. Henry, *Catalogue Houses: Eatons' and Others* (Saskatoon: Henry Perspectives, 2000).

35. J. A. G. Howe, "One Hundred Years of Prairie Forestry," *Prairie Forum* 11, no. 2 (fall 1986): 243–51.

36. L. Turner to family, 29 April 1906, Lillian Turner fonds, Glenbow Archives M8244.

37. Quoted in Turner, "Pioneer Farming Experiences," 51.

38. B. M. Barss, *The Pioneer Cook: A Historical View of Canadian Prairie Food* (Calgary: Detselig Enterprises, 1980), 93–94.

39. Quoted in D. P. Fitzgerald, "Pioneer Settlement in Northern Saskatchewan" (unpublished Ph.D. diss., University of Minnesota, 1965), 150.

40. Rees, *New and Naked Land*, 50.

41. J. Letkeman, "My Walk in Life," 26 November 1954, provided by S. Thiessen.

42. Sansom typescript.

43. Widdis, *With Scarcely a Ripple*, 306.

44. L. H. Neatby, *Chronicle of a Pioneer Prairie Family* (Saskatoon: Western Producer Prairie Books, 1979), 30.

45. Sansom typescript.

46. A. J. Wheeler, "Helping to Build the G. T. P.," *Saskatchewan History* 4, no. 1 (spring 1951): 27–28.

47. P. A. Mazzone, "An Immigrant Family in Saskatchewan 1903–1943," *Canadian Ethnic Studies* 12, no. 3 (fall 1980): 134.

48. E. Mitchell, *In Western Canada Before the War* (London: J. Murray, 1915), 47.

49. *Pioneer Surveys*, M. McManus, 1906, Saskatchewan Archives Board, 2110.

50. P. A. Maxwell, *Percy Augustus Maxwell: Letters Home* (Toronto: 1967), 120.

51. S. Rollings-Magnusson, "Canada's Most Wanted: Pioneer Women on the Canadian Prairies," *Canadian Review of Sociology and Anthropology* 37, no. 2 (May 2000): 225–29; S. B. Kohl, *Working Together: Women and Family in Southwestern Saskatchewan* (Toronto: Holt, Rinehart, and Winston, 1976): 32–36; A. C. Moffatt, "Experiencing Identity: British-Canadian Women in Rural Saskatchewan, 1880–1950" (unpublished Ph.D. diss., University of Manitoba, 1996), 111.

52. N. McClung, *In Times Like These* (Toronto: McLeod and Allen, 1915), 191.

53. Canada, House of Commons, *Debates*, 30 April 1910, 8489–90. In the United States, any woman (American-born or naturalized citizen) eighteen or older could claim a homestead.

54. G. Binnie-Clark, *Wheat and Women* (London: Heinneman, 1914), 395–96.

55. C. A. Cavanaugh, "'No Place for a Woman': Engendering Western Canadian Settlement," *Western Historical Quarterly* 28 (winter 1997): 505.

56. *Grain Growers' Guide*, 6 July 1910.

57. Ibid., 3 November 1915.

58. Ibid., 10 November 1915.

59. Ibid., 14 August 1909.

60. M. E. McCallum, "Prairie Women and the Struggle for a Dower Law, 1905–1920," *Prairie Forum* 18, no. 1 (spring 1993): 19–34; S. Rollings-Magnusson, "Hidden Homesteaders: Women, the State, and Patriarchy in the Saskatchewan Wheat Economy, 1870–1930," *Prairie Forum* 24, no. 2 (fall 1999): 171–83.

61. J. H. Gray, *The Roar of the Twenties* (Toronto: Macmillan, 1975), 45.

62. "Pioneer Days," Morton manuscript collection, C555/1/2.29.

63. *Pioneer Surveys*, Mrs. J. I. Anderson, no. 218, Saskatchewan Archives Board.

64. Quoted in Saskatchewan Women's Division, *Saskatchewan Women, 1905–1980* (Regina: Saskatchewan Labour Women's Division, 1980), 21.

65. B. Bent, "Latter Day Pioneering," Morton manuscript collection, C555/1/1.5.

66. LaDow, *The Medicine Line*, 165.

67. N. Langford, "Childbirth on the Canadian Prairies," in *Telling Tales: Essays in Western Women's History*, ed. C. A. Cavanaugh and R. R. Warne (Vancouver: University of British Columbia Press, 2000), 170.

68. Moffatt, "Experiencing Identity," 111.

69. Quoted in LaDow, *The Medicine Line*, 186.

70. Neatby, *Chronicle*, 4, 20.

71. W. Stegner, *Wolf Willow: A History, A Story, and a Memory of the Last Plains Frontier* (New York: Viking, 1962), 3–4.

72. N. L. Lewis, "Goose Grease and Turpentine: Mother Treats the Family's Illnesses," *Prairie Forum* 15, no. 1 (spring 1990): 67–84.

73. G. Swerhone, email communication to author, 24 June 2003.

74. E. C. Morgan, "Pioneer Recreation and Social Life," *Saskatchewan History* 18, no. 2 (spring 1965): 41–54; S. Mein, "The Aberdeen Association: An Early Attempt to Provide Library Services to Settlers in Saskatchewan," *Saskatchewan History* 38, no. 1 (winter 1985): 2–19; C. Tulloch, "Pioneer Reading," *Saskatchewan History* 12, no. 3 (summer 1959): 97–99.

75. *Pioneer Surveys*, T. E. Perry, no. 219, Saskatchewan Archives Board.

76. J. H. Archer, *Saskatchewan: A History* (Saskatoon: Western Producer Prairie Books, 1980), 163.

77. C. MacDonald, "Pioneer Church Life in Saskatchewan," *Saskatchewan History* 13, no. 1 (spring 1960): 16.

78. D. C. Jones, *Midways, Judges, and Smooth-Tongued Fakirs: The Illustrated Story of Country Fairs in the Prairie West* (Saskatoon: Western Producer Prairie Books, 1983).

79. D. G. Wetherell, "A Season of Mixed Blessings: Winter and Leisure in Alberta before World War Two," in *Winter Sports in the West*, ed. E. A. Corbet and A. W. Rasporich (Calgary: Historical Society of Alberta, 1990), 42–44; F. R. Holt, *Sharing the Good Times: A History of Prairie Women's Joys and Pleasures* (Calgary: Detselig Enterprises, 2000); R. Ellis and E. Nixon, *Saskatchewan's Recreation Legacy* (Saskatoon: Modern Press, 1986); Morgan, "Pioneer Recreation and Social Life," 47.

80. P. Hack and D. Shury, *Wheat Province Diamonds: A Story of Saskatchewan Baseball* (Regina: Saskatchewan Baseball Association, 1997), 8–10.

81. S. Ellis, *A Prairie as Wide as the Sea: The Immigrant Diary of Ivy Weatherall* (Markham: Scholastic Canada, 2001), 17.

82. Minifie, *Homesteader*, 29.

83. R. Jickling diary, Manuscript Division, National Archives of Canada.

CHAPTER SEVEN:
A VERY NICE FAIRY TALE

1. Craig Brown and Ramsay Cook contend that "the success of the Laurier government's western settlement policies bore the seeds of the Liberal's destruction." *Canada, 1896–1921: A Nation Transformed* (Toronto: McClelland and Stewart, 1974), 144.

2. F. G. Roe, "Early Agriculture in Western Canada in Relation to Climatic Stability," *Agricultural History* 26, no. 3 (July 1952): 104–23.

3. B. Stonechild and B. Waiser, *Loyal till Death: Indians and the North-West Rebellion* (Calgary: Fifth House, 1997), 29–37.

4. Quoted in D. C. Jones, *Empire of Dust: Settling and Abandoning the Prairie Belt* (Calgary: University of Calgary Press, 2002), 16.

5. The CPR also established showcase farms at six stations along the main line in southwestern Saskatchewan (Secretan, Rush Lake, Swift Current, Gull Lake, Maple Creek, and Forres) to try to dispel the notion that the area the railway ran through was little better than a desert. E. H. Oliver, "The Settlement of Saskatchewan to 1914," *Transactions of the Royal Society of Canada 20*, series 3, section 2 (1926): 68.

6. J. W. Morrison, "Marquis Wheat: A Triumph of Scientific Endeavour," *Agricultural History* 34, no. 4 (October 1960): 182–88.

7. S. Carter, *Lost Harvests: Prairie Indian Reserve Farmers and Government Policy* (Montreal: McGill-Queen's University Press, 1990), 50–72.

8. R. Widdis, *With Scarcely a Ripple: Anglo-Canadian Migration into the United States and Western Canada, 1880–1920* (Montreal: McGill-Queen's University Press, 1998), 33–34.

9. Agriculture Canada, *Indian Head Experimental Farm, 1886–1986* (Ottawa: Agriculture Canada, 1986), ch. 3.

10. G. Friesen, *The Canadian Prairies: A History* (Toronto: University of Toronto Press, 1984), 329–31; C. Danysk, *Hired Hands: Labour and the Development of Prairie Agriculture, 1880–1930* (Toronto: McClelland and Stewart, 1995), 93–96.

11. See D. De Brou and B. Waiser, *Documenting Canada: A History of Modern Canada in Documents* (Saskatoon: Fifth House, 1992), 185–94.

12. M. Knuttila, *That Man Partridge: E. A. Partridge, His Thoughts and Times* (Regina: Canadian Plains Research Center, 1994).

13. W. A. Mackintosh, *Prairie Settlement: the Geographical Setting* (Toronto: Macmillan, 1934), 53–56.

14. Quoted in T. D. Regehr, *The Canadian Northern Railway: Pioneer Road of the Northern Prairies, 1895–1918* (Toronto: Macmillan, 1976), 191.

15. Quoted in ibid., 190.

16. Quoted in J. Eagle, *The Canadian Pacific Railway and the Development of Western Canada, 1896–1914* (Montreal: McGill-Queen's University Press, 1989), 104.

17. Ibid., 101–104.

18. Regehr, *The Canadian Northern Railway*, 160. See table vii for a listing of Canadian Northern construction on the prairies between 1897 and 1916. G. R. Stevens, *History of the Canadian National Railways* (New York: Macmillan, 1973), 254.

19. J. Everitt, "The Line Elevator in Saskatchewan," *Saskatchewan History* 64, no. 2 (spring 1992): 41–47. For a history of the elevator in western Canada, see B. V. Silversides, *Prairie Sentinel: The Story of the Canadian Grain Elevator* (Calgary: Fifth House, 1997).

20. *Census of Population and Agriculture of the Northwest Provinces, 1906: Manitoba, Saskatchewan, Alberta* (Ottawa: King's Printer, 1907), xxii–xxix.

21. D. Spector, *Agriculture on the Prairies, 1870–1940* (Ottawa: Parks Canada, 1983), 5.

22. J. H. Thompson, "Bringing in the Sheaves: The Harvest Excursionists, 1890–1929," *Canadian Historical Review* 59, no. 4 (December 1978): 447–89; W. J. Cherwinski, "The Incredible Harvest Excursion of 1908," *Labour/Le Travail*, no. 5 (spring 1980): 57–79.

23. Friesen, *The Canadian Prairies*, 301; B. LaDow, *The Medicine Line: Life and Death on a North American Borderland* (New York: Routledge, 2001), 86.

24. For the historical background of the Hudson Bay railway idea, see D. Owram, *Promise of Eden: The Canadian Expansionist Movement and the Idea of the West, 1856–1900* (Toronto: University of Toronto Press, 1980), 180–90.

25. Brown and Cook, *Canada, 1896–1921*, 153–54.
26. W. L. Morton, *The Progressive Party in Canada* (Toronto: University of Toronto Press, 1950), 11.
27. Quoted in J. W. Brennan, "A Political History of Saskatchewan, 1905–1929" (unpublished Ph.D. diss., University of Alberta, 1976), 139.
28. Brennan, "Political History of Saskatchewan," 140–60; R. Irwin, "'The Better Sense of the Farm Population': The Partridge Plan and Grain Marketing in Saskatchewan," *Prairie Forum* 18, no. 1 (spring 1993): 35–48.
29. E. Porritt, *The Revolt in Canada Against the New Feudalism* (London: Cassell, 1911).
30. Brown and Cook, *Canada, 1896–1921*, 18–21, 157–58.
31. "Sir Wilfrid Laurier's Tour of the Western Provinces," *The Canadian Annual Review of Public Affairs, 1910* (Toronto: Annual Review Pub. Co., 1911), 264.
32. *Toronto Globe*, 25 July 1910.
33. "Laurier's Tour," 269.
34. Ibid., 271.
35. B. Robertson, *Wilfrid Laurier: The Great Conciliator* (Toronto: Oxford University Press, 1971), 123.
36. "Laurier's Tour," 272–74.
37. *Toronto Globe*, 5 August 1910.
38. National Archives of Canada, Government Archives Division, RG 46, v. 1419, f. 15381.
39. "Laurier's Tour," 282.
40. N. S. Elliott, "'We Have Asked For Bread, and You Gave Us a Stone': Western Farmers and the Siege of Ottawa" (unpublished M.A. thesis, University of Saskatchewan, 2004), 85–106.
41. Quoted in ibid., 107
42. Brown and Cook, *Canada, 1896–1921*, 161, 179–80.
43. Brennan, "A Political History of Saskatchewan," 164–65.
44. Just two decades earlier in the 1891 federal election, western farmers had supported the Conservative party and the National Policy. See J. R. Miller, "The 1891 Election in Western Canada," *Prairie Forum* 10, no. 1 (spring 1985): 147–67.
45. Brennan, "A Political History of Saskatchewan," 172–96.

CHAPTER EIGHT:
LIKE VAPOUR FROM A RIVER

1. P. Dederick and B. Waiser, *Looking Back: True Tales from Saskatchewan's Past* (Calgary: Fifth House, 2003), 22–24.
2. G. Abrams, *Prince Albert: The First Century, 1866–1966* (Saskatoon: Modern Press, 1966), 16–18.
3. Fort Livingstone is often referred to by several other names: Livingstone, Livingstone Barracks, Swan River Barracks, and Fort Pelly. It was not the first choice for the new territorial capital. The Mackenzie government originally designated Fort Ellice, a HBC post further south, as capital in May 1874, but then changed its mind two months later.
4. For a brief history of the selection and construction of the dominion telegraph line across western Canada and its relationship with the CPR, see W. A. Waiser, "The Government Explorer in Canada, 1870–1914," in *North American Exploration, v. 3: A Continent Comprehended*, ed. J. L. Allen, (Lincoln: University of Nebraska Press, 1997), 435–39.
5. Quoted in S. Hewitt, "Fort Livingstone: A History," unpublished Parks Canada report, Saskatoon office, n.d.
6. Ibid.
7. Ibid.
8. A. McPherson, *The Battlefords: A History* (North Battleford, SK: Battleford and North Battleford, 1967), 32–39.
9. Ibid., 44.
10. Ibid., 41–50.
11. Abrams, *Prince Albert*, 18.
12. Ibid., v; McPherson, *The Battlefords*, 131; C. Mair, "Open the Bay" from *Dreamland and other poems* (Montreal: Dawson Brothers, 1868), 170.
13. See T. Herriot, *River in a Dry Land: A Prairie Passage* (Toronto: Stoddart, 2000).
14. Quoted in R. Rees, *New and Naked Land: Making the Prairies Home* (Saskatoon: Western Producer Prairie Books, 1988), 127.
15. J. W. Brennan, *Regina: An Illustrated History* (Toronto: Lorimer, 1989), 12.
16. Ibid., 12–14.
17. H. Graham, *Across Canada to the Klondyke* (Toronto: Methuen, 1984), 24.
18. Brennan, *Regina*, 18–19, 29–31.
19. P. Voisey, "The Urbanization of the Canadian Prairies 1871–1960," *Histoire Sociale/Social History* 8, no. 15 (May 1975): 82.
20. A. Artibise, "The Urban West: The Evolution of Prairie Towns and Cities to 1930," *Prairie Forum* 4, no. 2 (fall 1979): 256 (table).
21. Voisey, "Urbanization," 78–85, see also table II; R. Rees, "The Small Towns of Saskatchewan," *Landscape* 18, no. 3 (fall 1969): 29.
22. M. B. Leyton-Brown, "The History of Estevan During the Territorial Period" (unpublished M.A. thesis, University of Regina, 1982).
23. Voisey, "Urbanization," 83.
24. D. G. Wetherell and I. R. A. Kmet, *Town Life: Main Street and the Evolution of Small Town Alberta, 1880–1947* (Edmonton: University of Alberta Press, 1995), 2–6.
25. Rees, "Small Towns," 30.
26. Quoted in G. R. Stevens, *History of the Canadian National Railways* (New York: Macmillan, 1973), 224.
27. B. Barry, *People Places: Saskatchewan and its Names* (Regina: Canadian Plains Research Center, 1997), 49–63. The CPR started to build an alphabet line south from Moose Jaw in 1912 (starting with the word Archive), but abandoned the naming approach at Expanse.

28. C. W. Bohi and H. R. Grant, "The Standardized Railroad Station in Saskatchewan: The Case of the Canadian National System," *Saskatchewan History* 29, no. 3 (autumn 1976): 81–102; C. W. Bohi and H. R. Grant, "The Standardized Railroad Station in Saskatchewan: The Case of the Canadian Pacific," *Saskatchewan History* 31, no. 3 (autumn 1978): 81–96.

29. Rees, "Small Towns," 31.

30. D. W. Holdsworth and J. C. Everitt, "Bank Branches and Elevators: Expressions of Big Corporations in Small Prairie Towns," *Prairie Forum* 13, no. 2 (fall 1998): 173–77.

31. C. Macdonald, "Pioneer Church Life in Saskatchewan," *Saskatchewan History* 13, no. 2 (winter 1960): 9.

32. J. M. Dewar, *Saskatchewan Soccer: A History* (Saskatoon: Saskatchewan Soccer Association, 1988), 1–2; B. Zeman, *Hockey Heritage: 88 Years of Puck-Chasing in Saskatchewan* (Regina: WDS Associates, 1983), 2.

33. W. Humber, *Diamonds of the North: a concise history of baseball in Canada* (Toronto: Oxford University Press, 1995), 75.

34. L. Stubbs, *Shoestring Glory: A Prairie History of Semi-Pro Baseball, 1886–1994* (Winnipeg: Turnstone Press, 1996), 26.

35. Quoted in P. Hack and D. Shury, *Wheat Province Diamonds: a story of Saskatchewan Baseball* (Regina: Saskatchewan Baseball Association, 1997), 24.

36. Quoted in ibid., p. 25.

37. A. Artibise, "Introduction," in *Town and City: Aspects of Western Canadian Urban Development*, ed. A. Artibise (Regina: Canadian Plains Research Center, 1981), 205–207; Voisey, "Urbanization," 84–89. See also A. Artibise, "Boosterism and the Development of Prairie Cities, 1871–1913," in *The Prairie West*, ed. R. D. Francis and H. Palmer (Edmonton: University of Alberta Press, 1992), 515–43.

38. D. S. Richan, "Boosterism and Urban Rivalry in Regina and Moose Jaw, 1902–1913" (unpublished M.A. thesis, University of Regina, 1981).

39. See J. Larsen and M. R. Libby, *Moose Jaw: People, Places, History* (Regina: Couteau, 2001).

40. Brennan, *Regina*, 55–58, 61.

41. Quoted in R. Rees, "The 'Magic City on the Banks of the Saskatchewan': The Saskatoon Real Estate Boom 1910–1913," *Saskatchewan History* 27, no. 2 (spring 1974): 512.

42. D. McGowan, *Grassland Settlers: the Swift Current region during the era of the ranching frontier* (Regina: Canadian Plains Research Center, 1975), 123–26.

43. McPherson, *The Battlefords*, 149.

44. Abrams, *Prince Albert*, 128, 140, 174–77.

45. D. Kerr and S. D. Hanson, *Saskatoon: The First Half-Century* (Edmonton: NeWest Publishers, 1982), 40–41, 49.

46. Quoted in Rees, "Magic City," 53.

47. Quoted in *A Prairie Memoir: The Life and Times of James Clinkskill, 1853–1936*, ed. S. D. Hanson (Regina: Canadian Plains Research Center, 2003), 150.

48. E. B. Mitchell, *In Western Canada Before the War* (London: J. Murray, 1915), 74–75.

49. E. R. Stuart, *The History of Prairie Theatre: The Development of Theatre in Alberta, Manitoba, and Saskatchewan, 1833–1982* (Toronto: Simon and Pierre Pub. Co., 1984), 36, 65–66, 74; P. B. O'Neill, "Regina's Golden Age of Theatre: Her Playhouses and Players," *Saskatchewan History* 28, no. 1 (spring 1975): 29–32.

50. B. Calder and G. Andrews, *Rider Pride: the story of Canada's best-loved football team* (Saskatoon: Western Producer Prairie Books, 1984), 6.

51. B. Zeman, *Hockey Heritage*, 31–33.

52. M. Boyle, *Ninety Years of Golf: An Illustrated History of Golf on the Prairie* (Regina: Saskatchewan Golf Association, 1987), 17–22.

53. Rees, *New and Naked Land*, 128–32.

54. Artibise, "Boosterism," 524.

55. Abrams, *Prince Albert*, 179–80.

56. Artibise, "Boosterism," 529.

57. Mitchell, *In Western Canada*, 114.

58. Artibise, "Boosterism," 526–28.

59. Kerr and Hanson, *Saskatoon*, 104–45.

60. Ibid., 57, 90–92; Brennan, *Regina*, 65–68, 82.

61. A. Artibise, "Patterns of Prairie Urban Development, 1871–1950," in *Eastern and Western Perspectives*, ed. P. Buckner and D. Bercuson (Toronto: University of Toronto Press, 1981), 124.

62. McPherson, *The Battlefords*, 163.

63. *The Globe and Mail*, 13 August 2002, A7.

64. Dederick and Waiser, *Looking Back*, 22–24.

65. Quoted in Brennan, *Regina*, 83.

66. Stuart, *History of Prairie Theatre*, 69–70.

67. Richan, "Boosterism and Urban Rivalry," 177; Brennan, *Regina*, 110; Abrams, *Prince Albert*, 203–19, 213, 236.

68. Brennan, *Regina*, 91.

69. Kerr and Hanson, *Saskatoon*, 145.

CHAPTER NINE:
PAGANISM IS DYING HARD

1. Quoted in M. K. Lux, *Medicine That Walks: Disease, Medicine, and Canadian Plains Native People, 1880–1940* (Toronto: University of Toronto Press, 2001), 159.

2. For a history of Saskatchewan treaties, see A. J. Ray et al., *Bounty and Benevolence: A History of Saskatchewan Treaties* (Montreal: McGill-Queen's University Press, 2000).

3. Lux, *Medicine That Walks*, 51.

4. Quoted in ibid., 51.

5. P. Erasmus, *Buffalo Days and Nights* (Calgary: Fifth House, 1999), 239–64; B. Stonechild and B. Waiser, *Loyal till Death: Indians and the North-West Rebellion* (Calgary: Fifth House, 1997), 59–60.

6. Ibid., 192–237.

7. S. Carter, *Lost Harvests: Prairie Indian Reserve Farmers and Government Policy* (Montreal: McGill-Queen's University Press, 1990), 248.

8. The situation was comparable to the mid-1880s and the death of four prominent Cree chiefs: Little Pine, Red Pheasant, Poundmaker, and Big Bear.

9. Quoted in Carter, *Lost Harvests*, 248.

10. D. Lee, "Foremost Man and His Band," *Saskatchewan History* 36, no. 3 (autumn 1983): 94–101.

11. D. M. Loveridge, *From Wood Mountain to the Whitemud: A Historical Survey of the Grasslands National Park Area* (Ottawa: Parks Canada, 1983), 105.

12. J. H. Richards and K.-I. Fung, eds., *Atlas of Saskatchewan* (Saskatoon: University of Saskatchewan, 1969), 94.

13. P. Martin-McGuire, *First Nation Land Surrenders on the Prairies, 1896–1911* (Ottawa: Indian Claims Commission, 1998), xxiii–xxv.

14. Lux, *Medicine that Walks*, 45, 51, 58.

15. Ibid., 142, 152–55, 181–84.

16. See D. Payment, *"The Free People—Otipemisiwak": Batoche, Saskatchewan, 1870–1930* (Ottawa: Parks Canada, 1990).

17. B. Waiser, "The North-West Rebellion," *Canada: Confederation to Present* (Edmonton: Chinook Multimedia, 2001), CD-ROM.

18. Payment, *"The Free People—Otipemisiwak,"* 204, 230–37, 281–88.

19. F. Tough, "Métis Scrip Commissions," in *Atlas of Saskatchewan*, ed. K.-I. Fung (Saskatoon: University of Saskatchewan, 1999), 61–62; *Regina Leader*, 21 June 1900. A total of 13,941 Métis claims (4,840 land, 9,101 money) were awarded in Saskatchewan and Alberta. Royal Commission on the Natural Resources of Saskatchewan, National Archives of Canada, Government Archives Division, RG 33, ser. 50, v. 10, f. 8, exhibit 120-S.

20. J. G. Diefenbaker, *One Canada: Memoirs of the Right Honourable J .G. Diefenbaker, v. 1* (Toronto: Macmillan, 1975), 26. Diefenbaker claimed to have met Dumont (1837–1906) when he was sixty-eight years old.

21. D. Smyth, "James Isbister," unpublished Historic Sites and Monuments Board Agenda Paper, 1996–52.

22. Payment, *"The Free People—Otipemisiwak,"* 78–79; F. L. Barron, *Walking in Indian Moccasins: The Native Policies of Tommy Douglas and the CCF* (Vancouver: University of British Columbia Press, 1997), 7; D. McLean, *Home from the Hill: A History of the Métis in Western Canada* (Regina: Gabriel Dumont Institute, 1987), 245–46.

23. M. Howlett, "The Forest Industry on the Prairies: Opportunities and Constraints to Future Development," *Prairie Forum* 14, no. 2 (fall 1989): 239–40; B. Waiser, *Saskatchewan's Playground* (Saskatoon: Fifth House, 1989), 11–12.

24. T. L. Strom, "When the Mounties Came: Mounted Police and Cree Relations on Two Saskatchewan Reserves" (unpublished M.A. thesis, University of Saskatchewan, 2000), 129.

25. *Department of Indian Affairs Annual Report, 1908* (Ottawa: King's Printer, 1908), xxx.

26. A. Gulig, "'We Beg the Government': Native People and Game Regulation in Northern Saskatchewan 1900–1940," *Prairie Forum* 28, no. 1 (spring 2003), 81–84.

27. See Carter, *Lost Harvests*.

28. R. Innes, B. Macdougall, and F. Tough, "Band Economies, 1897–1915," in *Atlas of Saskatchewan*, ed. K.-I. Fung, 59–60; Lux, *Medicine That Walks*, 160, 164.

29. E. Ahenakew, *Voices of the Plains Cree* (Toronto: McClelland and Stewart, 1973), 148.

30. See, for example, "Annual Report of the Department of Indian Affairs, 1913," *Sessional Papers*, 1914, no. 23, 127–28, 135, 140–61.

31. Payment, *"The Free People—Otipemisiwak,"* 59, 230.

32. "Annual Report, 1913," 161.

33. Quoted in K. Pettipas, *Severing the Ties that Bind: Government Repression of Indigenous Religious Ceremonies on the Prairies* (Winnipeg: University of Manitoba Press, 1994), 77.

34. Quoted in Lux, *Medicine That Walks*, 97.

35. H. Greyeyes, "Jim Greyeyes and the Doukhobors," in *And They Told Us Their Stories: A Book of Indian Stories*, ed. J. Funk (Saskatoon: Saskatoon District Tribal Council, 1991), 79–80.

36. N. Powers, *Personal Best: The History of Track and Field in Saskatchewan* (Regina: Saskatchewan Track and Field Association, 1997), 2–4.

37. Pettipas, *Severing the Ties*, 123–24, 141. See also C. Backhouse, *Colour Coded: A Legal History of Racism in Canada, 1900–1950* (Toronto: University of Toronto Press, 1999), 56–102.

38. Quoted in J. R. Miller, *Shingwauk's Vision: A History of Native Residential Schools* (Toronto: University of Toronto Press, 1996), 99.

39. Ibid., 100–103.

40. Canada, House of Commons, *Debates*, 7 April 1884, 1403.

41. The following schools were in operation in Saskatchewan in the first decade of the twentieth century: Battleford, Beauval, Crowstand, File Hills (Balcarres), Gordon, Île-à-la-Crosse, Lac la Ronge, LeBret (Qu'Appelle), Onion Lake (one Catholic, one Anglican), Prince Albert, Regina, Round Lake (Broadview), St. Michaels (Duck Lake), and St. Philips (Kamsack).

42. At Onion Lake, non-treaty children and even white students attended the Catholic boarding school for a fee. S. Marceau-Kozicki, "Onion Lake Indian Residential Schools, 1892–1943" (unpublished M.A. thesis, University of Saskatchewan, 1993), 78–79.

43. Quoted in Miller, *Shingwauk's Vision*, 134–35.
44. Ibid., 325.
45. E. B. Titley, *A Narrow Vision: Duncan Campbell Scott and the Administration of Indian Affairs* (Vancouver: University of British Columbia Press, 1986), 83–84.
46. J. F. Dion, *My Tribe, The Crees* (Calgary: Glenbow Museum, 1993), 129.
47. Quoted in Miller, *Shingwauk's Vision*, 133.
48. Pettipas, *Severing the Ties*, 81.
49. J. S. Milloy, *A National Crime: The Canadian Government and the Residential School System, 1879–1986* (Winnipeg: University of Manitoba Press, 1999), 155.
50. Quoted in Pettipas, *Severing the Ties*, 82.
51. Miller, *Shingwauk's Vision*, 145–48; E. Brass, "The File Hills Ex-Pupil Colony," *Saskatchewan History* 6, no. 2 (spring 1953): 66–69.
52. D. De Brou and B. Waiser, eds., *Documenting Canada: A History of Modern Canada in Documents* (Saskatoon: Fifth House, 1992), 167.
53. Quoted in W. P. Stewart, *My Name is Piapot* (Maple Creek, SK: Butterfly Books, 1981), 109.
54. Pettipas, *Severing the Ties*, 118–19.
55. Ibid., 117–18, 128–29.
56. F. L. Barron, "The Indian Pass System in the Canadian West, 1882–1935," *Prairie Forum* 13, no. 1 (spring 1988): 25; Pettipas, *Severing the Ties*, 111–12.
57. Quoted in Pettipas, *Severing the Ties*, 111.
58. Ibid., 127–35.
59. J. R. Miller, *Skyscrapers Hide the Heavens: A History of Indian-White Relations in Canada* (Toronto: University of Toronto Press, 1989), 193.
60. Quoted in Pettipas, *Severing the Ties*, 142.
61. "Notes of Representations Made by Delegation of indians from the West," National Archives of Canada, Government Archives Division, Department of Indian Affairs, RG 10, v. 4053, f. 379, 203-1.
62. Quoted in Carter, *Lost Harvests*, 257.
63. Quoted in Miller, *Skyscrapers*, 207.

CHAPTER TEN:
THE BLESSINGS OF WAR

1. Quoted in "Saskatchewan Provincial Affairs," in *The Canadian Annual Review of Public Affairs, 1914* (Toronto: Annual Review Pub. Co., 1915), 633.
2. For an examination of the symbolic significance of the war, see J. F. Vance, *Death So Noble: Memory, Meaning, and the First World War* (Vancouver: University of British Columbia Press, 1997).
3. D. Morton, *Canada and War: A Military and Political History* (Toronto: Butterworths, 1981), 54–55. In *The Harvests of War: The Prairie West, 1914–1918* (Toronto: McClelland and Stewart, 1978), J. H. Thompson suggests that Saskatchewan was oblivious to the impending war, while L. L. Begley in his 1998 unpublished University of Manitoba M.A. thesis, "The Foreign Threat: Nativism in Saskatchewan, 1896–1930," contends that war had been anticipated, as evidenced by the mobilization of local militia units before 1 August.
4. E. Drake, *Regina: The Queen City* (Toronto: McClelland and Stewart, 1955), 157; D. Kerr and S. D. Hanson, *Saskatoon: The First Half Century* (Edmonton: NeWest Publishers, 1982), 147–48.
5. Thompson, *Harvests of War*, 23–24.
6. Morton, *Canada and War*, 56.
7. J. H. Archer, *Saskatchewan: A History* (Saskatoon: Western Producer Prairie Books, 1980), 169–70.
8. Thompson, *Harvests of War*, 24.
9. *Toronto Globe and Mail*, 11 November 2002, 4 February 2003.
10. H. Baldwin, *Holding the Line* (Chicago: A. C. McClurg, 1918), vii.
11. Morton, *Canada and War*, 57.
12. Quoted in "Gleanings from the Sheaf, 1914–1919, on the Great War," *Green and White* (fall 1987): 17.
13. Quoted in S. Billinton, "The University at War: Professor Bateman on the Blessings of War," University of Saskatchewan *On Campus News*, 20 October 1995.
14. J. M. Hayden, *Seeking a Balance: The University of Saskatchewan, 1907–1982* (Vancouver: University of British Columbia Press, 1983), 82–83.
15. Quoted in Thompson, *Harvests of War*, 42.
16. J. Coggins, "A Chaplain's War: Edmund Oliver and the University of Vimy Ridge, 1916–1919," unpublished paper kindly provided to the author.
17. J. Dempsey, *Warriors of the King: Prairie Indians in World War One* (Regina: Canadian Plains Research Center, 1999), 15–16, 19–22, 31, 46–47, 62, 87–94.
18. J. W. Brennan, *Regina: An Illustrated History* (Toronto: Lorimer, 1989), 147.
19. G. Abrams, *Prince Albert: The First Century, 1866–1966* (Saskatoon: Modern Press, 1966), 220; J. Larsen and M. R. Libby, *Moose Jaw: People, Places, History* (Regina: Couteau, 2001), 36–37.
20. Kerr and Hanson, *Saskatoon*, 152–53.
21. Baldwin, *Holding the Line*, 36.
22. Gus Lambert to family, 10 April 1917, A. E. Lambert collection [M647], Glenbow Archives.
23. J. T. Jaspar to M. E. Lambert, 11 July 1969, ibid.
24. Archer, *Saskatchewan*, 170.
25. Dempsey, *Warriors of the King*, 87–94.
26. Hayden, *Seeking a Balance*, 330 n. 6.
27. J. L. McWilliams and R. J. Steel, *The Suicide Battalion* (Edmonton: Hurtig, 1978).
28. V. Clemence, *Saskatchewan's Own: People who Made a Difference* (Calgary: Fifth House, 2004), 156–60. The other five Saskatchewan recipients of the Victoria Cross were Arthur George Knight, William Johnstone Milne, George Harry Mullins, Michael O'Leary, and Ralph Louis Zengel.

29. For a list of Saskatchewan donations to the war effort, see "What Saskatchewan Has Done in the Great War" (Regina: Saskatchewan Department of Education, 1919), a government pamphlet for schoolchildren. The total provincial contribution to the Canadian Patriotic Fund, for example, was almost three million dollars.

30. For a list of funds raised by Saskatchewan reserves during the war, see Dempsey, *Warriors of the King*, 104–105.

31. Thompson, *Harvests of War*, 109.

32. M. M. C. Dirk, "Imperial Order Daughters of the Empire and the First World War: Combining Imperialism and the Cult of True Womanhood for the War Effort" (unpublished M.A. thesis, Carleton University, 1987), 70. See also N. Small, "Stand by the Union Jack: The Imperial Order Daughters of the Empire in the Prairie Provinces during the Great War, 1914–1918" (unpublished M.A. thesis, University of Saskatchewan, 1988).

33. Dirk, "IODE and the First World War," 118.

34. Quoted in ibid., 79.

35. According to the 1911 census, there were 957 Chinese in Saskatchewan (0.2 per cent of the total provincial population). Of these, 268 (or roughly 25 per cent) lived in the Moose Jaw district, the highest concentration in western Canada after Winnipeg and Calgary. *Fifth Census of Canada, 1911, v.* 2 (Ottawa: King's Printer, 1913), 371.

36. J. Walker, *Race, Rights and the Law in the Supreme Court of Canada: Historical Case Studies* (Waterloo: Wilfrid Laurier University Press, 1997), 51–121; C. Backhouse, *Colour Coded: A Legal History of Racism in Canada, 1900–1950* (Toronto: University of Toronto Press, 1999), 132–50.

37. *Fifth Census of Canada, 1911, v.* 2, 340.

38. E. B. Mitchell, *In Western Canada Before the War* (London: J. Murray, 1915), 167, 188.

39. Quoted in Thompson, *Harvests of War*, 94.

40. G. L. Barnhart, *Peace, Progress and Prosperity: A Biography of Saskatchewan's First Premier, T. Walter Scott* (Regina: Canadian Plains Research Center, 2000), 128.

41. B. Waiser, *Park Prisoners: The Untold Story of Western Canada's National Parks, 1914–1946* (Saskatoon: Fifth House, 1995), 4–8.

42. Quoted in ibid., 10.

43. Quoted in Begley, "The Foreign Threat: Nativism in Saskatchewan," 66–67.

44. Brennan, *Regina*, 113.

45. Thompson, *Harvests of War*, 76–77, 81.

46. For a list of name changes, see E. T. Russell, *What's in a Name?: The Story behind Saskatchewan Place Names* (Saskatoon: Western Producer Prairie Books, 1980), 170–71.

47. Quoted in Waiser, *Park Prisoners*, 6.

48. See ibid. for an examination of internment labour in western Canada's national parks.

49. G. Friesen, *The Canadian Prairies: A History* (Toronto: University of Toronto Press, 1984), 355.

50. Ratepayers were supporting schools (public or separate) with the lower assessment to avoid a higher tax bill, regardless of whether their children went to the public or separate school.

51. R. Huel, "Pastor vs. Politician: The Reverend Murdoch Mackinnon and Premier Walter Scott's Amendment to the School Act," *Saskatchewan History* 32, no. 2 (spring 1979): 61–62.

52. F. Stambrook and S. Hryniuk, "Who Were They Really?: Reflections on East European Immigrants to Manitoba before 1914," *Prairie Forum* 25, no. 2 (fall 2000): 232 n. 95.

53. Thompson, *Harvests of War*, 89–91. Replies to a 1918 questionnaire indicated that French was used in seventy-seven schools, German in seventy-one, and Ukrainian in thirty-seven. R. Huel, "The French Canadians and the Language Question, 1918," *Saskatchewan History* 23, no. 1 (winter 1970): 10. C. O. White argues that many more German Catholics were establishing and operating unilingual English public than bilingual parochial schools and that a majority of German Catholic children were receiving an elementary education comparable to that in Anglo-Celtic districts. "Pre-World War One Elementary Educational Developments Among Saskatchewan's German Catholics: A Revisionist View," *Prairie Forum* 18, no. 2 (fall 1993): 171–96.

54. Quoted in R. Huel, "The Public School as a Guardian of Anglo-Saxon Traditions: The Saskatchewan Experience, 1913–1918," in *Ethnic Canadians: Culture and Education*, ed. M. L. Kovacs (Regina: Canadian Plains Research Center, 1978), 300.

55. Ibid., 299–300.

56. Brennan, "Political History of Saskatchewan," 391–407.

57. Quoted in Barnhart, *Peace, Progress and Prosperity*, 139.

58. Quoted in Brennan, "Political History of Saskatchewan," 408.

59. Vance, *Death So Noble*, 37–40.

60. For a history of early government activity in this area, see K. Marschall, "Raising Juvenile Delinquents: The Development of Saskatchewan's Child Welfare Laws, 1905–1930" (unpublished M.A. thesis, University of Saskatchewan, 2003).

61. D. H. Bocking, "The Saskatchewan Board of Film Censors, 1910–1935," *Saskatchewan History* 24, no. 2 (spring 1971): 51–62.

62. J. H. Gray, *Red Lights on the Prairies* (Toronto: Macmillan, 1971), 9, 86–89, 99–110.

63. Brennan, "Political History of Saskatchewan," 225–27, 243–55.

64. J. Menzies, "Votes for Saskatchewan Women," in N. Ward and D. Spafford, *Politics in Saskatchewan* (Don Mills: Longmans, 1968), 79; C. MacDonald, "How Saskatchewan Women Got the Vote," *Saskatchewan History* 1, no. 3 (fall 1948): 1–8.

65. E. A. Kalmakoff, "Woman Suffrage in Saskatchewan" (unpublished M.A. thesis, University of Regina, 1993), 34–53.

66. Quoted in Menzies, "Votes," 81.

67. Ibid., 79–85; A. Moffatt, "Where the Emphasis on Sex was Less: The Women's Section of the Canadian Council of Agriculture" (unpublished M.A. thesis, University of Saskatchewan, 1990), 3.

68. Quoted in M. R. Marrus, *Mr. Sam: The Life and Times of Samuel Bronfman* (Toronto: Viking, 1991), 63.

69. Quoted in Brennan, "Political History of Saskatchewan," 260.

70. Thompson, *Harvests of War*, 102.

71. Quoted in Menzies, "Votes," 84.

72. Quoted in ibid., 90.

73. Quoted in ibid., 91.

74. Kalmakoff, "Woman Suffrage," 69–71, 99–103, 150.

75. S. Ramsland to her parents, 29 November 1919, Sarah Ramsland Papers, Saskatchewan Archives Board.

76. Brennan, "Political History of Saskatchewan," 377.

CHAPTER ELEVEN:
LITTLE SHORT OF MADNESS

1. A. Artibise, "Patterns of Prairie Urban Development, 1871–1950," in *Eastern and Western Persectives*, ed. P. Buckner and D. Bercuson (Toronto: University of Toronto Press, 1981), 124–29; J. H. Thompson, *The Harvests of War: The Prairie West, 1914–1918* (Toronto: McClelland and Stewart, 1978), 45, 48–49, 58; G. Abrams, *Prince Albert, The First Century, 1866–1966* (Saskatoon: Modern Press, 1966), 236; J. W. Brennan, *Regina: An Illustrated History* (Toronto: Lorimer, 1989), 128.

2. Thompson, *Harvests of War*, 51–59.

3. Quoted in ibid., 58.

4. Ibid., 13.

5. Quoted in D. C. Jones, "We'll All be Buried Down Here in this Dry Belt," *Saskatchewan History* 35, no. 2 (spring 1982): 41.

6. See "Report of the Ranching and Grazing Investigation Commission, 1913," Department of Interior, 1913.

7. Jones, "We'll All be Buried," 42.

8. Thompson, *Harvests of War*, 17–18.

9. J. W. Brennan, "A Political History of Saskatchewan, 1905–1929" (unpublished Ph.D. diss., University of Alberta, 1976), 217–18; Province of Saskatchewan, "A Submission by the Government of Saskatchewan to the Royal Commission on Dominion Provincial Relations," 1937, 148, table XI.

10. Jones, "We'll All be Buried," 42.

11. Quoted in B. Potyondi, *In Palliser's Triangle: Living in the Grasslands, 1850–1930* (Saskatoon: Purich Publishing, 1995), 85.

12. J. F. C. Wright, *Saskatchewan: The History of a Province* (Toronto: McClelland and Stewart, 1955), 174–75; J. H. Archer, *Saskatchewan: A History* (Saskatoon: Western Producer Prairie Books, 1980), 168.

13. C. Danysk, *Hired Hands: Labour and the Development of Prairie Agriculture, 1880–1930* (Toronto: McClelland and Stewart, 1995), 106.

14. B. E. Kelcey, "The Great Gopher War," *The Beaver* 79, no. 3 (June-July 1999): 17.

15. Danysk, *Hired Hands*, 102; Brennan, "Political History of Saskatchewan," 221.

16. B. W. Dawson, "Better Than a Few Squirrels: The Greater Production Campaign on the First Nations Reserves of the Canadian Prairies" (unpublished M.A. thesis, University of Saskatchewan, 2001), 4–5, 56.

17. Quoted in ibid., 67–68.

18. J. Dempsey, *Warriors of the King: Prairie Indians in World War One* (Regina: Canadian Plains Research Center, 1999), 34–35.

19. V. C. Friesen, "Seager Wheeler, Wheat King," *Saskatchewan History* 48, no. 2 (fall 1996): 17–25. In 1943, King George VI made Wheeler a member of the Order of the British Empire.

20. Quoted in G. L. Barnhart, *Peace, Progress and Prosperity: A Biography of Saskatchewan's First Premier, T. Walter Scott* (Regina: Canadian Plains Research Center, 2000), 72.

21. D. Spector, *Agriculture on the Prairies, 1870–1940* (Ottawa: Parks Canada, 1983), 163–67.

22. M. W. Hislop, "Trains took technical information to Saskatchewan farm communities," *Western People*, 18 December 1986.

23. R. B. Shepard, "Tractors and Combines in the Second Stage of Agricultural Mechanization on the Canadian Plains," *Prairie Forum* 11, no. 2 (fall 1986): 255–56. During the Great War years in the three prairie provinces, the total farm acreage increased by more than one-half, while the total improved farm acreage almost doubled. Thompson, *Harvests of War*, 59.

24. Brennan, "Political History of Saskatchewan," 316–17. In 1916, the rural/urban split was 72.79 per cent rural, 27.21 urban.

25. Quoted in R. G. Marchildon, "The Women's Section of the Saskatchewan Grain Growers' Association: A Study in Agrarian Activism" (unpublished M.A. thesis, University of Victoria, 1982), 88.

26. Ibid., 25, 57, 66–69, 90–114, 122–23.

27. J. M. Hayden, *Seeking a Balance: The University of Saskatchewan, 1907–1982* (Vancouver: University of British Columbia Press, 1983), 68, 124.

28. Thompson, *Harvests of War*, 109–10.

29. Quoted in *Saskatchewan Farmer* 4, no. 4 (January 1914).

30. Quoted in Thompson, *Harvests of War*, 61.

31. Quoted in Spector, *Agriculture on the Prairies*, 161.

32. Thompson, *Harvests of War*, 61; Spector, *Agriculture on the Prairies*, 113.

33. Saskatchewan, "Submission," 148, Table XI.

34. In an article entitled, "Always the Bridesmaid: The Development of the Saskatchewan Beef Production System," *Saskatchewan History* 42, no. 3, (autumn 1989), C. M. Williams claims that the war "did little for the beef industry" (114). But between 1908 and 1919, the production of beef cattle and swine increased 500 per cent, dairy cattle 400 per cent, and sheep 300 per cent. Spector, *Agriculture on the Prairies*, 5.

35. B. Anderson, *Beyond the Range: A History of the Saskatchewan Stock Growers Association* (Regina: The Association, 1988), 14.

36. D. H. Breen, *The Canadian Prairie West and the Ranching Frontier, 1874–1924* (Toronto: University of Toronto Press, 1983), 190–205.

37. H. E. Bronson, "The Saskatchewan Meat Packing Industry: Some Historical Highlights," *Saskatchewan History* 26, no. 1 (winter 1973), 24; S. Evans, "The Saskatchewan Range in 1906 and 1921," in *Atlas of Saskatchewan*, ed. K.-I. Fung (Saskatoon: University of Saskatchewan, 1999), 64–65.

38. J. H. Archer, "The Saskatchewan Stock Growers' Association," *Saskatchewan History* 12, no. 2 (spring 1959): 43–59. The six ranchers were John D. Simpson, Robert Cruikshank, Olaf Olafson, and John H. Grayson of Moose Jaw, William H. Ogle of Wood Mountain, and Treffle Bonneau of Willow Bunch.

39. Spector, *Agriculture on the Prairies*, 5, 58.

40. Quoted in Thompson, *Harvests of War*, 68.

41. Brennan, "Political History of Saskatchewan," 217–20; W. A. Mackintosh, *Prairie Settlement: the Geographical Setting* (Toronto: Macmillan, 1934), 128.

42. In 1917, there were 4,105 homestead entries and 3,588 cancellations. In 1918, there were 2,741 entries and 2,193 cancellations. See Danysk, *Hired Hands*, 184–86, table 3.

43. Thompson, *Harvests of War*, 61–62.

44. Danysk, *Hired Hands*, 102; Wright, *Saskatchewan*, 177.

45. Brennan, "Political History of Saskatchewan," 220–21.

46. Thompson, *Harvests of War*, 63–65.

47. Wright, *Saskatchewan*, 168–69.

48. Brennan, "Political History of Saskatchewan," 223–24. The following year, the province repeated the feat, even though the harvest had been poor.

49. D. De Brou and B. Waiser, eds., *Documenting Canada: A History of Modern Canada in Documents* (Saskatoon: Fifth House, 1992), 256–59.

50. Brennan, "Political History of Saskatchewan," 306–307.

51. Ibid., 307–46. The three MLAs found guilty by the three royal commissions were E. H. Devline, J. A. Sheppard, and H. C. Pierce; only Devline served time in jail. Two others, S. R. Moore and C. H. Cawthorpe, were purged from the party.

52. Quoted in Brennan, "Political History of Saskatchewan," 329.

53. Quoted in T. D. Regehr, "William M. Martin," in *Saskatchewan Premiers of the 20th Century*, ed. G. L. Barnhart (Regina: Canadian Plains Research Center, 2004), 40.

54. Ibid., 45.

55. Brennan, "Political History of Saskatchewan," 330–36; Regehr, "Martin," 44–49.

56. Quoted in Abrams, *Prince Albert*, 225.

57. G. Da Pont, "W. M. Martin and the Farmers' Movement in Saskatchewan, 1916–1922" (unpublished M.A. thesis, University of Saskatchewan, 1976), 18–20; Brennan, "Political History of Saskatchewan," 364–75.

58. Three new seats in the Saskatchewan legislature were set aside for soldier representatives to be elected in the fall of 1917 by Saskatchewan men serving in Belgium, France, and England. Brennan, "Political History of Saskatchewan," 369.

59. See E. Kalmakoff, "Naturally Divided: Women in Saskatchewan Politics, 1916–1919," *Saskatchewan History* 46, no. 2 (fall 1994), 3–18.

60. Quoted in Brennan, "Political History of Saskatchewan," 225.

61. Quoted in ibid., 379.

62. Ibid., 377–85; Thompson, *Harvests of War*, 124–31.

63. Da Pont, "Martin," 38–41.

64. Quoted in Abrams, *Prince Albert*, 227.

65. Brennan, "Political History of Saskatchewan," 388–91; Thompson, *Harvests of War*, 138–45.

66. Quoted in Thompson, *Harvests of War*, 152.

67. Ibid., 147–65.

68. For a description of the last months of the war and the Canadian role, see J. L. Granatstein and D. Morton, *Canada and the Two World Wars* (Toronto: Key Porter Books, 2003), 133–49.

69. C. Garbay, "My Fallen Hero," *Out Front*, CBC National Radio, 4 December 2001.

70. E. G. Drake, *Regina: the Queen City* (Toronto: McClelland and Stewart, 1955), 167; D. Kerr and S. D. Hanson, *Saskatoon: The First Half-Century* (Edmonton: NeWest Publishers, 1982), 184.

71. M. K. Lux, "The Impact of the Spanish Influenza Pandemic in Saskatchewan, 1918–19" (unpublished M.A. thesis, University of Saskatchewan, 1989), 12–15, 48–52, 61–80. The names of the volunteers who staffed the Emmanuel College emergency centre can be found today engraved in the bricks of the old College building. During the quarantine, President Murray deliberately attributed a student death from alcohol poisoning to the flu. See M. K. Lux, "The Bitter Flats: The 1918 Infuenza Epidemic in Sakatchewan," *Saskatchewan History* 49, no. 1 (spring 1997): 3–14.

72. Lux, "Spanish Influenza Pandemic," 119–21.

73. S. A. Keighley, *Trader, Tripper, Trapper: The Life of a Bayman* (Winnipeg: Watson and Dwyer, 1989), 37–8.

74. S. Marceau-Kozicki, "Onion Lake Indian Residential Schools, 1892–1943" (unpublished M.A. thesis, University of Saskatchewan, 1993), 131.

75. Lux, "Spanish Influenza Pandemic," 94–100, 122–24.

76. S. K. Thompson, "A Prairie Wife's Tale," *Saskatchewan History* 44, no. 1 (winter 1992): 29–30.

77. *Globe and Mail*, 5 November 2003.

78. J. F. Vance, *Death So Noble: Memory, Meaning, and the First World War* (Vancouver: University of British Columbia Press, 1997), 14, 47–48, 205–206.

CHAPTER TWELVE:
ABSOLUTE PERFECTION

1. Quoted in J. H. Thompson, *The Harvests of War: The Prairie West, 1914–1918* (Toronto: McClelland and Stewart, 1978), 168.

2. In 1913, ninety-nine unions were registered with the Saskatchewan Bureau of Labour: forty-four railroad; forty construction; six printing. Women at the time constituted roughly 7 per cent of the provincial workforce. W. J. C. Cherwinski, "Organized Labour in Saskatchewan: The TLC Years, 1905–1945" (unpublished Ph.D. diss., University of Alberta, 1972), 1–43. G. Makahonuk, "The Labouring Class in Saskatchewan's Economy, 1850–1912" *Saskatchewan History* 46, no. 1 (spring 1994): 29–32; G. Makahonuk, "The Regina Painters' Strike of 1912," *Saskatchewan History* 35, no. 3 (fall 1982): 108; C. Smillie, "The Invisible Workforce: Women Workers in Saskatchewan from 1905 to World War II," *Saskatchewan History* 39, no. 2 (spring 1986): 62–71.

3. *Moose Jaw Times*, 26 September 1908. The newspaper account does not jive with the one presented in J. Larsen and M. R. Libby, *Moose Jaw: People, Places, History* (Regina: Couteau, 2001), 31.

4. G. Makahonuk, "Class Conflict in a Prairie City," *Labour/Le Travail*, no. 19 (spring 1987): 98–101.

5. Quoted in ibid., 120.

6. Quoted in G. S. Kealey, "1919: The Canadian Labour Revolt," *Labour/Le Travail*, no. 13 (spring 1984): 15.

7. Makahonuk, "Class Conflict," 121–212.

8. Cherwinski, "Organized Labour," 66–73.

9. Ibid., 97–108; Makahonuk, "Class Conflict," 122–24.

10. For a discussion of Progressivism, see W. L. Morton, *The Progressive Party in Canada* (Toronto: University of Toronto Press, 1950); D. Laycock, *Populism and Democratic Thought in the Canadian Prairies, 1910 to 1945* (Toronto: University of Toronto Press, 1990); R. Allen, "The Social Gospel as the Religion of the Agrarian Revolt," in *The West and the Nation: Essays in Honour of W. L. Morton*, ed. C. Berger and R. Cook (Toronto: McClelland and Stewart, 1976), 174–86.

11. J. W. Brennan, "A Political History of Saskatchewan, 1905–1929" (unpublished Ph.D. diss., University of Alberta, 1976), 450–53.

12. Ibid., 474.

13. Ibid., 473.

14. Quoted in ibid., 497.

15. Ibid., 497–501.

16. D. E. Smith, *Prairie Liberalism: The Liberal Party in Saskatchewan, 1905–71* (Toronto: University of Toronto Press, 1975), 92.

17. T. D. Regehr, "William M. Martin, 1916–1922," in *Saskatchewan Premiers of the 20th Century*, ed. G. L. Barnhart (Regina: Canadian Plains Research Center, 2004), 62–66.

18. J. W. Brennan, "C. A. Dunning and the Challenge of the Progressives, 1922–25," *Saskatchewan History* 22, no. 1 (winter 1969): 1–12.

19. For a history of the SPP, see D. Robertson, "The Saskatchewan Provincial Police" (unpublished M.A. thesis, University of Saskatchewan, 1976).

20. Quoted in Brennan, "Political History of Saskatchewan," 441.

21. M. R. Marrus, *Mr. Sam: The Life and Times of Samuel Bronfman* (Toronto: Viking, 1991), 49–55, 66–70, 73–81, 102–105.

22. J. F. C. Wright, *Saskatchewan: The History of a Province* (Toronto: McClelland and Stewart, 1955), 193–95.

23. Brennan, "Political History of Saskatchewan," 589–606.

24. K. Marschall, "Raising Juvenile Delinquents: The Development of Saskatchewan's Child Welfare Laws, 1905–1930" (unpublished M.A. thesis, University of Saskatchewan, 2003), 62–63.

25. Quoted in C. Backhouse, *Colour-Coded: A Legal History of Racism in Canada, 1900–1950* (Toronto: University of Toronto Press, 1999), 157.

26. Ibid., 150–72.

27. *Sixth Census of Canada, 1921, v. 1* (Ottawa: King's Printer, 1924), 355; *Seventh Census of Canada, 1931, v. 1* (Ottawa: King's Printer, 1936), 719.

28. E. Ahenakew, *Voices of the Plains Cree* (Toronto: McClelland and Stewart, 1973), 123.

29. Quoted in J. F. Vance, *Death So Noble: Memory, Meaning, and the First World War* (Vancouver: University of British Columbia Press, 1997), 250.

30. M. Campbell, *Halfbreed* (Toronto: McClelland and Stewart, 1973), 7–8.

31. K. Pettipas, *Severing the Ties that Bind: Government Repression of Indigenous Religious Ceremonies on the Prairies* (Winnipeg: University of Manitoba Press, 1994), 154–59, 169–86.

32. Canada, House of Commons, *Debates*, 17 July 1924, 4705–4706.

33. J. R. Miller, *Shingwauk's Vision: A History of Native Residential Schools* (Toronto: University of Toronto Press, 1996), 169–70.

34. Quoted in J. S. Milloy, *A National Crime: The Canadian Government and the Residential School System, 1879–1986* (Winnipeg: University of Manitoba Press, 1999), 146.

35. Quoted in ibid., 109.

36. P. Hurly, "Beauval, Saskatchewan: An Historic Sketch," *Saskatchewan History* 33, no. 3 (autumn 1980): 105.

37. L. Meijer Drees, *The Indian Association of Alberta: A History of Political Action* (Vancouver: University of British Columbia Press, 2002), 12–13; F. L. Barron, *Walking in Indian Moccasins: The Native Policies of Tommy Douglas and the CCF* (Vancouver: University of British Columbia Press, 1997), 66–67.

38. Quoted in Vance, *Death So Noble*, 249.

39. S. Cuthand, "The Native Peoples of the Prairie Provinces in the 1920s and 1930s," in *Sweet Promises: A Reader on Indian-White Relations in Canada*, ed. J. R. Miller (Toronto: University of Toronto Press, 1991), 381–83.

40. K. Tischler, "The German Canadians in Saskatchewan with Particular Reference to the Language Problem, 1900–1930" (unpublished M.A. thesis, University of Saskatchewan, 1978), 113–14. For an assessment of the experience of those Mennonites who left Saskatchewan for Mexico, see D. Quiring, *The Mennonite Old Colony Vision: Under Siege in Mexico and the Canadian Connection* (Steinbach, MB: Crossway Publications, 2003).

41. M. Owen, "Building the Kingdom of God on the Prairies: E. H. Oliver and Saskatchewan Education, 1913–1930," *Saskatchewan History* 40, no. 1 (winter 1987): 22–34.

42. Quoted in K. Kaiser, "Protestant Home Missionaries in Saskatchewan and the Concept of Applied Christianity, 1918–30" (unpublished M.A. thesis, University of Saskatchewan, 1988). See also M. R. Nebel, "Rev. Thomas Johnson and the Insinger Experiment," *Saskatchewan History* 11, no. 1 (winter 1958): 1–17.

43. C. Melis, "J. T. M. Anderson, Director of Education Among New-Canadians and the Policy of the Department of Education, 1918–1923," *Saskatchewan History* 33, no. 1 (winter 1980): 1–12.

44. J. T. M. Anderson, *The Education of the New Canadian: A Treatise on Canada's Greatest Education Problem* (Toronto: Dent, 1918), 25, 34.

45. S. Wurtele, "Nation-building from the Ground Up: Assimilation Through Domestic and Community Transformation in Inter-War Saskatchewan" (unpublished Ph.D. diss., Queen's University, 1993), 141–43.

46. Robert England papers, MG 30, ser. C181, v. 5, f. 29, "Slawa School," Manuscript Division, National Archives of Canada.

47. C. J. Kitzan, "The Fighting Bishop: George Exton Lloyd and the Immigration Debate" (unpublished M.A. thesis, University of Saskatchewan, 1996), 59–61.

48. Brennan, "Political History of Saskatchewan," 677–79; A. S. Whiteley, "The Peopling of the Prairie Provinces of Canada," *American Journal of Sociology* 38, no. 2 (1932–33): 240–52.

49. Quoted in Brennan, "Political History of Saskatchewan," 679.

50. D. Avery, *Dangerous Foreigners: European Immigrant Workers and Labour Radicalism in Canada, 1896–1932* (Toronto: McClelland and Stewart, 1979), 101–12.

51. Quoted in Kitzan, "The Fighting Bishop," 812. Thirty years earlier, Agnes Deans Cameron, a Victoria school principal, said much the same thing about the "yellow" peril in British Columbia. "In their picturesque dresses and striking colouring they make pictures which please the eye and stimulate the imagination," she wrote in the 1901 pamphlet "To Young British Columbians," "But we today are not picking out a costume for a masquerade party: we are choosing a race and a nation to be born into … the British nation."

52. Quoted in M. Robin, *Shades of Right: Nativist and Fascist Politics in Canada, 1920–1940* (Toronto: University of Toronto Press, 1992), 36.

53. H. Palmer, *Patterns of Prejudice: A History of Nativism in Alberta* (Toronto: McClelland and Stewart, 1982), ch. 3; R. Huel, "J. J. Maloney: How the West was saved from Rome, Quebec, and the Liberals," in *The Developing West: Essays in Honour of L. H. Thomas*, ed. J. Foster (Edmonton: University of Alberta Press, 1983), 219–41.

54. Quoted in Brennan, "Political History of Saskatchewan," 679.

55. W. Calderwood, "Pulpit, Press, and Political Reactions to the Ku Klux Klan in Saskatchewan," in *The Twenties in Western Canada*, ed. S. M. Trofimenkoff (Ottawa: National Museums of Canada, 1972), 191–229.

... Leddy, "Real Estate Offer Drew Family West," *Saskatoon StarPhoenix*, 8 May 1982.

57. Brennan, "Political History of Saskatchewan," 694–706.

58. Quoted in ibid., 587. Anderson had been first chosen provincial Conservative leader in 1924, but stepped down two years later for health reasons. He was named leader again at the 1928 convention.

59. In school districts, the religious minority had the right to establish and support their own separate school. In some cases, though, there were not enough Protestant families to support their own school and hence the children had to attend the local Catholic school.

60. D. E. Smith, *Prairie Liberalism*, 194; Brennan, "Political History of Saskatchewan," 706, 761.

61. Quoted in Brennan, "Political History of Saskatchewan," 760.

62. N. Ward and D. E. Smith, *Jimmy Gardiner: Relentless Liberal* (Toronto: University of Toronto Press, 1990).

63. Brennan, "Political History of Saskatchewan," 647–51.

64. Gardiner was also the first premier to have served as a backbencher in the Saskatchewan legislature. The first two Saskatchewan premiers, Scott and Martin, simply assumed the position, while Dunning entered the government as a cabinet minister.

65. R. Huel, "The Anderson Amendments and the Secularization of Saskatchewan Public Schools," *Canadian Catholic Historical Association* 44 (1977): 61–76.

66. See *Report of the Saskatchewan Royal Commission on Immigration and Settlement, 1930* (Regina: Government of Saskatchewan, 1930). The commission collected fifty-two volumes of evidence during forty sittings.

CHAPTER THIRTEEN: WHERE WE LEFT OFF

1. Quoted in J. Pitsula, "Muscular Saskatchewan: Provincial Self-Identity in the 1920s," *Saskatchewan History* 54, no. 2 (fall 2002): 6–7.

2. Quoted in J. W. Brennan, "A Political History of Saskatchewan, 1905–1929" (unpublished Ph.D. diss., University of Alberta, 1976), 448.

3. J. H. Thompson with A. Seager, *Canada 1922–1939: Decades of Discord* (Toronto: McClelland and Stewart, 1985), 76–77.

4. T. D. Regehr, "William M. Martin, 1916–1922," in *Saskatchewan Premiers of the 20th Century*, ed. G. L. Barnhart (Regina: Canadian Plains Research Center, 2004), 57.

5. J. H. Archer, *Saskatchewan: A History* (Saskatoon: Western Producer Prairie Books, 1980), 187.

6. B. Potyondi, *In Palliser's Triangle: Living in the Grasslands, 1850–1930* (Saskatoon: Purich Publishing, 1995), 93, 181.

7. D. Breen, *The Canadian Prairie West and the Ranching Frontier, 1874–1924* (Toronto: University of Toronto Press, 1983), 2112.

8. Simon Evans, "The Saskatchewan Range in 1906 and 1921," in *Atlas of Saskatchewan*, ed. K.-I. Fung (Saskatoon: University of Saskatchewan, 1999), 64–65.

9. Quoted in D. C. Jones, "We'll All Be Buried Down Here in This Dry Belt," *Saskatchewan History* 35, no. 2 (spring 1982): 43.

10. Quoted in ibid., 44.

11. Quoted in Potyondi, *In Palliser's Triangle*, 94.

12. Quoted in D. M. Balkwill, "The Prairie Farm Rehabilitation Administration and the Community Pasture Program, 1937–1947" (unpublished M.A. thesis, University of Saskatchewan, 2002), 13.

13. Quoted in Saskatchewan, *Report of the Royal Commission of Inquiry into Farming Conditions* (Regina: Government of Saskatchewan, 1921), 44.

14. Ibid., 14.

15. D. P. Fitzgerald, "Pioneer Settlement in Northern Saskatchewan" (unpublished Ph.D. diss., University of Minnesota, 1965): 180, 195–98.

16. J. McDonald, "Soldier Settlement and Depression Settlement in the Forest Fringe of Saskatchewan," *Prairie Forum* 6, no. 1 (spring 1981): 40.

17. The surrendered lands were from the following reserves: Big River (980 acres), Mistawasis (17,000), Ochapowace (18,240), Piapot (16,960), Poorman's (8,080), Wood Mountain (5,760). *Regina Leader*, 18 July 1918.

18. Ibid.

19. J. Dempsey, *Warriors of the King: Prairie Indians in World War I* (Regina: Canadian Plains Research Center, 1999), 77–78; S. Carter, *Lost Harvests: Prairie Indian Reserve Farmers and Government Policy* (Montreal: McGill-Queen's University Press, 1990), 252–53; J. F. Vance, *Death So Noble: Memory, Meaning, and the First World War* (Vancouver: University of British Columbia Press, 1997), 259.

20. Fitzgerald, "Pioneer Settlement," 196.

21. Quoted in ibid., 222.

22. Quoted in ibid., 211.

23. McDonald, "Soldier Settlement," 40–412. By 1941, just over eight thousand soldier settlers of the approximately twenty-five thousand in Canada who took out loans remained on their land. D. Morton and G. Wright, *Winning the Second Battle: Canadian Veterans and the Return to Civilian Life, 1915–1930* (Toronto: University of Toronto Press, 1987), 266.

24. Saskatchewan, *A Submission by the Government of Saskatchewan to the Royal Commission on Dominion-Provincial Relations* (Regina: Government of Saskatchewan, 1937), 148, 175; Brennan, "A Political History of Saskatchewan," 575.

25. K. Cruikshank, *Close Ties: Railways, Government and the Board of Railway Commissioners* (Montreal: McGill-Queen's University Press, 1991), 142–66.

26. Regehr, "Martin," 58.

27. Brennan, "A Political History of Saskatchewan," 565–67, 613.

28. Quoted in *Building a Province: A History of Saskatchewan in Documents*, ed. D. E. Smith (Saskatoon: Fifth House, 1992), 218.

29. Quoted in Brennan, "A Political History of Saskatchewan," 565.

30. Quoted in J. H. Thompson, *Forging the Prairie West* (Toronto: Oxford University Press, 1998), 119. A few years later, an editorial in *The Western Producer* (15 September 1927) argued that "Pools may help weld many races into one people."

31. I. MacPherson, *Each for All: A History of the Co-operative Movement in English Canada, 1900–1945* (Toronto: Macmillan, 1979), 86–89.

32. Ibid., 89–99.

33. B. Fairbairn, *Building a Dream: The Co-operative Retailing System in Western Canada, 1928–1988* (Saskatoon: Western Producer Prairie Books, 1989), 20–22, 45–54.

34. D. De Brou and B. Waiser, *Documenting Canada: A History of Modern Canada in Documents* (Saskatoon: Fifth House, 1992), 175–77.

35. Ibid., 282–83.

36. W. L. Morton, *The Progressive Party in Canada* (Toronto: University of Toronto Press, 1950), 157.

37. Quoted in C. Hoffer and F. H. Kahan, *Land of Hope* (Saskatoon: Modern Press, 1960), 148.

38. Quoted in B. LaDow, *The Medicine Line: Life and Death on a North American Borderland* (New York: Routledge, 2001), 170.

39. A. Huelskamp to C. A. Dunning, 8 July 1922, Saskatchewan Archives Board, M13, v. 14, f. 1. See also Curtis McManus, "Happyland: The Agricultural Crisis in Saskatchewan's Drybelt, 1917–1927" (unpublished M.A. thesis, University of Saskatchewan, 2004).

40. Department of Agriculture memo, 10 November 1922, Saskatchewan Archives Board.

41. C. A. Dunning to C. Stewart, 31 May 1924, Saskatchewan Archives Board.

42. Saskatchewan, *Submission*, 148, 175.

43. Quoted in Potyondi, *In Palliser's Triangle*, 111.

44. Ibid., 110–11.

45. D. M. Loveridge and B. Potyondi, *From Wood Mountain to the Whitemud: A Historical Survey of the Grasslands National Park Area* (Ottawa: Parks Canada, 1983), 190–95.

46. Quoted in Potyondi, *In Palliser's Triangle*, 63.

47. Brennan, "A Political History of Saskatchewan," 434–38.

48. R. Schaeffer, "In the Public Interest: The Oil and Gas Industry of Saskatchewan, 1905–1950" (unpublished M.A. thesis, University of Saskatchewan, 1988), 41–43.

49. E. K. Cullity, "Gold Mining Claims," *Saskatchewan History* 27, no. 1 (winter 1974): 29–33.

50. *Regina Leader*, 29 November 1919.

51. Quoted in G. Abrams, *Prince Albert: The First Century, 1866–1966* (Saskatoon: Modern Press, 1966), 222.

52. B. Waiser, *Saskatchewan's Playground: A History of Prince Albert National Park* (Saskatoon: Fifth House, 1989), 16–19; M. Howlett, "The Forest Industry on the Prairies: Opportunities and Constraints to Future Development," *Prairie Forum* 14, no. 2 (fall 1989): 239–40.

53. Waiser, *Saskatchewan's Playground*, 21–22.

54. A. G. Gulig, "'We Beg the Government': Native People and Game Regulations in Northern Saskatchewan, 1900–1940," *Prairie Forum* 28, no. 1 (spring 2003): 84–85.

55. S. A. Keighley, *Trader, Tripper, Trapper: The Life of a Bay Man* (Winnipeg: Watson and Dwyer, 1989), 53.

56. A. J. Ray, *The Canadian Fur Trade in the Industrial Age* (Toronto: University of Toronto Press, 1990), 149–50, 160, 199–204, 211, 221, 227.

57. Gulig, "'We Beg the Government'," 87–91.

58. Charles Macdonald, the MP for Prince Albert who resigned his seat to Mackenzie King in 1925, was later appointed to the Senate. But the Liberal was too ill to attend the start of the next sitting. "He is the only person who was elected to the Commons and appointed to the Senate and never said a word in either chamber." Paul Park, "The Worst MPs in History," *Saturday Night* 111, no. 7 (September 1996): 14.

59. Waiser, *Saskatchewan's Playground*, 25–35.

60. A. Artibise, "Patterns of Prairie Urban Development, 1871–1950," in *Eastern and Western Perspectives*, ed. P. Buckner and D. Bercuson (Toronto: University of Toronto Press, 1981), 126–32.

61. J. W. Brennan, *Regina: An Illustrated History* (Toronto: Lorimer, 1989), 99–119.

62. Ibid., 101–102, 106.

63. G. T. Bloomfield, "'I can see a car in that crop': Motorization in Saskatchewan, 1906–1934," *Saskatchewan History* 37, no. 1 (winter 1984): 3–24; R. B. Shepard, "Tractors and Combines in the Second Stage of Agricultural Mechanization on the Canadian Prairies," *Prairie Forum* 11, no. 2 (fall 1986): 253–71; Brennan, *Regina*, 101–102; Brennan, "Political History of Saskatchewan," 664.

64. Shepard, "Tractors and Combines," 268.

65. C. Danysk, *Hired Hands: Labour and the Development of Prairie Agriculture, 1880–1930* (Toronto: McClelland and Stewart, 1995), 112–141.

66. S. Sliwa, "Standing the Test of Time: A History of the Beardy/Okemasis Reserve, 1876–1951" (unpublished M.A. thesis, Trent University, 1993), 117–18.

67. M. Barber, "Help for Farm Homes: The Campaign to end Housework Drudgery in Rural Saskatchewan in the 1920s," *Scientia Canadiensis* 9, no. 1 (1985): 3–26; L. C. Volk, "The Social Effects of Rural Electrification in Saskatchewan" (unpublished M.A. thesis, University of Regina, 1980), 19–23.

68. H. L. Jones, *O Little Town: Remembering Life in a Prairie Village* (Winnipeg: University of Manitoba Press, 1995), 28.

69. Quoted in ibid., 29.

70. Brennan, *Regina*, 146.

71. B. Willett, "Present at the Birth of Radio," *Western People*, 24 June 1993, 2.

72. W. Schmalz, *On Air: Radio in Saskatchewan* (Regina: Couteau, 1990), 31, 35–37.

73. R. Millar, "Martha Bowes: Saskatchewan's First Woman Radio Announcer," *Saskatchewan History* 52, no. 1 (spring 2000): 37–39.

74. Schmalz, *On Air*, 44–45.

75. See D. C. Jones, *Midways, Judges, and Smooth-Tongued Fakirs: The Illustrated Story of Country Fairs in the Prairie West* (Saskatoon: Western Producer Prairie Books, 1983).

76. R. Ellis and E. Nixon, *Saskatchewan's Recreation Legacy* (Regina: Modern Press, 1986), 23.

77. V. Pezer, *The Stone Age: A Social History of Curling on the Prairies* (Calgary: Fifth House, 2003), 127–37.

78. P. Hack and D. Shury, *Wheat Province Diamonds* (Regina: Saskatchewan Baseball Association, 1997), 75–77; J. Mortin, *Safe At Home: A History of Softball in Saskatchewan* (Regina: Softball Saskatchewan, 1997), 5.

79. W. Simpson, "Hockey," in *A Concise History of Sport in Canada*, ed. D. Morrow (Toronto: Oxford University Press, 1989), 190–93.

80. P. Dederick and B. Waiser, *Looking Back: True Tales from Saskatchewan's Past* (Calgary: Fifth House, 2003), 64–67.

81. D. E. Smith, ed., *Building a Province: A History of Saskatchewan in Documents* (Saskatoon: Fifth House, 1992), 49–50. The formal transfer took place on 1 October 1930 by Imperial statute (20 & 21 Geo. 5, c. 26, 1930). In 2003, the Saskatchewan government sued the federal government for compensation for minerals rights retained by the Soldier Settlement Board after 1930. *Saskatoon StarPhoenix*, 19 August 2003.

CHAPTER FOURTEEN: NOTHING OF EVERYTHING

1. J. H. Gray, *Men Against the Desert* (Saskatoon: Fifth House, 1996), 65.

2. Ibid.; G. Friesen, *The Canadian Prairies: A History* (Toronto: University of Toronto Press, 1984), 386.

3. Quoted in P. Dederick and B. Waiser, *Looking Back: True Tales from Saskatchewan's Past* (Calgary: Fifth House, 2003), 29.

4. J. H. Thompson with A. Seager, *Canada, 1922–1939: Decades of Discord* (Toronto: McClelland and Stewart, 1985), 193–221.

5. A. Lawton, "Urban Relief in Saskatchewan During the Years of the Depression, 1930–39" (unpublished M.A. thesis, University of Saskatchewan, 1969), 43–50; J. W. Brennan, *Regina: An Illustrated History* (Toronto: Lorimer, 1989), 102.

6. Saskatchewan, *A Submission by the Government of Saskatchewan to the Royal Commission on Dominion-Provincial Relations* (Regina: Government of Saskatchewan, 1937), 136, 148–49, 174–80.

7. J. Struthers, *No Fault of Their Own: Unemployment and the Canadian Welfare State, 1914–1941* (Toronto: University of Toronto Press, 1983), 12–43.

8. Quoted in *The Wretched of Canada: Letters to R. B. Bennett, 1930–1935*, ed. L. M. Grayson and M. Bliss (Toronto: University of Toronto Press, 1971), 112.

9. S. Sliwa, "Standing the Test of Time: A History of Beardy's/Okemasis Reserve, 1876–1951" (unpublished M.A. thesis, Trent University, 1993), 119–20; J. Funk, ed., *And They Told Us Their Stories* (Saskatoon: Saskatoon District Tribal Council, 1991), 88–89.

10. Quoted in A. Artibise, "Patterns of Prairie Urban Development, 1871–1950," in *Eastern and Western Perspectives*, ed. P. Buckner and D. Bercuson (Toronto: University of Toronto Press, 1981), 132.

11. Brennan, *Regina*, 104–106; G. Abrams, *Prince Albert: The First Century, 1866–1966* (Saskatoon: Modern Press, 1966), 311; J. Larsen and M. R. Libby, *Moose Jaw: People, Places, History* (Regina: Couteau, 2001), 98–101; D. Kerr and S. Hanson, *Saskatoon: The First Half Century* (Edmonton: NeWest Publishers, 1982), 303–304.

12. T. M. Healy, "Engendering Resistance: Women Respond to Relief in Saskatchewan, 1930–1932," in *"Other" Voices: Historical Essays on Saskatchewan Women*, ed. D. De Brou and A. Moffatt (Regina: Canadian Plains Research Center, 1995), 94–115.

13. M. Hobbs, "Equality and Difference: Feminism and the Defence of Women Workers During the Great Depression," *Labour/Le Travail*, no. 32 (fall 1993): 215.

14. Quoted in T. M. Healy, "'Trouble Enough': Gender, Social Policy, and the Politics of Place in Vancouver and Saskatoon, 1929–1939" (unpublished Ph.D. diss., Simon Fraser University, 1998), 178–79.

15. Quoted in ibid., 183.

16. Quoted in E. Strikwerda, "From Short-Term Emergency to Long-Term Crisis: Public Works Projects in Saskatoon, 1929–1932" (unpublished M.A. thesis, University of Saskatchewan, 2000), 70.

17. P. H. Brennan, "'Thousands of our men are getting practically nothing at all to do:' Public Works Relief Programs in Regina and Saskatoon, 1929–1940," *Urban History Review* 21, no. 1 (October 1992), 33–34.

18. Quoted in Strikwerda, "From Short-Term Emergency to Long-Term Crisis," 64.

19. Ibid., 54, 79–80.

20. Artibise, "Patterns," 132–34; Brennan, *Regina*, 135; Larsen and Libby, *Moose Jaw*, 105.

21. A. McPherson, *The Battlefords: A History* (North Battleford, SK: Battleford and North Battleford, 1967), 184; Abrams, *Prince Albert*, 327.

22. *Winnipeg Free Press*, 6 August 1932.

23. Kerr and Hanson, *Saskatoon*, 300–301; Healy, "Engendering Resistance," 94–95, 108–109; Strikwerda, "From Short-Term Emergency to Long-Term Crisis," 92–94.

24. Brennan, *Regina*, 128; Abrams, *Prince Albert*, 330.

25. Lawton, "Urban Relief in Saskatchewan," 90–91.

26. "C. W. Report re Unemployment and Relief in Western Canada, 1932," 29–30. Charlotte Whitton papers, v. 25, Manuscript Division, National Archives of Canada. The Whitton report was the only official investigation of the unemployment situation in western Canada commissioned by the Conservative government.

27. L. Rodwell, "The Saskatchewan Association of Music Festivals," *Saskatchewan History* 16, no. 1 (winter 1963): 1–21; Brennan, *Regina*, 148–49; M. Spain, *Augustus Kenderdine* (Calgary: Glenbow Museum, 1986).

28. G. Kelly, *Green Grit: The Story of the Saskatchewan Roughriders* (Toronto: Harper Collins, 2001), 102–103, 115.

29. Larsen and Libby, *Moose Jaw*, 124.

30. Dederick and Waiser, *Looking Back*, 80–82.

31. D. G. Matheson, "The Saskatchewan Relief Commission, 1931–34" (unpublished M.A. thesis, University of Saskatchewan, 1974), tables 1 and 4.

32. Quoted in Lawton, "Urban Relief," 37.

33. B. Neatby, "The Saskatchewan Relief Commission 1931–1934," *Saskatchewan History* 3, no. 2 (spring 1950): 41–56; Saskatchewan, *Submission*, 181–84.

34. Quoted in Dederick and Waiser, *Looking Back*, 7–9.

35. D. B. McRae and R. M. Scott, *In the South Country* (Saskatoon: Saskatoon StarPhoenix, 1934), 13, 18, 20, 23.

36. E. Wheaton, *But It's a Dry Cold: Weathering the Canadian Prairies* (Calgary: Fifth House, 1998), 79–101.

37. Sinclair Ross, *As For Me and My House* (Toronto: McLelland and Stewart, 1941), 96.

38. W. E. Wallace, "'All Else Must Wait': Saskatchewan Women and the Great Depression" (unpublished M.A. thesis, University of Victoria, 1988), 56–60.

39. *The Western Producer*, 1 April 1976.

40. Quoted in Wallace, "'All Else Must Wait'," 60.

41. P. W. Riegert, *From Arsenic to DDT: A History of Entomology in Western Canada* (Toronto: University of Toronto Press, 1980), 214–58.

42. Gray, *Men Against the Desert*, 47.

43. A. Criddle, *Criddle-de-diddle-ensis: a biographical history of the Criddles of Aweme* (Winnipeg: A. Criddle, 1973).

44. In 1930, about 75 per cent of Saskatchewan's retail trade was handled by 8,279 small businesses. D. Hande, "Saskatchewan Merchants in the Great Depression: Regionalism and the Crusade Against Big Business," *Saskatchewan History* 43, no. 1 (winter 1991): 21–33.

45. Wallace, "'All Else Must Wait'," 181–87. A Department of Education official claimed that the unemployment problem would be eased considerably if female teachers were replaced. A. M. Kojder, "The Saskatoon Women Teachers' Association: A Demand for Recognition," *Saskatchewan History* 30, no. 2 (spring 1977): 70–71.

46. H. L. Jones, *O Little Town: Remembering Life in a Prairie Village* (Winnipeg: University of Manitoba Press, 1995), 185–86.

47. Wallace, "'All Else Must Wait'," 3–8.

48. *The Western Producer*, 1 April 1976.

49. McRae and Scott, *In the South Country*, 18.

50. C. Bye, "A Friend to Woman: The Prairie Farm Garden During the Depression" (unpublished paper presented before Graduate Symposium on Gender Research, 2003).

51. *The Western Producer*, 8 February 1934.

52. Quoted in Wallace, "'All Else Must Wait'," 113.

53. Ibid., 102–104.

54. Gray, *Men Against the Desert*, 58–60. See also T. D. Isern, "Gopher Tales: A Study in Western Canadian Pest Control," *Agricultural History Review* 36, no. 2 (1988): 188–98.

55. B. Waiser, *All Hell Can't Stop Us: The On-to-Ottawa Trek and Regina Riot* (Calgary: Fifth House, 2003), 88–89.

56. "C. W. Report R. B. Bennett 1932," R. B. Simpson to C. Whitton, 24 June 1932, Whitton papers, v. 25.

57. Quoted in G. J. Hoffman, "The Saskatchewan Provincial Election of 1934: Its Political, Economic, and Social Background" (unpublished M.A. thesis, University of Saskatchewan, Regina Campus, 1973), 23.

58. Dederick and Waiser, *Looking Back*, 83–84.

59. Quoted in *Globe and Mail*, 27 June 1998.

60. Dederick and Waiser, *Looking Back*, 101–103.

61. A. W. Bailey, "The Year We Moved," *Saskatchewan History* 20, no. 1 (winter 1967), 24.

62. D. P. Fitzgerald, "Pioneer Settlement in Northern Saskatchewan" (unpublished Ph.D diss., University of Minnesota, 1965), 282, 314, 346.

63. Quoted in ibid., 316.

64. T. J. D. Powell, "Northern Settlement, 1929–1935," *Saskatchewan History* 30, no. 3 (autumn 1977): 91.

65. D. S. Bowen, "'Forward to a Farm': The Back-to-the-Land Movement as a Relief Initiative in Saskatchewan during the Great Depression" (unpublished Ph.D. diss., Queen's University, 1998).

66. Fitzgerald, "Pioneer Settlement in Northern Saskatchewan," 326–30, 337–39, 388–89, 432–37.

67. Some of the urban unemployed were placed on unoccupied land in southern Saskatchewan. See I. George, "Back-to-the-Land in the Moose Mountains in the 1930s," *Saskatchewan History* 33, no. 2 (spring 1980): 71–74.

68. Powell, "Northern Settlement," 94–95.

69. Quoted in Fitzgerald, "Pioneer Settlement in Northern Saskatchewan," 331.

70. B. Fawcett, "Farmers on the Move," *Western People*, 10 June 1999, 3.

71. Fitzgerald, "Pioneer Settlement in Northern Saskatchewan," 337.

72. Ibid., 355, 417.

73. A. L. Karras, *North to Cree Lake: The Rugged Lives of the Trappers* (Calgary: Fifth House, 2003).

74. Powell, "Northern Settlement," 95.

75. A. G. Gulig, "'Determined to Burn Off the Entire Country': Prospectors, Caribou, and the Denesuliné in Northern Saskatchewan, 1900–1940," *American Indian Quarterly* 26, no. 3 (summer 2002): 335–59.

76. Karras, *North to Cree Lake*, 210–11.

77. Quoted in McRae and Scott, *In the South Country*, 14.

CHAPTER FIFTEEN:
SWAPPING HORSES

1. B. Broadfoot, *Ten Lost Years, 1929–1939* (Toronto: Doubleday, 1973).

2. J. H. Gray, *The Winter Years* (Calgary: Fifth House, 2003), 215.

3. D. E. Smith, *Prairie Liberalism: The Liberal Party in Saskatchewan, 1905–71* (Toronto: University of Toronto Press, 1975), 199.

4. P. Kyba, "J. T. M. Anderson," in *Saskatchewan Premiers of the 20th Century*, ed. G. L. Barnhart (Regina: Canadian Plains Research Center, 2004), 124, 129–130.

5. B. Neatby, "The Saskatchewan Relief Commission," *Saskatchewan History* 3, no. 2 (spring 1950): 56.

6. P. A. Russell, "The Co-operative Government's Response to the Depression 1930–34," *Saskatchewan History* 24, no. 3 (autumn 1971): 81–100; G. J. Hoffman, "The Saskatchewan Provincial Election of 1934: Its Political, Economic, and Social Background" (unpublished M.A. thesis, University of Saskatchewan, Regina Campus, 1973), 41–46.

7. I. MacPherson, *Each for All: A History of the Co-operative Movement in English Canada, 1900-1945* (Toronto: Macmillan, 1979), 119–22.

8. Russell, "The Co-operative Government's Response to the Depression," 95–97.

9. Smith, *Prairie Liberalism*, 204–208.

10. J. Manley, "'Starve, Be Damned!': Communists and Canada's Urban Unemployed 1929–39," *Canadian Historical Review* 79, no. 3 (September 1998): 466–91.

11. D. Kerr and S. D. Hanson, *Saskatoon: The First Half Century* (Edmonton: NeWest Publishers, 1982), 298; J. W. Brennan, *Regina: An Illustrated History* (Toronto: Lorimer, 1989), 137.

12. *Regina Leader-Post*, 2 May 1931.

13. Quoted in S. D. Hanson, "Estevan 1931," in *On Strike: Six Key Labour Struggles in Canada, 1919–1949*, ed. I. Abella (Toronto: Lorimer, 1975), 38.

14. S. R. Hewitt, "September 1931: A Re-interpretation of the Royal Canadian Mounted Police's Handling of the 1931 Estevan Strike and Riot" *Labour/Le Travail*, no. 39 (spring 1997): 159–78.

15. Quoted in Hoffman, "The Saskatchewan Provincial Election of 1934," 48.

16. For an account of the struggle from the miners' perspective, see S. L. Endicott, *Bienfait: The Saskatchewan Miners' Struggle of '31* (Toronto: University of Toronto Press, 2002).

17. Quoted in J. Struthers, *No Fault of Their Own: Unemployment and the Canadian Welfare State, 1914–1941* (Toronto: University of Toronto Press, 1983), 52–53.

18. B. Roberts, *Whence They Came: Deportation from Canada, 1900–1935* (Ottawa: University of Ottawa Press, 1988), 159–94.

19. Kerr and Hanson, *Saskatoon*, 299–300.

20. B. Hunter, *Wild Bill: Bill Hunter's Legendary 65 Years in Canadian Sport* (Calgary: Johnson Gorman, 2000), 26.

21. Quoted in Hoffman, "The Saskatchewan Provincial Election of 1934," 49.

22. S. R. Hewitt, "Old Myths Die Hard: The Transformation of the Mounted Police in Alberta and Saskatchewan" (unpublished Ph.D. diss., University of Saskatchewan, 1997).

23. Quoted in L. and C. Brown, *An Unauthorized History of the RCMP* (Toronto: Lorimer, 1978), 63.

24. Smith, *Prairie Liberalism*, 211–12; Hoffman, "The Saskatchewan Provincial Election of 1934," 51.

25. J. C. Courtney and D. E. Smith, "Saskatchewan: Parties in a Politically Sensitive Province," in *Canadian Provincial Politics*, ed. M. Robin (Scarborough: Prentice-Hall, 1978), 293; Smith, *Prairie Liberalism*, 211–13.

26. G. Hoffman, "The Saskatchewan Farmer-Labor Party, 1932–1934: How Radical Was It At Its Origin?" *Saskatchewan History* 28, no. 2 (spring 1975): 52–64; L. H. Thomas, "The CCF Victory in Saskatchewan, 1944," *Saskatchewan History* 34, no. 1 (winter 1981): 1–16.

27. P. R. Sinclair, "Class Structure and Populist Protest: The Case of Western Canada," in *Society and Politics in Alberta: Research Papers*, ed. C. Caldarola (Agincourt: Methuen, 1979), 73–86.

28. Quoted in Hoffman, "The Saskatchewan Provincial Election of 1934," 1512.

29. Quoted in Hoffman, "The Saskatchewan Farmer-Labor Party," 57.

30. W. D. Young, "M. J. Coldwell, the making of a Social Democrat," *Journal of Canadian Studies* 9, no. 3 (August 1974): 50–60.

31. Quoted in Hoffman, "The Saskatchewan Farmer-Labor Party," 57.

32. Quoted in Hoffman, "The Saskatchewan Provincial Election of 1934," 167.

33. Ibid., 167–68.

34. Co-operative Commonwealth Federation, *Regina Manifesto* (Regina: CCF, 1933); the term "co-operative commonwealth" was coined by an American populist in the 1880s. J. H. Thompson, *Forging the Prairie West* (Toronto: Oxford University Press, 1998), 130.

35. Quoted in S. M. Jamieson, *Times of Trouble: Labour Unrest and Industrial Conflict in Canada, 1900–66* (Ottawa: Information Canada, 1968), 217.

36. Quoted in R. A. Wardhaugh, *Mackenzie King and the Prairie West* (Toronto: University of Toronto Press, 2000), 176.

37. Hoffman, "The Saskatchewan Provincial Election of 1934," 50; D. E. Smith, "James G. Gardiner, 1926–1929, 1934–1935," in *Saskatchewan Premiers of the 20th Century*, ed. G. L. Barnhart (Regina: Canadian Plains Research Center, 2004), 101.

38. Quoted in Hoffman, "The Saskatchewan Farmer-Labor Party," 60.

39. L. Meijer Drees, *The Indian Association of Alberta: A History of Political Action* (Vancouver: University of British Columbia Press, 2002), 180; F. L. Barron, *Walking in Indian Moccasins: The Native Policies of Tommy Douglas and the CCF* (Vancouver: University of Toronto Press, 1997), 68.

40. J. Goodwill and N. Sluman, *John Tootoosis* (Winnipeg: Pemmican Publications, 1984), 168–69.

41. See, for example, *Regina Leader-Post*, 23 July 1935, when the chief of the Fond du Lac band complained about the white invasion of Dene hunting grounds.

42. Goodwill and Sluman, *John Tootoosis*, 154–55.

43. D. McLean, *Home from the Hill: A History of the Métis in Western Canada* (Regina: Gabriel Dumont Institute, 1987), 255–56.

44. Quoted in Kyba, "Anderson," 114.

45. Smith, *Prairie Liberalism*, 198–99.

46. C. Dobmeier to B. Waiser, 10 March 2003.

47. Quoted in *Alameda Dispatch*, 8 March 1935.

48. Quoted in Hoffman, "The Saskatchewan Provincial Election of 1934," 2012.

49. Ibid., 236–37.

50. Courtney and Smith, "Saskatchewa

51. Smith, *Prairie Liberalism*, 199; Smit 84.

52. Kyba, "Anderson," 116–17.

53. Wardhaugh, *Mackenzie King and the Prairie West*, 181.

54. B. Waiser, *All Hell Can't Stop Us: The On-to-Ottawa Trek and Regina Riot* (Calgary: Fifth House, 2003).

55. N. Ward and D. E. Smith, *Jimmy Gardiner: Relentless Liberal* (Toronto: University of Toronto Press, 1990), 200–202; B. Bilson, "William J. Patterson," in *Saskatchewan Premiers of the 20th Century*, ed. Barnhart, 140–42.

56. Wardhaugh, *Mackenzie King and the Prairie West*, 163–64, 176–77.

57. Quoted in ibid., 206.

58. D. M. Balkwill, "The Prairie Farm Rehabilitation Administration and The Community Pasture Program, 1937–1947" (unpublished M.A. thesis, University of Saskatchewan, 2002), 22–38.

59. Wardhaugh, *Mackenzie King and the Prairie West*, 206–207.

60. Ibid., 200.

61. J. Kendle, *John Bracken: A Political Biography* (Toronto: University of Toronto Press, 1979), 149–54. See also B. Ferguson and R. Wardhaugh, "Impossible Conditions of Inequality: John W. Dafoe, the Rowell-Sirois Royal Commission and the Interpretation of Canadian Federalism," *Canadian Historical Review* 84, no. 4 (December 2003): 551–84.

62. Bilson, "William J. Patterson," 128.

63. Quoted in ibid., 126.

64. Ibid., 125–30.

65. Smith, *Prairie Liberalism*, 237–38, 241–42.

66. Ibid., 239.

67. Courtney and Smith, "Saskatchewan," 295.

68. Quoted in Smith, *Prairie Liberalism*, 241.

69. Quoted in P. Dederick and B. Waiser, *Looking Back: True Tales from Saskatchewan's Past* (Calgary: Fifth House, 2003), 90.

**CHAPTER SIXTEEN:
GETTING THINGS DONE**

1. D. E. Smith, "A Period of Waiting is Over: The Prairies in 1939," in *A Country of Limitations: Canada and the World in 1939*, ed. N. Hillmer et al. (Ottawa: Canadian Committee for the History of the Second World War, 1996), 94.

2. G. B. Buchanan, *The March of the Prairie Men: A Story of the South Saskatchewan Regiment* (Weyburn: S. Sask Regiment Orderly Rooms, 1957); G. Brown and T. Copp, *Look to Your Front ... Regina Rifles: A Regiment at War, 1944–45* (Waterloo: Laurier Centre for Military, Strategic, and Disarmament Studies, 2001).

3. R. Innes, "The Socio-Political Influence of the Second World War Saskatchewan Aboriginal Veterans, 1945–1960" (unpublished M.A. thesis, University of Saskatchewan, 2000), 19. The number of Métis enlistees is difficult to determine since they were never identified as Métis.

4. Quoted in D. Hutchinson et al., eds., *Remembrances: Métis Veterans* (Regina: Gabriel Dumont Institute, 1997), 38.

5. J. Summerby, *Native Soldiers, Foreign Battlefields* (Ottawa: Government of Canada, 1993), 29–30; L. J. Barkwell et al., eds., *Resources for Métis Researchers* (Winnipeg: Louis Riel Institute of the Manitoba Métis Federation, 1999), 27.

6. *Globe and Mail*, 15 January 2003.

7. H. G. Mayes, "Saskatchewan in the Auvergne," *The Beaver* 69, no. 4 (August/September 1989): 41–44.

8. P. Dederick and B. Waiser, *Looking Back: True Tales from Saskatchewan's Past* (Calgary: Fifth House, 2003), 25–27.

9. D. Chisholm, *Their Names Live On: Remembering Saskatchewan's Fallen in World War II* (Regina: Canadian Plains Research Center, 2001).

10. C. Gossage, *Greatcoats and Glamour Boots: Canadian Women at War, 1939–1945* (Toronto: Dundurn Press, 1991).

11. Dederick and Waiser, *Looking Back*, 85–86.

12. R. Millar, "Gladys Arnold: Second World War Correspondent and Free French Advocate," *Saskatchewan History* 52, no. 2 (fall 2000): 47–53.

13. A. Viel, *Lethbridge on the Homefront, 1939 to 1945* (Lethbridge: Lethbridge Historical Society, 1998); K. L. Burianyk, "The 'Home Front' in Regina During World War II" (unpublished M.A. thesis, University of Regina, 2003), 26–37; G. Bilson, *The Guest Children* (Saskatoon: Fifth House, 1988).

14. G. Kelly, *Green Grit: The Story of the Saskatchewan Roughriders* (Toronto: Harper Collins, 2001), 119; V. Pezer, *The Stone Age: A Social History of Curling on the Prairies* (Calgary: Fifth House, 2003), 145; W. Simpson, "Hockey," in *A Concise History of Sport in Canada*, ed. D. Morrow et al. (Toronto: Oxford University Press, 1989), 209; W. Humber, *Diamonds of the North: A Concise History of Baseball in Canada* (Toronto: Oxford University Press, 1995), 75–80.

15. Viel, *Lethbridge on the Homefront, 1939 to 1945*.

16. J. Bruce, *Back the Attack! Canadian Women During the Second World War at Home and Abroad* (Toronto: Macmillan, 1985); *Regina Leader-Post*, 5 October 1942.

17. J. Wagner, "The Deutscher Bund Canada, 1934–9," *Canadian Historical Review*, 58, no. 2 (June 1977): 176–200.

18. R. J. MacDonald, "The Silent Column: Civil Security in Saskatchewan During World War II," *Saskatchewan History* 39, no. 2 (spring 1986): 41–61.

19. Quoted in Smith, "A Period of Waiting is Over," 1012.

20. Burianyk, "The 'Home Front' in Regina," 18–19.

21. G. L. Toombs to L. Stewart, 15 November 1999, correspondence in possession of author.

22. B. Waiser, *Park Prisoners: The Untold Story of Western Canada's National Parks* (Saskatoon: Fifth House, 1995), 129–74.

23. Canada, *Report of the Department of Mines and Resources, 1942* (Ottawa: King's Printer, 1942), 111; W. Janzen, *Limits of Liberty: The Experience of Mennonite, Hutterite, and Doukhobor Communities in Canada* (Toronto: University of Toronto Press, 1990), 230–32; G. Abrams, *Prince Albert: The First Century, 1866–1966* (Saskatoon: Modern Press, 1966), 332–52.

24. Burianyk, "The 'Home Front' in Regina," 45.

25. Quoted in D. Morton, *Canada and War* (Toronto: Butterworths, 1981), 106.

26. Quoted in J. L. Granatstein and D. Morton, *Canada and the Two World Wars* (Toronto: Key Porter, 2003), 233.

27. R. H. Crone, "The Unknown Air Force," *Saskatchewan History* 30, no. 1 (winter 1977): 1–17. See also R. H. Crone, "Aviation Pioneers in Saskatchewan," *Saskatchewan History* 28, no. 1 (winter 1975): 9–28. The first successful flight in the province took place at the Saskatoon exhibition in May 1911, when American W. C. "Lucky Bob" Shaefer put on a short flying display before crashing his plane.

28. Quoted in R. L. Heide, "The Politics of the British Commonwealth Air Training Plan Base Selection in Western Canada" (unpublished M.A. thesis, Carleton University, 2000), 76–77.

29. The BCATP host communities were Assiniboia, Caron, Dafoe, Davidson, Estevan, Moose Jaw, Mossbank, North Battleford, Prince Albert, Regina, Saskatoon, Swift Current, Weyburn, and Yorkton. B. Greenhous and N. Hillmer, "The Impact of the British Commonwealth Air Training Plan on Western Canada: Some Saskatchewan Case Studies," *Journal of Canadian Studies* 16, nos. 3 & 4 (fall/winter 1981): 133. For an explanation of the different kinds of schools and the training process, see Granatstein and Morton, *Canada and the Two World Wars*, 236–37.

30. Greenhous and Hillmer, "Impact of BCATP," 135.

31. *Yorkton Enterprise*, 8 August 1940.

32. A. McPherson, *The Battlefords: A History* (North Battleford, SK: Battleford and North Battleford, 1967), 209–10.

33. *Yorkton Enterprise*, 19 June 1941.

34. S. Flood, "'A Prettier Dump You Never Did See': Excerpts from the H. Vernon Peters Letters," *Saskatchewan History* 53, no. 2 (spring 2001): 16.

35. Greenhous and Hillmer, "Impact of BCATP," 138.

36. Dederick and Waiser, *Looking Back*, 71–73.

37. Quoted in Greenhous and Hillmer, "Impact of BCATP," 142–43

38. *Globe and Mail*, 1 August 2003.

39. Quoted in P. C. Conrad, *Training for Victory: The British Commonwealth Air Training Plan in the West* (Saskatoon: Western Producer Prairie Books, 1989), 77.

40. Quoted in Smith, "A Period of Waiting is Over," 95.

41. D. E. Smith, ed., *Building a Province: A History of Saskatchewan in Documents* (Saskatoon: Fifth House, 1992), 50.

42. Quoted in I. MacPherson and J. H. Thompson, "An Orderly Reconstruction: Prairie Agriculture in World War Two," in *Canadian Papers in Rural History, v. 4*, ed. D. H. Akenson (Gananoque: Langdale Press, 1984), 12.

43. G. E. Britnell and V. C. Fowke, *Canadian Agriculture in War and Peace, 1935–50* (Stanford: Stanford University Press, 1962), 92–94, table iv.

44. MacPherson and Thompson, "An Orderly Reconstruction," 12–15, 18; Britnell and Fowke, *Canadian Agriculture in War and Peace*, table iv.

45. MacPherson and Thompson, "An Orderly Reconstruction," 16–17.

46. J. H. Archer, *Saskatchewan: A History* (Saskatoon: Western Producer Prairie Books, 1980), 251.

47. MacPherson and Thompson, "An Orderly Reconstruction," 21–24.

48. D. De Brou and B. Waiser, eds., *Documenting Canada: A History of Modern Canada in Documents* (Saskatoon: Fifth House, 1992), 390–91.

49. Quoted in MacPherson and Thompson, "An Orderly Reconstruction," 27.

50. D. Owram, "Canadian Domesticity in the Postwar Era," in *The Veterans Charter and Post-World War II Canada*, ed. J. L Granatstein and P. Neary (Montreal: McGill-Queen's University Press, 1998), 207–209.

51. D. E. Smith, *Prairie Liberalism: The Liberal Party in Saskatchewan, 1905–1971* (Toronto: University of Toronto Press, 1975), 242–46.

52. E. Eager, *Saskatchewan Government: Politics and Pragmatism* (Saskatoon: Western Producer Prairie Books, 1980), 3, 56–58.

53. A. W. Johnson, *Dream No Little Dreams: A Biography of the Douglas Government of Saskatchewan, 1944–1961* (Toronto: University of Toronto Press, 2004), 36–58.

54. T. H. McLeod and I. McLeod, "T. C. Douglas," in *Saskatchewan Premiers of the 20th Century*, ed. G. L. Barnhart (Regina: Canadian Plains Research Center, 2004), 175–78.

55. Quoted in R. A. Wardhaugh, *Mackenzie King and the Prairie West* (Toronto: University of Toronto Press, 2000), 247.

56. McLeod and McLeod, "Douglas," 168.

57. Quoted in ibid., 165.

58. Quoted in W. Stewart, *The Life and Politics of Tommy Douglas* (Toronto: McArthur and Company, 2003), 156.

59. Johnson, *Dream No Little Dreams*, 63–64.

60. Quoted in ibid., 3.

61. Smith, *Prairie Liberalism*, 246–52.

62. Wardhaugh, *Mackenzie King and Prairie West*, 246.

63. Smith, *Prairie Liberalism*, 230–31.

64. Quoted in B. Bilson, "William J. Patterson," in *Saskatchewan Premiers of the 20th Century*, ed. Barnhart, 153.

65. Quoted in Johnson, *Dream No Little Dreams*, 3.

66. Ibid., 66.

67. J. Richards and L. Pratt, *Prairie Capitalism: Power and Influence in the New West* (Toronto: McClelland and Stewart, 1979), 109.

68. Quoted in ibid., 98.

69. Quoted in D. M. Quiring, "Battling Parish Priests, Bootleggers and Fur Sharks: CCF Colonialism in Northern Saskatchewan" (unpublished Ph.D. diss., University of Saskatchewan, 2002), 27.

70. Johnson, *Dream No Little Dreams*, 71.

71. Quoted in Richards and Pratt, *Prairie Capitalism*, 127.

72. Quoted in Johnson, *Dream No Little Dreams*, 74.

73. Richards and Pratt, *Prairie Capitalism*, 103–105, 116–17.

74. Johnson, *Dream No Little Dreams*, 189.

75. Ibid., ixx–xx, 59, 95, 105–107, 118; McLeod and McLeod, "Douglas," 169, 179, 186.

76. Quoted in Richards and Pratt, *Prairie Capitalism*, 130.

77. Bilson, "Patterson," 154.

78. Johnson, *Dream No Little Dreams*, 126–33.

79. D. G. McGrath, "A Challenge to Tradition: Co-operative Farming in Saskatchewan, 1944–1960" (unpublished M.A. thesis, University of Saskatchewan, 1996); L. McNaughton, "There is No Land Suitable for Agriculture: Progress and Agriculture in Post-World War II Saskatchewan" (unpublished M.A. thesis, University of Saskatchewan, 2003); W. E. Hope, *Riverbend Revisited: Memories of Riverbend Co-operative Farm, 1947–1957* (n.p., n.d)., provided by J. Gow.

80. Quoted in L. H. Thomas, ed., *The Making of a Socialist: The Recollections of T. C. Douglas* (Edmonton: University of Alberta Press, 1982), 293, 349.

81. Quoted in Quiring, "Battling Parish Priests," 19.

82. Ibid., 23.

83. Ibid., 124–42.

84. J. Pitsula, "The CCF Government and the Formation of the Union of Saskatchewan Indians," *Prairie Forum* 19, no. 2 (fall 1994): 131, 137, 146–47; F. L. Barron, *Walking in Indian Moccasins: The Native Policies of Tommy Douglas and the CCF* (Vancouver: University of British Columbia Press, 1997), 64–78.

85. J. Goodwill and N. Sluman, *John Tootoosis* (Winnipeg: Pemmican Publications, 1984), 188–89.
86. Barron, *Walking in Indian Moccasins*, 37; M. Dobbin, *The One-And-A-Half Men* (Vancouver: New Star Books, 1981), 164–82; D. McLean, *Home From The Hill: A History of the Métis in Western Canada* (Regina: Gabriel Dumont Institute, 1987), 259–612.
87. Smith, *Prairie Liberalism*, 258.
88. Bilson, "Patterson," 135; McLeod and McLeod, "Douglas," 193.
89. Quoted in Smith, *Prairie Liberalism*, 257.
90. Ibid., 258–63.
91. T. H. McLeod and I. McLeod, *Tommy Douglas: The Road to Jerusalem* (Edmonton: Hurtig, 1987), 183–84.
92. Quoted in Thomas, ed., *The Making of a Socialist*, 256–57.
93. Richards and Pratt, *Prairie Capitalism*, 142–44.
94. Eager, *Saskatchewan Government*, 57–58.

CHAPTER SEVENTEEN:
MAKING DREAMS COME TRUE
1. Quoted in *Regina Leader-Post*, 21 June 1951.
2. A. Rae, "Back to the Drawing Board," *Western People*, 5 March 1998.
3. D. Owram, *Born at the Right Time: A History of the Baby Boom Generation* (Toronto: University of Toronto Press, 1996), 3–158; A. Finkel, *Our Lives: Canada after 1945* (Toronto: Lorimer, 1997), 3–79.
4. M. L. Szabo, *Demographic Trends in Saskatchewan, 1921–1959* (Regina: Saskatchewan Department of Public Health, 1962), 13.
5. Ninety-three of 422 Saskatchewan farm families who had participated in a federal survey in 1942 were no longer farming when the team returned to do a follow-up interview five years later. M. A. MacNaughton and M. E. Andal, *Changes in Farm Family Living in Three Areas of the Prairie Provinces from 1942–3 to 1947* (Ottawa: Department of Agriculture, 1949), 15, 54.
6. B. Y. Card, "Perspectives on Rural Western Canada in the 1950s," in A. W. Rasporich, ed., *The Making of the Modern West: Western Canada since 1945* (Calgary: University of Calgary Press, 1984), 154–56; J. W. Brennan, *Regina: An Illustrated History* (Toronto: Lorimer, 1989), 153, 159.
7. J. H. Archer, *Saskatchewan: A History* (Saskatoon: Western Producer Prairie Books, 1980), 270, 296–97.
8. Quoted in J. H. Thompson with A. Seager, *Canada, 1922–1939: Decades of Discord* (Toronto: McClelland and Stewart, 1985), 96.
9. A. W. Johnson, *Dream No Little Dreams: A Biography of the Douglas Government of Saskatchewan, 1944–1961* (Toronto: University of Toronto Press, 2004), 36.
10. Quoted in J. M. Pitsula, "The Saskatchewan CCF Government and Treaty Indians, 1944–64,"

Canadian Historical Review 75, no. 1 (March 1994): 26.
11. J. R. Miller, *Shingwauk's Vision: A History of Native Residential Schools* (Toronto: University of Toronto Press, 1996), 377.
12. Quoted in ibid., 378. In 1946, there were twenty-eight day schools and fifteen boarding or residential schools in Saskatchewan.
13. Quoted in Pitsula, "Saskatchewan CCF Government and Treaty Indians," 49.
14. Ibid., 23–30.
15. Quoted in ibid., 24.
16. Ibid., 30–38.
17. Quoted in D. M. Quiring, "Battling Parish Priests, Bootleggers, and Fur Sharks: CCF Colonialism in Northern Saskatchewan" (unpublished Ph.D. diss., University of Saskatchewan, 2002), 48.
18. Ibid., 72–96.
19. Quoted in ibid., 68.
20. Ibid., 94.
21. R. Bothwell, *Eldorado: Canada's National Uranium Company* (Toronto: University of Toronto Press, 1984), 278–302.
22. Ibid., 62, 67–68, 169–70.
23. Ibid., 68–69.
24. E. McLachlan, *With Unfailing Dedication: Rural Teachers in the War Years* (Edmonton: NeWest Publishers, 2001), 9–10.
25. D. L. Lloyd, "Woodrow S. Lloyd," in *Saskatchewan Premiers of the 20th Century*, ed. G. L. Barnhart (Regina: Canadian Plains Research Center, 2004), 214–18.
26. Quoted in Johnson, *Dream No Little Dreams*, 85.
27. W. Carlyle, "The Changing Geography of Administrative Units for Rural Schooling and Local Government on the Canadian Prairies," *Prairie Forum* 12, no. 1 (spring 1987): 11–12; Johnson, *Dream No Little Dreams*, 83–88.
28. D. R. Whyte, "Rural Canada in Transition," in *Rural Canada in Transition*, ed. M.-A. Tremblay and W. J. Anderson (Ottawa: Agricultural Economic Research Council of Canada, 1966), 68–71.
29. MacNaughton and Andal, *Changes in Farm Family Living*, 36.
30. Quoted in Archer, *Saskatchewan*, 290.
31. Quoted in D. E. Smith, ed., *Building a Province: A History of Saskatchewan in Documents* (Saskatoon: Fifth House, 1992), 190.
32. Quoted in Johnson, *Dream No Little Dreams*, 147.
33. Ibid., 208. Education spending per student rose from a base index of 100 in 1946 to 247 eight years later.
34. Ibid., 150–55.
35. Quoted in ibid., 153.
36. Ibid., 152–55.
37. Quoted in ibid., 142.

38. Quoted in D. E. Smith, *Prairie Liberalism: The Liberal Party in Saskatchewan, 1905–71* (Toronto: University of Toronto Press, 1975), 264.

39. T. H. McLeod and I. McLeod, *Tommy Douglas: The Road to Jerusalem* (Edmonton: Hurtig, 1987), 181.

40. J. Larmour, "The Douglas Government's Changing Emphasis on Public, Private, and Co-operative Development in Saskatchewan, 1944–1961," in *Building the Co-operative Commonweath*, ed. J. W. Brennan (Regina: Canadian Plains Research Center, 1984), 177.

41. D. B. Banks, "The Political Economy of Petroleum Development in Saskatchewan, 1940–1960" (unpublished M.A. thesis, University of Regina, 1986), 34–36, 70–74; R. Schaeffer, "In the Public Interest: The Oil and Gas Industry of Saskatchewan, 1905–1950" (unpublished M.A. thesis, University of Saskatchewan, 1988), 126–29, 194–97, 226–33; Archer, *Saskatchewan*, 300. By 1976, Saskatchewan oil (2.1 billion barrels) and natural gas (2.4 trillion cubic feet) discoveries represented 19 and 3 per cent, respectively, of the Alberta discoveries. J. Richards and L. Pratt, *Prairie Capitalism: Power and Influence in the New West* (Toronto: McClelland and Stewart, 1979), 178.

42. Johnson, *Dream No Little Dreams*, 183.

43. Archer, *Saskatchewan*, 269–70.

44. G. E. Britnell and V. C. Fowke, *Canadian Agriculture in War and Peace, 1935–50* (Stanford: Stanford University Press, 1962), 446–47.

45. J. Whalen, "Marked for Death," *Western People*, 9 January 1997: M. Foran, "It Could Have Been Much Worse: The 1952 Outbreak of Foot and Mouth Disease in Saskatchewan," in *Harm's Way: Disasters in Western Canada*, ed. A. Rasporich and M. Foran (Calgary: University of Calgary Press, 2004), 179–202.

46. N. Ward and D. E. Smith, *Jimmy Gardiner: Relentless Liberal* (Toronto: University of Toronto Press, 1990), 293–315.

47. Quoted in ibid., 312.

48. Quoted in ibid., 309.

49. Banks, "Political Economy of Petroleum Development," 131–33.

50. Brennan, *Regina*, 155–57.

51. Johnson, *Dream No Little Dreams*, 159–60.

52. P. F. Rein, "These Changing Conditions: A Study of the Saskatchewan Royal Commission on Agriculture and Rural Life" (unpublished M.A. thesis, University of Regina, 1994), 74–100, 117–18, 126–28, 131–33, 165–71.

53. J. M. Hayden, *Seeking a Balance: The University of Saskatchewan, 1907–1982* (Vancouver: University of British Columbia Press, 1983), 229–32.

54. Johnson, *Dream No Little Dreams*, 223–24; Archer, *Saskatchewan*, 300–301.

55. See B. C. Wagner, "We Proudly Begin Our Broadcast Day: Saskatchewan and the Arrival of Television, 1954–69" (unpublished M.A. thesis, University of Saskatchewan, 2004).

56. It would take until 1965, when Regina handed over the keys to its powerhouse, before one single, integrated system was finally in place. C. O. White, *Power for a Province: A History of Saskatchewan Power* (Regina: Canadian Plains Research Center, 1976), 265–90; W. Chabun, "Meet Penny Powers," *Folklore* 23, no. 4 (autumn 2002): 6–7.

57. Quoted in L. Blashill, *Remembering the '50s: Growing Up in Western Canada* (Victoria: Orca Book Publishers, 1997), 20.

58. C. Dobmeier to B. Waiser, 17 May 2004.

59. White, *Power for a Province*, 295–310.

60. MacNaughton and Andal, *Changes in Farm Family Living*, 39.

61. Johnson, *Dream No Little Dreams*, 226–28.

62. Quoted in Blashill, *Remembering the '50s*, 141.

63. *Regina Leader-Post*, 28 December 1949.

64. Quoted in Macleod and Macleod, *Tommy Douglas*, 186.

65. Ibid., 181–82.

66. Johnson, *Dream No Little Dreams*, 183.

67. G. Kelly, *Green Grit: The Story of the Saskatchewan Roughriders* (Toronto: Harper Collins, 2001), 119–20, 131–46; W. Simpson, "Hockey," in *A Concise History of Sport in Canada*, ed. D. Morrow (Toronto: Oxford University Press, 1989), 211; V. Pezer, *The Stone Age: A Social History of Curling on the Prairies* (Calgary: Fifth House, 2003), 234–35.

68. *Regina Leader-Post*, 16 May 1955.

69. D. E. Smith, "Celebrations and History on the Prairies," *Journal of Canadian Studies* 17, no. 3 (fall 1982): 50–52.

70. F. McGuinness, *Letters from Section 17: A Collection of Morningside Essays* (Winnipeg: Great Plains, 1999), 56–58.

71. Smith, *Prairie Liberalism*, 264–70.

72. Canada, House of Commons, *Debates*, 22 May 1956, 4196.

73. Quoted in R. Tyre, *Douglas in Saskatchewan: The Story of a Socialist Experiment* (Vancouver: Mitchell Press, 1962), 99.

74. Quoted in ibid., 123.

75. For a fresh assessment of Diefenbaker, see D. Smith, *Rogue Tory: The Life and Legend of John G. Diefenbaker* (Toronto: Macfarlane, Walter and Ross, 1995).

76. Johnson, *Dream No Little Dreams*, 203.

77. Macleod and Macleod, *Tommy Douglas*, 195.

CHAPTER EIGHTEEN: BOTH SIDES NOW

1. Quoted in A. W. Johnson, *Dream No Little Dreams: A Biography of the Douglas Government of Saskatchewan, 1944–1961* (Toronto: University of Toronto Press, 2004), 50–51.

2. For Douglas' account of the story, see T. H. McLeod and I. McLeod, *Tommy Douglas: The Road to Jerusalem* (Edmonton: Hurtig, 1987), 145.

3. Quoted in L. H. Thomas, ed., *The Making of a Socialist: The Recollections of T. C. Douglas* (Edmonton: University of Alberta Press, 1982), 59.

4. C. S. Houston, *Steps on the Road to Medicare: Why Saskatchewan Led the Way* (Montreal: McGill-Queen's University Press, 2002), 26–64; A. Ostry, "Prelude to Medicare: Institutional Change and Continuity in Saskatchewan, 1944–1962," *Prairie Forum* 20, no. 1 (spring 1995): 91; *Globe and Mail*, 18 May 2002.

5. Johnson, *Dream No Little Dreams*, 78–81.

6. J. Feather, "From Concept to Reality: Formation of the Swift Current Health Region," *Prairie Forum* 16, no. 1 (spring 1991): 59–80.

7. D. Mombourquette, "'An Inalienable Right': The CCF and Rapid Health Care Reform, 1944–1948," *Saskatchewan History* 43, no. 3 (autumn 1991): 101–16.

8. Houston, *Steps*, 89–92, 115–20.

9. E. Dyck, "Prairie Psychiatry Pioneers: Mental Health Research in Saskatchewan" (unpublished paper presented before the Canadian Historical Association, Dalhousie, 2003).

10. Ibid., 240–42.

11. Quoted in McLeod and McLeod, *Tommy Douglas*, 195.

12. Johnson, *Dream No Little Dreams*, 250–51.

13. Ibid., 251–55.

14. Quoted in D. E. Smith, *Prairie Liberalism: The Liberal Party in Saskatchewan, 1905–1971* (Toronto: University of Toronto Press, 1975), 277.

15. Quoted in J. Richards and L. Pratt, *Prairie Capitalism: Power and Influence in the New West* (Toronto: McClelland and Stewart, 1979), 198.

16. Quoted in D. Eisler, "W. Ross Thatcher," in *Saskatchewan Premiers of the 20th Century*, ed. G. L. Barnhart (Regina: Canadian Plains Research Center, 2004), 241.

17. J. C. Courtney and D. E. Smith, "Saskatchewan: Parties in a Politically Sensitive Province," in *Canadian Provincial Politics*, ed. M. Robin (Toronto: Prentice-Hall, 1978), 303.

18. Quoted in Johnson, *Dream No Little Dreams*, 252.

19. J. Saywell, "Saskatchewan," *Canadian Annual Review 1960* (Toronto: University of Toronto Press, 1961), 24–27; E. A. Tollefson, "The Medicare Dispute," in *Politics in Saskatchewan*, ed. N. Ward and D. Spafford (Toronto: Longmans, 1968), 241–45.

20. Quoted in Tollefson, "The Medicare Dispute," 245, 272 n. 67.

21. Quoted in Johnson, *Dream No Little Dreams*, 263–64.

22. Tollefson, "The Medicare Dispute," 249.

23. Quoted in D. L. Lloyd, "Woodrow S. Lloyd," in *Saskatchewan Premiers*, ed. Barnhart, 223.

24. Quoted in McLeod and McLeod, *Tommy Douglas*, 225.

25. J. H. Archer, *Saskatchewan: A History* (Saskatoon: Western Producer Prairie Books, 1980), 309.

26. Tollefson, "The Medicare Dispute," 263–64.

27. Quoted ibid., "The Medicare Dispute," 276–77, 277 n. 130.

28. Quoted in ibid.

29. Quoted in ibid.

30. Johnson, *Dream No Little Dreams*, 288–301.

31. Quoted in Lloyd, "Lloyd," 226.

32. F. B. Roth, "Health," *Canadian Annual Review, 1962* (Toronto: University of Toronto Press, 1963), 318. For a critical assessment of Premier Lloyd's handling of the issue, see K. Brownsey, "Policy, Bureaucracy, and Personality: Woodrow Lloyd and the Introduction of Medicare in Saskatchewan," *Prairie Forum* 23, no. 2 (fall 1998): 197–210.

33. J. W. Brennan, *Regina: An Illustrated History* (Toronto: Lorimer, 1989), 180, 188; Archer, *Saskatchewan*, 310–12; Johnson, *Dream No Little Dreams*, 229–32.

34. V. Pezer, *The Stone Age: A Social History of Curling on the Prairies* (Calgary: Fifth House, 2003), 206–207, 241–49.

35. Agriculture Canada, "Selected Statistical Information on Agriculture in Canada," 1968, 2–3.

36. Quoted in J. Harbron, "Agriculture," *Canadian Annual Review, 1960*, 229. In 1961, the total net income of Saskatchewan farm operations was $100 million compared with $402 million in 1956. R. Daviault, "Selected Agricultural Statistics for Canada," Agriculture Canada, 1976, table 51.

37. P. Kyba, *Alvin: A Biography of the Hon. Alvin Hamilton, PC* (Regina: Canadian Plains Research Center, 1989), 160–79.

38. D. B. Banks, "The Political Economy of Petroleum Development in Saskatchewan, 1940–1960" (unpublished M.A. thesis, University of Regina, 1986), 135–36.

39. N. Ward, "Saskatchewan," *Canadian Annual Review, 1964* (Toronto: University of Toronto Press, 1965), 157.

40. N. Ward, "Saskatchewan," *Canadian Annual Review, 1963* (Toronto: University of Toronto Press, 1964), 147.

41. Quoted in Richards and Pratt, *Prairie Capitalism*, 198.

42. T. R. Weir, "The Population," in *The Prairie Provinces*, ed. P. J. Smith (Toronto: University of Toronto Press, 1972), 86–87.

43. J. Saywell, "Saskatchewan," *Canadian Annual Review, 1962*, 65.

44. Smith, *Prairie Liberalism*, 298.

45. Ward, "Saskatchewan," *Canadian Annual Review, 1964*, 159–62; Smith, *Prairie Liberalism*, 280–302.

46. Quoted in Smith, *Prairie Liberalism*, 299.

47. McLeod and McLeod, *Tommy Douglas*, 203.

48. Smith, *Prairie Liberalism*, 280–85.

49. D. Eisler, *Rumours of Glory: Saskatchewan and the Thatcher Years* (Edmonton: Hurtig, 1987), 135–38.

50. Johnson, *Dream No Little Dreams*, xii–xiii.

51. Smith, *Prairie Liberalism*, 303; Eisler, *Rumours of Glory*, 153.

52. Quoted in Ward, "Saskatchewan," and J. Harbron, "Agriculture," *Canadian Annual Review, 1964*, 165, 312.

53. E. Eager, *Saskatchewan Government: Politics and Pragmatism* (Saskatoon: Western Producer Prairie Books, 1980), 60.

54. Smith, *Prairie Liberalism*, 279–82.

55. Quoted in Eisler, *Rumours of Glory*, 155.

56. Richards and Pratt, *Prairie Capitalism*, 137–39, 187–93.

57. Quoted in ibid., 201.

58. N. Ward, "Saskatchewan," in *Canadian Annual Review, 1965*, 177.

59. R. Robson, "Wilderness Suburbs: Boom and Gloom on the Prairies, 1945–1986," *Prairie Forum* 13, no. 2 (fall 1988): 201–203; N. R. Seifried, "Growth and Change in Prairie Metropolitan Centres after 1951," *Prairie Forum* 7, no. 1 (spring 1982), 49–67.

60. Gerald Friesen, email communication to author, 28 September 2004; Helen Dimitroff, email communication to author, 16 August 2004.

61. D. Quiring, "Battling Parish Priests, Bootleggers, and Fur Sharks: CCF Colonialism in Northern Saskatchewan" (unpublished Ph.D. diss., University of Saskatchewan, 2002), 167.

62. P. Mathias, *Forced Growth: Five Studies of Government Involvement in the Development of Canada* (Toronto: J. Lewis and Samuel, 1971), 81–94.

63. Quoted in ibid., 93.

64. Eisler, *Rumours of Glory*, 162–69.

65. Quoted in Mathias, *Forced Growth*, 92.

66. J. M. Pitsula, "The Saskatchewan CCF Government and Treaty Indians, 1944–64," *Canadian Historical Review* 75, no. 1 (March 1994): 40–41.

67. H. Buckley, *From Wooden Ploughs to Welfare: Why Indian Policy Failed in the Prairie Provinces* (Montreal: McGill-Queen's University Press, 1992), 69.

68. E. J. Peters, "'Our City Indians': Negotiating the Meaning of First Nations Urbanization in Canada, 1945–1975," *Historical Geography* 30 (2002): 78. The numbers might actually be higher because respondents may not have identified themselves as Aboriginal at census time.

69. Ibid., 79–81.

70. P. Gzowski, "This is Our Alabama," *Maclean's*, 6 July 1963, 20–21, 46–49.

71. Quiring, "Battling Parish Priests," 198–205, 231–36; see also R. M. Bone, "Colonialism to Post-Colonialism in Canada's Western Interior: The Case of the Lac La Ronge Indian Band," *Historical Geography* 30 (2002): 59–73.

72. A. K. Davis, ed., *A Northern Dilemma: reference papers*, 2 v. (Calgary: s.n. 1965–67).

73. Eisler, "Thatcher," 243–44.

74. Quoted in J. M. Pitsula, "The Thatcher Government in Saskatchewan and Treaty Indians, 1964–1971," *Saskatchewan History* 48, no 1 (spring 1996): 5.

75. Quoted in ibid., 4.

76. Ibid., 5.

77. J. M. Pitsula, "The Thatcher Government in Saskatchewan and the Revival of Métis Nationalism, 1964–1971," *Great Plains Quarterly* 17, no. 3-4 (summer/fall 1997): 221–22; M. J. Dobbin, "The Métis in Western Canada Since 1945," in *The Making of the Modern West: Western Canada Since 1945*, ed. A. W. Rasporich (Calgary: University of Calgary Press, 1984), 187–90.

78. Eisler, "Thatcher," 243.

79. A. Norman, "The Women's Web: Networking in Saskatchewan and the Royal Commission on the Status of Women in Canada" (unpublished M.A. thesis, University of Saskatchewan, 1997), 54–76.

80. Quoted in ibid., 60.

81. Ibid., 73.

82. Ibid., 75.

83. Mary Batten (Liberal), 1956–64; Marjorie Cooper (CCF), 1952–67; Sally Merchant (Liberal), 1964–67; Sarah Ramsland (Liberal), 1919–25; Gladys Strum (CCF), 1960–64; Beatrice Trew (CCF), 1944–48.

84. See G. M. Taylor, "'Should I Drown Myself Now or Later?' The Isolation of Rural Women in Saskatchewan and Their Participation in the Homemakers' Clubs, the Farm Movement, and the Co-operative Commonwealth Federation, 1910–1967," in *Women: Isolation and Bonding*, ed. K. Storrie (Toronto: Methuen, 1987), 85–88.

85. Eisler, *Rumours of Glory*, 180–81.

86. K. Peacock, "CA-NA-DA: The Song That Sold The Centennial," *The Beaver* 84, no. 3 (June-July 2004): 14–19.

87. N. Ward, "Saskatchewan," *Canadian Annual Review, 1967* (Toronto: University of Toronto Press, 1968), 173.

88. N. Ward, "The Contemporary Scene," in *Politics in Saskatchewan*, ed. Ward and Spafford, 300–302.

89. Eisler, *Rumours of Glory*, 208–32.

90. See H. Adams, *Prison of Grass: Canada from the Native Point of View* (Toronto: New Press, 1975).

91. Quoted in Pitsula, "Thatcher Government and Revival of Métis Nationalism," 221.

92. Quoted in N. Ward, "Saskatchewan," *Canadian Annual Review, 1970* (Toronto: University of Toronto Press, 1971), 289.

93. Pitsula, "Thatcher Government and Treaty Indians," 3–10.

94. "Fate of an Indian Shrine," *Regina Leader-Post*, 4 January 1967.

95. Archer, *Saskatchewan*, 327–28; J. J. Gunn, "The Political and Theoretical Conflict over Saskatchewan Uranium Development" (unpublished M.A. thesis, University of Regina, 1983), 67–69; Banks, "The Political Economy of Petroleum Development in Saskatchewan, 1940–1960," 135–36.

96. Richards and Pratt, *Prairie Capitalism*, 202–10; B. M. Barr, "Reorganization of the Economy since 1945," in *The Prairie Provinces*, ed. Smith, 65–82.

97. Archer, *Saskatchewan*, 319–20, 326–27; B. Proudfoot, "Agriculture," 60–64; Ward, "Saskatchewan," *Canadian Annual Review, 1969*, 159, 168; Ward, "Saskatchewan," *Canadian Annual Review, 1970*, 284.

98. Lloyd, "Lloyd," 232–33.

99. Eisler, *Rumours of Glory*, 261–65.

100. D. Gruending, "Allan E. Blakeney," in *Saskatchewan Premiers,* ed. Barnhart, 281–82.

101. Quoted in Eisler, "Thatcher," 249.

CHAPTER NINETEEN: NEXT YEAR COUNTRY

1. Quoted in N. Ward, "Saskatchewan," in *Canadian Annual Review of Politics and Public Affairs, 1971* (Toronto: University of Toronto, 1972), 199.

2. D. Gruending, "Allan E. Blakeney," in *Saskatchewan Premiers of the 20th Century*, ed. G. L. Barnhart (Regina: Canadian Plains Research Center, 2004), 289.

3. Ibid., 273. The Waffle dubbed Blakeney "the civil servant's ideal ... more competent as a bureaucrat than any bureaucrat will ever be." Quoted in N. Ward, "Saskatchewan," *Canadian Annual Review of Politics and Public Affairs, 1972* (Toronto: University of Toronto Press, 1973), 223.

4. A. E. Blakeney, "Reflections on Innovations I Hoped to See," in *Policy Innovation in the Saskatchewan Public Sector, 1971–82*, ed. E. D. Glor (North York: Captus Press, 1997), 254.

5. Quoted in Gruending, "Blakeney," 277.

6. For a discussion of Blakeney's philosophy of governance, see P. Barker, "Decision Making in the Blakeney Years," *Prairie Forum* 19, no. 1 (spring 1994): 65–79.

7. B. Wilson, *Beyond the Harvest: Canadian Grain at the Crossroads* (Saskatoon: Western Producer Prairie Books, 1981), 119, 122, 136; J. F. Conway, "The Decline of the Family Farm in Saskatchewan," *Prairie Forum* 9, no. 1 (spring 1984): 107. A 1977 Science Council of Canada report found that the number of people aged between twenty and twenty-four and living on Canadian farms had dropped 62 per cent between 1966 and 1976.

8. Quoted in J. H. Thompson, *Forging the Prairie West* (Toronto: Oxford University Press, 1998), 155.

9. Wilson, *Beyond the Harvest*, 7, 19–20, 89–94; R. Gibbins, *Prairie Politics and Society: Regionalism in Decline* (Toronto: Butterworths, 1980), 66, 78–82; G. Skogstad, *The Politics of Agricultural Policy-Making in Canada* (Toronto: University of Toronto Press, 1987), 44–45; B. Proudfoot, "Agriculture," in *The Prairie Provinces*, ed. P. J. Smith (Toronto: University of Toronto Press, 1972), 61–62.

10. Wilson, *Beyond the Harvest*, 59–61, 121–22; E. Gordon, "Stress in the Farm Family: Implications for the Rural Human Service Worker," in *The Political Economy of Agriculture in Western Canada*, ed. G. S. Basran and D. A. Hay (Toronto: Garamond Press, 1988), 144.

11. 25th Street Theatre, *Paper Wheat: The Book* (Saskatoon: Western Producer Prairie Books, 1982), 75.

12. Quoted in D. Perkins, "Necessary Adjustments: The Problem of Community Solidarity in *Paper Wheat, The Fighting Days* and *The Shipbuilder*," *Prairie Forum* 21, no. 1 (spring 1996): 43.

13. J. C. Stabler et al., *The Changing Role of Rural Communities in an Urbanizing World: Saskatchewan, 1961–1990* (Regina: Canadian Plains Research Center, 1992), viii.

14. Quoted in B. Broadfoot, *Next-Year Country: Voices of Prairie People* (Toronto: McClelland and Stewart, 1988), 156.

15. M. R. Olfert and J. C. Stabler, "Rural Communities of the Saskatchewan Prairie Landscape," *Prairie Forum* 25, no. 1 (spring 2000): 124–25; J. C. Stabler and M. R. Olfert, *Restructuring Rural Saskatchewan: The Challenge of the 1990s* (Regina: Canadian Plains Research Center, 1992), 3; G. Hodge, "The Prediction of Trade Center Viability in the Great Plains" (unpublished Ph.D. diss., Massachusetts Institute of Technology, 1965), 36–37.

16. S. Butala, "Time, Space and Light: Discovering the Saskatchewan Soul," *NeWest Review* 13, no. 6 (February 1988): 4.

17. T. R. Weir, "The Population," in *The Prairie Provinces*, ed. Smith, 97–98.

18. N. R. Seifried, "Growth and Change in Prairie Metropolitan Centres after 1951," *Prairie Forum* 7, no. 1 (spring 1982): 53, 61, 65.

19. Quoted in Gibbins, *Prairie Politics and Society*, 95.

20. D. E. Smith, "Western Politics and National Unity," in *Canada and the Burden of Unity*, ed. D. J. Bercuson (Toronto: Macmillan, 1977), 149.

21. Skogstad, *The Politics of Agricultural Policy-Making in Canada*, 27–28.

22. Quoted in D. E. Smith, *Prairie Liberalism: The Liberal Party in Saskatchewan, 1905–71* (Toronto: University of Toronto Press, 1975), 318.

23. J. H. Archer, *Saskatchewan: A History* (Saskatoon: Western Producer Prairie Books, 1980), 338.

24. Quoted in N. Ward, "Saskatchewan," *Canadian Annual Review of Politics and Public Affairs, 1972,* 219.

25. Wilson, *Beyond the Harvest,* 85–87, 96, 103.

26. Quoted in D. Spafford, "Saskatchewan," *Canadian Annual Review of Politics and Public Affairs, 1974* (Toronto: University of Toronto Press, 1975), 254–55.

27. Conway, "Decline of the Family Farm," 106–107.

28. D. Spafford, "Saskatchewan," *Canadian Annual Review of Politics and Public Affairs, 1973* (Toronto: University of Toronto Press, 1974), 187–88; J. C. Courtney, "Saskatchewan," *Canadian Annual Review of Politics and Public Affairs, 1976* (Toronto: University of Toronto Press, 1977), 260–61; Conway, "Decline of the Family Farm," 106–11; Wilson, *Beyond the Harvest,* 94.

29. J. R. Miller, *Skyscrapers Hide the Heavens: A History of Indian-White Relations in Canada* (Toronto: University of Toronto Press, 2000), 328–41.

30. J. Hammersmith and B. Hauk, "Indian and Native Policy in Southern Saskatchewan," in *Policy Innovation,* ed. Glor, 109.

31. J. M. Pitsula, "First Nations and Saskatchewan Politics," in *Saskatchewan Politics: Into the Twenty-first Century,* ed. H. A. Leeson (Regina: Canadian Plains Research Center, 2001), 359; see also J. M. Pitsula, "The Thatcher Government in Saskatchewan and Treaty Indians, 1964–1971," *Saskatchewan History* 48, no. 1 (spring 1996): 16.

32. D. Cuthand, "Indian Control of Indian Education: A Brief History," *Saskatchewan Indian* (September 1988): 18; J. R. Miller, *Shingwauk's Vision: A History of Native Residential Schools* (Toronto: University of Toronto Press, 1996), 402–405.

33. Hammersmith and Hauk, "Indian and Native Policy in Southern Saskatchewan," 106–107.

34. Quoted in E. J. Peters, "'Our City Indians': Negotiating the Meaning of First Nations Urbanization in Canada, 1945–1975," *Historical Geography* 30 (2002): 85.

35. Quoted in J. M. Pitsula, "The Saskatchewan CCF Government and Treaty Indians, 1944–64," *Canadian Historical Review* 75, no. 1 (March 1994): 52.

36. K. Collier, "Social Democracy and Underdevelopment: The Case of Northern Saskatchewan," in *Social Policy and Social Justice: The NDP Government in Saskatchewan During the Blakeney Years,* ed. J. Harding (Waterloo: Wilfrid Laurier University Press, 1995), 323.

37. G. R. Weller, "Provincial Ministries of Northern Affairs: A Comparative Analysis," in *Resources and Dynamics of the Boreal Zone,* ed. R. W. Wein et al. (Ottawa: Association of Canadian Universities for Northern Studies, 1983), 483.

38. *Saskatoon Star-Phoenix,* 7 June 1974; *Regina Leader-Post,* 7 June 1974.

39. D. Spafford, "Saskatchewan," in *Canadian Annual Review of Politics and Public Affairs, 1974,* 255–56.

40. Weller, "Provincial Ministries," 496.

41. Quoted in T. Waller, "Framework for Economic Development: The Role of Crown Corporations and the Crown Investments Corporation of Saskatchewan," in *Policy Innovation,* ed. Glor, 32.

42. Quoted in J. Richards and L. Pratt, *Prairie Capitalism: Power and Influence in the New West* (Toronto: McClelland and Stewart, 1979), 258.

43. What was somewhat puzzling about the court case is why the industry chose to take on Saskatchewan, when neighbouring Alberta, with much larger reserves, had introduced similar royalty charges. But the industry apparently suspected that the Saskatchewan legislation was the first step towards eventual nationalization and wanted to throw up a roadblock before the province went down that road. Ibid., 258–59, 263–64, 287–88.

44. Ibid., 294–98

45. Quoted in Spafford, "Saskatchewan," *Canadian Annual Review, 1973,* 197.

46. D. Spafford, "Saskatchewan," *Canadian Annual Review, 1974,* 251–52; Richards and Pratt, *Prairie Capitalism,* 259–60.

47. Quoted in "Crises in Agriculture in Western Canada: A Theoretical Explanation," in *The Political Economy of Agriculture in Western Canada,* ed. Basran and Hay, 43.

48. For a debate about the creation of the University of Regina, see M. Hayden et al., *Saskatchewan Universities: A Perception of History,* Saskatchewan Institute of Public Policy, policy paper 15, May 2003.

49. Quoted in J. C. Courtney, "Saskatchewan," *Canadian Annual Review of Politics and Public Affairs, 1975* (Toronto: University of Toronto Press, 1976), 207.

50. Quoted in ibid., 207.

51. Quoted in N. Ward, "Saskatchewan," *Canadian Annual Review of Politics and Public Affairs, 1972,* 222.

52. B. Wilson, *Politics of Defeat* (Saskatchewan: Western Producer Prairie Books, 1980), 96–97.

53. E. Eager, *Saskatchewan Government: Politics and Pragmatism* (Saskatoon: Western Producer Prairie Books, 1980), 64; Wilson, *Politics of Defeat,* 83–85.

54. Quoted in Courtney, "Saskatchewan," *Canadian Annual Review, 1975,* 210.

55. J. K. Laux and M. A. Molot, "The Potash Corporation of Saskatchewan," in *Public Corporations and Public Policy in Canada,* ed. A. Tupper and G. B. Doern (Montreal: Institute for Research on Public Policy, 1981), 192–94.

56. Ibid.

57. Courtney, "Saskatchewan," *Canadian Annual Review, 1975,* 213.

58. Quoted in Wilson, *Politics of Defeat*, 106.

59. Quoted in Richards and Pratt, *Prairie Capitalism*, 143.

60. J. C. Courtney, "Saskatchewan," *Canadian Annual Review of Politics and Public Affairs, 1976* (Toronto: University of Toronto Press, 1977), 263.

61. Richards and Pratt, *Prairie Capitalism*, 271.

62. G. Kelly, *Green Grit: The Story of the Saskatchewan Roughriders* (Toronto: Harper Collins, 2001), 275.

63. Quoted in J. J. Gunn, "The Political and Theoretical Conflict over Saskatchewan Uranium Development" (unpublished M.A. thesis, University of Regina, 1983), 76.

64. One estimate pegs the amount that the Blakeney government spent on uranium development during its period in office at $850 million. D. P. M. Gullickson, "Uranium Mining, the State, and Public Policy in Saskatchewan, 1971–1982: The Limits of Social Democratic Imagination" (unpublished M.A. thesis, University of Regina, 1991), 2–3, 69–73.

65. B. Harding, "The Two Faces of Public Ownership: From the Regina Manifesto to Uranium Mining," in *Social Policy and Social Justice*, ed. Harding, 291–92.

66. Gruending, *Promises to Keep*, 166–68.

67. Ibid., 163.

68. J. R. Miller, "Saskatchewan," in *Canadian Annual Review, 1978* (Toronto: University of Toronto Press, 1979), 217.

69. Quoted in Richards and Pratt, *Prairie Capitalism*, 279.

70. Eager, *Saskatchewan Government*, 186.

71. Quoted in ibid., 186.

72. Quoted in Wilson, *Politics of Defeat*, 150.

73. *Regina Leader-Post*, 11 March 1980, 12 March 1980.

74. D. M. Jackson, "Political Paradox: The Lieutenant-governor in Saskatchewan," in *Saskatchewan Politics: Into the Twenty-First Century*, ed. H. A. Leeson (Regina: Canadian Plains Research Center, 2001), 63.

75. Archer, *Saskatchewan*, 352.

76. Quoted in D. E. Smith, "Celebrations and History on the Prairies," *Journal of Canadian Studies* 17, no. 3 (fall 1982): 46.

77. Quoted in J. R. Miller, "Saskatchewan," *Canadian Annual Review of Politics and Public Affairs, 1979* (Toronto: University of Toronto Press, 1980), 366.

CHAPTER TWENTY:
IN A MUDHOLE

1. Quoted in D. Smith, *Rogue Tory: The Life and Legend of John G. Diefenbaker* (Toronto: Macfarlane, Walter and Ross, 1995), 577. The Diefenbaker funeral was the most expensive state funeral in Canadian history.

2. *Saskatoon Star-Phoenix*, 23 August 1979.

3. T. D. Regehr, "Western Canada and the Burden of National Transportation Policies," in *Canada and the Burden of Unity*, ed. D. J. Bercuson (Toronto: Macmillan, 1977), 132.

4. Ibid., 131–35.

5. G. Skogstad, *The Politics of Agricultural Policy-Making in Canada* (Toronto: University of Toronto Press, 1987), 123–28.

6. B. Wilson, *Beyond the Harvest: Canadian Grain at the Crossroads* (Saskatoon: Western Producer Prairie Books, 1981), 127.

7. T. Waller, "Framework for Economic Development: The Role of Crown Corporations and the Crown Investments Corporation of Saskatchewan," in *Policy Innovation in the Saskatchewan Public Sector, 1971–82*, ed. E. D. Glor (North York: Captus Press, 1997), 35.

8. J. Keet, "Matrimonial Property Legislation: Are Women Equal Partners," in *The Political Economy of Agriculture in Western Canada*, ed. G. S. Basran and D. A. Hay (Toronto: Garamond Press, 1988), 175–84. One of the most unusual legal documents in Saskatchewan history, dating from 1948, is found in the law library at the University of Saskatchewan. Pinned under his overturned tractor in the field, a mortally injured C. G. Harris scratched on his fender with his pocket knife, "In case I die in this mess I leave all to the wife." The court ruled the will valid.

9. See A. M. Iheduru, "Conservation Planning in the South Saskatchewan River Valley and Recent Changes in Saskatoon's Urban Landscape," *Prairie Forum* 27, no. 2 (fall 2002): 221–37.

10. Quoted in J. MacKinnon, *Minding the Public Purse: The Fiscal Crisis, Political Trade-offs, and Canada's Future* (Montreal: McGill-Queen's University Press, 2003), 19.

11. Quoted in B. Wilson, *The Politics of Defeat: The Decline of the Liberal Party in Saskatchewan* (Saskatoon: Western Producer Prairie Books, 1980), 125.

12. Quoted in MacKinnon, *Minding the Public Purse*, 14.

13. *Toronto Globe and Mail*, 26 April 1982; MacKinnon, *Minding the Public Purse*, 18–19.

14. D. Gruending, *Promises to Keep: A Political Biography of Allan Blakeney* (Saskatoon: Western Producer Prairie Books, 1990), 221–22.

15. Quoted in L. Biggs and M. Stobbe, "An Examination of the Conservative Years, 1982–1990," in *Devine Rule in Saskatchewan: A Decade of Hope and Hardship*, ed. Biggs and Stobbe (Saskatoon: Fifth House, 1991), 10.

16. Wilson, *Politics of Defeat*, 151.

17. *Saskatoon Star-Phoenix*, 10 May 1982.

18. Quoted in J. M. Pitsula, "Grant Devine," in *Saskatchewan Premiers of the 20th Century*, ed. G. L. Barnhart (Regina: Canadian Plains Research Center, 2004), 322.

19. B. Waiser, "Saskatchewan," *Canadian Annual Review of Politics and Public Affairs, 1982* (Toronto: University of Toronto Press, 1983), 287–90.

20. J. R. Miller, "Saskatchewan," *Canadian Annual Review, 1981* (Toronto: University of Toronto Press, 1982), 429–30.

21. G. R. Weller, "Managing Canada's North: the case of the provincial north," *Canadian Public Administration* 27, no. 2 (summer 1984): 208.

22. P. Prebble, "Protecting God's Country," in *Devine Rule in Saskatchewan*, ed. Biggs and Stobbe, 128–29.

23. Quoted in J. R. Miller, "Saskatchewan," *Canadian Annual Review of Politics and Public Affairs, 1984* (Toronto: University of Toronto Press, 1985), 289.

24. M. Goldstick, *Wollaston: People Resisting Genocide* (Montreal: Black Rose Books, 1987); see also D. McLeod, "From Exploitation to Marginalization: The Aboriginals of Northern Saskatchewan in Relation to the National and International Political Economy" (unpublished M.A. thesis, University of Regina, 1991).

25. Prebble, "Protecting God's Country," 129–30.

26. Quoted in Miller, "Saskatchewan," *Canadian Annual Review, 1984*, 288.

27. J. R. Miller, "Saskatchewan," *Canadian Annual Review of Politics and Public Affairs, 1986* (Toronto: University of Toronto Press, 1987), 320.

28. *Saskatoon Star-Phoenix*, 30 December 1989.

29. Pitsula, "Devine," 319.

30. T. Pugh, "Cultivating the Corporate Agenda," in *Devine Rule in Saskatchewan*, ed. Biggs and Stobbe, 72–77, table 4.2; *Saskatoon Star Phoenix*, 30 December 1989.

31. D. Kerr, "In Defence of the Past: A History of Saskatchewan Heritage Preservation, 1922–1983," *Prairie Forum* 15, no. 2 (fall 1990): 294–95.

32. P. Smith, "Murdoch's, Becker's, and Sorochan's Challenge: Thinking Again About the Roles of Women in Primary Agriculture," in *The Political Economy of Agriculture in Western Canada*, ed. Basran and Hay, 157–74.

33. Pugh, "Cultivating the Corporate Agenda," 75.

34. A. C. Moffatt, "Experiencing Identity: British-Canadian Women in Rural Saskatchewan, 1880–1950" (unpublished Ph.D. diss., University of Manitoba, 1996), 111 n. 16.

35. J. Martin, "From Bad to Worse: Day Care in Saskatchewan, 1982–1989," in *Devine Rule in Saskatchewan*, ed. Biggs and Stobbe, 240.

36. Quoted in J. R. Miller, "Saskatchewan," *Canadian Annual Review of Politics and Public Affairs, 1987* (Toronto: University of Toronto Press, 1988), 335.

37. MacKinnon, *Minding the Public Purse*, 24.

38. Quoted in Waiser, "Saskatchewan," *Canadian Annual Review, 1982*, 290.

39. Quoted in Miller, "Saskatchewan," *Canadian Annual Review, 1984*, 292.

40. M. Stobbe, "Political Conservatism and Fiscal Responsibility," in *Devine Rule in Saskatchewan*, ed. Biggs and Stobbe, 15–17.

41. Quoted in Pitsula, "Devine," 332.

42. J. R. Miller, *Lethal Legacy: Current Native Controversies in Canada* (Toronto: McClelland and Stewart, 2004), 81–85, 206.

43. Quoted in *Globe and Mail*, 27 March 1987.

44. Quoted in *Saskatoon Star-Phoenix*, 28 March 1987.

45. T. B. Krywulak, "The Free-Trade Debate in Saskatchewan, 1985–1988" (unpublished M.A. thesis, University of Regina, 2000).

46. *Saskatoon Star-Phoenix*, 2 April 1987.

47. P. Martin-McGuire, "Treaty Land Entitlement in Saskatchewan: A Context for the Creation of Urban Reserves," in *Urban Indian Reserves: Forging New Relationships in Saskatchewan*, ed. F. L Barron and J. Garcea (Saskatoon: Purich, 1999), 62–64; J. M. Pitsula, "The Blakeney Government and the Settlement of Treaty Indian Land Entitlements in Saskatchewan, 1975–1982," *Canadian Historical Association Historical Papers*, 1989, 190–209.

48. F. L. Barron and J. Garcea, "The Genesis of Urban Reserves and the Role of Governmental Self-Interest," in *Urban Indian Reserves*, ed. Barron and Garcea, 22–36.

49. Quoted in D. Yeo, "Municipal Perspectives from Prince Albert," in *Urban Indian Reserves*, ed. Barron and Garcea, 177.

50. Quoted in Barron and Garcea, "The Genesis of Urban Reserves," 28.

51. MacKinnon, *Minding the Public Purse*, 26.

52. Quoted in Miller, "Saskatchewan," *Canadian Annual Review, 1986*, 324.

53. Ibid., 323.

54. Quoted in ibid.

55. Pitsula, "Devine," 311.

56. Biggs and Stobbe, "An Examination of the Conservative Years, 1982–1990," 11–12.

57. Quoted in B. Waiser, "Saskatchewan," *Canadian Annual Review of Politics and Public Affairs, 1989* (Toronto: University of Toronto Press, 1990), 212.

58. *Globe and Mail*, 5 May 1990.

59. Ibid., 21 March 1987.

60. K. Rosaasen et al., "Federal Government Relief Programs for Grain Farmers: Rewards for Late Adjusters?" (unpublished paper presented before Soils and Crops Workshop, Saskatoon, 1990).

61. Bill Waiser, "Saskatchewan," *Canadian Annual Review of Politics and Public Affairs, 1988* (Toronto: University of Toronto Press, 1989), 292.

62. Quoted in D. E. Smith, "Saskatchewan," *Canadian Annual Review of Politics and Public Affairs, 1990* (Toronto: University of Toronto Press, 1991), 221.

63. Quoted in *Globe and Mail*, 21 March 1987.

64. I. Anderson, "An Overview of the Development of a Natural Resource-Based Economy: the supply of output in Saskatchewan" (unpublished paper presented before All-European Canadian Studies Conference, The Hague, 1990).

65. *Saskatoon Star-Phoenix*, 19 September 1992.

66. Quoted in Waiser, "Saskatchewan," *Canadian Annual Review, 1988*, 289.

67. For an examination of gays rights in Saskatchewan at the time, see V. J. Korinek, "The Most Openly Gay Person for at least a thousand miles: Doug Wilson and the Politicization of a Province, 1975–83," *Canadian Historical Review* 84, no. 4 (December 2003): 517–50.

68. MacKinnon, *Minding the Public Purse*, 47–51.

69. J. M. Pitsula and K. A. Rasmussen, *Privatizing a Province: The New Right in Saskatchewan* (Vancouver: New Star Books, 1990), 63–64.

70. Quoted in Waiser, "Saskatchewan," *Canadian Annual Review, 1989*, 203.

71. Waiser, *Canadian Annual Review, 1988*, 280, 284.

72. Quoted in Waiser, *Canadian Annual Review, 1989*, 204.

73. Ibid.

74. Ibid., 206.

75. Ibid.

76. Ibid., 209.

77. Pitsula and Rasmussen, *Privatizing a Province*, 285–86.

78. Quoted in Waiser, "Saskatchewan," *Canadian Annual Review, 1989*, 212.

79. Pugh, "Cultivating the Corporate Agenda," 68.

80. *Poverty Profile 1988* (Ottawa: National Council of Welfare, 1988), 10, 28; Waiser, "Saskatchewan," *Canadian Annual Review, 1989*, 217.

81. *Saskatoon Star-Phoenix*, 14 September 1988.

82. G. N. Hood, *Against the Flow: Rafferty-Alameda and the Politics of the Environment* (Saskatoon: Fifth House, 1994).

83. Quoted in Biggs and Stobbe, "An Examination of the Conservative Years, 1982–1990," 9.

84. Quoted in MacKinnon, *Minding the Public Purse*, 39.

85. Quoted in G. Jones, *SaskScandal: The Death of Political Idealism in Saskatchewan* (Calgary: Fifth House, 2000), 188.

CHAPTER TWENTY-ONE:
OUR SHARED DESTINY

1. *Regina Leader-Post*, 23 September 1992; *Saskatoon StarPhoenix*, 23 September 1992.

2. Quoted in G. P. Marchildon, "Roy Romanow," in *Saskatchewan Premiers of the 20th Century*, ed. G. L. Barnhart (Regina: Canadian Plains Research Center, 2004), 367.

3. J. MacKinnon, *Minding the Public Purse: The Fiscal Crisis, Political Trade-offs, and Canada's Future* (Montreal: McGill-Queen's University Press, 2003), 56.

4. Ibid., 98, 101–102.

5. Ibid., 61.

6. Quoted in D. E. Smith, "Saskatchewan," *Canadian Annual Review of Politics and Public Affairs, 1993* (Toronto: University of Toronto Press, 1994), 215.

7. Marchildon, "Romanow," 370–71; J. Praud and S. McQuarrie, "The Saskatchewan CCF-NDP from the Regina Manifesto to the Romanow Years," in *Saskatchewan Politics into the 21st Century*, ed. H. Leeson (Regina: Canadian Plains Research Center, 2001), 162–63.

8. MacKinnon, *Minding the Public Purse*, 110, 123–24.

9. Marchildon, "Romanow," 374–76; MacKinnon, *Minding the Public Purse*, 75–76; Praud and McQuarrie, "The Saskatchewan CCF-NDP," 158.

10. *National Post*, 5 February 2000.

11. Marchildon, "Romanow," 379–85.

12. V. Clemence, *Saskatchewan's Own: People Who Made a Difference* (Calgary: Fifth House, 2004), 219.

13. D. E. Smith, "Saskatchewan," *Canadian Annual Review of Politics and Public Affairs, 1994* (Toronto: University of Toronto Press, 1995), 202.

14. H. A. Leeson, "The Rich Soil of Saskatchewan Politics," in *Saskatchewan Politics*, ed. Leeson, 11; D. E. Smith, "Saskatchewan Perspectives," in *Saskatchewan and Aboriginal Peoples in the 21st Century: Social, Economic, and Political Changes and Challenges* (Regina: PrintWest Publishing, 1997), 9.

15. F. Nault et al., *Population Projections of Registered Indians, 1991–2015* (Ottawa: Indian Affairs and Northern Development, 1993), 49.

16. A. Blakeney, "Reflections on Innovations I Hoped to See," in *Policy Innovation in the Saskatchewan Public Sector, 1971–82*, ed. E. D. Glor (North York: Captus Press, 1997), 267.

17. Marchildon, "Romanow," 354–55.

18. Ibid., 378; Leeson, "The Rich Soil of Saskatchewan Politics," 8–9.

19. P. Martin-McGuire, "The Importance of the Land: Treaty Land Entitlement and Self-Government in Saskatchewan," in *Aboriginal Self-Government in Canada*, ed. J. H. Hylton (Saskatoon: Purich Publishing, 1999), 274–88.

20. *Regina Leader-Post*, 26 May 1992.

21. For an examination of race relations in the Punnichy area, see M. Mandryk, "Uneasy Neighbours: White-Aboriginal Relations and Agricultural Decline," in *Writing Off the Rural West: Globalization, Governments, and the Transformation of Rural Communities*, ed. R. Epp and D. Whitson (Edmonton: University of Alberta Press, 2001), 205–21.

22. Ipsos Reid, "Public Views Regarding Aboriginal People 2002," Saskatchewan only results.

23. *Regina Leader-Post*, 19 October 1994.

24. *Regina Leader-Post*, 11 September 1995.

25. Quoted in Mandryk, "Uneasy Neighbours," 216.

26. *Saskatchewan Indian* 22, no. 2 (February 1993).

27. *Regina Leader-Post*, 9 February 1995.

28. A. G. Gulig, "Yesterday's Promises: The Negotiation of Treaty Ten," *Saskatchewan History* 50, no. 1 (spring 1998): 25; Section 12 of the act explicitly stated that "Indians shall have the right, which the Province hereby assures them, of hunting, trapping, and fishing game and fish for food at all seasons of the year on all unoccupied Crown lands and on any other lands to which the said Indians may have a right of access." Quoted in A. G. Gulig, "'We Beg the Government': Native People and Game Regulation in Northern Saskatchewan 1900–1940," *Prairie Forum* 28, no. 1 (spring 2003): 91.

29. A. G. Gulig, "Whales, Walleyes, and Moose: Recent Case Studies in a Comparison of Indian Law in the United States and Canada," *Native Studies Review* 16, no. 1 (2005), 87–114.

30. C. Chartier, "Aboriginal Self-Government and the Métis Nation," in *Aboriginal Self-Government in Canada*, ed. J. H. Hylton, 112–128.

31. *Saskatoon StarPhoenix*, 16 June 1993.

32. C. Chartier, "Métis Perspective on Self-Government," in *Continuing Poundmaker and Riel's Quest*, ed. R. Gosse et al. (Saskatoon: Purich Publishing, 1994), 86.

33. B. Stirling, "Transitions in Rural Saskatchewan," in *Saskatchewan Politics into the Twenty-First Century*, ed. Leeson, 325.

34. I. Boyens, *Another Season's Promise: Hope and Despair in Canada's Farm Country* (Toronto: Viking, 2001), 49.

35. Quoted in C. Harder, "Overcoming Cultural and Spiritual Obstacles to Rural Revitalization," in *Writing Off the Rural West*, ed. Epp and Whitson, 231.

36. Quoted in Boyens, *Another Season's Promise*, 49.

37. Stirling, "Transitions in Rural Saskatchewan," 323, 330–31.

38. Boyens, *Another Season's Promise*, 50–51.

39. *Regina Leader-Post*, 18 June 1993.

40. Stirling, "Transitions in Rural Saskatchewan," 329.

41. M. R. Olfert and J. Stabler, "Rural Communities of the Saskatchewan Prairie Landscape," *Prairie Forum* 25, no. 1 (spring 2000): 123–38; G. Lawrence et al., "Globalization, Neo-Liberalism, and Rural Decline," in *Writing Off the Rural West*, ed. Epp and Whitson, 98.

42. D. E. Smith, "Saskatchewan," *Canadian Annual Review of Politics and Public Affairs, 1992* (Toronto: University of Toronto, 1993), 236.

43. Ibid., 232.

44. MacKinnon, *Minding the Public Purse*, 216–18.

45. Praud and McQuarrie, "The Saskatchewan CCF-NDP," 159–59.

46. MacKinnon, *Minding the Public Purse*, 143; Smith, "Saskatchewan," *Canadian Annual Review, 1992*, 236.

47. D. Adams, "The White and the Black Horse Race: Saskatchewan Health Reform in the 1990s," in *Saskatchewan Politics*, ed. Leeson, 278–79; Smith, "Saskatchewan," *Canadian Annual Review, 1993*, 213–14.

48. Quoted in J. Garcea, "Saskatchewan," *Canadian Annual Review, 1995*, 200.

49. Quoted in L. Haverstock, "The Saskatchewan Liberal Party," in *Saskatchewan Politics*, ed. Leeson, 237.

50. K. Wishlow, "Rethinking the Polarization Thesis: The Formation and Growth of the Saskatchewan Party, 1997–2001," in *Saskatchewan Politics*, ed. Leeson, 170–73.

51. Quoted in ibid., 175.

52. Ibid., 175–80.

53. D. E. Smith, "Saskatchewan: A Distinct Political Culture," unpublished paper.

54. MacKinnon, *Minding the Public Purse*, 261.

55. C. Voyageur and J. Green, "From Many Peoples, Strength: Demographics and Democracy in Saskatchewan's 1999 'Harvest Election'," in *Saskatchewan Politics*, ed. Leeson, 343–46.

56. Quoted in Smith, "Saskatchewan," *Canadian Annual Review, 1993*, 218.

57. Quoted in Smith, "Saskatchewan Perspectives," 26.

58. Quoted in C. Sampson, *Buried in the Silence* (Edmonton: NeWest Publishers, 1995), 186.

59. *Saskatoon StarPhoenix*, 6 November 2003, 14 November 2003; Smith, "Saskatchewan: A Distinct Political Culture."

60. *Saskatoon StarPhoenix*, 29 October 2003.

EPILOGUE:
A ROAD TO THE FUTURE

1. Quoted in D. R. Owram, ed., *The Formation of Alberta: A Documentary History* (Calgary: Alberta Records Publication Board, 1979), 183, 185.

2. D. E. Smith, "Saskatchewan Perspectives," in *Saskatchewan and Aboriginal Peoples in the 21st Century: Social, Economic, and Political Changes and Challenges* (Regina: PrintWest Publishing, 1997), 12.

3. T. Mountjoy, "Municipal Government Perspectives on Aboriginal Self-Government," in *Aboriginal Self-Government in Canada*, ed. Hylton (Saskatoon: Purich Publishing, 1999), 326.

4. This negative population growth may become the norm, especially when nearly three-quarters of all new immigrants to Canada between 1991 and 2001 settled in Canada's three largest cities (Toronto, Montreal, and Vancouver). *Globe and Mail*, 19 August 2004.

5. *Saskatoon StarPhoenix*, 26 August 2004.

6. In 2000, the average rural family income in Saskatchewan was almost $5,000 below the national rural average. J. J. Azmier, "Fighting the Odds: Rural Development Strategies for Western Canada," Canada West Foundation, March 2004; J. J. Azmier, "The Rural West: Diversity and Dilemma," Canada West Foundation, June 2003.

7. Quoted in *National Post*, 5 February 2000.

8. A similar reduction in farm receipts had devastating consequences in the 1930s, but the most recent drought did not even produce a blip on the province's economic monitor. Ibid.

9. *Globe and Mail*, 8 September 2004.

10. Even if global warming does not trigger a drought, it is an unavoidable natural occurrence. Researchers at the University of Regina, looking at layers of algae, pollen, and tree rings preserved in prairie sloughs, have determined that the last century has been abnormally wet and that frequent, persistent dry cycles, lasting decades, have been more common over the last two millennia. T. Herriot, "Overdrawn at the water bank," *Canadian Geographic* 123, no. 3 (May/June 2003): 48–50.

11. C. Evans, "Flawed Science and Good Husbandry," *The Beaver* 84, no. 4 (August/September 2004): 11–12.

12. "Saskatchewan in the West: An Economic Profile," Canada West Foundation, January 1999.

13. I. Peach and D. Hovdebo, "Righting Past Wrongs: The Case for a Federal Role in Decommissioning and Reclaiming Abandoned Uranium Mines in Northern Saskatchewan," Saskatchewan Institute of Public Policy, paper 21, December 2003.

14. *Saskatoon StarPhoenix*, 1 September 2004.

15. Between 1996 and 2002, the rural Saskatchewan workforce was reduced by 6 per cent or eleven thousand jobs; it was the only rural region in the four western provinces to suffer a decrease in rural employment. J. J. Azmier, "The Rural West."

16. This situation is made worse by the fact that Saskatchewan is almost four times as likely to lose a university graduate to another province than a blue-collar worker or retired person. J. Stokes, "Demographic Trends and Socio-Economic Sustainability in Saskatchewan: Some Policy Considerations," Saskatchewan Institute of Public Policy, paper 19, October 2003.

17. *National Post*, 5 February 2000.

18. Smith, "Saskatchewan Perspectives," 25.

19. According to the 2003 Saskatchewan Child Poverty Report, almost 60 per cent of Aboriginal children lived in poverty—that's three times the rate for all children in the province. Almost half of Aboriginal adults have less than a grade twelve education and can be expected to work less and earn less. Aboriginal people also have poorer health, have more one-parent families, and

experience greater domestic violence. Eighty per cent of the inmates in the province's correctional facilities are Aboriginal, twenty times the incarceration rate for non-Aboriginals. Perhaps the most significant statistic is that First Nations children currently account for one in five children entering kindergarten. C. Hanselmann, "Urban Aboriginal People in Western Canada: Realities and Policies," Canada West Foundation, September 2001.

20. Quoted in *National Post*, 4 April 2002.

21. R. Blake and A. Nurse, "The Rural Problematic: An Introduction to the Rural Trajectories of Life," in *The Trajectories of Rural Life: New Perspectives on Rural Canada*, ed. Blake and Nurse (Regina: Canadian Plains Research Center, 2003), vii–xi.

22. R. Gibbins, "The Rural Face of the New West," in ibid., 142–44.

23. *National Post*, 10 October 2000.

24. A. Scholz, *Don't Turn Out The Lights: Entrepreneurship in rural Saskatchewan* (Saskatoon: University Extension Press, 2000).

25. R. M. Bone, "Colonialism to Post-Colonialism in Canada's Western Interior: The Case of the Lac La Ronge Indian Band," *Historical Geography* 30 (2002): 69–71.

26. *Globe and Mail*, 14 December 2004.

27. *Saskatoon StarPhoenix*, 1 December 1994.

28. See E. J. Millions, "Ties Undone: A Gendered and Racial Analysis of the Impact of the 1885 North-West Rebellion in the Saskatchewan Territory" (unpublished M.A. thesis, University of Saskatchewan, 2004).

29. Quoted in C. L. Nicholat, "Exploring a Shared History: Indian-White Relations Between Fishing Lake First Nation and Wadena, 1882–2002" (unpublished M.A. thesis, University of Saskatchewan, 2002), 107–108.

30. *Saskatoon StarPhoenix*, 9 August 2004 (special "Moving Beyond" report); Mandryk, "Uneasy Neighbours," 210–13.

31. Mandryk, "Uneasy Neighbours," 217.

32. E. H. Oliver, "The Settlement of Saskatchewan to 1914," *Transactions of the Royal Society of Canada* 20, series 3, section 2 (1926): 87.

33. D. M. Jackson, "Political Paradox: The Lieutenant-governor in Saskatchewan," in *Saskatchewan Politics into the Twenty-First Century*, ed. H. Leeson (Regina: Canadian Plains Research Center, 2001), 60–61.

34. J. R. Miller, "Aboriginal Peoples and the Academy," in *Reflections on Native-Newcomer Relations: Selected Essays* (Toronto: University of Toronto Press, 2004), 279–95.

35. Smith, "Saskatchewan Perspectives," 26.

36. G. Scholz, *Gold on Ice: The Story of the Sandra Schmirler Curling Team* (Regina: Couteau, 1999), i.

37. Canadian Press stories, 4 March 2000, 6 March 2000.

Acknowledgements

Preparing *Saskatchewan: A New History* has been an extremely gratifying experience, all the more so because of the assistance and support of many individuals and agencies. Peter MacKinnon, president of the University of Saskatchewan, readily embraced the idea of a new provincial history as a university centennial project and helped find ways to make it happen. His efforts were generously complemented by Michael Atkinson, vice-president (Academic); Ken Coates, former dean of the College of Arts and Science; Tom Wishart, acting dean of Arts and Science and now dean of the College of Graduate Studies; Gary Kachanoski, former dean of Graduate Studies; Barb Geib of Financial Reporting; and Larry Stewart, Dave De Brou, and Brett Fairbairn of my home department.

In addition to university support, funding for the project was kindly provided by the Government of Saskatchewan (through the efforts of Murray Langgard, Brent Cotter, and Olivia Shumski), the federal Department of Canadian Heritage (Norman Moyer and Andrea Sebastian), and the Celebrate Canada! Committee for Saskatchewan (Joy Pelling). How the history of the province was handled was left completely to me.

The research team of Christa Nicholat, Nathan Elliott, and Bonnie Wagner did a tremendous job. They not only located good material, but took great interest in how it was presented in the book. Nathan also prepared the tables, with some of the data provided by Jean Barman. Bonnie identified possible photographs and confirmed the accuracy of the references. Cheryl Loadman and Tom Novosel assisted this work. Some of the research material was also collected by Jacki Andre as part of a Social Sciences and Humanities Research Council grant on the twin forces of distance and isolation in prairie history.

A number of professional friends read the manuscript in its various stages and provided helpful suggestions and expert direction: Ann Leger-Anderson, Gordon Barnhart, Beth Bilson, Bill Brennan, Craig Brown, Gerry Friesen, Gerry Hallowell (not the Spice Girl), Jim Miller, James Parker, David Smith, Randy Widdis, and Glenn Wright. In particular, Bill, Jim, and David were regularly called upon and responded with helpful feedback. Glenn also chased down sources at Library and Archives Canada. Any errors are my own.

John Perret drew on his photographic skills to assemble a stunning collection of images. Library and Archives Canada also contributed visual material, as did Charles Hou from his vast cartoon collection. Finn Andersen of the

Saskatchewan History and Folklore Society granted access to the Everett Baker photographs. Tim Novak recommended several gems from the Saskatchewan Archives Board photograph collection. The story of Gus and Tony Lambert and related visual material is reproduced with the permission of the family.

Mike McCoy and Brian Smith of Articulate Eye devised an elegant design for the book; they also did the maps. Their work was ably facilitated by Marilyn St. Marie and the gang at St. Solo Computer Graphics.

Fifth House Publishers shared my desire to write an engaging but informed history of the province. Charlene Dobmeier asked me to call her weekly to talk about the project and reciprocated with family stories and lots of laughter. Lesley Reynolds gently wrung excess words out of the manuscript to ensure that the provincial story was told well. Meaghan Craven carefully shepherded the book through production with her infectious cheerfulness. Simone Lee worked tirelessly to generate public interest in the book. The handsome publication is a testament to their hard work, energy, and dedication to the project.

My family (Marley, Jess, Mike, and Kate) was a constant source of support. They had great confidence that the book would get done and helped wherever they could along the way. Marley deserves special recognition for patiently listening to my Saskatchewan tales, offering critical advice when needed most, and sharing the journey with me. The cats, Bits and Baby, kept me company and reminded me to take time to play.

My last thank-you goes to the many people over the past few years who expressed interest in the project, provided warm words of encouragement, and made helpful suggestions or supplied material for the book. I hope the wait has been worthwhile.

Index

Note: Numbers in italics refer to pages with photographs or illustrations.

556 | SASKATCHEWAN: A NEW HISTORY

On-to-Ottawa Trek, *319,* 319–20
One Big Union movement, 234, 235
Onion Lake, 172, 243, 515n. 42
Onion Lake Reserve, *181,* 227–28
Ontario, 104, 263, 272, 331
    Aboriginal population, 501, 502
    Ontario settlers, 60–61, 66, 102, 106, 107, 142,
      152
Opawoscikan Reserve, 445
Orange Lodge, 199
Osmond, Humphry, 382
O'Soup, Louis, 182
Otterson, Harry, 53, 56, 57
Oxbow, 67, 120

P
P. Lyall and Sons of Montreal, 94
Paddockwood, 259
Palliser expedition (1857-60), 42
Palliser's Triangle, 42, 58, 294
Pangman, 381
Paper Wheat (play), 408–9
Paradise Hill, 67
Parker, Peter, 274
Parker, Reginald J. M., 491
Parsons and Whittemore Inc., 394, 403
Partridge, Edward Alexander (Sage of Sintaluta), 127,
    131, 137, 312
    and "Partridge Plan," 131–33
Pascal, Émile, 30, 32, 38
Pasqua Forest Reserve, 300
Pasqua Indian Reserve, 243
Patience Lake mine, 392
Patriotic Acre Fund, 221
patriotic funds, 185, 192, 193, 212
Patterson, William J., *322,* 323–24, 332, 340, 343, 346,
    491
    Sask. premier, 321
Peake's Butte, 55
Pearce, William, 62
Pearson, Lester, 398–99
Pederson, Martin, 390–91
Pedley, Frank, 169, 182
Peepeekisis Reserve, 180
Pelican Narrows, 25, 28
Pelly, *170*
Pepin, Jean-Luc, 433
Perry, Jessie, 17
Perry, Tom, 119
Peter Pond Lake, 269
Peters, Vernon, 335
Peterson, Eric, 394
Peterson, Warren, 394
Petrofka, 176
Pezer, Vera, 388
Pheasant's Rump band, 166
Phelps, Joe, 344, *345,* 347–48, 349, 350, 359, 363, 364, 373

Piapot, Chief, 13, *14,* 48, 166, *168,* 180
Piapot Reserve, 243
Pierce, H. C., 519n. 51
Pile of Bones, 146
Pinto Creek area, 75
Pipestone Creek, 62
Pipestone Valley, 67
political parties, list of, 491
Pollard, W. C., 105
Poor Man, 78
Pope Commission, 209–10, 218
population, 354, 500
    Aboriginal, 501–2
    baby boom, 354
    decline, 452, 461, 480, 539n. 4
    demographics, 497–503
    in early 1900s, 59, 148
    ethnic origin and composition, 502–3
    rural depopulation, 355–56, 368, 373, 405, 406–9,
      413, 433, 467
Porcupine, 260
Porcupine Forest Reserve, 259
Porritt, Edward, 133
Portage La Loche, 24, 30, 32, 34–35, 36, *36*
Porteous, George, 491
Potash Corporation of America, 392, 423–24, 438,
    460
Potash Corporation of Saskatchewan, 430, 450, 452
potash mining, 392, 401, 419–20, 422–24, 430, 438,
    450, 452, 460
Pound-Maker Agventures, 483
Poundmaker, Chief, 46–47, 165, 182, 316
Poundmaker Reserve, 164, 180, 182, 416
poverty
    of Aboriginal children (2003), 540n 19
    of Aboriginals, 70, 170, 173, 188, 242, 243, 290,
      358–59, 396, 416, 444, 476, 486
    of immigrants, 65, 111
    poverty rate (1988), 452
    in Regina (1988), 452
    in 1930s, 297, 313
    in WWI, 233
Poverty Profile 1988 (report), 452
Prairie Farm Rehabilitation Administration (PFRA),
    321
Prairie River, 174
Prelate, 197
premiers
    list of Sask. premiers, 491
    See also specific names of premiers
Presbyterian Theological College, Saskatoon, 244
Price, George, 226
Primrose Lake Air Weapons Range, 466
Prince Albert, 60, 85, 91, 155, *155,* 363, 368, 411, 415
    Aboriginal peoples, 290–91, 445, 476
    beginnings, 141, 145–46, 156, 173
    and British Commonwealth Air Training Plan
      (BCATP), 335

ABOUT THE AUTHOR

A specialist in western and northern Canadian history, Bill Waiser joined the Department of History at the University of Saskatchewan in 1984.

Bill is the author, co-author, or co-editor of eight books, including *Park Prisoners: The Untold Story of Western Canada's National Parks* and (with Blair Stonechild) *Loyal till Death: Indians and the North-West Rebellion*, which was a finalist for the 1997 Governor General's Literary Award for non-fiction. His most recent book, *All Hell Can't Stop Us: The On-to-Ottawa Trek and Regina Riot*, won the 2003 Saskatchewan Book Award for non-fiction.

Between 1998 and 2001, Bill hosted a weekly history series, *Looking Back*, on CBC Saskatchewan Television during the early evening news. It is also available in book format from Fifth House Publishers.

Bill has served on the council of the Canadian Historical Association and the board of directors of Canada's National History Society, publisher of *The Beaver* magazine. He was named the university's Distinguished Researcher at the spring 2004 convocation, and received the College of Arts and Sciences Teaching Excellence Award in 2003. When not teaching or writing, Bill is a recreational runner and also likes to garden, hike, and canoe.